S0-BPZ-471

The Journals and Miscellaneous Notebooks

of

RALPH WALDO EMERSON

WILLIAM H. GILMAN *Chief Editor*

ALFRED R. FERGUSON *Senior Editor*

HARRISON HAYFORD RALPH H. ORTH

J. E. PARSONS A. W. PLUMSTEAD

Editors

The Journals and Miscellaneous Notebooks of

RALPH WALDO EMERSON

VOLUME XI

1848–1851

EDITED BY

A. W. PLUMSTEAD WILLIAM H. GILMAN

RUTH H. BENNETT
ASSOCIATE EDITOR

THE BELKNAP PRESS
OF HARVARD UNIVERSITY PRESS
Cambridge, Massachusetts
and London, England
1975

Library of Congress Catalog Card Number 60–11554
ISBN 0–674–48474–6

Typography by Burton J Jones
Printed in the U.S.A.

Preface

This volume has been a collaborative effort; both editors have shared in the labors on text and notes, and each has critically reviewed the other's work.

The editors wish to thank a number of institutions and persons for help of various kinds. The Ralph Waldo Emerson Memorial Association, through the medium of David Emerson, has continued to provide regular grants-in-aid which have been indispensable to the progress of the edition. The University of Massachusetts at Amherst provided a semester's leave for Professor Plumstead and two graduate assistant grants. The University of Rochester provided four half-year leaves both for this volume and for the work of the Chief Editor on the edition as a whole. The Center for Editions of American Authors of the Modern Language Association of America provided generous financial support for the work of both editors from grants made by the National Endowment for the Humanities of the National Foundation on the Arts and Humanities.

The full and exact debt of the editors to particular individuals can hardly be expressed. Mrs. John A. Leermakers has given several years of voluntary service. Professors Wallace Williams and James Justus, present editors of the later Emerson lectures, have provided us with nearly 2,000 pages of transcripts of Emerson's lectures, without which we would not have been able to locate lecture uses. Mary R. Leonard skillfully transcribed most of the texts from the original manuscripts in Houghton Library. Niki Plumstead constantly brought her keen intelligence to bear on the notes as she typed them. Linda Kellner drew upon her long service to the Journals to assist in innumerable ways. Katherine Quill detected editorial errors as she checked the hundreds of notes. Amy Lezberg and Martha Blaisdell were valuable in researching materials in the Houghton and Widener libraries, and the Boston Public Library, and in the Emerson house and the Concord Antiquarian Society. Marcy Chambers, a research librarian of unparalleled skill, was responsible for rooting out some of the most esoteric allusions, and William Lucey located many hard to find uses in *Conduct of Life*. Professor Cyrus Hoy prevented the editors from making well-intended but ignorant references to Ben Jonson and others. Shirley Ricker located and translated most of the remote classical allusions. Patricia Fischler and Margaret B. Heminway typed the Index.

Other valuable help was supplied by Professors Peter Moes and Joel Myerson, and by Russell Brubaker, Joseph McCarthy, Ben Bowman, Margaret R., Christopher and Lucia Gilman.

For other assistance and courtesies we wish to thank Miss Carolyn Jakeman, Professor William H. Bond, and others of the staff of the Houghton Library; the staffs of the University of Rochester Library, the University of Massachusetts Library at Amherst, and Widener Library; Mrs. John Dempsey of the Emerson House in Concord; and the staff of the Concord Antiquarian Society.

Unless otherwise noted, translations of quotations in Latin and Greek are from the Loeb Classical Library and are reprinted by permission of Harvard University Press and the Loeb Classical Library. Letters of Caroline Sturgis are used by permission of Harvard College Library.

All the surviving editors named on the edition title page have responsibilities of various kinds for the edition as a whole. The Chief Editor has the primary responsibility for the edition and for certification of individual volumes.

W. H. G.

Alfred Riggs Ferguson

1915–1974

Alfred Riggs Ferguson died on May 5, 1974. One of the original three founders and editors of this edition of Emerson's Journals and Notebooks in 1954, he worked with matchless vigor as editor or co-editor on five of the eleven volumes now in print. As Senior Editor since 1966, he helped with other volumes; he was especially kind and thoughtful to inexperienced junior editors. In the last month of his life, when he had to go into Houghton Library in a wheelchair, he nearly finished the collation of volume XIII, of which he is coeditor.

To do full justice to him as student, athlete, naval officer, teacher, administrator, scholar, and person is not an enviable task. At the College of Wooster he won letters in track, football, and swimming, was elected to Phi Beta Kappa, and graduated summa cum laude in 1937. He took his M.A. degree at Yale, taught at Middlebury College, and became a lieutenant in military intelligence in World War II; after attending a Japanese language school, he became an interpreter and served in the Far East. He returned to finish his Ph.D. at Yale in 1948.

For eighteen years he taught at Ohio Wesleyan University and also acted as chairman of the departments of English and the humanities. In 1957–1958 he was a Fulbright Lecturer at the University of Hamburg. In 1966 he joined the faculty of the new University of Massachusetts in Boston and served as chairman of the English department and of the division of the humanities. In 1969–1972 he was professor of American Literature and Director of the Textual Center at Ohio State University. He returned to teach at the University of Massachusetts, Boston, in 1972 and served as faculty cochairman of the University Senate. In his honor the University has established a

Prize Fund for distinguished undergraduate work in American literature. All his work as teacher and administrator was marked by devotion, sound judgment, and brilliant learning.

His first published work was *Edward Rowland Sill: the Twilight Poet* (1955). In addition to his indispensable and lengthy work on *The Journals and Miscellaneous Notebooks of Ralph Waldo Emerson* (1960–), he became General Editor of the new *Collected Works* of Emerson in 1966. He established the text of volume I (*Nature, Addresses, and Lectures*, 1971), prepared copy for volume II, and completed much of the text of volume III. But he was not an Emersonian only. He had published scholarly articles on Dickens, Howells, Henry James, and Robert Frost, and edited several texts used in high schools. His essay "Frost and the Paradox of the Fortunate Fall" appeared in *Frost: Centennial Essays* (University of Mississippi, 1974). It arose out of an introduction of Frost to a college audience; afterwards Frost said to him, "You understand me better than anyone I know."

It was a sign of affection and recognition of his human warmth and good humor that Professor Ferguson was known to his fellow editors, his many, many other friends and colleagues, assistants in the Emerson projects, and even some students, as "Fergie," or "Ferg." Those who knew him best were also aware of his stern sense of duty, which led him to take on unpopular offices, his combination of courage, decisiveness, and utter lack of pompousness, his fabulous memory (it seemed as if he knew the Bible word for word), and his fondness for poetry, from the Psalms, Herbert, and Wordsworth to Hopkins, Yeats, Eliot, Roethke, and Stevens.

We who knew him best remember his hearty laugh, his jokes, his hospitality, his earnest prayers before dinner. We saw him bounding up the stairs in Houghton Library, rushing through the stacks in Widener, yet doing his research with thoroughness and accuracy and tireless energy. At home, he was a loving husband and father. It is said that no man is indispensable; to his fellow editors, and to many others, the loss of Fergie, as friend and scholar, is irreparable.

Contents

Illustrations

Following page 390

Foreword to Volume XI

THE JOURNALS FROM 1848 TO 1851

The Emerson who emerges from the 1848–1851 Journals and Notebooks is a familiar figure, while at the same time he pushes into new territory—in person, as he travels further west to lecture than he had before, and intellectually, as he reacts to the increasing scientific and technological advancements of his age, and to the darkening political trauma of slavery in America. As the first journal in this volume opens, he had been home only a few months from a successful lecture tour in England and a visit to France. By the time of the latest dated entry in the volume, he had prepared a new lecture series on "The Conduct of Life," seen two books through the press—*Nature, Addresses, and Lectures* and *Representative Men*—and traveled as far as St. Louis to lecture.

Familiar topics recur in these journals: "The Central Man," the philosopher, the scholar, and his relationship to his age, the Times (variously called the Age, or the Nineteenth Century). He reflects on his English experiences in many entries, some of which are later used in *English Traits*. Scattered comments also show that his usual distaste for the French has been softened only slightly by his recent visit to revolutionary Paris; safely back in Concord he can suppose that all Saxons would agree it "an unspeakable misfortune to be born a Frenchman." Here also are new or more thoroughly developed topical concerns, later metamorphosed through lecture and rewriting into *Conduct of Life*—Wealth, Power, Fate, Culture—and a new "Chapter on Intellect." Many entries attest to Emerson's desire to keep abreast of the expanding scientific and technological discoveries and inventions of his day; he would see what laws of time, place, race, and power combine to create a Crystal Palace or Lawrence,

Massachusetts, or the exceptional man — a railroad builder, an astronomer, a mathematician, a paleontologist. He is pleased that the nineteenth century is seeing "new importance" in reinterpreting and editing the masters — Dante, Shakespeare, Michelangelo. Thirteen years after *Nature*, he is still fascinated with analogies and parallels between "mechanical laws" and the "kingdom of the mind."

Emerson continues to be challenged by his inadequacies, to admit the bafflements and polarities facing him as a scholar and interpreter of man. "I affirm melioration," he writes; "I affirm also . . . that only that is true which is always true. . . . But I cannot reconcile these two statements." "I am, of course, at ebbtide" he writes at the age of forty-five, perhaps already aware of the tremendous psychic strain his established habits of study and continual writing were making on his life. Protecting himself for such study is a continual difficulty: "I retreat & hide. . . . When I bought a house, the first thing I did was to plant trees. I could not conceal myself enough," he confides to his journal. Periodic disillusion over the inactivity of his life bothers him. If he finds a "fault" with Henry Thoreau, that he is not more ambitious, "that he is insignificant here in the town," the "captain of a huckleberry party" instead of "the head of American Engineers," he feels a similar sting himself. "If I should be honest, I should say, my exploring of life presents little or nothing of respectable event or action, or, in myself, of a personality." Almost as if to console and reinforce himself, he writes a few days later: "I confine my ambition to true reporting, though I only get one new fact in a year."

Local and family scenes are here — though not in abundance — glimpses of Emerson as father, husband, friend, farmer, and gentleman. There is talk of starting a new literary journal, which depresses him. He plays a role in forming and selecting members for the Town and Country Club. He prunes his trees: "we all have expensive vices; you play at billiards, & I at pear trees." Hawthorne is gone, Caroline Sturgis married and moved away, Margaret Fuller is in Italy, to return in 1850 to within sight of the American shore before being drowned with her family in a shipwreck. Other friends whose names dotted earlier journals are hardly mentioned, if at all — Samuel Ward, Jones Very, Elizabeth Hoar, George P. Bradford. But there are Alcott, William Ellery Channing the younger, and Thoreau—the three closest local friends of these years, if the journals are taken as sole evidence. Here are records of several walks and rides with Channing, who interprets nature for Emerson. "Saturday afternoon professors" Emerson quips of his rambles with Channing when they talked of "books & lands & arts & farmers" on visits to Sudbury Inn, White Pond, or the old Marlborough Road. Two visits by Charles Newcomb leave Emerson peevish: "Destroyed three good days for me!" he writes after one of them. But it is Alcott who is the most fully described local figure in the journals for these years, almost as if Emerson were collecting material for a biography. (Either now or later he does collect materials, in Notebook Amos Bronson Alcott.) A combination of the bizarre and the divine, Alcott "can as little as any man separate his drivelling from his divining." In the comic, eloquent, and Platonic sides of Alcott, Emerson sees an image of a pure Transcendentalist manqué.

Emerson's reading in the years covered in this volume follows his usual eclectic pattern. He returns to the ancients: Taylor's translation of *Phaedrus* and *Proclus*, Henry Cary's translation of volume I of *The Works of Plato*, Thomas Stanley, *The History of Philosophy*, William Sewell's *An Introduction to the Dialogues of Plato*, J. A. St. John, *The History of the Manners and Customs of Ancient Greece*, Arnold Heeren, *Reflections on the Politics of Ancient Greece*. With the thought of working his lectures on England into a book, eventually titled *English Traits*, he read about modern and ancient England, including books he brought home with him from abroad (some at Carlyle's suggestion): Sturleson's *Heimskringla*, translated by Samuel Laing, Huber's *The English Universities*, Macaulay's *History of England* (in which he found "low merits"), Anthony à Wood's *Athenae Oxonienses*. He was delighted with Arthur Clough's recent poem *The Bothie of Toper-na-Fuosich*. Other works read in these years are George Sand's *Lettres d'un Voyageur*, *Jeanne*, and *Le Compagnon du Tour de France*, Wilkinson's Introduction to Swedenborg's *Economy of the Animal Kingdom*, Quételet's *Treatise on Man*, von Hammer's *Geschichte der schönen Redekünste Persiens*, Stallo's *General Principles of the Philosophy of Nature*, Goethe's

Letters from Italy and *Conversations with Eckermann*, van Helmont's *Oriatrike*; Lord Mahon's *Life of Condé*, Brewster's *The Life of Sir Isaac Newton*, William Beattie, *Life and Letters of Thomas Campbell*. Political tensions between slave and free factions and the passage of the Fugitive Slave Law turned Emerson toward books on political liberty and the law — Michel de Bourges' *Révision de la Constitution*, John Adams' *Works*, Campbell's *Lives of the Chief Justices of England*, Blackstone's *Commentaries*.

Of his experiences lecturing in the west "across the Alleganies for the first time," as he reported to Carlyle, there is hardly a trace in the regular journals, save scattered addresses of people he met. "I have made no note of . . . long weary absences," he writes; "I am a bad traveller." But he did keep a separate notebook, Journal at the West, included in the present volume, in which he recorded observations on his three western trips, in 1850, 1852, and 1853. Here we find what one might expect in an Emerson travel notebook — a meticulous accounting of his expenses (with his usual penchant for bad addition), lists of addresses, records of bits of conversation or local stories, and facts which might become useful symbols for a lecture or essay: "at night it was very easy to see the two volumes of water by their different colour, one muddy, & one black, & the force with which from its mighty mouth the Missouri drove the Missisippi towards the Illinois bank. . . . How deep is the water here? 'From 20 to 50 feet.' How fast is the current? 'Three miles an hour.'" In addition to such matter, however, the little notebook attempts to capture the flavor of the new or wild west, a part of America Emerson until now had only heard about. There are two worlds here, the New England one (rarely so designated, but present by implication in the contrasts) and the new one which Emerson doesn't quite know how to take, though he is obviously attracted to it. When the St. Louis papers announce that "only two men were killed in the streets during the last week," Emerson muses on Missourians (or is it on all westerners?) that "their eyes are all dangerous. . . . They are made of sulphur & potash." "Every one has the mud up to his knees," he acknowledges in another entry, "the coal of the country dinges his shirt collar. How can he be literary or grammatical?" But if these are not the types for Harvard Square or Boston's Athenaeum, there are compensations: "The people are all kings. . . . No holding a hat for opinions." The tall tales of western humor Emerson finds especially attractive, and he records several, perhaps, in places, improvising on his own, compacting a yarn into an aphorism of dry Yankee wit: "They had a boat drawing so little water that they said it would sail in a heavy dew." "Steamboat disasters are as common as musquitoes." "And they are confident of graduating a class of Ten by the time green peas are ripe."

The second notebook included in the present volume, Margaret Fuller Ossoli, is a source book Emerson drew up for his part in *Memoirs of Margaret Fuller Ossoli* (1852), on which he collaborated with William Henry Channing and James Freeman Clarke. Less than a month after her death, William Henry Channing urged Emerson to write a Life, and soon negotiations were underway to collect and report on her papers. Most of the notebook is a transcript of Margaret's ideas taken from her letters and journals, and the memories by friends, though it includes original matter by Emerson. Journal CO also has several passages on Margaret Fuller, some of which are used in *Memoirs*.

"The principal thing that occurs now," Emerson wrote in December, 1850, "is the might of the law which makes slavery the single topic of conversation in this Country." "Slavery. We eat it, we drink it, we breathe it." Before the Fugitive Slave Law went into effect in September, 1850, the journals have scattered entries on slavery, the plight of black people Emerson has seen or known, freedom, liberty, comments on specific political acts, elections, speeches relating to the slavery issue, and snapshots of politicians—especially Webster—as Emerson sees them from Concord. After passage of this law, however, something snapped within the usual poise and cool eclecticism of Emerson's journalizing, resulting in a continuous cluster of entries for eighty-six manuscript pages in Journal BO—a concentration unique, in length and tone, in all of Emerson's journals. He had written before in the white heat of emotion; he had been caustic and satirical. Here, he becomes angry, bitter, ironical, and holds this mood for days. He was deeply touched in areas he held inviolate: the higher law's superior claim over political expediency; pride in Harvard's, Boston's, if not New England's, moral superiority; the responsible conduct of American gentlemen-politicians as protectors of the weak and unfortunate. Such bastions of faith lay at the heart of Emerson's concept of America's political structure; now all seemed to be crumbling. Sensitive to charges of aloofness and inactivity — which not only came from others but which he leveled at himself — he decided to act in the most effective way he knew: to give a lecture. "I make no secret of my intention to keep [the injured American people] informed of the baseness of their accustomed leaders."

"Bad times" are the simple but potent words that open this sequence, like Paine's more famous opening: "These are the times that try men's souls." Emerson writes "I cannot read longer with any comfort the local good news." House and land have lost their sunlight; men wake with pain and look gloomily on their children. "The College, the churches, the schools, the very shops & factories are discredited" by "this nefarious business." The new law robs "the day of its beauty." "Pardon the spleen of a professed hermit," he writes amidst passages of bitter satire. Liberty in Webster's mouth "sounds like the word *love* in the mouth of a courtezan." "It was a little gross, the taste for boiling babies" in the south, "but as long as this kind of cookery was confined within their own limits, we could agree for other purposes, & wear one flag." Now, however, cannibalism spreads to the local table. "And this filthy enactment was made in the 19th Century, by people who could read & write. I will not obey it, by God."

Analogous to Tennyson, Arnold, and other Victorians in England at mid-century who were troubled by the dying of old worlds and the changing into new in religion, science, manners, Emerson in Journals BO and CO reacts to the Fugitive Slave Law as symbolic evidence that the world he knew and had often heralded seems to be breaking apart. The higher law is derided as a joke by influential gentlemen. Transcendentalism is attacked. A rift appears; previously trusted scholars now appear to be rogues; Harvard men seem to have sacrificed moral law to economic interests. Eloquent defenders of liberty bow to proslavery pressure. "Everett is ornamental with liberty & dying Demosthenes, &c. but when he acts, he comes with the planter's whip in his buttonhole — & Eliot writes 'history of liberty' & votes for South Carolina." Emerson had devoted his life to the eloquent persuasion of men through rhetoric, in the belief that minds must be changed before constitutions and hierarchies. Was it all a hopeless dream?

Final analysis of Emerson and the slave question must await the publication of the WO Liberty notebook in *JMN*, XIV, and the "American Slavery" lecture, in the later lectures. With publication of the present volume, however, it will be possible to compare the heated journal entries with the often toned-down use in the two Fugitive Slave Law speeches, especially that of 1851, where Emerson drew heavily from Journal BO. This 1850 law stirred Emerson to an outpouring in his journals unmatched by any other event in his country's history up to that time.

Editorial technique. The editorial process follows that described in volume I and the slight modifications introduced in subsequent volumes of the edition. In volume XI there is relatively little erased pencil writing, but in each case every effort has been made to recover the text. Use marks in the journals and notebooks comprising volume XI have been carefully described, and uses in *English Traits, Conduct of Life*, and other lectures and printed essays have been noted where possible, often with help from the locations supplied by Edward W. Emerson in the manuscripts.

Referring the reader properly to passages in the journals used in the lectures proved a formidable and ultimately an impossible task. The editors located journal passages in the 2,000 typewritten pages of the later lectures provided by the editors, Professors Wallace Williams and James Justus. But since the Williams'-Justus' texts and titles are not final, and some lectures as printed may not contain passages from journals in volume XI (Emerson often scrambled his lectures when he reused them, adding, shifting, and substituting), and since it would have been virtually impossible for the interested scholar to track down many of the used passages in the manuscripts in Houghton Library, the editors decided not to print their list of used passages. The list will be turned over to Williams and Justus, who will use the major information it contains. It is significant that the editors of volume XI found 241 passages in the journals that are used in the Williams'-Justus' typewritten versions of the lectures. There are probably many more.

There is a major departure in volume XI from earlier editorial practice. Indexer *remarquable*, Emerson continually cross-referenced his journals, reminding himself that for one reason or another a certain passage in one journal is to be associated with another passage in another journal. For the first ten volumes of this edition the editors have indicated in a note where the cross-reference may be found in the printed text of an earlier volume. Thus Emerson's "O 41" is annotated in *JMN*, X, "See *JMN*, IX, 372." Beginning with the present volume, such notes will no longer be provided. Replacing these hundreds of notes is a table, in the Appendix, which shows the reader where all of the journals published up to the volume in hand appear in the Harvard edition. Because the edition carries Emerson's manuscript pagination as well as its own, the reader can easily locate any cross-reference to a journal already printed. If Emerson should cross-reference a passage in a journal in the present volume to "D, 71," for example, a glance at the table in the Appendix, where the titles of his journals and notebooks are listed alphabetically, will show that Journal D appears in *JMN*, VII, between pages 3 and 262; locating page [71] in that volume will be almost as easy as locating printed page 71.

Notebook Margaret Fuller Ossoli contains much copying from her letters, journals, and other memorabilia, as has been mentioned. Apparently without significant reason, Emerson puts quotation marks around some of this copied material, but not around other copied material. The editors have decided to follow Emerson exactly in this matter, instead, as is the usual practice, of normalizing silently. In cases of certainty that matter in this notebook was not original with Emerson, even though not set off by quotation marks, it has been set in extract size type.

In the manuscripts, Emerson's topical headings are sometimes underlined, sometimes set off by a rule or by enclosing or partly enclosing straight or wavy lines; unless he seems to have intended something more than marking to identify the matter as a heading, the various forms are interpreted by setting the heading in italics. Whenever one of Emerson's hyphens coincides with the compositor's end-of-line hyphenation, two hyphens have been set, one at the end of the line and one at the beginning of the following line. When the text is quoted in the notes, no silent emendations are made; hence there are occasional variations between notes and text.

Numbering of "Fragments on Nature and Life" and "Fragments on the Poet and the Poetic Life" follows that assigned by Edward Emerson or by George S. Hubbell, *A Concordance to the Poems of Ralph Waldo Emerson.*

In accordance with the policies of the Center for Editions of American Authors, a list of silent emendations has been prepared; copies are to be deposited in the Rush Rhees Library of the University of Rochester, the Library of Congress, Houghton Library, Huntington Library, and Newberry Library. The following statement describes the silent or mostly silent emendations. These range from numerous—as with punctuation of items in a series, supplying periods at the ends of sentences if the next sentence begins with a capital, or expansion of contractions—to occasional, as with supplying quotation marks, dashes, or parentheses missing from intended pairs.

Emendation of prose. A period is silently added to any declarative sentence lacking terminal punctuation but followed in the same paragraph by a sentence beginning with a capital letter. If a declarative sentence lacking a period is followed by a sentence beginning with a small letter, either a bracketed semicolon is supplied, or a bracketed period is supplied and the small letter is silently capitalized. In the second instance the reader will automatically know that the capital was originally a small letter. If a direct question lacking terminal punctuation is followed by a sentence in the same paragraph beginning with a capital, the question mark is silently added. Punctuation of items in a series, since Emerson habitually set them off, is silently inserted. Small letters at the beginning of unquestionable paragraphs or of sentences which follow a sentence ending with a period are silently capitalized. Where indispensable for clarity a silent period is added to an abbreviation. Quotation marks, dashes, and parentheses missing from intended pairs have been silently supplied; so have quotation marks at the beginning of each of a series of quotations. Apostrophes have been silently inserted or normalized in possessives and contractions. Superscripts have been lowered and double or triple underscorings have been interpreted by small or large capitals. Common Emersonian contractions like y^t for *that*, y^e for *the*, *wh* for *which*, *wd* and *shd* for *would* and *should*, and *bo't* for *bought*, are silently expanded. His dates have been regularly normalized by the silent insertion of commas and periods.

Emendation of poetry. On the whole, Emerson's poetry has been left as it stands in the manuscripts; apostrophes and some commas, periods, and question marks have been supplied, in accordance with the rules for emending prose, but only where Emerson's intention was unmistakable.

Certain materials are omitted, either silently or with descriptive annotation; these will not be reported in the list of emendations. Omitted silently are slips of the pen, false starts at words, careless repetitions of a single word, and Emerson's occasional carets under insertions (assimilated into the editor's insertion marks). Underscoring to indicate intended revisions is not reproduced. Omitted, but usually with descriptive annotation, are practice penmanship, isolated words or letters, and miscellaneous markings.

CHRONOLOGY 1848–1853

1848: October, Emerson receives sheets of John Carlyle's translation of Dante and sends them to Harper & Bros., in New York, who publish the *Inferno* in June, 1849; November, he lectures at Lowell twice; November 22, Theodore Parker asks Emerson if he has anything for the *Massachusetts Quarterly Review*; December, Emerson lectures at Boston, Concord, Providence, Newport, Newburyport, Lowell, Waltham, and New Bedford.

1849: January, Emerson lectures at Boston, Woburn, West Newton, Salem, Roxbury, Albany, and Portland; January and February, he gives five lectures at Boston on "Mind and Manners in the Nineteenth Century"; February, he lectures at Chelmsford, Charlestown, Concord, West Newton, Gloucester, Worcester, Framingham, Northampton, Cabotville, Providence, and East Lexington; March, he lectures at Chelmsford, Manchester, Cambridge, Worcester, Concord, Andover, Milton, Portland, and Fitchburg; March 20, at a meeting at Alcott's house, Emerson discusses plans for a clubroom for the Town and Country Club of which he becomes a member of the executive committee; April, Emerson lectures at Concord, Fitchburg, and Worcester; April–May, he is an interested observer of the Jackson-Morton controversy over the discovery of ether, siding with his brother-in-law; May, he works in the "Warren lot," setting out trees and weeding; Emerson's wife Lidian suffers ill health; he lectures at Boston, Worcester, Lynn, Providence, Harvard (Mass.), and Groton; June 12–15, Emerson visits New York with his wife and daughter Ellen and meets Catherine Sedgwick and Henry James, Sr.; July, the weather is so hot he has to use a pump to keep his shrubs and young pear trees from dying; September 11, *Nature, Addresses and Lectures* is published by James Munroe in 1,500 copies; October 17, Charles Newcomb visits Emerson in Concord; October, Emerson weighs the pros and cons of selling his mother's equity in the Haskins estate; December, Emerson lectures at Lynn, Providence, Groton, and Harvard (Mass.); December, he is probably proofreading sheets of *Representative Men*, published by John Chapman in London and Phillips, Sampson and Co. in Boston, early in January, 1850.

1850: January, Emerson lectures at Concord, Albany, Woonsocket, Attleborough, New York City, and Bridgeport between January 30 and February 3; February, he lectures at South Danvers, Saco, South Berwick, Newburyport, Gloucester, and Brookline; February 18, he offers a sketch of topics for Conversations at Town and Country Club meetings; March, he lectures at New York City, Brooklyn, Newark, and Paterson; March 24, he apparently meets Washington Irving while dining with the Bancrofts in New York City; April 3–11, he gives six lectures at Philadelphia; April 5, he dines with Lucretia Mott in Philadelphia; before May 6, he receives a request signed by 100 Cincinnati residents that he present a lecture series there; April 19, Emerson attends the annual Concord celebration of the Battle; May 15–16, en route from Buffalo to Cincinnati, Emerson's steamer catches fire and forces him to land at Cleveland where, on a spur-of-the-moment invitation, he lectures on England to the Library Association; May 20–June 3, he gives eight lectures to the Cincinnati Literary Club; June 9–10, he visits the Mammoth Cave in Kentucky, then begins a circuitous trip home via Hopkinsville, Paducah, Cairo, St. Louis, Galena, Chicago, Detroit, Buffalo, Niagara, Syracuse, Albany, and Worcester; July 19, Margaret Fuller Ossoli, her husband, and child, are drowned in the wreck of the *Elizabeth* off Fire Island on their trip to America from Italy; July 23, Emerson helps fund a trip for Thoreau to search the scene of the *Elizabeth* wreck for Margaret Fuller manuscripts and other property; August 26–September 12, the Fugitive Slave Bill passes Congress and goes into effect September 18; September 18, Emerson declines an invitation to attend a Woman's Rights Convention in Worcester but agrees to let his name be listed as a sponsor; November, Emerson lectures at Clinton and Haverhill; November 15, Emerson receives Margaret Fuller's letters to Caroline Sturgis and is busy reviewing other Fuller documents in preparation for collaborating on her *Memoirs*; December, he lectures at Great Falls, Concord, Saco, Harvard (Mass.), Brighton, Shirley, and Andover; December 22, at Theodore Parker's request, Emerson invites Hawthorne to help out with a proposed literary magazine, an invitation declined.

1851: January, Emerson lectures at Reading, New Bedford, Salem, Gloucester, and Brookline; February, he lectures at Rochester, Buffalo, Syracuse, Concord, Clinton, Newburyport, and Waltham; February–March, he drafts a tentative list of lecture titles for a new series, "Conduct of Life"; he begins a continuous sequence of journal entries on his indignant response to the Fugitive Slave Law and Webster and decides to lecture on the topic; March 4–11(?), he lectures at Stoughton, Randolph, and Bedford; March 20–April 1, he gives six lectures to the Young Men's Mercantile Library Association in Pittsburgh; May 3, he addresses the citizens of Concord on the Fugitive Slave Law and repeats the speech at two Free Soil campaign meetings in Fitchburg and Cambridge; September, James Freeman Clarke replaces Samuel Ward as an editor of Margaret Fuller's *Memoirs*; October 3, Emerson gives Mrs. Thoreau fifty cents to help a fugitive slave; October 7, he declines an invitation from Lucy Stone to speak at the Woman's Rights Convention in Worcester, on the grounds that he is preoccupied with the Fuller memoir; October 20(?), he lectures at Reading; November, he lectures at Augusta, North Adams, Leominster, and Waltham; November 10, though an undeclared candidate, he receives a single vote in the Concord election for representative to the General Court of Massachusetts; December, he lectures at Waltham, Concord (on Margaret Fuller Ossoli), at Lowell, Woburn, Concord (N.H.), Leominster, Woburn, Randolph, Gloucester, Worcester, and Lawrence; December 22–January 26, 1852, he gives six lectures in the "Conduct of Life" series at Boston's Masonic Temple.

1852: Emerson lectures eighty-two times, from Boston to St. Louis to Montreal, including several lectures in the "Conduct of Life" series; February, *Memoirs of Margaret Fuller Ossoli* is published in two volumes in Boston.

1853: Emerson lectures fifty-six times, from Springfield (Ill.) and St. Louis to Lewiston Falls (Me.) and Fairhaven (Vt.).

SYMBOLS AND ABBREVIATIONS

⟨ ⟩	Cancellation
↑ ↓	Insertion or addition
/ /	Variant
|| . . . ||	Unrecovered matter, normally unannotated. Three dots, one to five words; four dots, six to fifteen words; five dots, sixteen to thirty words. Matter lost by accidental mutilation but recovered conjecturally is inserted between the parallels.
⟨|| . . . ||⟩	Unrecovered canceled matter
||msm||	Manuscript mutilated
[ ]	Editorial insertion
[. . .]	Editorial omission

[ ]	Emerson's square brackets
⌊ ⌋	Marginal matter inserted in text
⌈ ⌉	Page numbers of original manuscript
n	See Textual Notes
--	Two hyphens are set when the compositor's end-of-line hyphen coincides with Emerson's.
^	Emerson's symbol for intended insertion
[R.W.E.]	Editorial substitution for Emerson's symbol of original authorship. See volume I, plate VII.
*	Emerson's note
epw	Erased pencil writing
☞ ☜ ☟	Hands pointing

ABBREVIATIONS AND SHORT TITLES IN FOOTNOTES

CEC	*The Correspondence of Emerson and Carlyle.* Edited by Joseph Slater. New York: Columbia University Press, 1964.
E t E	Kenneth W. Cameron. *Emerson the Essayist.* Raleigh, N.C.: The Thistle Press, 1945. 2 vols.
J	*Journals of Ralph Waldo Emerson.* Edited by Edward Waldo Emerson and Waldo Emerson Forbes. Boston and New York: Houghton Mifflin Co., 1909–1914. 10 vols.
JMN	*The Journals and Miscellaneous Notebooks of Ralph Waldo Emerson.* William H. Gilman, Chief Editor; Alfred R. Ferguson, Senior Editor; Harrison Hayford, Ralph H. Orth, J. E. Parsons, A. W. Plumstead, Editors (Volume I edited by William H. Gilman, Alfred R. Ferguson, George P. Clark, and Merrell R. Davis; volumes II–VI, William H. Gilman, Alfred R. Ferguson, Merrell R. Davis, Merton M. Sealts, Jr., Harrison Hayford, General Editors). Cambridge: Harvard University Press, 1960–
L	*The Letters of Ralph Waldo Emerson.* Edited by Ralph L. Rusk. New York: Columbia University Press, 1939. 6 vols.
Lectures	*The Early Lectures of Ralph Waldo Emerson.* Volume I, 1833–1836, edited by Stephen E. Whicher and Robert E. Spiller; volume II, 1836–1838, edited by Stephen E. Whicher, Robert E. Spiller, and Wallace E. Williams; volume III, 1838–1842, edited by Robert E. Spiller and Wallace E. Williams. Cambridge: Harvard University Press, 1959–
Life	Ralph L. Rusk. *The Life of Ralph Waldo Emerson.* New York: Charles Scribner's Sons, 1949.

SYMBOLS AND ABBREVIATIONS

W — *The Complete Works of Ralph Waldo Emerson.* With a Biographical Introduction and Notes, by Edward Waldo Emerson. Centenary Edition. Boston and New York: Houghton Mifflin Co., 1903–1904. 12 vols. I — *Nature Addresses and Lectures*; II — *Essays, First Series*; III — *Essays, Second Series*; IV — *Representative Men*; V — *English Traits*; VI — *Conduct of Life*; VII — *Society and Solitude*; VIII — *Letters and Social Aims*; IX — *Poems*; X — *Lectures and Biographical Sketches*; XI — *Miscellanies*; XII — *Natural History of Intellect.*

YES — *Young Emerson Speaks.* Edited by Arthur C. McGiffert, Jr. Boston: Houghton Mifflin Co., 1938.

PART ONE

The Journals

RS

1848–1849

Journal RS, a regular journal, covers the period from October, 1848, to May, 1849, following chronologically after Journal LM, whose last dated entry is [October 1, 1848] (*JMN*, X, 360). The first dated entry, on page [5], is for October, 1848, and the last, on page [274], is for May 3, 1849.

Journal RS is written in a copybook bound in black boards and black leather spine. The cover measures 16.5 x 20 cm, and has a vertical gold band where the boards and spine meet. The spine has three pairs of horizontal lines in gold. Pasted on the front cover is a square piece of white paper inscribed "RS / 1848", the letters in ink, the date in pencil. The pages, faintly ruled, measure 16.2 x 19.4 cm; the edges are green. The pages are numbered in ink except for the following 10 in pencil: 12, 37, 50, 51, 60, 64, 112, 154, 155, 214. Pages 62, 66, 68, 70, 96, and 215 are numbered in pencil overwritten in ink. Fifteen pages are unnumbered: i, ii, 2, 4, 55, 71, 74, 105, 149, 189, 243, 247, 264, 265, 286 (verso of flyleaf); 33 are blank: 3, 4, 6, 7, 15, 19, 26, 38, 55, 56, 71, 74, 77, 85, 104, 105, 115, 138, 148, 149, 151, 162, 169, 197, 206, 207, 211, 218, 237, 258, 261, 264, 265. One leaf has been torn out (pages 83–84). Five pages were misnumbered and corrected: ⟨57⟩ 51, 5⟨0⟩2, 9⟨6⟩5, 12⟨4⟩6, 12⟨5⟩7. Laid in between pages 76 and 77, and numbered 77_a by the editors, is a loose sheet, 12.8 x 20 cm; the inscription, on one side only, tabulates the genealogy of Emerson's ancestor Peter Bulkeley. Glued to the bottom left corner of page 124 is a newspaper clipping describing the naming of Lake Cochituate.

[front cover]

RS

1848

[front cover verso] [Index material omitted]

Pittsburgh

In Lect on "Culture", at close, insert Xy[Christianity]
p. 142 p 20

[i] [Index material omitted]

R. W. Emerson
October, 1848.

RS[1]

To Intellect the Guardian.

"Μελετη το παν." *Periander.*[2]

[ii][3] Manners

[1] Intellect

[1] "RS" is enclosed by a circular line in ink.

[2] Translated by Thomas Stanley as "*Thought is all in all*" in *The History of Philosophy* . . . (London, 1701), p. 54, bound with Thomas Stanley, *The History of the Chaldaick Philosophy* (London, 1701), in Emerson's library.

[3] Pp. [ii]–[2] are in pencil.

[3]–[4] [blank]

[5] ↑*Juries.*↓ ↑1848 October.↓

Judge Allen said, "that, in his experience, juries had given a just verdict in nine cases out of ten." He appealed to Mr Hoar, who stood by, and he said, "he should not state it quite so high; he should say five out of six." [4]

[6]–[7] [blank]

[8] *Immortality*

The engaged soul incurious of immortality

⟨RS⟩LM 11

[9] "God's having tasted the sweet of Eternity occasions him⟨self⟩ to[n] demean himself enviously ⟨of⟩in it,"[n] says the old translator of Plutarch, quoting Herodotus, Thalia.[5]

[4] The references here are to Charles Allen (1797–1869), Judge of the Court of Common Pleas, 1842–1844, and Ebenezer Rockwood Hoar (1816–1895), lawyer, congressman, 1873–1875, and later attorney general. See *JMN*, X, 475.

[5] *Plutarch's Morals: translated from the Greek by several hands*, 3rd ed., 5 vols. (London, 1694), II, 249.

"Enlarge not thou thy Destiny," says the Chaldaic oracle.[6] And yet ⟨we aim above the mark to hit the mark; and⟩ the exhilarations & expansions of spirit which come to us, & the entertainment ⟨f⟩in happy hours of dreams of a superior life are needed to balance the weight of earth[.] [7]

"Endeavour not to do more than is given thee in charge for thou wilt not be able" [8]

⟨Steep & craggy is the path of the gods⟩ [9]

———

Is my future related to my present only as my present to my past? say all. O 125

[10] *Immortality*

The Central ⟨m⟩Man. O 130

I think, he only is righ↑t↓ly Immortal to whom all thing are immortal. O 332

[11] "Fear, ere thou sin, thy self, tho' none be nigh:
Life fades; a glorious death can never die:
Let not thy tongue discover thy intent:
'Tis misery to dread, & not prevent:
He helps his foes, who justly reprehends;
He who unjustly praiseth, harms his friends:
That's not enough, that to excess extends." [10]

[12] Education and the Universities, Alcott proposes for a theme, and it would be a good Essay. And he would provide every fine soul & only every fine soul, ⟦dropping as democratic nonsense all pretence that every soul is fine⟧ with such culture that it shall not at 30 or 40

[6] This sentence, struck through in ink with a vertical use mark, is used in "Power," *W*, VI, 73. The quotation appears in Thomas Stanley, *The History of the Chaldaick Philosophy*, 1701, p. 52. See *JMN*, VII, 456.

[7] "And yet . . . mark;", struck through in ink with a vertical use mark, is used in "Nature," *W*, III, 185. See *JMN*, VIII, 87.

[8] Thomas Stanley, *The History of the Chaldaick Philosophy*, 1701, p. 52. The sentence is in pencil.

[9] This entry is used in "Culture," *W*, VI, 163. See *JMN*, X, 325, where the author is identified as Porphyry.

[10] Thomas Stanley, *The History of Philosophy* . . . , 1701, p. 12.

years have to say, This which I might do, is made hopeless through my want of weapons.

"More are made good by exercitation than by nature." *Democritus.*[11]

—— ☞

Once they thought every thing depended on the election of Ames to prevent the election of Jarvis; & if J. had been elected, the world would not have come to an end.[12]

A boy is the most difficult to manage of all wild beasts[.] *Laws* p 203 [13]

[13] Ah if a model person would remain a model person for a day! but no, his virtues only serve to give a currency to his foolish acts & speeches.

It is plain that some men may be spared from politics. The salvation of America & of the human race depends on the next Election, if we believe the newspapers. But so it was last year, & so it was the year before, and our fathers believed the same thing forty years ago. And these elections depend ⟨the⟩ on the general bias & system of the people,—on their religion, interest, appetite, & culture,—and not on the particular information that is circulated in one or another set of handbills. The whole action of the scholar is mediate & to remote ends, and voting is not for him. ⟨T⟩His poem is good because it is not written to any person or moment, but to life [14] generalised & perspectived↑.↓ ⟨, to distilled water & polarised light.⟩ He does not live by the same calender as the banker,[n] but by the ⟨slow celestial⟩ ↑sidereal↓ time of cause & consequen⟨s⟩ce.

[11] "And he . . . *Democritus.*" is struck through in ink with a vertical use mark. The first stentence is used in "Culture," *W*, VI, 141; the quotation, from Thomas Stanley, *The History of Philosophy* . . . , 1701, p. 466, is used in "Power," *W*, VI, 79.

[12] This sentence is in pencil. Fisher Ames (1758–1808), first elected to Congress in 1789, was opposed by Charles Jarvis (b. 1748), member of the Massachusetts State legislature, in the election of 1795.

[13] *The Works of Plato* . . . , trans. Floyer Sydenham and Thomas Taylor, 5 vols. (London, 1804), in Emerson's library. See *JMN*, X, 473. The quotation, struck through in ink with two vertical use marks, is used in "Culture," *W*, VI, 139.

[15] [blank]

[16] All my knowledge of mathematics is ⟨a⟩the story of Thales who measured the Pyramid by its shadow, & of ↑Pythagoras,↓

"When the famed lines Pythagoras devised,
For which a ⟨snow-white ox⟩ ↑hecatomb↓ he sacrificed"; [14]

and of ⟨the Multiplication table which seems to me⟩ the Decimal Notation, the invention of Zero, which seems to me one of the triumphs of human wit; and of the Multiplication Table which ranks with astronomy, & lastly of the Science of Fractions as taught by Warren Colburn, for which I even him with Stephenson and Leverrier among our modern benefactors: [n] ↑ˣand I add the beautiful command of the Delphian oracle to the Athenians that they should double his altar.—See p 18.↓ [15]

"⟨C⟩*A child is better unborn than untaught.*" [16] *Certainly he is.* Great cities, enormous populations, if they be paddy populations, are disgusting, like the [17] population of cheese, like hills of ants, or swarms of fleas[,] the more the worse.[17] But if they contain Merlins & Corneliuses, Friar Bacons, & Crichtons, if roadmakers, mathematicians, astronomers, chemists; good kings like Alfred; poets, like Chaucer, inventors, farmers, & sailors, who know the elements, & can make them work, memories, imaginations, combinings, persever-

[14] Emerson may be recalling, though imperfectly, "That Noble Scheme *Pythagoras* devis'd, / For which a Hecatomb he sacrific'd" in Stanley, *The History of Philosophy* . . . , 1701, pp. 9 (chapter on Thales) and 391 (chapter on Pythagoras). Stanley cites Plutarch's insistence that Pythagoras sacrificed "only an Ox" (p. 391), but does not mention a "snow-white" ox.

[15] Warren Colburn (1793–1833), American educator and author of *First Lessons in Arithmetic, on the Plan of Pestalozzi* (1821), a standard textbook, gave up teaching to superintend cotton mills in Waltham and later at Lowell, Mass.; in 1847 Emerson met in England George Stephenson (1781–1848), English inventor and founder of railways; the calculations of Urbain Jean Joseph Leverrier (1811–1877), French astronomer, led to the discovery of Neptune in 1846; for the story of doubling the cube at Delos, see p. [18] below.

[16] This sentence, struck through in ink with one diagonal and three vertical use marks, is used in "Culture," *W*, VI, 139, where Emerson attributes it to the English poet Gascoigne (as he does in *JMN*, X, 294, and Journal TU, p. [91], below). Stevenson, *The Home Book of Quotations*, attributes the saying to Symon Simeonis, *Lessons of Wysedome for All Maner Chyldryn* (c. 1322).

[17] This sentence, struck through in ink with a vertical use mark on p. [16] and two diagonal use marks on p. [17], is used in "Uses of Great Men," *W*, IV, 4.

ances, arts, music, architecture, nations of Spartans, of ⟨a⟩Athenians, of English, aristocratic men, & not maggots; then the more the merrier.[18] Open the gates, let the miracle of generation go on.

[18] The story of doubling the cube at Delos, is in Plutarch's "Demon of Socrates", and in ⟨"⟩ Valerius Maximus VII. 13 and in Webster's Orations p 443 and in ⟨Tholml⟩ [n]Tennemann's Life of Plato p 339 [19]

[19] [blank]
[20] ⟨A great man⟩ A[n] successful man is a good hit, a lucky adjus↑t↓-ment to the men about him, & their aims, as Goodrich, as Weld, as Brown, ↑Belknap,↓ & all that company are.[20] In another age & temper of the majority, each of these would be an odd ⟨a⟩one, an imbecile. Well, what is a great man, but the ⟨sam⟩like felicity of adjustment on a higher platform? And when society is advanced, the ruder strengths will be no more organizable, than are now the first Sauri whose bones lie in the coal-beds.

[21] ⟨Every Englishman is an island.⟩ [21]
The world is a glass dictionary. Nineteen⟨th⟩ twentieths, mark it well, of their Nourishment & of their substance do ⟨these⟩ trees owe to the air. Plant the pitch pine in the sandbank, where is no food, & it grows & thrives, & presently makes a wood of pine trees. Well, the powers

[18] Among Emerson's references in this sentence are, undoubtedly, John Cornelius (1557–1594), Jesuit exorcist, executed in 1594, and James Crichton (1560?–1582), Scottish prodigy of learning.

[19] Except for the Webster reference, Emerson's source was William G. Tennemann, "Life of Plato," in *Selections from German Literature*, ed. B. B. Edwards and E. A. Park (Andover, 1839). In a footnote, Tennemann (or the editors) cites "Plutarch De Socratis Daemonio, VII. 228. Valer. Maxim. VII. 13." No reference to doubling the cube has been found in any of the nine books in *Valerii Maximi Factorum et Dictorum Memorabilium* (Stuttgart, 1966). See also Daniel Webster, *Speeches and Forensic Arguments*, 3 vols. (Boston, 1839–1843), I, 443.

[20] Among Emerson's references, Belknap is undoubtedly the Sewel F. Belknap of *JMN*, IX, 428, otherwise unidentified. Brown may be the Concord merchant John Brown with whom Emerson had a dry-goods account, according to several entries in Account Book 5 (1850). Goodrich and Weld are unidentified.

[21] Cf. "Manners," *W*, V, 105: "In short, every one of these islanders is an island himself, safe, tranquil, incommunicable."

that make a capitalist are metaphysical; the force of method, & the force of will makes banks, & builds towns.[22]

Behmen & Swedenborg & Fox & Luther do with the old nearly effete Christianity what good housewives do with their pies & bread⟨.⟩ when they are a little old⟨.⟩—put them into the oven, & check [22] the fermentation which is turning them sour & putrid.

———

A book very much wanted is a "Beauties of Swedenborg," or a judicious collection of sentences and symbols & pictures from his diffuse & wearisomely repetitious pages.

I find a vulgarity in his mind of /reading/thinking/ always the popular sects of his time.

[23] C[harles]. N[ewcomb]. came with his fine perceptions, his excellent instincts, his beautiful learning, his catholic mind, but ⟨I found⟩ I grudged him the time I gave him.[23] He has become the spoiled child of culture; the *roué* of Art & letters; *blasé* with too much Plato, Dante, Calderon, & Goethe; tickled with music; pampered by ↑this narrow↓ society; amused by ballets; reading novels "like my bible;" and so jealous of partialism, so fearful of losing the level of life, that he has not written for three years, and now communicates nothing, but lies like a bit of bibulous paper. It was very melancholy to see that what I once esteemed [24] the highest privilege, his conversation, was now sloth & weariness and a consumption of my time. What with the unwillingness to disgust him with questions & with "intellectuality," & the entire absence of any demonstration on his part, there was no frankness, no pleasure; there is nothing now but unmixed pain. Farewell my once beautiful genius! I have learned a sordid respect for uses & values: & must have them. I must send him a peat-knife. Are we to [25] say, a man shall not go out to the shed to bring

[22] "Nineteen⟨th⟩ . . . towns." is used in "Instinct and Inspiration," *W*, XII, 80–81. With the first sentence, cf. "Concord Walks," *W*, XII, 178: " 'Nineteen twentieths of the timber are drawn from the atmosphere.' "

[23] Charles King Newcomb was an idiosyncratic mystic whose insights Emerson respected in 1845 (see *JMN*, IX, 222), but who was now growing tedious in his demands on Emerson's time; see also Journal BO, p. [105] below.

an armful of wood, lest this violence of action hurt the balance of his mind?

[26] [blank]

[27] Ενтελεχεια, εν, τελος, & εχω.
perpetuity, continuation, perfection.

Cicero interprets Aristotle's εντελεχεια, *a continued & perpetual motion.* (Tuscul. Quaest. 1) [x. 22][24]

Entelecheia, form; the form which the soul gives the body.
perfection of the body
causative form.

All knowledge is assimilation to the object of knowledge; —[25]

[28] "Intellect is a god through a light which is more ancient than intellectual light & intellect itself."

Proclus
Theol of Plato
Vol 1. p 115[26]

Intellect the guardian.[27]

Nature: her forces are emulous of mental processes.

"All conquests that history tells of, will be found to resolve themselves into the superior mental powers of the conquerors." Laing.
Vol 1, p 14[28]

"The powers that make a capitalist are metaphysical," I just wrote, p. 21,[29]

[24] For a note on Cicero's possible confusion of two similar Greek words, see Cicero, *Tusculan Disputations*, Loeb ed. (London, 1927), p. 28, n. 1.

[25] See *JMN*, VII, 430, and *JMN*, X, 135: "All knowledge assimilation."

[26] *The Six Books of Proclus . . . on the Theology of Plato*, trans. Thomas Taylor, 2 vols. (London, 1816), in Emerson's library. See *JMN*, VI, 331.

[27] See p. [i] above.

[28] *The Heimskringla; or, Chronicle of the Kings of Norway*, trans. from the Icelandic of Snorro Sturleson by Samuel Laing, 3 vols. (London, 1844). The quotation is used in "Instinct and Inspiration," *W*, XII, 81.

[29] I.e., p. [21] above.

[29] Writing selects only the eminent experiences; poetry, the supereminent.

[30][30] Inaction disgusts; activity[n] is contagious.[31] The inaction is treated with a bow like a rich man, but it is a farewell bow. He who bows makes his quittance so. That one he henceforth avoids, & will never pay him again the high↑est↓ compliment of summoning him to help in manly work.[32]

[31] Inspiration & Talent

"Je n'étais pas en peine de votre succès; je savais que les hommes comme vous imposent tout ce qu'ils veulent, et, que, quand l'inspiration leur échappe, la science y supplée."

She proceeds,

"Mais pour les poetes, pour ces êtres incomplets et maladifs qui ne savent rien, qui etudient bien peu de choses, mais qui pressentent et devinent presque tout, il est difficile de les tromper, et de l'autel où le feu sacré n'est ↑pas↓ descendu, nulle chaleur n'émane."

Lettres d'un Voyageur. Vol 1. p. 226.[33]

[32] Detachment

I value men as they can complete their creation. One man can hurl from him a sentence which is spheral, and at once & forever disengaged from the author. Another can say excellent things, if the sayer & the circumstances are known & considered; but the⟨y⟩ ↑sentences↓ need a ⟨long⟩ ↑running↓ commentary, and are not yet independant individuals that can go alone.

Thales called the Soul *κινητικον apt to move*.[34]

Detachment of Goethe. GH 30 Artist natures do not weep.

↑Concentration & detachment. *RS* 86,↓

[30] The page number is struck through in ink with a slash mark, as if to cancel it.

[31] "Activity is contagious." is used in "Uses of Great Men," *W*, IV, 13.

[32] In his Notebook OP Gulistan, Emerson lists under Charles K. Newcomb "RS 30".

[33] George Sand, *Lettres d'un Voyageur*, 2 vols. (Brussels, 1837), II, 226. The passages, which are continuous, are in Letter XI, to Giacomo Meyerbeer.

[34] Thomas Stanley, *The History of Philosophy . . .* , 1701, p. 7.

[33] [35] 17 Oct English compliment to Miss B
sacrifice to the immortals
South wind trustless, says he will rain & doesn't
Brilannique [Britannique?]
Superior ||profession?||
Ox & ass but not the driver
I ||coul?||d not have ||con?||trived ⟨|| ... ||⟩us ⟨|| ... ||⟩
scheme as that ||AL?|| hindered into
Tuilleries d jardins [36]

[34] If I wrote a novel, my hero should begin a soldier & rise out of that to such degrees of wisdom & virtue as we could paint; for that is the order of nature.

What pity that the insanities of our insane are not complemental or compensating, so that we could house two of them together.

[35] Nature loves a joke, for she made the ape.

Her forces are emulous of mental processes.[37]

Nature uniformly does one thing at a time: if she will have a perfect hand, she makes head & feet pay for it. So now, as she is making railroad & telegraph ages, she starves the ⟨|| ... ||⟩*spirituel*, to stuff the *materiel* & *industriel*.

[36] χρως δηλοει, the skin showeth, said the rotting Pherecydes.[38]

[35] This page is in erased pencil writing.

[36] These notes on p. [33] are an example of Emerson's frequent practice in his journals of jotting down ideas, often in pencil, to be elaborated on later. Sometimes he erases the notes after the later entries are made, sometimes he doesn't; usually he does not elaborate on all the notes, only a few. For "English . . . Miss B", see p. [51] below; for "sacrifice . . . immortals", p. [63] below; for "South . . . doesn't", p. [64] below; for "Ox . . . driver", p. [51] below.

[37] See p. [28] above.

[38] Pherecydes was "eaten up with Lice"; he showed his friends "the condition of his whole Body: Saying 'χερι δήλα, the skin sheweth' " (Stanley, *The History of Philosophy* . . . , 1701, p. 59). Emerson apparently corrected the original Greek. In the lecture "Essential Principles of Religion" (Houghton bMs Am 1280.207(4), Emerson has "Χρως δηλωει".

Every thing comes to the face also.

Old rogues soon show themselves.[39]

Life a surface phenomenon *O* 185
Skim with a dipper

---

[37] Who are you that speak of these men? Have you a title to sit in judgment on industrious, effective, producing men who have not indulged themselves by sitting in a corner & year by year surrounding themselves with new screens from dust, & light, & noise, & vulgarity, but have exposed themselves by labor in the open air to your ↑inspection &↓ criticism? [n] ⟨&⟩ How dare you mention their names to me?

Once these were your mates. Now you are a gentleman. Away with you! These are no gentlemen, but servants,—earnest, muscular, toilsome, reliable servants, whom God & man must serve & hono⟨u⟩r.[40]

[38] [blank]
[39] A. bears wine better than B. bears water.
↑*Accommodation*↓
Did you give Athens the best laws?
Solon. "No, but the best it would receive."[41]

[40] The transfer.

I am struck with joy whenever genius makes the transfer from one part of nature to a remote part, & betrays ⟨(its knowledge of)⟩ the rhymes & echoes that pole makes with pole.

↑On kicking up our heels.↓

We have a ridiculous wisdom like that which a man has of his corns, or of his gouty foot, & has become by experience cunning in

[39] See *JMN*, VIII, 122: "Old rogues soon show themselves said Dr J."
[40] In his Notebook OP Gulistan, Emerson lists under Charles K. Newcomb "RS 37".
[41] Thomas Stanley, *The History of Philosophy* . . . , 1701, p. 19.

setting it down so as not to hurt him, so we of our limitations. We have learned not to strut or talk of our wings, or affect angelic moods, but to keep the known ways, knowing that at the end of these fine streets is the Lunatic Asylum.

[41] The Spirit of Knowledge is serious, honest & trustworthy[.]
We say nothing against astronomy & vegetation, because we are roaring here in our bed with rheumatism, we doubt not there are bounding fawns, & lilies with graceful springing stem; so neither do we doubt or fail to love the eternal law of which we are such shabby practisers. A cripple was o⟨r⟩ur father & an Ethiop was our mother. And we worship the Liberty which we shall not see with our eyes, nor help but with our prayer.

[42] Our philosophy is to *wait*. We have retreated on patience, transferring our oft shattered hope now to larger & eternal good. We meant well, but our uncle was crazy & must be restrained from waking the house. The roof leaked, we were out of wood, our sisters were unmarried & must be maintained; there were taxes to pay, & notes, and, alas, a tomb to build: we were obliged continually to postpone our best action, and that which was life to do, could only be smuggled in to odd moments of the month & year. Then we say Dear God, but ⟨we⟩ [42] the life of man is not by man, it is consentaneous & far-related, it came with the sun & nature, it is cresc⟨ent⟩ive & vegetative, and it is with it as with the [43] sun and the grass. I obey the beautiful Necessity. The powers that I want will be supplied, as *I* am supplied, and the philosophy of waiting is sustained by all the oracles of the Universe.

God never made such a bungler as I am at any practical work, therefore I keep clear of the garden and the phalanstery.

H[enry]. T[horeau]. sports the doctrines of activity: but I say, What do *we*? We want a sally into the regions of wisdom & do we go out & lay stone wall or dig a well or turnips? No, we leave the

[42] Canceled in pencil.

children, sit down by a fire, compose our bodies to corpses, shut our hands, shut our eyes, that we may be entranced & see truly. ↑Sir D. Brewster gives exact directions for microscopic observation, thus; "lie down on your back & hold the single lens & object over your eye", &c↓ [43]

[44] Do you think ecstasy is ever communicable?

[45] The most powerful means are the cheapest, fire, water, fresh air, the stroke of the hand, a kind eye, a serene face, these are the drugs of ⟨Hippocrates⟩ ↑Æsculapius↓ & Galen ⟨Aesculapius But inferior & busier doctors⟩ and these leave the whole apothecary's shop to inferior & busier doctors.

"Peu de moyens, beaucoup d'effet." [44]

[46] "Wherein do philosophers excel other men?"—"Though all laws were abolished, we should lead the same lives," [n] answered Aristippus.[45]

"For we should dare to affirm the truth, especially when speaking concerning the truth." Phaedrus

Taylor Vol III p 323 [46]

Immortality

"Le besoin de specifier, la persistance tenace de tout ce qui est une fois arrivé à la réalité, force centripète, a laquelle aucune condition extérieure ne saurait rien changer: le genre *Erica* en est la preuve." *Goethe* ap. *Martins* p 334 [47] ⟨I find⟩ "Is individuality the preached immortality?"

[43] This sentence is used in "Wealth," *W*, VI, 116. Cf. Sir David Brewster, *A Treatise on Optics* (Philadelphia, 1839), pp. 287–288.

[44] George Sand, *Le Compagnon du Tour de France* (Paris, 1843), p. 208. This sentence, struck through in ink with single vertical and diagonal use marks, is used in "Uses of Great Men," *W*, IV, 6.

[45] Thomas Stanley, *The History of Philosophy* . . . , 1701, p. 137.

[46] *The Works of Plato* . . . , 1804. See *JMN*, IX, 275.

[47] *Oeuvres d'Histoire Naturelle de Goethe* . . . traduits et annotés par Ch. Fr. Martins (Paris, 1837). Emerson borrowed this volume from Harvard College Library March 14, 1849; this third entry on p. [46] may have been added after this date.

[47] Immortality.

That, death takes us away from ill things, not from good.

Immortality⟨.⟩—'Tis an intellectual quality. He has it, who gives life to all names, persons, things, so that Greek mythology dies not for him, nor any art is lost.[48]

I read or heard that Schiller said, that, Death could not be an evil, since it was universal.[49]

Raffaelle had no need of more originality than to watch the clouds [n] ↑& the men.↓

Boston or Unitarian immortality, compared with the Platonic, Scaldic, Indian.

[48] When Anaximander sung, the boys derided him; whereupon he said, "We must learn to sing better for the boys." [50]

The boys & the journals are always right.

[49] ↑Doctrine of leasts↓

A dance which represented the seasons & the solar system.[51]

Malpighi said, "Cum tota in minimis existat natura." [52]

Homoiomeria.

"The principle of all things, entrails made
Of smallest entrails; bone of smallest bone;
Blood of small sanguine drops reduced to one;

[48] This entry is used in "Immortality," *W*, VIII, 347; see *JMN*, VIII, 458.

[49] This sentence is in pencil. "That, death takes . . . universal." is struck through in pencil with a diagonal use mark. "I read . . . universal." is used in "Immortality," *W*, VIII, 329.

[50] Thomas Stanley, *The History of Philosophy* . . . , 1701, p. 60.

[51] See *JMN*, VIII, 458; cf. *JMN*, IX, 452.

[52] Emerson translates this as "nature works in leasts" in "Swedenborg," *W*, IV, 104; cf. the same essay, *W*, IV, 114, and "Works and Days," *W*, VII, 176. See *JMN*, IX, 410.

Gold of small grains; earth of small sands compacted;
Small drops to water; sparks ⟨to⟩ to fire contracted.
Lucretius, ap. *Stanley* [53]

Every director is also a bank.[54]

Every poem must be made up of lines that are poems.[55]
Every hose in nature fits every hydrant; every atom screws to every atom; so only is crystallization, chemistry, vegetable, ⟨or⟩ and animal, possible.[56]

[50] Lectures
1 The Superlative
2 Reading
3 Natural Aristocracy
4 I Nat Hist Intellect
5 II
6 III
7 ⟨of⟩Spirit of the Age [57]

I went out by invitation of some societies to read lectures in Lancashire & Yorkshire; yet I could ⟨hardly⟩ ↑not↓ have contrived ↑so ingenious↓ a⟨ny⟩ scheme for seeing towns & cities, men & things with thoroughness, as that I blundered into.[58]

[⟨57⟩ 51] England
not to see a knife made, but to see the country of success I who delighted in success departed

[53] Thomas Stanley, *The History of Philosophy* . . . , 1701, p. 63. "Malpighi said . . . contracted.", struck through in ink with a vertical use mark, is used in "Swedenborg," *W*, IV, 113–114.

[54] See *JMN*, IX, 245.

[55] With this sentence, cf. "Poetry and Imagination," *W*, VIII, 54: "the poem is made up of lines each of which fills the ear of the poet in its turn. . . ."

[56] "Every hose . . . possible." is used in "Powers and Laws of Thought," *W*, XII, 20. "Every hose . . . hydrant;", struck through in ink with vertical use marks, is used in "Swedenborg," *W*, IV, 121. See *JMN*, IX, 347.

[57] "Lectures . . . Age" is in pencil. This list, which includes titles of lectures given in England, may be a preliminary grouping for Emerson's American series, "Mind and Manners," 1849.

[58] On his English tour, Emerson lectured in the Lancashire cities of Manchester, Liverpool, Preston, and Rochdale and in the Yorkshire cities of Leeds, Sheffield, Bradford, and Beverley. For his engagements, and the lectures given, including "Reading," "The Superlative in Manners and Literature," and "Natural Aristocracy," see *JMN*, X, 437–442, and *passim*.

In England ⟨b⟩Beggar is a term of reproach
A poor lord is none
An adventurer[59]

An Englishman's adjective of climax is "so *English*," and, when he wishes to pay you the highest compliment, he says, I should not know you from an Englishman.[60]

L[idian?]. asks if I saw the spiritual class? O no, I saw the ox & the ass, but rarely the driver.

[5⟨0⟩2] Oct.

Alcott is a certain fluid in which men of a certain spirit can easily expand themselves & swim at large, they who elsewhere found themselves confined. He gives them nothing but themselves. Of course, he seems to them the only wise & great man. But when they meet people of another sort, critics & practical, & ⟨they⟩ ↑are↓ asked concerning Alcott's wisdom, they have no books to open, no doctrines to impart, no sentences or sayings to repeat, and they find it quite impossible to communicate to these their good opinion.

Me he has served now these twelve years in that way; he was the reasonable creature to speak to, that I wanted.

[53] There is in California a gold ore in great abundance ⟨with⟩ in which the gold is in combination with such elements that no chemistry has yet been able to separate it without great loss. Alcott is a man of unquestionable genius, yet no doctrine or sentence or word or action of his which is excellent can be detached & quoted.

He is like C[hanning]., who possesses a painter's eye, an appreciation of form & especially of colour, that is admirable, but who, when he bought pigments & brushes & painted a landscape on a barrel head could not draw a tree so that his wife could know it was a tree. So Alcott the philosopher has not an opinion or an apothegm to produce.

[59] The entries on p. [51] to this point are in pencil.

[60] This sentence, struck through in ink with two diagonal use marks, is used in "Cockayne," *W*, V, 145. For this and the following entry, see p. [33] above.

[54] I shall write on his tomb, *Here lies Plato's ⟨only⟩ reader.* Read he can with joy & naiveté inimitable, and the more the style rises, the more natural & current it seems to him. And yet his appetite is so various that the last book always seems to him the best. *Here lies the amateur.*

[55]–[56] [blank]

[57] The Age

Among the marks of the ⟨mechanic age⟩ ↑age of cities↓ must be reckoned conspicuously the universal adoption of cash-payment. Once it was one of many methods. People bought, but they also borrowed, & received much on various claims of goodwill, on hospitality, in the name of God, in the interest of party, of letters, of charity. Young men made essay of their talents for proof, for glory, for enthusiasm, on any ↑reasonable↓ call, ⟨without much calculation in the good assurance⟩ nothing doubting that in one or another way their hazarded bread would return to them after many days. But now ⟨no service is thought⟩ ↑in the universal expansion of the city by railroads the stock exchange infects our country fairs, & no service is thought↓ reasonable which does not see [58] a requital in money. Yet where is the service which can by any dodge escape its remuneration? For grandeur, at least, let us once in a while serve God. ↑See p. 63↓ [61]

[59] ↑*City*↓ ↑Gardner Brewer said to me,↓ "To be a salesman you must have splendid talents⟨,⟩." ⟨says G Brewer.⟩ [62]

[60] American Literature

We have not had since ten years a pamphlet which I have saved to bind! and here at last is Bushnell's; and now, Henry Thoreau's Ascent of Ka⟨tat⟩tahdin.[63]

[61] Wisdom is like electricity. There is no permanent wise man, but

[61] "See p. 63" is in pencil. With "bread . . . days.", cf. Eccles. 11:1.

[62] Gardner Brewer (1806–1874) was a wealthy Boston merchant and philanthropist; a fountain on the Boston Common, his gift, was named Brewer Fountain.

[63] Emerson's reference is probably to Horace Bushnell's *An Argument for "Discourses on Christian Nurture," Addressed to . . . Massachusetts Sabbath School Society* (Hartford, 1847), and undoubtedly to Thoreau's "Ascent of Ktaadn," the *Union Magazine of Literature and Art*, III, 4 (Oct. 1848), 177–182.

men capable of wisdom, who, being put into certain company or other favorable conditions, become wise for a short time, as glasses rubbed acquire electric power for a while.[64]

↑See p 13↓

Days days in Mull. AB 74 GH 66 R 140
You must be a day yourself. O 10
Days like muffled figures CD 4[65]
A good day. Index 206,[66]

The worst day is good for something, &c. Y 112

↑To deal erect with the Days TU [194]↓

[62] Literary men in the same vein of thought must use each other's society sparingly, for they are soon fulsome.

I think it indispensable that we should converse both with our superiors & our inferiors in intellect. With the first, for new aim & correction; & with the last, for self possession & talent[.]

[63] Let us sacrifice to the immortal gods.[67] The killers of oxen & sheep did not in old or later times, but they do who in their action respect a sentiment, and not cash-payment. ↑See p. 57↓

[64] Ellery C[hanning]. declared that ⟨a⟩wealth is necessary to every woman, for then she won't ask you as you go out, whether you won't call a hack. Every woman has a design on you—all—all—if it is only just a little message. But Mrs H. rings for her black servant.

[64] This paragraph, struck through in ink with a vertical use mark, is used in "Clubs," *W*, VII, 250, and in "Powers and Laws of Thought," *W*, XII, 27. See *JMN*, VIII, 457. "See p 13", below, is added in pencil.

[65] This and the preceding two entries are struck through in ink with vertical use marks; "You must . . . figures" is used in "Works and Days," *W*, VII, 180, 168. With "Days like . . . figures", cf. "Days," *W*, IX, 228.

[66] Index II, p. [206]: "The ascetic of every day is how to keep me at the top of my condition. Because a good day of work is too important a possession to be risked for any chance of good days to come."

[67] See p. [33] above.

The Southwind is trustless; he often says, 'I will bring rain', & he does no such thing.[68]

↑C.↓L. said, "'Tis so many years since we met, & you have passed over such stages!"[69]—Ah, my friend, I must think so often of Capt. Franklin's Company in the Arctic regions travelling laboriously for six weeks to the north & then discovering by observation that they were south of their starting point. The ice had floated and so with us.[70]

[65] ↑Conceit↓[71]

I notice that people who wash much, have a high mind about it, & talk down to those who wash little. Carlyle washes, & he has come to believe that the only religion left us is ablution, and that Chadwick[,] the man who is to bring water for the million[,] is the priest of these times.[72] So at home I find the morning bathers are proud & haughty scorners, and I begin to believe that the composition of water must be one part hydrogen, & three parts conceit.

Graveyard Walker
Music ruin of Engd LM 9[73]

[66] There are quick limits to our interest in the personality of people, they are as much alike as their pantries & barns, & are soon as stupid & musty. Therefore at the second or third encounter, we have nothing more to learn, & they have grown fulsome. But the true genius does not fear the fortieth encounter, for he has the royal expedient to thrust nature between him & you, & perpetually to divert at-

[68] See p. [33] above.

[69] Emerson's reference is probably to the English educator and friend of Alcott, Charles Lane.

[70] Sir John Franklin (1786–1847) led an expedition in 1845 to discover a northwest passage and died in the Arctic. See *JMN*, V, 25.

[71] Added in pencil.

[72] Sir Edwin Chadwick (1800–1890), English economist, was well known for his public sanitary reform measures. See *JMN*, X, 234.

[73] This and the preceding entry are in pencil. Emerson is referring to George Alfred Walker (1807–1884), who became known as "Graveyard Walker" after he published *Gatherings from Graveyards* (1839) and *Graveyards of London* (1841), and to a "Mr Phillips in London who tho't the ruin of England lay in Musical Concerts." See *JMN*, X, 292–293, and Journal BO, p. [87] below.

tention from himself by the unfailing stream of thoughts & laws & images[.] [74]

[67] When Nature removes a great man, people explore the horizon for a successor, but none comes, & none will. In some other & quite different field, the next man will appear. Not Jefferson, not Franklin, but now a great salesman[,] the Lawrences; then a road--contractor[,] Belknap; then a student of fishes, Agassiz; then a buffalo[-]hunting Fremont, or rowdy Andrew Jackson or Benton or Sam Houston; [75]

[68] ↑Races↓

Who can doubt the fate of races, who sees the position of English, French, & Germans planting themselves thus on South America, & monopolizing the commerce of that country? [n] But America is the commercial nation. With what resources & power, & space, & taste, & head, & all but heart! [76]

↑Races LM 152 RS 96 CD 82↓

[69] "One touch of nature makes the whole world kin," in talk or in public eloquence.[77]

Merchant

In the distribution of lots, the merchant seems to me often enviable, his social position is so good. He mixes with people on a ground so free from all hypocrisy. He has no part to play, but stands on the strength of things. He acquires facility, knowledge of

[74] This paragraph is struck through in pencil with a diagonal use mark. "There are . . . learn," is used in "Powers and Laws of Thought," *W*, XII, 57–58; "But the . . . images" is used in "Instinct and Inspiration," *ibid.*, p. 70.

[75] This paragraph, struck through in ink with a vertical use mark, is used in "Uses of Great Men," *W*, IV, 19. Of those listed who have not been previously identified or are not easily recognizable, Abbott Lawrence (1792–1855) founded Lawrence, Mass., where he was associated with his brother Amos (1786–1852) in textile manufacturing.

[76] This paragraph is struck through in ink with a diagonal use mark; the first sentence is used in "Fate," *W*, VI, 16.

[77] The quotation is from Shakespeare, *Troilus and Cressida*, III, iii, 175.

things, knowledge of modes, knowledge of men, knows that which all ↑men↓ gladly hear.

[70] Superstition

"For there as wont to walken was an elf,
Th⟨r⟩ere walketh now the limitour himself."

↑[Editor]↓ [Chaucer, "The Wife of Bath's Tale," ll. 873–874]

[71] [blank]

[72] October

Edith, who until now has been quite superior to all learning, has been smitten with ambition at Miss Whiting's school and cannot be satisfied with spelling.[78] She spells at night on my knees with fury & will not give over; asks new words like conundrums with nervous restlessness and, as Miss W[hiting] tells me, "will not spell at school for fear she shall miss."

Poor Edie struggled hard to get the white card called an "approbation" which was given out on Saturdays but one ⟨day⟩week she lost it by ⟨losing⟩ ↑dropping out of a book on her way home↓ her ↑week's↓ card on which her marks were recorded. This she tried hard to get safe home but she had no pocket so she put it in her book as the safest place. When half way home she looked in her book [73] & it was there; but when she arrived at home it was gone. The next week she tried again to keep a clean bill but Henry Frost pointed his jack-knife at her; Edie said, "Don't!" & lost her "approbation" again.

↑infallible C↓[79]

How long does it take you to go to school? [n]
"Twenty minutes, but if we go with our hoops we can go in ten," says Edie.

Every gas is a *vacuum* [n] to every other gas.[80]

[74] [blank]

[75] "The right hon. gentleman (Pitt) had sitten so long, that, like

[78] Edith, Emerson's third child, was born in 1841.

[79] Added in pencil.

[80] This sentence is used in "Resources," *W*, VIII, 149.

Hercules, when he arose, he left the sitting part of the man behind him,"[n] said Sheridan of the Addington ministry.[81]

[76] France
I sought in vain in Paris for a daguerrotype or some print of my favourite Tour S⟨t⟩aint-Jacques de la Boucherie.[82]

It was curious what objects they do daguerrotype⟨.⟩& hang in windows.

[77] [blank]
[78] ↑Woman
——————↓

"A woman moved is like a fountain troubled,
Muddy, ill seeming, thick, bereft of beauty."
Shakspeare [*The Taming of the Shrew*, V, ii, 142–143]

[77a]

Peter Bulkeley[83]
Peter
his daughter [Rebecca]
m. Jona Prescott
Jona Prescott's
daughter married
Rev David Hall of Sutton Mas
2 daughters
1. married Gen Chase Cornish NY
2. Capt. Saml Paine Cornish NY
his ⟨father⟩ son was Saml Paine
his son Francis B Paine

[81] Thomas Moore, *Memoirs of the Life of . . . Richard Brinsley Sheridan* (Paris, 1835), pp. 398–399.

[82] The Tour St. Jacques, the only remaining portion of the church of St. Jacques-de-la-Boucherie, was in the Square at the corner of the Rue de Rivoli and the Boulevard de Sébastopol.

[83] Peter Bulkeley (1582/3–1658/9), clergyman and founder of Concord, was one of Emerson's ancestors.

[79] The penalty of scholarship is that solitariness which hangs a certain wolfish look on the face at the approach of the best people, if they do not converse in a manner exactly to fit him[.] [84]

[80] Again must I make cheap what I adore,
And play the mountebank one winter more.[85]

[81] [86] Stevenson to Devonshire
Nat hist of Intel
Selden's allusion to pocket bible
battery
men who know no event but new books
as much thought in his head as there is water in a pump
Solitude of Anthony Wood [87]

Three sons 1. Kickthehousedown, and there were always gentle insinuations that he dear little soul was pining to come & see us. 2 Eatusup 3 Stealit, Sly
Eaton Salop

Then there was Mrs Dieaway herself ↑padded high↓ in her balloon chair & water-bed & ⟨towels made of⟩ thistledown ↑towels↓ & suffering such tortures from the in⟨su⟩tolerable heat of a wax candle that it became necessary to light her chamber with fireflies, ↑sitting on the register,↓ [88]

[84] This sentence, struck through in ink with a vertical use mark, is used in "Culture," *W*, VI, 138.

[85] Undoubtedly Emerson's own couplet, as he contemplated the coming winter season of lecturing, which would include the new lectures "England," "London," and the "Mind and Manners" series.

[86] Pp. [81] and [82] are in pencil.

[87] "George Stephenson, the inventor of the locomotive, in his delight at the overflowing conveniences . . . of this villa [Chatsworth], said to the Duke [of Devonshire], 'When your grace goes to Heaven, I don't see that you will have much more' " (Emerson's ms. lecture, "Wealth"). In the Westminster Assembly of 1643, John Selden disdainfully silenced those divines who quoted from little English pocket bibles in supporting their assertions, by quoting the original Hebrew. Anthony à Wood secluded himself in his garret rooms in Oxford for a lifetime of study.

[88] "Mrs Dieaway" is probably the "G H" referred to on p. [154] below. With this entry, cf. "Culture," *W*, VI, 154: "people . . . who coddle themselves, who toast their feet on the register, who intrigue to secure a padded chair and a corner out of the draught."

Her son Abner wrote a poem, he called it a myth.[n] It was the production he ⟨said⟩ modestly said, not of himself but of the Age. He called it The Ode & if any one did not perceive as many did not the melody of the piece, he [82] smiled ⟨pl serenely⟩ at his own success in concealing the secret rhythm. It begun

"How beautiful in the morning are human beings
getting up to breakfast!"

to which the Academy at their next meeting furnished a second line, running thus,

⟨They⟩ Headforemost tumbl⟨e⟩i↑ng↓ out of bed ⟨&⟩ ↑grumbling↓ ↑they↓ wash their ⟨head⟩ ↑face & neck first↓
You⟨ve⟩ only ⟨to⟩ ↑must↓ put one leg out of bed
And draw the other after it, he said [89]

[83]–[84] [leaf torn out] [90]
[85] [blank]

[86] There must be connexion, every state represented, every mortal & immortal element represented in the eye that sees, a concentration,—(one element failing, the experiment fails,)—and the result is a perfect mixture. Then, as there has been perfect connexion, there must be instant & perfect detachment; th⟨en⟩us only we have creation, a man from a man!

[87] Memory

"It is best knocking in the nail over night, & clinching it ↑the↓ next morning" Fuller.[91]

[89] Emerson may have originally meant to have "head" end the first line, to rhyme with "bed" and "said". "Headforemost" is actually inscribed below "⟨They⟩ tumbl⟨e⟩ing"; the editors conjecture that Emerson intended it as an insert before "tumbl⟨e⟩ing".

[90] Emerson indexed p. [83] under Rustics and p. [84] under Individualism, Intellect, and Quetelet. P. [84] apparently contained references to "graveyard Walker" and Mr. Phillips of London; in Notebook S (Salvage), p. [33], Emerson wrote "add Walker the graveyardman & the music man. See BO 86 RS 84". See p. [65] above.

[91] Thomas Fuller, *The Holy and Profane States* (Cambridge, Mass., 1831), p. 180, in *The Library of the Old English Prose Writers*, ed. Alexander Young, 6 vols.

See St Augustine's analysis of Memory pp 172——187 of the Boston Edition[92]

"How they entered into me, let them say if they can, ⟨"⟩for I have gone over all the avenues of my flesh, & cannot ↑find↓ by which they entered." p 175

"The memory is, as it were, the belly of the mind; and joy & sadness, like sweet & bitter food, which, when committed to the memory, are, as it were, passed into the belly, where they may be stowed, but cannot taste. Ridiculous is it to imagine these to be alike; & yet they are not utterly unlike." p 177

We remember that we forget[.]

[88] ↑Memory↓

One of the chief faculties which Plato like other ancient philosophers proposed to exercise & develop was memory, *μνημονικην αυτην γητωμεν δεῖν εἶναὶ* —

See *clouds* passim, & ↑v.↓ 465 and Republic lib. vi.

Sewell p 215[93]

[89] The Beatitude of Conversation.

I am afraid books do stand in our way; for the best heads are writers, and when they meet & fall into profou[n]d conversation, they never ⟨do⟩ quite lose all respects of their own ⟨pen⟩ ↑economy↓ & pour out the divinest wine, but each is a little wary, a little checked, by thought ↑of the↓ rare helps this ⟨happy⟩ hour might afford him to ⟨this & that other⟩ ↑some↓ page ⟨in⟩ which he has written↑.↓ ⟨his thought on the subject now before us. I observe that⟩ Each[n] is apt to become abstracted & lose the remark of the other through too much attention to his own[.]

Yet I have no book & no pleasure in life comparable to this. Here I come down to the shore of the Sea & ⟨l⟩dip my hands in its miraculous

---

(Cambridge, Mass., 1831–1832), in Emerson's library. "the", between "it" and "next", has been added in pencil. This sentence, struck through in ink with two vertical use marks, is used in "Memory," *W*, XII, 107.

[92] *Confessions* (Boston, 1843).

[93] William Sewell, *An Introduction to the Dialogues of Plato* (London, 1841), borrowed from the Harvard College Library November 8, 1848. See *JMN*, X, 469.

waves. Here I am assured of the eternity, & can spare all omens, all prophecies, all religions, for I see & know that which they obscurely announce. I seem rich with earth & air & heaven, but the next morning I have lost my keys. To escape this economy of writers, women would be better friends; but they have the drawback of the perplexities of sex.

[90] ↑"There is always a cloud on an American's brow."↓ [94]

Every American is made anxious & restless by the exposure ⟨to change⟩ to be ↑suddenly↓ rich⟨er⟩ or poor⟨er⟩; but thus is the solid fund of calamity, misanthropy, malignity, robbery, & murder of Europe,—the monumental mass—distributed into ounce loads, an ounce to every man.

"40 per. cent of the Eng. people cannot write their names. One half of one per cent of the Massachusetts people cannot, & these are probably Britons born." [95]

American Education tends, I am told, to Arithmetic: At least, I hear it complained that all the public schools teach Arithmetic chiefly.

↑Mary Russell↓ [96]

[91] Another walk this Saturday afternoon with Ellery through the woods to the shore of Flint's Pond.[97] The Witchhazel was in full bloom and from the highland we saw one of the best pictures of the New Hampshire Mountains. But E. said that when you come among them they are low & nothing but cowpastures. I say, let us value the woods; they are full of solicitation. My woodlot ⟨I⟩has no price. I could not think of selling it for the money I gave for it. ⟨V⟩It is full of unknown mysterious values. What forms, what colours, what powers, null, it is true, to our ignorance, but opening inestimably to human wit.

The crows filled the landscape with a savage sound; the ground was

[94] Alexis de Tocqueville, *Democracy in America*, Pt. II, trans. Henry Reeve (N.Y., 1840), p. 144. See *JMN*, VII, 440, and cf. "Lecture on the Times," *W*, I, 284, and "Success," *W*, VII, 292.

[95] See *JMN*, X, 251.

[96] Added in pencil. Mary Russell had taught Emerson's son Waldo "for two summers" (*JMN*, VIII, 165).

[97] Flint's (or Sandy) Pond was in Lincoln, about a mile east of Walden Pond.

covered with new fallen leaves which rustled so loud as we tramped through them that we could hear nothing else.

[92] One thing our Concord wants, a Berkshire brook which falls, & now beside the road, & now under it, cheers the traveller for miles with its loud voice. C. asks whether the mullein is in England?[98] I do not remember it. It is so conspicuous in our pastures with its architectural spire (especially where it grows with the pokeweed in the ruined shanties of the Irish in my woods) that it must not be forgotten[.]

E. was witty on Xantippe & the philosophers old & new, & compared one to a rocket with two or three millstones tied to it, or, to a colt tethered to a barn. Channing celebrates Herrick as the best of English poets, a true Greek in [93] England, a great deal better poet than Milton, who, he says, is too much like Dr Channing. I think that the landscape before us would ⟨have⟩ give Herrick all he needed; he who sung a cherry, Julia's hair, Netherby's pimple, his own hen partlet, and Ben Jonson; we have a wider variety here among the maples; — but[n] the prose & the poetry of that Age was more solid & cordial than ours. I find myself always admiring single twigs & leaves of that tree & for a chance example found in Wood's A⟨l⟩thenae Oxon Vol 1 p 225 a quotation from *Edmund Campi⟨a⟩↑o↓n's Hist. of Ireland*, that was a proof of the wit of that age.[99]

[94] The past with me turns to snakes.[100]

[9⟨6⟩5] How impossible to find Germany! Our young men went to the Rhine to find the genius which had charmed them, and it was not there. They hunted it in Heidelberg, in Gottingen, in Halle, in Berlin, ⟨it escaped their pursuit; & then⟩ ↑no one knew where it was.↓ From[n] Vienna to the frontier, it was not found, and they very slowly &

[98] "C.", and "E." below, are Emerson's references to William Ellery Channing, the younger.

[99] Anthony à Wood, *Athenae Oxonienses . . .* , 2 vols. (London, 1721). The "o" in "*Campi⟨a⟩↑o↓n's*" has been added in pencil.

[100] This sentence, marked by two vertical pencil lines in the left margin, is used in "Works and Days," *W*, VII, 177.

mournfully learned that in the speaking it had escaped, and as it had charmed them in Boston, they must return & look for it there.[101]

[96] History ↑Community. Morals.↓
Better ↑that↓ races should perish, if thereby a new principle be taught.[102]

All the world may well be bankrupt if they are driven so into a right socialism.

[97] It is necessary that you should know the people's facts. If you have no place for them, the people absolutely have no place for you. You may prove your theory by all syllogisms & all symbols, but heaven & earth, the constitution of things is on the people's side, & that is a reasoner not liable to a fallacy.[103]

In politics, all are dilettanti. No man makes a duty ⟨|| . . . ||⟩there, but he votes on a magnified whim. Our politics are an affectation.

Politics 'Tis plain that our people will vote for him who gives them rum. Polk & Cass stand nearer to the barrel, than Webster, Clay, or Taylor possibly can.[104]

[98] Love is necessary to the righting the estate of woman in this world. Otherwise nature itself seems to be in conspiracy against her dignity & welfare; for the cultivated, high thoughted, beauty-loving, saintly woman finds herself unconsciously desired for her sex, and even enhancing the appetite of her savage pursuers by these fine ⟨things⟩ ↑ornaments↓ she has piously laid on herself. She finds with indignation that she is herself a snare, & was made such. I do not wonder at her occasional protest, violent protest against nature, in fleeing to nunneries, & taking black veils. Love rights all this deep

[101] "Our young . . . there." is struck through in pencil with a diagonal use mark; see Appendix I.

[102] This sentence is marked in the left margin with two vertical pencil lines.

[103] This paragraph is struck through in pencil with a vertical use mark.

[104] James Polk was the incumbent President, Lewis Cass, the Democratic candidate for President in 1848.

wrong, but who ever knew in real life a genuine instance of seasonable love?

[99] What are Kant's views of History? Tell me that, Master Brook.[105]

[100] I find out in an instant if my companion does not want me; I cannot comprehend how my visiter does not perceive that I do not want him.[106] It is his business to find out that. I, of course, must be civil. It is for him to offer to go. I certainly shall not long resist. I must pardon much to English exclusiveness when I see how life is left by the swainishness of our fellows. ↑See CD 100↓

Another vice of manners which I do not easily forgive is the dulness of perception which talks to every man alike. As soon as I perceive that my man does not know me, but is making his speech to the [101] man that happens to be here, I wish to gag him.

"The frieze of the Parthenon with its long moving line of procession was necessary to balance the repose & stillness of its unbroken colonnades. And, if they preserved in their sculpture the severest quietness & simplicity, they relieved it, though in a mode not quite reconcileable with modern taste, by filling the lifeless eyes, ομματων αχηνίας, with precious stones." Sewell's[n] Introduction to the Dialogues of Plato, [p]p [148–]149

They are quick, says Thucydides, to devise fresh plans, οξεῖς επινοησαι.

See the sequel ap Sewell [*ibid.*,] p. 160[107]

[102] *Anthony Wood: Athenae Oxonienses* [1721]
In the article "George Peele," Wood writes, "This person was living in his middle age in the latter end of Qu. Elizabeth; but when or where he died, I cannot tell; for so it is, & always hath been, that most poets die poor, & consequently obscurely, & a hard matter it is to trace them to their graves." [I, 300]

[105] With this sentence, cf. Shakespeare, *The Merry Wives of Windsor*, III, v, 124: ". . . Think of that, Master Brook!"

[106] "I find . . . me;" is used in "Society and Solitude," *W*, VII, 15.

[107] See *JMN*, VI, 364.

Shakspeare see Wood, A.O. vol 1 p 333, 338, 366, 398
Marlow, vol 1.p. 338

Albert Alaskie, Prince of Sirad, a noble Polonian who in 1583 came into England to do his devotions to and admire the wisdom of Qu. Elizabeth. A[*thenae*]. O[*xonienses*]. vol.1, p.366,
Jo Rainolds the miracle of memory wrote in 1593 "*Overthrow of Stage Plays*"

See A. ↑th.↓ O. ↑Oxon.↓ vol.1, p. 366

[103] *Wood's A. O.*
Albericus Gentilis relieved & maintained by the University

Vol.1, p, 367.

[104]–[105] [blank]
[106] The German reads a literature, whilst we are reading a book.[108] We read only that which interests us, he reads conscien⟨s⟩tiously the whole hundred volumes.

Books are worth reading that settle a principle, as lectures are. All others are tickings of a clock. And we have so much less ↑time↓ to live,—the Robbers! [109]

[107] Alcott learned to write on the sand & on the snow, when paper & pens were dear.
His journal must be stablished. He sits ⟨st⟩here & plots an invasion of Cambridge Library, which, he says, has never been reported. He proposes to Thoreau to go down & spend a fortnight there, & lay it open to the day.

Education

It was a right course which Brisbane indicated when he told me of his visit to Paris, & went, he said, to the first men in name & credit in science. I said, Is there any man here who, for any price, will teach me the principles of music? I found the learnedest in the science & put myself diligently down to learn.— And young Ward tells me he went to Von Waagen to hear ↑private↓ lectures on art.[110]

[108] See *JMN*, VI, 372.
[109] See *JMN*, IX, 214.
[110] Albert Brisbane (1809–1890), journalist and prominent Fourierist, studied

[108] I cannot tell you how many chatterers I see who exercise on me their airy genius for one real observer & honest reporter like my two or three friends. I should be very short & decisive with my visiters, but that I am not sure that I have private employment, when I shall have got rid of them. If my inspiration were only sure, I should disembarrass myself very fast of my company.

[109] Laissez faire. No bounties. Secure life & property, and you need not give alms.

George Minott thinks the cattle used to live much longer, in old times, than they do with modern farmers.[111]

[110] ↑Dreams↓
I knew an ingenious honest man who complained to me that all his dreams were servile, and, that, though he was a gentleman by day, he was a drudge, a miser, and a footman, by night. Civil war in our atoms, mutiny of the sub-daemons not yet subdued.

[111] ⟨I have⟩ The university clings to us.

The universities give a certain mechanical integrity & make it impossible to make a mistake[.]

These men are paid to read.

[112][112] These men are paid to read, who is
benefitted by their reading?

[. . .][113]

in Paris under Cousin, Guizot, and Fourier before his return to America in 1834. Samuel Gray Ward (1817–1907), Harvard graduate and Boston banker, was a close friend of Emerson; since 1838 Ward had tried to further Emerson's education in art through conversations, tours of art exhibitions, and by lending him prints. Ward's lecturer on art was undoubtedly Gustav Friedrich Waagen.

[111] The frequency of journal entries about George Minott suggests that Emerson had many conversations with his neighboring farmer who lived across the road; they were mutually respectful of, and interested in, each other's occupations.

[112] P. [112] is in pencil.

[113] Omitted here is a pencil version of the ink entry on p. [113] below: "I wonder . . . fed? —", with "wise," for "wise;". This pencil version is struck through in pencil with a vertical use mark; see the note on the ink entry below.

I believe in the admirableness of art. I ⟨would⟩ expect it to be miraculous, & find it so. The combinations of the Gothic building are not now attainable & the Phidian friezes with reason affect us as the forest does.

[113][114] I wonder the melioration is not more. The One is wise; but he has a great many foolish faces. The men remain ridiculous under the beautiful cap of the sky. Why not Platonised? Why do they not assimilate the arts & natural beauties on which they have fed? ——[115]

It fell in well enough with what I had written ↑p. 84↓ of repeating one's self, & H[enry]. D[avid]. T[horeau].'s complaint, that Æschylus & the Greeks in describing Apollo & Orpheus had given no song, or no good one. "These ought to have moved not trees, but to[n] have sung to the gods such a hymn as would have sung all their old ideas out of their heads, & have brought new ones in."[116]

[114] *Morals* ↑Printed↓[117]

It is a sort of proverbial dying speech of scholars, which I find e. g. in the mouth of Nath'l Carpenter, ap. Wood's A[*thenae*]. O[*xonienses*, 1721]. vol. 1. p 517 "⟨i⟩It did repent him that he had formerly so much courted the Maid instead of the Mistress, meaning, that he had spent his time on philosophy & mathematics, & neglected ⟨a⟩divinity."[118]

[115] [blank]

[116] When I am walking in Boston, I think how much better had it been if I had stayed at home, & read such or such a book, written such letters, disposed of such affairs, &c. But if I stay at home, I do not those things.
Why?

[114] On the top quarter of p. [113], underlying the ink inscription, is erased pencil writing; "defining" and "sing" are the only recovered words.

[115] For the use of "The men . . . sky.", see Appendix I.

[116] "It fell . . . in.' ", struck through in pencil with a vertical use mark, is used in "Thoreau," *W*, X, 475.

[117] Added in pencil, probably by Edward Emerson.

[118] This paragraph, struck through in pencil with a vertical use mark, is used in "The Sovereignty of Ethics," *W*, X, 186.

Yesterday, 28 October, another walk with Ellery well worth commemoration if that were possible; but no pen could write what we saw: it needs the pencils of all the painters that ever existed, to aid the description. We went to White-Pond, a pretty little Indian basin, lovely now as Walden once was; we could almost see the sachem in his canoe in a shadowy cove.[119] But making the circuit of the lake on the shore, we came at last to see some marvellous [117] reflections of the coloured woods ⟨of the shore⟩ in the water, ⟨which were⟩ of such singular beauty & novelty that they held us fast to the spot, almost to the going down of the sun. The water was very slightly rippled, which took the proper character from the pines, ⟨& the⟩ birches, & few oaks, which composed the grove; & the submarine wood ⟨was⟩ ↑seemed↓ all made of Lombardy poplar, with such delicious green, stained by gleams of mahogany from the oaks, & streaks of white from the birches, every moment growing more excellent, it was the world seen through a prism, & set Ellery on wonderful Lucretian theories of "law" & "design".

[118] Ellery, as usual, found the place with excellent jud⟨e⟩gment "where your house should be set," leaving the woodpaths as they ⟨where⟩were, which no art could make over; and, after leaving the pond, & a certain dismal dell, whither a man might go to shoot owls, or to do selfmurder in, we struck across an orchard to a s↑t↓eep hill of the ↑right↓ New Hampshire slope, newly cleared of wood, & ⟨then⟩ came ⟨in sight of the⟩ ↑presently into↓ rudest woodland landscapes, unknown, undescribed, & hitherto *unwalked* by us Saturday afternoon professors. The sun was setting behind terraces of pine⟨,⟩s disposed ⟨as no⟩ ↑in ⟨ways⟩ ↑groups↓ unimaginable by↓ Downings, or Loudons, or [119] ⟨Landscap⟩Capability Browns↑;↓[120] ⟨ever imagined,⟩ but we kept our way & ⟨came⟩ ↑fell↓ into the Duganne trail, as we ⟨s⟩had already seen the glimpse of his cabin in the ↑edge of the↓ barbarous district we had traversed. Through a clump of apple-trees, over a long ridge (qu. what Dr. Jackson calls such ridges? ↑*osars,*↓)[n] with fair outsight of the river, & across the ⟨n⟩Nutmeadow brook, we

[119] White Pond is in Concord, near Sudbury.

[120] Charles Downing (1802–1885) and his brother Andrew Jackson Downing (1815–1852) were both American horticulturists; John Claudius Loudon (1783–1843) was a Scottish horticultural writer, and Lancelot Brown (1715–1783), known as "Capability Brown," an English landscape gardener.

came out upon the banks of the river just below James Brown's.[121] Ellery proposed that we should send the Horticultural Society our notes, 'Took an apple near the White Pond fork of the Duganne trail,—an apple of the *Beware of this* variety, a true [120] /*Seek no further of this*.'/ *Touch me if you dare*!/[122] We had much talk of books & lands & arts & farmers. We saw the original *tumulus* or first barrow, which the fallen pine tree makes with its upturned roots, & which, after a few years, ⟨is⟩precisely resembles a man's grave. ⟨At⟩ We talked of the great advantage which he has who can turn a verse, over all the human race. I read in Wood's A. Oxoniensis a score of pages of learned nobodies, of whose once odoriferous reputations not a ⟨whiff⟩ trace remains in the air, & then I came to the name of some Carew, [121] Herrick, Suckling, Chapman, whose name is as ↑fresh &↓ modern as those of our friends in Boston & London, and all because they could turn a verse. Only write a dozen lines, & rest on your oars forever, you are dear & necessary to the human race & worth all the old trumpery Plutarchs & Platos & Bacons of the world. I quoted Suckling's line, "a bee had stung it newly" to praise it, & E. said, "Yes, every body's poetry is good but your own."[123] He declared that the modern books, Tennyson, Carlyle, Landor, gave him no standard, no measure of thought & life [122] and he fancies that the only writing open for us is the Essay. He arrived at three rules, ↑1.↓ that no mercy is to be shown to poetry, ↑2.↓ none to artists, ↑3. lost↓. I defended Boston people from his charges of bottomless stupidity, by the wit they have shown in these two things I have read today [—] Fitchburg Road Report, & Hale & Quincy speeches at the Water celebration.—[124] What an use is their arithmetic turned to! For

[121] From the information Emerson supplies, and from H. F. Walling's and Herbert W. Gleason's maps of Concord (1852, 1906), it appears that Emerson and Channing circled White Pond, went through some dreary territory, followed a trail probably named after an E. Dugan, continued toward the town, and arrived at the Sudbury River near the residence of a J. P. Brown.

[122] See *JMN*, X, 360: "The apples were of the kind which I remember in boyhood each containing a barrel of wine & half a barrel of cider. —↑ Touch-me-if-you--dare↓".

[123] Sir John Suckling, "A Ballad upon a Wedding," stanza 11, l. 63, *The Poems, Plays and Other Remains*, 2 vols. (London, 1874), I, 44.

[124] Emerson undoubtedly received a copy of the Fitchburg Road Report by virtue of his being a stockholder in the company. Josiah Quincy, Jr., mayor of Boston, 1845–1849, and Nathan Hale (1784–1863), chairman of the Water Com-

four millions of dollars, (and in any street you can pick up forty men worth a hundred thousand ↑each↓) they have in two years finished this splendid & durable toy, a strong aqu⟨a⟩aduct to last forever, [123] running down Snake-⟨b⟩Brook bed, placed under navigable salt water, & arriving in Boston, feeding every chamber & closet as well as the Frog Pond fountain. And then, by their judicious ciphering, the sale of city lands, new made, (& rendered available by the water) for the next few years will pay all these four millions, & give the water free, as it is pure, to all.

E. said, he had once fancied that there were some amateur trades, as politics, but he found there were none; these too were fenced by Whig barricades. Even walking could not be done by amateurs, but by professors only. In walking with Ellery you shall always [124] see what was never before shown to the eye of man. And yet for how many ages of lonely days has that pretty wilderness of White Pond received the sun & clouds into its transparency, & woven each day new webs of birch & pine, shooting into wilder angles & more fantastic crossing of these coarse threads, which, in the water, have such momentary elegance.[125]

[125] ↑*Socrates*.↓ "Like those who make a hungry animal follow them by holding up to him a green bough or some fruit, so you, whilst you hold in your hand that roll of paper, could draw me without difficulty to the end of Attica, & farther, if you would."[126]

Ph⟨r⟩aedrus.
Cousin. p. 11-
Vol.VI.[127]

[12⟨4⟩6][128] Every man is entitled to be measured ⟨b⟩ or characterised by his best influence.

---

mission, both gave addresses at a celebration on Boston Common, October 25, 1848, to mark the opening of a new water line from Lake Cochituate to Boston.

[125] Pasted to the bottom left half of p. [124] is a newspaper clipping describing the choice of the Indian name Cochituate for a recently purchased pond intended to service Boston with "an ample supply of pure, soft water."

[126] See *JMN*, X, 472.

[127] Victor Cousin, trans., *Oeuvres de Platon*, 13 vols. (1822–1840).

[128] This page is in pencil.

Every loafer knows the way to the rum shop, but every angel does not know the way to his nectar. Why can we never learn our proper economy? Every youth & maid should know the road to prophecy as surely as the cookmaid to the baker's shop.

[12⟨5⟩7] October 31

A good deal of thought & reading is no better than smoking, yet we give ourselves airs thereon, & not on our cigars. The difference between labor & indolence in the world of thought certainly points at a code and scale of reward as emphatic as the Christian heaven & hell. Yet with this difference, that Inspiration is very coy & capricious, we must lose many days to gain one,[129] and, in order to win infallible verdicts from the inner mind, we must indulge & humour it in every way, & not too exactly task & harness it.[130]

[128] It is a finer thing to hold a man by his ears, than by his eyes, as the Beauty does; by his belly, as the rich man does; by his fears, as the State does.

[129] The man whom we have not seen is the rapt lover in whom no regards of self degraded the ⟨Inamorato⟩ ↑adorer↓ of the Laws. There is a pretension about our gasping dilettant⟨s⟩i, and we tax them with imbecility; but if I discovered in an obscure country boy, halfwitted perhaps, that his sole pleasure was in finding certain spots of beautiful wilderness, that he had the truest taste in this selection, & it was all his passion & employ, a new ⟨Endymion⟩ ↑Narcissus↓, seeing the reflection of man in Nature & dying of its beauty,—must I not respect him?

I think the true solace of the philosopher is in the perfections of the law which ruins him. Proud is [130] he that he is a Spartan, & that Sparta can easily spare him.

[129] In October, 1839, Emerson wrote Samuel Gray Ward that "Margaret Fuller showed me not long ago a sentence of De Vigny—that the poet must lose a good many days in order to have a great one" (*L*, II, 227).

[130] "Yet with . . . it.", struck through in ink with a vertical use mark, is used in "Instinct and Inspiration," *W*, XII, 75.

[131] The Scholar posts his books. The world is arithmetical. In this numbered system the Scholar is a numberer, and so adds nature's soul to nature. The tree Igdrasil grows, but grows geometrically. It is not Plato but the world that writes "Let none enter but a geometer." [131]

Passion is logical, as vine is geometrical[.] [132]

"He found that nature is no other than philosophy & theology embodied in mechanics," ⟨m⟩&c

Wilkinson
Econ An. K.
See AB 55 lxxvii [133]

Greek architecture is geometry. Its temples are diagrams in marble, & not appeals to the imagination like the Gothic powers of the square & cube[.] [134]

[132] What is indispensable to inspiration? —⟨the door without which I cannot enter the temple of Thought?⟩ Sleep. There are two things, both indispensable; ⟨One is⟩ sound sleep; & ⟨the other⟩, the provocation of a good book or a companion.

[133] The rules of the game are paramount, & daunt the genius of the best players. Webster does not lead, but always plays a reverential second part to some ancestors, or Whig party, or Constitution, or other primary, who ⟨was⟩ ↑is much↓ his inferior, if he had ↑but↓ courage & a calling.

[131] With the quotation, cf. *JMN*, X, 484: " 'Who knows not geometry, enter not here.' "

[132] With "Passion is logical," cf. *JMN*, VI, 185, where the source is either William Hazlitt's "Cymbeline," or Francis Jeffrey, "Hazlitt on Shakespeare," in the *Edinburgh Review*, XXVIII (Aug. 1817), 477.

[133] Emanuel Swedenborg, *The Economy of the Animal Kingdom . . .*, trans. Augustus Clissold, 2 vols. (London and Boston, 1845–1846), in Emerson's library. A statement in the Preface, which is bound along with the Introductory Essay at the end of vol. II, indicates that James John Garth Wilkinson, who had translated *The Animal Kingdom*, "is responsible for the . . . Introductory Remarks." See *JMN*, X, 26.

[134] This paragraph is struck through in pencil with a wavy diagonal use mark. See *JMN*, X, 15.

[134] ↑*Plymouth*↓

Lidian says, that when she was a child, her mother never bought any *crash*, but that kitchen towels & coarse cloths were made from old sails brought home from her father's vessels, & were called *sail*--towels[.]

[135] ↑Wit in Trade↓

There is no good story in the books to show how much better is wit, liberal wit, in trade, than pennywisdom, & yet, one would think, we should have many. The school text is Thales, who, foreseeing the plenty of olives that would be that year, before the winter was gone, bought up all the ⟨places for oil⟩ ↑oil casks↓ at Miletus & Chios, which he did with little money, &, when the time came that many were sought for in haste, he, setting what rates on them he pleased, by this means got together much money.[135] ↑It might be as the orchardist who cuts open the fruitbud of the peach in winter & observes the black germ.↓ Our common instances are, private information communicated by men in power of measures in progress which affect markets; accidental discoveries, as of a ↑copper, coal, lead↓ mine, or of a new material likely to be useful; pigeon expresses;

The famous Coffee speculation is a good instance, & I should like [136] better to know the true history of that, & the reasons of its failure, than to have many volumes of Political Economy.[136] The wit that elects the site of ⟨a⟩ new mills & a new city, finds the path & ↑true↓ terminus of a new railroad, perceives well where to buy ↑wild↓ land in the western country, judging well where the confluence of streams, the change of soil, climate, or race, will make thoroughfares & markets,

[137] ↑*American Climate*↓

When it is warm, 'tis a sign that it is going to be cold.[137]

[135] Thomas Stanley, *The History of Philosophy* . . . , 1701, p. 11.

[136] Emerson's reference is perhaps to those coffee speculators who bought up coffee in 1823, believing a war between France and Spain imminent; many of them lost large sums of money when the price of coffee fell.

[137] This sentence is used in "Country Life," *W*, XII, 139.

[138] [blank]

[139] ↑*How nature* ↑*to*↓ *keep her balance true invented a cat.*↓ What phantasmagoria in these animals! Why is the snake so frightful, which is the line of beauty, & every resemblance of it pleases? See what disgust & horror of a rat, loathsome in its food, loathsome in its form, & a tail which is villanous, formidable by its ferocity; yet interposed between this horror and the gentler kinds, is the cat, a beautiful horror, or a form of many bad qualities but tempered & ⟨m⟩thus strangely ⟨set⟩ ↑inserted↓ as an offset, check, & temperament, to that ugly horror. See then the squirrel strangely adorned with his tail, which is his ⟨recommendation &⟩ saving grace in human eyes.

[140] I went to see the dwarf of dwarfs, Tom Thumb[,] 28 inches high and 16 years old[.] [138]

In the hotels the air is buttered and the whole air is a volatilized beef-steak[.] [139]

[141] Our poetry is an affectation, but read Chaucer, & the old lays in which Merlin & Arthur are celebrated, & you will find it as simple as the speech of children.

[142] Christianity in all the Romantic Ages signified *european culture*[,] this grafted or meliorated tree in a crab forest; and to marry a paynim wife or husband, was to marry Beast, & voluntarily to take a step backward towards the negro & baboon.

"Hengist had verament
A daughter both fair & gent;
But she was heathen Sarazine;
And Vortigern, for love fine,
Her took to fere & to wife,
And was cursed in all his life!

[138] Tom Thumb, whom P. T. Barnum advertised c. 1842–1843 as "General Tom Thumb, a dwarf eleven years of age," was touring the United States.

[139] This sentence is in pencil.

For he let Christian wed heathen
And meynt* (?) [140] our blood as flesh & mathen." [141]
(maggots)

So Olaf punished eating horseflesh with death[.] [142]

[143] What awe would not the smallest exaltation of the intellectual processes awaken, as we see in Safford or Colburn's case, and the unproved pretensions of som⟨me⟩nambulists.[143] ↑The boy↓ Merlin laughs three times, &, in each instance, because he foresees or second--sees what is future or distant. We are always on the edge of this, but cannot quite fetch it.

[144] A. & M. J & so many honest bourgeois in our population vote on the expectation & assurance of a specific reward. It is as honest & natural ⟨for⟩ ↑in↓ them to expect the *place*, as ⟨for⟩ ↑in↓ an ox to expect his hay & stalks; & they are as legitimately angry & implacable, i⟨n⟩f they are baulked of it. This is the true *wild*, the Hengist & Horsa, unchristianised still, in so many ages. The same brutish naïveté appears in all their story, in their family quarrels on wills, &c.

[145] Nature trains us on to see illusions & prodigies with no more wonder than our toast & omelet at breakfast. Talk of memory & I think how awful is that power & what privilege & tyranny it must confer. Then I come to a bright school girl who remembers ⟨thousands of lines⟩ all she hears, carries thousands of nursery ⟨v⟩rhymes & all the poetry in the Readers in her mind, & it seems a mere drug. She carries it so carelessly, it seems like the profusion of hair on ⟨a⟩the shock heads of all these village children, grows like dogs.[144]

* mixed

[140] The asterisk written below the line between "meynt" and "(?)", and the asterisk and "mixed" at the bottom of p. [142], are in pencil.

[141] George Ellis, *Specimens of Early English Metrical Romances* (London, 1848), p. 80. "Christianity . . . mathen.'", struck through in ink with a discontinuous vertical use mark, is used in "Worship," *W*, VI, 206.

[142] *The Heimskringla*, 1844, I, 330n.

[143] Emerson's references are undoubtedly to Truman Henry Safford (b. 1836), known as the "Vermont boy-calculator" because of his remarkable powers of calculation (see Journal TU, p. [10] below), and Warren Colburn (see p. [16] above).

[144] This paragraph is used in "Memory," *W*, XII, 106. The "bright school

[146] Channing thinks it the woe of life that ⟨our⟩ natural effects are continually crowded out & ⟨conventional⟩ artificial arrangements substituted. He remembers when an evening, any evening, grim & wintry like this, was enough for him, the houses were in the air; now it takes a very cold winter night to overcome the common & mean.

And this, no doubt, as we agreed is the poet-state. As long as the evening is sufficient, as long as the youth is in the capability of being imparadised by the sights & sounds of common day, he is poet; but as soon as he begins to use them well, knows how to parse & spell, ⟨|| . . . ||⟩ & turns ⟨in⟩ⁿartist, ⟨&⟩he ceases to be poet.

[147] C. said, drive a donkey & beat him with a pole with both hands; —that's action.[145] But poetry is, revolution on its own axis.

[148]–[149] [blank]

[150] It is curious & universal that the first symptom of madness is to bite. ⟨A⟩Insanity makes insanity.

Cockneyism & so much that passes as costly English Culture, is fancy--stock merely; great by our allowance. W[illiam].E[llery].C[hanning]. said that a cockney was a horse-louse curried from a horse.

[151] [blank]

[152] I used to value Newton's theory of transparency, that transpar⟨e⟩ant bodies were homogeneous, & the ray entering being attracted equally in every direction, was as if it were not attracted at all, & passed directly through; but opaque were heterogeneous, and the ray, being drawn this way & that way, was diverted, & did not traverse. I think it is so with books. Cram people with your books, furnish them with a ⟨flo⟩ constant river of books & journals, & you may be sure they will remember as little as if they read none.

[153] The laws (the statute book) are only the wishes of the majority

girl" may refer to a prodigy of memory Emerson had read about in Donne's *Five Sermons upon Special Occasions* (London, 1626), p. 54. See *JMN*, III, 180.

[145] "C." is undoubtedly William Ellery Channing, the poet, as in the entries on p. [146] above.

of the people: there will be great deduction to be made for the performance. ⟨It is always⟩ Just[n] so much private ⟨life⟩ ↑volition↓ as there is, ⟨that⟩ makes the reliable force of the law[.]

faces that resemble like hollyhocks & roses manyheaded ⟨trail⟩

they all have it they all know what is good for them they & not the learned the

Socrates said, as they lead animals with a few dry leaves, so with a few thoughts you can draw one over attica.[146]

Woman said, Nature does with us as N.Y. villains[.]

A[lcott] would fain know the sweet of having done some service to thoughtful men. How to catch them, how to catch these fine boys who dress & shave & trade & dance & vote[.] ⟨Cd⟩Could we not have morning hymns? The new pagan[.] The Old Church opens all its days with solemn hymns[.] [147] [154] Where are ours? The rising sun, the road, business[.]

↑Of the last importance must generation be, if nature will stab the mind of her own daughters↓[.]

The arrested development & the powers of the brain are squandered in generation[.]

Laissez faire the only way. Meddle, & I see you snap the sinews with your sumptuary laws.[148] Rum.[149] The finest philanthropi[e]s &c are jobs like the Smithson & Girard. Values for values. Rum rules. Piety bequeaths but Rum administers[.] [150]

The true safety in the prodigious energy ↑of good↓ born with energy of evil. The ecstasies of devotion appear with the exasperations of vice. Get energy & you get all[.]

[146] With "Socrates said . . . attica.", cf. p. [125] above.

[147] "faces that . . . solemn hymns" is in pencil. "Socrates said . . . attica." is partially erased. The entries on p. [154] below are also in pencil.

[148] "Laissez faire . . . laws.", struck through in ink with one vertical and two diagonal use marks, is used in "Wealth," *W*, VI, 105.

[149] This word is struck through in pencil with a wavy diagonal line; it is not clear whether this is a cancellation, or a use mark.

[150] With these last two sentences, cf. p. [97] above. James Smithson (c. 1754–1829), philanthropist, left property for the Smithsonian Institution; Stephen Girard (1750–1831) was a Philadelphia merchant and philanthropist.

A good cook, a good gizzard, that can digest religions, railroads, revolutions & make poetry of them all ⟨are sure to be known for good in the next age⟩

———

G H sits on the register[.] [151]

———

[155] Plato called the powers of the mind gods; a beautiful personification.[152]

[156] I see no security in laws, but only in the nature of men; & in that reactive force which develops all kinds of energy at the same time; energy of good with energy of evil; the ecstasies of devotion with the exasperations of debauchery. The sons of democrats will be whigs, and the fury of ⟨advocacy⟩ ↑republicanism↓ in the father is only the immense effort of nature to engender an intolerable tyrant in the next age. [153]

⟨For Montaigne⟩

J.H. said his ⟨yo⟩son might, if he pleased, buy a gold watch.[154] It did not matter much what he did with his money; he might put it on his back; for his part, he thought it best to put it down his neck, & get the good of it.[155] ↑Old Garfield was never happy but when he could fight. Goodwin was the right person to marry into his family. He was not the worst ⟨p⟩man you ever saw, but brother to him.↓ [156]

[157] Those faculties will be strong which are used, fancy, reasoning, numbering, just as Indian legs are strong & arms weak. See LM 113

[151] See p. [81] above.

[152] This sentence, in ink, overlies the same sentence written in pencil. See *JMN*, X, 480.

[153] This paragraph, struck through in pencil with a vertical use mark, is used in "Power," *W*, VI, 64.

[154] Emerson refers, perhaps, to John Hosmer, a neighbor in Concord.

[155] The paragraph to this point, struck through in ink with single vertical and diagonal use marks, is used in "Montaigne," *W*, IV, 153.

[156] An 1852 map of Concord shows a Daniel Garfield living in the town; Goodwin, otherwise unidentified, may be the "felon in Concord" referred to in Journal CO, p. [57] below.

⟨For Montaigne again⟩
⟨faith in suspenders D 330⟩[157]
⟨and ginger⟩

[158] November 9, 1848.

The whig party are what people would call *firstrate* in opposition, but not so good in government. Perhaps they have not sufficient fortitude. The same thing happens often in England.

Here has passed an Election, I think, the most dismal ever known in this country. Three great parties voting for ⟨c⟩three candidates whom they disliked. Next Monday there will be more heart.

↑Van Buren? Taylor?↓ [158]

[159] "Sister Lucy," said the lady, "How do you enjoy your mind lately? I have put up a great many petitions for you."

"Why I don't ⟨mu⟩ expect much enjoyment," said the other, who was quilling skeins, "I have such a bad heart." [159]

[160] ↑*ninth pen*↓

In Plato's Republic, Book III, see a sentence which might be an introduction to a friendly biography of Alcott.

"We must seek ⟨out⟩ for those who are to supply us with the forms of art, men who by instinct can trace out the springs of grace & beauty, that, dwelling as in a sanctuary ↑of↓ health, the young may imbibe good from all around them, from every work & sight & sound whence aught may strike their sense,— [160] like airs that are wafting health from purest climes, &, step by step, from childhood, are changing them into the image of goodness, & into [161] likeness & love & harmony with the beauty of truth." [161]

[157] Journal D, p. [330]: "The man I saw believed that his suspenders would hold up his pantaloons & that his straps would hold them down.", used in "Montaigne," *W*, IV, 153.

[158] Zachary Taylor (Whig), Lewis Cass (Democrat), and Martin Van Buren (Free Soil) were the candidates of the "great parties" in the Presidential election, Tuesday, November 7, 1848.

[159] In Notebook Phi Beta, p. [242], Emerson notes "Mrs. Haskell & Mrs. L. J. See RS 159". The ladies are unidentified.

[160] After this word Emerson has written, slanting down diagonally, "tenth pen".

[161] Emerson's exact source is unlocated; it is not Thomas Taylor's edition of the

↑2d pen↓ "It was the peculiar genius of the Athenian to anticipate." ↑Thucyd.↓ "Before the orator had finished ⟨the⟩his first clause they could tell the end"

Novels. Heliodorus Christian bishop in his Æthiopica, containing Theagenes & Chariclea, is the founder of Novels. From this source comes the Romance of the Middle ages, & the modern novel.

See *Sewell* [*An Introduction to the Dialogues of*] Plato [1841,] p 154

[162] [blank]

[163] Laissez fa↑i↓re the only way. Meddle, & I see you snap the sinews with your sumptuary laws. The finest philanthropies &c are jobs, like the Smithson & Girard bequests. Demand & Supply are as true as thermometer.[162]

[164] Dr Johnson said, he always went into stately shops, ⟨to bu⟩ and good travellers seek always the best hotels in every ⟨city⟩ town; for though they cost more, ⟨yet⟩ ↑they do not cost much more, &↓ there is the good company, the best information, & the scholar knows that the best books contain first & last the best thoughts & facts.[163] Now & then by rarest luck in some foolish ⟨pamphlet⟩ grubstreet ⟨publication⟩ lies the gem we want. But, in ⟨great company⟩ the best circles is the best information, as I thought when I found what I wanted in "Wykeham's Life".[164] ↑You can get phosphate from cowdung; but better from bones. ⟨|| . . . ||⟩ oxygen best from *conferva rivularis.*↓

Works, I, 244, nor the translation of the *Works* by Henry Davis and others in the Bohn edition, II, 83, though both editions are in Emerson's library.

[162] This paragraph is used in "Wealth," *W*, VI, 105. Cf. p. [154] above.

[163] For the Johnson allusion, see James Boswell, *The Life of Samuel Johnson* . . . (London, 1827), p. 530, in Emerson's library.

[164] "Dr Johnson . . . found what", struck through in pencil and in ink with vertical use marks, is used in "Books," *W*, VII, 196. Emerson borrowed Robert Lowth, *The Life of William of Wykeham, Bishop of Winchester* (London, 1759) from the Harvard College Library Nov. 8, 1848. See *JMN*, VIII, 564.

[165] ⟨↑Fifth pen loose↓⟩[165]

It is one convenience of culture that it has no enemies. The finished man of the world holds his hatreds also at arm's length, so that he can, whenever is fit occasion, receive his foe with all the world at his house, & ⟨ex⟩ associate with him in public or in private affairs, unencumbered by old quarrel. But country people are like dogs or cows that quarrel, & remember their spite. William of Wykeham quarreled with the Duke of Lancaster. All Wykeham's temporalities were sequestered, & he excluded from parliament. William managed to get ⟨th⟩all back, & the Duke was for the time worsted. It does not hinder that the Duke should be solemnly received at William's College at Oxford on the Visitation.[166]

[166] ⟨Tenth pen⟩ This fast & loose belongs to the Intellect, belongs to that power of detachment which the Intellect introduces.

The other lesson I learned in *Wykeham's* Life was certainly a confirmation of my respect for the solidity of English national genius. What men that isle yields! What gravity; what liberality, & nobleness; what tenacity of purpose; what lofty religion! Here is a man so allied to the material world, that he is sure to become rich & great under any government & times, & whose aims are so public & disinterested that he can [167] easily be prudent & not too much mixed with bad politics, though, by greatness of nature, he must necessarily be mixed with great men & affairs. He is a man of the Washington type, and it is by many such men as Wykeham that England is great & free[.]

Ah these fine solitudes around me in ⟨Middlesex⟩ Massachusetts could easily become dear & enviable to the human race if once they were the homes of grave, religious, forcible men.

[168] Englishmen *1848*

I went to England to know who were the e⟨|| . . . ||⟩xcellent men of that country. Some of them I know personally[,] some only by name[.]

165 "loose⟩" is in pencil. Underlying the ink writing "convenience . . . enemies. The" in the paragraph which follows below is "Roxbury", in pencil.

166 Robert Lowth, *The Life of William of Wykeham* . . . , 1759, pp. 129–130, 148–151, 205.

Wordsworth
Landor
Carlyle
Tennyson
Wilkinson
Stephenson
Hallam
Faraday
Owen
Edw. Forbes
Samuel Brown
⟨T⟩De⟨q⟩Quincey
David Scott
P[hilip].J. Bailey
J.S. Mill
Arthur H. Clough
⟨T. Carlyle⟩

W[illiam]. Sewell
James Moseley
Henry Taylor
Edwin Chadwick
Duke of Wellington
Robert Peel
Richard Cobden
Robert Browning
Matthew Arnold
John Bright
⟨J.S. Mill⟩

All these I have seen
except Chadwick, Browning,
Taylor & Sewell,
↑& Moseley↓ [167]

[169] [blank]

[170] What difference in the hospitality of minds! Some are actually hostile, & imprison me as in a hole. A blockhead makes a blockhead of me: [168] Whilst for my Oriental friend here, I have always claimed for him, that nothing could be so expansive as his ele-

[167] Of those listed who have not been previously identified or are not easily recognizable, James John Garth Wilkinson (1812–1899) was a translator of Swedenborg; Edward Forbes (1815–1854), a naturalist and lecturer; Dr. Samuel Brown (1817–1856), a research chemist. Emerson met the Scottish painter David Scott in February, 1848, in Perth, when Scott painted the portrait which now hangs in the Public Library in Concord. Philip James Bailey (1816–1902) was a poet and author of *Festus, A Poem*, which Emerson had read before his English trip (*JMN*, VII, 325); William Sewell (1804–1874) was a divine, a Plato scholar, and prominent Oxford lecturer; James Bowling Mozley (if this is the person to whom Emerson refers) was a writer for the London *Times*; Sir Henry Taylor (1800–1886) wrote *Philip Van Artevelde*, in Emerson's library; John Bright (1783–1870), physician, was also a classical scholar.

[168] The paragraph to this point is used in "Considerations by the Way," *W*, VI, 269.

ment is. The Atlantic Ocean is a tub compared with the atmosphere in which I float, at once inspiring the air & upborne by it.

My friends begin to value each other, now that A[lcott]. is to go;[169] & Ellery declares, "that he never saw that man without being cheered," & Henry says, "He is the best natured man he ever met. The rats & mice make their nests in him."

[171] The apple is our national fruit, & I like to see that the soil yields it; I judge of the country so. The American sun paints himself in these glowing balls amid the green leaves. Man would be more solitary, less friended, less supported, if the land yielded only the useful maize & potato, & withheld this ornamental & social fruit.

I have planted a Pumpkin Sweeting near my summerhouse,—I believe out of agreeable recollection of that fruit in my childhood at Newton. It grew in Mr Greenough's pasture, and I thought it solid sunshine.[170]

"Ere boyhood with quick glance had ceased to spy
The doubtful apple 'mid the yellow leaves."

[172] There are always a few heads & out of these come the mythology & the machinery of the world. Whence came all these books, laws, inventions, parties, kingdoms⟨,⟩? Out of the invisible world, through a few brains:[171] and, if we should pierce to the origin of knowledge, & explore the meaning of memory, we might find it some strange mutilated roll of papyrus, on which only a strange disjointed jumble of universal traditions of ⟨angelic⟩heavenly scriptures, of angelic biographies, were long ago written, relics of a foreworld.

Let us have the experiences of Metternich, of Humboldt, of General Taylor, of Trelawney.[172]

[169] In November, 1848, the Alcott family moved to Dedham St., Boston.

[170] Rev. William Greenough of Newton married Emerson's maternal aunt, Lydia Haskins.

[171] The paragraph to this point, struck through in pencil with a vertical use mark, is used in "Instinct and Inspiration," *W*, XII, 80.

[172] Emerson's references are probably to Prince Klemens Wenzel Nepomuk Lothar von Metternich (1773–1859); Baron Alexander von Humboldt (1769–

[173] In my chapter on Intellect, I should wish to catalogue those high commandments which in all the mental history elevate themselves like towers; as, not until our own day, did Herschel go to the Cape, & publish the catalogue of the stars of the Southern Hemisphere.[173]

↑*Midsummer*↓

'Tis very certain that this almanack of the soul may be written as well as that of Greenwich. We have had our heights of sun & depths of shade, & it would be easy in the soul's year to recall & fix its 21 of June. Moses had his Ten Commandments; but[n] we have ours.

[174] ⟨The circumstance fits; i⟩In the first age, they wrote on stone, & what ⟨they wrote⟩ was fit to be written on stone. Lycurgus, his laws; Moses, his Decalogue; but we write novels & newspapers. You would not have Bulwer ↑& D'Israeli↓ publish ⟨his⟩their novel ⟨so?⟩ on stone?

There is a sort of climate in every man's speech running from hot noon, when words flow like steam & perfume,—to cold night, when they are frozen.

↑Library↓

A ⟨lib⟩man's library is a sort of harem. I observe they have a great pudency in showing their books to a stranger.[174]

[175] We must accept a great deal as Fate. We accept it with protest, merely adjourning our experiment, and not squander our strength in upheaving mountains. Mountain is conquerable also, to be sure; but, whilst you cannot quarry it, let it be a mountain.

1859), traveler and statesman; Edward John Trelawny (1792–1881), English sailor, adventurer, and friend of Shelley and Byron.

[173] This sentence, struck through in pencil with a vertical use mark, is used in "Ability," *W*, V, 91. Emerson refers to Sir John Frederick William Herschel, *Results of Astronomical Observations, Made During the Years 1834–8 at the Cape of Good Hope* . . . (London, 1847).

[174] This paragraph, struck through in pencil with a vertical use mark, is used in "Books," *W*, VII, 209.

Action & idea are man & woman[,] both indispensable; why should they rail at & exclude each other?

Yes, we must call the anatomist & physiologist to counsel. The human body is undoubtedly the true symbol, true & highest & most instructive; human body & not sun or galaxy.

———

—

↑Library↓

Every house should be an athenaeum.
There is no privacy that is not penetrable.

[176] ↑Teutonics.↓

I still return, or did last night, to the eulogy of those natural priests who, in every condition of life have yielded us some token of having read the laws of heaven —[n] beginning as usual with my poor churl Tarbox at Newton. These are the small Behmens, or, the Teutonic school; & one farmer or labourer of that sort is worth ⟨a⟩whole towns full of plausible farmers, traders, & sele⟨t⟩ctmen. It is the outcropping of the granite which is the core of the world. I seem to meet no more such. Very & Rebecca Black were the last; & yet perhaps Hermann knows something. In England, how few! & yet there was Sylvester, [177][n] & Fletcher, & Sutton, & David Scott[.][175]

[178] ↑Alcott.↓

It occurred in the conversation yesterday repeatedly, that Alcott wants a certain rigour in playing his game of conversation. He shifts

[175] The Methodist laborer Tarbox helped Emerson understand prayer when they worked together in 1825 (*JMN*, II, 388, n. 91); Emerson met Mrs. Rebecca Black in New York in March, 1842 (*L*, III, 23, n. 82). Hermann may be Charles Frederick Hermann (1804–1855), German classical scholar; in 1847 Emerson had read a review of Hermann's *A Manual of the Political Antiquities of Greece* (see *JMN*, X, 7). "Fletcher" and "Sylvester," otherwise unidentified, appear in a list of names in Journal London, p. [202], following two newspaper clippings entitled "The British Aristocracy." and "British Royalty." (*JMN*, X, 280–281); "Sylvester" is probably the same person referred to in Journal TU, p. [9] below. Henry Sutton, the English religious poet, quoted Emerson on the title page of his *Evangel of Love* (1847; see *JMN*, X, 189); for David Scott, see p. [168] above.

his purpose nimbly, &, when you thought you were speaking to one point, lo! he has changed it. It is the same vice for which my Boston Pilot lost his Branch.[176] Then a good deal of the talk has no design, & it is like the curvetting, prancing, arching of the neck, & pawing, of a play-horse.

[179] ↑*The Club*↓ ↑*Examiners*↓

How long shall we sit & wait to be challenged by the Examiners? If the Kings of thought came together & asked for results, we too should have our pregnant formulas to give. That occasion would be the iron girdle we want. We should cast off our long holiday, & quit us like men. As much result would be given & received in intellectual & moral science, as in the Section rooms of the British Association at the annual assembling of the chemists & geologists.[177]

[180] ⟨To one⟩Jack says, he must & will have the law go in hat & boots ⟨&⟩ if he is to believe & obey it; none of your mathematics, astronomy, & abstract law, for him. Bring in your mythology, or don't expect to hold him.

[181] *Sewell.* [*An Introduction to the Dialogues of Plato*, 1841] good story of a copy of a portrait of Rembrandt. p. 217

⟨|| . . . . ||⟩[178]

shop window

[182] ↑*Few fables*↓

In the pedigree of thoughts, in the alleged paucity of fables, a striking instance is our good Munchausen story of the tune which thawed out of the horn, when it was hung in the chimney.[179]

[176] For the story of the Boston pilot who lost his "Branch" after an accident caused by his changing his plan, see *JMN*, IX, 297, and VIII, 366.

[177] The meeting of the British Association for the Advancement of Science, held at Swansea beginning August 9, 1848, broke into sections, such as "Chemical Science" and "Geology and Physical Geography" (*Athenæum*, Aug. 19, 1848).

[178] Of the approximately eight canceled words the only meaningful ones or parts of ones recovered are "of the clea".

[179] For this anecdote, see *The Travels of Baron Münchausen* . . . , ed. William Rose (London, 1923), p. 55.

"Antiphane, un des amis de Platon, comparait, en riant, ses écrits à une ville, òu les paroles se gel⟨e⟩↑i↓sent en l'air dès qu'elles etaient prononcées, et, l'été suivant, quand elles venaient à etre echauffées et fondues par les rayons du soleil, les habitans* entenda↑i↓ent — ce qui avait été dit, l'hiver. —[180]

Dacier. Doctrines de Platon
Vol. I, p.79
ap Sewell, [*An Introduction to the Dialogues of Plato*, 1841,] p.201

↑printed in "Quotation & Originality"↓
* Sic

[183] I find Sewell's "Introduction to the Dialogues of Plato," London 1841, a good book full of the be⟨c⟩st Oxford Culture, and full of English sense. The sole deduction is in the avowed devotion to the English Church system, which, in deed, is the motive of the book, in opposition to modern movements of London University, & Diffusion of Knowledge. Against this heresy, he is as bitter as Thomas Taylor.

[184] In every family a system settles itself which is paramount & tyrannical over master & mistress, servant & child, ⟨a⟩ ⟨relati⟩ cousin & acquaintance. 'Tis in vain that genius or virtue or energy of character strive & cry against this. This is fate; and 'tis very well that the poor husband reads in a book of a new way of living, & resolves to adopt it at home; let [n] him go home & try it if he dare.[181]

"Days are dam long," said Colombe.[182]

[185] The mechanical laws might as easily be shown pervading the kingdom [n] of mind, as the vegetative. The facts & thoughts which the traveller has found in Spain, will gradually settle themselves

[180] "In the pedigree . . . l'hiver. — ", struck through in ink with a vertical use mark, is used in "Quotation and Originality," *W*, VIII, 186–187.

[181] This paragraph, struck through in ink with a vertical use mark, is used in "Wealth," *W*, VI, 123–124.

[182] The French-Canadian laborer Antoine (Anthony) Colombe worked for Emerson, Edmund Hosmer, and others in Concord. See *JMN*, VIII, 9.

into a determinate heap of one size & form, & not another. And that is what he knows & has to say of Spain. He cannot say it truly, until a sufficient time for the settling & fermenting has passed, & for the disappearing of whatever is accidental & not essential.[183]

[186] Nov. 19.

'Tis the coldest November I have ever known. This morning the mercury is at 26. Yesterday afternoon cold fine ride with Ellery to Sudbury Inn, & mounted the side of Nobscot.[184] Finest picture though wintry air of the russet Massachusetts. The landscape is democratic, not gathered into one city or baronial castle, but equally scattered into these white steeples, round which a town clusters in every place where ⟨f⟩six roads meet, or where a river branches or falls, or where the ↑pan of↓ soil is a little deeper. The horizon line marked by hills tossing like waves in a storm: firm indigo line. 'Tis a pretty revolution which is [187] effected in the landscape by simply turning your head upside down, or, looking through your legs: an infinite softness & loveliness is added to the picture.[185] It changes the landscape at once from November to June. Or as Ellery declared makes *Campagna* of it at once; so he said, Massachusetts is Italy upside down.

"When Nature is forsaken by her lord be she ever so good she does not survive." [186]

[188] William of Wykeham was born at Wykeham in 1324 in the 18th year of Edward II. and died 1404 aged 80 years[.]
is said to have been brought to Court & employed by Edward III at 23[.]

In October 1356, he is made surveyor ⟨at⟩of the king's works at the Castle & in the Park of Windsor[.]

[183] This paragraph is used in "Powers and Laws of Thought," *W*, XII, 27.

[184] The "Sudbury Inn" was known as "Howe's Tavern," after its original builder, until 1863, when Longfellow published *Tales of a Wayside Inn.* Sometime later it became known as "The Wayside Inn."

[185] With this sentence, cf. "Nature," *W*, I, 51: "Turn the eyes upside down, by looking at the landscape through your legs, and how agreeable is the picture, though you have seen it any time these twenty years!"

[186] *The Hĕĕtōpădēs of Vĕĕshnōō-Sărmā, in a Series of Connected Fables, Interspersed with Moral, Prudential, and Political Maxims . . . ,* trans. Charles Wilkins (Bath, 1787), p. 230, altered, in Emerson's library. See *JMN*, VIII, 14.

By his advice, the king was induced to pull down great part of the Castle, & to rebuild it in the magnificent manner in which, upon the whole, it now appears.
Warden, justiciary, privy counsellor, sent to treat of the ransom of the King of Scotland, 1365,
All his ⟨liv⟩ ecclesiastical livings together amounted to 873 pounds a year, in 1366[.]

Froissart says "At this time reigned a priest called William of Wykeham in favour with the King of England, that every thing was done by him, & nothing was done without him."
[189] made bishop of ⟨V⟩W⟨e⟩inchester Oct. 1367
Then Chancellor of England
He /explored/inquired into/ the abuses & embezzlements of the funds of the Bishopric & of the charities & foundations Hospital of St Cross, &c & had them redressed.[187]

[190] 26 November.

Yesterday walked over Lincoln ⟨p⟩hills with Ellery, & saw golden willows, savins with two foliages, old ches↑t↓nuts, apples as ever, E. said, "Old Bass & Abrams were come upon us; Bass at Stow, and Abrams at Weston 'had a comfortable situation.' Ah! when they went out, we ought to have had the Athenaeum: Bradford for head librarian, and I for Abrams. Bradford could have done Bass, & come up the trapdoor; & I could have done the stiff heel very well, with a pair of high shoes."[188]

[191] I understand Dr C[harles].T.J[ackson]. that a piece of ⟨s⟩ordnance may usually be fired 1000 times before it will burst, & only so many times; [n] that it is the rule in the U.S. service, that one piece of each new kind of fire arm should be burst; and that Jen⟨n⟩ks's Rifle was fired by a sergeant & man⟨,⟩ ↑appointed to that service↓ 66000 times, when last heard from, & was not yet burst.[189]

[187] Emerson's notes on Wykeham on pp. [188]–[189] derive from Robert Lowth, *The Life of William of Wykeham . . .* , 1759, pp. 3, 4, 18–21, 28–29, 36, 37, 40, 49, 72–92.

[188] Bass and Abrams are unidentified; Emerson's third reference is probably to George P. Bradford, a lifelong friend since they were students together at the Harvard Divinity School.

[189] "appointed to that service" is written above "& man⟨,⟩ 66000 times," perhaps

The Doctor described the wonderful mirage of Lake Superior; and the analysed sounds; and the aurora borealis. ↑the air in the woods at 100, the water at 38.↓
The osars or horsebacks, so familiar in our woods, are made, he says, by the combing of waves?

A ⟨man is⟩robin, says Agassiz, (embryonic), is a gull; a gull is a duck; a duck is a fish; add[n] now what I suppose is omitted, pro causa conciliandi gratiam,[190] that a man [192] is a robin,—and the chain is perfect, a man is a fish.[191]

We all like a good superlative. Mitchell in Nantucket showed me a nebula in Orion with his telescope, and assured me it was a great way off.[192] At the Bank of England they are accustomed to put a million of money into the hand of the visiter.[193] Every body climbs Mont Blanc,—if he can; nor will travellers rest until they have looked off Himalaya. We go under the flood of Niagara at Table Rock. The Flying Childers who ran a mile a minute, must be seen, is[?] to see; and General Thumb, the smallest man that ever grew,—or grew not.[194]

[193] 1. I wrote above p. 97, that, once for all, you must honour the people's facts, or, in other words, make largest allowance for Fate, or you arrive at absurdity, with what talent or genius soever. It is not for nothing, that ↑very↓ few heads are sent into the world busy with

---

as an alternate reading for "& man⟨,⟩". Dr. Charles T. Jackson, brother of Lidian Emerson, chemist and mineralogist, made a geological survey of the mineral lands around Lake Superior, the source of his observations reported in the paragraph immediately below.

190 "for the sake of winning favor" (Ed.).

191 In the winter of 1848–1849, Emerson may have heard Louis Agassiz lecture at the Lowell Institute on his recent findings concerning fish and other specimens at Lake Superior; at least, by 1850, Emerson knew of these lectures (see Journal AZ, p. [49] below).

192 Henry Mitchell (1830–1902), born in Nantucket, was a hydrographer.

193 The paragraph to this point is used in "The Superlative," *W*, X, 172.

194 Flying Childers, a horse bred by Leonard Childers and later owned by the Duke of Devonshire, was known to have run the course at Newmarket at a speed of one mile in a minute. Emerson records his seeing Tom Thumb on p. [140] above.

abstractions, & very many heads busy with making money. Accept the order of the world, though it make you a shopkeeper.
2. That is one thing; the second thing which comes often to mind, lately, is, the conviction that our security is in the reactive force which develops all kinds of energy at the same time, the ecstasies of devotion with the exasperations of debauchery. Get energy, & you get all.[195]
See p. 156

[194] ↑*Drill*↓

December 10. Great is drill. I read somewhere without surprise, that John P. Kemble said, that the worst provincial company of actors would go through a play better than the best amateur company. I am sure it is true; and that the worst regular troops would beat the best volunteers; and that for performance, for net result, your man must have become a tool.[196]

"None any work can frame,
Until himself become the same." [197]

See p 164, ↑& ⟨1⟩280.↓

H[enry] T[horeau] is still falling on some bold volunteer like his Dr Heaton who discredits the regulars; but HT, like all the rest of sensible men, when he is sick, will go to Jackson & Warren.[198]

[195] T.W. Higginson at Newburyport urged the establishment of such a journal as the Dial for the comfort & encouragement of

[195] "That is . . . all.", struck through in ink with a vertical use mark, is used in "Power," *W*, VI, 64.

[196] "Great is . . . tool." is struck through in ink with single diagonal and vertical use marks; "Great is . . . volunteers;" is used in "Power," *W*, VI, 77–78. John Philip Kemble (1757–1823) was a noted English actor.

[197] Thomas Stanley, *The History of Philosophy* . . . , 1701, p. 179 [the second p. 179, which is an error for p. 197 in this edition]. The couplet is used in "Poetry and Imagination," *W*, VIII, 43. See *JMN*, IX, 262.

[198] James Jackson (1777–1867), Hersey Professor of Medicine at the Harvard Medical School, was a founder of the Massachusetts General Hospital, along with John Collins Warren, professor of anatomy and surgery at Harvard. Dr. Heaton is unidentified.

young men, who, but for that paper had felt themselves lonely & unsupported in the world.[199]

[196] Punch notices, ↑that↓ in the ↑late↓ hard times, ⟨that⟩ Saturn has lately appeared without his rings, and that the other planets openly accuse him of having pawned them.

⟨"Perfidious Albion"⟩ [200]

The "Freeman's Journal" (?) advises England to ↑make haste &↓ sell Ireland to the Americans, whilst islands are in fashion; for, in a short time, Jonathan won't look at any thing but continents.[201]

[197] [blank]

[198] Carlyle looks for such an one as himself. He would willingly give way to you & listen, if you would declaim to him as he declaims to you: but he will not find such a mate; but the only talk I care for, short plain dealing, the communication of results, (as when Dalton & Dana met, & communicated by scratching down chemical formulas on bits of paper, each surprising the other with authentic proof of a chemist,) *that* [n] he does not care for.[202]

[199] ↑George Sand↓ ↑(See LM 130, 145, 162,)↓

Admirable ⟨ce⟩expressions of George Sand. In "*Jeanne*," vol.II p. 51, "M. Harley ⟨w⟩voulut [n] répondre, mais il fut bientôt contredit et battu par Marsillat, qui avait la parole plus facile, et qui était à cheval sur une logique plus claire."

[199] Thomas Wentworth Higginson (1823–1911), reformer, author, soldier, became pastor of the First Religious Society in Newburyport, Mass., in 1847.

[200] This phrase is used in "Truth," *W*, V, 123. Quoted by Napoleon, and current in French pamphlets and the press during the French Revolution, its source is apparently Jacques Bossuet, *Sermon on the Circumcision* (1652).

[201] Emerson's Account Book 5 (1849–1853) lists a subscription to the Concord "Middlesex Freeman" for one year, "from Oct. 1 [1849]"; originally the *Concord Freeman*, it changed its name in 1848 and is possibly the "Freeman's Journal" of this entry.

[202] The story of the meeting between the English chemist, John Dalton (1766–1844), and the American chemist, Samuel L. Dana (1795–1868), is expanded in "Clubs," *W*, VII, 238–239.

Mais si ça m'ôte un plaisir, ça m'ôte aussi une peine.[203]

Compagnon du Tour de France

Qui peut le plus, peut le moins.

La grandeur n'est pas dans l'étendue, mais dans la proportion, et que l'on peut faire mesquinement un colosse d Architecture, tandis qu'on peut donner l'apparence de ↑la↓ hauteur et de la force à un modèle de quelques pouces.

Ces arabesques semées avec tant de richesse et de sobriété a la fois, car ceci est encor⟨l⟩e la meme question; *peu de moyens, beaucoup d'effet.* ⟨vol⟩ p 208 [204]

[200] *Action rare.*

Men live on the defensive, and go through life without an action, without one overt act, one initiated action. They buy stock, because others do, and stave off want & pain the best they can, defending themselves; but to carry the war into the enemy's country↑;↓ to live from life within, & ⟨express⟩ impress on the world their own form, they dare [n] ⟨never⟩ ↑not↓.[205] Thousands & thousands vegetate in this way, streets full, towns full, & never an action in them all.

All the talk that goes on is like chat on the way to church, to pass the time. When that is spoken which has a right to be spoken all this chattering will gladly stop.[206]

[201] Nature ↑Printed in May-Day↓ [207]

The earth takes the part of her children so quickly & adopts our

[203] The two quotations are from *Jeanne*, 2 vols. (Brussels and Leipzig, 1844), II, 50–51 and 56.

[204] George Sand, *Le Compagnon du Tour de France*, 1843. For "*peu . . . d'effet.*", see p. [45] above.

[205] The semicolon after "country", the cancellation of "never", and the addition of "not" are in pencil. Also in pencil are the numbers "2" below the canceled "never", and "1" below "dare", indicating that Emerson intended "they dare never" before his final change to "they dare not."

[206] This paragraph and the entries below on p. [201] are in pencil.

[207] Added in pencil, probably by Edward Emerson.

thoughts, affections, & quarrels.* The schoolboy finds every step of the ground on his way to school acquainted with his quarrel, & smartly expressing it. The ground knows so well his top & ball, the air itself is full of hoop-time, ball-time, swimming, sled, & skates. So ductile is the world. The rapt prophet finds it not less facile & intelligent. 'Tis Pentecost all, the rose speaks all languages[,] the sense of all affections[,] Parthians, Jews, Mesopotamians, Greeks, ↑French,↓ English[.] [208]

[202] [209] Courage of Archimedes[.] If he had courage of heart he would be a gone Archimedes; it [n] is by pounding on his problem, ↑by↓ being pure brain, that he suffers the soldier to kill him without a pang,[210]

Fate in the mixture of the children, one having life in, the other life outside herself, the best antidote to fortune is the religious determination[.] Fate Fate. Well settle this then[;] the nobility of the sentiments is in resisting that or in accepting it.

[203] Here is a blessed piece of realism from George Sand's joiner Pierre.

"Content d'avoir acquis les talents qu'il avait ambitionnés, il attendait que l'occasion de les faire apprecier vint d'ellemême, et ⟨ell⟩il savait bien qu'elle ne tarderait pas."

Le Compagnon du tour de France [1843,]
p. 24

£1000,000,000 Eng capital [211]

---

* The girl finds her chamber enchanted and all her walks with the dear dream[.] [212]

[208] With the entry to "skates", cf. "May-Day," ll. 66–69, *W*, IX, 165. For "the rose . . . languages", see *Nature*, *W*, I, 1, epigraph, l. 4.

[209] P. [202] is in pencil.

[210] With this entry, cf. "Courage," *W*, VII, 270. Plutarch's account of Archimedes' courage and death during the defense of Syracuse is noted in *JMN*, VI, 56.

[211] Cf. "Wealth," *W*, V, 160: "A thousand million of pounds sterling are said to compose the floating money of commerce."

[212] Emerson turned this sentence into a couplet in his Notebook NP, a couplet which Edward Emerson points out was omitted from "May-Day" (*W*, IX, 456): "Her cottage chamber, wall and beam, / Glows with the maid's delicious dream."

⟨no corporat⟩ stock companies in mills

———

you might pick up in the street richer men than ⟨L⟩A.L.

———

Konghele

———

Beckford

———

Hope [213]

Dr Johnson thought you would remember who kicked your shins last [214]
James Northcote
King Réné [215]

[204] Dec. 22, 1848.

Directly on the dreadful calamity of young George Emerson's death, comes to me one of my highest prosperities. I received Clough's poem at the bookstore, whilst pondering the dare or dare not of a visit to Pemberton Square.[216]

[213] A. L. could be Abbott Lawrence (1792–1855), who gave or willed large sums to Harvard, the Boston Public Library, and poor Irish for housing; or his brother Amos (1786–1852), who gave an estimated $700,000 to worthy causes. In "Race," *W*, V, 62, Emerson says that "Konghelle, the town where the kings of Norway, Sweden and Denmark were wont to meet, is now rented to a private English gentleman for a hunting ground." William Beckford (1760–1844), author of *Vathek*, expended enormous sums in decorating his residence, Fonthill. In a letter to Lidian, "London, April 2 and 6, 1848," Emerson spoke of a "Mr Hope, reputed the richest commoner in England. . . ." He is identified as James Robert Hope, later Hope-Scott (1812–1873), who married Sir Walter Scott's granddaughter (*L*, IV, 47).

[214] This entry is used in "Memory," *W*, XII, 105.

[215] "£1000,000,000 . . . Réné" is in pencil. James Northcote (1746–1831) was an English portrait painter; René I (1409–1480), Duke of Anjou and Lorraine, Count of Provence and Piedmont, and King of Naples, was a poet, painter, and patron of troubadour poets and artists (see *JMN*, VIII, 370).

[216] George Samuel Emerson was the son of Emerson's lifelong friend and second cousin, George Barrell Emerson. The poem from Arthur Hugh Clough, whom Emerson had met in England, was *The Bothie of Toper-na-Fuosich* (1848). Perhaps Emerson's "dare or dare not of a visit to Pemberton Square." was to see Nathaniel

'Tis, I think, the most real benefit I have had from my English visit, this genius of Clough. How excellent, yet how slow to show itself! He gave no hint of all this to me, & I learned to esteem him for reticent sense, for solidity, & tenacity, after he had given proof of his apprehensiveness & of his thorough Oxford culture, which was manifest enough. An Oxonian is a kind of nobleman, of course. Then he had that [205] interest in life & realities in the state of woman & the questions so rife in Paris through Communism, and through the old loose & easy conventions of that city for travellers,—he talked so considerately of the Grisette estate, that I found him the best *pièce de resistance*, & tough adherence, that one could desire. But I never surmised that this flowing all-applicable expression belonged to him. Where had he concealed it? And now Tennyson must look to his laurels. And now ⟨we⟩I have a new friend, & the world has a new poet.

[206]–[207] [blank]
[208] Tests
Have you given any words to be the current coin of the country? Carlyle has.
What all men think, he thinks better.

Carlyle is thought a bad writer. Is he? Wherever you find good writing in Dorian or Rabelaisian, or Norse Saga, or English Bible, or Cromwell himself, 'tis odd, you find resemblance to his style.

[209] ↑Superlative↓
The bray of the ass is our symbol of stupid noise.

[210] English wit See p 196, 75,
Lord H⟨a⟩ervey(?) said, that villa was too small for a house, & too large to hang at your watch chain.[217]

I. Bowditch who lived there; a trustee of the Massachusetts General Hospital, Bowditch was currently involved in the dispute over the development of anesthesia between William Morton and Emerson's brother-in-law, Dr. Charles T. Jackson (see Journal TU, p. [67] below).

[217] Emerson has left a space after "said, that", presumably to fill in later the name of the villa. Hervey may be John Hervey (1696–1743), Baron Hervey of Ickworth, author of *Memoirs of the Reign of George II.*

[211] [blank]

[212] The older Edda of which Snorro Sturleson's is but an epitome, is attributed to Saemund[,] born A.D. 105⟨6⟩7, in Iceland. Only three fragments of it are extant; Voluspa, Havamal, Magic. The Younger Edda, 120 years later, by Snorro Sturleson, is a commentary on the Voluspa.

[213] Where there is a common language between the authors & the mob, "the intellectuality of the educated class works down," ⟨th-r⟩ to use Laing's word.
He says, "no sentiment, p⟨r⟩hrase, popular idea, or expression from the works of Lessing, Goethe, Schiller, Richter or any other German writer is ever heard among the lower classes ⟨of⟩ ↑in↓ Germany" because of the wide difference between their Plat-Deutsch ⟨f⟩and the written language.[218]

I should say, that, in English, only those sentences stand, which ⟨t⟩are good both for the scholar & the cabman, Latin & Saxon; half & half; perfectly Latin & perfectly English.

[214] [219] Iceland was civilised & learned. Thence came the Scalds. ⟨It was the⟩ ↑What↓ New England is to South[,] that was Iceland to Norway. The Christian Iceland filled out no viking expeditions; but[n] young Icelanders sometimes joined the Northmen's. So ⟨Am⟩ Mass & R Island fit out no slavetrade yet the Dewolfs go[.] [220]
Rise of Hanseatic ⟨towns⟩ League & wealth of west of Europe ⟨pu⟩ extinguished these pests of Vikings[.]
And Scald fell before clerk with his pen & ink as ⟨P⟩Viking before Eng. Trade[.]
And as stage coach before railroad

[218] "He says . . . language.", struck through in ink with a vertical use mark, is used in "Ability," *W*, V, 100. Cf. Samuel Laing, *Notes of a Traveller on the Social and Political State of France, Prussia, Switzerland, Italy* . . . (Philadelphia, 1846), pp. 261, 256.

[219] The entries on p. [214] are in pencil except that the dotting of the "i" and the crossing of the "t" in "with" in "clerk with his pen" are added in ink.

[220] James DeWolf (1764–1837) was a U.S. senator, manufacturer, and slave-trader from Rhode Island.

[215] Iceland 63 or 64 000 souls

"The enterprising & restless spirits found occupation abroad in the roving viking expeditions of the Norwegians; for the Icelanders fitted out no viking expeditions: while the equally ambitious but more peaceful & cultivated appear to have acquired property & honor as Scalds, in no inconsiderable number. But the rise of the Hanseatic League, & the advance of the West of Europe in civilization, trade & naval power, had extinguished the Vikings on the sea. They were no longer in public estimation exercising an allowable or honorable profession, but were treated as common robbers, & punished.
The diffusion of Xy[Christianity] & of a lettered clergy over the Scandinavian Peninsula had, in the same age, superseded the Scalds, even as recorders of law ⟨or⟩ & history. The Scald, with his saga & his traditional verses, gave way at once before the clerk with his paper, pen, & ink. Both occupations, viking & Scald, fell in one generation, in end of 12 & beginning of 13th Century."

Heimskringla Vol1p[p.] 196[–197, trans.] *Laing* [1844]

[216] *Heimskringla.*
Edda

Odin's people↑, the Asalanders,↓ n & the V⟨i⟩analanders "made peace & exchanged hostages. The Vanaland people sent their best men, Niord & Frey. The people of Asaland sent Haener a stout & very handsome man, and with him they sent a man of great understanding called Mimir.

Now when Haener came to Vanaheim, he was immediately made a chief & Mimir came to him with good counsel on all occasions. But when Haener stood in the Things, ⟨&⟩ ↑or↓ other meetings, if Mimir was not near him, & any difficult matter was laid before him, he always answered in one way, 'Now let others give their advice', so that the Vanaland people got a suspicion that the Asaland people [217] had deceived them in the exchange of men."

Heimskringla, [trans. Laing, 1844,] Vol. 1, p. 218—

So it seems that in early ages a man is valued for intrinsic qualities, as a horse or a dog is, & not for his name or accidents; and that it was the wise policy of contending tribes, to adopt each a firstrate man from the other, & make him a chief, & so weave friendly relations between tribes.[221]

↑choice of a dog
& of Olaf by Q. G⟨u⟩yda↓ [222]

Scald craft, see an important paragraph in *Heimskringla*, [trans. Laing, 1844,] Vol. I, p. 221.[223]

[218] [blank]

[219] ↑*1849*↓ [224]

The word God is the algebraic × in morals, and the Hebrews with right philosophy made it unspeakable. But the stupid world finding a word, assumes this scientific for a baptismal name, and talks of him as easily as of Captain Gulliver.

[220] Quetelet

Circumstance

Napoleon said, "View man as we may, he is as much the result of his physical & moral atmosphere, as of his own organization." *Quetelet.* p 82 [225]

Destiny

"Every thing which pertains to the human species considered as a whole, belongs to the order of physical facts." Quetelet. [*A Treatise on Man* . . ., 1842,] p 96

[221] "So it . . . tribes.", struck through in pencil with a diagonal use mark, is used in "Aristocracy," *W*, X, 41.

[222] "choice . . . G⟨u⟩yda" is in pencil. In *The Heimskringla*, an Irish peasant asked Olaf Tryggvesson to return the cows that belonged to him. Olaf agreed, if the peasant could distinguish his cows. The peasant sent his dog into the herd of many hundred, and the dog drove out the exact number the peasant asked for. Olaf wished to buy the dog; the peasant preferred to give the dog to him and did so; and Olaf gave the peasant a gold ring (I, 400–401). Queen Gyda, sister of the king of Dublin and daughter of the king of Ireland, asked Olaf if he would have her if she chose him for husband. Olaf said, "I will not say no to that," and the two were betrothed (I, 399–400).

[223] Emerson copied most of the paragraph on p. [224] below.

[224] Added in pencil, probably by Edward Emerson.

[225] Lambert A. J. Quételet, *A Treatise on Man and the Development of his Faculties*, trans. Dr. R. Knox (Edinburgh, 1842).

"the greater", he continues, "the number of individuals, the more does the influence of individual will disappear, leaving predominance to a series of general facts, dependent on causes by which society exists & is preserved." [*Ibid.*]

[221] *Quetelet*

"The people are almost always richer in nations called *poor*, than in those called *rich*," said M. de Tracey. [*Ibid.*, p. 38]

Quetelet's problem is to write the biography of the Average Man.

---

[222] Art is the power to execute details without losing the view of the whole.

[223] [226] *Tickets to*

x	E[douard] Desor — Cabot —	2		Boston Post	I
	C[harles] T Jackson	2		Transcript	I
	J[ohn] S[ullivan] Dwight	I		Journal	I
	G[eorge] B[arrell] E[merson]	3	x	Traveller	I
	Mrs [E.C.] Goodwin	2		Atlas	I
	G[eorge] P Bradford	I			
	A[mos] B[ronson] Alcott	3	x		
	Scherb	I			
	⟨Bangs⟩				
	E[lizabeth]. Prichard	2			
	J[ames] F[reeman] Clarke	2	x		
	S[arah]. Clarke	I	x		
	E[lizabeth]. P[almer]. Peabody	2	x		
	W[illiam] H[enry] Channing	I	x		
	E[lizur] Wright	I			
	E[lizabeth] Hoar	2			
	R F[rederic] Fuller	I			
	A[bel] Adams [227]	3			

[226] P. [223] is in pencil.

[227] The "*Tickets*" for the recipients in this list were undoubtedly to the lectures in the series "Mind and Manners in the 19th Century," given in Boston beginning January 15, 1849. Of those listed who have not been previously identified or are

[224] *Heimskringla*

"Odin spoke everything in rhyme such as now composed, & which we call scaldcraft. He & his temple-gods were called song-smiths," &c. "Odin could make his enemies in battle blind, or deaf, or terrorstruck, & their weapons so blunt that they could no more cut than a willow twig. ⟨On the other hand,⟩ His [n] men rushed forwards without armour; were ⟨as⟩ mad as ⟨dogs, or⟩ wolves, bit their shields; were as strong as bears or wild bulls; & killed people at a blow; ⟨&⟩ neither fire nor iron told on them. These were called Bersaerkers"

Heimskringla [trans. Laing, 1844,] vol. 1, p.221

"He (Odin) taught these arts in Runes & songs, which are called incantations, & therefore the Asaland people are called *incantation-smiths*." [*Ibid.*,] p. 222,

[225] ↑Heimskringla↓

"for there were many seakings who ruled over many people, but had no lands; & he might well be called a seaking, who never slept ⟨under⟩beneath sooty roof timbers."

[*Ibid.*,] vol. 1. p 246

[226] *Chartism*

At Sheffield, the humour of the operatives was particularly bad, nor would they suffer any mason or carpenter to come from London to build the Mechanics' Institute; and they themselves had entered into some ten-hour covenant, which the Managers of the Mechanics' Institute thought unjust.

At Leicester, Mr Cobden himself was unable to obtain a hearing at a public meeting.

---

not easily recognizable, Edouard Desor was a geologist; John Sullivan Dwight, a music critic and member of Brook Farm; George Barrell Emerson, a second cousin and teacher; Mrs. E. C. Goodwin, a cook in Emerson's house. Emmanuel Vitalis Scherb was a German patriot, exile, and poet from Basel, living apparently in Concord. Emerson heard him lecture in 1851 (Journal CO, p. [202] below). Edward Bangs was a young Harvard graduate of Boston, studying law; Elizabeth, the daughter of Moses Prichard of Concord; James Freeman Clarke, Unitarian clergyman, writer, founder and pastor of the Church of the Disciples, Boston; Sarah Freeman Clarke, sister of James. Elizabeth Palmer Peabody operated a bookshop in Boston. William Henry Channing, nephew of William Ellery Channing the elder, was a Unitarian minister; Elizur Wright, editor of the associationist *Daily Chronotype* of Boston; Elizabeth Hoar, daughter of the Concord lawyer, Samuel; Richard Frederic Fuller, younger brother of Margaret. Abel Adams was a Boston banker and Emerson's financial adviser.

At Leicester, Mr Biggs told me that it was sufficient that a man should be a manufacturer or master, to deprive him of all voice or right to be heard at a public meeting.

Foster ⟨at⟩of Rawdon, said [227] something like that at Bradford.[228]

[228] XIX Century
Peculiarities
Its great miscellany requires longevity.

'tis the age of tools[229]

and of cash payment RS 57, 63,

California
Newspapers

[229] Energy is all. Indian rule shames graham rule. Thrifty tree & not arts of cure. Manure the best scraper.
E 165
Human nature in its wildest forms most virtuous V 132
Friction of the social machine absorbs all the power W 17[230]
Antony's diet.[231]

[230] Whatever is good is effective, ⟨productive⟩ generative. An apple reproduces seed, a hybrid or monster does not. If a man is a man, working ↑there↓ by authority, I shall find, that, as the river makes its shores, so he has made grand institutions, weapons, disciples, to work by & live on, harvests, also, to eat, that he may work more. But DIsraeli still stands in his shoes, & has no planet under him.[232] Call you that a man, or natural power? 'Tis a dandy, a frippery.

[228] Joseph Biggs entertained Emerson when he lectured at Leicester in December, 1847. "Foster" is probably William E. Forster, Emerson's host in Rawdon in January, 1848 (*L*, IV, 3).

[229] "tis . . . tools" is used in "Works and Days," *W*, VII, 157.

[230] "Friction . . . W 17" is in pencil.

[231] Emerson may possibly refer to: "Thou didst drink / The stale of horses and the gilded puddle / Which beasts would cough at." Shakespeare, *Antony and Cleopatra*, I, iv, 61–63.

[232] "Whatever is . . . more." is struck through in ink with a vertical use mark; "Whatever is . . . him." is used in "Uses of Great Men," *W*, IV, 7.

[231] F. went to Father Taylor's prayer-meeting, & an old salt told his experiences, and how intemperate he had been for many years; "but now, dear brother," said he, "Jesus Christ is my grog shop". Father Taylor, ↑thereupon,↓ recommended to his brethren to be short, & sit down when they had done.[233]

[232] The new electrical light in London puts out the gas. The old yellow oil light is avenged. What gas did for that, is now done for gas, by this new lustre. There is no night longer for London. 'Tis time the Nelson column was finished; its defects were charitably hidden for twelve hours, hitherto; but now, it stares in broad light, without an interval. There is no more night. A good lamp is ⟨better⟩ the best police. I wrote formerly what seemed the experience of some of our rural Socialists, [233] that the purity of the sexes depended on plainspeaking, and that to redress the wronged pudency, it needed— to come nearer. A good lamp is the best police.[234]

Extirpation is the only cure.
↑Amputation for headache↓ [235]

The proof of his humanity amounts to this, that ↑driving out↓ on one occasion he did ↑not↓ run over a child, when he had a good opportunity.

---

[234] Perhaps one of the most real advantages of railroads & now of California, to the people of New England, will be, the knowledge of geography which they diffuse.

If a man is going to California, he announces it with some hesitation; because it is a confession that he has failed at home.

"A locomotive engine must be put together as carefully as a watch," says Robert Stephenson.[236]

[233] Edward Taylor (1793–1871) was the pastor of the Seamen's Bethel in Boston.

[234] This sentence is used in "Worship," *W*, VI, 224. With "I wrote . . . police.", cf. *JMN*, X, 377.

[235] Added in pencil.

[236] Robert Stephenson (1803–1859), English engineer and son of George

[235] You tell me they are hospitable in Germany; yes,[n] but I do not travel to find hospitable people. If I knew of any magnet that would ⟨show⟩ point to that quarter where are the people whom I wish to see, I would sell all to buy it, & to travel in the direction it indicated, though to Samarcand, ⟨a⟩or to Timbuctoo.[237]

[236] It is the policy of the English to plant a clearheaded, generous, & energetic gentleman at every important point all along their immense colonial territory in islands or on the main, in the shape of a ⟨diplomatic⟩ military, or diplomatic⟨e⟩, or, at least, commercial agent. These Clives, Hastingses, Brookes, Cannings, Ponsonbys, Hardinges,   carry the eye & heart of the best circles of London into the extremities of the earth & the homes[n] of almost bestial barbarism.[238]

[237] [blank]

[238] From "*a Treatie of humane learning.*"

Music instructs me which be lyric moods,
Let her instruct me rather how to show
No weeping voice for loss of Fortune's goods.
Geometry gives measure to th' earth below;
  Rather let her instruct me how to measure
  What is enough for need, what fit for pleasure.
[ll. 187–192]

She teacheth how to lose nought in my bounds,
And I would learn with joy to lose them all;
The Artist shows which way to measure Rounds,
But I would know how first man's mind did fall,
  How great it was, how little now it is,
  And what that knowledge was which wrought us this.
[ll. 193–198]

Fulke Greville, Lord Brooke.[239]

Stephenson, was manager of the Newcastle locomotive works. Cf. "Eloquence," *W*, VIII, 117: "He is put together like a Waltham watch, or like a locomotive just finished at the Tredegar works."

[237] This paragraph is struck through in ink with a vertical use mark.

[238] This paragraph is struck through in pencil with a vertical use mark; see Appendix I.

[239] See *The Works in Verse and Prose Complete* . . . , 4 vols. (1870), II, 18–19.

[239] "For which respects, learning hath found distaste
In governments of great & glorious fame,
In Lacedaemon scorned & disgrac⟨e⟩'d
As idle, vain, effeminate, & lame:
Engines that did unman the minds of men
From action, to seek glory in a den.
Lord Brooke ["A Treatie of Humane Learning," ll. 247–252]

———

"So words must sparks be of those fires they strike"
[*Ibid.*, l. 660]

———

"Since to be reverenced, loved, obeyed, & known,
Man must effect with powers above his own."
Lord Brooke, [*An Inquisition upon*] *Fame & Honor* [ll. 227–228]

———

"All what the world admires comes from within;
A doom whereby the sin condemns the sin."
Ld. Brooke [*An Inquisition upon*] *Fame & Honor* [ll. 503–504]

[240] In Europe, every church is a kind of book or bible, so covered is it with inscriptions & pictures.[240]

I saw on Saturday at Ward's the Ludovisi Juno, which is again one of the miracles of old sculpture, & indeed of human art, as ⟨ra⟩unaccountable as Shakspeare's drama. There was never that face or figure in nature, from which it could be modelled. I am sure that the artist [241] drew from a cloud when he ⟨fas⟩moulded these features. Then the Jove's head was a combed mountain.[241]

[242] Trivium included Grammar, Logic, & Rhetoric; Quadrivium,—Arithmetic; Geometry; Astronomy; & Music. Maxim, "that the University has its foundation in Arts."[242]

[240] This sentence, struck through in ink with two diagonal use marks, is used in "Religion," *W*, V, 218.

[241] Samuel Gray Ward may have shown Emerson a print of a sculpture in the Ludovisi Palace in Rome.

[242] Victor Aimé Huber, *The English Universities* . . . , trans. Francis W. Newman, 2 vols. in 3 (London, 1843), I, 34, 4n. The entry is struck through in pencil with a diagonal use mark.

[243] When Cambridge was a barn—

"Monks of Croyland 1109–1124 under then abbot Goisfred taught at a farm called Cottenham near Cambridge & afterwards in a barn at Cambridge itself"[243] Huber [*The English Universities* . . . , 1843,] vol 1 p[p. 61–]62

[244] We never think much of those who think much of us.

Perhaps the French Revolution of 1848 was not worth the trees it cut down on the Boulevards of Paris.

Huber, the German.

"The English universities content themselves with producing the first & most distinctive flower of the national life a well educated Gentleman. I cannot enter into any exact definition of the Old English Gentleman, but I hope no one need be offended by my saying, that, *we* have nothing of the kind. A gentleman must possess ⟨the⟩a political character, an independent & public position or, at least, the right of assuming it. He must farther have average opulence, with landed property, [245][244] either of his own, or in the family, a condition not very easily fulfilled among us. He should also have bodily activity & strength, unattainable by our sedentary life in public offices. The race of English Gentlemen, certainly presents, or rather did present an appearance of manly vigour & form not elsewhere to be found among an equal number of persons, no other Nation produces the stock, and, in England itself, it has already been much deteriorated.[245]
What comes nearest to the English Gentlem⟨e⟩an, is, the Castilian Cavallero.

↑xxx↓ The University was a decisive *presumption* in any man's favor, &, as it were, his final stamp. The cultivation of the faculties was more thought of than [246] the amount of knowledge acquired."[246]

[Huber, *The English Universities* . . . , 1843, II, 320–322]

[243] "When Cambridge . . . itself'" is struck through in pencil with two diagonal use marks.

[244] "Huber" is written in the top margin of p. [245] as an index heading.

[245] Victor Aimé Huber, *The English Universities* . . . , 1843, II, 320–321. "'The English universities . . . deteriorated.", struck through in ink with single diagonal and vertical use marks on p. [244] and a vertical use mark on p. [245], is used in "Universities," *W*, V, 208–209.

[246] "Huber", an index heading, is written in ink in the top margin of p. [246] and underlined in ink with a circular line curving up to the top of the page. "The

"If we include all the members *on the books*, excluding those who only once belonged to the university, we find the ⟨me⟩numbers to be not less than 3000 ⟨at⟩in Oxford, & nearly as many ⟨in⟩at Cambridge, among whom, are some hundreds of the most celebrated or most exalted personages in the kingdom, clerical & lay. In fact, a glance at the university calendars may convince us, that in all the world one cannot be in better company, than on the books of one of the larger Oxford or Cambridge Colleges." [247]

[*Ibid.*,] vol II, p[p]. [323–]324

[247] ↑*Huber*↓

"The Body of Fellows comprises from two to three ⟨t⟩hundred [n] men who pass ⟨t⟩several years, & sometimes their whole lives, at the University, in a position of great respectability, ⟨&⟩ even externally, & in whose sentiment & cultivation, the real support of the corporate spirit is found." [*Ibid.*, II, 325]

[248] "Seculum hoc humanum non est seculum." [248]

"⟨Tres⟩Quatuor (tres) in hominibus distinxi conditiones apertas evidentes. Est cui vita haec arcta, quem gloriosa altera consequitur. Est cui vita haec est excellens, ast postea non erit vita sequens. Est qui utramque amittens, nec hanc, nec sequentem vitam, habea⟨n⟩t." [249]

Ali Ben Abu Taleb

[249] ↑*Spirit of the Age*↓

Now th⟨e⟩at the man was ready, the horse was brought. The timeliness of this invention of the locomotive must be conceded. To us Americans, it seems to have fallen as a political aid. We could not else have held the vast North America together, which now we engage to do. It was strange, too, that when it was time to build a road across to the Pacific [—] a railroad, a shiproad, a telegraph, & in short a perfect communication ⟨for⟩in every manner for all nations [—] 'twas strange to see how it is secured. The good World-Soul under-

---

University . . . acquired.'" is struck through in ink with a vertical use mark on p. [245] and three diagonal use marks on p. [246]. "The University . . . favor," is used in "Universities," *W*, V, 209.

[247] This paragraph is struck through in ink with two diagonal use marks; the last sentence is used in "Universities," *W*, V, 209.

[248] "This human age is not an age" (Edward Emerson).

[249] "Among men, I have noticed three obvious and evident conditions: he who finds the present life narrow, but followed by another glorious one; he who finds this life splendid, but followed by no other; he who, wasting both, enjoys life neither here nor hereafter" (Ed.).

stands us well. How simple the means. Suddenly the Californian soil is spangled with a little gold [250] dust here & there, in a mill race, in a mountain cleft, an Indian picks up a little, ⟨a⟩ a farmer, & a hunter, & a soldier, each a little; the news flies here & there, to New York, to Maine, to London, and an army of a hundred thousand picked volunteers[,] the ablest & keenest & boldest that could be collected instantly organize & embark for this desart bringing ⟨not only all⟩ tools, instruments, books, & framed houses, with them↑.↓ ⟨to⟩ Such a⟨s⟩ ↑well appointed↓ Colony as ⟨was⟩never was planted before [251] arrive with the speed of sail & steam on these remote shores, bringing with them ⟨the pledge &⟩ the necessity ⟨& the means⟩ that their government shall ⟨hasten⟩ instantly proceed to make the road which they themselves are all intimately engaged to assist.

It was strange too that all over the world about the same moment mineral treasures were uncovered. We heard of gold in various parts of the United States; in ⟨Russia,⟩ ↑Siberia; in Africa on the Tomat river near Cassan↓ & in other parts of Europe. Silver, quicksilver, [252] platina, copper, lead, iron, & coal, all appeared in new quarters about the same time ↑i.e.↓ in the year 1848. Peu de moyens, beaucoup d'effet.[250]

[253] *Contradictions*
We remember that we forget.[251]
Our freedom is necessary.[252]
The preacher of eternity dates our chronology.

[254] March 19
Gravitation is the operator in what we call mechanical division. Gravitation is Nature's Grand Vizier & prime favourite. Much that we call chemical, even electrical action, is really, at last, his deed. Look at the sponge-like foliaceous forms which wet sand & clay take when falling with the water, in spring, on the steep sides of "the deep cut" in the RailRoad. And one will suspect that Gravity, too, can make a

[250] For this last sentence, see pp. [45] and [199] above.
[251] See p. [87] above.
[252] This sentence is used in "Fate," *W*, VI, 23. See also *JMN*, IX, 335.

leaf. In morals, again, Gravity is the Laissez faire principle, or Destiny, or Optimism, [255] than which nothing is wiser or stronger.

That nature works after the same method as the human Imagination.
That nature makes flowers, as the mind makes images.
that metaphysics might anticipate Jussieu
that organic matter, & mind, go from the same law, & so correspond

[256] Our science is very shiftless & morbidly wise; wise where it is not wanted; blind where we most wish to see. What ⟨geologi⟩a pother in the last twenty years about geology! Geologists were crossing all seas & lands, like so many squibs. Well, why did not they find California? They all knew what all men most wanted. Why did not they find the copper mines? There is no Columbus in these sciences with an anticipating mind; but they are like critics & amateurs; when the heel of a trapper's foot has turned up gold or copper [257] or quicksilver, they come & give it a name.

———

24 March

The Indians were a sort of money, it seems, in Spanish colonies. And the poor Lucayans were treated according to the proverb "the kid was seethed in its mother's milk."[253] Columbus seems to have been the principal introducer of American slavery. See Helps, History of the Conquerors of America & their Bondmen.[254]

[258] [blank]
[259] ↑*Town & Country Club.*↓
At Alcott's last Tuesday (20 March) we had a meeting of thirty men, and discussed the expediency of a Club & Clubroom. Alcott was festal & Olympian, as always, when friends come; his heart is then too great; his voice falters & chokes in his throat. Every newcomer seems large, sacred, & crowned ↑to him↓. It was proposed that the Club should rent the room in which we sat, (Alcott's,) & that he should be declared perpetual secretary.[255]

[253] Cf. Exod. 23:19.

[254] Arthur Helps, *The Conquerors of the New World and their Bondsmen* . . . , 2 vols. (London, 1848–1852), in Emerson's library. Several details in the first volume (1848) would justify Emerson's assumption (see, e.g., pp. 121–123, 129, 151–152).

[255] The meeting was held in Alcott's rooms at 12 West St., Boston, next to Eliza-

It is much wanted by the country scholars a café or Reading Room in the city, where, for a moderate subscription, they can find a place to sit in, & [260] find their friends, when in town, & to write a letter in, or read a paper. Better still, if you can add certain days of meeting when important questions can be debated, ⟨papers⟩ ↑communications↓ read, &c. &c. It was proposed by Hale & others, sometime since, to form in Boston a "Graduate⟨'⟩s' Club." This would be that. Then the ministers have a "Hook & Ladder," or a "RailRoad Club." ↑Club, see above, p 179↓

[261] [blank]

[262]

		H[enry] D Thoreau	Concord
		J[ohn]. L. Russell	Hingham
A[mos]. B. Alcott		T[homas]. W. Higginson	Newbury Port
W[illiam]. H. Channing		Rufus Ellis	Northampton
W[alter] F. Channing		Geo. Simmons.	Springfield
W[illiam]. E. Channing		[William] White	W. Newton
E[dward]. Bangs		[Thomas H.] Dorr	E. Lexington
J[ames]. F. Clarke		S[amuel]. Johnson	Salem
W[illiam] B Greene	Brookfield	R[alph]. W Emerson	Concord
T[homas]. Hill	Waltham	J[ohn] W Brown	Boston
J[ames]. E. Cabot		S[amuel]. G. Ward.	Lenox
C[harles]. C. Shackford.	Lynn	Wood	
S[amuel]. Robbins.	Chelsea	⟨S⟩J. G. Dwight	
E[dward]. E. Hale	Worcester	O[liver]. Johnson	
H[arrison]. G. O. Blake	Worcester	H[enry]. C. Wright	
W. H. Knapp	Nantucket	John Orvis.	Jamaica Plains
J[ohn]. Weiss	N. Bedford	Saml Longfellow	Fall River
Starr King		C[harles]. T. Brooks	Newport
T[homas]. T. Stone	Salem	Chandler Robbins	Boston
O[ctavius]. Frothingham.	Salem	J[ohn]. G. Whittier	Amesbury
J[ames]. R. Lowell	Cambridge	Dr Parsons	Boston
[James T.] Fisher.		F[rederic]. H. Hedge	Bangor
T[homas]. Davis.	Providence	C[aleb]. Stetson,	Scituate
[Samuel] Osgood	Providence	C[harles]. Sumner	Boston
[Cyrus] Bartol			
G[eorge]. P. Bradford			

beth Peabody's bookshop. It led to the founding of the Town and Country Club (a name bestowed by Emerson), with a constitution, a membership of over 100, and fairly regular monthly meetings at which papers were often read. The Club dissolved in the spring of 1850 for lack of financial support from the members. See Kenneth W. Cameron, "Emerson, Thoreau, and the Town and Country Club," *Emerson Society Quarterly* (III Quarter, 1957), 2–17.

[263]

Wyman [John C.] Worcester
Brown Worcester
F[rancis]. Cunningham Milton
F[rederic]. Eustis Milton
Dr [Convers] Francis
Dr Gregerson
E[dward]. Tuckerman [256]

[264]–[265] [blank]

[266] You cannot have ⟨a good⟩ ↑one first-rate↓ newspaper ↑like the Times,↓ without you ↑have↓ a good many good ones; they keep each other up. It is so with women. It requires a great many cultivated women, in order that you should have ⟨th⟩Mme. de Stael.[257]

[256] Most of the persons mentioned on pp. [262] and [263] became members of the Town and Country Club. Of those listed who have not been previously identified or are not easily recognizable, Dr. Walter F. Channing was Dean of the Harvard Medical School and father of the poet, William Ellery Channing (1818–1901); William Batchelder Greene (1819–1878), a Unitarian minister and author of a pamphlet, "Transcendentalism" (1849); Thomas Hill (1818–1891), a Unitarian minister and mathematician; Charles C. Shackford, Harvard graduate, 1835, a minister. Harrison Gray Otis Blake, William H. Knapp, John Weiss, and Thomas Starr King were all Unitarian ministers. Thomas Treadwell Stone was a liberal minister and antislavery lecturer; Thomas Davis, a member of the Chardon Street Convention; Samuel Osgood, a Unitarian minister and member of the Transcendental (or "Hedge's") Club. Cyrus Bartol, also a member of the Transcendental Club, was a Unitarian minister in Boston; John Lewis Russell, a naturalist; Rufus Ellis became pastor of Boston's First Church in 1853. George Frederick Simmons was a minister; William Abijah White, an editor of temperance journals and lecturer on antislavery. Thomas H. Dorr and Samuel Johnson were both liberal ministers. "Wood" may refer to Nathaniel Wood (1797?–1876), Harvard graduate and sometimes representative of Fitchburg in the state legislature in the 1840's and 1850's. Chandler Robbins became the minister of Boston's Second Church when Emerson resigned his pulpit there in 1832. Thomas William Parsons was a dentist and poet; Frederic Henry Hedge and Caleb Stetson were Unitarian ministers; Charles Sumner was a lawyer and later leader of the antislavery forces in the U.S. Senate; Francis Cunningham and Frederic Augustus Eustis were ministers; Convers Francis was professor of "Pulpit Eloquence & Pastoral Duty" at the Harvard Divinity School (*JMN*, VIII, 502). Edward Tuckerman, brother of Frederick Goddard Tuckerman, the poet, was a botanist and later professor at Amherst College. S. Robbins, Fisher, J. W. Brown, Dwight, O. Johnson, Wright, Orvis, Brooks, Wyman, Brown, and Gregerson are not further identified. "Alcott" through "Wright" (p. [262]) is in one kind of pen; "Orvis" through "Brown" (p. [263]) is in a second kind and probably added; "Cunningham" through "Tuckerman" is in a third kind and probably added after the second group.

[257] This paragraph is used in "Culture," *W*, VI, 149.

It is plain that domestic-economy & political-economy, as well as natural-history, are the symbols from which the new religion must draw its illustration. Wilkins ⟨the⟩ ⟨paper⟩deals in paper: When I complained to him of the price & quality of the specimens of paper for my new book, he said, he could furnish me with ⟨better or worse⟩ ⟨v⟩thicker or thinner paper to any variety of pattern, cheaper or dearer, with a list of [267] prices annexed.[258] It was entirely indifferent to the manufacturer what kind you buy. The pound always sells for so much. I find the same fact in the renting of my house. I can reduce the rent, certainly, but that incapacitates me to make proper repairs, & the tenant gets ⟨a worse⟩ not the house I would let him, but a worse one: besides that a relation a little injurious, is established between the ⟨parties⟩ landlord & tenant.[259] ↑/ See below, p 277↓

Enthusiasm is a fine thing, my son, so it be guided by prudence; says Grocer: which is like W[illiam] E[llery] C[hanning]'s saying of [Burrill] Curtis, that, "Yes, he would draw very well, if he had any talent for it."[260]

[268] April 4

Mr Phillips, bookseller, tells me, that he knows, that, from 75 to 100 000 copies of the two first volumes of Macaulay's History have been already *sold in this country*.[261]

Imbecility & Energy

The key to the age is this thing, & that thing, & that other, as the young orators describe. I will tell you the key to all ages, Imbecility: imbe↑c↓ility in the vast majority of men at all times & in every man, even heroes, in all but certain eminent moments victims of mere

[258] Emerson was preparing to get *Nature, Addresses, and Lectures* printed. According to the *Boston Directory*, 1849–1850, J. H. Wilkins was a member of a firm, Wilkins, Carter, and Co., 16 Water Street, which dealt in wholesale paper supplies.

[259] "Wilkins . . . & tenant.", struck through in ink with single vertical use marks on pp. [266] and [267], is used in "Wealth," *W*, VI, 107.

[260] Burrill Curtis, a brother of George William Curtis, was a member of Brook Farm and later moved to Concord.

[261] Emerson's reference is probably to Moses Dresser Phillips of Phillips, Sampson and Company, Boston publishers.

gravitation, custom, fear, & sense. This gives force to the strong, that the others have no habit of selfreliance or original action.[262]

[269] England

One of my chief lessons in England as I have probably written already * was the confirmation of a frequent experience at home that in literary circles the men of the most trust & consideration, bookmakers, editors, university deans & professors, bishops too, were by no means men of the ⟨most⟩ ↑largest↓ literary talent, but usually of a low & ordinary intellectuality but of a sort of mercantile activity & working talent. Jared Sparks, Griswold, Greeley, Bowen here; and ⟨Hen‖ . . . ‖⟩Morell, Newman, Lyell, there, down to the Oxenfords & Howitts, are examples.[263]

[270] *England*

The other lesson I learned from England, was, the power of the religious sentiment, the belief in the immortality of the Soul, & the rest, which inspired the Crusades, inspired the Religious Architecture, York, Newstead, Westminster, Winchester, Beverley, & Dundee [n] (works to which the key is lost with the sentiment that created them,) & inspired the English Bible [and] the Chronicle of Richard of Devizes[.] [264]

[271] ↑*England*↓

⟨O⟩The striking difference between English & our gentlemen is their thorough drill; they are all Etonians, they know prosody, & tread securely through all the humanities. The University is felt. It needs that our people should have ⟨n⟩closer association as scholars, that

* See LM 26

[262] This paragraph, struck through in pencil and in ink with vertical use marks, is used in "Power," *W*, VI, 54.

[263] This paragraph is struck through in pencil with a vertical use mark; "One of . . . Morell," is struck through in ink with a vertical use mark; "One of . . . working talent." is used in "Power," *W*, VI, 79–80. Emerson's references are probably to Rufus Wilmot Griswold, Horace Greeley, Francis Bowen (see Journal TU, p. [67] below), J. D. Morell, John Henry Newman, Sir Charles Lyell, John Oxenford, and William Howitt.

[264] This sentence, struck through in pencil with a vertical use mark and in ink with a wavy vertical use mark, is used in "Religion," *W*, V, 215–216. See *JMN*, X, 279.

they may have their grammar, gazetteer, & Dibdin, not so dusty & cobwebbed; and I wish our Club to be dignified with literary exercises[.]

[272] In my childhood, some peering eyes of boys discovered that the oranges hung on the boughs of Gov. Gray's orange tree were tied on with a thread. — I fear it is so with the novelist↑'s↓ ⟨wh⟩events. Nature has a magic by which she accurately suits the man to his fortunes by making these the fruit of his own character. ⟨But⟩ Ducks take to water & eagles to the sky, and every man to his liking, Lord Palmerston to foreign affairs, hunters to the forest, gardeners to the hothouse, sailors to the sea[.] [265]

[273] Some temperaments would spoil any success, men of no grasp, whose example & atmosphere enervates all who work for them[.]

Thus events grow on the same stem with persons, are sub[-]persons.[266]

But the novelist rashly plucks this event & fortune here & there & applies them with little consideration to his figures simply to tickle the fancy of his readers with a visionary prosperity or to scare them with visionary tragedies.[267]

[274] Men. *1849*

⟨4⟩3 May I set out in the Warren lot a couple of pears, seedlings from my ⟨b⟩Bartlett, which I budded myself. The best had died in the Heater Piece & these two poor old looking young things remained. Let us see if they can thrive.[268]

[265] "Gov. Gray's . . . sky," is struck through in pencil with a vertical use mark. "In my childhood . . . character." is used in "Books," *W*, VII, 216; "Nature has . . . sea" is used in "Fate," *W*, VI, 40–41.

[266] "Thus events . . . subpersons.", struck through in ink with a diagonal use mark, is used in "Fate," *W*, VI, 41.

[267] This sentence is used in "Books," *W*, VII, 216.

[268] Emerson purchased nearly three acres from Cyrus Warren, a neighbor who occasionally worked for him, on January 6, 1847, and subsequently kept records of plantings in the "Warren Lot" (see *JMN*, X, 489–493); the land he called "the Heater Piece," site of tht present Concord Antiquarian Society building, was purchased in December, 1838.

[275] In Richard of Devizes' Chronicle of Richard I's Crusade, p. 62, (Bohn) is a good specimen of the religious opinions of the 12th Century. Richard taunts God with forsaking him; "O fie! O how unwilling should I be to foresake thee in so forlorn & dreadful a position, were I thy lord & advocate, as thou art mine! In sooth, my standards will in future be despised, not through my fault but through thine; in sooth, not through any cowardice of my warfare, art thou thyself, my King & my God, conquered this day, & not Richard thy vassal." [269]

———

Remember Chaucer's Queen Dido.[270]

[276] Our columns are drums.[271] Mr Webster's son E asked his father, Who shall say *wis wis* at table when you are gone to Washington? [272] and today I observe that my correspondent R H D, tired, I suppose, of signing *Yours truly*, has a sterotyped form which cannot be read[:] Yur ‖ . . . ‖ R H D [273]
And at Philadelphia, W H Furness showed me, that the masons, who had long been renowned for their solid marble structures, had now learned of the New Yorkers to veneer in marble also.[274]

[277] ↑(See above, p 267)↓
I dismiss my labourer with saying "Well, Malachi, I shall send for you as soon as I cannot do without you." [275] Malachi goes off con-

[269] *Chronicles of the Crusades . . . of Richard Coeur de Lion, by Richard of Devizes and Geoffrey de Vinsauf; and of the Crusade of Saint Louis, by Lord John de Joinville* (London, 1848), in Emerson's library. This paragraph, struck through in ink with a vertical use mark, is used in "Worship," *W*, VI, 206.

[270] With this sentence, cf. "Worship," *W*, VI, 207.

[271] See *JMN*, IX, 416: "In the city of Makebelieve all the marble edifices were veneered & all the columns were drums."

[272] For this anecdote, see *JMN*, VIII, 100.

[273] Following "Yur" is Emerson's playful version of an unreadable salutation, which looks like "Ut Ust"; an elliptical line in ink, open on the left end, is drawn around "Yur Ut Ust". Emerson's correspondent is probably Richard Henry Dana.

[274] William Henry Furness, a friend since boyhood, was minister of the First Unitarian Church in Philadelphia when Emerson lectured there in 1843. With this sentence, cf. *JMN*, IX, 416: "In the city of Makebelieve all the marble edifices were veneered. . . ."

[275] Emerson's Account Books 4 (1849) and 5 (1850) have several entries of payment for labor to "Malachi Garity," variously spelled "Garrity" and "Garroty."

tented with that assurance, for he knows well that the potatoes will grow & the weeds with them; the melons & squashes must be planted week after next. And however unwilling to pay his high wages I must send for him. I wish that all labour should be as real & valuable as his, & should stand on the same simple & surly market. If it is the best of its kind, it will. I want & must have painter, stable-keeper, locksmith, poet, gentleman, priest, doctor, cook, confectioner, carpet weaver, chairmaker, & so on each in turn in course of the year. [278] If each really knows his craft, he cannot be spared. Political Economy rightly read, would be a consolation, like Christianity.[276]

οι ρεοντες[277]

A master in each art is required because the practice is never with still or dead subjects, but they change in your hands. A cockney talks of taking a cottage in the country, & ⟨buying⟩keeping a cow. ⟨Yes but⟩ He thinks a cow is a creature who is fed on hay, ↑&↓ gives a pail of milk every day. But a cow gives milk only for a certain time, then her bag dries up. What to do now with a dry cow? Sell her: but who [279] will buy a dry cow? Helpless cockney! Perhaps he bought farther also a ⟨p⟩yoke of oxen, to do his work. But they get lame & blown. What to do with lame & blown oxen! The farmer fats them usually, after the spring work is done, & kills them as fat oxen in the fall. But what can a townsman, leaving his cottage daily in the cars at business hours, do? He plants trees, but then there must be crops to keep the trees in ploughed land.—What shall be the crops? He will have nothing to do with trees, but will have grass: after two or three years the grass must be turned up & ploughed. Now what crops?[278]

οι ρεοντες ↑*TU* p. 11↓
See Economy O 195

[280] Teschemacher rejected the suggestion of a quickness or

[276] This paragraph is struck through in ink with single vertical use marks on pp. [277] and [278]; "I dismiss . . . year." is used in "Wealth," *W*, VI, 107–108.

[277] The phrase is translated as "the flowing philosophers" by Thomas Taylor in *The Works of Plato* . . . , 1804, IV, 56. See *JMN*, X, 159.

[278] This paragraph, struck through in ink with single diagonal use marks on pp. [278] and [279], is used in "Wealth," *W*, VI, 119–120.

scientific genius as being any substitute for constant industry in analysis & experiment.[279]

See what is said of Drill p. 194

Martial gave me to think of the faculty of writers. He can detach the object with unerring taste, & knows he can: sees that the power perfect in him differs infinitely from the imperfect approaches to the same power in ordinary scribblers. It is chemical mixture & not mechanical, which makes the writer. The others have not intelligence enough [281] to know they are not writers. One thing more. Martial suggests again, as every purely literary book does, the immortality. We see we are wiser than we were: We are older: Can nature afford to lose such improvements? Is Nature a suicide?

See W 127

Macaulay

The historian of England or France seems to be compelled to treat of England as of an Englishman; the nation has a continuous existence, memory, history in his head, knows his rights[.]

[282] Who buys Channing's house buys a sunset. It should be sold in a fair day, then the purchaser gets rivers, ⟨v⟩mountains, villages, in the bargain. I would not, ⟨I⟩if I owned that place, ⟨I⟩ sell it. I would hold onto it as long as I could see.[280]

[283] ↑*Life*↓

We must not think that all the charm is in the employment. Life itself is an ecstasy: life is sweet as nitrous oxide; and the fisherman standing dripping all day over a cold pond, the ⟨boil⟩switchman at the railroad intersection, the labourer in the field, the Irishman in the ditch, the flaneur in the street[,] all ⟨aleg⟩ascribe a certain pleasure

[279] Cf. James Englebert Teschemacher, *A Concise Application of the Principles of Structural Botany to Horticulture*, . . . (Boston, 1840), p. iv: "It cannot be denied that many of the advantageous practices in Horticulture and Agriculture have been discovered by the mere practical man, without any deductions from science, or the laws of Vegetation."

[280] William Ellery Channing, the poet, lived with his family in a cottage on Punkatasset Hill in Concord until 1849, when he moved onto Main Street.

to their employment which they themselves give it. It is health & appetite that gives sweetness to sugar, & bread, & meat,[281]
And it is easy to see that as insane persons are rendered [284] indifferent to their dress, diet, & other accommodations, & as we do in dreams with great equanimity the most unusual & surprising things, so a drop more of wine in our cup of life will reconcile us to strange company & work.[282]

↑[See *TU* p 247]↓

I meet in the street people full of life. I am, of course, at ebbtide; they at flood; they seem to have come from the south or from the west or from Europe. I see them pass with envy at this gift which includes all gifts.

[285]–[286] [Index material omitted]
[inside back cover] [Index material omitted]

[281] "We must not . . . meat," struck through in ink with a vertical use mark, is used in "Illusions," *W*, VI, 311. "Life itself . . . ecstasy:" is also used in "Fate," *W*, VI, 41.

[282] "And it [p. [283]] . . . work." is used in "Fate," *W*, VI, 41.

TU

1849

Journal TU, a regular journal except for one short sequence of pages, covers the period from May, 1849, to probably early November, 1849, following chronologically after Journal RS, whose last dated entry is for May 3, 1849. The first dated entry, on p. [65], is for May 25, 1849, and the last, on p. [250], is for October 19, 1849. A short sequence of pages, [17]–[25], is devoted to outlines and notes which assemble under different headings references to entries elsewhere in the journals, a frequent practice of Emerson's in composing lectures and essays. Pages [26]–[64], while containing much original journal matter, also show a continuous, if sporadic, pattern of listing, under topic headings, references to journal entries elsewhere.

Journal TU is written in a hard-cover copybook. The cover, 17.8 x 21.1 cm, is of predominantly brown paper marbled with blue and yellow over boards, with a tan leather margin at the binding and forming two triangles at the top and bottom outer edges. The spine, of brown leather, now cracked and peeling, has "849" barely visible at the top, beneath which is "TU". There appears to have been an ink inscription on the bottom of the spine, but it is now illegible. The front cover is inscribed "TU", centered in ink on the upper portion of the marble paper, and "1849", inscribed in ink on the upper leather triangular corner. The back cover is inscribed "TU", also in ink, on the lower leather triangular corner. The unruled pages measure 17.3 x 20.2 cm. The pages are numbered in ink except for the following six in pencil: 15⟨2⟩0, 152, 153, 154, 155, 265. Nineteen pages are unnumbered: i, ii, 2, 4, 37, 43, 81, 93, 95, 151, 185, 197, 199, 201, 205, 207, 225, 263, 290 (verso of flyleaf); twenty pages are blank: 1, 2, 4, 37, 42, 43, 54, 55, 56, 72, 86, 93, 185, 187, 199, 215, 225, 229, 232, 263. Ten leaves have been either torn out (with fragments of the stubs still in the binding) or are missing: pp. 99–100, 143–144, 163–164, 165–166, 167–168, 179–180, 241–242, 271–272, 275–276, 277–278. The stub of the leaf bearing pages 271–272 is loose from the binding. The leaf bearing pages 113–114 is loose from the binding. The leaves bearing what would have been pages 9–10 and 11–12 in sequential pagination have been cut out before pagination, as there is no gap at this point in Emerson's numbering. Four pages were misnumbered and corrected: 10⟨0⟩2, 10⟨1⟩3, 15⟨2⟩0, 21⟨2⟩1. Tipped in between pages 46 and 47 is a newspaper clipping containing articles on "Cultivating Marsh Land" and "Plaster for Potatoes."

[front cover] TU 1849

TU

[front cover verso] [Index material omitted]
↑Examined March '77↓

[i] R.W.Emerson.

TU[1]

1849

"Parcite, dum propero; mergite, dum redeo."[2]

Martialis. [*Epigrams*, *XXV*]

[ii]–[2] [blank]

[3] Valour pays rents as surely as land. Up heart, & dispose of the day's duty first, and the dividend of peace & power will be paid. The proverb of "*Business before friends*," is God's truth too.[3]

[4] [blank]

[5] The way to wealth of every kind is plainly along the *upper road*,[n] & not by State Street. Convert yourself into wealth, ⟨& kings' daughters shall be your women, &⟩ ↑you shall buy↓ kings↑.↓ ⟨your men.⟩ Sordid calculations convert you into punk & abhorrence. The doctrine that genius takes its rise out of the mountains of Rectitude,—that all beauty & power, which men covet, are born out of that /egg/ humility/ which they disdain,—is alternately concealed & suggested.[4] How we love nobility! priest, poet, [6] or republican cannot keep his eyes off it. Yet how rare! The whole society and every member of it is first or last adjudged to be "snobbish." Why, but because every member is referring or looking up to others, who, in their turn, are referring; and[n] only one in ten thousand is a person of elevated sentiments whose condition flows from his character,—secure, serene, & his own friend. From a better man than myself, (I used to ⟨write,⟩ ↑say,↓) I can easily expect ⟨more⟩a finer [7] thought: ↑—↓⟨F⟩from a

[1] "TU" is enclosed by a circular line in ink.

[2] "Spare me while I hasten, o'erwhelm me when I return." The Latin is used in "Quotation and Originality," *W*, VIII, 186.

[3] See *JMN*, III, 316.

[4] "The doctrine . . . disdain,—", struck through in ink with single vertical and diagonal use marks, is used in "Worship," *W*, VI, 216.

worse, I am incredulous. But that *Better* we so slowly believe↑.↓ (See GH 118)

Plato suggested after Pythagoras thorough Culture. 'Tis pity our dismasted rudderless hulks drifting about on the sea of life should not be taken into port. Pity that the Commonwealth should not set its Horace Manns on applying the stern Culture suggested in the "Republic" to the adults, & so keep them up. When the school & college drop them, let Plato take them up, & life would no longer be forlorn, & they left to the stock quotations by day, & cards at night.

[8] I was about to add just now, in speaking of Morals, as the ⟨origin⟩fountain of nobility, that we do with that as our farmers, who carry all their best peaches & apples to market & feed their families with the refuse. We parade our nobilities in poems, instead of working them up into happiness.[5] Then we must bring the day about with dross & prose[.]

[9] *Feats*

⟨Equally master of his feet & of his hands,⟩ He [n] ⟨could⟩ wr⟨i⟩ote ⟨beautifully on paper⟩ ↑a fair hand↓, & he could draw the same lines ⟨with⟩ in capitals with his skates on the ice.

Giotto, the painter, could draw with his pen a perfect circle. *Tu sei piu tondo che l'O di Giotto.*[6]

Mr Sylvester told me that Farie the engineer could draw a model of any loom or machine, after once seeing it. He went through Mr Strutt's mills, & drew from memory designs of the machinery, which were printed in Rees' Cyclopaedia, to the great indignation of Mr Strutt.[7]

[5] This sentence, struck through in ink with one diagonal and three vertical use marks, is used in "Behavior," *W*, VI, 191.

[6] The incident and the Italian quotation occur in Giorgio Vasari, *Lives of the Most Eminent Painters, Sculptors, and Architects*, which Emerson had read at least by 1839 (*JMN*, VII, 291). See the London, 1890, ed., trans. Mrs. Jonathan Foster, vol. I, pp. 102–103.

[7] In Charles Sylvester's *The Philosophy of Domestic Economy* (Nottingham, 1819), the Strutt family figures prominently; Jedediah Strutt (1726–1797) built a cotton mill at Nottingham. John Farey (1791–1851) drew illustrations for Abraham Rees's *The Cyclopaedia; or An Universal Dictionary of Arts and Sciences* (London, 1786). See *JMN*, X 260.

[10] Story of Descartes. ↑See *this book* p. 44,↓

Romeo, Middlebury Address.[8]

Columbus & his course to Veragua, BO 162 [9]
Sculptor's feat — AZ 194
Pook's ship — [10]
Ben Jonson can the paper stain. AZ 183
Thoreau can pace 16 rods accurately [11]
E B Bigelow can invent you a machine to do any work you wish.[12]
Giotto can draw a circle TU 9
Farie a model of a loom [TU 9]
Safford can compute 15 figures by 15 in his head [CD 3–4]
Doubling the Cube at Delos. *RS 18*
Leverrier's discovery of Neptune
Thales' measure of Pyramid } *RS* 16, *18*,
Pythagoras's "*lines*"
Stephenson's locomotive
Byron's three feats. TU 139
Nantucket feats CD 10
Decimal notation & Zero. *RS* 16
Ojeda could throw an orange from the bottom of the Giralda to the top, 250 feet; & walk swiftly out on a plank at the top of the building & back again. *Helps*.[13]

[8] For the story of Romeo, from Dante, *The Paradiso*, Canto VI, see *JMN*, VII, 478. Emerson delivered a discourse at Middlebury College, 22 July, 1845, in which he referred to Romeo.

[9] This, and four of the topics listed below on p. [10], are developed in "Success," *W*, VII; seven of the topics in this list are developed in the lecture "Economy" (see Appendix I). As those entries in Journals AZ and BO cross-referenced below postdate 1849, the list from at least this point must have been drawn up later than the regular entries in Journal TU.

[10] Samuel Hartt Pook (1827–1901) designed the first New England clipper, *Surprise*, launched October 5, 1850; when on its maiden voyage to California it beat the record of the *Sea-Witch*, Pook's reputation was established.

[11] Cf. "Works and Days," *W*, VII, 157, and "Thoreau," *W*, X, 461.

[12] The American inventor and economist Erastus Brigham Bigelow (1814–1879) invented a power loom for his factory in Clinton.

[13] Cf. Arthur Helps, *The Spanish Conquest in America* . . . , 4 vols. (New York, 1856–1857), I, 282–283. A 4-volume London edition of 1855–1861 is in Emerson's library.

Sculptor's feat AZ 194 [Richard Owen, *NY* 132,[14]

[11] ↑*Swedenborg*↓

I look on Swedenborg as on Kant, Newton, Leibnitz, Goethe, Humboldt, men of a larger stature than others, & possessing very great advantages in that preternatural size. He & Newton were both cracked or bursten; yet 'tis easier to see the reflection of the sphere in globes of this magnitude, cracked or not, than in the common minute globe[.]

Οι ρεοντες, οι ρεοντες. He knows, if he only, the flowing of nature.[15] And it was wise—that ⟨the⟩ old answer of Amasis to him who bade him drink up the sea,—"Yes, willingly, if you will stop the rivers that run in."[16]

Οι ρεοντες RS.p.279
Tu 19

[12] One must study Quetelet to know the limits of human freedom. In 20,000, population, just so many men will marry their grandmothers. Doubtless, in every million, there will be one astronomer, one mathematician, one comic poet, & one mystic. Thus Mahometans & ⟨T⟩Chinese know all that we know of leap year, of the Precession of ⟨the⟩ equinoxes & Gregorian Calendar, for they too had millions, & so had one or two astronomical Skulls. In a barrel of cypraeas, there shall be one orangia.[17]

[14] This Owen entry may be very late—1860 at least, the first publication date of Richard Owen's *Palaeontology, or A Systematic Summary of Extinct Animals and their Geological Relations*, which Emerson appears to be reading at the time of the entry in Journal NY, p. [132].

[15] See Journal RS, p. [278] above.

[16] It was Bias, not Amasis, who gave the answer: "Why then, let Amasis require the Æthiopian king to stop the streams which from all parts flow." *Plutarch's Morals: in Five Volumes. Translated from the Greek, by Several Hands . . .*, 5th ed. (London, 1718), II, 11. A broken set of this edition is in Emerson's library (see *JMN*, VII, 78, n. 218). The entries on p. [11] are struck through in ink with a vertical use mark. "he knows . . . in.'" is used in "Swedenborg," *W*, IV, 112.

[17] "In 20,000 . . . orangia." is struck through in ink with a vertical use mark; "Doubtless . . . orangia." is used in "Fate," *W*, VI, 18. For Emerson's reading of Quételet, see Journal RS, pp. [220]–[221] above.

[13] There is always so much lime, so much iron, so much carbon, so much azote, to keep the balance of things. Is there not, then, in every age so much Platonism, so much holy passion, so much contemplative & ascetical nature, in the men? —that is, so much friendship for thee, O prophet! Then fear not but thou shalt find, in the midst of the crucifiers, some loving minority.
↑See how white souls are born W 127½↓[18]

[14] Clough's Beautiful Poem I read again last night in the sitting room.[19] 'Tis a kind of new & better Carlyle; the Homeric Iteration is one secret; the truly modern question & modern treatment another; and there is abundance of life & experience in it; good passages are, the prayer to the sun & moon & hours to pass slowly over Philip & Elspie. And good youth in it, as E[lizabeth]. H[oar]. says.

[15] The wisdom of words every day might surprise us. After a man has made great progress, & has come, as he fancies, to heights hitherto unscaled, the common words still fit his thought; nay, he only now finds for the first time how wise they were. "*Macrocosm*," *Reason*, *Conscience*, *Substance*, *Accidence*, *Nature*, *Relation*, *Fortune*, *Fate*,[n] *Genius*, Element, Person, 'twill be long before he needs a new coat.[20]

The old mythology still serves us, not of Jove, Mars, &c but of Nature, Destiny, Fortune.[n] Words therefore seem wiser than any man, & ↑to be↓ tools provided by the Genius of Humanity. After ↑t↓he ↑student↓ has waked all night speculating on his analogies &

[18] "See how . . . W 127½" is in pencil.

[19] *The Bothie of Toper-na-Fuosich*, undoubtedly the poem Emerson says he received "at the bookstore" in Journal RS, p. [204] above, under the date "Dec. 22, 1848". Emerson could hardly have been aware of the meaning of the Gaelic — "the hut of the bearded well" — or have known that the last part was a bawdy Highland toast to the female pudenda. When Clough discovered the truth, he was amused; in 1855 he changed the title to *The Bothie of Tober-na-Vuolich*, of which the last part sounds Gaelic but is concocted and meaningless. See Richard M. Gollin, "The 1951 Edition of Clough's *Poems*: A Critical Re-examination," *Modern Philology*, LX (Nov. 1962), 123n.

[20] Emerson left approximately a two-inch space between "Person," and "twill", perhaps to add words to his catalog.

ties to the world & to the starry heaven, the first words he meets in the morning book, are, *microcosm macrocosm.*

[16] "Nature tells everything once."[21] Find each organ & function somewhere in *great bodies.*

[17] *Morals*

Maid & mistress RS 114
Lover of laws RS 129, 46
Thales' Verses.
Nor do we love law less, because of our sickness *RS* 40, 41,[22]
Hafiz & Edda on Freedom *AB* 129.
Zoroaster, Herodotus, Porphyry. *RS* 9,
Solace of the philosopher in the law that ruins him. *RS* 129,
Greatness of Fate. Well; the nobility of the sentiments is in resisting it, or in accepting it. *RS* 202,
Realism from G. Sand *RS*. 203,
Cash payment & Sacrifice to the gods. *RS* 57. 63,
Perish Races for the teaching a principle. *RS*. 96
Always so much virtue. The proportions are constant. TU 1⟨7⟩3
Origin of thought *GH* 118, *TU* 5,

[18] ↑MORALS.↓

"Heaven kindly gives our blood a moral flow."[23]
Young [*Night Thoughts*, "Night Seventh," l. 347]
"No noble virtue ever was alone."[24]
Ben Jonson [*Epicœne, or The Silent Woman*, II, iii, 34]

[21] A paraphrase of Goethe's remark in Sarah Austin, *Characteristics of Goethe*, 3 vols. (London, 1833), I, 64. See *JMN*, V, 259. Emerson used the paraphrase in his 1834 lecture, "On the Relation of Man to the Globe" (*Lectures*, I, 29), and in "Country Life," *W*, XII, 160.

[22] The "w" of "law" is joined to the "l" of "less,"; a vertical pencil line separates these letters.

[23] This sentence, struck through in ink with three vertical use marks, is used in "Worship," *W*, VI, 202. See *JMN*, *V*, 20.

[24] See *JMN*, VII, 219, and VI, 386.

When was an act of goodness & virtue,—when was a sentiment of bene⟨o⟩v↑o↓lence & love, not greater than the conquest of the Universe? *Oegger. B* 63,[25]

"For Virtue's whole sum is to know & dare." [26]

Donne. ["To the Countess of Bedford," l. 33, misquoted]

[19] *Results*

Self poise; nature has it in all her works, certain proportions in which oxygen & azote combine. &c. *GH* 38, ↑48,↓ *CD* 51 [27]

Οι ρεοντες,[28] Transition, *GH* 73 *W* 86, *RS* 278, *TU* 11,
the artist,[n] LM 70.

[20] *Results*

There must be a relation between power & probity; or, we have as much power as we can be trusted with. *LM* 51

There will be no revolution 'till we see new men. *LM* 50,

⟨Bigger incomes do not help any body.⟩ LM 75

True safety in the Reaction which increases centrifugence with centripetence.

RS 156, 193
LM 123, 118
AB 5
E 90. RS 268.

Men begin & begin. *LM* 102

Expression large & bounteous & healthful. River makes its shores; blood makes the walls of vein & artery. Shakspeare all pores. CD 20, 21, 22, 23, 24,

[25] In 1835 Emerson read a manuscript translation of G. Oegger, *Le Vrai Messie* (Paris, 1829), probably by Elizabeth Peabody, and recorded this quotation in Journal B.

[26] See *JMN*, IX, 367.

[27] This entry is struck through in ink with a vertical use mark.

[28] See Journal RS, p. [278] above.

[21] In history the great moment is the transit of the savage to civility. *CD* 48 [29]

Races CD 82, R.S 68, 96, *LM* 152

↑The↓ man [n] gets out of the railroad car in every respect the same as he got in. *CD* 90,

---

On the progressive value of money *AB* 15, *O* 10 324, *41*

You must honour the people's facts. *RS* 97, 193,

You shall not intermeddle with *Laissez faire*, & the fine thermometer of demand & supply. *RS* 154, 163,

---

The Battery, or man of aplomb. *LM* 1

Greatest effect by cheapest means. *RS* 45 199

God is a reality & his method is illusion[.] [30]

Conduct of life. *LM* 3,

[22] Results *continued*

We should kill ourselves if we thought men were free, & could derange the Order of Nature.[31] But the inference from Nature A Beautiful Necessity. Lect. on Humanity of Science

---

Identity of man's mind with nature's for he is a part of nature, & the vegetable prin[c]iple pervades him.[32] *Idem*

---

[29] This entry is struck through in ink with a vertical use mark.

[30] This entry, struck through in ink with a vertical use mark, is used in "Montaigne," *W*, IV, 178. See *JMN*, X, 355.

[31] This sentence, struck through in ink with a vertical use mark, is used in "Fate," *W*, VI, 48–49.

[32] With this sentence, cf. *JMN*, IX, 335.

In astronomy, vast distances; but we never go into a foreign system:[33]
In geology, vast duration; but here, too, we are never strangers. Same functions slower performed — many races it cost then, to achieve the completion⟨,⟩ that is⟨,⟩ now in the life of one: life had not yet so fierce a glow —[34]

"All difference is quantitative." Schelling[35]

[23] *Results.*

Everything will come home[n] at last, & a man also; &, if long held back, the more fiercely. *O* 337,

---

Let us think the grief of others as slight & medicable as our own. *F* [No. 2] 122.

Form always stands in dread of power *R* 48,

Everyone would make the daregod & daredevil experiment. *N* 102

What is good is effective: a real man makes ground for himself — : D'Israeli none. *RS* 230,[36]

That mass which ruins Europe, is divided & borne as ounce loads by every American[.] *RS* 90,

---

The new electrical light the best police. *RS* 232,[37]

---

[33] "In astronomy . . . system:", struck through in ink with a diagonal use mark, is used in "Fate," *W*, VI, 49, and in "Powers and Laws of Thought," *W*, XII, 5.

[34] "In geology . . . races" is struck through in ink with a diagonal use mark; it thickens to a blot from directly after "strangers." into "races". "In geology . . . strangers." is used in "Fate," *W*, VI, 49, and "Powers and Laws of Thought," *W*, XII, 5. "Same functions . . . glow — " is used in "Powers and Laws of Thought," *W*, XII, 49–50.

[35] John Bernhard Stallo, *General Principles of the Philosophy of Nature . . .* (Boston, 1848), p. 222, in Emerson's library. The quotation, struck through in ink with a diagonal use mark, is used in "Literature," *W*, V, 242.

[36] This entry is struck through in ink with three vertical use marks.

[37] This entry is struck through in ink with a vertical use mark.

Cockney scrapes his trees, scrapes the bark to the quick; but manure is the best scraper.[38]

---

[24] Indirection *O* 255, *GH* 36,

Whip for our top. *GH* 14,

Men are loyal. *GH* 38, *BO* 17.

---

[25] Realism, or Circulating Decimals,
pole rhymes with pole RS[39]

No man has learned anything until he knows that every day is the Judgment Day.

[26] Realism

The American workman who strikes ten blows with his hammer, whilst the foreign workman only strikes one, is as really vanqu⟨s⟩ishing that foreigner, as if the blows were aimed at & told on his person.[40]

Character not to know oneself defeated W 13⟨0⟩9[41]

[27] Corinne CD 79[42]
Your own verdict LM ⟨3⟩79
Bigger incomes don't help any body[43]

[38] For "manure . . . scraper.", see Journal RS, p. [229] above.

[39] "pole . . . RS" is in pencil; cf. Journal RS, p. [40] above.

[40] This sentence, struck through in ink with a vertical use mark, is used in "Worship," *W*, VI, 225. See *JMN*, X, 305.

[41] "Character not . . . W 13⟨0⟩9" is in pencil. Cf. "Worship," *W*, VI, 234–235.

[42] For an explanation of "Corinne" as Margaret Fuller, and an earlier version of the "CD 79" entry, see *JMN*, VIII, 524, and n. 18.

[43] "Corinne . . . any body" is in pencil and is struck through in ink with a diagonal use mark; "Yr own . . . any body" is also struck through in ink with two diagonal use marks. Material referred to in the Corinne entry in Journal CD, p. [79], is used in "Uses of Great Men," *W*, IV, 6. The "verdict" entry in Journal LM, p. [79], is used in "Worship," *W*, VI, 241. "Bigger incomes . . . any body" is expanded in "Wealth," *W*, VI, 117.

Whoever knows what happens in the getting & spending of a loaf of bread, & a pint of beer; that no wishing will change the somewhat rigorous limits of pints & penny loaves; that for all that is consumed, so much less remains in the basket & pot; but what is gone out of these is not wasted, but well spent, if it nourishes his body,—knows all of political economy that ⟨all⟩ the ↑budgets of↓ empires ⟨of Europe & Asia⟩ can teach him.[44] This ⟨is a⟩ wisdom ⟨which⟩ I find every day helpful in the street, when I compare the libertinism of France, with the staidness of Massachusetts. —The Grisette institution particularly interests the young men, [28] but everything is as broad as it is long, —and grisettes also.[45]

When men feel & say, "Those men occupy my place," the revolution is near. So we say. But I never feel that any men occupy my place; but that the reason I do not have what I wish, is, that I want the faculty which entitles. All spiritual or real power makes its own place. Revolutions of violence, then, are scrambles merely.[46]

All for thee therefore all against thee G 28 [47]

[29] *Realism*

Happy is he who looks only into his work, to know if it will succeed, never into the times, or the public opinion; and who writes from the love of imparting certain thoughts, & not from the necessity of fate,—who writes always to *the unknown friend*.[48]

[44] "Whoever knows . . . him.", struck through in pencil and in ink with single vertical use marks, is used in "Wealth," *W*, VI, 106. See *JMN*, X, 330.

[45] For this sentence, see *JMN*, X, 329. "vulgar man licentious when he travels G 26" is written in pencil at the bottom of p. [27]. "Realism", which may be an index heading for the entry below on p. [28] beginning "When men feel", is written in the top left margin of p. [28] and set off from "but everything is" by a short rule.

[46] This paragraph is lined in pencil in the left margin; "But I . . . place." is used in "Aristocracy," *W*, X, 47. For " 'Those men occupy my place,' " see *JMN*, IX, 109. "Pr. Aristocracy" is written in pencil above "feel & say," probably by Edward Emerson.

[47] "All . . . 28" is in pencil.

[48] This sentence is struck through in pencil with a vertical use mark. "Happy is . . . opinion;" is struck through in pencil with two vertical use marks and in ink

"Pierre, content with having acquired the talents he had aspired to possess, waited when the occasion of making them appreciated should come of itself, and he knew well that it would not loiter." *Geo. Sand.*[49]

[30] *Realism* ☞ [50]

Do it. Bridge the gulf well & truly from edge to edge, & the dunces will find it out.[51] There is but one verdict needful, & that is mine.[52] If I do it, I shall know it.

Happy is he who finishes his work for its own sake; & the state & the world is happy that has the most of such Finishers. The world will do justice to such. It cannot otherwise: but never on the day when the work is newly done & presented. ⟨But forever it is true that⟩ ⟨e⟩Every man settles his own rate.[53]

[31] *Realism*

⟨The way to make⟩ ↑We must realize↓ our rhetoric & our rites↑.↓ ⟨sublime, is to make them real.⟩ Our ↑national↓ flag is not affecting, because it does not represent the population of the United States, but some Baltimore or Philadelphia Caucus: not uni⟨s⟩on & sentiment, but selfishness & cunning. If we never put on the liberty cap, until we were freemen by love & self denial, the liberty-cap would mean something.

Over ☞

[32] *Realism* [54]

One would think, from the talk of men, that riches & poverty were a

---

with a vertical use mark. The sentence is used in "Worship," *W*, VI, 225. See *JMN*, X, 315.

[49] The quotation, presumably Emerson's translation of a passage from *Le Compagnon du Tour de France* inscribed in Journal RS, p. [203] above, is struck through in pencil and in ink with two vertical use marks.

[50] A line in ink extends along the top right margin of verso p. [30] to the top left margin of recto p. [31], leading into the heading "*Realism*".

[51] "Do it . . . to edge," is struck through in ink with a diagonal use mark. For the whole paragraph, see *JMN*, X, 156.

[52] With this sentence, cf. p. [27] above.

[53] This paragraph, struck through in ink with a diagonal use mark, is used in "Worship," *W*, VI, 225–226. See *JMN*, X, 386–387.

[54] "*16*" is written in pencil in the top margin to the right of this heading.

great matter, — whilst they are really a thin costume,* & our life, the life of all of us, is identical. For we transcend circumstance continually, & taste the real quality of existence; as, in our employments, which only differ in the manipulation, but express the same laws; or, in our thoughts, which wear no broadcloth, & taste no ice cream↑s↓. We see God face to face, every hour, & know the savour of nature.[55]

[33] Realism

——— ↑Culture.↓

In good conversation, the parties do not speak to the words, but to the meanings & characters of each other. ↑probably printed↓ [56]

———

That the thing done, that the quality avails, & not the opinion entertained of it, is a lesson which all things teach, & no man can sufficiently learn.[57] W 139

———

I met no gods, — I harboured none.[58]

———

If what we hate was murderable, that were some comfort. But, unhappily, no knife is long enough to reach to the heart of any enemy we have.[59]

our whole existence subjective. What we are[,] that we see & love & hate. "He who has 1000 friends," &c [60]

* See *Electra*, in *Potter's Euripides*, p. [61]

[55] This paragraph, struck through in ink with a vertical use mark, is used in "Illusions," *W*, VI, 323–324. See *JMN*, IX, 206–207. For "We see . . . face," see 1 Cor. 13:12. An ink line is drawn below "& know . . . nature.", separating the entry from the note "See . . . *Euripides*, p.", which is written in the bottom margin.

[56] Added in pencil, perhaps by Edward Emerson. The entry is used in "Social Aims," *W*, VIII, 99. See *JMN*, IX, 213.

[57] This sentence is used in "First Visit to England," *W*, V, 9. See *JMN*, X, 387.

[58] This sentence is used in "Worship," *W*, VI, 230. See *JMN*, IX, 206.

[59] This sentence is used in "Character," *W*, X, 120. See *JMN*, IX, 88, 224.

[60] "our whole . . . &c" is struck through in ink with two diagonal use marks; the quotation is used in "Considerations by the Way," *W*, VI, 272–273, where Emerson attributes it to "An Eastern poet, Ali Ben Abu Taleb." See also "From Ali Ben Abu Taleb," *W*, IX, 302.

[61] Possibly the passage, "This truth unknown . . . lifts her head."; see *The Plays of Euripides*, trans. R. Potter (London and Toronto, 1906), p. 185.

[34] Realism

Do not throw up your thought because you cannot answer objections to it.[62]

Putting off butchering on to the butchers does not save the society: it returns to them in the brutality of those they have brutalized.

No history true but what is always true. *G* 91 *H* 75, *N* 96. J 108[63]

Qui s'excuse s'accuse.[64]

I met myself *F* [No. 2] 27[65]

The ⟨things⟩ ↑acts↓ of a man for which I visit him, were done in the dark & in the cold.[66]

[35] Malachi[67]

"Malachi, I shall not send for you until I cannot do without you." With this arrangement, employer & employed are both contented. *RS* [277][68]

Fruitur fama?[69] — no never. The poet is least a poet when he sits crowned. The transcendental & divine has the dominion of the world, on the sole condition of ⟨not having⟩ ↑declining↓ it.[70]

The girl insisted on living at home. She was right, though the parents were poor. Work grows like grass everywhere. And labor is

[62] This sentence is used in "Worship," *W*, VI, 230. See *JMN*, IX, 282.

[63] "No history . . . J 108" is in pencil. See *JMN*, X, 329.

[64] This epigram first occurs apparently in Gabriel Meurier, *Trésor des Sentences* (c. 1575), p. 63. See *JMN*, VII, 430.

[65] "I met . . . 27" is in pencil.

[66] This sentence, struck through in ink with a vertical use mark, is used in "Behavior," *W*, VI, 189. See *JMN*, X, 376.

[67] Emerson first wrote what appears to be "Michael", then finger-wiped it and superimposed upon it "alalc[?]i" in the apparent attempt to produce "Malachi".

[68] " 'Malachi, I . . . contented.", struck through in ink with a vertical use mark, is used in "Wealth," *W*, VI, 107. See Journal RS, p. [277] above. "*RS*" is underlined in pencil.

[69] "Delights he in fame?" (Ed.).

[70] See *JMN*, IX, 420.

capital, wherever created, & exchangeable for every coin on the globe. See *CD* 77[71]

[36] *Realism*

In heaven, when a man wants a horse, a horse wants a man.

Every day is the best in the year.[72] For all the elements are co--present in every moment, patent or latent.

↑See AZ 21↓

---

[37] [blank]

[38][73]

			essence
harbinger	porter	courier	centre
	chalice		sparkle

parasite
pursuivant
darling
envoy

[39] "I have found
More sweets in one unprofitable dream,
Than in my life's whole pilgrimage."
Ford's Sun's Darling.[74]

[40] *Weather*

"So exquisite is the structure of the cortical glands," says Malpighi, "that when the atmosphere is ever so slightly vitiated or altered, (as Hippocrates intimates in his book De Morbis Sacris) the

[71] See also *JMN*, VIII, 523, and n. 17. "The girl" is almost certainly Louisa May Alcott. "*CD*" is underlined in pencil.

[72] This sentence is used in "Works and Days," *W*, VII, 175.

[73] P. [38] is in pencil.

[74] The play is by John Ford and Thomas Dekker. The lines are I, i, 70–72. Drawn in pencil on the lower two-thirds of p. [39] are outlines of several implements: a hoe and shovel, forming an X, an axe, a large hammer (or sledge hammer), and what appears to be a long-handled cleaver.

brain is the first part to sympathize, & to undergo a change of state." [75]

↑Part II p 81↓

Ap. E[conomy]. [of the] A[nimal]. K[ingdom,
1845–1846,]. vol. II.
[pt. II, sec. 81, 119]
Animal Kingdom [76]

See Plutarch

"Ah! Could I hide ⟨myself⟩ ↑me↓ in my song
And kiss thee when it flows from thy lips!"
Ammar *Ammar.*[77]

[41] ↑*Days*↓

There is the least deliberation in our life. We worry through the world, & do not unfold ourselves with leisure & dignity, & adorn our days suitably. Especially I observe that we have not ↑learned↓ the art to ⟨m⟩ avail ourselves of the virtues & powers of our Companions. The day is gloomy with politics or bitter with debt.

"In vain thou runnest from death on two days,
The day which God fixes, & the day God fixes not:
On the first, no physician can save thee;
On the second, you cannot give up the ghost."
Pindar of Rei in Cuhistan [78]
[Von Hammer, *Geschichte der schönen Redekünste Persiens* . . . , 1818, p. 43]

[42]–[43] [blank]

[75] "(as Hippocrates . . . Sacris)" is struck through in ink with a vertical use mark.

[76] "Animal Kingdom" is in pencil.

[77] Emerson translated Ammar's lines from Joseph von Hammer-Purgstall, *Geschichte der schönen Redekünste Persiens, mit einer Blüthenlese aus zweyhundert persischen Dichtern* (Wien, 1818), p. 41, in Emerson's library. The quotation, struck through in pencil with a diagonal use mark, is used in "Persian Poetry," *W*, VIII, 260, where the lines are wrongly attributed to Hafiz. "See Plutarch . . . *Ammar.*" is in pencil.

[78] " 'In vain . . . Cuhistan", in pencil and struck through in pencil with a vertical use mark, is used in "Fate," *W*, VI, 5, and in "Translations," *W*, IX, 302.

[44] *Intellect*

Feats of talent

Plato called the faculties gods.

Pythagoras, Thales, Delos. *RS* 16

Safford

Awe of new powers *RS* 143

Educated powers *LM* 157 [79]

Descartes. "Such was the Superiority of Descartes over all the geometers of his age, that questions which most perplexed them, cost him but an ordinary degree of attention." [80]

Montucla

Exchange of best men as hostages betwixt Asalanders & Vanalanders. RS 216 [81]

[45] King Olaf could run across the oars outside of the vessel, while his men were rowing the Serpent.[82] He could play with three daggers, so that one was always in the air, & he took the one falling by the handle. He could walk all ⟨a⟩round upon the ship's rails; could strike & cut equally well with both hands, & could cast two spears at once.[83] —merry, frolicsome man, gay & social, great taste in dress, very ⟨soci⟩generous, in battle exceeded all in bravery.

Heimskringla, [1844] vol. 1. p[p]. [454–]455

[46] Intellect

Origin of Intellect in the Moral. TU ⟨p⟩ 5
GH 118
J 95
U 109

[79] The underlinings of "*RS* 16", "*RS* 143", and "*LM* 157" are in pencil.

[80] A short rule is drawn below the "De" of "Descartes.", probably inadvertently.

[81] This sentence is struck through in ink with a vertical use mark.

[82] This sentence, struck through in ink with a vertical use mark, is used in "Success," *W*, VII, 284.

[83] "He could walk . . . once." is struck through in ink with a vertical use mark.

[47][84] Intellect

[48] *Intellect*
Byelaws

Thought is interval[.]

Thought is a power.
↑Intellectuality works down.↓[85]
Every one leads in another.
Every truth universally applicable
Every one ranks itself. Ascension JK 106
O 359
Motive force ↑Selfmoved; or its own currents.↓
Mnemonic force of ideas
Conversation mother, & solitude father of thought.
Inaccessibleness of every thought but that you are in. *F* [No. 2] 111.
↑The used faculties bright. *RS* 157

All kinds of power develop simultaneously. *AZ* 9,[86]

Indisputable talent does not rightly affect us if it do not obey the natural determination [49][87] of character. ↑*AZ* 159 *O* 337 GH 39↓

The transit moment in all things. *CD* 48

Genius takes its rise from the mountains of rectitude *TU* 5

By always intending my mind. *Y* 210[88]

---

[84] Tipped in between pp. [46] and [47] is a newspaper clipping containing two items entitled "Cultivating Marsh Land" and "Plaster for Potatoes."

[85] See *JMN*, X, 314.

[86] This entry is struck through in ink with four diagonal use marks.

[87] "*Intellect*", an index heading, is written at the top of the page.

[88] "Genius takes . . . mind." is struck through in ink with a vertical use mark. "Genius . . . rectitude" is used in "Worship," *W*, VI, 216; "By always . . . mind." is used in "Power," *W*, VI, 75. In Journal Y, Emerson attributes this quotation to Newton. See *JMN*, IX, 335; see also *JMN*, X, 133.

Strict ⟨conversation⟩ ↑discourse↓ with a friend is the magazine out of which all good writing is drawn.[89]

---

[50] "Essence of mind consists in thinking, and that of matter in extension," said Descartes.

[51] *Intellect* [n]

Miscellanies

Arithmetic science of surfaces; probity, of essences. *W* 125

Want of insight the reason why we are so slow. *W* ⟨171⟩75,

Identity. *T* 111,

Others may build cities, he should understand them, & keep them in awe. *W* 93,

"Man feels that he has been what he is from all eternity."

⟨T⟩*V* 13,[90]

Order of Wonder *E* 147, *W* 80, *Y* 142,

All knowledge is assimilation to the object of knowledge.[91]

Common sense is the wick of the candle.[92]

---

[52] *Intellect*

Descartes being asked, where was his library? showed a calf wh⟨e⟩ich he was dissecting, & said, "This is my library." [93]

We may well ask 'What is the effect of thoughts?' Hafiz very properly inquires,

[89] The cancellation line through "conversation" and the added word "discourse" are in pencil.

[90] "Others may . . . eternity.' " is struck through in ink with a vertical use mark. For a possible source of the quotation, from Schelling, see *JMN*, IX, 101, n. 25; it is used in "Fate," *W*, VI, 13.

[91] This sentence is struck through in ink with a vertical use mark; see *JMN*, X, 135, Journal RS, p. [27] above, and Appendix I.

[92] See *JMN*, IX, 164.

[93] Henry Hallam, *Introduction to the Literature of Europe in the Fifteenth, Sixteenth, and Seventeenth Centuries*, 4 vols. (Paris, 1839), III, 142.

"Why changes not the inner mind
Violet earth into musk?"[94]

Hafiz. vol. I. 316

Identity

"Fletcher, whose wit
Was not an accident to the soul, but it,
Only diffused; thus we the same sun call
Moving i' th sphere, & shining on a wall"
[Edward] Powell ["To the Memorie
of Master Fletcher," ll. 21–24][95]
"Durer's pencil, which first knew
The laws of faces, & then faces drew."
[William Cartwright, "Another," ll. 35–36]

Gates of thought slow to show. *K* 96

[53] ↑*Intellect*↓
"Man feels that he has been what he is from all eternity" V 13[96]
Schelling.

Reason of the aversation from metaphysics is the voice of nature. Nature made the eye to see other things, but not itself. If you have sharp eyes, use them, not brag of them.

---

[54]–[56] [blank]
[57] *Beauty*

"Things that are natural are never without a certain grace & excellence. The cracks & rents of a well-baked loaf induce a desire to partake of it.

[94] Emerson's English version of two lines from *Der Diwan von Mohammed Schemsed-din Hafis*, trans. Joseph von Hammer-Purgstall, 2 vols. (Stuttgart and Tübingen, 1812–1813), I, 326. The lines are used in "Poetry and Imagination," *W*, VIII, 18.

[95] One of the "Commendatory Poems" at the beginning of Francis Beaumont and John Fletcher, *Comedies and Tragedies. Never Printed Before. And Now Published by the Authours Originall Copies . . .* (London, 1647). See *JMN*, VII, 186. The quotation beginning " 'Durer's pencil . . .' " below, is also from the "Commendatory Poems" of this edition.

[96] This entry is struck through in ink with a vertical use mark. See p. [51] above.

So likewise the cleft fig, the luscious olive, the spiked grain" &c Marcus Antoninus. p. 16 McCormac, Translater [97]

[58] *Beauty*

"*It was for Beauty that the World* was made."

Ben Jonson
vol 3. 297p. [98]

Inamorato of laws, & new Narcissus. RS 129

What a privilege is not that of a beautiful person, who knows that whenever he sits, or moves, or leaves a shadow on the wall, or sits for a portrait to the artist, or to the Daguerrotype,—he confers a favor on the world.[99]

[59] *Beauty*

Archimedes' devotion to it. *See* V 3 [100]

"For 'tis the eternal law,
That first in beauty should be first in might." [101]
Keats ["Hyperion," II, 228–229]

Death in love. D 51[–52]

"To feel a joy in what is fair,
And o'er it to have power," is Meno's definition of Virtue.[102]

See Y 31

[97] *The Meditations of Marcus Aurelius Antoninus, with the Manual of Epictetus, and a summary of Christian morality*, trans. Henry McCormac (London, 1844).

[98] "The Second Masque, Which was of BEAUTY," *The Works of Ben Jonson*, 5 vols. (London, 1716). This edition, except for vol. 2, is in Emerson's library. The title actually reads "*The Works of Ben. Johnson.*" "'*It was* . . . made.'", struck through in ink with a vertical use mark, is used in "Beauty," *W*, VI, 301.

[99] This sentence, struck through in ink with a vertical use mark, is used in "Beauty," *W*, VI, 299. Cf. "Friendship," *W*, IX, 301.

[100] "3" may be an error; p. [2] of Journal V would seem more appropriate. See *JMN*, IX, 95–96.

[101] The quotation, struck through in ink with a vertical use mark, is used in "Manners," *W*, III, 147.

[102] Victor Cousin, *Oeuvres de Platon*, 1822–1840, VI, 159.

The sky looks indignantly on all that is doubtful & obscure in man.

Beauty fluxional. Beauty is the medium state; balance of expression; what is just ready to flow, & be metamorphosed into other ⟨states⟩forms. Any fixedness, or heaping, or concentration on one feature, a long nose, a sharp chin, a humpback, is the reverse of flowing.[103]

↑— On to p. 61 —↓

[60] Those who painted angels & nativities and descents from the cross, were also writing biographies & satires, though they knew it not. ↑The history of humanity is ↑no↓ hopping squib, but all its discoveries in science, religion & art, consecutive & correlated.↓

Narrowness has been thy bane.

He makes me rich, him I call Plutus, who shows me that every man is mine, & every faculty is mine; who[n] does not impoverish me in praising Plato, but, contrariwise, is adding assets to my inventory. ↑See p. 119↓

[61] *Beauty*
The mountains in the horizon acquaint us with more exalted relations to our friends than any we sustain. — from old MS

R 140,

"Position is necessary for perfecting beauty," said Sir C. Wren.[104]
See *B* 255
Gracefulness given by high thoughts. *B* 138

---

[103] "Beauty fluxional . . . flowing.", struck through in ink with a vertical use mark, is used in "Beauty," *W*, VI, 292. See *JMN*, VIII, 388.

[104] Quoted in [H. B. Ker], "Sir Christopher Wren; with Some General Remarks on the History and Progress of Architecture," *Lives of Eminent Persons* (1833), p. 30.

"By beauty, I mean that melting of human lineaments into simple concord, which resembles the union of musical notes into simple melody."
Thos. Campbell.[105]

[62] "Il faudrait pour bien faire
Que tout le monde fût millionnaire." [106]

Froude's "Nemesis" had a remarkable formula[.] [107]

"I had rather go a fishing," said the chimneysweep at ⟨m⟩Marblehead,—when it [n] was proposed to abate his price a little,—& enraged the whole town.

⟨The slaughterhouse style of thinking & the carving knife style of education⟩ [108]

---

[63] *Immortality.*
I notice that as soon as writers broach this question they begin to ⟨quote⟩quote. I hate quotation. Tell me what you know.

[64] Heimskringla [1844,] Vol.II p. 195 ↑*Eloquence*↓
Every reader has a taste for kings' speeches not kings' speeches of modern Eng. & France Moniteur & Times,—but good royal brag & insult, such as the Richards & Charlemagnes & Henri Quatres & Canutes & Olafs & Sweyns & Haralds made, speeches of royal pirates. Olaf says, "Does K. Canute wish to rule over all the countries of the North? Will he eat up all the Kail in England? He shall do so, & reduce that country to a desart before I lay my head in ⟨his⟩ his hands, or show him any sign of vassalage. Now ye shall tell him these my words. I will defend Norway with battleaxe & sword as long as life is given me,—& will pay scott to no man for my kingdom." [109]

[105] *Life and Letters of Thomas Campbell*, ed. William Beattie, 3 vols. (London, 1849), III, 305.

[106] Augustin Eugène Scribe, *Le Mariage d'Argent*, I, iv, 99, in *Oeuvres Choisies*, 5 vols. (Paris, 1845), V, in Emerson's library. See *JMN*, X, 63.

[107] For the formula, and its source, see Journal AZ, p. [162] below.

[108] "⟨The slaughterhouse . . . thinking" is used in "Immortality," *W*, VIII, 332.

[109] *The Heimskringla*, 1844, II, 195.

King Hake's — death vol I [110]

Good speech full of rough churl strength of Sweinke Steinarson vol III, 125 [126–128] [111]

↑See TU p 66↓

[65] 25 May 1849. Two gravestones have been planted in my path within the year, Ellen Hooper's and David Scott's. Ellen Hooper connected herself with all the noblest & most loved figures that have cheered & enriched me in my own land ⟦or with all but one: my own Ellen she never knew⟧. And she gave a value by her interest to all my writings.[112]

[66] You like these pirate kings. You like these men who are kings or captains, because they are the best, i.e. the worst of the gang. One talent they have, viz. the power of doing what the others also think is desireable, — of beating their enemies, & of beating their friends too; in short, of restoring order among these ⟨farmers⟩roarers.[n] Well now they have brought it so far that the ⟨is⟩ order is good, — so good that a child or a woman can sit on the pirate's ⟨throne⟩seat. Well, are you pleased? You have got what you wanted? O no. Now you are wishing for your pirate again. Do you want Bloodyaxe again? Do you not see, that, if the pirate tames the crew, the tamed crew tame the Pirate again?

[67] I find ⟨the⟩ ↑my↓ peartree a ⟨perfect⟩ key to the world. I find that each man, like each plant, has his own parasite, & Dr J. has very different & formidabler & more vivacious enemies than any slugs that are on my leaves. H⟨enry⟩ JB is his curculio & F & W his borers & knifeworms. ↑C. ⟨B⟩ ↑Brown↓ eat him first; then Morse;

[110] This line is struck through in ink with a vertical use mark; cf. "Race," *W*, V, 59, where Emerson paraphrases, and borrows directly from, *The Heimskringla*, 1844, I, 237–238.

[111] Sweinke Steinarsson's speech to King Magnus occurs in vol. III of *The Heimskringla*, 1844, 126–128.

[112] Ellen Sturgis Hooper (1812–1848), Caroline Sturgis' sister and contributor to *The Dial*, died on November 3, 1848. David Scott (see Journal RS, p. [168] above) died on March 5, 1849.

then Morton. Bowditch, Bigelow; then Forster & Whitney; then Pierce & Bowen.↓ [113]

England. Pertinacity a prime element of English power & grandeur. What an eminent example is this catalogue of Stars by

[113] Except for the first sentence, this paragraph, struck through in ink with a diagonal use mark, is used in "Fate," *W*, VI, 45, where Dr. J. becomes "A strong, astringent, bilious nature," C. Brown a "swindler," Morse a "client," Morton a "quack," and the rest "smooth, plausible gentlemen, bitter and selfish as Moloch." Emerson firmly believed, with some evidence, that his brother-in-law, Dr. Charles T. Jackson, had discovered sulphuric ether as an anesthetic in 1842 and passed the information on to Dr. William T. G. Morton in 1846, who then used it in a surgical case at Massachusetts General Hospital and won fame as the discoverer (*L*, IV, 57n; V, 317, 367). The controversy was fierce and bitter. Dr. Henry J. Bigelow, of the Massachusetts General Hospital, persuaded fellow doctors to allow Morton to administer the ether, read a paper describing Morton's process and criticizing Jackson, and, when Jackson sought money, asked him if he expected to be rewarded for letting people suffer all the time from 1842 to 1846. Jackson considered Bigelow a "very conceited young surgeon." Nathaniel I. Bowditch, a trustee of Massachusetts General, was chairman of the Hospital's board of inquiry to determine who discovered ether anesthesia. Jackson denied the authority of the board; Bowditch asked if it was to conclude that Jackson had no case; the board ultimately decided in favor of Morton. Later, in a letter apparently to a member of Congress, Bowditch attacked Jackson's probity.

In 1844, Jackson was the first man to explore and reveal the extensive mineral resources of the southern shore of Lake Michigan. In 1847, he was appointed to superintend a geological survey of mineral lands in Michigan; John W. Foster and Josiah D. Whitney were among his associates. Their discontent with Jackson, and that of others in the survey, led to Jackson's resignation in 1849; he later rescinded it and declared that it was extorted. When Whitney was nominated for admission to the American Academy of Arts and Sciences, of which Jackson was a member, Jackson tried to block it. Francis Bowen, who had earlier attacked Transcendentalism in a review of Emerson's *Nature*, coauthored a resolution to expel Jackson from the Academy; it was passed, but subject to an investigation of Jackson, which was never held. The role of anyone named Pierce (or Peirce) as a Jackson enemy has not been determined. Interestingly, Emerson does not mention Dr. Martin Gay, one of Jackson's major proponents, who had fascinated Emerson at Harvard (see *JMN*, I, 22, 39, 52–53, 54). (The story of the Morton-Jackson controversy comes largely from L. J. Ludovici, *The Discovery of Anaesthesia* [New York, 1962]; the author is blatantly hostile to Jackson.)

Charles Brown, Jackson's brother-in-law, failed in business, lost his reputation, and left his wife and children. Jackson claimed to have told Samuel F. B. Morse the basic principle of the telegraph. In 1845 Emerson wrote, "Dr [Charles T.] J[ackson]. invented Morse's Magnetic Telegraph" (*JMN*, IX, 172). Emerson originally drew the long rule below "& F & W . . . knifeworms", intending to set off the entry from the one which follows, beginning "*England.*"; later he added the remaining names above and below the rule.

younger Herschel. His father had done it for the northern hemisphere. He expatriates himself & family 4 years among bushmen & dutchmen at Cape of Good Hope, & finishes his inventory, comes home, & redacts it in 8 years more(?) and it will not begin to be useful for 30 years, & then will forever be precious.[114] That is true nobility of use. . . . I give you, ↑gentlemen,↓ Pertinacity, & not too much pertinacity.

[68] *England*
I find the Englishman to be he of all men who stands firmest in his shoes.[115]

———

"The people of England have always been of an eminently practical turn, especially in politics, — very little given to mere theory, & looking mainly to the immediate comforts & decencies of life, as the objects which they desire to secure."

(Jeffrey) ? (Edinburgh Review of Macaulay)
July 1849 [116]

———

↑See *TU*, 210. Englishman departmental↓

———

Every Englishman capable of bad manners, thought A.

———

Cleverness is the new word the nation has introduced.

[69]

Spring.

How comes it Winter is so quite forced hence
And locked up under ground? that every sense
Hath several objects? Trees have got their heads,
The fields their coats; that now the shining meads
Do boast the /paunce,/pan⟨s⟩zy/ [117] the lily, & the rose,

[114] "*England* . . . precious.", struck through in ink with single vertical and diagonal use marks, is used in "Ability," *W*, V, 91. Sir John Herschel (1792–1871), astronomer, was the son of Sir William Herschel.

[115] This sentence, struck through in ink with a vertical use mark, is used in "Manners," *W*, V, 102.

[116] From a review of "The History of England from the Accession of James the Second, by Thomas Babington Macaulay," vol. XC, No. CLXXXI, 141.

[117] "panzy" is in pencil, written above "paunce,".

And every flower doth laugh as Zephyr blows.
The seas are now more even than the land,
The rivers run as smoothéd by the hand.

Ben Jonson (*Vision of Delight*) [*The Works of Ben Jonson*, 1716,] Vol 5 p 334

Ford The Sun's Darling.[118]

Spring. "My youngest girl, the violet breathing May,
Is come to do you service." [II, i, 85, 87]

Spring. "A girdle make whose buckles stretched to the length
Shall reach from arctic to the antarctic pole.
What ground so e'er thou canst with that enclose
I'll give thee freely." [II, i, 224–227]

↑*Humour*. "Poor spring, goody herbwife!"↓ [II, i, 213]

[70] *Spring*

The Sportive Sun[119]

"May makes the cheerful sure, May breeds & brings new blood;
May marcheth throughout every limb, May makes the merry mood."[120]

Richd. Edwards. b. 1523, d. 1566.

See for Spring, *V* 143 and S 270[121]

See for an eastern poem on Spring, *Von Hammer*. p. 259[122]

---

[71] Some minds are forever restrained from descending into

[118] "The Sun's Darling." is enclosed by an oval line in ink. Ford and Dekker wrote the play.

[119] This phrase, struck through in ink with two diagonal use marks, is used in "Song of Nature," l. 3, *W*, IX, 244. See *JMN*, IX, 292.

[120] "M[aster] Edwardes May," *The Paradise of Dainty Devices* (London, 1812), p. 1, misquoted. See *JMN*, VII, 24.

[121] In Notebook S Salvage, pp. [270]–[271], Emerson copied almost verbatim under the heading "Spring" the passage from his letter to Margaret Fuller of February 21, 1840, beginning "These spring winds" and ending with "self commanding." He labeled the passage "To M F Feb 1840". See *L*, II, 254–255.

[122] Joseph von Hammer-Purgstall, *Geschichte der schönen Redekünste Persiens* . . . , 1818.

nature: Others, & much the largest class, are forever prevented from ascending out of it. Plotinus & Alcott cannot know it.[123]

↑See p 136↓

[72] [blank]

[73] A man's giving should not degenerate into a diabetes which ⟨converts⟩ ↑sends↓ all the food & sugar in the body into the urinary discharge[.]

[74] Bonaparte had burglars to deal with. "When the battle of Eylau was fought, 60 000 men were wanting in the ranks, of which only half were in hospital. Les autres étaient en maraude, plundering three times more food than they used,—30 000 vagabonds living at discretion on the peasantry,—les uns vrais lâches, dont une armée même héroique a toujours une certaine quantité dans les rangs; les autres ↑fort↓ braves, au contraire, ma↑i↓s pillards par nature, aimant la liberté et le désordre, et prêts à revenir [75] au corps dès qu'ils apprenaient la reprise des opérations."

The dealing with this monstrous evil did not monopolize his energy. Nothing was too minute for his searching curiosity, for a suspicious habit, as his admirer observes satirically, "ne peut manquer ⟨'⟩d'arriver chez un maitre absolu et nouveau."

Lord Lovelace's Review of Thiers'
Histoire du Consulat et de L'Empire.[124]

Remember that only the light characters travel; and there is no moral deformity but is a good passion out of place.[125] (See *O* 40)

---

[123] This paragraph, struck through in ink with a vertical use mark, is used, except for the last sentence, in "Swedenborg," *W*, IV, 143.

[124] The paragraph, struck through with single discontinuous use marks in ink on pp. [74] and [75], and with a vertical pencil mark on p. [74] and a diagonal pencil mark on p. [75], is used in "Power," *W*, VI, 72. From "Eylau" on, the language is identical with the review of Thiers' *Histoire* in both the American and the English editions of the *Westminster Review*, XLIX, 1848, p. 221 or 416, but in neither edition is Lovelace mentioned as the author.

[125] This sentence, struck through in ink with a vertical use mark, is used in "Considerations by the Way," *W*, VI, 258.

And remember Pillsbury's use of the Comic.[126] See *O* 112.

Timing, *Y* 207.

Cannot trust men, can trust their natures.

[76] Luther's famed verse is

"Wer nicht liebt Wein, Weib, und Gesang,
Der bleibt ein Narr, sein Leben lang." [127]

See also *CD* 109

Which has the homely sense of Propertius's "Salvo grata puella viro." [128]

[77] Words

The Collegians have seldom made a better word than *Squirt* for a showy sentence. So I find *tin* for money always comic.
Lubber is a well marked genus.

In conversation, the game is, to say something new with old words. And you shall ⟨hear⟩ ↑observe↓ a man of the people picking his way along, ⟨from⟩ step by step, using every time an old boulder, yet never setting his foot on an old place.

"Honey-pie," says Statestreet when there is ⟨fondness or any too much show of good fortune⟩ ↑flattery;↓ "All my eye," when any exaggeration[.]
Fiddle faddle *C* 161

[78] Wilkinson[,] Swedenborg's pupil after 100 years[,] a

[126] Parker Pillsbury (1809–1898) was a reformer, abolitionist, lecturer, and editor of the *Herald of Freedom*, an antislavery magazine published at Concord, New Hampshire, by William Lloyd Garrison.

[127] The two lines of poetry, struck through in ink with a vertical use mark, are used in "Montaigne," *W*, IV, 153. The quotation, written in the Luther room in Wartburg Castle, is attributed to Luther without proof of authorship.

[128] "The thankoffering of a grateful wife for her husband's safety," *The Elegies of Propertius*, Bk. IV, iii, 72.

philosophic critic with a brain like Bacon.[129] Why not read in England? Are there no mornings in England? Do they read Dickens when they first get up as well as overnight?

———

Swedenborgian Church an imprisonment in the letter; never a hero stirs out of it.

———

Ah the Imagination has a flute that sets the ⟨m⟩atoms of our frame in a dance like planets, and once so flagellated, the whole man reeling drunk to the music, they never ↑quite↓ subside to their old marble.[130]

———

In Swedenborg, the Spirits have the dumps.

———

In the Conclave⟨,⟩ ↑⟨at Rome,⟩↓ the mendicant orders had their cardinal,—and in man, mouse & midge[,] chalk & marl must be represented. Every affinity & quality[,] sour & bitter, slime & reek must come to [79] the day. There is no low & high in real being. Each of these things has its translation into the spiritual & celestial ⟨sp⟩ & necessary sphere where it plays a part as indestructible as any other. But it is plain that each of these qualities, chlorine, iodine, & what not becomes pronounced in a man. That is their first ascension. He knows what to do with them. Their quality makes his career. And he ⟨understands &⟩ [n] can variously publish their virtues because he is made of that thing.[131]

[80] Nature

"As large a demand upon our faith is made by nature as by miracles, themselves."[132] Swedenborg E[conomy].[of the]A[nimal].K[ingdom, 1845–1846,]. Vol 1 p 188

[129] This sentence, struck through in ink with two vertical use marks, is used in "Swedenborg," *W*, IV, 111.

[130] This sentence, struck through in ink with a diagonal use mark, is used in "Poetry and Imagination," *W*, VIII, 18.

[131] This paragraph, struck through in ink with single vertical use marks on pp. [78] and [79], is used in "Uses of Great Men," *W*, IV, 11.

[132] This sentence, struck through in ink with a vertical use mark, is used in "Swedenborg," *W*, IV, 112, and "Demonology," *W*, X, 12. See *JMN*, X, 27.

He found, says Wilkinson, that Nature is no other than philosophy & theology embodied in mechanics, or, more reverently speaking, she is the mechanism or means ↑of↓ which truth & good are the end.[133]

E.A.K.

Introd. Essay lxxvii [134]

Show me thy face, dear Nature, that I may forget my own.[135]

[81] ↑Boon↓

Nature shows ⟨us⟩ /every/each/ day somewhat we now first behold
⟨Nature⟩ ↑And↓ trains us on to see the new as if it were the old,
And blest is he who sees ↑the same↓ & ↑haply↓ [n] asks not why
⟨The fool of nature & his eyes.⟩
Imparadised in crowded hours nor afraid to live or die [136]

Kinde was the old English, which however only filled half the range of our fine Latin word, with its delicate future tense, *Natura, About to be born.*

But nothing expresses that power which seems to work for beauty alone.

Stars. AB 4

Her forces are emulous of mental processes.

[82] That nature works after the same method as the human Imagination.

that nature makes flowers as the mind makes images.

that metaphysics might anticipate Jussieu.

That organic matter & mind ⟨s⟩go from the same law, & so correspond.[137]

---

[133] "He found . . . mechanics," is struck through in ink with a vertical use mark.

[134] The Introductory Essay occurs in volume II, following a new title page for volume I, dated 1846. See Journal RS, p. [131] above.

[135] See *JMN*, IX, 398.

[136] "Boon . . . die", in pencil and struck through in pencil with a diagonal use mark, is used in "Quatrains: Nature," *W*, IX, 294.

[137] For "That nature works . . . correspond.", see Journal RS, p. [255] above.

Aristotle's Definition of Nature E A K. II; [p. 225][138]

[83] ↑Boon↓ Nature shows each day a brag which we now first behold
And trains us to see the new as if it were the old
And blest who ⟨sees the same⟩ ↑deeply playing deep yet↓ yet haply asks not why
⟨Imparadised in crowded ⟨|| . . . ||⟩⟩ ↑Too ⟨|| . . . ||⟩ ↑busied↓ with the crowded↓ fears to live or die.[139]

Boon Nature yields each day a brag which we now first behold,
And trains us on to slight the new, as if it were the old,
And blest is he who playing deep, yet haply asks not why,
Too busied with the crowded day to fear to live or die.[140]

[84] Can't[n] forgive Swedenborg the confusion of planes. ⟨There⟩ We will pardon a popular orator for a mistake in Categories, but not a categorist, not Aristotle, Kant, or Swedenborg.[141] Has not the Intellect sins? He shall be degraded out of Olympus for a thousand years, & shall not eat ambrosia for that term. Let him be tried by the law of his tribe. High cr↑i↓me & misdemeanour. He carried the law of surface into the plane of substance; he carried individualism & its fopperies into the realm of Essences & generals. & so introduces chaos & dislocation.[142]

[85] Swedenborg could so easily cosmologize because of his

[138] Emanuel Swedenborg, *The Economy of the Animal Kingdom* . . . , 1845–1846. The definition is "Nature . . . is that, by the primary inexistence of which anything is generated; also the *materia prima* [?]; that exist in nature. . . . It is a principle and cause of motion and rest in that thing in which it is . . . *per se*." The bracketed question mark and suspension dots are in the original. See *JMN*, VI, 329.

[139] "Boon Nature . . . die." is in erased pencil writing; the rule across the page following this erased entry is also in pencil.

[140] The poetry written in ink below the pencil rule overlies the same version written in pencil. See p. [81] above.

[141] "C'ant . . . categorist,", struck through in ink with a vertical use mark, is used in "Swedenborg," *W*, IV, 140.

[142] "He carried the . . . dislocation.", struck through in ink with a vertical use mark, is used in "Swedenborg," *W*, IV, 140.

habitual ↑insensibility to↓ perception of ⟨quality⟩ the insignificance of mere magnitude: alike to him the magnetic atom, & the astronom⟨er⟩ic spaces, so concentrated was his insight of quality. & that was easy to him which would be hard to another.[143]

Nearness[144]

And really the soul ↑is *near* things, because it↓ is centre of the universe. So that Astronomy & history & nature & theology date from where the observer stands. There is no quality in nature's vast magazines he cannot touch; no truth in science he cannot see; no act in will he cannot verify; —↑there↓ where he stands.

Swedenborg was the last Christian.

[86] [blank]

[87] *Reaction* | *Energy*

See *TU* p. 20, *RS* 156, 193

The ⟨very⟩ rancour of the disease denotes the strength of the Constitution[.][145]

The senators who dissented from the President's war, were not those who knew better, but those who could afford to. See O 196[146]

Micah Ruggles was a good example of personal force. O 267 & Davis & Capt. Rhynders[147]

See O 268

[143] This paragraph is struck through in ink with a vertical use mark; "Swedenborg could . . . quality." is used in "Swedenborg," *W*, IV, 106.

[144] This index heading for the paragraph which follows is enclosed by an ink line forming a box.

[145] "The ⟨very⟩ . . . Constitution", struck through in pencil and in ink with single vertical use marks, is used in "Power," *W*, VI, 62. See *JMN*, IX, 137.

[146] This entry is struck through in pencil and in ink with single vertical use marks and is also marked in the left margin with a vertical pencil line.

[147] Emerson heard Ruggles "of Fall River" in a Lyceum Conversation; see *JMN*, IX, 427. Davis is probably Andrew Jackson Davis (see p. [145] below). Isaiah Rynders was a United States marshal and Tammany leader in New York City.

Tigers. O 289
Fremont
Democratic rabble. O 315
Abel Moore CD 94
Imbecility RS 268 156 193 [148]
The Devil Steward of the Communities, & of the Shakers; &, ⟨c⟩when poets paint God, they draw the Energy from hell. See LM 118 [149]

[88] "And all that Cowards have is mine"

Leyden
ap Scott [150]

Buonaparte's Energy. TU. p. 74 [151]

The pirate & his men. TU, p. 66

Pawnees

[89] I conceive the value of railroads to be this, in education, namely, to unite the advantages of town & country life, neither of which we can spare. A man should live in or near a large town; because, let his own genius be what it may, it will repel quite as much of agreeable & valuable talent as it draws; &, in a city, the total attraction is sure to conquer first or last every repulsion, & ⟨win⟩ ↑drag↓ the most improbable hermit within its walls, some day in the year. In the town, he can find the swimming school, the gymnastic teacher, the chemist, the music, the dancing master, the shooting gallery. Opera, ballet, & panorama, Agassiz, Lyell, Webster, & Lafayette⟨.⟩ [n] ↑& the Club.↓ In the country, he can find solitude & reading, manly labor, & cheap living, moors for game, hills for geology, & [90] groves for devotion.

A great deal that is not set down in the bill. I pay the Schoolmaster, but 'tis the school-boys that educate ⟨h⟩my son.[152]

[148] "156" and "193" are in pencil.

[149] "Imbecility . . . hell." is struck through in ink with a vertical use mark. Heavy, stubby ink marks partly cover the second "of" and "Energy".

[150] See Sir Walter Scott, *Minstrelsy of the Scottish Border* (London, 1868), p. 44. John Leyden (1775–1811) helped Scott prepare early volumes of the "Border Minstrelsy."

[151] This entry is struck through in ink with a vertical use mark.

[152] "I conceive . . . son." is struck through in pencil and in ink with single

[91] Education. Ancora imparo
TU 7, 89, ↑124, 243↓ I carry my satchel still.[153]
AB 112
AB 4
Y 102
GH 35 63

⟨"A child is better unborn than untaught" Gascoigne.⟩ [154]

A man who can make hard things easy.
My children go to ⟨|| . . . ||t's school,⟩ ↑the schoolmaster,↓ but the ↑school↓ boys ⟨in the street have the⟩ educat⟨ing⟩↑e↓ ⟨of⟩ them ⁿ↑.↓ [155] ⟨|| . . . ||⟩

The children divide their waking time between school, fruit, & the cats.

I like to see them learn the use of cats; then 'tis worth while to suffer a dog in the house a little while; & after, be sure to let them learn the use of horses.

"a boy is ↑the↓ most difficult to manage of all wild beasts" Plato *Laws* [Taylor, *The Works of Plato* . . . , 1804, II,] 203 [156]

[92] *Americans*

Americans would sail in a ship built of lucifer matches.— [157] Yes, & the walls of our 2000 ton boat were of thickest pasteboard, & our timbers the biggest jackstraws.

---

diagonal use marks on pp. [89] and [90]. "I conceive . . . devotion." is used in "Culture," *W*, VI, 148; "A great . . . son." is used in "Culture," *W*, VI, 142.

[153] "Ancora imparo" ("I still learn") is the motto of a Michelangelo sketch. See *JMN*, X, 6, 7, and n. 10. "I carry . . . still." is used in "Poetry and Imagination," *W*, VIII, 14.

[154] See Journal RS, p. [16] above.

[155] "A man . . . them⟨,⟩." is struck through in pencil and in ink with vertical use marks; the second sentence is used in "Culture," *W*, VI, 142. See p. [90] above.

[156] The quotation, struck through in ink with a vertical use mark, is used in "Culture," *W*, VI, 139. See Journal RS, p. [12] above, and *JMN*, X, 473.

[157] See *JMN*, X, 320.

[93] [blank]

[94] The tree needs water & digging about & pruning & protection from its enemies the slug, the ⟨aphis⟩louse, the borer, & so on, &, more than all, ⟨fo⟩it needs food; it will die without food, if you want fruit, you must give manure. Well, then, a pretty Case you make out for the Cultivator. Well, it is not gainful, & yet it seems to me much, that I have brought a skilful chemist into my ground & keep him there overnight, all day, all summer, for an art that he possesses of cooking pears; he can take common water & clod, & by means of sunshine, manufacture the handsomest & most delicious [95] Bonne de Jerseys, Bartletts, bergamots, & brown beurrés in an inimitable manner which no confectioner can approach & his method of working is ⟨a⟩no less beautiful than his result.[158]

In the drought, the peartree roots murmured in the dark, & said, they were sorely put to it for water, & could not go on another day, supplying food to the tree above them. But there is the kind old master who so tendered us, & visits the tree daily, we hear his footsteps every morn. If we could only give him a sign of our condition. Be it so. I will instantly, said the taproot, hang him out a signal on the highest bough of the tree, & we will see if he can understand us. So the taproot ceased working, & the top bough wanting food, drooped & hung its head. The master, you may be sure, was not long in seeing ⟨with alarm⟩ the withering of his favourite, & [96] much alarmed he ran in haste & brought a ⟨pail of⟩ water↑-pot↓ & soon after a barrel of water, & abundantly refreshed the roots, whi↑c↓h, thus restored, showed their good humour to the very top of the tree.

Who climbs best? the monkey; no, the squirrel goes higher. No; ⟨the s⟩sap climbs ⟨far⟩ better, & will go into the top bough, & to the ⟨top⟩ ↑last↓ vein & edge of the highest leaf on the tree. Yes; but a drop of water climbs higher, for look, there is a cloud ⟨high over⟩ ↑above↓ the tree. Well, heat climbs higher than water, & space higher than heat.

———

Your pears, ↑which you raise,↓ cost you more than mine, which

[158] "Well, it [p. [94]] . . . result." is used in "Country Life," *W*, XII, 146.

I buy. — Yes, they are costly, but we all have expensive vices; you play at billiards, & I at pear trees.

[97] *Riches*

Neither will poverty suit every complexion. Socrates & Franklin may well go hungry & in plain clothes, if they like it; but there are people who cannot afford this, but whose poverty of nature needs wealth of food & clothes to make them decent. See *LM* 21

I do not drink wine, but would have the name of drinking wine

[98] ↑Printed↓ [159]

Carlyle is a man of force, of burly, vivacious, aggressive temperament and unimpressionable. The literary man & the fashionable man, & the political man, each fresh from triumphs in his own sphere comes eagerly to see & unite with this man whose fun they so heartily enjoy, but they are struck with despair at the first onset. His cold, victorious, scoffing, sneering, vituperative declamation strikes them with coldness & hestitation ⟨at am⟩on the instant. ↑The↓ Malleus mediocritatis.[160]

[99]–[100] [leaf missing] [161]

[101] *Boston* ↑See *BO* 53↓

Boston, since its railroads opened, has advanced on New York in point of property, &, I am surprised to learn, exceeds it in personal property. The figures stand thus:

	1848 Real	Personal
New York	$193,029 076	$61 164 451
Boston	$100,403 200	$67,374 800

Increase in 8 years, real & personal.

---

[159] Added in pencil, perhaps by Edward Emerson.

[160] "A hammer against moderateness" (Ed.). See *JMN*, X, 553. The paragraph, struck through in pencil with a vertical use mark, is used in "Carlyle," *W*, X, 493.

[161] Emerson indexed p. [99] under Woman and p. [100] under Meteorology. In Notebook S Salvage, p. [82], Emerson records: "Village negatives and malefactors will not let the high-meaning maiden mean highly TU 99".

⟨Boston⟩New York $1,350 373
Boston $73,146 400[162]

[Boston 1849. Aug
Real Estate 102 890 800
Personal 71 218 100
Bost. Transcript
Aug.

[10⟨0⟩2] *Martial*
Ad Sophronium.

Tanta ⟨est⟩tibi est animi probitas orisque, ↑Sophroni,↓
Ut mires fieri te potuisse patrem[163]
[*Epigrams*,] Lib XI. ciii.

——

Difficilis, facilis, jucundus, acerbus, es idem:
Nec tecum possum vivere, nec sine te.[164]
[*Epigrams*,] Lib. XII. Ep. xlvii

——

[10⟨1⟩3] Martial is the literature of Aristocracy. See the famous Epigram De Porsenna et Mu⟨t⟩cio Scaevola. ↑(Lib 1.22).↓ And now read this

De Porcia Uxore Bruti:

Conjugis audisset fatum cum Porcia Bruti,
Et subtracta sibi qu⟨e⟩aereret arma dolor:
Nondum scitis, ait, mortem non posse negari?
Credideram satis hoc vos docuisse patrem.
Dixit, et ardentes avido bibit ore favillas.
I nunc, et ferrum, turba molesta, nega.[165]
————[*Epigrams*,] Lib. I. Epig. 43

[162] In a letter to his brother William, June 18, 1849 (*L*, IV, 152–153), Emerson says the figures on real and personal property in New York and Boston were furnished him by Robert B. Storer, a Boston merchant who married Sarah Sherman Hoar, sister of Elizabeth.

[163] "Such is your modesty in mind and aspect, Safronius, that I wonder you have managed to become a father." The Loeb text has "Safroni".

[164] "Difficult and easy-going, pleasant and churlish, you are at the same time: I can neither live with you nor without you." For "Nec . . . te.", see *JMN*, VI, 124.

[165] "When Porcia had learned the fate of her husband Brutus, and grief looked for the weapons that had been stolen from it, 'Know ye not yet,' she said, 'that death

"The wisdom & the arts of Athens form in all polished communities a principal object of study, &, to comprehend & to enjoy them, is to be a gentleman." *St John* [misquoted] [166]

[104] Martial. (continued)

See the Epigram De Leandro.[167]

De Rusticatione Lib IV 90
Ad Regulum de fama poetarum V, 10,
In Cinnam, VII, 43
Ad Avitum. IX, 1.

De Cleopatra Lib IV, 22,
De vipera electro inclusa IV 59
De ape electro inclusa IV 32
De fragmento Argus [VII, 19]
De Villa Faustini [III, 58]
To Horatio Greenough I sent *Faustinus* Lib. 1. 26

[105] "Ille ego sum nulli nugarum laude secundus," says[n] this ancient Herrick in the ode *ad Avitum*.[168] And all the English lyrists are much indebted to him; Herrick chiefly. Here is the original Doctor Fell

↑
Ad Sabidium.
↓

Non amo te, Sabidi, nec possum dicere quare;
Hoc tantum possum dicere, non amo te.[169]

Martial, like Aesop, or Horace, or Homer, or a Bible, shows that one book can avail to touch all the points in the circle of daily manners, & furnish a popular literature,—as well as a hundred[.]

---

cannot be denied? I had believed my sire by his fate had taught you this!' She spake, and with greedy throat drank down the glowing embers. Go to now! officious throng: deny the steel!"

[166] James Augustus St. John, *The History of the Manners and Customs of Ancient Greece*, 3 vols. (London, 1842), I, xi–xii, in Emerson's library.

[167] See p. [i] above. All references below, on p. [104], are to the *Epigrams*.

[168] "Lo! he am I whose light verse yields to none." Martial, *Epigrams*, IX, 1.

[169] "I do not love you, Sabidius; and I can't say why. This only I can say: I do not love you." Martial, *Epigrams*, I, 32.

↑(To Beau Brummel) In Posthumum.↓

Posthume, non bene olet, qui bene semper olet.[170]
[Martial, *Epigrams*, II, 12]

In Priscum.

Cum te non nossem, dominum regem que vocabam;
Cum bene te novi, jam mihi Priscus eris.[171]

I should make it complimentary to a friend, & write *Ad Priscum*[.]

At mihi succurrit pro Ganymede manus[172]
[Martial, *Epigrams*, II, 43]

---

[106] 20 June.

At our sad fire⟨,⟩ last night, ↑at the Old Court House & the store on the East side,↓[173] which[n] burned the Court house, James Conner found a door among the Chattels of one family, &, carrying off that prize, he & Sam Staples protected their backs by means of it from the scorching heat, whilst they directed the engine-pipe against the ten-footer under the elm tree. I had not seen a door perform such good extra service, since its famed feat of the Coverlet.[174]

At New York, ↑June 13 14 15↓ I read Saint Antony's sermon to the fishes, full of bonhommie in the idea & the expletives, but ludicrously inapt in some of the points, ⟨a⟩e.g. reminding them how much our Lord loved to eat them; [107] but kindly considered in remind-

[170] "Postumus, he is not well scented who always is well-scented!"

[171] "When I did not know you, I called you my master and my king. Now I know you well, henceforth you shall be to me Priscus." Martial, *Epigrams*, I, 112.

[172] "But my own hand is Ganymede to serve me."

[173] Emerson first turned the comma after "fire" into a caret, then inscribed another caret after "night,"; the editors have inserted his added matter at the more likely place.

[174] The Court House at Concord was destroyed by fire early in the morning of June 20, 1849. The "feat of the Coverlet." probably refers to the anecdote about a poor woman who covered her children with an old door; see *JMN*, V, 282. "James Conner" is perhaps a relative of the E. Conner shown on an 1852 map of Concord as living on the Lexington Road, two houses away from Nathaniel Hawthorne. Sam Staples was the local constable, tax collector, and jailer.

ing them how safe they were from rain, wind, dust, & deluges, not afraid of crevasses, &, let us add, ↑of↓ conversation; no talking permitted in that atheneum[.] He should have reminded them of their few duties,—they have the vacation we men sigh for; suggested a piscine philosophy in view of pike & grampus, that if a soldier of the kingdom of Ci has lost a buckler, a soldier of Ci has found it, & not failed to throw in an effective hint of transmigration & ascent to the inconveniences of pantaloons & Westminster Catechism one of these days.[175]

New England Catholics disgusting. And the spread of Popery futile. As to fearing the Pope, we in America should as ⟨soon⟩ soon think of fearing a muskmelon.

[108] In N.Y. I saw Catherine Sedgwick daughter of ⟨Robert⟩ ↑Roderick↓ S.; and Henry James.

[109] As Culture enables a man to live well with his enemies, ⟨also,⟩ ↑⟨even⟩↓ so it checks the excess of individual genius, "half his strength he put not forth, but checked his thunder in mid volley[.]"

"For philosophy↑,↓ ⟨is an⟩O Socrates, is an elegant thing, if any one moderately meddles with it; but if he is conversant with it more than is becoming, it corrupts the man," [n] said Callicles[.]

Taylor's[n] [The Works of] Plato, [1804,] IV. 400

[110] ---

I think it a consideration of ⟨m⟩some importance,—that the Federal Union takes away from its members the power of declaring peace & war: so that, let Texas, & California, & Minesota, & Oregon, be never so quarrelsome, once in the Union, their hands are tied. ↑??↓

[175] Emerson went to New York for a few days on June 12, with Lidian and Ellen, apparently for no specific engagements (*L*, IV, 150, 152). For "Saint Antony's sermon", see Joseph Addison, *Remarks on Several Parts of Italy, &c., In the Years 1701, 1702, 1703* (London, 1705), pp. 62–74. In a letter of 1855, Emerson writes, "I would quote Confucius's sentence to you: 'A soldier of the Kingdom of Ci has lost a buckler. Well, a soldier of the Kingdom of Ci has found the buckler' " (*L*, IV, 509). The source may be *The Phenix; a Collection of Old and Rare Fragments* (New York, 1835), p. 83; see *JMN*, VI, 338.

England. My friend said what is true, that a man arriving in England finds ⟨to⟩ himself protected to a wonderful degree; a hundred grandfathers & grandmothers he has; the old mansionhouse, with a witness. The pictures on the chimney-tiles of his nursery were the pictures of these people. He belongs to an old nation[.] [176]

[111] 1 July. I find England again this summer in Macaulay's two volumes, as I found it, last summer, in London.[177] The same country of wealth, of birth, of precedent, of decorum. The story is told with all that ability which one meets so abundantly in England, & in no other country,—full of knowledge of books, & men, & customs, which it is creditable to know. The story is quite full of *bon ton.* ⟨There is not⟩ It is written with extreme diligence & is very entertaining & valuable from the amount of good information & curious anecdote, & really has claims to be a [112] history of the people of England, as the author has studied to make it. The second volume is far the best, the ⟨history⟩ ↑character↓ of James is so ⟨bad⟩dramatically bad, & the character & conduct of William so excellent. At last, in the success of William, tears almost come to the eyes. ⟨But⟩ The persons & incidents are so fine that it seems strange this period has been neglected so long. ⟨But⟩ One sad reflection arises on all the course of the narrative, of wonder, ↑namely,↓ at the depravity of men in power, & ⟨of⟩ ↑at↓ the shocking tameness with which [113] it is endured. One would think the nation was all tailors, & mince-pie-makers. The writer has a great deal of talent, but no elevation of mind. There is not a ⟨single⟩ novel or striking thought in ⟨all⟩ the book, not a ⟨single⟩ new point of view from which to consider the events, & never one thrill or pulse of moral energy imparted. He is always a fine artificial Englishman, ↑& keeping the highway invariably;↓ well-bred, but for sale. ⟦all dated *Windsor Castle.*⟧ Here is good black blood, English pluck, but no philosophy.—A ⟨great⟩ deal of ⟨good⟩ pamphlet⟨eering⟩s now well bound.

[176] "*England.* My . . . has;" is struck through in ink with a diagonal use mark; the complete entry is struck through in ink with a second diagonal use mark. "My friend . . . people." is used in "Race," *W*, V, 65.

[177] Thomas Babington Macaulay, *The History of England from the Accession of James II*, 2 vols. (London and Philadelphia, 1849), is in Emerson's library.

[114] I cannot get enough alone to write a letter to a friend. I retreat & hide. I left the city, I hid myself in the pastures. When I bought a house, the first thing I did was to plant trees. I could not conceal myself enough. Set a hedge here, set pines there, trees & trees, set evergreens, above all, for they will keep my secret all the year round.[178]

[115] I am afraid A[lcott]. can as little as any man separate his drivelling from his divining.[179]

[116] ↑Brag↓

The feeling of Boston & Massachusetts for a few years past has been like that of the shopmen & of a village on the morning of a Cattle Show, or other holiday, which is to bring a crowd of strangers into t⟨heir⟩he town; every body is building booths, or arranging shop windows, or laying tables; everywhere a small ⟨trap⟩ ↑pan↓ to gather some rill of the expected silver shower. So feels Boston & Massachusetts on the eve⟨r⟩ of a prodigious prosperity; & we build, & plant, & ⟨|| . . . ||⟩lay roads, & set up signposts, [117] to attract our share of the general blessing.[180]

In New York, they characterise our hats & books & beauties as Frogpondish; but we, on the other hand, pity the whole *uncochituated* creation.[181]

The Kentuckian said, his country "was bounded ⟨nor⟩on the east by the rising sun, on the north by the aurora borealis, on the west by the

[178] This paragraph, struck through in ink with a vertical use mark, is used in "Society and Solitude," *W*, VII, 4; cf. *JMN*, VIII, 204.

[179] In Notebook Amos Bronson Alcott, p. [1], TU, p. [115], is listed under "Alcottiana".

[180] "Brag", an index heading, is added in the top left margin of p. [117].

[181] A pond on Boston Common was called the Frog Pond long after it deserved the name. Poe was apparently the first to use the term "frog-pond," in relation to Boston or Bostonians, in the *Broadway Journal*, November 1, 1845. In "The Rationale of Verse," he refers to Professors Longfellow and Felton, "or the Frogpondian Professors collectively" (*Southern Literary Messenger*, Nov. 1848, p. 681). Beginning in 1848, Lake Cochituate in Natick, Mass., provided Boston with its chief water supply. "Uncochituated" may be Emerson's coinage.

precession of the equinoxes, & on the south by the Day of Judgment."[182]

———

Mountain air better than gas of tobacco.

———

[118][183] Entsagen
The sun casts his image in all places[.]
Swedenborg will fight no battle but count the dead[.]
Genius of humanity the point of view of history
Our great men will be to the inspired a parade of rags[.]
Swedenborg's peruke
Depravation of men in Martial, in Macaulay, & in Peter the Great
'Tis very certain that the man must yield who has omitted inevitable facts in his view of life. Has he left out marriage & the σπερματος ουσιης συντηρησιν,[184] he [119][185] has set a date to his fame. We are expe⟨t⟩cting another.

Insert this under Criticism in Salvage

I fear I cannot recall the light I had for a just conclusion of the section on Morals in my Essay on Eloquence.[186] But we must not impoverish the audience, but ennoble & endear mutually the orator & the hearer.

See TU p. 60

[182] From a review of an Autobiography of Jonathan Romer, *Kaloolah, or Journeyings to the Djebel Kumri*, ed. W. S. Mayo, M.D., *Athenæum*, No. 1134 (July 21, 1849), 736. The "Autobiography," of course, is fictional satire, written by Mayo.

[183] P. [118] is in pencil. "Entsagen", the first item, may refer to "the high meaning of Renunciation by which alone the first real entrance into life is conceivable," in Goethe's *Wilhelm Meister's Travels*, trans. Thomas Carlyle, ch. 14. See *JMN*, IV, 301.

[184] "observation of one's own offspring" (Ed.).

[185] The first entry on p. [119], in ink, is the "I fear . . . TU p. 60" entry below. This is followed by a pencil line across the page, below which is the entry "has set . . . Salvage", in pencil, which completes the pencil entry on p. [118]. The entries are arranged to follow Emerson's intended order.

[186] It would be hard to say exactly where Emerson would have placed his "just conclusion" (the section on morals in the printed version begins on *W*, VII, 97). "Eloquence," first a lecture, was delivered in Boston February 10, 1847, and several times thereafter in 1847 and 1850 before its publication in the *Atlantic Monthly*, II (Sept. 1858), 385–397. Although he calls it an "Essay" in this entry, it was still in lecture form and, it would appear, still open to revision.

[120] 13 July. Yesterday, the day before, & today, another storm of heat, like that three weeks ago. The day is dangerous, the sun acts like a burningglass, on the naked skin, & the very slugs on the pear leaves seem broiled in their own fat. ↑Mercury at 94° at 3 p.m.↓

When a man dies in Concord the neighbors sum his epitaph[:] "he was a good provider," or a bad.

One of the first works of good sense is to build a good dwellinghouse, yet a good house is rare.

[121] Μελετη το παν.[187] I took my hoe & waterpail & fell upon my ⟨pear⟩ sleepy pear trees, ⟨&⟩ broke up the soil, ⟨&⟩ ⟨dra⟩pulled [n] out the weeds & grass, I manured, & mellowed, & watered, ⟨&⟩ pruned, & washed, & staked, & separated the clinging boughs by shingles covered with list: I killed every slug on every leaf. The detestable pear worm, ⟨I detected⟩ which mimics a twig, I detected & killed. The poor tree ⟨was⟩ tormented by this excessive attention & industry, ⟨it⟩ must do something, & ⟨at last it⟩ began to grow[.]

My pears & apples were well favoured as long as I did not go beyond my own hedge: but if I went down to Edmund's farm, his trees were three stories high, & high up in the air hung a harvest of fruit.

[122] "Isn't [n] it too bad, father!" says Eddy, "there's a letter from Ellen for me, & none for Edie."[188]

I find Swedenborg to have no future. It is the best sign of a great nature that it opens heaven for you, &, like the breath of morning mountains, invites you onward. Swedenborg is retrospective only. Nor can we divest him therefore of this charnel house odour. With a force of ten men, he could never yet break the umbilical cord which held him to nature, & he did not rise to the platform of pure genius.[189]

[187] "Care for the whole." See Journal RS, p. [i] above.

[188] Edward, Emerson's fourth child, was born in 1844; Ellen, his second, in 1839; and Edith, his third, in 1841.

[189] "It is . . . genius.", struck through in ink with a vertical use mark, is used in "Swedenborg," *W*, IV, 143.

[123] ↑*Swedenborg.*↓

'Tis curious that he should be entangled with Calvinism. 'Tis curious that all the great mathematicians, be they never so grand, should be unable to pass the materialism barrier. Newton is ⟨poor⟩ ↑rusty↓ with Calvinism. Cuvier is calvinistic. All the science of England & France is, all but Goethe & Oken.[190] ↑& ⟨Goethe⟩Plato & Kepler only have united geometry to the poetic spirit.↓

I find what L. read me this morning from "Conjugial Love" ↑to be↓ in a Goody-Two-Shoes taste, the description of gold houses, & Sinbad Sailor fruit trees,—all tinsel & gingerbread. Mr Cushing's Watertown garden would ⟨b⟩out-paradise ↑t↓his French Eden.[191] What to do with the stupendous old prig?

[124]

⌈Education⌉

In Dante pleases the friendly conversation with Brunetto Latini, Inferno XV, 82.

—in la mente m'è fitta, ed or⟨'⟩ m'accuora
La cara buona imagine paterna
Di voi, quando nel mondo ad ora ad ora
M'insegnavate come l'uom s'eterna.

I think if I were professor of Rhetoric,—teacher of the art of writing ↑well↓, to young men, I should use Dante for my text-book.[192] Come hither, youth, & learn how the brook that flows at the bottom of your garden, or the farmer who [125] ploughs the adjacent field, ↑—↓

[190] Lorenz Oken (1779–1851), German naturalist and philosopher, was a theorist of cellular structure and protoplasm.

[191] Lidian was doubtless reading from Emanuel Swedenborg, *The Delights of Wisdom concerning Conjugial Love: after which follow Pleasures of Insanity concerning Scortatory Love* (Boston, 1843), in Emerson's library. On p. 20, Swedenborg describes a palace with a gold roof and gold windowframes; on p. 21, he describes one tree with "fruits of gold" and others "laden with most delicious fruits. . . ." John Perkins Cushing (1787–1862), wealthy Boston merchant, opened once a week to the public the grounds of his estate in Watertown, celebrated for its horticultural taste.

[192] Emerson brought back with him from England, in 1848, unbound sheets of *Dante's Divine Comedy: The Inferno. A Literal Translation*, by J. A. Carlyle (London, 1849), from which the first American edition (New York, 1849) was set, following Emerson's negotiations with Harper & Brothers. See n. 196 below.

your father & mother, your debts & credits, & your web of habits are the very best basis of poetry, & the material which you must work up. Dante knew how to throw the weight of his body into each act, and is, like Byron, Burke, & Carlyle, the Rhetorician. I find him full of the *nobil volgare eloquenza*;[193] that he knows "God damn", & can be rowdy if he please, & he does please. Yet is not Dante reason or illumination & that ⟨thing⟩essence [126] we were looking for, but only a new exhibition of the possibilities of genius.[194] Here is an imagination that rivals in closeness & precision the senses. But we must prize him as we do a rainbow, we can appropriate nothing of him. Could we some day admit into our oyster heads the immense figure which these flagrant ⟨examples⟩ ↑points↓ compose when united, the hands of Phidias, the conclusion of Newton, the pantheism of Goethe, the all wise music of Shakspeare, [127] the robust eyes of Swedenborg⟨—⟩↑!↓[195]

M. was like a vigorous cock let in↑to↓ ⟨among a brood of hens⟩ ↑the coop of a farm house↓. He trod the hundred hens of the barnyard, and the very partridges for a mile round, and for the next fortnight the whole country side was filled with cackle over the eggs which they laid.

Dante

[128] Sent copies of ↑John↓ Carlyle's Dante[196] to
Dr [John A.] Carlyle — London
A[lexander].Carlyle — Brantford, Canada West
H[enry] W Longfellow
T[heodore] Parker

[193] The Italian, translated as "noble vulgar speech," is used in "Literature," *W*, V, 234.

[194] "we were . . . genius." is struck through in ink with two diagonal use marks.

[195] "Could we . . . compose when" (p. [126]) is struck through in ink with a vertical use mark.

[196] *Divine Comedy: The Inferno. A Literal Prose Translation with the Text of the Original Collated from the Best Editions, and Explanatory Notes* (New York, 1849).

S[amuel].G. Ward
J[ames].E Cabot
Mrs. S[arah] A Ripley
Geo P Bradford
H[enry]. D Thoreau
W[illiam]. E. Channing
A[mos]. B. Alcott
J[ohn]. S. Dwight
W[illiam]. Emerson N.Y.
G[eorge]. S. Hillard
⟨17⟩ E[dwin]. Whipple
⟨18⟩ R.W.Emerson
1⟨9⟩7 Sarah [Freeman] Clarke [197]

[129] Plato.
The irony of Socrates in calling the dulness of Gorgias & Polus shamefacedness. *Cary* I, 185
the Buddhism or transcendental Ethics in teaching that the sinner ought to covet & seek punishment. (Cary I, 178.) [198]

How much wit in finding that word "cookery" & "adulatory art" for rhetoric, in Gorgias. It is, as I have written elsewhere, only in good names that the battle is won.[199] Booby, granny, sweepstakes, catamite, puppy, dandy, cocktail, lubber,

[197] Of those listed who have not been previously identified or are not easily recognizable, Alexander Carlyle, brother of Thomas and John in England, emigrated to Canada to farm in 1843; Sarah Alden Ripley was a scholar of several languages and wife of Reverend Samuel Ripley of Waltham; Emerson's brother, William, a lawyer in New York; George S. Hillard, graduation orator in the class of 1828 along with Emerson's deceased brother Charles, a Boston lawyer; Edwin Percy Whipple, an essayist and critic.

[198] *The Works of Plato. A New and Literal Version Chiefly from the Text of Stallbaum* . . . , Bohn ed., 6 vols. (London, 1848–1854), in Emerson's library. Vol. I is translated by Henry Cary. "the Buddhism . . . punishment.", struck through in ink with a vertical use mark, is used in "Plato: New Readings," *W*, IV, 84.

[199] "the Buddhism . . . won." is struck through in ink with a vertical use mark; "How much . . . won." is used in "Plato; or, the Philosopher," *W*, IV, 59–60. For "How much . . . Gorgias.", cf. *Gorgias*, in *The Works of Plato* . . . , 1804, IV, 374, and *JMN*, X, 113.

Pillsbury is a ram's horn[.]

Plato

[130] Plato
The admirable earnest comes not only at intervals in the perfect yes & no of the dialogue, but in bursts of light like (Cary I, 231) "I therefore, Callicles, am persuaded by these accounts & consider how I may exhibit my soul before the judge in a healthy condition. Wherefore, disregarding the honours that most men value, & looking to the truth, I shall endeavour in reality to live as virtuously as I can, & when I die, to die so. And I invite all other men to the utmost of my power, & you too, I in turn invite to this life, & this contest, which, [131] I affirm, surpasses all contests here," &c &c (which see) [200]

Now hearken with all your ears; — "All the great arts require a subtle & speculative research into the law of nature: for that loftiness of thought & perfect mastery over every subject seems to be derived from some such source as this; which Pericles possessed in addition to a great natural genius. For, meeting, I think, with Anaxagoras, who was [132] a person of this kind, & being filled with speculative research, & having arrived at the nature of intelligence & want of intelligence, about which Anaxagoras made that long discourse, he drew from thence to the art of speaking whatever could contribute to its advantage." [201] Phaedrus

[*The Works of Plato* . . . , trans.] Cary. [1848,] I. 349.

[133] In the summersaults, spells & resurrections wrought by the imagination a central power which seems [202] to infuse a certain volatility & intoxication into all nature. Yet is that too only an arm or weapon of an interior energy pre[c]ursor of the Reason[.] [203]

[200] This paragraph, struck through in ink with single vertical use marks on pp. [130] and [131], is used in "Plato; or, the Philosopher," *W*, IV, 60–61. Emerson's reference is to vol. I of *The Works of Plato* . . . , 1848–1854, trans. Henry Cary.

[201] This paragraph, struck through in ink with two diagonal use marks on each of pp. [131] and [132], is used in "Literature," *W*, V, 241.

[202] "In the . . . seems", struck through in ink with a vertical use mark, is used in "Uses of Great Men," *W*, IV, 17.

[203] "volatility . . . Reason" is struck through in pencil with a diagonal use

I think Hindoo books excellent gymnastic for the mind as showing treatment. All European libraries might almost be read without the swing of this gigantic arm of the mind being suspected. But those orientals deal with worlds & pebbles very freely.[204]

[134] Passion is logical; and I note that the vine, symbol of the Bacchus which intoxicates the world, is the most geometrical & tractable of all plants.[205]

↑See of *Heat BO* 67↓

	1	Cheap Press
The Times.[206]	2	Natural Science
	3	No prayer

The cheap press & the universal reading, which have come in together, have caused a great many translations to be made from ↑the↓ Greek, ↑the↓ German, ↑the↓ Italian, & ↑the↓ French. Bohn's Library now furnishes me with a new [135] & portable Plato, as it had already done with new Goethes.[207] And John Carlyle translates Dante. To me the command is loud to use the time by reading these books. And I should as soon think of foregoing the railroad & the telegraph, as to neglect these. With these belong the Mediaeval Chronicles,—Richard of Devizes, Asser's Life of Alfred, & the rest in Bohn.[208]

———

———

A feature of the times is this, that when I was born, private & family prayer was in the use of all well-bred people, & now it is not known.

———

mark; "the imagination . . . intoxication" is used in "Books," *W*, VII, 213; "Yet is . . . Reason" is used in the same essay, *W*, VII, 214.

[204] "I think . . . freely.", struck through in pencil with a vertical use mark, is used in "Poetry and Imagination," *W*, VIII, 15.

[205] This sentence is struck through in pencil with a vertical use mark. See Journal RS, p. [131] above.

[206] An ink line below "Times." curves up above "1 Cheap".

[207] Both the Bohn edition of Plato's *Works*, 1848–1854, and of *The Auto-biography of Goethe. Truth and Poetry: From My Own Life . . .* , [trans. John Oxenford], 2 vols. (London, 1848–1849) are in Emerson's library.

[208] *Chronicles of the Crusades . . .* , 1848.

Another feature of the Age is the paramount place of Natural History.

[136] ↑*Men-in-nature*↓

⟨I see⟩ ↑Some↓ persons ⟨who⟩ have such determination or tendency, that, ⟨I think,⟩ if by any heat their particles could be set free, so as to obey it, they would at once assume ⟨certain⟩ ↑the↓ forked or horned or clubbed or scal⟨ed⟩y forms, which they now suggest. See p. 71

"Mr Hosmer's thoughts always come in season; mine come afterwards," said Mrs H.[209]

[137] ↑*What presents shall we give?*↓

Camera obscura ⟨T⟩Writing desk, at 6.00, for sale at E. Stearns's
30 Washington St

a pistol —
a paperknife —
a hand to hold papers. bronze
a framed print

shells at Warren's[210]
Compass
microscope
Silver fruit knives, that shut like penknives
a lamp
a basket
a stereoscope
a pair of steps
a mustardpot
a padlock
a burned or branded bracket

[209] Mrs. H. is probably a reference to the wife of Emerson's neighboring farmer and agricultural adviser, Edmund Hosmer.

[210] Above the "h" in "shells" is the capital letter "V", preceded by a faint "g" or "q" and followed by a faint "6", both apparently in erased ink.

The dime-gifts, as, the needlethreader, the cent ring, the pencil-cutter, the pen-maker,

---

Aeolian harp

---

[138] 1 August 1849

Correcting MSS & proofs for printing, makes apparent the value of perspective as essential to good writing. Once we said genius was health; but now we say genius is Time. ↑See TU 190↓[211]

This doctrine results too from that which shows genius also to be geometrical & mechanical, or, that Gravitation reaches up into the sacred soul.

[139] "On the Rhine, Dr Polidori said to Byron, 'After all, what is there you can do that I cannot?' 'Why, since you force me to say,' answered the other, 'I think there are three things I can do which you cannot.' Polidori defied him to name them. 'I can,' said Lord Byron, 'swim across that river; — I can snuff out that candle with a pistol shot at the distance of twenty paces; & I have written a poem, of which 14000 copies were sold in one day.' "

Moore's Life of Byron
Vol II. p. 30.[212]

[140] Mr ↑H[arrison].G[ray].↓ Otis said, "that it was of no use to tie up a woman's property; by kissing or kicking, her husband would get it away from her."[213]

The loves of flint & iron are naturally a little rougher than those of the nightingale & the rose.

Flagrat anhela silex et amicam saucia sentit
Materiam, placidosque chalybs cognoscit amores.[214] [Claudian, *Carminum Minorum Corpusculum*, xxix, ll. 42–43]

[211] Added in pencil.

[212] Thomas Moore, *Letters and Journals of Lord Byron*, 2 vols. (London, 1830).

[213] Harrison Gray Otis (1765–1848) had been a member of the House of Representatives, U.S. Senator, and mayor of Boston.

[214] "The stone sighs and burns, and smitten with love recognizes in the iron the object of its desire, while the iron experiences a gentle attraction for the stone."

[141] There is no remedy for the musty self[-]conceited English life made up of fictions, hating ideas, — like ⟨⟨E⟩Hindu fictions⟩ [n] Orientalism. That astonishes & disconcerts English decorum. For once there is thunder he never heard, light he never saw, & power which trifles with time & space[.] [215]

England

"It is in bad taste," is the most formidable word an Englishman can pronounce.[216]

That is ruined in England which is made disrespectable, and in France which is made ridiculous.

[142]

Read at Chelmsford 1849
2. Lectures on England
1. Domestic Life
1. Eloquence
1. New England
1 Books [217]

[143]–[144] [leaf torn out] [218]
[145] Aug. 6, 1849 —

The rose is the only wild flower that appears to be improved by culture. ↑See AZ 276↓

↑The Times↓
The ideas of the time shine out so brightly that even the nightmares

[215] This paragraph, struck through in pencil with a diagonal use mark, is used in "Literature," *W*, V, 258.

[216] This sentence is struck through in pencil with a diagonal use mark; "There is . . . pronounce." is struck through in ink with two diagonal use marks. " 'It is . . . pronounce." is used in "Manners," *W*, V, 111. See *JMN*, X, 515.

[217] Emerson's lecture schedule for 1849 included five lectures from the "English Traits" series at Chelmsford, Mass., between February 1 and March 8.

[218] Emerson indexed p. [144] under Conduct of Life.

as they go discern them. What other account shall I give of Davis's Revelations?[219]

Revolution is

"lord of the visionary eye whose lid
Once raised, remains aghast, & will not fall."
[Wordsworth, "Dion," ll. 92–93]

↑Nature never reproduces the fossil strata↓[.][220]

[146] There are three degrees in philosophy. Plato came with geometry; that was one degree. Plotinus came with mythology, Zoroastrian or magian illumination, &c[,] an exalted or stilted Plato: that was the second degree. But now comes my friend with palmistry, phrenology, mesmerism, & Davisian revelation; this is the third degree; & bearing the same relation to Plotinism which that bore to Platonism.[221]

[147] "Les Francais sont la nation la plus sensée dans ses plaisirs, et la plus folle dans ses affaires."
Théophile Gautier.[222]

⟨Tigre Singe⟩
Singe tigre[223]
Comment vous portez vous?

The French follow the course of rivers, the English hug the seashore.

"M. Dupin, comment vous assassinez vous?"[224]

[219] Andrew Jackson Davis (1826–1910), American spiritualist, published *Principles of Nature, Her Divine Revelations, and a Voice to Mankind* in 1847.

[220] "Nature . . . strata" is in pencil.

[221] In his Notebook Amos Bronson Alcott, Emerson lists p. [146] under Alcottiana.

[222] See *JMN*, VI, 354.

[223] See *JMN*, VI, 25: "Voltaire said, 'a Frenchman is a mixture of monkey & tiger.'" See Voltaire's *Oeuvres Complètes*, 52 vols. (Paris, 1877–1885), XLIV, 505.

[224] In the lecture "France" Emerson wrote: "When it was rumored once and again M. Dupin's life was threatened, he was greeted, on entering the assembly, '*Comment vous assassinez vous.* M. Dupin.'" André-Marie-Jean-Jacques Dupin (1783–1865) was president of the Chamber of Deputies and of the Legislative Assembly.

La France est capable du tout selon qu'il est conduit.

The French change their Constitution as often as their shirt. *L'inconstance immortelle du Francais.*[225]

---[226]

[148] Will you spend your income, or ↑will you↓ invest it? 'Tis worth seeing how far this question holds good. All your bodies & organs are jars in which the liquor of life is stored. Will you spend it for pleasure? You are a sot. Will you husband it? It passes through the sacred fermentations, & at last comes out imagery & thought, &, higher still, courage & magnanimity. Compound interest; capital doubled; man raised to a cube; Angelic.[227]

[149] In Mr Levi Bartlett's farm every slope & duct was so arranged that you could not so much as spit without its being carried off to the muck-heap.[228]

Trade is the lord of the world nowadays—& government only a parachute to this balloon.

[15⟨2⟩0][229] Eustach⟨us⟩ius Boerhaave
Mr P died of too much perspiration[.]
Buna was engaged in writing a book on the conduct of life, & today in the chapter on Crickets. It could not be said of Buna, that she ⟨was entir⟩ lived entirely for her dinner, though she was tenderly patiently absorbed in that capital event of the day, no, for she was not less dedicated to her supper, nor less to her breakfast. He had studied her character imperfectly who thought she lived in these. ⟨|| . . . ||⟩No[,]

[225] See *JMN*, X, 262.

[226] Emerson inadvertently drew this short rule one line high, in the left margin between the ms. lines beginning "as often" and "*immortelle*".

[227] This paragraph, struck through in ink with a curved vertical use mark, is used in "Wealth," *W*, VI, 126.

[228] An L Bartlett is listed on H. F. Walling's map of Concord Town, 1852; he lived on the Lexington Road, about 1½ miles from Emerson.

[229] Pp. [150]–[152] are in pencil.

she wished to keep her feet warm, & she was ⟨passionately fond of⟩ ↑addicted to↓ a ⟨warm &⟩ [n] soft seat ⟨what⟩ ↑& expended a↓ skill & generalship ⟨she expended⟩ on securing the ⟨best⟩ ↑red↓ chair & ⟨the best⟩ ↑a↓ [n] corner out of the draft & in the air worthy of a higher ⟨place⟩ seat in heaven[.]

[151] Neither on these was she exhausted her ample genius insisted on he

In a frivolous age Buna was earnest. She screamed, she groaned, she watched at night, she waited by day for her omelet & her lamp with smooth handle & when she went out of the house it was a perfect *row* for half an hour[.]

Buna had catarrh, pleurisy, rush of blood to the head, apoplexy, diabetes, diarrhea, sunstroke, atrophy, worms, palsy, erisypelas, consumption & dropsy.

[152] ↑see page 155↓

Swedenborg born	1688	died 1772
Linnaeus born	1707	1783
Christian Wolff	1679	1754
Malpighi	1628	1694
De⟨c⟩sCartes		
Tschirnhausen [230]	1651	
Newton	1642	1726
Copernicus	1473	1543
Kepler	1571	1630
Galileo	1564	1642
Tycho Brahe	1546	1601
Shakspeare	1564	1616
Grotius		

[153] Swedenborg's antediluvian leisures

Magnet was thrown into Europe & all philosophy has taken a direction from it. Men have studied its currents & got the vortex & the spiral & the polarity which now inundate all low thinking & all

[230] Emerson's reference is to Count Ehrenfried Walter von Tschirnhaus (1651–1708), German mathematician, physician, and philosopher.

language & end in the charlatanism of Tractors, of Mesmerism, & ⟨a⟩Phrenology, Pathetism, & Davis[.] [231]

Shakspeare's fun is as wise as his earnest. Its foundations are below the frost. His is a moral muse simply from its depth, and I value the intermixture of the common & the transcendental, as in nature.[232]

Then also his ⟨s↑t↓ructural⟩ knowledge of structure & complexion; — he knows what is in a blue eye, and ⟨in⟩ what in an adust skin, & does justice to both. He is all pulverized into proverbs, & dispersed into human discourse[.]

[154] *Greatness*

The difference is immense to appearance certainly between man & man. ⟨The⟩Plato or Swedenborg is just ready to make a world, if he do not like this; he is Krish⟨a⟩na[.]

Luther born 1483 [233]
died 1546

Eustachius, Swammerdam, Leeuwenhoek, Lancisi
Boerhaave, Winslow,[234]

[155]

Copernicus	1473	1543
Tycho B[r]ahe	1546	1601
Galileo	1564	1642

[231] "Swedenborg's antediluvian . . . Davis" is in pencil. For Davis, see p. [145] above.

[232] This paragraph is used in "Art and Criticism," *W*, XII, 294.

[233] This and the remaining entries on p. [154] are in pencil; those on p. [155] are also in pencil.

[234] Bartolommeo Eustachius (d. 1574) was an Italian anatomist; Jan Swammerdam (1637–1680), a Dutch naturalist known for his biological research with the microscope; Anton van Leeuwenhoek (1632–1723), a Dutch naturalist known for his work with red corpuscles; Giovanni Bernardo Moschieri Lancisi (1654–1720), an Italian anatomist and author of a work on diseases of the heart; Hermann Boerhaave (1668–1738), a Dutch physician and professor of medicine; Jakob Benignus Winslow (1669–1760), a Danish naturalist and author of a work on human anatomy.

	Shakspeare	1564	1616
	Kepler	1571	1630
	↑Harvey	1578	1658↓
Grotius 1583	Des Cartes	1596	1650
d 1645	Malpighi	1628	1694
	Locke	1632	1704
	Newton	1642	1726
	Tschirnhausen	1651	
	Christian Wolff	1679	1754
	Swedenborg	1688	1772
	Linnaeus	1707	1783

[156] It is no matter how fine is your rhetoric, or how strong is your understanding, no book is good which is not written by the Instincts. A fatal frost makes cheerless & undesireable every house wh⟨ich⟩ere ⟨vital heat⟩ animal heat is not. Cold allegory makes us yawn whatever elegance ⟨&⟩it may have. Of Heat, see TU 134, ↑BO 67↓

An oil mill to express oil from hickory nuts. Lubberland. Life [n] wasteful cheap, & must establish the singsong club or sonneteers to spend the evening, or go ⟨down⟩ ↑down↓ [235] in three hours to Flint's Pond to see the new cotton grass [157] carex, & rush. But plainly the novel is not written. We must write the women in. The Indian Squaw with a decisive hat has saved herself a world of vexation. The tragedy of our women begins with the bonnet. Only think of the whole Caucasian race damning the women to cover themselves with this frippery of rye straw & tags, that they may be at the mercy of every shower of rain. A meetinghouse full of women & a shower coming up,—it is as if we had dressed them all in paper. Put on the squaw's man's hat, & you amputate so much misery.

[158] Aug. 18—Yesterday a ⟨w⟩ride & walk with Thoreau to Acton. We climbed to the top of Nagog hill, & afterwards of Nashobah, the old domain of Tahatawan & his praying Indians.[236] The ⟨f⟩wide land-

[235] A first "down" was canceled, then a second "down" was written over the first, then it was canceled, and the third "down" was written above the line.

[236] Tahatawan was the Sachem of Musketaquid, the site of Concord, when Reverend Peter Bulkeley bought the six-mile square of the original township.

scape is one vast forest skirted by villages in the horizon.[237] We saw ↑Littleton,↓ Acton, Concord, Westford, Carlisle, ↑Bedford,↓ Billerica, Chelmsford, Tyngsboro, Dracut. On the western side, the old mountains ending with Uncanoonuc in the North. The geology is unlike ours & the granite ledges are perpendicular. Fort Pond is a picturesque sheet with a fine peninsula scattered park[-]like with noble pines on the western side — Grass Pond a pretty lake: Nagog seen from Nagog-hill is best, & Long Pond [159] we came to the shore of. These four ponds dictated, of course, ⟨Ac⟩Tahatawan's location of his 600 acres. ↑Also we visited the top of Strawberry hill; & a big chestnut tree.↓

I thought the Concord Society should meet & assign its business to Committees; thus —
Mr Channing presented a report on Baker Farm.
Mr Thoreau a Report on Fort Pond, the Cromlech, & the remains of a swamp fort near the Pond.
Mr E. called attention to the Ebbahubba↑r↓d park[.][238]
Miss E. Hoar presented a bunch of Linnaea Borealis found in Concord.
Mr C read a paper on the foliaceous & spongelike formations by spring-thaw in the argillite of the Deep Cut in the Rail Road[n] — & so forth.

[160] There is something finer in our sky & climate than we have senses to appreciate; it escapes us: & yet is only just beyond ⟨a⟩our reach. Tantalus must have finer senses.

I suppose the apple or the whortleberry to have this adaptation ⟨oc⟩to the human palate, because they are only the palate inverted; one is man eating, & the other man eatable. Each fruit must occur in the sphere wherever two circles intersect.

[161] Fort Pond Brook was represented as an industrious miller & machinist who lost no time & no space[.][239]

[237] "skirted" is followed by a pencil mark representing the closing of a bracket, but without the horizontal mark at the top (like a large capital "L" turned around); this is followed by "73", also in pencil, written above the "b" of "by".

[238] Probably Ebenezer Hubbard's property on the Walden road.

[239] Fort Pond Brook runs through Boxboro, Acton, and Concord.

The houses in Acton seemed to be filled with fat old people who looked like old tomatos[,] ↑their faces crumpled into red collops,↓ fatting & rotting at their ease[.]

———

L., at cat's cradle, was pronounced a good needle, but with the polarity reversed[.]

[162] [blank]
[163]–[168] [3 leaves torn out] [240]
[169] *Eyes & No Eyes.* One man sees the fact or object & another sees the power of it; ↑one the triangle, & the other the cone which↓ ⟨As a cone⟩ is generated by the revolution of a triangle,[241]

[170] 29 August. A long sad strange dream last night in which I carried E. to Naples & lost her.[242]

———

We are struck if a more powerful & swifter horse than ordinary goes by. A man is not allowed to be so very clever as to browbeat or outwit all other men. No giants. Nature has made up her mind on

[240] The stub of the leaf bearing pp. [163]–[164] contains only a few letters at the margin of what were probably the last two lines on p. [164]. The stubs of the leaves bearing pp. [165]–[168] are larger and contain the following words and parts of words: "[165] & unit|| . . . || of|| . . . || p|| . . . || ⟨d⟩|| . . . || t|| . . . || is || . . . || an|| . . . || ci[t?]|| . . . || the || . . . || wi|| . . . ||[-]ces || . . . || sera|| . . . || wha|| . . . || send|| . . . || [166] || . . . || that || . . . || house || . . . ||d's || . . . ||an || . . . ||ole || . . . || of || . . . || the || . . . ||ull || . . . ||[n?]en) || . . . ||ow || . . . ||[s?]ed." The stub of the leaf bearing pp. [167]–[168], approximately two inches in width between the tear and the binding, contains the following words and parts of words: "[167] Shakspea|| . . . || describe || . . . || the only || . . . || that to [lo?]|| . . . || I think || . . . || the crops || . . . || rock || . . . || strat|| . . . || was wr|| . . . || man || . . . || I can || . . . || well || . . . || througho ["t" crossed in pencil]|| . . . || by Shaks|| . . . || like the N|| . . . || in his || . . . || [168] || . . . ||liments to || . . . || not ⟨good⟩". Emerson indexed p. [163] under Fame, Genius, and Poet, p. [164] under Tavernkeeper, and p. [167] under Shakspeare.

[241] The editors conjecture that "⟨As a . . . triangle,", in a lighter ink than "*Eyes &* . . . it;", was inscribed first with the thought left unfinished. At a later time Emerson added "*Eyes &* . . . it;", then canceled "As a cone" and added "one the . . . which".

[242] "E." could be Emerson's first wife, Ellen, or either of his two daughters, Ellen or Edith.

this point, & is republican in her politics. If he have a transcendent talent, it draws so lavishly on his forces as to lame him.[243]

Love is the bright foreigner, the foreign self[.]

[171] The paddy period lasts long. Hungary, it seems, must take the yoke again, & Austria, & Italy, & Prussia,[n] ↑& France.↓ Only the English race can be trusted with freedom.

The French proclamations are hysterical.

If I had a barn-fowl that wanted a name, I should call him *France*. Never was national symbol so comically fit.

↑The Cagliostro revolution of ↑Dec.↓ 1851.↓ [244]

[172] Plato's fame does not stand on ⟨some demonstration or single thesis⟩ a syllogism, or on any specimen of the Socratic argumentation. He ⟨represents⟩ is much more than an expert, or a schoolman, or a geometer. He represents the privilege of the human mind, the power of ascending to new platforms with every subject, & so giving to every sub⟨b⟩ject an expansion. The Republic of Plato anticipates inasmuch as it requires the astronomy of Laplace. But the naturalist would never help us to these expansions [173] but is as poor when cataloguing the ↑resolved↓ nebula of Orion as when surveying his own street.
⟨B⟩These expansions are organic. The mind does not create that which it perceives, any more than the eye creates the flower; but the distinction of Plato is, that he could apply the ⟨s⟩whole scale; of the senses, of the understanding, & of the ↑high↓ intellect.[245] For we do not listen with much respect to the verses of a man who is only a poet, nor to the calculations of a man who is only an algebraist[,]

[243] "Nature has . . . him." is struck through in ink with a vertical use mark; "If he . . . him." is used in "Fate," *W*, VI, 35.

[244] Emerson is evidently poking fun at the coup d'état by Louis Napoleon, December 1–2, 1851, by linking it with the name of the famous fraud and adventurer, Alexandre, Comte de Cagliostro (1743–1795).

[245] "Plato's fame . . . intellect.", struck through in ink with single vertical use marks on pp. [172] and [173], is used in "Plato: New Readings," *W*, IV, 81–82.

but if a man is at the same time acquainted with the geometrical foundations of things & with their moral purposes & sees the festal splendour of the [174] day, his poetry is ⟨oracular⟩ ↑exact↓; & his arithmetic ⟨venerable⟩ ↑musical↓. His poetry & his mathematics accredit each other.[246]
I look upon ⟨Plato's emphatic⟩ the stress laid by Plato on geometry as highly significant. He saw that the sensible world was not more lawful & precise than was the supersensible, that a celestial geometry was in place there, as a logic of lines & angles ⟨bel⟩here below[.]

Mathematicalness of the world; the proportions constant of oxygen & azote & lime; &, not less, of moral elements.[247] TU 13, 19,

[175] He wrote on the scale of the mind itself, & put in all the past without weariness, & descended into detail with a courage like that which he witnessed in nature.[248] Of course, he cannot often find a reader; but of course h⟨o⟩e ought to have ⟨done so⟩ written so[.]

Parker thinks, that, to know Plato, you must read Plato thoroughly, & his commentators, &, I think, ⟨he⟩ ↑Parker↓ would require a good drill in Greek history too. I have no objection to hear this urged on any but a Platonist. But when erudition is insisted on to Herbert [176] or Henry More, I hear it as if to know the tree you should make me eat all the apples. It is not granted to one man to express himself adequately more than a few times: and I believe fully, in spite of sneers, in interpreting the French Revolution by anecdotes, though not every diner out can do it. To know the flavor of tanzy, must I eat all the tanzy that grows by the Wall? When I asked Mr Thom in Liverpool—who is ⟨this⟩ ↑Gilfillan↓? & who is ⟨that⟩ ↑⟨Forbes⟩MacCandlish↓? he began at the settlement of the Scotch Kirk in 1300 ? & came down with the history to 1848, that I might understand what was Gilfillan, or what was Edin. Review &c &c.[249] But if a man cannot answer me in ten words, he is not wise.

[246] This sentence is struck through in ink with a diagonal use mark.

[247] "I look . . . elements.", struck through in ink with a vertical use mark, is used in "Plato: New Readings," *W*, IV, 84–85.

[248] "He wrote . . . nature.", struck through in ink with a vertical use mark, is used in "Plato: New Readings," *W*, IV, 86.

[249] Reverend David Thom entertained Emerson at his home in Liverpool, November 30, 1847 (*JMN*, X, 259); George Gilfillan (1813–1878), Scottish Presbyterian

[177] Plato's vision is not illimitable, but it is not self limited by its own obliquity, or by fogs & walls which its own vices create.

Plato is to mankind what Paris or London is to Europe. Europe concentrates itself into a capital. He has not seen Europe, who has not seen its cities. Plato codifies & catalogues & distributes. ⟨By⟩ ↑In↓ his broad daylight things reapp↑e↓ar as they stood in the sunlight, hardly shorn of a ray, yet now portable & reportable[.]
Before, all things st⟨an⟩ood enchanted,—not tangible. He comes, & touches them, & henceforth anybody may.

[178] My Edinburgh critic of Shakspeare &, it seems, Gervinus also, think no criticism valuable that does not proceed purely on the dramatic merit.[250] He is falsely judged as poet, ↑or↓ philosopher, &c. I think ⟨it not less perfect than they,⟩ ↑as highly as they of↓ his dramatic merit, but ↑still↓ think it ⟨still⟩ secondary. He was a full man who liked to talk; a brain ⟨full of⟩ ↑exhaling↓ thoughts & images, which↑,↓ ⟨looked about for the readiest⟩ ↑seeking↓ vent, ⟨&⟩ found the drama next to his hand; just as a young Bostonian with a taste for Ethics falls ⟨nowadays⟩ into an Unitarian pulpit, and his more muscular brother is engineer on the railroad. Had he been less than he is, we should have had to consider how well[251] [179]–[180] [leaf torn out][252]

---

clergyman and writer, wrote an essay on Emerson's British reputation in *Tait's Edinburgh Magazine*, XV (Jan. 1848), 17–23; Emerson heard Edward Forbes (1815–1854), geologist, lecture in England. MacCandlish is unidentified.

[250] Georg Gottfried Gervinus (1805–1871) was a German historian and commentator on Shakespeare.

[251] "My Edinburgh . . . well", struck through in ink with a vertical use mark, is used in "Shakspeare," *W*, IV, 210.

[252] Words and parts of words remaining on the stub are: "[179] he fill|| . . . || he w|| . . . || but || . . . || he ha|| . . . || ⟨enter⟩ || . . . || ⟨into⟩ ↑to↓ || . . . || and || . . . || wh|| . . . || lang|| . . . || into || . . . || the || . . . || ⟨as⟩ ↑meani|| . . . ||↓ a c[o]|| . . . || com|| . . . || of it|| . . . || [180] || . . . || to || . . . || whole || . . . || all || . . . ||pples. || . . . || paddies || . . . ||ads || . . . ||orks || . . . ||hite || . . . || ⟨[s]he is⟩ || . . . || [i]s her || . . . ||e turns || . . . ||tury, || . . . ||. The matter on p. [179] seems to be a continuation of the entry on p. [178], and is probably used in "Shakspeare," *W*, IV, 210–211 (words and parts of words corresponding to those in the ms. are italicized): ". . . *he fill*ed his place, how good a dramatist *he was*,—and he is the best in the world. *But* it turns out that what *he ha*s to say is of that weight as *to* withdraw some attention from the vehicle; *and* he is like some saint whose history is to be rendered into all *lang*uages,

[181] *Doctrine of degrees*

The excellence of men consists in the completeness with which the lower system is taken up into the higher,—a process of much time & delicacy, but in which no point or ray of the lower should be left untranslated. So that the warfare of beasts should be renewed in a finer field, for more excellent victories. Savage war gives place to that of Turenne & Wellington, which has limitations & a code. This ⟨rude⟩ war ↑again↓ gives place to the finer quarrel of property, where the victory is wealth, & the defeat is poverty. But the ruin here is how much less! instead of being killed or mangled, a man is behindhand in paying his notes, lives in a cheaper street, & walks instead of riding to his work.

↑See p 221↓

[182] Nature

In the last days of August, & the first of September, the woods are full of agarics[.]

[183] The manners of the eye reveal all the interiors of the man[,] yet is our language inadequate to paint them.

[184] ↑*Sept. 2, 1849.*↓

I read, in the London Lit. Gazette, that the Sacrificial stone at Stonehenge, was the only one in all the stones there that could resist the action of fire; and, I believe, it was added, that it was probably brought 150 miles.—[253]

---

into verse and prose, *into* songs and pictures, and cut up into proverbs; so that *the* occasion which gave the saint's *meaning* the form of a conversation, or of a prayer, or of a *co*de of laws, is immaterial *com*pared with the universality *of its* application." Emerson indexed p. [180] under Nature and Paddy and in Notebook BO Conduct, p. [5], he notes, "Nature hits the white as seldom as we. TU 180,". The matter on p. [180] is probably used in "Considerations by the Way," *W*, VI, 250 (words and parts of words corresponding to those in the ms. are italicized): "Nature makes fifty poor melons for one that is good, and shakes down a tree full of gnarled, wormy, unripe crabs, before you can find a dozen dessert a*pples*; and she scatters nations of naked Indians and nations of clothed Christians, with two or three good he*ads* among them. Nature w*orks* very hard, and only hits the w*hite* once in a million throws. In mankind s*he is* contented if she yields one master in a cen*tury*."

[253] The *Literary Gazette and Journal of the Belles Lettres, Arts, Sciences, Etc.*, July 28, 1849, p. 554.

England[254]

I suppose all the Saxon race at this day, Germans, English, Americans, all to a man regard it as an unspeakable misfortune to be born a Frenchman.[255] See *B* 115,

Melancholy cleaves to the Saxon mind as closely as to ⟨y^e^⟩ ↑the↓ tones of an ↑A↓Eolian Harp.[256]

[185] [blank]

[186] 4 September, 1849. Dante's imagination is the nearest to hands & feet that we have seen. He clasps the thought as if it were a tree or a stone, & describes it as mathematically. I remember I found Page the painter modelling his figures in clay, (Ruth & Naomi), before he painted them on canvas. Dante, ↑one would say,↓ did the same thing before he wrote the verses.[257]

[187] [blank]

[188] It is true that Webster has never done any thing up to the promise of his faculties. He is unmistakeably able, & might have ruled America, but he was cowardly, & has spent his life on specialties. ↑When shall we see as rich a vase ⟨of wine⟩ [n] again!↓ Napoleon, on the other hemisphere, obeyed his instincts with a fine audacity, dared all, went up to his line, & over his line, found himself confronted by Destiny, & yielded at last.

[189] I have many metres of men, one is, ⟨that⟩their perception of identity. 'Tis a good mark of any genius [—] a single novel expression of the identity. Thus Lord Brooke's

> "So words ↑should↓ sparks ⟨should⟩ be of those fires
> they strike"

[254] An ink line beginning at the left margin, curls above and around this heading, underscoring it.

[255] This sentence, struck through in ink with a vertical use mark, is used in "Cockayne," *W*, V, 146. See *JMN*, X, 499.

[256] The entries on p. [184] are struck through in pencil with a diagonal use mark; "I read . . . miles. —" is used in "Stonehenge," *W*, V, 278. "Melancholy . . . Harp." is used in "The Tragic," *W*, XII, 406; see *JMN*, V, 107, 391.

[257] The American portrait painter William Page (1811–1885), painted "Ruth and Naomi." This paragraph is used in "Powers and Laws of Thought," *W*, XII, 49.

or Donne's

"That one would almost say her body thought." [258]

I hold that ecstasy will be found mechanical, if you please to say so, or, nothing but an example on a higher field of the same gentle gravitation by which rivers run.

Experience identifies. Shakspeare seems to you miraculous. But these wonderful juxtapositions, parallelisms, transfers, which his genius effected were all to him mechanical also, [190] & the mode precisely as conceivable & familiar as the index-making of the literary hack is to him. The result of Mr Hack is inconceiv⟨e⟩able also to the Printer's Devil who waits for it.[259] So that ↑Walter↓ Scott, — I think it was, — who defined Genius as Perseverance.[260] And Newton said, "By always intending my mind." [261]

[191] Rhymes

The iterations or rhymes of nature are already an idea or principle of science, & a guide. The sun & star reflect themselves all over the world in the form of flowers & fruits & in the human head & the doctrine of series which takes up again the few functions & modes & repeats them with new & wondrous result on a higher plane. What rhymes are these which Oken or Agassiz show, in making the head only a new man on the shoulders of the ⟨one⟩old, the spine doubled over & putting out once more its hands & feet, the upper jaw being the hands, the lower jaw the feet; & the teeth being fingers & toes respectively.[262] [192] This too only leads on the anatomist to the

[258] Fulke Greville, Lord Brooke, "A Treatie of Humane Learning," stanza 110, l. 6, misquoted; John Donne, "The Second Anniversarie," l. 246 (see *JMN*, V, 340).

[259] "I hold [p. [189]] . . . it." is used in "Inspiration," *W*, VIII, 275–276.

[260] See *JMN*, VI, 196: "Genius, Sir Walter Scott defined to be, the power of sustained intellectual exertion."

[261] The quotation, struck through in ink with two diagonal use marks, is used in "Power," *W*, VI, 75; see p. [50] above, and *JMN*, X, 41.

[262] "the few functions . . . respectively." is struck through in ink with a vertical use mark; "What rhymes . . . respectively." is used in "Swedenborg," *W*, IV, 108. Emerson is undoubtedly recalling John Bernhard Stallo's summary of Oken in *General Principles of the Philosophy of Nature*, 1848, p. 292. For Oken's full concept, see his *Elements of Physiophilosophy* (London, 1847), p. 408.

anatomy of the Understanding, which is the material body of the mind, whilst Reason is its soul; and the ⟨phenomena⟩ ↑law↓ of Generation is constant, & repeats on the higher plane of intellect every fact ⟨of⟩ in the animal. The true Economy of man, then, is always to prefer spending on the higher plane; always to invest & invest, with holy avarice, that he may spend in spiritual creation & not in begetting animals.[263]

[193] Then, as I have written before, Astronomy is not yet astronomy, until it is applied to human life; & all our things are to be thus exalted or ⟨r⟩echoed & re⟨c⟩echoed in finer & higher rhymes.——

The snake or the span-worm is the horizontal spine. Man is the erect spine. Between these two lines which form a quadrant, all beings find their place. Body of man is a spine with appendages which are new spines. On its top the upper vertebra transforms itself into a new spine bending over like a spanworm & constituting a skull. Within that in a new & higher ⟨form⟩ ↑plane↓ the same thing repeats itself[.][264]

[194] I think it as much a disease to be silenced when I do not wish it, as to have the measles when I do not wish it.

———

How difficult to deal erect with the Days! Each of these events which they bring,—this Concord thieving, the muster, the ripening of plums, the shingling of the barn, all throw dust in your eyes, & distract your attention. He is a strong man who can look them in the eye, see through this superficial juggle, feel their identity & keep his own; know ⟨y⟩surely that one will be like another to the end of [195] the world, nor permit bridal or funeral, earthquake or church, ⟨to⟩ ↑election or revolution↓ to draw him from his task.[265]

↑Printed in "*Works & Days*"↓

[263] "This too . . . animals." is struck through in ink with a vertical use mark; "The true . . . animals." is used in "Wealth," *W*, VI, 126.

[264] The entries on p. [193] are struck through in ink with a vertical use mark. With "Then, as . . . rhymes.——", cf. "Swedenborg," *W*, IV, 110; "The snake . . . itself" is used in the same essay, *W*, IV, 107–108.

[265] "How difficult . . . task.", struck through in pencil with single vertical use

[196] *1849*
Garden Diary Aug. 15 Apricot plums
⟨W⟩September 7 We are so late this year that I picked the first muskmelons today—four;—today the first ripe tomato; and all the Bartlett pears to ripen in the house[.]

———

The whole product of my Bartlett at the corner of the garden might count 45 pears.

———

The gages yield every day a supply, and the two ↑purple↓ plum-trees[.]

———

Today, too, we dig seven bushels of excellent chenangoes.

———

12th. Today Tomatoes for the first time on table.

———

September is the month of melons
↑melons last with us till 15th October.↓
[197] I think the Seckle pears should hang on the tree till 15 September. ↑or 20th↓

———

1850 1 October
Apricot [266]
1850 Plums first gathered in baskets on August 23d

Sopsavines 10 Aug
Sweet corn 22 & not well ripe

Sept 6 ⟨P⟩Horseplum & Blue plum ripe
Sept 5 Parkman apple ripe

———

marks on pp. [194] and [195], is used in "Works and Days," *W*, VII, 173–174. "Printed in . . . *Days*' ", below, is in pencil.

[266] Beginning with "Apricot", the remaining entries on p. [197] are in pencil, undoubtedly added a year later.

[198] 1849
7 ⟨D|| . . . ||⟩September, was published "Nature, Addresses, & Lectures."
[1500] copies.
and [250] copies of "Nature" separate

Sent presentation copies to[267]
My mother
Lidian
Elizabeth Hoar
G[eorge]. P. Bradford
H[enry]. D. Thoreau
Mrs [Almira] Barlow
W[illiam]. E. Channing
S[amuel]. G. Ward
J[ames]. E. Cabot
E[lizabeth] P Peabody
O[liver] W Holmes
N[athaniel]. Hawthorne
W[illiam]. Emerson
Edw. Bangs
H[enry]. W. Longfellow
N Y Tribune
Boston Post
Daily Advertiser
Chronotype
Lit. World
Phila.
Christn Examiner

W[illiam].H. Channing
C[harles]. T. Jackson[269]

11 Sept
paid S G W 37
1 37
38 37
for B[ill]. of Exchge. for
£13. 17. 3d payable
to C Lane[268]

[267] Between "to" and "My mother", a line in ink runs down the left side of the list to "H. W. Longfellow". To the left of this line, the entry "11 Sept . . . Lane" is in pencil.

[268] The figures undoubtedly record one of the transactions (probably an interest payment on a note) by which Emerson was acting as agent for Charles Lane in the sale of Fruitlands to Joseph Palmer in 1846. Although Emerson has clearly written "37" and "38 37" here on p. [198], in Account Book 5 (1849–1853), p. [27], he records under the same date the dollar amount as "58.37½", the more likely figure.

[269] Of those listed who have not been previously identified or are not easily

[199] [blank]

[200] Nature is likest herself. At the end of the spine she projects two ⟨s⟩little spines for arms; at the other, two more for legs; at the end of these, she repeats the gift, each time a little modified to suit the want. Nature is likest herself. ⟨i⟩In the brain, which she prepared by bending over a spine, she recites her lesson once more, the well known tune in a higher key. Here are male & female faculties of mind, here is marriage, here is fruit.[270] There is also constant relation to the lower & a stern Nemesis binds the [201] farthest series in her divine grasp.

[202] The Aristotelian method was the athletic training of the scholars of [the] 17th Century, & a method so wide & respective of such universal relations that ⟨we⟩ ↑our education↓ seems narrow, linear, & indigent.[271] ⟨Th⟩Aristotle easily maintained his ground as master, by virtue of this real superiority, until it was found that his Physics were unsound; then his Metaphysics were discredited, & he was tumbled from his throne of a thousand years. But the Schoolmen were his pupils, & the Abelards, then the Galileos, Keplers,[n] Des Cartes, Grotiuses, Harveys, Malpighis, Tschirnhausens [203] & Christian Wolffs, that preceded Swedenborg, show their rough training. Like Roman soldiers they were required to carry more weight in their daily discipline than they would need in war. And so well born of stark Norwegian Berserkirs, & with this iron training comes Swedenborg, & shows a power of performance incredible to the Dryasdusts of the present day. Nobody is entitled ⟨|| ... ||⟩to ask for new great men, who has not tested his strength on this anthropometer. Wilkinson is the only man I know who is ⟨fit⟩ ↑broad chested enough↓ to cope with him. Humbol⟨t⟩dt ⟨the⟩& Goethe only rivals of their universality. The men of science so called[,] [204] the scholars are fops by the side of these colossi.

recognizable, Emerson's mother, Ruth Haskins Emerson, lived with him in Concord; Almira Penniman Barlow was a friend of Margaret Fuller's and wife of Reverend D. H. Barlow of Lynn, Mass.

[270] The entry on p. [200] to "is marriage," is struck through in ink with a curved vertical use mark. The use mark extends to "There is" in the next sentence below, but is canceled with a finger wipe beyond "marriage,". The entry to "fruit." is used in "Swedenborg," *W*, IV, 108.

[271] This sentence is used in "Swedenborg," *W*, IV, 104.

Maxillary music

[205] True Bramin in the morning meadows wet
Expound the Vedas of the violet
↑Or↓ hid [n] in ⟨the⟩ vines peeping thro' many a loop
See my plums redden & my beurrés stoop [272]

[206] *Representative*
It is my belief that every animal in our scale of creatures leans upward on man, & man leans ↑downward↓ on it; that lynx, dog, tapir, lion, lizard, camel, & crocodile, all find their perfection in him; all add a support & some essential contribution to him. He is the grand lion, he the grand lynx, he the grand worm; ↑the fish of fishes, & bird of birds,↓ so that if one of these ⟨creatures⟩ tribes were struck out of being he would lose some one property of his nature. And I have no doubt that to each of these creatures [207] Man appears as of ⟨his⟩its own kind; to a lion, man appears the archlion; to a stork, the archstork; He is the masterkey for which you must go back, to open each new door in this thousand gated Thebes.[273]

[208] It was fine when the paleontologist learned that the frog's egg on the thirteenth day, added the gills; & on the fourteenth day, lengthened the tail; & then, referring to the fossils, showed that this type of animals with gills, must have ⟨been created⟩ flourished in the thirteenth [n] ⟨age⟩ geologic age, & these with the long tails in the fourteenth period.

[209] It is clear that immense advantage comes from a superior ⟨survey⟩ simultaneous survey of all the kingdoms of nature. How different is the attitude of Linnaeus, Cuvier, & Agassiz, from that of Leewenhoeck or our estimable Dr Harris or Professor Peck! [274]

[272] "True Bramin . . . stoop" is in pencil. See "Quatrains: Gardener," *W*, IX, 292; for the first two lines, see *JMN*, VII, 386.

[273] With this sentence, cf. "Powers and Laws of Thought," *W*, XII, 29.

[274] Emerson's references here are probably to Thaddeus William Harris (1795–1856), Harvard librarian and author of *A Report on the Insects of Massachusetts* (Cambridge, Mass., 1841), and William Dandridge Peck (1763–1822), Boston

The comparison of ⟨kingdo⟩ tribes & kingdoms & the procession of structure in sunfish & mammal is open to one, whilst Peck & Harris count the cilia & spines on a beetle's wing.

The like value have ethnological & glossological researches, Prichard & Kraitsir, over the historian of a town or Lindley Murray[.] [275]

[210] It takes a long time to mature a race to the right temper & culture for philosophy. ⟨I⟩ We want a catholic genius able to embrace & distribute wholes. The English are departmental. Owen is. He sticks to the ⟨physician surgeon⟩ scalpel. He is the great surgeon. Yet the English have such excellent feet & legs, body & blood. The great idealist should come from them. The Americans are vulgar[.]

[21⟨2⟩1] Go to the end of gravitation, & it fails to interest. We are interested in nothing that ends, &, no matter how vast the extension, if it comes to an end somewhere within our sense, we desire not that, but somewhat better, & endless.[276] It

[212] ↑See O 348↓ [277]

An individual body is the momentary fixation of a portion of the solids or fluids of the universe, which, after performing ⟨this⟩ compulsory duty to this enchanted statue, ⟨for a time,⟩ are released, & again flow in the currents of the world. An individual soul, in like manner, is a fixation or momentary ⟨⟨whirl⟩vortex⟩ eddy in which certain affections, ↑sciences,↓ & powers of immaterial Force are taken up, & work & minister, ⟨for a time,⟩ in petty circles & localities, & then, being released, return to the Unbounded Soul of the World.[278] The tenacity of retention must be in exact proportion to the rank of

---

naturalist, professor of natural history at Harvard, and author of several articles on economic entomology.

[275] James Cowles Prichard (1786–1848), British physician and ethnologist, wrote several works on racial theory; Charles Kraitsir (1804–1860), Hungarian physician, became professor of modern languages and history at the University of Virginia; Lindley Murray (1745–1826), American lawyer, was the author of a popular grammar text used in American schools.

[276] "Go to . . . endless.", struck through in ink with two diagonal use marks, is used in "Swedenborg," *W*, IV, 109, and "Immortality," *W*, VIII, 335.

[277] Added in pencil.

[278] "An individual body . . . World." is used in "Powers and Laws of Thought," *W*, XII, 27–28.

the idea which the individual represents. So a fixed idea is the unit of this.

[213] In dreams, last night, a certain instructive race-horse was quite el⟨r⟩aborately shown off ⟨to me⟩, which seemed marvellously constructed for violent running, & so mighty to go, that he stood up continually on his hind feet in impatience & triumphant power. But my admiration was checked by some one's remarking behind me, that, "in New York they could not get up the smallest plate for him." Then I noticed, for the first time, that he was a show-horse, & had wasted all the time in this rearing on the hind legs, & had not run forward at all.[279] I hope they did not mean to be personal.

[214] "And that we may know all things that all men know, speech is given us; also the memory of the past; & perpetual experience: wonders too familiar, & too closely environing us, to allow us to wonder at them."
Swedenborg
E[conomy].[of the]A[nimal].K[ingdom]. [1845–1846] II, 312.

[215] [blank]
[216] ↑Swedenborg Shakspeare↓

Some minds ⟨bring forth⟩ are viviparous like Shakspeare & Goethe. Every word is a poem. Others are oviparous, alive though incomplete; and others are like trees which leave seeds & fruits on which the living can feed.[280]

It is strange that Swedenborg ↑is↓ never lyric; never a sweet sound; no muse ever breathed in all that vast architecture. 'Tis a kind of Petra, a city of the dead, a palace of catacombs. I find his exclamations those of a country parson.[281]

Shakspeare the only writer who has had the honour of a Concordance.↑? ? Cicero has, & the Bible Saints.↓[282]
[217] ↑Swedenborg (Christ)↓

Modern Philosophy has not yet attempted the portrait of the

[279] With this sentence, cf. Journal RS, p. [178] above.

[280] With this paragraph, cf. "Powers and Laws of Thought," *W*, XII, 18.

[281] This paragraph, struck through in ink with a wavy, discontinuous, diagonal use mark, is used in "Swedenborg," *W*, IV, 142, 144.

[282] Added in pencil.

Blessed Jew, that wonderful youth who fascinated Asia & Europe. Swedenborg has attempted it,[n] but he is obviously not the person to do it. He showed his incapacity by binding himself hand & foot, & flinging himself at his feet by way of first salutation.

The preacher of eternity dates our chronology.[283]

Our freedom is necessary.[284]

[218] The highest compliment that can be conferred, better than a garter, or order of the Sacred Fleece, or laurel crown, is the addressing to a human being thought out of a certain region, & presupposing his intelligence.[285]

I send my children to the Schoolmaster, but the schoolboys educate them.[286]

[219] I figure to myself the world as a hollow temple, & every individual ⟨a⟩mind as an exponent of some sacred part therein, as if each man were a ⟨phosphorescence⟩ ↑jet of flame↓ affixed to some capital, or node, or angle, or triglyph, or rosette, or spandyl, bringing out its beauty & symmetry to the eye by his shining. But when the ⟨man⟩ ↑jet of light↓ is gone, ⟨& the phosphorescence,⟩ the groined arch ↑⟨& fluted pillar⟩ & fluted column↓ remain⟨s as⟩ beautiful, & can in an instant be lighted again & vindicated.
Actinism. ⟨a⟩A portion of the ray has the property of insinuating itself into the molecular structure of bodies, & so revealing their secret architecture[.]

[220] Aunt Mary never liked to throw away any medicine; but, if she found a drop of laudanum here, & a pill or two there, a little

[283] See Journal RS, p. [253] above.

[284] This sentence, struck through in ink with two diagonal use marks, is used in "Fate," *W*, VI, 23. See Journal RS, p. [253] above.

[285] This sentence, struck through in ink with a vertical use mark, is used in "Uses of Great Men," *W*, IV, 16.

[286] This sentence, struck through in ink with a vertical use mark, is used in "Culture," *W*, VI, 142. See pp. [90] and [91] above.

quinine & a little antimony, mixed them up & swallowed them. So when she came to the tea-table — "O, no, she never took tea;" — "Can you get a little shells?" The cocoa came, & Aunty took cocoa, because it was soothing, & put a little tea in it to make her lively, & if there was a little coffee, that was good for getting rid of the taste.

[221] I said that the ⟨fec⟩least acceleration of thought would add indefinite longevity to the man.[287] And we are to go to the best examples in each faculty to take notes for the creation of the complete brain. Plato insists much on "those who can without ⟨the⟩ aid ⟨of eyes⟩ from the eyes, or any other sense, proceed to truth & to Being."[288] Dante ↑(See TU 126)↓ is the best example of tenacity in the intellectual senses; his fancy grasps with the hold of *hands*, and he describes from his imagination, as if from his retina. But we all have the like grasp of intellectual objects in ⟨s⟩dreams.
What differences! Some men cannot see the house till it is built,[289] — cannot see the machine till the model is placed before their eyes. Moody the machinist, when Colburn described an improvement to him, cried immediately ↑"ah but↓ ⟨I⟩it hits, [222] it hits *somewhere*;"[290] a fatal objection. Plato says, choose those "who can ⟨see⟩ ↑proceed↓ without aid from their eyes, or any other sense, ⟨from⟩with truth to being."[291] (See above p. 181)

Well, now it seems as if this Plato's power of grading or ranking all that offers itself at sight was as good as a duration of a thousand years. The reason why life is short, is, because we are confounded by the dazzle of new things, & by the ↑seeming↓ equal↑ity↓ which custom sheds on great & small; & we are obliged to spend a large part of life in ⟨watching comparison &⟩ corrections which we [223] should save, if our judgment was sure when we first beheld things.

[287] With this sentence, cf. "Memory," *W*, XII, 108.

[288] This sentence is used in "Uses of Great Men," *W*, IV, 17.

[289] See *JMN*, IX, 23, 210, 212.

[290] An ink line, interpreted here as italics, strikes through the first two letters of "somewhere;'", then curves down so as to underscore the rest of the word; Emerson may have intended to cancel "somewhere;'". Paul Moody (1779–1831), mechanic and inventor of machinery for the manufacture of cotton, worked in Lowell, Mass., with Warren Colburn (see Journal RS, p. [16] above).

[291] See p. [221] above.

Plato is like those Tamers who have ⟨curbed the⟩ charmed ⟨a⟩down the ferocity of vicious animals, or who by some virulence ↑or ferocity↓ in their own nature have terrified frantic madmen. He looks ⟨at⟩ through things at ⟨the first⟩ ↑a↓ glance, & they fly into place. & he walks in life with the security of a god. It seems as if [292] the winds of ages swept through this universal thinking, so wide, so just, yet so minute, that it is impossible that an air of such calmness & long maturity can belong to the hasty,   crude, experimental blotting [224] of one lifetime.[293]

——

Art

——

I read in Ellery Channing's manuscript,—"He who is not naturally great, may acquire some taste for this style by art."

[225] [blank]

[226] Some minds are incapable of skepticism; the doubts they profess to entertain are rather a civility or accommodation to the common language of their company & of society. But they have no valves of interruption: the blood of the Universe ⟨f⟩rolls at all times through their veins without impediment. Others there are to whom the heaven is brass, & perhaps it shuts down for them to the very surface of the earth[.] [294]

[227] Dr Patten of New York was challenged to continue the verses in the Primer; — In Adam's Fall
We sinned all.

Dr Patten proceeded; In Cain's murder,
We sinned furder.

[292] A pencil line, resembling the capital letter "Z" turned backwards, occurs between "as" and "if", with "96" in pencil written above "if".

[293] There is space for a word of approximately eight letters after "hasty", suggesting that Emerson intended later to add another word. "It seems . . . blotting" is struck through in ink with a diagonal use mark on p. [223]; "It seems . . . lifetime." is used in "Plato: New Readings," *W*, IV, 87.

[294] This paragraph, struck through in ink with a vertical use mark, is used in "Montaigne," *W*, IV, 180, 181.

In Tubal Cain,
We sinned again.

Dr Ashbel Green In Doctor Green,
Our sin is seen.[295]

[228] A[lcott] was nettled at railroads & telegraphs. He thought with impatience, that if those jobs were once done & ended, the intellect of America could be won to some worthy occupation,[n 296] ↑as Goldsmith did not like to hear a pretty woman praised.↓[297]

[229] [blank]

[230][298] The celestial mind incapable of offence, of haste, of care, of inhospitality, of peeping, of memory, incapable of being embarrassed, incapable of discourtesy, treating all with a sovereign equality.[299]

A man must not have a fixed idea, or any condescension, but a publicity, & put his peculiarities in his pocket, when his fellow approaches.[300]

"I stand here for humanity,—to make humanity beautiful to you," said J. P.[301]

[231] *Positive degree.* J⟨.⟩↑onathan↓ P⟨.⟩↑hillips↓ said of Dr Channing; "I have known him these many years, & I think him capable of virtue."—

---

[295] "Dr Patten" may be William Patton (1798–1879), New York clergyman and author, one of the founders of Union Seminary, which he directed until 1849. Ashbel Green (1762–1848) was a Presbyterian clergyman, president of the College of New Jersey, 1812–1822, and editor of the *Christian Advocate* until 1835.

[296] Emerson's Notebook Amos Bronson Alcott lists TU, p. [228], "nettled at railroads" on p. [1], and quotes this passage on pp. [4] and [11].

[297] "A was . . . praised." is struck through in pencil with a vertical use mark.

[298] In Notebook Amos Bronson Alcott, p. [1], under "Alcottiana" Emerson lists TU, p. [230], "courtesy".

[299] There is a space for a word of approximately ten letters after "memory," suggesting that Emerson intended to add another word later.

[300] This sentence is struck through in ink with a vertical use mark.

[301] This sentence, struck through in ink with a vertical use mark, is used in "Behavior," *W*, VI, 197. Emerson's reference is undoubtedly to Jonathan M. Phillips (1778–1861), close friend of the family, philanthropist, and early member of the Transcendental Club.

Today, carpets; ⟨w⟩yesterday, the aunts; the day before, the funeral of poor S; & every day, the remembrance in the library of the rope of work which I must spin; — in this way life is dragged down & confuted.[302] We try to listen to the hymn of gods, & must needs hear this perpetual co⟨a⟩ck-a-doodle-doo, & ⟨ca⟩ke-tar-kut, right under the library windows. They ↑the gods↓ ought to respect a life, you say, whose objects are their own: But steadily they throw mud & eggs at us, roll us in the dirt, & jump on us.[303]

[232] [blank]
[233] Solitary Imprisonment is written on his coat & hat, on the lines of his face, & the limbs of his body, on his brow, & on the leaves of laurel on his brow. He wrestles hard with the judge, & does not believe he is in earnest. "Solitary Imprisonment," replies the Judge. Yet with some mitigation. Three times a day his keeper comes to the window, & puts bread & water on the shelf. The keeper's dog he may play with, if he will. Bow-wow-wow, says the dog. People may come from Asia to see him, if they like. He is only permitted to become his own friend.

[234] M[ary]. M[oody]. E[merson].

⟨E⟩When E[lizabeth]. H[oar]. was at Waterford, & had gone out to walk in the woods with Hannah, Aunt Mary feared they were lost, & found a man in the next house & begged him to go & look for them.[304] The man went & returned, saying, that he could not see them. Go & ⟨call⟩ ↑cry↓ "Elizabeth." The man rather declined this service, as he did not know her. Aunt Mary was highly offended, & exclaimed, "God has given you a voice that you might use it in the service of your fellow creatures. Go instantly, & call 'Elizabeth,' 'till you find them." The man went immediately, & did as he was bid, &, having found them, apologised for calling thus, by telling what Miss Emerson said to him.[305]

[302] Emerson's aunts "Betsey & Fanny" Haskins were visiting him as of September 25; Rusk describes Fanny as excessively religious (*L*, IV, 165; *Life*, p. 55).

[303] This paragraph, struck through in ink with four diagonal use marks, is used in "Culture," *W*, VI, 153.

[304] "Hannah" is probably Mary Moody Emerson's niece Hannah V. Haskins (Mrs. Augustus Parsons), who was devoted to, and cared for, Miss Emerson.

[305] This paragraph is used in "Mary Moody Emerson," *W*, X, 410.

[235] For good reading, there must be, of course, a yielding, sometimes entire, but always ⟨a⟩some yielding to the book. Then the reader is refreshed with a new atmosphere & foreign habits. But many minds are incapable of any surrender; they are like ⟨no⟩ knights of a Border Castle, who

"Carve at the meal
In gloves of steel,
And drink the red wine thro the helmet barred."[306]

&, of course, their ⟨eating⟩ ↑dining↓ is very unsatisfactory. How admirable a ⟨discipline is⟩ University is Plato's *Republic*; yet set ⟨|| . . . ||⟩ ↑P.↓ to read it, he would read nothing in it but P.

[236] In the conduct of life, let us not parade our rags, let us not, moved by vanity, confess, & tear our hair, at the corners of streets, or in the sitting room; but, as age & infirmity steal on us, contentedly resign the front seat & the games to these bright children, our better representatives, nor expect compliments or inquiries,—much less, gifts or love—any longer, (which to expect is ridiculous,) and, not at all wondering why our friends do not come to us, much more wondering when they do,—decently withdraw ourselves into modest & solitary resignation & rest.

[237] *Genius of Humanity*

The genius of humanity—his biography only can we read. There are few,—fewest individuals. Most men have no sharp edges, but blend insensibly on all sides with the race; Custom, Tendency, Gravitation, they exhibit; that is, the history of Humanity. Well; he is handsome, strong, musical, & eloquent, & has a part to play, as his predecessors in paleontology, (say, the Saurian, & the Plant,) had before him. He has the forest in his rear. And something is achieved. His arts & sciences, the easy [238] issues of his brain, look glorious from the distant brain of ox & lion, crocodile, & fish.[307]
On the other side, he has only generic possession of the best things.

[306] Sir Walter Scott, *The Lay of the Last Minstrel*, Canto I, ll. 31–33.

[307] "the Saurian . . . fish.", struck through in ink with single vertical use marks on pp. [237] and [238], is used in "Plato: New Readings," *W*, IV, 80.

He speaks of ⟨the lustre⟩ that which is the united lustre of all the sages, as if it were light orbed already in some ⟨man⟩ human eye.

[239] And it seems as if nature, contemplating the long geologic night behind her, when at last in five or six millenniums she had turned out five or six men,—say, Phidias, Plato, ⟨Jesus, Shakspeare⟩ ↑Menu, Columbus↓, was nowise impatient of the millions of ↑disgusting↓[308] blockheads she had spawned along with them, but was well contented with these few. These samples, she said [240] attested the virtue of the tree, these were a clear amelioration of trilobite & saurus, and a good basis for further proceeding. The next advancements should be more rapid. With this artist time & space are cheap, & she is insensible to what you say of tedious preparation. Her manners & modes are secular. And she busies herself with quite other measures.[309]

[241]–[242] [leaf torn out][310]

[243] Believers give themselves most leave to speculate, as they are secure of a return:[311] ⟨and this too for skepticism, that⟩ Nature does not work for classes, but for the whole; so she ↑absorbs them↓[,] occupies the adult masses with the care of providing for themselves & ↑their↓ families, to the exclusion of every other thought. Nothing but the brandy of politics will wake them from their brute life. No song of any muse will they hear. But it is plain that the adult education should be undertaken. When our Republic, O Plato! shall begin, the education shall not ⟨stop⟩ ↑end↓ with the youth, but shall be as vigorously continued in maturity. We have in nowise exhausted [244][n] the books. Astronomy invites, and Geology & Geometry & Chemistry. See how Humboldt, & Agassiz, & Berzelius, & Goethe, & Faraday, & Brown, & Lindley, work! Let our state be provided with

[308] Added in pencil.

[309] Except for the last two sentences, this paragraph, struck through in ink with single vertical use marks on pp. [239] and [240], is used in "Plato: New Readings," *W*, IV, 80–81.

[310] Emerson indexed p. [242] under Dreams, Morals, and Skeptic. In Notebook S Salvage, p. [45], Emerson records: "Dreams make dreadful revelations & leave Locke & Hegel little to tell you TU 242".

[311] The sentence to this point, struck through in ink with two vertical use marks, is used in "Montaigne," *W*, IV, 180.

proctors who shall drive the old fellows to school. Let our games ⟨p⟩ offer competition & prizes, & let us keep the ⟨people⟩ ↑fathers↓ up to as high a point of aim as we do the children. Then you will have a state. Now nothing can exceed the disappointment & despondency of such of the [245] people as have arrived at maturity without marriage, in finding themselves absolutely without proper task, and compelled to be either brooms & dusters, or else drones & ⟨sots⟩ ↑gourmands.↓ [312] Yet Nature selfishly puts them all to marrying & providing, & leaves the exceptions (which, she, to be sure, winks at,) to the care of higher power. I mean she always lets higher power look out for itself, &, if any soul has seen anything of truth, she knows it will [246] revolt against all this musty housekeeping of hers & dedicate itself to sacred uses. "Every one for himself," says Nature.

I look then at a soul born with a task, as happy.

☞ In youth we clothe ourselves with rainbows, with hope & love, & go as brave as the Zodiack. In age we put out another sort of perspiration; gout, fever, rheumatism, caprice, doubt, fretting, and avarice.

[247] ↑*Life* (See *R.S* 283↓

Some of the sweetest hours of life, on retrospect, will be found to have been spent with books.—Yes; but [n] the sweetness was your own. Had you walked, or hoed, or swum, or sailed, or kept school, in the same hours, it would have endeared those employments & conditions. Nature has taught each creature to put out from itself its own condition & sphere, as the slug sweats out its own slimy house in the pear leaf; & the wooly aphides in the apple, perspire their own bed; & the fish, its shell.

see p. 246 ☜ [313]

[312] "sots" has been canceled, and "gourmands." added, both first in pencil, then, after "gourmands." was partially erased, in ink.

[313] This hand points across to p. [246] where, just below the rule, a pointing hand appears in the left margin, followed by "In youth . . . avarice.", undoubtedly indicating that Emerson wished "In youth . . . avarice." to follow "its shell.". "to put out . . . avarice.", struck through in pencil with single vertical use marks on pp. [247] and [246], is used in "Fate," *W*, VI, 41, in the order designated here.

[248][314] ⟨Character. We conceive some men as⟩ It is the high doctrine that the events are in the same chain as persons; are only part & parcel of persons. A man's fortunes are the print of his character: A man's friends are his magnetisms. If I ⟨found⟩ ↑did not find↓ him ⟨not⟩ at home, I repelled him. And, accordingly, as I have noticed elsewhere, a man likes better to be complimented on his ⟨co⟩position, (as the proof of the most ultimate or total excellence), than on his other merits.[315] ↑N 107↓

[249] *Macaulay again*

Macaulay's History is full of low merits: it is like English manufactures of all kinds, neat, convenient, portable, saleable, made on purpose for the Harpers to print a hundred thousand copies of. So far can Birmingham go.

Macaulay is the Banvard of English history, good at drawing a Missisippi Panorama, but 'tis cheap work.[316] No memorable line has he written, no sentence. He is remembered by flippancy on one occasion against Plato & Bacon, but has no affirmative talent: he can write quantities of verses, too, to order, wrote "Lays," or something. No doubt wrote good nonsense verses at Eton, better than Virgil. His chef d'oeuvre was a riddle on the Cod-fish. That was really good.[317] see 111

[314] A canceled hand pointing across to p. [249] appears in the center top margin of p. [248].

[315] "It is . . . merits.", struck through in pencil with a discontinuous vertical use mark and in ink with a diagonal use mark, is used in "Fate," *W*, VI, 41, 42. With "It is . . . of persons.", cf. Journal RS, p. [273] above.

[316] John Banvard (1821–1891) painted a half-mile-long panorama of the Mississippi on canvas and exhibited it throughout the United States and abroad.

[317] In Notebook NQ, p. [276], Emerson entered the riddle:

Enigma. by T. B. Macaulay.

Cut off my head, and singular my act;
Cut off my tail, and plural I appear;
Cut off both head and tail, most curious fact,
Altho' the middle's left, there's nothing there.
What is my head cut off? a sounding sea;
What is my tail cut off? a flowing river;
Amidst their foaming depths, I fearless play,
Parent of softest sounds, though mute forever.

"Enigma" has not been located in Macaulay's works.

[250] Oct 19
Two meters, I have assumed lately, will measure men, the perception of identity, & the perception of reaction. Shakspeare, Plato, Swedenborg, Goethe's eyes never shut on either of these laws. The⟨y⟩se indicate men of great calibre: The little are little by failure to see them.[318]

George Shorey 17 Oct

[251] Charles Newcomb came, but we grow incapable of events & influences. He too turns the conversation, if I try a general remark. His MSS, which he brought, were six years old, but full of subtle genius.[319] Intense solitude appears in every sentence. They are soliloquies, & the abridged stenographic wit & eloquence, like that or better than that we are wonted to in M[ary].M[oody].E[merson]. He is a Bramin existing to little use, if prayer & beauty are not that. Yet he humiliates the proud & staggers the dogmatist, & subverts all the mounds & fortification lines of accustomed thought, [252_1] eminently[320] aristocratic beyond any person I remember to have met, because self centred on a deep centre of genius,—easy, cheerful, condescending, [253] condescending to the greatest, & mortifying Plato & Jesus, if it were possible, by his genuine preference of children, & ladies, & the first piece of nature, to all their fame & sanctity. If one's centrality is incomprehensible to us, we can do nothing with him. We may as well affect to snub the sun.[321] One will shine as the other. But though C.'s mind is unfounded, & the

[318] This paragraph, struck through in ink with two diagonal use marks, is used in "Uses of Great Men," *W*, IV, 17–18.

[319] In a letter to Caroline Sturgis Tappan, November 8, 1850 (ms. Houghton Library), Emerson writes that he has had Newcomb's " 'Edith' or 'Cleone' or 'Caroline' now for a year"; it is not clear whether these are alternate titles for a single work or three divisions or chapters.

[320] Emerson first ended this entry at "accustomed thought," at the bottom of p. [251], then changed the period after "thought" to a comma, added "emi-" to the end of the line, and "see bottom of next page" in the bottom margin with a line curving up over the clause to set it off from the entry. He continued the passage below a rule across the bottom third of p. [252_1], beginning his continuation with the complete word "eminently". It is printed here as one continuous passage.

[321] "If one's . . . sun." is used in "Greatness," *W*, VIII, 303.

walls actually taken out, so that he seems open to nature, yet he does not accumulate his wisdom into any amounts of thought: rarely arrives at a result,—perhaps does not care to, so that [254] I say, it seems as if instead of my bare walls your ⟨house was hung with fine perspective-paper or frescoed with landscapes but though these are⟩ [322] ↑surrounding ⟨has⟩ is↓ really landscapes & perspectives of temples: ⟨you⟩ ↑yet↓ they avail no more to you than if they were landscape-paper-hangings or fresco pictures of temples.

"Will Fortune never come with both hands full?
She either gives a stomach & no food,
——— ——— or else a feast
And takes away the stomach."
[Shakespeare, 2] *Henry IV.* [iv, 103–107] [323]

[252₂] We have Virginians, Carolinians, Western men, New Yorkers & Yankees, but no Americans as yet; no man up to the grandeur of the geographic lines, and to the immense Future of this Country. But great things enforce great administration, & sea & land have a miraculous organ & speak out through lawyer & pedant.[324]

---

[255] Ah dear old Swedenborg, and is thy saw good, "*The perfection of man is the love of use.*"? [325] And this fine luminary, brightest of all, can ill conceal his dislike of a general remark, spends his mornings at Newport, all summer, in walking; his afternoons, "in society;" & has read but one book, this year, namely, an old novel by Lord Normanby! [326] Dear Swedenborg, if you can catch this American sprig, will you not whip him soundly!

[322] "fine perspective-paper . . . are⟩" is struck through in pencil and in ink with single vertical use marks.

[323] From the spacing in the ms., it is not clear whether this quotation belongs with the Newcomb entry above or whether it is a separate entry. The editors believe it belongs with the Newcomb entry.

[324] This paragraph is struck through in pencil with a diagonal use mark and in ink with two diagonal use marks. For "miraculous organ", see Shakespeare, *Hamlet*, II, ii, 622.

[325] *The Delights of Wisdom concerning Conjugial Love* . . . , 1843, p. 245. The quotation is used in "Swedenborg," *W*, IV, 126.

[326] Constantine Henry Phipps (1797–1863), first Marquis of Normanby, MP, lord lieutenant of Ireland, and minister to the court of Tuscany, was the author of romantic novels and sketches.

[256] Yet it is very true, as Napoleon said, that you must not fight too often with one enemy, or you will teach him all your art of war. Talk with Alcott, or Very, or Carlyle, or Newcomb, & you quickly come to their talent, new eyes bud in your brow, & you see what they see.[327]

[257] ↑C[harles].K[ing].N[ewcomb]↓

C N had a fine subtlety like this, "that, it is not what the thought is, but how he stands to his thought, that ⟨qualifies for⟩ ↑we value in↓ friendship." ↑*See below*↓ [328]

"Spiritual persons have an unactual effect by their dependence on the spiritual nature in them. They are only as it is & their outward position is from action for their deeper nature."

"A deep & delicate person is apt to shun strangers, because knowing them so readily, they come in suddenly upon him, & are nea↑r↓ him as fellow natures, while he does not recognise them [n] as congenial ones, or as of the same sphere. & he sees commonness of life, without the identity of nature underneath: for, it is how men are to their thought, not what thought they have, which makes friendship." *C.K. Newcomb.*

[258] Shakspeare was the farthest bound of subtlety & universality compatible with individuality; the subtilest of authors, and only just within the possibility of authorship.[329] C.K.N. is my best key to him, & he is just beyond authorship.—The impartiality of Shakspeare is like that of the light itself, which is no aristocrat, but shines as mellowly on gipsies as on emperors, on bride & corpse, on city & swamp.

[259] ↑"I believe that there is no true theory of disease that does not at once suggest cure." Wilkinson.↓ [330]

---

[327] This paragraph, struck through in ink with a vertical use mark, is used in "Uses of Great Men," *W*, IV, 13.

[328] Although the quotation appears in Journal AZ, p. [159] below, "*below*" here undoubtedly refers to the passage on p. [257] below, " 'A deep . . . friendship.' " A line, beginning just below the "*w*" of "*below*", curves down through the next entry " 'Spiritual persons . . . nature." and ends in a pointing hand just above "deep &".

[329] This sentence, struck through in ink with a vertical use mark, is used in "Shakspeare," *W*, IV, 212.

[330] This sentence is used in "The Preacher," *W*, X, 232.

Mrs R. suggests that *cholera* is a signal of new life forming, as always death & life are observed to be convertible in nature. The decomposition of the potato or pear is the composition ⟨& growth⟩ & flourishing of plants not less necessary to Nature in her inscrutable laboratories.[331]

Bigendians	*Littleendians*
Plato	Alcott
Swedenborg	Very
Shakspere	Newcomb
Montaigne	Channing
Goethe	RWE
Napoleon	Thoreau[332]

[260] Devil is the fag-end.

[261] Melioration[333]

[262] ⟨"Concentration is the secret⟩ ↑of strength↓[334] ⟨of politics as of war."

London Times⟩

— one of those things which men hear gladly. —

[263] [blank]

[264] ⟨At f⟩At this time we fell upon the design of establishing a club of the readers of Shakspeare's Sonnets, as the only Church still possible. The questions to be announced for the debate of this parliament, were; Who is the author? To whom were they written? What do they mean?

[331] Emerson's reference is to Mrs. Sarah Alden Ripley, according to his own identification in a reference to "TU 259" in Notebook OP Gulistan, p. [73]. "The decomposition . . . composition" is struck through in ink with two diagonal use marks; cf. "Plato: New Readings," *W*, IV, 82.

[332] The left-column list is that of the men whose biographies appear in *Representative Men*. Whether Emerson intended to set up parallels with the names in the right-hand column isn't clear, but either in interests or manner, there are demonstrable relationships between all pairs except Napoleon and Thoreau.

[333] This word is centered in the middle of p. [261].

[334] Added in pencil. Emerson neglected to cancel the insert.

The Malone sentence in my "Shakspeare" is to be found in *Vol. 18, p. 572 Malone's Shakspeare, Lond. 1821.*[335] Dissertation at the end of Third Part of Henry VI.

[265][336] Concord

the barberry trade

There is not a fox or a crow or a partridge in Concord who knows the woodlands better than Thoreau[.]

The Indian rule that Sannup and Squaw should not both get drunk on the same day, is worthy of all acceptation, & of various application.

Identity philosophy makes swinging a chair every whit as good as ⟨clin⟩ a journey to Oregon, but great is the illusory energy of Vishnu[.]

How can a man ↑with capital↓ afford to go into any business when the market offers so many investments at 12 per cent?

[266] You cannot make a statue out of punk.

I found I could not interest my children & gave up clubs[337]

Live in a large town. In a small one though you draw never so much, you will repel more valuable & agreeable talent of all kinds than you draw.[338]

[335] *The Plays and Poems of William Shakspeare . . . comprehending a life of the poet . . . by the late E[dmond] Malone* . . . , 21 vols. (London, 1821). Vol. 18, p. 572: "The total number of lines in our author's Second and Third Part of King Henry VI, is Six Thousand and Forty-three: of these, as I conceive, 1771 lines were written by some author or authors who preceded Shakspeare; 2373 were formed by him on the foundation laid by his predecessors; and 1899 lines were entirely his own composition." Cf. "Shakspeare," *W*, IV, 195.

[336] P. [265] is in pencil. "The Indian . . . application." has been traced over in ink.

[337] This and the above entry on p. [266] are in pencil. Erased pencil writing underlies the next two ink entries below, but recovered words indicate that the ink entries are copies of the erased pencil matter.

[338] "Live . . . draw." is used in "Culture," *W*, VI, 148. See p. [89] above.

I supposed the landscape to be full of a race of Daemons who move at a faster rate than men,—so fast as just to escape our organ of sight.

---

[267][339] *A⟨d⟩sdschedi of Merw* / on the march of the Sultan Mahmoud

It draws the Shah to Sumenat,
Sticks on his banner the Wonder deed

[Von Hammer, *Geschichte der schönen Redekünste Persiens*, 1818, p. 44]

On a Melon.

Colour taste & smell, Smaragdus sugar & musk
Amber for the tongue coloured stuff for the eye
When thou cuttest in slices every slice is a new moon
When thou leavest it whole, stands the full moon there[340]

They talk of repentance of glad drinking bouts,
Of repentance of the love of beautiful idol /pictures, /images/[341]
In sin burns the heart, the mouth speaks repentance,
Not seldom is it that such repentance repents.

See Von Hammer p 44
Geschichte der Schönen Redekünste Persiens[342]
Wien 1818

[268] "Perhaps when our good days no longer last
The mind runs backward & enjoys the past;"

[339] P. [267] is in pencil.

[340] With Emerson's translation of the poem to this point, cf. "Persian Poetry," *W*, VIII, 244:

"Color, taste and smell, smaragdus, sugar and musk,
Amber for the tongue, for the eye a picture rare,
If you cut the fruit in slices, every slice a crescent fair,
If you leave it whole, the full harvest moon is there."

[341] Emerson drew a line under "images", apparently to separate it from "pictures,".

[342] Emerson's umlauts look like Greek iotas.

says (Rowe's) Lucan when ⟨Cae⟩Pompey's soldiers have happy dreams ⟨one⟩the night before the battle of Pharsalia.[343]

The children say, "Don't you know how we used to," &c with alarming quickness[.]

[269] Michel Angelo paints with more will; Raffaelle, with the obedience of water & flame. Every body would paint like Raffaelle, if the power of painting were added to everybody.

[270] Two or three things ⟨were⟩ ↑I have↓ just now observed of Swedenborg. That his distinction of shunning evils as sins is a pounding or preaching distinction, or snuffle. That his Inferno is mesmeric, and, as in dreams we s↑c↓ratch the ground like dogs, grope, watch, & sneak about the stable yards & leavings of creation, imbeciles, underlings, &, when we wake up, do stand erect on our feet, aiming from year to year to be decent & honest people, so is it here; his Spiritual World bears the same relation to the generosities & joys of truth as bad dreams do to each man's ideal life. His whole book is libellous & mere undigested potato.[344]

[271]–[272] [leaf torn out] [345]

[343] Lucan, *Pharsalia*, trans. Nicholas Rowe, Book VII, ll. 25–26. See *JMN*, VI, 45.

[344] This paragraph, struck through in ink with a vertical use mark, is used in "Swedenborg," *W*, IV, 137, 141.

[345] The leaf bearing pp. [271]–[272] has been torn out about 1¼ inches from the binding; the stub, which has worked free of the binding, is inserted between pp. [270] and [273] with "Journal T.U. This is the remaining part of p. 271–p 272 not enough to type" written across the inner margin, obviously not by Emerson. Words or parts of words remaining are: "[271] I re|| . . . || goodne|| . . . || this || . . . || laby|| . . . || prev|| . . . || to the || . . . || cask || . . . || the || . . . || befor|| . . . || here || . . . || sails || . . . || rely || . . . || prud|| . . . || sense || . . . || of m|| . . . || keep || . . . || nor || . . . || noth|| . . . || forev|| . . . || that || . . . || studies || . . . || [272] || . . . || this || . . . || him || . . . ||ting || . . . || I be || . . . ||mire || . . . || dimmest || . . . || cleave || . . . || that || . . . || God || . . . || that || . . . ||trality || . . . || as sins || . . . || untunes || . . . ||tive was || . . . || element || . . . || But || . . . ||" The matter on pp. [271] and [272] is probably used in "Swedenborg," *W*, IV, 144–145, 137 (words and parts of words corresponding to those in the ms. are italicized): "He elected *goodne*ss as the clue to which the soul must cling in all this *laby*rinth of nature. Many opinions conflict as to the true centre. In the shipwreck, some cling *to* running rigging, some to *cask* and barrel, some to spars, some to mast; *the* pilot chooses

[273] ↑*Swedenborg*↓

⟨h⟩He does not know what evil is, or what good is, who thinks any ground remains to be occupied after saying that evil⟨s are⟩is to be shunned as evil. One man, you say, dreads erysipelas. Show him, then, that this dread is evil: or ↑one dreads↓ hell; show him that *dread* is evil. He who loves goodness, ⟨loves⟩ ↑harbours↓ angels, reverences reverence, ↑&↓ lives with God↑.↓ [346] ⟨& cannot sin.⟩

Once more, as⟨,⟩ I have somewhere written, ↑(above p 118)↓ he who addresses himself to modes or wants that can be dispensed with, goes out of fashion, ↑builds his house off the road.↓ But he who addresses himself to [274] problems that every man must come to solve, builds his house on the road, & every man must come to it. Jesus's problems are mine, & therefore to Jesus & through Jesus must we go, & Swedenborg had the like wisdom. Swedenborg is the poet of the spine.

Nature pays no respect to those who pay any respect to her; was H. J.'s doctrine[.] [347]

---

[275] [348] The Chapter ||msm||
great is pa||msm||
painter, ||msm||

with science, — I plant myself here; all will sink *before* this; 'he comes to land who *sails* with me.' Do not *rely* on heavenly favor, or on compassion to folly, or on *prudence*, on common *sense*, the old usage and main chance *of men*: nothing can *keep* you, — not fate, nor health, *nor* admirable intellect; none can keep you, but rectitude only, rectitude *for ever* and ever! And with a tenacity *that* never swerved in all his *studies*, inventions, dreams, he adheres to *this* brave choice. I think of *him* as of some transmigra*ting* votary of Indian legend, who says 'Though *I be* dog, or jackal, or pis*mire*, in the last rudiments of nature, under what integument or ferocity, I *cleave* to right, as the sure ladder *that* leads up to man and to *God*. . . . His cardinal position in morals is *that* evils should be shunned *as sins*. . . . I doubt not he was led by the desire to insert the *element* of personality of Deity. *But* nothing is added."

[346] This paragraph, struck through in ink with a vertical use mark, is used in "Swedenborg," *W*, IV, 137–138.

[347] Emerson saw Henry James, Sr., in New York between June 13 and 15 (see pp. [106] and [108] above). It is not known when Emerson picked up James's "doctrine", but the hostility of nature to man is a theme in a later lecture, "The Scientific Accord of Natural and Revealed Religion," in *Lectures and Miscellanies* (New York, 1852), pp. 262, 263, 266, and elsewhere.

[348] The leaf bearing pp. [275]–[276] has been torn out approximately two

one who ||msm||
'Tis strong ||msm||
all my ||msm||
of orations ||msm||
of books ||msm||
with so ||msm||
am still ||msm||
new pag||msm||
or any ||msm||
new p||msm||
I fancy ||msm||
be all ||msm||
in these ||msm||

[276]

||msm|| Then at
||msm||ub with
||msm|| But it
||msm|| like the
||msm|| the pedlar
||msm||; he makes
||msm|| ⟨stick⟩ with
||msm|| never
||msm|| ⟨stick of it⟩ ↑of the cement↓
||msm|| stick when
||msm|| more
||msm|| element
||msm||sion.
||msm|| through
||msm||ow dare
||msm||ol, — pluck

[277]–[278] [leaf missing] [279] Versailles, & borrows of his memory to trick out the tree.

Momentum

---

inches from the binding. Emerson indexed p. [275] under Illusion, and p. [276] under Woman. The matter on both pages is probably used in "Illusions," *W*, VI, 313, 315–317.

"Gases, however compressed, act as vacua with respect to each other" n is Dalton's law[.] [349]

——

Miss —— of New Haven, after reading Ruskin, said, that Nature was *Mrs Turner*.[350]

[280] Swedenborg strange, scholastic, didactic, passionless, bloodless, fishy man, who describes classes of souls as a botanist would a carex, ⟨& perambulates⟩ ↑or shall I say geologizes↓ hells as ⟨a geologist crosses⟩ a stratum of chalk or hornblende. ⟨The n⟩ He goes up & down the world of men ⟨in ↑gold↓ cane & peruke⟩ a sort of R↑h↓adamanthus in gold↑-headed↓ cane & peruke, & with the utmost disengagedness & air of ↑a↓ referee distributes souls. The warm many-weathered passionate peopled world is to him [281][351] only a grammar of hierogly[p]hs, or an emblematic free-mason's procession. Jacob Behmen how different! he is tremulous with emotion, & ⟨when actually seems to⟩ listens awestruck ⟨to the Teacher⟩ with the gentlest humanity, ↑to the Teacher whose lessons he conveys;↓ & when he explains that "love is greater than God," his heart beats so high that ⟨you can hear⟩ the thumping ⟨is audible⟩ against ⟨the⟩ ↑his↓ leathern coat ↑is audible↓ across the centuries. This makes [282] the greatest difference in their effect. Behmen is healthily & beautifully wise, notwithstanding the mystical narrowness & incommunicableness. Swedenborg is disagreeably wise, and for all his worlds I would not be he.[352] His Inferno too affects me as when a delicate young girl falls into lunacy, & instantly ⟨begins⟩ ↑falls↓ to curs⟨e⟩ing & swear⟨e⟩ing & pollut⟨e⟩ing her⟨self⟩ ↑lips↓ with profane & obscene speech.

He is so painful that I should break with him forever [283] but that I find him really scientific.

[349] John Bernhard Stallo, *General Principles of the Philosophy of Nature*, 1848, p. 46. Cf. Journal RS, p. [73] above, and "Resources," *W*, VIII, 149.

[350] See *JMN*, X, 528.

[351] "printed" is written in the bottom right margin of p. [280] and again in the bottom left margin of p. [281].

[352] "Swedenborg strange . . . he.", struck through in ink with a vertical use

Of all Englishmen, Wilkinson seems fittest by his learned & imaginative style, by breadth & vigour to introduce Swedenborg to ⟨th⟩ his countrym⟨a⟩en, & to this century. It is wonderful that his books have not yet startled the sleep of the contemplative power in England. TU 78

This reappearance ⟨of S⟩after a century of Swedenborg in his pupil is a more startling fact in psychology than any of his Revelations[.] [353]

[284] ↑In heaven,↓ when [n] a man wants a horse, a horse wants a man.[354]

Symbolism
⟨That which⟩ ↑What↓ I want to know, is, the meaning of what I do; believing that any of my ↑current↓ Mondays or Tuesdays is /bible/ Fatebook/ ↑⟨of eternity⟩↓ for me; & believing ⟨&⟩that hints & telegraphic signals are ⟨tormenting⟩ ↑arriving to↓ me ⟨out of these days⟩ ↑every moment out of the interior eternity,↓ I am tormented with impatience to make them out. We meet people who seem to overlook our game, & read us with a smile, but [285] they do not tell us what they read.

This is one kind of Symbolism. A more limited one is Swedenborg's fancy that certain books of Scripture were exact allegories or written in the angelic & ecstatic speech, as other books are not[.] [355]

———

Of what corn was his bread made? Of what bread had he eaten?

[286] *Swedenborg* was apt for cosmology because of that native perception of identity, which made magnitude of no account to him.

mark on p. [280], two vertical use marks on p. [281], and a vertical use mark on p. [282], is used in "Swedenborg," *W*, IV, 142–143.

[353] This sentence, struck through in ink with a curved vertical use mark, is used in "Swedenborg," *W*, IV, 111.

[354] See p. [36] above.

[355] This sentence is used in "Swedenborg," *W*, IV, 120.

In the atom of magnetic iron he instantly saw the quality which would generate the spiral motion of suns & planets.[356]

——

The ⟨us⟩style of his philosophic works is lustrous with points & shooting spicula of thought & reminds me of one of those frosty winter mornings when the air is sparkling with crystals[.] [357]

——

For the skeptic, Yes, we may give ourselves what allowance we will, for, once admitted to the heaven of thought, I see no return to Night, but infinite in⟨f⟩vitation on the other side. Heaven is within heaven[,] [287] sky over sky, and we are encompassed with divinities.[358] To what purpose dark ages & barbarous Irish, if I know, as I know, five or six men, without hardly going out of my village, to whom & with whom all is possible; who restore to me Plato, Shakspeare, Montaigne, Hindoo ⟨yes⟩ [n] cosmology, yea Buddh himself with their audacious intellectual adventure. We are as elastic as the gas of gunpowder, & small & tame as we walk here with our hands in our pockets, an imaginative book sets free our fancy, and in a moment our head is bathed in the Galaxy, & our feet tread on the ⟨C⟩hells.[359]

[288] ↑Our↓ Indeterminate Size is the delicious secret which books of imagination reveal to us.[360]

O endless ends, o living child! how can you fail! to you I open the ill kept secret that you are Hari, divine & invincible,—cousin to the four elements & the four hundred gods. You were concealed in an egg for thirty millenniums, the↑n↓ born on the side of a brook, confided to a shepherd who brought you up in a shanty, but your enemies have no longer power. It is time you should show yourself,

[356] With this paragraph, cf. p. [85] above.

[357] "*Swedenborg* was . . . crystals", struck through in ink with three diagonal use marks, is used in "Swedenborg," *W*, IV, 106.

[358] "once admitted . . . divinities.", struck through in ink with two vertical use marks on each of pp. [286] and [287], is used in "Montaigne," *W*, IV, 180–181.

[359] "We are . . . hells.", struck through in ink with a vertical use mark, is used in "Uses of Great Men," *W*, IV, 17.

[360] This sentence, struck through in ink with a vertical use mark, is used in "Poetry and Imagination," *W*, VIII, 18. Cf. "Uses of Great Men," *W*, IV, 17: "It [imagination] opens the delicious sense of indeterminate size and inspires an audacious mental habit."

fate is in your eye. You will ⟨be⟩yet be a horse, a lizard, a dragonfly, & a swamp full of alligators, but time & space are cheap to you, Hari; you can afford to be multiplied & divided, to bite & to be bitten, to be a bankrupt trade⟨r⟩sman, or [289] an acre of Sand; divided you will reunite, & ⟨dying⟩ you thrive by dying; do not care o Hari for the speech of men, do not ⟨call⟩care for a shabby appearance! [361]

[290] [Index material omitted]
[inside back cover] [Index material omitted]

[361] The apostrophe to Hari ought to be in *The Vishńu Puráńa*, like other references to the god in *JMN*, IX, 309 and 322, but it has not been located. Some of the metaphors have the ring of Emerson's style.

AZ

1849–1850

Journal AZ, a regular journal, begins about a month after the last dated entry for 1849 in Journal TU. Dated entries run from November 17, 1849 (p. [5]), to October 24, 1850 (p. [288]). Between mid-May and mid-June, Emerson visited Cincinnati, Ohio, to lecture—his first trip to the "west." He kept notes and observations in a separate book, Journal at the West, the first 35 pages of which record this 1850 trip. Journal at the West is printed on pp. 510–540 below.

Journal AZ is written in a hard-cover copybook, virtually identical to the one Emerson designated TU. The cover, 17.7 x 21.2 cm, is of predominantly brown paper marbled with blue and yellow over boards, with a tan leather margin at the binding and forming two triangles at the top and bottom outer edges. The spine, of brown leather, now peeling, has what appears to be "AZ" barely visible in the upper portion. The front cover is inscribed "1849" centered in ink on the upper portion of the marbled paper, below which is "1850", also in ink, in smaller numbers and perhaps inscribed later than the larger "1849". "AZ" is inscribed in ink on the upper leather triangular corner. The unruled pages measure 17.3 x 20.3 cm. The pages are numbered in ink except for the following four in pencil: 37, 132, 238, 258. Eight pages are numbered in pencil, then overwritten in ink: 36, 38, 39, 40, 240, 254, 255, 266_1. Seven pages are unnumbered: 51, 200, 201, 218, 243, 283, 292 (verso of flyleaf); fourteen pages are blank: ii, 2, 3, 32, 41, 50, 51, 55, 72, 74, 95, 131, 242, 243. Seven leaves have been torn out, with fragments of the stubs still in the binding: pp. 29–30, 79–80, 97–98, 187–188, 231–232, 273–274, 275–276. One page was misnumbered and corrected: 10⟨2⟩1. Page numbers 266 and 267 were repeated. Laid in between pages 230 and 233 (231–232 are torn out) is a newspaper clipping of a poem, "On the Death of S. Margaret Fuller" by G. P. R. James. Matching indentation and rust tracing marks show that it was at one time attached to page 233 with a paper clip, the poem facing up. Laid in between the back cover and page 292 is a cardboard sheet measuring 21.5 x 8.6 cm, written in ink on both sides in Edward Emerson's handwriting; the sheet bears a printed announcement of a bank stock dividend, dated November 14, 1903; the ink inscriptions are of various subject headings followed by journal references and "Look up".

[front cover] AZ

1849

1850

[front cover verso] ↑Examined Apr 77↓
[Index material omitted]

[i] Gulistan[1]

R.W. Emerson
Nov.:1849.

AZ

[Index material omitted]

"I hearing get, who had but ears,
And sight, who had but eyes before,
I moments live, who lived but years,
And truth discern, who knew but learning's lore."
H. D. Thoreau. ["Inspiration," ll. 25–28]

Hunc solem, et stellas, et decedentia certis
Tempora momenti⟨r⟩s, sunt qui formidine nulla
Imbuti spectant.[2] *Horace.* [*Epistles*, I, vi, 3–5]

[ii] [blank]

[1] Chemists say, *Corpora non agunt nisi soluta*: or, Others burn by fire, we by water.[3]

[2]–[3] [blank]

[1] Saadi, *The Gûlistân; or, Rose Garden*, trans. Francis Gladwin (London, 1808), is in Emerson's library.

[2] "Yon sun, the stars and seasons that pass in fixed courses — some can gaze upon these with no strain of fear." (The Loeb text reads "spectent" where Emerson has "spectant.") See *JMN*, V, 18. The quotation is used in "Progress of Culture," *W*, VIII, 225.

[3] The Latin is used in "The Fortune of the Republic," *W*, XI, 533. See *JMN*, X, 112, where it is translated "They do not exert themselves unless unfettered" (Ed.), or "Bodies only act when freed" (*J*, VII, 307, n. 1).

[4] They told Edmund Kean, the boxes applauded: "The boxes! a fig for the boxes! *the Pit rose to me*," he replied.[4]

[5] 1849

November 17. Yesterday saw the fields covered with cobwebs in every direction, on which the wake of the setting sun appeared as on water. Walked over hill & dale with Channing, who ⟨was⟩ found wonders of colour & landscape everywhere, but ⟨was⟩complained of the want of invention. "Why, they had frozen water last year; why should they do it again? Therefore it was so easy to be an artist, because *they* [n] do the same thing always, & therefore he only wants time to make him perfect in the [6] imitation.⟨"⟩ And I believe, too, that *pounding* is one of the secrets." C. thought the cause of cows was, that they made good walking where they fed. All summer, he gets water *au naturel*, and, in winter, *they* serve it up *artist↑i↓cally* [n] in this crystal johnny-cake; and he had observed the same thing at the confectioners' shops, that he could never get but one thing there, though [they] had two ways of making it up.[5]

[7] Roomy Eternity
Casts her schemes rarely,
⟨A completed⟩ ↑And a rounded↓ age allows
To every quality & part
In the multitudinous
⟨a⟩And many-chambered heart.[6]

Poet of poets
Is Time the distiller;
⟨Chemist,⟩ ↑Time the↓ refiner,
He hath a vitriol

[4] This anecdote appears in a review of Bryan Waller Procter's *Life of Edmund Kean* (London, 1835) in the *Quarterly Review*, LIV (July 1835), 115.

[5] With "he had observed . . . up.", cf. "Illusions," *W*, VI, 314: "And I remember the quarrel of another youth with the confectioners, that when he racked his wit to choose the best comfits in the shops, in all the endless varieties of sweetmeat he could find only three flavors, or two."

[6] These six lines are apparently the first version of "Fragments on Nature and Life," VI, *W*, IX, 350.

Which can dissolve
Towns into melody.
Burn up the libraries,
Down with the colleges,
Raze the foundations,
Drive out the doctors,
Rout the philosophers,
[8] Harry the critics, —
Men of particulars,
Narrowing niggardly,
Something to nothing;
All their ten thousand ways
End in the néant.

All thro' the countryside
Rush locomotives;
Prospering grocers
Poring on newspapers
Over their shop-fires
Settle the State.
But for the poet, —
Seldom in Centuries
Comes the well-tempered
Musical man.
He is the waited-for
He is the complement
Of one man & all men
The ⟨chance-⟩ ↑random↓ wayfarer.

↑p 18↓

[9] ↑*Intellect*↓

An affirmative talent is always safe. Th⟨is⟩e critics may do their worst; it is victory.

As for Germany, we have had no interest in it since the death of Goethe. All kinds of power usually develop themselves at the same time, and I look in the most active race for the idealism.[7] The

[7] "All kinds . . . time,", struck through in ink with a vertical use mark, is used in "Power," *W*, VI, 64. See Journal TU, p. [48] above.

Americans went to Heidelberg to find Germany, & discovered with surprise that they had left it behind them in New York. Mr Scherb attempted last night [10] to unfold Hegel for me and I caught somewhat that seemed cheerful & large, & that might, & probably did, come by Hindu suggestion.[8] But all abstract philosophy is easily anticipated,—it is so structural, or necessitated by the mould of the human mind. Schelling said, "the Absolute is the union of the Ideal and the Real."[9]

[11] The world, the universe, is a gigantic flower,—but the flower is one function or state of the plant, and the world but a stage or state of the Pan. As I have written long ago, the Universe is only in transit, or, we behold it shooting the gulf from the past to the future.[10]

[12] A[mos].B[ronson].A[lcott]. is like a slate-pencil which has a sponge tied to the other end, and, as the ⟨pencil dra⟩ point of the pencil draws lines, the sponge follows ⟨just⟩ as fast, & erases them. He talks high & wide, & expresses himself very happily, and forgets all he has said. If a Skilful operator could ⟨insert⟩ ↑introduce↓ a lancet & sever the sponge, ABA would be the prince of writers[.][11]

[13] ⟨C⟩J's vanity is like a bad sleeper who again & again loses himself in reveries but reappears to his own dismay & the general injury, & cannot die.

[14] I envied a young man in the cars who when his companion told him they had arrived at Waltham, ↑by Massasoit H[ouse]↓ was asleep, & his friend shook him, lifted him up, & called in his ear, in vain, he could not wake him, & the cars went on again to the next station before he could be fully aroused.[12] Then I came home & counted every hour the clock struck all night.

[8] For Scherb, see note 227 to Journal RS, p. [223] above.

[9] Cf. John Bernhard Stallo, *General Principles of the Philosophy of Nature . . .*, 1848, p. 221.

[10] For this sentence, see "Powers and Laws of Thought," *W*, XII, 59.

[11] This paragraph is struck through in ink with a diagonal use mark.

[12] Massasoit House stood at the corner of Main and Linden Streets, Waltham.

[15] *Goethe*

Nature told everything once.[13]

Angel song & chorus at opening of Faust is magazine or "*squirt*" poetry.

Goethe as a man who wished to make the most of himself was right in avoiding the horrors.

[16] ↑To describe adequately is the high power & one of the highest enjoyments of man.↓

She was beautiful & he fell in love with her. The thing has happened to millions, yet how few can tell the story. Try some of them, set them at the painting; each knows it all & can communicate nothing. Then comes Shakspeare, & tells it point for point as it befel, or better; and now we have two things, Love & literature.[14]

↑See *IT* 28↓

[17] I sent Chapman orders to send copies of "Representative Men" to

T[homas]. Carlyle
J[ohn].A. Carlyle
Earl of Lovelace
Arthur Helps
Mrs [Elizabeth] Paulet
W[illiam]. E[dward]. Forster
John Forster
Arthur H. Clough
Miss Ellen Randall
Dr Samuel Brown. Edinburgh
Edwin Field
J[ohn] J[ames] G Wilkinson[15]

I must add to the list by the next steamer
Miss [Harriet] Martineau

[13] See Journal TU, p. [16] above.

[14] "She was . . . literature." is struck through in ink with a discontinuous vertical use mark; "She was . . . her." is used in "Books," *W*, VII, 216.

[15] "Edwin Field" and "J J G Wilkinson" were first written in pencil, then traced in ink.

Dr [William] Jacobson
C[harles]. E. Rawlins Jr
John Kenyon Esq[16]
[18] Copies to be ⟨sent⟩given to

My Mother x
L[idian] E[merson] x
M[ary] M[oody] E[merson]
W[illiam] E[merson] x
E[lizabeth] H[oar] x
W[illiam] E[llery] Channing x
H[enry] D[avid] Thoreau x
A[mos] B[ronson] Alcott x
G[eorge] P[artridge] Bradford x
S[amuel] G[ray] Ward x
Caroline [Sturgis] Tappan x
H[arrison] G[ray] O[tis] Blake x
G[eorge] B[arrell] Emerson x
A[bel] Adams x
H[enry] W[adsworth] Longfellow x
Theodore Parker x
Edw Bangs x
J[ames] E[lliot] Cabot
C[harles] K[ing] Newcomb
B[arzillai]. Frost x
J[ohn] M[ilton] Cheney x
E[benezer] R[ockwood] Hoar x
E[lizabeth] P[almer] Peabody x
S[arah]. [Freeman] Clarke

Mrs [Sarah Bradford] Ripley x
Mrs [Almira] Barlow x
N[athaniel] L[angdon] Frothingham x
Martha Bartlett x
Mrs [Calvin C.] Damon x
Mrs L[ucy] C Brown x
N[athaniel] A Hawthorne x
W[illiam] H[enry] Furness x
C[harles] T[homas] Jackson x
E[mmanuel] V Scherb x[17]

[16] Of those listed who have not been previously identified or are not easily recognizable, William King, first Earl of Lovelace, entertained Emerson in England in June, 1848, as did the historian Arthur Helps on July 8 and 9; Elizabeth Paulet, socialite wife of a Swiss merchant, was a friend of the Thomas Carlyles; William Edward Forster (1818–1886), Quaker, reformer, and statesman, was also a friend of the Carlyles; John Forster (1812–1876) was a historian and biographer; Edwin Wilkins Field (1804–1871), a law reformer and artist; William Jacobson (1803–1884), a bishop of Chester and, in 1848, Regius Professor of Divinity at Oxford. Charles E. Rawlins, Jr., befriended Emerson in Liverpool and encouraged his friendship with Arthur Clough. John Kenyon, English poet and philanthropist, traveled with Emerson to various English towns in July, 1848. Ellen Randall is unidentified.

[17] "Copies to . . . Scherb" is in pencil, much of it erased. The "x" beside a

Continued from p. 8
Compare X p. 45 [18]

Thinks the poet of his kin
This is he that should come
Tongue of the secret
Key of the caskets
Of past & of future.
Sudden the lustre
That hovered round cities,
Round ⟨the chamber⟩ ↑closets↓ of power,
Or Chambers of Commerce,
Round banks, or round beauties,
Or State-rending factions,
Has quit them, & perches
Well pleased on his form.

The bard never cared
To pave his ⟨way⟩ ↑welcome↓ to the great
⟨It⟩ Costs [n] ↑him↓ time to live with them
Which ⟨a⟩ ↑the↓ genius ill supplies
Preengaged to woods & skies

[19] 1 Every man a ||fragment?||
The wholeness only to|| . . . || bud
|| . . . . ||

---

name probably indicates that a copy was sent. The poem below, beginning "Thinks the poet" is written in ink over the partially erased pencil list on p. [18]. Of those listed who have not been previously identified or are not easily recognizable, Caroline Sturgis, close friend of Emerson's since 1838, had recently married William Tappan of New York; Barzillai Frost was minister of the First Parish Church in Concord; John Milton Cheney, Emerson's classmate at Harvard, cashier of the Middlesex Institution for Savings in Concord; Nathaniel Langdon Frothingham, pastor of Boston's First Church and translator of the *Phaenomena* of the Greek poet Aratus; Martha Bartlett, apparently one of the Concord Bartletts, perhaps Josiah Bartlett's daughter; Mrs. Calvin Damon, wife of a Concord fabric manufacturer; Lucy C. Brown, sister of Lidian Emerson.

[18] "Continued . . . 45" is written diagonally upwards in ink under the page number [18]. There is little connection between the verse which follows and that in Emerson's poetry Notebook X, p. [45].

One man wrote all books, made all pictures municipal laws[19]
5 Art is preference of Wholes with sight of details
6 Thus we settle it, yet
Nature drives us into heed of singulars or parts.
7 G|| . . . || ad|| . . . || too.[20]

The poet received[21]
Foremost of all
Badge of nobility,
Charter of earth,
Free of the city,
Free of the field
Knight of each order
⟨Dubbed Staunch to⟩ ↑Mate of↓ each class
Fellow of monarchs,
And, what is better,
Fellow of all men.

But ↑over all↓ his crowning grace
Wherefor thanks ⟨g⟩God his daily praise
Is the purging of his eye
To see the people of the sky
↑2)↓ Friendly hands stretch forth to him
↑1)↓ From blue mount & headland dim
Him they beckon, him advise
Of heavenlier prosperities,
And a more excelling grace[22]

↑See p. 23↓

[19] "One man wrote all books," is used in "Powers and Laws of Thought," "Instinct and Inspiration," and "Celebration of Intellect," *W*, XII, 34, 72, 122. See also *JMN*, IX, 42, and Appendix I.

[20] "Every man . . . too." is in erased pencil writing, overwritten in ink by "The poet . . . sky" below.

[21] This and the following lines are apparently a continuation of the verse begun on p. [8] and continued on pp. [18] and [23].

[22] The preceding nine lines are apparently the first version of "Fragments on the Poet and the Poetic Gift," XI, ll. 1–9, *W*, IX, 329.

[20] Many after thoughts, as usual, with my printing, come just a little too late; & my new book seems to lose all value from their omission.[23] Plainly one is the justice that should have been done to the unexpressed greatness of the common farmer & labourer. A hundred times I have felt the superiority of George, & Edmund, & Barrows,* & yet I continue the parrot echoes of the names of literary notabilities & mediocrities, which, bring them (if they dared,) into presence [21] of these Concord & Plymouth Norsemen, would be as uncomfortable & ridiculous as mice before cats.[24] I believe, ⟨that every day is the finest day of the year⟩ when I hear people celebrating a particular sunset, that every day is the finest day in the year:[25] For, ⟨e⟩the same elements, & all elements, are always present, only sometimes, these conspicuous; & sometimes, those; ⟨the⟩ what ⟨of⟩was, yesterday, foreground, being today background; what was surface, playing now a not less effective part as basis.[26]

[22] So it is rare to have ⟨a⟩ ↑the↓ hero & professor united as in Montaigne. Or, I might say, churl & professor. I value Hyde & Therien because ⟨Mr ↑|| . . . ||↓ Ticknor⟩[n] would shrivel in their presence, they solid & unexpressed, he expressed into gold leaf.[27] And yet the whole human race agree to value a man precisely in proportion to his power of expression, & to the most expressive man that

*See p 25

[23] Emerson's "new book" is *Representative Men*, published in January, 1850, but undoubtedly in page proof by late November or early December, 1849. The last previously recorded date in Journal AZ is November 17 (p. [5], above); the next, December 14 (p. [24], below).

[24] "George," and "Edmund," are probably Emerson's neighboring farmers George Minott and Edmund Hosmer; "Barrows," could be one of several of this name — farmers, rope makers, a shoemaker and an ironworker — listed in the Plymouth County Register.

[25] See Journal TU, p. [36] above.

[26] "& all elements . . . basis.", struck through in ink with a vertical use mark, is used in "Power," *W*, VI, 64.

[27] Emerson's references are possibly to James F. C. Hyde, president of the Massachusetts Horticultural Society, and undoubtedly to Alek Therien, the French Canadian woodsman who figures anonymously in *Walden*, and whom Emerson hired for sawing, splitting, and piling wood, according to entries in Account Book 4 (1845–1849). "I value . . . leaf.", struck through in erased pencil with vertical and diagonal use marks, is used in "Farming," *W*, VII, 153.

has existed, namely Shakspeare, they have awarded the highest place.[28]

[23] ↑Swedenborg↓

Then again I have to regret that I have not ⟨said⟩ ↑stated↓ of Swedenborg the most important defect, this namely, that he does not awaken the sentiment of piety. Behmen does; St Bernard does; Thomas A Kempis; Herbert; and that Moravian hymn-maker do.[29]

[continued from p. 19]

And a truer bosom-glow
Than the wine-fed feasters know.
They turn his heart from lovely maids
And make the darlings of the earth
Swainish, coarse, & nothing worth
Teach him gladly to postpone
⟨His⟩ Pleasures [n] to another ↑st↓age
Beyond the scope of human age
Freely as task at eve undone
Waits unblamed tomorrow's sun [30]

[24] 1⟨2⟩4 December. Every day shows a new thing to veteran walkers. Yesterday ⟨shadows⟩ ↑reflections↓ of trees in the ice; snow-flakes, perfect rowels, on the ice; beautiful groups of icicles all along the eastern shore of Flint's Pond, in which, especially where encrusting the bough of a tree, you have the union of the most flowing with the most fixed. Ellery all the way squandering his jewels as if they were icicles, sometimes not comprehended by me, sometimes not heard. How many days can Methusalem go abroad & see [25] somewhat new? When will he have counted the changes of the kaleidoscope[?]

↑FARMERS↓

---

[28] "And yet . . . place." is used in "The Superlative," *W*, X, 173.

[29] The "Moravian hymn-maker" is perhaps Nikolaus Ludwig, Count von Zinzendorf (1700–1760); see *JMN*, III, 92n.

[30] These lines are apparently the first version of "Fragments on the Poet and the Poetic Gift," XI, ll. 10–19, *W*, IX, 329.

When I see ⟨Tuttle or⟩ one of our young farmers in Sunday clothes, I ⟨hold⟩feel [n] the greatest respect for & joy in them, because I know what powers & utilities are so meekly worn.[31] What I wish to know they know, what I would so gladly do, they can do. The cold gloomy day, the rough rocky pasture, the swamp, ⟨these⟩ are invitations & opportunities to them. And yet there is no arrogance in their bearing, but a perfect gentleness, though they know how to take care of cattle, how to raise & ⟨t⟩ cure & keep their crops.[32] Why a writer should be vain, & a farmer not, though the writer admires the farmer, & the farmer does not admire the writer, does not appear.

[26] ↑*Japanning.*↓

The Englishman is finished like a sea-shell. After the spines & convolutions are all formed, or, with the formation, the hard enamel varnishes every part.[33] Pope, Swift, Johnson, Gibbon, Goldsmith, Gray. We get good men sometimes in this country; but Everett & Irving are the only persons I think of who have pretensions to finish, & their enamel will not rival the British. It seems an indemnity to the Briton for his precocious maturity. He has no generous daring in this [27] age; the Platonism died in the Elizabethan; he is shut up in French limits; the practical & the comfortable oppress him with inexorable claims, so that the smallest fraction of power remains disposable for poetry. But Birmingham comes in, & says, 'Never mind; I have some patent lustre that defies criticism'; and Moore made his whole fabric of the "lustre," & Tennyson supplied defects with it. Only Wordsworth bought none.[34]

[28] England [35]

The dinner, the wine, the homes of England look attractive to the

[31] Emerson's reference is probably to his neighbor, Augustus Tuttle, but could be to "Mr John L. Tuttle of Concord" (*JMN*, IX, 30).

[32] "When I . . . gentleness," is used in "Farming," *W*, VII, 153.

[33] The paragraph to this point, struck through in ink with two vertical use marks, is used in "Manners," *W*, V, 111. See *JMN*, X, 511.

[34] "the Platonism . . . poetry." is struck through in ink with a vertical use mark; for the use of "Pope, Swift [p. [26]] . . . none.", see Appendix I. For "The Englishman . . . Gray. [p. [26]]", "It seems [p. [26]] . . . limits;" and "But Birmingham . . . the 'lustre,' ", see *JMN*, X, 511–512.

[35] This heading is set off by an ink line forming a three-sided box, open at the top.

traveller, but they are the poor utmost that illiberal wealth can perform. Alas! the halls of England are musty, the land is full of coal--smoke & carpet-smell: not a breath of mountain air dilates the languishing lungs,—and the Englishman gets his amends by ⟨driving⟩ ↑weaving↓ his ⟨affair⟩ ↑web↓ very fine. He is bold & absolute in his narrow circle; he is versed in all his routine, sure & elegant; his stories are good, his sentences solid, and all his statesmen, lawyers, men of letters, & poets, finished & solid as the pavement.[36]

[29]–[30] [leaf torn out] [37]
[31] ↑*Rich & Poor.*↓

The rich man has 1200 acres of land; the poor man has the universe, and much has he to say of it.—But when he, too, comes to hold 1200 acres, we never hear any more about the Universe.

Like the New England soil, my talent is good only whilst I work it. If I cease to task myself, I have no thoughts. This is a poor sterile Yankeeism. What I ⟨love &⟩ admire & love is the generous spontaneous soil which flowers & fruits at all seasons.

[32] [blank]
[33] ↑*Superlative.*↓

People like exaggerated event, & activity,—like to run to a house on fire, to a murder, an execution;—like to ⟨to⟩ tell of a bankruptcy, of a death, of a crime, or of an engagement. They like a rattling town, where a great deal of business is done. The ⟨n⟩student shuns all this. Mr Pickens "would go to the Church when the *interesting Sundays* were *over*." [n 38]

They like to be in a state of exaggeration. Of course, manly greatness consists in being so much that the mere wash of the sea, the observed passage of the stars, or the [34] *almost heard* current of Time, is

[36] "not a breath . . . pavement." is struck through in ink with a vertical use mark; "not a breath . . . languishing" and "he is bold . . . pavement." are also struck through in ink with single vertical use marks. See Appendix I.

[37] Emerson indexed p. [30] under Religion.

[38] This paragraph is used in "The Superlative," *W*, X, 174. For the last sentence, see *JMN*, VIII, 92.

event enough, & the full soul cries, Let not the noise of what you call events disturb me!

[35] Here is a right bit of Ellery C[hanning].

⟨"(*Helps*) Helps' book called 'Friends in Council' is inexpressibly dull.⟩ ↑"Helps' book called 'Friends in Council' is inexpressibly dull"↓[.] [39]
"In this manufacture, the modern English excel. Witness their Taylors, Wordsworths, Arnolds, and Scotts, (not Walter).[40] Wise, elegant, moderate, & cultivated, yet unreadable."

Ellery says of T↑thoreau,↓ "His effects can all be produced by cork & sand: but the substance that produces them is godlike & divine": and of C[urtis].—"Yes, he would make a very good draughtsman, if he had any talent for it." [41]

[36] *Learning by negatives*

A man's power is straitly hooped in by a necessity, which, by constant experiments, he touches on every side, until, at length, he learns its arc, which is learning his own nature.[42]

Every great fact in Nat. Science has been divined by the presentiment of somebody. ↑See p 282↓

[37] ↑*Natural Aristocracy*↓

It is a vulgar error to suppose that a gentleman must be ready to fight. The utmost that can be demanded of the gentleman is that he be incapable of a lie. There is a man who has good sense, is well-

[39] Arthur Helps, *Friends in Council: A Series of Readings and Discourse Thereon* . . . , 2 vols. (London, 1847–1849), is in Emerson's library. Emerson originally wrote this sentence in ink, canceled it in ink, then wrote it in pencil. The quotation marks which open the passage immediately below are also in pencil.

[40] Channing's references are undoubtedly to Sir Henry Taylor and the English poet and painter William Bell Scott (1811–1890), whom Emerson met in England (*JMN*, X, 361–362).

[41] "Curtis?" is written in pencil below "C.—", probably by Edward Emerson. See Journal RS, p. [267] above.

[42] This sentence, struck through in ink with a vertical use mark, is used in "Fate," *W*, VI, 19–20.

-informed, well read, obliging, cultivated, capable, and has an absolute devotion to truth. He always means what he says, & says what he means, however courteously. You may spit upon him;—nothing[n] could induce him to spit upon you,—no praises, & no possessions, ↑no compulsion of public opinion.↓ You may kick him; he will think it the kick of a brute: [38] but he is not a brute, & will not kick you in return. But neither your ⟨pis⟩knife & pistol, nor your gifts & ⟨kindness⟩ ↑courting↓ will ever make the smallest impression on his vote or word; for he is the truth's man, & will speak & act the truth until he dies. He is the truth's Thug, & goes willingly to ruin for his Thuggee. Is not he a gentleman?

[39] There is great interest taken lately in reforming thieves, &c. in England, & here. In London, a boy was selected who had been in prison 26 times, & a sovereign was confided to him to get changed, and he was told that if he chose to decamp with it, no process would be commenced against him. In a few minutes he returned with the full change, which he gave to the sender amidst the cheers of his companions.

[40] Eddy reads his fairy tales by the help of his memory, (having heard them read by Ellen) as the ⟨s⟩ostrich runs by help of his wings.

[41] [blank]
[42]

Nature

Van Helmont's definition of Nature, (p 171) is,—"Nature is that Command of God whereby a thing is that which it is, & doth ⟨that⟩what ⟨which⟩ it is commanded to do."[43]

[43] ↑*Bias.*↓
Nature has as seldom a success in her machines, as we in ours. There

[43] Jean Baptiste van Helmont, *Oriatrike or, Physick refined. The Common Errors therein Refuted, and the Whole Art Reformed & Rectified* . . . Now faithfully rendered into English by J[ohn]. C[handler]. . . . (London, 1662). This folio volume also contains other works, with appropriate title pages: works on the stone, fevers, the humors, and the plague.

is almost never good adjustment ⟨in⟩between the spring & the regulator, in a man. He only is a well made man, who has ↑a good↓ determination.[44] Now, with most men, it does not appear for what they were made, until after a long time. It is, of course, to be presumed, that they have a determination, but they ripen too slowly than that it should distinctly appear in this brief life. ⟨Like my⟩As [n] with my Catawbas, the season [44] not quite long enough for them. This determination of each man, too, is *from* all the others, like that of each tree up into free space.[45]

———

Duties are as much impediments to greatness, as cares. If a man set out to be rich, he cannot follow his genius; neither can he any more, if he wishes to be an e⟨t⟩stimable son, brother, husband, nephew, & cousin.

———

↑Neither is↓ life ⟨is not⟩ long enough [n] ⟨either⟩ for friendship. That is a solemn & majestic ⟨element⟩ ↑affair↓, surrounded [45] with ceremonies & respects, like a monarch, or like religion; & not to be crushed into corners, or, like a postillion's dinner, eaten on the run.[46]

———

The smallest ⟨increments⟩ ↑increments↓ of animal, much more, of mental power in the ⟨sailor⟩ ↑man↓ countervail the largest accumulations of physical impediment in the enterprise. Thus, if Eric has slept well, & is at the top of his condition, & 30 years old,—he will reach Greenland, & then Labrador: But, if you take out Eric, & put in a better man, namely, Thorfin, ↑Biorn↓ [46] he makes nothing of 600, a thousand, fifteen hundred miles more, & coasts along New England.[47]

[44] This sentence, struck through in ink with a diagonal use mark, is used in "Culture," *W*, VI, 134.

[45] This sentence, struck through in ink with a vertical use mark, is used in "Society and Solitude," *W*, VII, 8.

[46] This paragraph, struck through in ink with single vertical use marks on pp. [44] and [45], is used in "Considerations by the Way," *W*, VI, 273.

[47] "Biorn" is written in the bottom margin of p. [45], below "namely, Thorfin," and is here interpreted as an insert after "Thorfin,". "Thus, if Eric . . . England.", struck through in ink with single vertical use marks on pp. [45] and [46], is used in "Power," *W*, VI, 55.

[47] ——
I have entirely omitted to record L.'s exquisite ⟨a⟩plot for the edification of the expressman.[48] "How much will you do an errand for?" *Expressman.* "Nine pence if it do not take ⟨to⟩extra time, and I do not need to go in my wagon." *L.* "Excellent! Well, I want you to go to the Thursday Lecture ↑in Chauncy Place↓: go about 11:30, when the sermon begins, & you need not stay longer than you would ⟨to be⟩ wait⟨ing⟩ sometimes for an answer, & do you bring me home the text, & as much as you can remember of the sermon. You will not need your wagon, & I will pay you ninepence."

---

[48] 'Tis easy to see that the people will get Science as well as State.[49] *Schelling's* [n] aperçu & its statement was a forlo⟨n⟩rn hope, and all but fell into the pit. Yet just on the eve of ruin, *Oken* seized & made the most of it. Of course, he was ridiculous, & no⟨body⟩where but in Germany could have survived. Yet *Hegel*, a still more robust dreamer, clung to this identical piece of nonsense. Then it came rebounding to them in melody from songs of Goethe, &, strange to say, from *Geoff↑r↓oi Saint Hilaire's* [49] Memoires to the Institute in France.[50] Agassiz brought it to America, & tried it in popular lectures on the towns. It succeeded to admiration, the lecturer having of course the prudence to disown these bad names of his authors. The idea was that the form or type became transparent in the actual forms of successive ages as presented in geology.

[50]–[51] [blank]
[52] *Stallo*

Geologic strata "whose supraposition in space is a sufficient warrant for their succession in time."
[*General Principles of the Philosophy of Nature*, 1848, p. 7]

[48] According to a cross-reference to "AZ 47" in Emerson's Notebook OP Gulistan, p. [112], L. in this entry is his wife, Lidian.

[49] "the?", enclosed in square brackets, is written in pencil before "state.", probably by Edward Emerson.

[50] Emerson may refer here to Geoffroy Etienne Saint-Hilaire's *Funérailles de M. le Baron Cuvier* (Paris, 1832). A paleontologist, Cuvier studied animal and reptile fossils.

"The configurations of nature are more than a symbol, they are the gesticular expression of nature's inner life." [*Ibid.*, p. 17]

"Whatever exists, exists only in virtue of the life of which it is the expression." [51] [*Ibid.*,] p 35

"Every individual existence is but a living history" [52] [*ibid.*, p. 58]

[53] "The development of all individual forms will be spiral." [*Ibid.*, p. 16]

"State the sun, & you state the planets, & conversely." [53]
Stallo. [*Ibid.*, p. 69]

"Matter is only by its relativity." [*Ibid.*, p. 93]

"⟨a⟩The quantitative & qualitative existence of matter [, even when considered without any higher views,] is an uninterrupted flight from itself, a never-terminating whirl of evanescence." *Stallo.* [*Ibid.*,] p 93

"Animals are irregular men." [*Ibid.*, p. 285]
"Animals are but foetal forms of man." [*Ibid.*, p. 304]
"The limbs are emancipated ribs." [*Ibid.*, p. 291]
"Extension is petrified succession, or, space is dead time."

[54] *Stallo*
Oken

"The whole bird is a respiratory organ."
"The bird is an animal of song in full organization: in it nature attains to a complete hearing & speaking" [54]
[Stallo, *General Principles of the Philosophy of Nature*, 1848, p. 322]

"In the song of birds, the animal kingdom celebrates its constitutional day with trumpets & fifes." [*Ibid.*, pp. 322–323]
Feuerbach. [55]

---

[55] [blank]

[51] This entry is marked in the left margin with a vertical pencil line, perhaps a use mark.

[52] This quotation is struck through in ink with a diagonal use mark.

[53] This sentence is used in "Progress of Culture," *W*, VIII, 224.

[54] "N" is written in pencil above the "n" of "nature", perhaps by Edward Emerson.

[55] Ludwig Andreas Feuerbach (1804–1872), German philosopher, published *Das Wesen des Christentums* in 1841.

[56]

⟨See to it that you d⟩Do not make life hard to all around you. Egotism does.

↑*Genius*↓

Pegasus in Pound is an accident so common lately, that it may be classed among our epidemic diseases. 'Tis as common as goitres in Switzerland, or measles in Massachusetts. In every house occurs one case,—a rare boy or girl with wondrous aspiration for the parents know not what; whom the cruel parents [57] nevertheless condemn to daily drudgery, which he scorns,[n] & very badly performs. He goes out every morning, & throws up his pebble for an hour together, but can in no wise teach it by the habit to go up easilier.

[58] I easily distinguish three eras;—

1. *the Greek*; when men deified nature; Jove was in the air, Neptune in the sea, Pluto in the earth, Naiads in the fountains, dryads in the woods, oreads on the mountain; happy beautiful beatitude of nature.
2. *the Christian*; when the Soul became pronounced, and craved a heaven out of nature & above it,—looking on nature now as evil,—the world was a mere stage & school, a snare, and the powers that ruled here were devils hostile to the soul.

[59] and now lastly,

3. *the Modern*; when the too idealistic tendencies of the Christian period running into the diseases of cant, monachism, and a church, demonstrating the impossibility of Christianity, have forced men to retrace their steps, & rally again on Nature; but now the tendency is to ⟨make⟩ m⟨e⟩arry ⟨man⟩ mind to nature, to put nature under the mind, convert the world into the instrument of Right Reason. Man goes forth to the dominion of the world by ⟨science⟩ commerce, by science, & by philosophy.

[60] *Greek*

"How those inimitable artists (the Greeks) proceeded in their successful attempts to evolve from the human form their system of divine types, which is so perfect & complete, that, neither any leading character nor any intermediate shade or transition is wanting." *Goethe. Letters from Italy. Bohn* p 394[56]

[61] *England*

Some English felons who have been arrested here, on the evidence of their accomplices, expressed great indignation ⟨at⟩ that their associates were not staunch.[57]

---

[62] ↑Intellect↓

Bias.

"It is better for a man to be disposed or inclined, than to be knowing by description (books)." Aristotle quoted by Van Helmont [*Oriatrike* . . . , 1662, p. 22.] ↑See AZ p 117↓

Van Helmont's distribution is, Understanding, Will, Memory. [*Ibid.*, p. 23]

↑*Affirmative.*↓

"The soul understands in peace & rest, & not in doubting." [*Ibid.*,] p 9

The understanding transforms itself into the image of the thing understood.[58]

"Indeed study for eternity smiled on me"[59] [*ibid.*,] p. 12

[63] M[ary] M[oody] E[merson]'s imp like ↑W[illiam]. E[llery].↓ C[hanning].'s was exasperated by the presence of well dressed people, & drove her into all manner of *sottises*.[60]

---

[56] Emerson is quoting A. J. W. Morrison's translation of Goethe's *Letters from Italy* in *The Auto-biography of Goethe* . . . , 1848–1849. The title page lists *Travels in Italy*, but the Table of Contents and the left running head in the appropriate section show "Letters from Italy."

[57] This sentence, struck through in ink with a diagonal use mark, is used in "Ability," *W*, V, 101.

[58] The original reads: "Wherefore, whether the understanding be transformed, or whether it doth transform it self into the Image of the thing understood, surely it had need of help from God. . . ." van Helmont, *Oriatrike* . . . , 1662, p. 23.

[59] The quotation is used in "Celebration of Intellect," *W*, XII, 131.

[60] "W. E." is written in pencil above "C.'s", perhaps by Edward Emerson, in-

"Hippocrates had knowledge to cure the devouring plague, & with him that knowledge slept, the Most High so willing it." *Van Helmont* [*Oriatrike* . . . , 1662, p. 8]

"A nobleman of Ireland gave land to his household physician, not who had returned from the Universities, but who had healed the sick. For he had a book left him by his ancestors ⟨in which⟩filled with remedies. And so the heir of the book is always heir of that land. That book deciphers the signs of diseases, & the proper remedies of that country." *Van Helmont* [*ibid.*,] p. 8 —

"A duality of sex is required for the production of every plant." [*Ibid.*,] p 475

[64] ↑Music Eloquence↓

Chladni's experiment seems to me central. He strewed sand on glass, & then struck the glass with tuneful accords, & the sand assumed symmetrical figures.[61] ⟨w⟩With discords the sand was thrown about amorphously. It seems, then, that Orpheus ⟨out⟩is[n] no fable: You have only to sing, and the rocks will crystallize; sing, and the plant will organize; sing, & the animal will be born.

[65] Cat & mouse, hawk & hen, Austrian emperor & Hungarian serf, eater & eaten, Poverty & genius,—I see but one sad fact

Culture, the height of Culture, highest behaviour consist in the identification of the Ego with the universe, so that when a man says, I think, I ⟨intend,⟩ ↑hope,↓ I f⟨ound⟩ind,—↑he might properly say, the human race thinks, hopes, ⟨o⟩& finds,↓—[n] he states a fact which commands the understandings & affections of all the company, and yet, at the same time, he shall be able continually to keep sight of his biographical *ego*,—I had a↑n↓ ague, I had a fortune; ⟨I⟩my father had black hair; &c. as rhetoric, fun, or footman, [66] to his grand & public *ego*, without impertinence or ⟨con⟩ ever confounding them[.][62]

---

dicating that the reference is to William Ellery Channing; the identification is confirmed in Notebook OP Gulistan, p. [4].

[61] Ernst Florens Friedrich Chladni (1756–1827), German physicist, performed such experiments, also with thin metal plates.

[62] "Culture, the . . . them" is used in "Powers and Laws of Thought," *W*, XII, 62.

To M[argaret]. F[uller]. March 1840[63]

The Denon plates are a rich spectacle after my Heereniana last summer. "And Kings for such a tomb /would/might/ wish to die." What a fine thing has your demoniacal Shelley said about the tombs of Pompeii, "that these white marble cells so delicately carved contrasted so strongly with the plain dwelling houses, that they seemed not so much tombs,[n] as voluptuous chambers for immortal spirits, &c."

[67] January 13[64] I saw at Albany, in the State Library, Zahn's drawings after the frescoes, &c. of Herculaneum & Pompeii; a sumptuous work given to the State of New York by the King of Prussia, by the hands of ↑A.↓ Vattemare.[65] It is a sufficient document of the Greek art. Those people had bolder & completer senses than we. Their art is inventive, yet so secure. We can only in a quite feminine way approve what they have done, owning that it is good as far as we can ⟨see⟩judge, & we ⟨trust therefore that⟩ ↑doubt not↓ it is correct where we are not judges.

[68] ⟨N⟩The Times newspaper attracts the American in London more & more, until at last he wonders that it ⟨is not⟩ does not more pique the curiosity of the English themselves. They all repeat what it says; it[n] is their own understanding & day's ideal daguerrotyped. Yet they know nothing about it.[66] He never sees any person capable of writing these powerful paragraphs: and, though he hears up & down in society now & then some anecdote of a Mr Bailey or Mr Moseley [69] who sent his paper to the Times, & received in return

[63] "(An old letter)" in pencil follows "1840", perhaps inscribed by Edward Emerson. For the letter and sources of the quotations from Milton's "On Shakespeare" and Shelley's letter to Thomas Love Peacock, see *L*, II, 259, and nn. 53 and 54.

[64] "1850" is written in pencil in the top margin, perhaps by Edward Emerson.

[65] Alexandre Vattemare (1796–1864) was a Parisian who arranged international exchanges of books, including a gift from Paris to Boston in 1843 which became the nucleus of the Boston Public Library in 1848. See p. [71] below. Emerson's reference is to Wilhelm Zahn, *Les Plus Beaux Ornaments et les Tableaux le Plus Remarquables de Pompei, d'Herculanum* . . . , 2 vols. (Berlin, 1829–1842), listed in the 1850 *Catalogue of the New-York State Library*.

[66] "of the English . . . know nothing", struck through in ink with a vertical use mark, is used in "The Times," *W*, V, 268.

twenty guineas, with a request that he would write again, & so, that he did, in due time, become one of the Staff of the Journal,[67] — yet ⟨he⟩ ↑one↓ never hears among well informed men as Milnes, Carlyle, Helps, Gregg, Forster, any accounts of this potentate at all adequate to the fact.[68]

They may well affect not to know or care who wrote it, at the moment when I observe that all they know or say, they read in it.

[70] English propriety is felt much more in what they do not say than in what they say.

An Englishman of fashion is ⟨as⟩like one of these Souvenirs bound in gold & vellum, ⟨&⟩ enriched with delicate engravings, thick hotpressed vellum paper ↑fit for ladies & princes↓ but nothing in it worth reading or remembering.[69]

---

[71] ↑*Janus. Shopfront & Housefront.*↓
Goethe's Indian Legend of the Bramin head joined to the Pariah body, is significant of our inconveniences.[70] M. Vattemare is National Envoy, international, cosmopolitan, high historical ambassador of the learning of all nations, by day. By night, he puts off his citizen's cloak, & puts on a conjuror's harlequin cap, &, as M. Alexandre, juggles & ventriloquizes for his bread. Abellino (in the story,) the Robber, is the noble Flodoardo in the palaces of Venice.[71] But the flagrant instance of horse of the sun & old hack misyoked together

[67] Emerson's reference is presumably to Reverend Thomas Mozley (1806–1893) with whom he associates Bailey, unidentified, as writers for the *Times*, in *JMN*, X, 211–212, where the twenty-guinea anecdote is related of Bailey (it's ten guineas in the original anecdote).

[68] Emerson's references are probably to Richard Monckton Milnes, Thomas Carlyle (or possibly Dr. John Carlyle), Sir Arthur Helps, William Rathbone Greg, and John Forster, all mentioned in his journals during his 1848 trip to London.

[69] The entries on p. [70] are struck through in pencil and in ink with single, discontinuous, vertical use marks; the second entry is also struck through in ink with a wavy diagonal use mark. For "English propriety . . . say.", see Appendix I. "An Englishman . . . remembering." is used in "Manners," *W*, V, 112; see *JMN*, X, 514–515.

[70] See Goethe's poem "Paria."

[71] The story is Johann H. D. Zschokke's *Abällino der grosse Bandit*; it had been translated into English by M. G. ("Monk") Lewis, William Dunlap, and others.

is in the expansive contemplation & the despicable fawning of *Lord Bacon.*

[72] [blank]

[73] *Eloquence*

"Farewell, Thomas, I wende my way,
I may no longer stand with thee;"
"Give me some token, my ladye gay,
That I may say I spake with thee."

(The Fairy Queen ⟨gives him an apple.⟩ ↑holds out to him a harp-string & a drop of honey.↓)

—"To harp & carp, wher⟨eso⟩e'er thou go,
Thomas, take thou these with thee! —"
—"Harping," he said, "kepe I none,
For tongue is chief of minstrelsy." —

(The Fairy Queen ⟨gives him⟩ ↑pours↓ a drop of water ↑in↓to his eye.)

"If thou will spell, or tales [n] tell,
Thomas, thou shall make never lye;"
I have hung thy tongue by the middell,
To speak right after thy searching eye.⟨"⟩ [72]

[74] [blank]

[75] There are two or three Englands and it is difficult to speak emphatically of ⟨an⟩England without finding that we are saying that which is true of only one of these, ↑—↓ false of the others. I found in England plenty of well-marked Englishmen, English types, the ruddy complexion, fair & plump, robust men, with faces cut like a die, with a strong island speech & accent,—the *Norman* type,[n] with the complacency that belongs to that constitution. Others I found, ⟨in⟩who might have been [76] Americans, for anything that appeared in their complexion or form; and their speech was much less marked, and their thought much less bound. These were probably Saxons.

[72] Thomas of Erceldoune ("Thomas the Rhymer"), "True Thomas, and the Queen of Elfland: The Second Fytte," in Robert Jamieson, ed., *Popular Ballads and Songs* (1806), II, 27, and in Scott's *Minstrelsy of the Scottish Border*. See *JMN*, X, 22–23.

Then, there is besides the Celt, who has established his dark complexion in the trinity of the unity of this island.[73]

[77] E[lizabeth]. H[oar]. thinks that we do not sufficiently honour the English hero. There is an English hero superior to the French, the German, the Italian, or the Greek; when he is brought to the strife with fate, & dies for his faith, it is a more sublime act than of another martyr, because he knows what he does, & lives with a breadth that makes man & nature interested in his ⟨fate.⟩ ↑days.↓ He knows what he sacrifices; he sacrifices, too, a more truly rich material ⟨prosperity⟩ possession, & does it on more purely metaphysical grounds. ⟨H⟩It is not, as in France, circumstances that have[74] ↑[[pass on to p. 80]]↓

[78][75] At Attleborough the jewellers say, art does much, but luck does more; yet they believe that art may yet beat luck. They say sometimes the devil is in the gold, and it will not be malleable. They point in the boiling crucible to a point of light darting about like electricity & as long as that stays there, it will not be malleable. This is specially true of California gold, wh↑i↓ch cracks when worked up into small bars, & rolled into rings[.]

[79]–[80] [leaf torn out][76]

[81] and Arundel, & Cobham, and Sir Thomas More are the English heroes.—

Sir ⟨c⟩Charles Fellowes ↑Nelson↓
Sir John Herschel
Dr Layard[77]

[82] In ideal faces I notice unity of expression. In portraits,

[73] This paragraph, struck through in pencil with single vertical use marks on pp. [75] and [76], is used, except for the first sentence, in "Race," *W*, V, 54.

[74] "There is . . . have", struck through in ink with a diagonal use mark, is used in "Character," *W*, V, 136.

[75] P. [78] is in pencil.

[76] Fragments of inscription in the margins show that the entry on p. [79] was in pencil and that on p. [80] in ink. Emerson indexed p. [79] under Impressionable.

[77] The entry on p. [81] is struck through in ink with a vertical use mark; cf. "Ability," *W*, V, 91.

variety & compromise; as if in each individual were four or five rival natures, one of which was now in the ascendant, & compelled at certain hours to yield the lead to the suppressed rival. ↑(Perhaps↓ every face finds room for all its ancestors↑)↓ [78]

———

Every man finds room in his face for all his ancestors.[79]

———

Every face an *Atrium*.

———

[83] N. Y. Jan. 23.

What cunning magnets these boys are,—to draw all the iron out of the hour!

[84] [80] *Nisami* Von Hammer [*Geschichte der schönen Redekünste Persiens*, 1818,] p 105 [107–108]

Whilst on the plain the roses bloomed,
The nightingale to the falcon said,
Why of all birds must thou be dumb
Nor let thy comrades hear from thee?
With closed mouth thou utterest
Tho dying, no last word to man.
Yet sit'st thou on the hand of princes,
And feedest on the grouse's breast;
Whilst I, who hundred thousand jewels
Squander in one single tone,—
Lo, I feed myself with worms,
And my dwelling is the thorn.
The falcon answered; "Be all ear:
Thou seest I'm [n] dumb, be thou too dumb;
I, experienced in affairs,

[78] There is a short rule in the left margin separating "suppressed rival." from the sentence which originally began "Every face". It appears that Emerson then added "(Perhaps" and closed the parenthesis after "ancestors" without canceling the short rule or changing the "E" in "Every" to lower case, as the editors have done.

[79] This sentence is used in "Behavior," *W*, VI, 181.

[80] P. [84] was originally written in pencil, then lightly erased; several wavy use marks are struck through the entry. On p. [85] below, Emerson has transcribed an ink version of his translation from von Hammer, but as there are significant changes in that ink version, the erased pencil version is here fully printed.

See a hundred things, say never one;
But thee the people prizes not
Who do not one thing, say a thousand.
To me predestined to the chase
The king's hand gives the grouse's breast,
Whilst a chatterer like thee
Gnaws worms in the thorns. Farewell.[”]

[85] [81] *Nisami* See Von Hammer p 105 [107–108]
Whilst roses bloomed along the plain,
The nightingale to the falcon said,
“Why of all birds must thou be dumb.
With closed mouth thou utterest,
Though dying, no last word to man:
Yet sit'st thou on the hand of princes,
And feedest on the grouse's breast;
Whilst I, who hundred thousand jewels
Squander in one single tone,
Lo! I feed myself with worms,
And my dwelling is the thorn.”
The falcon answered, “Be all ear:
Thou seest, I'm dumb; be thou too dumb.
I, experienced in affairs,
See fifty things, say never one:
But thee the people prizes not
Who, doing nothing, say a thousand.
To me appointed to the chase,
The king's hand gives the grouse's breast,
Whilst a chatterer like thee
Must gnaw worms in the thorns. Farewell! [”]

[86] ↑Jan. 1850.↓

H Greeley told me that the circulation of the Tribune was

[81] The ink version of the poem on this page overlies an erased pencil version of the same poem; the erased version is struck through with at least two diagonal use marks, also erased. The ink version is used in “Persian Poetry,” *W*, VIII, 261–262, except that the printed version omits the line “Thou seest, I'm dumb; be thou too dumb.”

60 000. Yet there are ⟨20⟩twenty millions in the United States and until his circulation reaches one million it must not be accounted great.

↑1855. July It is now 130,000.
1856 170 000↓

[87] ↑*The two statements or Bipolarity.*↓

My geometry cannot span the extreme points which I see.[82] I affirm melioration,—which nature teaches, in pears, in the domesticated animals, and in her secular geology, & this development of complex races. ⟨But⟩ I affirm also the self-equality of nature; or, that ⟨wh⟩ only that is true which is always true;[83] and, that, in California, or in Greece, or in Jewry, or in Arcadia, existed the same amounts of private power, as now, & the same deductions, ⟨U⟩however differently distributed. But I cannot [88] reconcile these two statements. I affirm the sacredness of the individual, the infinite reliance that may be put on his determination. I see also the benefits of cities, and the plausibility of phalansteries. But I cannot reconcile these oppositions. I affirm the divinity of man; but, as I know well how much is my debt to bread, & coffee, & flannel, & heated room,—I shun to be Tartuffe, & ↑do↓ affirm also with emphasis [89] the value of these fomentations. But I cannot reconcile that absolute with this conditional. ↑My ancient Companion in Charleston, S.C. Mr Martin Luther ⟨Woodbridge⟩ ⟦⟨no that is not quite the name⟩⟧ ↑Hurlbut↓, used to reply to each statement of mine, "Yes, to a certain extent[.]"—↓[84]

[90] I am struck ⟨every⟩ now & then with a ⟨poem⟩passage of poetry or prose, which, especially if written some hundred years ago, amazes me by the fortitude or selfreliance it discovers in the man who dared thus firmly to trust his rare perception, as to write it elaborately out. Such a piece is Donne's "Ecstasy." Another is Attar (Ferideddin Attar) the Persian poet's mysticism in the "Bird-Logic"

[82] This sentence is used in "Fate," *W*, VI, 4.

[83] For "that ⟨wh⟩ only . . . true;", see Journal TU, p. [34] above.

[84] Reverend Martin Luther Hurlbut, graduate of Williams College in 1804, was a teacher and Unitarian clergyman.

or "Bird-Talk," which [91] I find in Von Hammer, [*Geschichte der schönen Redekünste Persiens*, 1818,] p. 153[.]
The three birds appear before the throne of the Simorg.

The bird-Soul was ashamed,
Their body was quite nullified,
They had cleared themselves from dust,
And were by the light ensouled.
What was, & was not, — the Past, —
Was wiped out⟨,⟩ from their breast.
The sun from near-by beamed
⟨Clearest⟩ ↑Pure↓ light into their soul:
The resplendence of the Simorg beamed
As one, back from all three.
They knew not, amazed, if they
Were either this or that.
They saw themselves all as Simorg,
Themselves in the eternal Simorg.
When they looked to the Simorg up,[85]
They beheld him among themselves;
[92] And, when they looked on each other,
They saw themselves [n] in the Simorg.
⟨The Simorg⟩A single look grouped the two parties,
The Simorg emerged, the Simorg vanished,
This in that, & that in this,
As the world has never heard.
So remained they, sunk in wonder,
Thoughtless in deepest thinking,
And quite unconscious of themselves,
Speechless prayed they to the Highest
To open this secret,
And to unlock *Thou* & *We*.
There came an answer without tongue,
"The highest is a sun-mirror;
Who comes to him, sees himself therein,

[85] Emerson originally wrote "When to the Simorg up they looked,"; he then drew an oval line around "to the Simorg up", curving it down under "they looked", indicating the order should be reversed.

Sees body & soul, & soul & body;
When you came to the Simorg,
Three therein appeared to you,
[93] And had fifty of you come,
So had you seen yourselves as many.
Him has ⟨no⟩ none of us yet seen.
Ants see not the Pleiades.
Can the gnat grasp with his teeth
The body of the elephant?
What you see, is HE not;
What you hear, is HE not.
The valleys which you traverse⟨d⟩,
The actions which you perform,
They lie under our treatment,
And among our properties.
You as three birds are amazed,
↑Impatient↓ shelterless,[n] heartless, confused:
Far over you am I raised,
Since I am in act Simorg.
Ye blot out /(my)/your/ highest being
That ye may find yourselves on my throne,
Forever ye blot out yourselves,
As shadows in the sun. Farewell! [86]

[94] *Greece affirmative.*

"She (Athens) could not indeed lead countless armies into the field, but she knew how with a little band to defeat those who could." J.A. St John [*The History . . . of Ancient Greece*, 1842,] vol I p. xii

"Barbarians destroy but create nothing: the delight & glory of the people of Athens consisted in the exercise of creative power," &c [*ibid.*, I, xii]

"Men are everywhere exactly what their mothers make them" [87] [*ibid.*, I, xv]

[86] "The bird-Soul [p. [91]] . . . Farewell!" is used in "Persian Poetry," *W*, VIII, 264–265.

[87] This sentence, struck through in ink with a vertical use mark, is used in "Fate," *W*, VI, 10.

[95] [blank]

[96] Love is temporary & ends with marriage. Marriage is the perfection which love aimed at, ignorant of what it sought. Marriage is a good known only to the parties. A relation of perfect understanding, aid, contentment, possession of themselves & of the world,—which dwarfs love to green fruit.[88]

[97] [89] Mada||msm||
C||msm||

Reconcile ||msm||
"Fate is ||msm||
in a ||msm||
This is th||msm||
"There is ||msm||
ing ||msm||
what ||msm||
& by no ||msm||
in ti||msm||

[98] ||msm||eely, or
||msm||ach
||msm|| its
||msm||dience
||msm|| theirs,

[88] "possession of . . . fruit." is struck through in ink with a diagonal use mark which is canceled by three sets of horizontal bars.

[89] The leaf bearing pp. [97]–[98] is torn away about two inches from the binding. Most of the entries on pp. [97]–[98] are undoubtedly used in "Fate," *W*, VI, 3–4, 12–13 (words and parts of words corresponding to those in the ms. are italicized): "It was a poetic attempt to lift this mountain of Fate, to *reconcile* this despotism of race with liberty, which led the Hindoos to say, '*Fate is* nothing but the deeds committed *in a* prior state of existence [see *JMN*, VIII, 489] . . . . *There is* in every man a certain feel*ing* that he has been *what* he is from all eternity, *& by no* means became such *in ti*me' " (*W*, VI, 12–13; see Journal TU, p. [51] above, and *JMN*, IX, 101). "By obeying each thought frankly, by harping, *or*, if you will, pounding on e*ach* string, we learn at last *its* power. By the same obe*dience* to other thoughts we learn *theirs*, and then comes some r*easonable* hope of harmonizing the*m*" (*W*, VI, 4). "After many experiments we *find* that we must begin earlier,—*at school*. But the boys and girls are n*ot docile*; . . . W*e must* begin our reform earlier still,—at ge*neration*" (*W*, VI, 3–4).

||msm||easonable
||msm||m.
||msm|| but find
||msm|| at school;
||msm||ot docile,
||msm||e must
||msm||neration.
||msm|| each
||msm||erence.

[99] ↑The Times↓
That is to say, there is Fate; Laws of the world; what then? w⟨ere⟩e are thrown back on Rectitude, forever & ever. Only rectitude: to mend one; that is all we can do. But that the world stigmatises as a sterile, chimney-corner, ⟨shin-roasting⟩ philosophy.[90]

[100] They who govern themselves ⟨may⟩ ↑⟨will⟩↓ govern others.[91]

[10⟨2⟩1] ↑*Fame*↓
What you say of another man to any person, you say to him↑self. It will reach him as by telegraph tomorrow.↓

[102] The English journals ⟨as⟩snub my new book; as indeed they have all its foregoers. Only now they say, that this has less vigour & originality than the others.[92] Where then was the degree of merit that entitled my books to their notice? They have never admitted the claims of either of them. The fate of my books is like the impression of my face. My acquaintances, as long back as I can re-

[90] This paragraph is struck through in pencil with a vertical use mark. "That is . . . of the world;" is used in "Fate," *W*, VI, 4; "w⟨ere⟩e are . . . philosophy." is used in "The Sovereignty of Ethics," *W*, X, 208.

[91] This sentence is used in "Greatness," *W*, VIII, 320.

[92] Though the *Athenæum*, No. 1160 (Jan. 19, 1850) ended a review of *Representative Men* by calling it "unsubstantial filagree work" (p. 69), Emerson may refer here to a brief notice in the *Eclectic Review*, New Series, XXVII (Feb. 1850), 261: "The 215 pages before us contain the essence of many a 'folio;' but how far such matter is wholesome, or calculated to sustain the life and vigour of the spiritual man, is, alas! quite another question."

member, have always said, "Seems to [103] me you look a little thinner than when I saw you last."

[104] ↑*The Times*↓

At Alcott's conversation each person who opened his lips seemed in snuffing the air to snuff nitrous oxide, & away he went — a spinning dervish, — pleasing himself, annoying the rest. A talent is a nuisance.[93] Each rode his nag with devotion round the walls of the universe; I found no benefit in this jar & jangle. There was much ability & good meaning in the room, but some persons present who should not have been there, & these, like an east wind, checked every growth.

[105] ↑⟦See too of Byron, *Y* p.35.⟧↓

Byron's life suggests that a partnership of authors would have the same immense advantage for literature, that concert has in war, in music, and in trade⟨,⟩: Byron's, because in his case, as in so many, (in mine, for example, who am hardly a writer,) his talent is conspicuously partial, & needs a complement. But if one with solid knowledge, — a man of massive mind, or a man of ideas, powerful generalizations, or both, had united with Byron, with his unmatched

---

↑turn to p. 107↓

[106] Sketch of topics offered by me at Mr Alcott's Conversation at T↑own↓. & C↑ountry↓. club last night (18 Feb.y 1850.)[94]

The Times.

Events in the same chain as persons; part & parcel of persons; fortunes are part of character. As the slug on the pear leaf exudes a slime which makes his shell & climate, so each creature sweats out his own.[95]

[93] This sentence is marked in the left margin in pencil with two vertical lines, possibly use marks.

[94] "T. & C." is expanded in pencil, perhaps by Edward Emerson. Alcott's Conversation was probably at the Club's room, 15 Tremont Row, Boston.

[95] This paragraph, struck through in ink with two diagonal use marks, is used in "Fate," *W*, VI, 41; see Journals RS, p. [273], and TU, pp. [247] and [248] above. "cf 92" is inscribed in ink diagonally upwards in the left margin from "part & parcel" to "Events".

Degrees of man. 1. suit of clothes. 2. aptitude, equal aptitude & indifferency to many pursuits. 3. Taste passing (by surcharge) into Art or Talent. 4. Creation of circumstance. 5. Following, & Contagion, Apotheosis, Literature, & Laws.

[107] ——
continued from p 10⟨4⟩5

---

expressiveness, his heat, his firm ductile thread of gold,—a battery had been built, against which nothing could stand. But, in his isolation, ⟨he⟩ ↑Byron↓ is starved for material, has no thoughts; & his fiery affections are only so many women, ⟨va⟩though rigged out in men's clothes, ↑garnished, too,↓ with beards & mustachios. They vapour.

⟨T⟩It is well worth thinking on. Thus, if Thoreau, Ellery, & I, ⟨instea⟩could, (which is perhaps impossible,) combine works heartily, [⟨&⟩being fired by such a desire to carry one

---

↑turn to p. 111 —↓

[108] *The Times*

That we are here, is proof we ought to be here. We have as good right, & the same sort of right as Boston Bay & Cape Cod; the same fitness, or the like fitness, must be presumed between a man & the time & event, as, between the sexes, or, between a race of animals & the food it eats, or the inferior races it uses, ⟨—⟩(e.g. man & horse.) Turtles are found in swamps; fishes in water; waders on seabeaches; camels in sand; goats on mountains; and, not less, Pericles or St John, Bonaparte & Webster to their time & geography.[96] Again, Why set up for professors? The only reason [97]

[109] ————
The secret of the world is the tie of person and event. Person makes event, & event person, and therefore a man likes better to be com-

[96] The paragraph to this point is struck through in ink with a vertical use mark; "the same fitness . . . horse.)" is used in "Fate," *W*, VI, 39–40.

[97] See n.100 below.

plimented on his position, than on his merits, as talent, or beauty, or other personal advantage,—because, this seems a tribute to more intimate merit[-]creating circumstance.[98]

↑See T⟨u⟩U 248↓

Yet I concede that we are much more impressed by a fact, than by the state of mind that caused it. O. 262

'Tis curious that the Times are always abridged into a few persons. Astor, Webster, Fremont, Garrison, Calhoun, Vanderbilt, ↑Collins,↓ Rothschild, Brunel, Peel, Stephenson, Cobden, Guizot, are the Times.[99]

[110] *The Times*

of misery is disproportion of power to the task.[100]

"The times are out of joint, O cursed spite,
That ever I was born to set them right."
[Shakespeare, *Hamlet*, I, v, 189–190]

A country parson said to another, in the street, "O Brother San⟨born⟩-ger, What shall we do with France?"

You are a pedant for your pains. When God has pirates to punish, he sends pirates to put them down. Let country squires mind their villages, & good boys their books, & never transcend. Not to ⟨mind⟩ ↑meddle with↓ other people's facts, is the rule.

[111] continued from p. 107

point as to fuse all our repulsions & incompatibilities.] I doubt not

[98] This paragraph is struck through in ink with a vertical use mark; "The secret . . . & event person," is used in "Fate," *W*, VI, 39; "and therefore . . . circumstance." is used in the same essay, *W*, VI, 42. See Journal TU, p. [248] above, and *JMN*, VIII, 291–292.

[99] This paragraph, struck through in ink with a vertical use mark, is used in "Fate," *W*, VI, 39.

[100] This entry may be a continuation of the one on p. [108] above which ended, "The only reason".

⟨an ⁿ effect⟩ we could ⟨accomplish⟩ ↑engender↓ something ⟨far⟩ superior ⟨in⟩ ↑for↓ quality & ⟨in⟩for effect to any of the thin cold-⟨p⟩blood⟨ed⟩ creatures we have hitherto flung into the light.

The "Times" Newspaper is an independent power, a third power, in England, — counterpoise to Throne & Parliament, — and is the best example I can cite of a concert of wits.

[112] The Times

The question of the Times is to each one a practical question of the Conduct of Life. How shall I live? Plainly we are incompetent to solve the riddle of the Times. Our geometry cannot span the huge orbits of the prevailing Ideas, & behold their return, & reconcile their opposition. We can only obey our own polarity, — every mind has a polarity, — & that will finally guide us to the sea. I see no choice. 'Tis mighty fine for us to affect to speculate & to elect our course. We have only to accept an irresistible dictation.[101]

[113] Certain ideas are in the air. We are all impressionable, for we are made of them. We are all impressionable, but some more than others, & these first express them. So Women, as most impressionable, are the best index of the coming hour.[102]

I am part of the solar system. Let the brain alone & it will keep time with that as the shell with the sea-tide.

We are made of ideas. Let the river roll which way it will, cities will rise on its banks.[103]

[114] The Times

Go to the corner of the street. You read the fate & possibility of each passenger prescribed on the dome of his brow, in the complexion, in

[101] This paragraph, struck through in ink with two diagonal use marks, is used in "Fate," *W*, VI, 3.

[102] This paragraph, struck through in ink with two vertical use marks and what appears to be a third diagonal use mark, smudged, as if canceled, is used in "Fate," *W*, VI, 44.

[103] See *JMN*, X, 374. In Notebook NP, p. [78], Emerson turned the sentence into verse:

And roll the river where it will,
Towns on its banks will rise.

the depth of his eye. His parentage determines it. You may as well ask a loom which weaves muslin, why it does not make lobsters, as expect poetry from this engineer, or a model farm from that linen-draper. Why pretend to be something else? [104] Let us be glad to breathe the great air, &, if we ar⟨t⟩e born in the geographical age, when the Niger & Sacramento are explored, & the N. & S. pole touched, [115] roads built, seas sounded, & charts drawn, let us do these with good will.

[116] *The Times*

There is something to be done now, and be sure they who have it in charge,↑—↓He who has it in charge,↑—↓will know how to ⟨make⟩ get it done.[105]

There is a curious shame in our faces. The age is convict, confessing, sits on the anxious benches.

We say there is no religion, no poetry, no heroism, no rage; death is unperfumed; age of debility; correctness; levity; of the looking-glass; not to be bruised by the bruisers, not to despond in cities, is a mark of merit.

But I hold that all the elements are ever co-present, that [106]

[117] H Greeley
Turtle Bay East River
Harlem at 61st Street Stage
Bowery ⟨at⟩to 49th Street
down a lane (N. Y.) [107]

"How we look!" says Col. Fremont [108]

[104] The paragraph to this point is struck through in ink with three vertical use marks; "Go to . . . linendraper." is used in "Fate," *W*, VI, 10.

[105] This sentence, struck through in ink with a vertical use mark, is used in "Fate," *W*, VI, 39.

[106] "But I . . . that" is struck through in ink with a vertical use mark; see p. [21] above. This entry is continued on p. [118] below.

[107] "H Greeley . . . (N. Y." is in pencil. Horace Greeley lived in a house at Turtle Bay, almost opposite the southern tip of Blackwell's Island in the East River.

[108] Apparently Emerson's recollection of earlier impressions he had of John Charles Frémont's *Report of the Exploring Expedition to the Rocky Mountains in*

[118] The Times

what is once true is always true; that Every day is the finest in the year.[109] What was background once, is foreground now. You say, there is no religion now. 'Tis like saying, in rainy weather, there is no sun; when the rain is one of his superlative effects. Religion consists now in ⟨the⟩ avoidance of forms it once created. All kinds of power usually develope at the same time.[110]

[119] Plainly, the Times make a great many people sick. *See*, Y 46

[120] *Times*

Above, I have written (p. 98 ↑87↓) of the necessity of leaving much to the Supreme Geometer, nor being annoyed if we cannot demonstrate the theorem. We are sure, that, though we know not how, Necessity does comport with liberty, the Individual with the World, my polarity with the Spirit of the Times.[111] Goethe said, "Every man loves to be distinguished, and loves also to be entirely melted into the crowd." We men are necessary to each other, yet every one stands on the top of the world. Over the nadir, & under the Zenith. So the riddle of the Age has always a private solution.[112] Pass to p. 122

[121] ⟨One insight⟩The difference between the saint & the scholar intellectually, is, that, whilst the scholar too has many divine thoughts, he uses them to a convenient & conventional purpose, for a "Treatise," for a "history:" but the other not only has thoughts, but the copula that joins them is also a thought.

---

the Year 1842, and to Oregon and North California in the Years 1843–'44 (Washington, D.C., 1845); see *JMN*, IX, 431.

[109] For "what is . . . always true;", see p. [87] above; for "that Every . . . year.", see p. [21] above.

[110] "that Every . . . time." is struck through in ink with a diagonal use mark. "You say . . . created." is used in "Worship," *W*, VI, 213. "All kinds . . . time." is used in "Power," *W*, VI, 64; see p. [9] above and Journal TU, p. [48] above.

[111] "We are . . . Times.", struck through in ink with two wavy vertical use marks, is used in "Fate," *W*, VI, 4.

[112] "every one . . . solution." is struck through in ink with a vertical use mark; "So the . . . solution." is used in "Fate," *W*, VI, 4.

[122] Read in Goethe's "Winckelmann" ↑Vol 37, p. 20↓ our cheerful Franklin-like philosopher's friendly view of the world. He is considerate & patronizing a little, be sure, to the gods.

"When the healthy nature of man works as a whole; when he feels himself, in the world, as in a large, beautiful, worthy, & solid whole; when the harmonious well-being assures him a clear free joy; then would the Universe, if it could be conscious, exult as arrived at its aim, and admire the summit of its own becoming [123] & being. Since, whereto serves all the expense of suns, & planets, & moons; of stars, & ⟨comets⟩galaxies: of comets & nebulae; of worlds being & to be; if at last one happier man cannot unconsciously rejoice in his existence?" *Goethe.*[113]

⟨Tis claimed for⟩ ↑I value↓ the clergy that it is the planting of a qualified man in every town whose whole business is to do good in every form.[114]

[124] "Knowledge subsists according to the nature of that which knows, & not according to the nature of that which is known." *Proclus* [*The Six Books of Proclus on the*] Theol[ogy of]. Plato [1816,] Vol II. 496.

———

↑but is original with Iamblichus See Taylor Proc[lus]. Vol II p 498↓

"The understanding transforms itself into the image of the thing understood."

Van Helmont[115]

"Reason is by no means a cause, part, or essence of a thing Caused; much less doth the rational faculty in man reach unto things. For a thing is that in itself which it is, without the reflexion of it on any discourse, & invention of human reason." [van Helmont, *Oriatrike* . . . , 1662, p. 19]

[113] *Werke*, 55 vols. (Stuttgart and Tübingen, 1828–1833), XXXVII, 20.

[114] The question mark after "existence", and the cancellation and insertion in this sentence, are in pencil.

[115] See p. [62] above.

[125] [*Ibid.,*] ↑*p. 25*[116] *Van Helmont.*↓

"The very understandingness of a thing is nothing but a coming to, & immediate approach of the unity of the understanding & of the thing understood."

↑[and afterwards p 26] "So as the things themselves seem to talk with us without words."↓

"The understanding intellect is no otherwise different from the thing understood, than as a beam of light which is direct, differs from itself being reflexed. Therefore the essence of a thing understood in the light of understanding is made a spiritual & essential splendour. Yea, by a co--passing unto a unity, it is after some sort made the light of the understanding itself." [*Ibid.,*] p. 25

[126] *Beauty*

Paule de Viguiere[117] ↑(See C p 30)↓ was no doubt a beauty ⟨but⟩ such as there are few; but I have heard, that it is not often beauty that ⟨awakens⟩ ↑inspires↓ the profoundest passion. It was s⟨u⟩aid of Mirabeau, that he had an ugly face on a handsome ground. And that is my commentary on the generality of faces; they all seem entitled to a beauty they have not; as if the type were good, but there was an accident in the casting. I see the fine face peering out in happy moments from the plain mask.[118]

↑I remember that when I read a lecture in New York in which I inserted some notices of Paule de Viguiere Mr Bartlett in his book--store inquired where I found her story, and I having forgotten what German book it was,—he believed that I had invented them.[119]

[116] "*p. 25*" is partially enclosed by an ink line forming a half oval, open on the left.

[117] The terminal "e" is canceled in pencil.

[118] This paragraph, struck through in ink with two vertical use marks, is used, except for the final sentence, in "Beauty," *W*, VI, 298, 299.

[119] The lecture "The Eye and Ear" (1837) contains a reference to de Viguier (*Lectures*, II, 276), and though Emerson apparently did not give this lecture in New York City, he could easily have "inserted" the de Viguier passage into any of his New York lectures of March, 1840 or February–March, 1843. John Russell Bartlett (1805–1886) was associated with Bartlett & Welford, a bookstore in New York City. The source of the de Viguier story recorded in Journal C and used in the lecture "The Eye and Ear" is *Briefe an Johann Heinrich Merck von Göthe, Herder, Wieland und andern bedeutenden Zeitgenossen* (Darmstadt, 1835), p. 494

[127] The stories I told were all from ⟨g⟩German books which I have never met with since.

September, 1877.↓ [120]

---

[128] *Journal*
1. Dr Frothingham's Astronomical Paper
2. Translation of Goethe's Legend.
3. Nisami, Falcon & Nightingale
4. Essay on Books [121]
5.

[129] Οι ρεόντες

We postpone our literary work until we shall have more ripeness & skill to write, and we one day discover that our literary talent was a youthful effervescence which we have now lost! [122]

[130] ↑*Samuel Hoar, Esq.*↓ [123]

Mr Hoar is & remains an entire stranger all his life long, not only in his village, but in his family. He might bow & touch his hat

---

and note (*JMN*, V, 299–300, n. 76). In Notebook NQ, p. [14], Emerson says he found all he knew about Paule de Viguier "in a note to one of the letters of Goethe to Camper . . . in a large German octavo volume of *Correspondence of Goethe*"; evidently Emerson's memory played him false. The confusion may account for his reference to "German books" below. For a long account of Paule de Viguier, see Edward Emerson's note, *W*, VI, 416–418.

[120] Presumably, the entries on pp. [126] below the line and on [127] were made on this date.

[121] The entry on this page is struck through in ink with a vertical use mark. In this list Emerson may be considering items for a new periodical, perhaps the *Town and Country Magazine* as planned by Emerson, Alcott, and Lowell, recorded in an Alcott journal entry of February 12, 1850 (*The Journals of Bronson Alcott*, ed. Odell Shepard [Boston, 1938], p. 223). Conjecturally, they are: Nathaniel Langdon Frothingham's version of the "Phenomena of the Stars," from the Greek of Aratus, in *Metrical Pieces, Translated and Original* (Boston, 1855), a collection of verses contributed to magazines; Goethe's legend of Paria (see p. [71] above); the "Nisami" poem copied on pp. [84] and [85] above from von Hammer-Purgstall's *Geschichte* . . . , pp. 107–108; and possibly Emerson's lecture on Books, printed in the *Atlantic Monthly* (Jan. 1858).

[122] This sentence, struck through in ink with a vertical use mark, is used in "Old Age," *W*, VII, 319.

[123] Concord lawyer, close friend of the Emerson family, onetime congressman, father of Charles Emerson's fiancée, Elizabeth.

to his wife & daughter as well as to the President. He does the same thing in politics & at the bar. It is not any new light that he sheds on the case, but his election of a side, & ↑the↓ giving ⟨th⟩ his statuesque dignity to that side, that weighs with juries, or with conventions. For he does this naturally.

See B 83

[131] [blank]

[132][124] Books for C[aroline]. S[turgis]. T[appan].

Ellis
Bohn — Mallet
Six English Chronicles
Ockley
Bede & Ang Sax Chron
Plato
Chronicles of Crusaders
Goethe's Autobiography

Stallo
D R Hay

Bhagavat
Kurroglou

Heimskringla
Dasent's Edda

Bothie

[133] Jacobson's Æschylus
Carlyle's Dante
Lodge's Winckelmann[125]

[124] Pp. [132] and [133] are in pencil except for "*Carlyles List*" on p. [133], written and underlined in ink, above the same words in pencil.

[125] Emerson's references in the list of books on pp. [132] and [133] are undoubtedly to the following: George Ellis, *Specimens of Early English Metrical*

Carlyle's List
Kennett's History of Eng
Camden's Brittannia translated by Holland
7 or 8 s
Britton's beauties of Eng & Wales
Hainault Abrege Chronologique de l'histoire de France
Bede
Collins' Peerage 1745 12/6
Wood's Athenae Oxoniensis[126]

[134] Bettine said, "If I cannot do as I have a mind in our poor Frankfort, I shall not carry it far."[127] So I would have a man of large designs use our little Boston & ⟨sprawling⟩ ↑noisy↓ New York as suburbs & villages, to try his pieces on, & find their faults, & supply a good hint, if they can. Then let him take them to London or to Paris, to whatever Rome his age affords him, & read them tentatively there

---

Romances, 1848; Paul Henri Mallet, *Northern Antiquities* . . . (London, 1847); *Six Old English Chronicles* . . . , ed. John Allen Giles (London, 1848); Simon Ockley, *The History of the Saracens* . . . , (London, 1848); Beda Venerabilis, *Ecclesiastical History of England. Also the Anglo-Saxon Chronicle* . . . , ed. J. A. Giles (London, 1847); *Chronicles of the Crusades* . . . , 1848; *The Auto-biography of Goethe* . . . , 1848–1849; John Bernhard Stallo, *General Principles of the Philosophy of Nature*, 1848; David Ramsay Hay, *The Laws of Harmonious Colouring* . . . (Edinburgh, 1847); *The Bhăgvăt-Gēētā; or, Dialogues of Krēēshnă and Ărjŏŏn* . . . , trans. Charles Wilkins (London, 1785); *Specimens of the Popular Poetry of Persia, as Found in the Adventures and Improvisations of Kurroglou* . . . , trans. Alexander Edmund Chodzko (London, 1842); *The Heimskringla*, 1844; *The Prose or Younger Edda* . . . , trans. George Webbe Dasent (Stockholm and London, 1842); Arthur Hugh Clough, *The Bothie of Toper-na-Fuosich*, 1848; Aeschylus, *The Seven Tragedies of Aeschylus* . . . (Oxford, 1843); Dante, *Divine Comedy: The Inferno* . . . (New York, 1849); Johann Joachim Winckelmann, *The History of Ancient Art among the Greeks*, trans. G. H. Lodge (London, 1850). Emerson's library contained many Plato items. The Mallet, *Six* . . . *Chronicles*, Bede, *Chronicles of the Crusades*, Goethe, Stallo, Hay, *Bhăgvăt-Gēētā*, *Heimskringla*, Dasent's *Edda*, Aeschylus, and Dante are in Emerson's library. There were Bohn library editions of the first eight items in Emerson's list.

[126] With the exception of the last item, a reference to Anthony à Wood's *Athenae Oxonienses* . . . , 1721, the books in this list are recorded and annotated in *JMN*, X, 283, and n. 304.

[127] Emerson is paraphrasing from a letter of Bettina von Arnim to Goethe's mother, in *Goethe's Correspondence with a Child*, 2 vols. (Lowell, 1841), I, 24, in Emerson's library. The sentence is used in "Culture," *W*, VI, 163.

too, not trusting his [135] audience much, since "non é nel mondo, se non volgo,"[128] with a reference still to his ultimate tribunal, namely, the few scattered sensible men, two or three in the world at a time, who, scattered thinly over the ages are called by excellence *posterity*, because they determine its opinion.[129]

[136] *Superlative*

The talent sucks the substance of the man. How often we repeat the disappointment of inferring general ability from conspicuous particular ability. But the accumulation on one point has drained the trunk. Blessed are those who have no talent! [130] The expressors are the gods of the world,—Shakspeare & the rest, but the sane men whom these expressors ⟨secretly⟩ revere, are the ⟨sound⟩ ↑solid↓ balanced undemonstrative [137] citizens who make the reserved guard, the central sense of the world.[131]

'Tis because he is not well mixed, that he needs to do some feat by way of fine or expiation. See AB 19

I have never met a person superior to his talent; one who had money in his pocket, & did not use it.[132]

[138] *Carlyle.*

Carlyle is wonderful for his rhetorical skill. This trick of rhyme, burden, or refrain, which he uses so well, he not only employs in each new paragraph, suddenly treating you with the last ritornello, but in each new Essay or Book quoting ⟨to you⟩ the Burden or Chorus of the last book.—You know me, & I know you;—or,—

[128] Inaccurately quoted from Coleridge, *On the Constitution of the Church and State . . .*, (see *The Complete Works of Samuel Taylor Coleridge*, ed. W. G. Shedd, 7 vols. [New York, 1853], VI, 70), where it is attributed to Machiavelli. See *JMN*, VI, 128.

[129] This paragraph is struck through in ink with single vertical use marks on pp. [134] and [135]; "Bettine said . . . far.'" is used in "Culture," *W*, VI, 163.

[130] With this sentence, cf. *JMN*, VII, 414: "'Blessed,' said the Review which pleased me so well, 'is the man who has no Powers.'"

[131] "The talent . . . man." and "The expressors . . . sense of the world." are used in "The Superlative," *W*, X, 173. The paragraph is incorporated into a long disquisition in Notebook Amos Bronson Alcott, pp. [34]–[35], on the limitations of some men of genius.

[132] For this sentence, see *JMN*, X, 318.

Here we are again, come take me up again on your shoulders; — is the [139] import of this. 'Tis curious, the magnificence of his genius, & the poverty of his aims. He draws his weapons from the skies, to fight ⟨for⟩ ↑the cause of↓ some wretched English ⟨crotchet⟩ property or monopoly ⟨or He takes no expansive view⟩ or prejudice or whim. A transcendental John Bull delighting in the music of Bow-bells, who cannot see across the channel, but has the skill to make divine oratorios in praise of the ⟨s⟩Strand, Kensington & Kew. I was to have said just now that he contrives in each piece to make out of his theme or lucky expression, [140] [n] a proverb before he has done; and this conclusion of the last is the exordium of the next Chapter.[133]

He is no idealist in opinions. He is a protectionist in Political Economy, ⟨a tory⟩ ↑aristocrat↓ in politics, epicure in diet, goes for ↑slavery,↓ murder, money, punishment by death, & all the pretty abominations, tempering them with epigrams.[134]

[141] If a pear sells for a shilling, it costs a shilling to raise it. If the "best securities" offer 12 per cent for money, they have just 6 per cent of insecurity.[135]

↑"the worth of any thing
Is so much money as t'will bring."↓
[Butler, *Hudibras*, II, Canto I, 465–466, misquoted]

Politics.

Mr E[dward].T[yrrel]. Channing told W[illiam]. E[llery]. C[hanning]. that, ⟨the⟩ as soon as Bowen began to abuse them, he told Sparks they must have him in. So they made him professor.[136]

[133] "Carlyle is . . . Chapter." is struck through in pencil with single diagonal use marks on pp. [138], [139], and [140]. For "Tis curious . . . Kew.", see *JMN*, X, 553.

[134] "He is no . . . epigrams.", struck through in pencil with a diagonal use mark, is used in "Carlyle," *W*, X, 491.

[135] This paragraph, struck through in ink with a vertical use mark, is used in "Wealth," *W*, VI, 108.

[136] Of the three Harvard professors, Edward Tyrrel Channing became Boylston Professor of Rhetoric and Oratory in 1819; Francis Bowen, McLean Professor of History in 1850; Jared Sparks, McLean Professor of History in 1838, and later president of the College.

[142] It is not the least characteristic ↑sign↓ of the Times, that Alcott should have been able to collect such a good company of the best heads for two Monday Evenings, for the expressed purpose of discussing the Times.[137] What was never done by human beings in another age, was done now; there they met to discuss their own breath, to speculate on their own navels, with eyeglass & solar microscope, and no man wondered at them. But these very ⟨many⟩men came in the cars by steam-ferry & locomotive to the meeting, & sympathized [143][n] with engineers & Californians. Mad contradictions flavor all our dishes.

Putnam, Whipple, Dewey, W.H. Channing, & I,—and I know not how many more,—are lecturing this winter on the *Spirit of the Times*! And now Carlyle's first pamphlet is "The Present Age."[138]

[144] ↑*Commonsense Eloquence*↓

Lord Mansfield's merit is like that of Plato, Montaigne, Sam Johnson, Socrates, & Shakspeare, namely, in his commonsense. Each of those decisions contains a level sentence or two, which hits the mark. His sentences are not finished outwardly, but are inwardly. His sentences are involved, but ⟨the⟩a solid proposition is set forth; a *true* distinction is drawn.[139]—But Alcott can never finish a sentence, but revolves in spirals, until [145] he is lost in air. And it is true that Johnson earned his fame. His reported conversation is up to his reputation.

---

[137] Emerson's reference is presumably to Alcott's second "Conversation" at the Town and Country Club; if the first Conversation was held on Monday, February 18, 1850 (see p. [106] above), then this entry may postdate February 25, a week later.

[138] George Putnam, D.D. (1807–1878), minister of Roxbury's First Unitarian Church, gave several addresses and orations in the Boston area in addition to his regular sermons; Edwin Percy Whipple, a young critic, was one of the original members of the Saturday Club; Reverend Orville Dewey, Unitarian minister, lectured at Lyceums in Boston and Baltimore; William Henry Channing was also a Unitarian minister. Emerson lectured on the "Spirit of the Times" in January, 1850, and had given a course of lectures "On the Present Age" in the 1839–1840 season (*JMN*, VII, 338).

[139] The underlining of "*true*" is in pencil. The paragraph to this point is used in "Eloquence," *W*, VII, 88.

↑Lords Camden & Kenyon↓ sneered at Mansfield's "*equitable* decisions," meaning thereby to disparage his learning.[140]

[146] St Augustine. *Oxford Edition.*
Of Memory admirable analysis
p 188—203

And with an admirable conclusion p 212

"But where in my memory residest thou, O Lord, &c"

and next page, 203,

"Too late ⟨I⟩ loved ↑I↓ thee, O thou Beauty of Ancient days, yet ever new! too late I loved thee!" &c

p 121 See a passage for the Doctrine of inspiration[141]

[147] ↑*Seven years in the Vat.*↓[142]

Ellery C[hanning]. thinks the merit of Irving's "Life of Goldsmith," is, that he has not had the egotism to put in a single new sentence. It is nothing but an agreeable repetition of Boswell⟨s⟩, Johnson, & Company. And so Montaigne is good, because there is nothing that has not already been in books. A good book being a Damascus blade made by the welding of old nails & horseshoes. Every thing has seen service, & been proved by wear & tear in the world for centuries, & yet now the article is brand-new.

[140] Emerson first drew a horizontal line at the beginning of the sentence; later he filled in "Lords . . . Kenyon". The exact source is unlocated. For Kenyon's sneering at Mansfield's decisions, see John Lord Campbell, *The Lives of the Chief Justices of England*, 3 vols. (London, 1849, 1857), III, 36.

[141] The passage represents God as "the Light Unchangeable" and as speaker to the soul of divine truth. Emerson's references on p. [146] are to *The Confessions of S. Augustine; Rev. from a Former Translation by E. B. Pusey, with Illustrations from S. Augustine Himself* (Oxford, 1840), in Emerson's library.

[142] "*Seven . . . Vat.*" is used in "Ability," *W*, V, 89: "Their [the Germans'] leather lies tanning seven years in the vat." See *JMN*, X, 282.

So Pope had but one good line, & that he got from Dryden, & therefore Pope is the best & only readable English poet.

---

[148] *The Age.*

God flung into the world in these last ages two toys, a magnet, & a looking glass; and the children of men have occupied themselves wholly with one or the other, or with both. Swedenborg, Des Cartes, and all the philosophers both natural & moral turned themselves into magnets, & have not ceased to express in every way their sense of polarity; — Schelling, and the existing thinkers, most of all. The most unexpected splendid effects are produced by this [149] principle, as a cone is generated by the revolution of a triangle.
Religions, philosophies, friendships, loves, poetries, literatures, are all hid in the horseshoe magnet. As galvanism, electricity, chemistry, light, heat, and LIFE & ⟨are all and at last⟩ Thought, are at last only /corollaries/powers/ of this fruitful ⟨Un⟩phenomenon.[143]
A single example occurs for a thousand. Society disgusts and the poet resolves to go into retirement & indulge this great heart & feed his thought henceforwards with botany & astronomy. — [150] Behold, on the instant, his appetites are exasperated: he wants dinners & concerts, scholars & fine women, theatre & club. And life consists in managing adroitly these antagonisms to ⟨excite⟩ ↑intensate↓ each other. Life must have continence & abandonment.

For the lookingglass, the effect was scarcely less. ↑⟨The⟩ Poor dear↓ Narcissus pines on the fountain side. Col. Fremont, on the Rocky Mountains, says, "*How we look*!"[144] And all cities & all nations think what the English, what [151] the French, what the Americans will say. Next, the trick of *philosophising* is inveterate, & reaches its height; and, last, *Symbolism* is the lookingglass raised to the highest

[143] Emerson originally wrote "chemistry, galvanism, electricity,"; he then wrote "1" below "galvanism," and "2" below "chemistry,"; finally, he scratched out "1", changed the "2" to a "3", and wrote "2" below "electricity," thus indicating his final preference for the order of the second two words. The editors have assumed that he wished "galvanism" to come first.

[144] See p. [117] above.

power. I wrote above "what I want to know, is, the meaning of what I do; believing that any of my current Mondays or Tuesdays is Fatebook enough for me; believing that hints & telegraphic signals are arriving to me, every moment, out of the interior eternity, I am tormented with impatience to make them out." See *TU*

[152] Still one thing more occurred in yesterday's conversation, —old hobnails all, that may yet one day help to make a blade,— That, there are not one or two, but six or seven, nay, nineteen or twenty things, that must be considered⟨,⟩ &⟨,⟩ had. You wish & must have a good poise, self-equality, or the fine adjustment to the world that enables you to do something well, some piece of work to your own & the world's satisfaction. Very good: 'Tis a great blessing, to be humbly [153] thankful for. Yes, but can you live with other people? Your work is done alone: But when you come into ⟨society,⟩ ↑the street,↓—do you come entire?— —Yes.—Excellent; Then you have two things. But there are new relations; to Women; to cultivated Society; to the Economist; to the Great, to the leaders & to the ideas of the time. There is living for the day, and living for the whole; and all the merits it is impossible to combine. (see what is written above—p 44)

[154] Garrison is venerable in his plan, like the tart Luther; but he cannot understand anything you say, and ne↑i↓ghs like a horse when you suggest a new consideration, as when I told him, that, the *fate*-element in the negro question he had never considered.

[155] *Eloquence*

Eloquence is like money, of no use ⟨to those who⟩ for the most part to those who have it, but inestimable it would be to such as have something to say. A course of mobs was recommended to me by N. P. Rogers to correct my quaintness & transcendentalism.[145] And I might have found it as good ↑for me,↓ as the water cure for paralysed stomachs.

[145] With this sentence, cf. *JMN*, X, 28; "Power", *W*, VI, 78; "Considerations by the Way," *W*, VI, 261; "Eloquence," *W*, VII, 96–97. Nathaniel P. Rogers (1794–1846) was, until December of 1844, editor of the antislavery magazine *Herald of Freedom*.

[156] "So that the state only exists, I shall never want anything," said the great Condé, & paid the army himself.[146]

Lord Mahon. p. 48

He opened the trenches before Lerida to the sound of violins.

"2 July 1652. Battle of St Antoine. At midday, fatigue & insupportable heat put a stop to the fight for some moments. Condé wore a breastplate, & was so soaked by sweat, & stifled by his armour, that he was forced to have himself unbooted, & to throw himself quite naked on the grass in a field where he rolled & [157] wallowed like a tired horse. Then he dressed himself, & was armed, & returned to end the conflict."

Lord Mahon's Life of Condé, p 231

Au coeur vaillant rien impossible.

To a stout heart[147]

[158] ——

Abuse is a pledge that you are felt. If they praise you, you will work no revolution.

Language is a quite wonderful city, which we all help to build. But each word is like a ⟨work⟩work of nature, determined a thousand years ago, & not alterable. We confer & dispute, & settle the meaning so or so, but it remains what it was in spite of us. The word [159] beats all the speakers & definers of it, & stands to their children ⟨as⟩ ↑what↓ it stood to their fathers.

How often indisputable talent does not affect us as such, for want of following the natural determination of character, or some-

[146] For this and the following two entries, see Philip Henry Stanhope, Lord Mahon, *The Life of Louis, Prince of Condé, Surnamed the Great*, 2 vols. in 1 (New York, 1845), I, 50, 47, and II, 77. The edition Emerson used is not located; it may have been the one-volume London edition, 1845. See *JMN*, VI, 355, and VIII, 117, for earlier accounts of the stories in the second and third entries.

[147] These four words are in pencil. The French motto, "Au coeur . . . impossible." is attributed to Jeanne d'Albret of Navarre, mother of Henry IV, and was adopted by him as his own *devise*.

what superior to itself! "For, it is not what ⟨we think,⟩ ↑our thought is,↓ but how we are to our thought that makes friendship."[148]

We practise our art in unsuspected ateliers.

---

[160] As far as I know, the misfortune of New England is,—that the Southerner always beats us in Politics. And for this reason, that it comes at Washington to a game of personalities. The Southerner has personalit⟨i⟩y, has temperament, has manners, persuasion, address & terror. The cold Yankee has wealth, numbers, intellect, material power of all sorts, but has not fire or firmness, & is coaxed & [161] talked & bantered & shamed & scared, till he votes away the dominion of his millions at home. ↑⟨&⟩He never comes back quite the same man he went; but has been handled, tampered with.↓ What is the remedy? Plainly I think, that we ↑must↓ borrow a hint from the military art. The Hungarians said, they could have easily beaten the Russians, if in any manner they could have made them run: but the Russian soldier is more afraid of his officers, than of the enemy: if he runs, he will assuredly be shot: if he fights, he has a chance of escape, and therefore he is cut down & butchered, but dares not run. So let our representative know that if he ⟨barters⟩ misrepresents his constituency there is no recovery from social damnation at home.

[162] ↑*Poverty & Riches*↓

The formula I hunted for in Froude's Nemesis, was, "⟨an⟩the grave moral deterioration which follows an empty exchequer." (*Nemesis*. p. 40)[149]

Majority. "The army of Unright is encamped from pole to pole, but the road to victory is known to the Dervish."[150]

[148] For the quotation (from Charles King Newcomb), see Journal TU, p. [257] above. " 'For, it . . . friendship.' ", struck through in ink with three vertical use marks, is used in "Behavior," *W*, VI, 193. Originally, the middle use mark extended through the whole paragraph, beginning at "How often", but the upper portion was canceled with a finger wipe.

[149] J. A. Froude, *The Nemesis of Faith* (London, 1849). "The formula . . . exchequer.' ", struck through in pencil with a vertical use mark, is used in "Wealth," *W*, V, 154.

[150] The quotation is used in "The Fugitive Slave Law" (1854), *W*, XI, 235.

"Friends he must have, but in no one could find
A tally fitted to so large a mind." [151]

[163] *England*

The good of England is that one soon learns to know that there is ↑all around you↓ an infinite number of educated & thoughtful people, ⟨there⟩ all quietly [n] & calmly carrying forward their /own/elegant/ studies with the best ⟨w⟩ aids & materials, & wholly independent of & unacquainted with the rest.[152]

[164] *Greek Art*

Goethe ⟨remarks⟩ ↑notes↓ that the horses of St Mark look heavy, if closely inspected; but, seen from below, look as fleet as greyhounds; —which agrees well with the foreshortening of the old inscriptions, and the curving of the lines of the Parthenon to compensate for the defects of the human eye.[153]

[165] *Women.*

Women are relative in their nature. They exist to take care of men, & when they take up bookmaking, o↑r↓ painting, or shopkeeping, with good earnest, it is only as a resource or substitute,[n] & is not with them a legitimate primary object, as it is with men.[154]
↑Their Conventional Devil. R [93]
no rudder BO 180↓ [155]

[166] *Intellect*

Lagrange thought Newton fortunate in this, that the law of uni-

In Notebook Morals, p. [282], Emerson attributes it to Hafiz. For a different translation, see *Persian Literature, Comprising the Sháh Námeh, The Rubáiyát, The Divan, and The Gulistan*, 2 vols. (New York and London, 1900), I, 387 (in *The Divan*, Ode XXIX, ll. 11–12).

[151] John Dryden, "Eleonora," ll. 255–256, slightly altered. See *JMN*, VI, 160. The couplet, struck through in ink with a vertical use mark, is used in *Memoirs of Margaret Fuller Ossoli*, 2 vols. (Boston, 1852), I, 280—hereafter cited as *Memoirs*.

[152] This paragraph is struck through in ink with a vertical use mark; see Appendix I.

[153] With "the curving . . . eye.", cf. *JMN*, X, 253.

[154] This paragraph is used in "Woman," *W*, XI, 407, 409.

[155] "Their Conventional . . . BO" is in pencil.

versal gravitation could be discovered but once, whilst the discoverer of Cape of Good Hope had a rival in the discoverer of Cape Horn, of Arctic Sea & land[,] in Antarctic Sea & land. And yet in metaphysics there is no terminus, & therefore no final discovery. Hegel, or Oken, or whosoever shall enunciate the law which necessitates gravitation as a phenomenon of a ⟨law⟩ larger law, embracing mind & matter, diminishes Newton.

How many centres we have fondly found, which proved soon to be circumferential points! How many conversations or books seemed epochs, at the moment, which we have now actually forgotten!

[167] *Nat. History of Intellect* must remember that all ⟨is⟩that is called genius, inspiration *par excellence*, though it appear to ⟨me⟩the auditor a miracle, is not that to the Poet or orator, but all these cunning juxtapositions, allusions, transitions, ↑&↓ symbols admit of being followed & explained by a snailish arithmetic ⟨& af⟩after usual laws.

↑Cause & Effect forever!↓

———

Memory.

A drowning man has ↑long minutes or↓ long seconds which ⟨a Com⟩recapitulate all his biography.[156]

[168] *The Undertaker.* There is obviously room for a new trade, namely, the *Undertaker* or *Social Factor.* A man of common sense intimately acquainted with good society, & with fashion, & the best modes, in all departments of life. The Scholar just released from college, & entering cities, & wishing to push his way, shall pay this Factor his commission, & the Factor shall lead him to a good tailor, & see to it that he is properly & becomingly dressed, shod, & hatted; then, that he is put to a proper gymnasium & riding school; then that he is properly advised in [169] all the etiquette of morning & evening visits, dinner, & ballroom,[n] properly joined to a club, & well instructed in the best economies of lodging & dieting[.]

A man of taste & sense who should open such an office as this, would easily make his fortune⟨.⟩, ↑& perhaps the fortune of his clients.↓

[156] With this sentence, cf. "Memory," *W*, XII, 109.

↑*Books*↓

I expect a great man to be a good reader, or in proportion to the spontaneous power, should be the assimilating power.[157] &c, See *N* 17

[170] As I read of Wolsey yesterday the Boy-bachelor at Oxford (where afterwards he built the beautiful tower of Magdalen-College--Chapel,) and his early success with the wise old Henry VII., it seemed that the true distinction & royalty of kings consists in this privilege of having pure truth in business spoken to them. They have the telegraphic dispatch. No man dare lie to them.

↑For good account of Wolsey, see
Wood's Athenae Oxiensis, [1721,] Vol. 1, p. 666↓

Truth & virtue will come to be the aristocratic diamond.

---

[171] These Children of fashion have found no more satisfaction in their element than the[n] other experimenters, & they are sallying into our pastures to see if (may-be) it is not there. I think how many superstitions we have. Patrick Jackson did not go to college, & therefore never quite felt himself the equal of his own brothers who did.[158] Dancing & equitation which poverty denied to me, I beheld in all my youth with awe & unquestioning respect.

Of occasion. [George Sand,] Compagnon du tour de France[1841,] p ⟨84⟩ ↑24↓

[157] This sentence is used in "Culture," *W*, VI, 142; "Quotation and Originality," *W*, VIII, 178; and "Address at the Opening of the Concord Free Public Library," *W*, XI, 504.

[158] "Patrick Jackson . . . did.", struck through in ink with a vertical use mark, is used in "Culture," *W*, VI, 144. Emerson's reference is perhaps to the Boston industrialist, Patrick T. Jackson (1780–1847), whose real estate speculations collapsed in the panic of 1837.

[172]
T. & C. Club

1849 [Caleb] Stetson
[Thomas] Hill
T[homas]. Davis
S[amuel]. Osgood
C[harles].T. Brooks
S[amuel]. Longfellow
G[eorge]. Simmons
F[rancis]. Cunningham
F[rederick]. Eustis
C. Farrar
T[ristram].B. Mackay
Thoreau
[Nathaniel?] Gage
⟨Eustis⟩ [Benjamin?] Thompson
[Joseph] Angier
[Horace] Bushnell
T[homas] S King
W B Greene
J.R. Lowell
H[enry].W. Longfellow
W[illiam] A Tappan
L B Russell
S G Ward
G[eorge] B E[merson]
S[amuel] K L[othrop]
G P B[radford]

T[homas?] Lee
G[eorge] Russell [160]

Honorary
[Christopher] Cranch
Bushnell
W[illiam].H. Channing
Duggan
[Thomas?] Hicks
[Hiram?] Powers
[Horatio] Greenough
[Nathaniel] Hawthorne
H[enry].W. Beecher
J[ames D.?] Whelpley
H[enry]. James
R[obert] M S Jackson
J P[eter] Lesley

Bangs
Cabot
W B Greene
E E Hale
Shackford [159]

1850
S[amuel] G Ward
J.W. Browne
Edw Bangs
A[mos] B Alcott
W[illiam] E Channing
J[ames] E Cabot
J[ames] R Lowell
T S King
L[e] B[aron] Russell
W[illiam] B Greene
E[dward] E Hale
C[harles] C Shackford
T[heodore]. Parker
J[ohn] S Dwight
W.E. Goodson
G[eorge] P Bradford
J[ames] F Clarke
W H Channing
E[dwin]. P. Whipple
G. Loring
W.F. Channing

[159] The list in the left-hand column, beginning with "Stetson" at the top and running down through "G Russell", and the list "Bangs . . . Shackford" are struck through in ink with vertical lines.

[160] Of those listed who have not been previously identified or are not easily recognizable, Tristram Barnard Mackay was a Concord neighbor; Benjamin Thompson, congressman from 1845–1847, was elected again in 1851 (see Journal CO, p. [41] below); William Aspinwall Tappan, a New York broker, married Caroline

[173] *Spring* from *Enweri* V[on].H[ammer,]. [*Geschichte der schönen Redekünste Persiens*, 1818,] p 96

In the garden goes now the wind over the water
⟨That by filing he may⟩ ↑To file & to↓ polish
the cheeks of the pond.
On tulips plays now the reflection [n] of fire
Which plays now no more in chimney & hearth [161]
⟨W⟩He who yesterday withdrew himself from affairs
Him now desire sets again in activity

[George] Bemis [Fred] Howes
Gould
Whipple
W[illiam] F. Chan[ning]
Walter C[hanning]
Lothrop
King
Ward
Burlingame
List
Homer
Shackford
Fisher
Emerson [162]

Sturgis in December, 1847, after Emerson encouraged their introduction; Thomas Hicks was a New York painter; James Davenport Whelpley, a physician, moved to New York in 1847 to edit the *American Whig Review*; the Pennsylvania physician Robert Montgomery Smith Jackson (1815–1865) was also a botanist and geologist; J. Peter Lesley (1819–1903), geologist, lectured at the Concord Lyceum in 1850; Le Baron Russell was a physician; Dr. George B. Loring sailed for America with Emerson in July, 1848 (*L*, IV, 101). Although Farrar, Gage, Angier, Duggan, Browne, Goodson, and Lee are otherwise unidentified, first names have been supplied in the text for some on the authority of Edward Emerson, in *J*, VIII, 103–104.

[161] With Emerson's translation to this point, cf. "Persian Poetry," *W*, VIII, 258.

[162] The lists of persons on p. [173], associated with the Town and Country Club, are in pencil. In the absence of Emerson's supplying initials, the editors have identified these names only where there is reasonable certainty from membership lists in the *Emerson Society Quarterly*, no. 8 (III Quarter, 1957), 17. George F. Bemis was publisher of the *Yeoman's Gazette* in Concord until 1843, when he went to Boston

[174] *Jane Eyre*

In novels, the most serious questions are really discussed. What made the popularity of Jane Eyre but that a ↑central↓ question was answered in some sort. The question there answered will always be treated according to the habit of the party. A person of great breadth of individualism will answer it as Rochester does, as Cleopatra, as George Sand, as Milton does; magnifying the exception into a rule, dwarfing the world into an exception. A person of less courage, that is of less constitution, will answer it as Jane does, giving importance to Fate, to the conventionalism, [175] to the actual state & doings of men & women.[163]

[176] "It is certainly a gigantic step to raise epic poetry to the unity of the chief action; but the idea springs from the very nature of a narration; & therefore it did not stand in need of a theory which was foreign to the age; genius was able of itself to take this step."

Heeren
Greece p. 115[164]

[177] The part that is built teaches the architect how to build the rest. The streets compress the mob into battalions. Who taught Raffaelle & Corregio how to draw? Was it ⟨M⟩Signor Quadro, the perspective-master, with his rule & dividers? No, it was the weather-stains on the wall; the cloud over the house-roof yonder, with that shoulder of Hercules, & brow ↑o↓f⟨or⟩ Jove; it was marbled paper; it was a lucky scratch with a bit of charcoal, which taught the secret of possibility, & confounded & annihilated ⟨M⟩Signor Quadro, & themselves also.

[178] ↑*Commonsense*↓

I heard a good speech, & a bad one, yesterday, at the town school; one boy in the name of the school presented the master with an escritoire of rosewood, & some books, & made a long speech to him, in which I remember something about "our posterity" that is, the boys'

---

and established a printing office; "Homer" may refer to the Boston merchant Sidney Homer.

[163] "In novels . . . women.", struck through in pencil with two vertical use marks on each of pp. [174] and [175], is used in "Books," *W*, VII, 215–216.

[164] Arnold H. L. Heeren, *Reflections on the Politics of Ancient Greece*, trans. George Bancroft (Boston, 1824), in Emerson's library.

posterity! Another boy, Tolman, in the name of his schoolmates also, ⟨gav⟩presented a portfolio & a book to the assistant, Miss Buttrick, and said, "he only hoped [179] that she would have as much pleasure in receiving it, as they had in giving it." [165]

[180] ↑*Eyes & No eyes.*↓

In Nat. Hist of Intellect Goethe becomes a sample of an eye, for he sees the site of Rome, its unfitness, he sees the difference between Palermo & Naples; he sees rivers, & which way they run. Henry Thoreau, too. An advancing eye, that like the heavens journeys too & sojourns not[.] [166]

[181] The great man is the impressionable man, ⟨who⟩ most irritable, most delicate, like iodine to light, so he feels the infinitesimal attractions. He obeys the main current, that is all his secret, the main current is so feeble a force as can be felt only by bodies delicately poised.[167] He can ⟨i⟩orient himself. In the woods, I have one guide, ↑namely,↓ to follow the light,—to go where the woods are thinnest; then at last I ⟨c⟩am sure to come out. So he cannot be betrayed or misguided, for he knows where the North is, knows painfully when he ⟨a⟩is going in the wrong direction.

[182] Memory, Imagination, Reason, are only modes of the same power, as Lampblack & diamond are the same chemical matter in different arrangement.[168]

"Animus habet, non habetur." [169] *Sallust.*

↑Abandon.↓

---

[165] Tolman is perhaps Adams Tolman, member of an old Concord family.

[166] This paragraph is in pencil. With "the heavens journeys too & sojourns not", cf. "For the heavens journey still, and sojourn not," from Coleridge's translation of *The Piccolimini; or, the First Part of Wallenstein*, IV, i, 43, in vol. VII of *The Complete Works of Samuel Taylor Coleridge*, 1853. See *JMN*, VI, 79.

[167] "The great . . . poised.", struck through in ink with a vertical use mark, is used in "Fate," *W*, VI, 44–45.

[168] For this sentence, see *JMN*, VI, 226.

[169] "The mind possesses, it is not possessed" (Ed.). See *JMN*, VI, 185. Cf.

⟨"⟩Men of genius "give out oracles when they are agitated, but are no more than men, when they are calm." *De Stael*[170]

[183] *Concentration* *Pericles*
"There was in the whole city," says Plutarch, "but one street in which ⟨Plut⟩Pericles was ever seen; the street which led to the market place & the council-house. He declined all invitations to banquets & all gay assemblies & company. During the whole period of his administration he never dined at the table of a friend."[171] &c apud *Heeren* [*Reflections on the Politics of Ancient Greece* . . . , 1824,] p[p. 267–]268

"I only can the paper stain,
Yet with a dye that fears no moth,
But scarlet-like out lasts the cloth."
Ben Jonson ["To Master John Burges,"
The Works . . . , 1716,] V 220

[184] *Eloquence*
Pericles was accustomed, whenever he was to speak in public, to entreat the gods, that he might not utter against his will ⟨one syllable⟩ ↑any word↓ that did not belong to the subject.[172] [Heeren, *Reflections on the Politics of Ancient Greece* . . . , 1824, p. 271]

Cobden, the "Unadorned One," makes the same prayer.[173]

Parliaments, Peers, Conne⟨e⟩ction, make it necessary that he who has points to carry should hire a great man. So Charles Austin makes ↑£↓ 30000 per annum in speaking to Rail Road Committees of H. of C↑ommons.↓[n] His clients pay for "*pluck*,"—pay for accomplishments,—pay for a gentleman.[174]

Sallust, *Bellum Iugurthinum*, 2, 3: "animus incorruptus, aeternus rector humani generis agit atque habet cuncta neque ipse habetur."

[170] See *JMN*, VI, 196.

[171] This paragraph, struck through in pencil with a vertical use mark, is used in "Power," *W*, VI, 75.

[172] "utter against . . . word" is struck through in ink with two diagonal use marks. With the whole sentence, cf. *JMN*, X, 164.

[173] In the House of Commons, June 29, 1846, Sir Robert Peel referred to Richard Cobden's eloquence as "unaffected and unadorned." See John Morley, *The Life of Cobden* (London, 1906), p. 388.

[174] "Parliaments . . . gentleman." is used in "Eloquence," *W*, VII, 80. Emerson met the English lawyer Charles Austin (1799–1874) in London. See *JMN*, X, 242.

[185] "To stand on one's own feet" is the maxim of Demosthenes, as of Chatham, says Heeren, in all his orations; & it is in the oration of the συμμοριαι or classes.[175] See *Heeren* [*Reflections on the Politics of Ancient Greece . . .*, 1824,] *p* 277

[186] *Phalanstery* means, the use which a wise man makes of a large city.

[187]–[188] [leaf torn out][176]

[189] He has the best sense whose sense is not good ⟨for⟩ only for one particular thing, but, as Rose Flammock[n] says of her father's, it is like his yardstick, which will measure dowlas & also cloth of gold.[177] Shakspeare was like a looking glass carried through the street[.]

For no man wishes to be a scarlet feather. It is odious to be a jester, or a poet.
"I stamp in the mire with wooden shoes," said Madame de Stael, "When they would force me into the clouds."[178]

[190] "Did I not drum⟨i⟩ well?" said Mr Gray to somebody who taunted him with being a drummer's boy.

His face was so constantly varied by expression, that I could not get a single chance to see his face.

It takes present & pas[179]

---

[175] This sentence is used in "Eloquence," *W*, VII, 99. See *JMN*, VI, 325.

[176] Emerson indexed p. [187] under Englishman and Superlative.

[177] Sir Walter Scott, *The Betrothed*, ch. XII, in *Waverley Novels*, 54 vols. (Boston, 1829–1834), XXXV, 133. With the following sentence, cf. *JMN*, IX, 76–77.

[178] Francis Jeffrey, "Madame de Staël," the *Edinburgh Review*, XXXVI (Oct. 1821), 61. This sentence, struck through in ink with a vertical use mark, is used in "Literature," *W*, V, 232–233. See *JMN*, VI, 80; "The Age of Fable," *Lectures*, I, 264.

[179] "His face . . . pas" is struck through in ink with a vertical use mark; cf. "Beauty," *W*, VI, 301.

Addresses

W[illiam]. B[urnet]. Kinney, Esq. Newark, N. J.
Mrs E[lizabeth]. C[lementine]. Kinney
F[rederick]. W[illiam]. Ricord ⟨N|| . . . ||⟩Library Association
S. P. Huntoon, Paterson, N. J.
Lewis S. Morris 63 State Street Brooklyn
Dr E. MacFarlan. corner 4th & South 5th Streets.
Williamsburgh [180]

[191] *Addresses in New York*

Gideon Nye 19 Fi⟨t⟩fth Avenue
Rev. H[enry]. W[hitney]. Bellows 32 Twentieth Street
George Bancroft 32 W. Twenty First Street
Henry James 58 West Fourteenth Street
J[oseph]. Woodward Haven, 31 Washington Square
Miss Anne C. Lynch 45 Ninth Street
Mrs Van Zandt, 80 Beekman Street.
John Jay, 124 Ninth Street.
Marcus Spring 51 Exchange Place
Henry P[hilip]. Tappan 4[?] Carroll Place
↑C[harles] A[nderson] Dana, & C.P. Cranch, 75½ MacDougal Street↓
Geo. Ripley Amity Street
C. C. Leeds 45 William⟨s⟩ Street
Mrs Mary H Hewes 30 Twentyfourth St near 4th Avenue
D[avid] D[udley] Field 328 Fourth Street
George Ripley
W[illiam]. L. Haskins, Esq. 6 Wesley Place South Second St
Williamsburgh
J[ohn] R[omeyn] Brodhead 32 Bond Street.
Mc Symon & ↑(Francis)↓ Macdonald, 1 Beaver St. New York [181]

[180] Emerson was in New York and Brooklyn to deliver 10 lectures between March 14 and April 2, 1850. William Burnet Kinney (1799–1880) was a journalist and diplomat; his wife, Elizabeth Clementine Dodge Stedman Kinney (1810–1889), a poet and essayist. Frederick William Ricord (1819–1897) was a man of letters, librarian, and author of textbooks; Lewis Morris was later, during the Civil War, a member of the Christian Commission for Brooklyn and Long Island. Huntoon and Dr. MacFarlan are unidentified.

[181] Of those listed who have not been previously identified or are not easily recognizable, Henry Whitney Bellows (1814–1882) was a Unitarian minister;

[192] *Beauty*

Did one ever see a beautiful woman, & not wish to look again? Could one ever see enough of a beautiful woman?

Personality

The reason why the highwayman masters the traveller is not his pistol but his personality. If the party attacked had really the superiority in character & in love ⟨it ^{n}⟩he could really conquer without arms. ⟨I⟩But he must be so charged & surcharged with love that he is as good a highwayman as the highwayman. You shall not match the pirate with a ⟨spooney⟩ ↑goody↓, but with a pirate (i.e. in natural [193] force) & more determined & absolute by dint of his heart than the other by help of his arms.

Col. Forbes ↑who ⟨fought⟩ ↑served↓ in Garibaldi's army, (Englishman)↓ told me of his being stopped by brigands in the night in carriage in Italy.[182] He ⟨y⟩got out of the coach & walked up to them. What do you want? no answer. Do you want money? Yes. Their guns were aimed. He walked directly up to them & they drew up their guns. My good fellows you have made a mistake. We are soldiers sent by the government to Sienna. We have no money, not even to pay our fare or dinner. It is all paid by order of the government. I wish you better luck the next time. Get in, get in, (to his companions) & tied in the horses, & off with "addio, a rive⟨r⟩derc⟨i⟩[.]"

Joseph Woodward Haven, brother of Susan who married Emerson's brother William in 1833; Anne C. Lynch (1820–1891), poet, and hostess for soirées for the New York literati; John Jay (1817–1894), lawyer, abolitionist, diplomat, one of the organizers of the Republican party; Marcus Spring, a Quaker and philanthropic merchant; Henry Philip Tappan (1805–1881), a Congregational minister and educationalist, who became the first president of the University of Michigan in 1852; Charles Anderson Dana (1819–1897), newspaperman and editor of the New York *Tribune*; George Ripley, founder of Brook Farm, a literary critic for the New York *Tribune*; David Dudley Field (1805–1894), a jurist; William L. Haskins, a merchant; John Romeyn Brodhead (1814–1873), a lawyer, diplomat, and historian; Francis MacDonald, a merchant. Nye, Van Zandt, Leeds, Hewes, and McSymon are unidentified.

[182] "(Englishman)" is in pencil. Colonel Hugh Forbes, an Englishman, commanded a regiment under Garibaldi at Terni in July, 1849. Where and when Emerson met Forbes has not been determined — possibly in England or Paris, 1848, or in New York, March, 1850.

[194] Brown's Indian, I saw in clay at Brooklyn. Good.[183]

I should like to set a sculptor to put a face on a church door that should draw & keep a crowd about it all the daytime by its character, good nature, & inscrutable meaning.[184]

They used to paint the heads on Bellows' Church every night a new colour[.]

[195] Concentration is that which distinguishes practical & successful people from others. Miserable Newmans & Bowens & Jenkses, & all sort of mediocrities, tower, by means of pushing their forces to a point, over multitudes of superior men, in Old & New England.[185]

See

Watson Haynes, the sailor, testifies that when he attempted to enlist the Clergy in his crusade against flogging in the navy, they replied, that their business was to preach the gospel, & not to interfere with the regulations of the navy.
And Webster thinks the gospel was to touch the heart, & not to abolish slavery.

[196] Washington Allston, when he painted blue sky, be⟨cam⟩gun as nature does, with a ground of deep black, & painted the light on that. And when he had occasion to paint a gem, he wrought on it as long as a lapidary.

[183] Henry Kirke Brown (1814–1886), best known for his equestrian statues, especially that of George Washington in Union Square, had done "Indian and Panther" in bronze in 1846. Emerson may have seen a replica in clay.

[184] This sentence, struck through in ink with a vertical use mark, is used in "Beauty," *W*, VI, 302.

[185] "Miserable Newmans . . . England.", struck through in ink with a vertical use mark, is used in "Power," *W*, VI, 80. Originally the use mark extended through the entire entry, but the mark through the first sentence is canceled with a finger wipe. Emerson's references are probably to John Henry Newman, Francis Bowen (see Journal TU, p. [67] above), and William Jenks (1778–1866), Congregational minister, orientalist, and author of *Comprehensive Commentary on the Holy Bible*, 6 vols. (1835–1838). Cf. Journal RS, p. [269] above.

Personality

Every body expects ↑the arrival of↓ a greater man, & will apologize for his own existence as soon as he comes. Every man is *his* [n] lieutenant.

---

[197] 1850 April

New York Tribune has a circulation of 60 000, Horace Greeley told me[.] [186]

C'est un père de famille; il faut vous en méfier. *Fourier.*

Fourier's walking stick was marked off into feet & inches[.]

La Série distribue les harmonies.

1. All the harmonies of the Universe are distributed in progressive series.
2. Les attractions sont proportionelles aux destinées.[187]
3. Analogie Universelle.

---

[198] *Philadelphia.* / April 6/ 1850 / [188]

I think a novel like "Shirley," must cultivate its readers.[189] It is very useful to each in ⟨its⟩his kind. I saw at once how a treati⟨s⟩se on the conduct of life would draw men to the exclusion of caucus & theatre. Describe & allow for the excessive virility of the mob in the hotels.

[186] See p. [86] above.

[187] This sentence, translated, is used in "Montaigne," *W*, IV, 183, 184, and "Poetry and Imagination," *W*, VIII, 41–42. See *JMN*, IX, 116. According to E. Silberling, *Dictionnaire de Sociologie Phalanstérienne* . . . (Paris, 1911), p. 308, "Ch. Fourier a résumé ces lois [re Passion] dans les deux formules suivantes: 1. Les attractions sont proportionelles aux destinées. 2. La série distribue les harmonies."

[188] Emerson lectured in Philadelphia on "England," "Eloquence," "Natural Aristocracy," "Instinct and Inspiration," and "Books" between April 3 and 11.

[189] Emerson wrote Lidian from Philadelphia that he read Charlotte Brontë's *Shirley* (1849) on April 5, and delighted "to think how it must cultivate its tens of thousands of readers" (*L*, IV, 194).

[199] Philadelphia

Market, Mulberry, Race, & Vine,
Chestnut, Walnut, Spruce, & Pine [190]

I read on a tombstone of "Elizabeth Roe died aged 25. She was,— Words is wanting to tell what she was,—Think what a true friend can be,—she was that." [191]

Pickering [192]

Did William Hazlitt say ("There is room enough in human life to crowd almost every art & science into it. If we pass no day without a line, visit no place without the company of a book, we may with ease fill libraries, or empty them of their contents. The more we do, the more we can do; the more busy we are, the more leisure we have.")[?] *Phila. paper.*

[200] "*Chinese upper ten arrived.* A lady belonging to the first class ⟨in⟩of society in China, arrived at N. Y. on Tuesday, with her maid servant, a distinguished Chinese Musical professor, & two very pretty Chinese children, in the ship I⟨ndi⟩anthe, from Canton, *via* Singapore"

[201] Addresses in Philadelphia
W[illiam]. H[enry]. Furness Pine Street above Broad
Walter Langdon
S[amuel] Bradford, Walnut St. between Schuylkill 6th and 7th
Dr Gouverneur Emerson
Judge W[illiam]. D Kelley
James Mott
Mrs Morrison 300 Mulberry St.[193]

[190] For a slightly different version of this couplet made up of street names in Philadelphia, see *JMN*, VIII, 334.

[191] Underlying the last two ms. lines of this entry, and continuing below them, is written in pencil: "⟨words⟩ She was — words cannot tell what she was — think what a friend can be, she was that". According to an entry in Notebook RT, p. [26], Emerson saw Elizabeth Roe's tombstone at Philadelphia.

[192] This word and the short rules above and below it are in pencil. Emerson's reference is probably to Charles Pickering (1805–1878) of Philadelphia and Boston, zoologist, author of *The Races of Man . . .* (Philadelphia, 1848).

[193] Of those listed who have not been previously identified, Walter Langdon was

[202] *Mem.* Dartmouth College commencement, 24 July next. Lewis W. Clark, sec.y

[203] I have made no note of these long weary absences at New York & Philadelphia. I am a bad traveller, & the hotels are mortifications to all sense of well being in me. The people who fill them oppress me with their excessive virility, and would soon become intolerable, if it were not for a few friends, who, like women, tempered the acrid mass. Henry James was true comfort,—wise, gentle, polished, with heroic manners, and a serenity like the sun.

[204] The worst symptom I have noticed in our politics lately is the attempt to make a gibe out of Seward's appeal to a higher law than the Constitution, & Webster has taken part in it.[194] I have seen him snubbed as "*Higher-law*-Seward." ↑And now followed by Rufus Choate, in his phrase, "the trashy sentimentalism of our lutestring enthusiasts."↓ [195]

Idealistic tendency of the Americans, Pegasus in Pound.

AZ 56

[205] *Higher Law* [196]

C. Sumner [197]

---

a Philadelphia merchant; Samuel Bradford, a lifelong friend from Boston and treasurer of two Philadelphia coal companies; Gouverneur Emerson, a physician and agriculturist. On his visit to Philadelphia in 1843, Emerson met William Kelly, then a young lawyer (*JMN*, VIII, 334), and Mrs. Morrison (*ibid.*, pp. 519 and 520, n. 3). The Philadelphia home of James Mott (1788–1868), Quaker abolitionist and husband of Lucretia, was a refuge for escaping slaves after passage of the Fugitive Slave Law.

[194] With this sentence, cf. "Worship," *W*, VI, 209: "In this country . . . the phrase 'higher law' became a political gibe."

[195] Rufus Choate (1799–1859) was a Boston lawyer and U.S. senator from Massachusetts.

[196] Below "Higher" is a tear with the remains of some red wax around it, showing that something was once attached to the page.

[197] Charles Sumner contributed several articles against slavery to newspapers, including the Boston *Courier*, in which he could have anticipated or recalled William Henry Seward's "Higher Law" speech of March 11, 1850.

[206] Lucretia Mott is the flower of Quakerism.[198] That woman has a unity of sense, virtue, & good-meaning perfectly impressed on her countenance which are a guarantee of victory in all the fights to which her Quaker faith & connection lead her. She told exceedingly well the story of her contest with the mob at Dover & Smyrna in Delaware, she and the wife of Mr[199] attending him down to the place where the mob were to tar & feather him, & it was perfectly easy to see that [207] she might safely go & would surely defend herself & him. No mob could remain a mob where she went. She brings domesticity & common sense, & that propriety which every man loves, directly into this hurly-burly, & makes every bully ashamed. Her courage is no merit, one almost says, where triumph is so sure.[200]

[208] ↑D. *Webster.*↓

I think there was never an event half so painful occurred in Boston as the letter with 800 signatures to Webster.[201] The siege of Boston was a day of glory. This was a day of petticoats, a day of imbecilities, the day of the old women La Veille. Many of the names very properly belong there,—they are the names ⟨of ideots,⟩ of aged & infirm people, who have outlived everything but their night cap & their ⟨co⟩tea & toast. But I observe some names of men under forty! I observe that very few lawyers have set their names. They are a ⟨‖ . . . ‖⟩prudent race though not very fond of liberty.

[209] D Webster

It seems 'tis now settled that men in Congress have no Opinions; that they may be had for any opinion, any purpose.[202]

[198] Lucretia Coffin Mott (1793–1880) was an American Quaker minister, abolitionist, and feminist lecturer.

[199] Following this word Emerson left a space of approximately 1¼ inches, undoubtedly for adding the name at a later date.

[200] In the lower right-hand portion of p. [207] are 2 pencil drawings of skeleton keys.

[201] Toward the end of March, 1850, nearly a thousand leading citizens of Boston, including Oliver Wendell Holmes, addressed a letter to Webster praising his Seventh of March speech in Congress supporting the Compromise of 1850, which included the infamous Fugitive Slave Law.

[202] This sentence, struck through in ink with a vertical use mark, is used in "Power," *W*, VI, 65.

Understanding is the one thing required in a member. Virtue is very good in country places, but impertinent in public men.

[210] "'Tis Virtue which they want, &, wanting it,
Honour no garment to their backs can fit."[203]
Ben Jonson. Cynthia's Revels [V, xi, 117–118, *The Works* . . . , 1716, I, 396.]

Raro antecedentem Scelestum
Deseruit pede poena claudo.[204]

The badness of the times is making death attractive.[205]

Andrew Fletcher "would give his life to serve his country, ↑but↓ would not do a mean act to save it."[206]

[211] At the Concord Celebration, I was struck with the talent of Everett & Choate, and the delight of the people in listening to their eloquence.[207] In the London ⟨C⟩Lord Mayor's banquet lately, Lord Lansdown & Lord Stanley are distinguished, I observe, in like manner. It is of great worth this stumporatory, (though much decried by Carlyle & others,) & very rare. There have been millions & millions ⟨&⟩of men, and a good stumporator only once in an age. There have been but a few since history began; Demosthenes, & Chatham, & Daniel Webster, & Cobden, [212] and yet all the human race are competitors in the art. Of course the writers prefer their own art. Stumporatory requires presence of mind, heat, spunk, continuity, humanity,

Governor Briggs is an excellent middle man, he ⟨speaks well⟩ looks

[203] See *JMN*, VI, 212.

[204] "Rarely does Vengeance, albeit of halting gait, fail to o'ertake the guilty, though he gain the start." Horace, *Odes*, III, ii, 31–32. See *JMN*, VI, 216.

[205] See *JMN*, VI, 203.

[206] Sir James Mackintosh, *A General View of the Progress of Ethical Philosophy* . . . (Philadelphia, 1832), p. 205, in Emerson's library. See *JMN*, VI, 205.

[207] At the Concord celebration, April 19, 1850, attended by several thousand persons, the speakers included Robert Rantoul, Ebenezer Rockwood Hoar, Rufus Choate, and Edward Everett. This annual Concord affair usually included a mock battle, and dinner given in a large pavilion.

well when speaking, & seems always just ready to say something good, but never said anything. He is an *orateur manqué*.

Rantoul had an inestimable advantage in belonging to the "locofoco party."[208] All his tediousness, [213][n] all his wearisomeness about "Ionic melody of the Father of History," a⟨ll⟩nd about the history of Islamism, indeed all those painful exertions which Collegians call "squirts," were patiently & even proudly heard by the mult⟨u⟩itude, who were proud of the College learning of *their*[n] man. In a Whig, the⟨y⟩se would have been intolerable, & all Scholars would have suffered from the supposed impatience of the company. Now, we sat quite at ease & irresponsible.

[214] *Superlative*

We used to hear of the bandying of compliments between Doctor Barrow & the Earl of Rochester, "Doctor, Your Servant."

"My lord, I am Yours to the shoe-tie."

"Doctor, I am Yours to the centre."

"My lord, I am Yours to the antipodes."

"Doctor, I am Yours to the lowest pit of hell."

"There, my lord, I leave you."[209]

Well; Oriental poetry seems to be in a perpetual spiral of this kind, the ambitious panegyrist ever striving to fetch one circle higher, to work one circle higher in his sweep toward the sun, & add one superlative more. See for abundant proof the panegyric ⟨of⟩by Ewhadeddin Enweri addressed to Shah Sandschar in Von Hammer p. 93,[210] ↑translated in my manuscript, "*Orientalist*," p [33]↓

[208] George Nixon Briggs (1796–1861), a Whig, was governor of Massachusetts, 1844–1851; Robert Rantoul, Jr. (1805–1852), political reformer and opponent of the extension of slavery, was elected to the senate in 1851 to fill Webster's unexpired term. He delivered an oration at the "Concord Celebration" referred to in the previous entry, on the 75th anniversary of the battle at Concord; it must have taken about two hours to deliver.

[209] Emerson's source for this dialogue between John Wilmot, 2nd Earl of Rochester, and Isaac Barrow, a recognized wit of the Restoration Court, is unlocated.

[210] Joseph von Hammer-Purgstall, *Geschichte der schönen Redekünste Persiens* . . . , 1818, pp. 92–93.

[215] ↑*Superlative*↓

To this style of Enweri's panegyric belongs also Chaucer's praise of Dido, & Richard of Devises' expostulation of Coeur de Lion with God[.][211]

[216] A bag of old copper coins. What can be more unpromising? And yet, being untied & poured out on the table, the company very soon became interested. Romulus & Remus suckled by the wolf were on one coin; *conservator*, with a warrior, and a goose by his side, on another; then Roman heads in a⟨n⟩ heroic style, and the sternness of the countenances, & the aquiline nose w⟨as⟩ere remarkable[.]

[217] The Elephantiasis or conceit, which destroys so many fine wits, as Brownson, Beecher, Mitchell, Jackson, & the rest, sends us back with new thankfulness to the Socratic wisdom, that the Pythian oracle pronounced him the wisest, because he knew that he knew nothing.[212] It is an organic distinction of intellects. "In reality, he is truly wise, who knows that he is not truly wise." Proclus.[213] [*The Six Books* . . . , trans. Thomas Taylor, 1816, II, p. 477]

[218] [blank]

[219] ↑Account of the Ionic Trophy Monument, excavated at Xanthus. By Sir Charles Fellows. London, Murray, 1848.↓

"Lycians were by the early inhabitants of the country known as Termelae or Termilians. [p. 1]
Xanthus, chief city, was called in the country itself, Arina, stood on a rock rising from river Xanthus." [p. 2]

"Early in the reign of Cyrus the Great, & during his conquest of the northern provinces of Asia Minor, his general Harpagus was employed in subduing Ionia & the southern provinces. Having conquered the maritime cities of Ionia, Harpagus landed at Halicarnassus, & proceeded to attack

[211] For Chaucer's "praise of Dido," see "The Legend of Dido," *The Legend of Good Women*, ll. 1004–1014, and Journal RS, p. [275] above, where Emerson also records the Richard of Devizes allusion.

[212] Emerson's references are probably to Orestes Brownson, Henry Ward Beecher, Francis Jackson (1789–1861), Boston businessman active in the Underground Railway movement, and the hydrographer Henry Mitchell (see Journal RS, p. [192] above).

[213] "Proclus." is circled in ink.

the Pedassians, at the foot of Mount Lida, ↑the↓ only Carians who opposed him. They submitted, & Harpagus, having incorporated the Ionians, Æolians, & Carians, with his forces, proceeded against the Lycians." [p. 3]

"In 1838 Sir⟨e⟩ C. F. ↑Charles Fellows↓ discovered Xanthus capital of Lycia. To the east on a high rock ½ a mile from the acropolis found the base of an important structure formed of blocks of scaglia; base measuring 33 ft in length, by 22 in width, was shown by a Turk the end of a slab of white marble with figures in relief. further researches in 1839, 1842, 1843, brought the whole ruins of the Monument to light" [pp. 4–5]

[220] Ten cities of Ionia supplied Harpagus with troops & we have between the columns ten statues of Venus, ↑Ionian Deity,↓ each borne by an emblem and these are all found on the coins of the maritime cities of Ionia crab of Cos, dove of Cnidus, snake of Miletus, dolphin of Myrina, phoca of Phocaea, shell of Pyrnus. Four lions at the angles represent the whole country of the Milesians [p. 10]
loose trowsers of Persians
a group on the apex of the pediment of 3 boys, representing, perhaps, Cares, Lydus, Mysus, the legendary founders

---

erected by the followers of Harpagus probably not later than, 500 B. C. [pp. 11–12]

[221] French Metre is ⟨$\frac{91}{100}$ of a yard⟩ 1.093633 yd.
or

La Madeleine is 100 metres long by 42 wide or, 109 yds by 45

The Parthenon is 72 yds. ↑1 ft↓ long, by 32 yds 2 ft

[222] ↑*Common Sense*↓

The Indians want interpreters & "blacksmiths to do such smith work as the Indians may require for those who by their good conduct entitle themselves to this favour."

Indian Agent's
Report p 954[214]

[214] *Annual Report of the Commissioner of Indian Affairs*, 1849, bound with the *Index to Executive Documents . . . 1849–1850*, 14 vols. (Washington, 1850).

Affirmative. Yes we must have the advancing foot. We see those who weakly repeat↑,↓ ⟨their⟩ or would repeat, their one experience, as, for example, their first love, their ↑boarding-↓school tie to one or two mates: it makes their conversation for the remainder of their life; or their college frolics, like poor [223] Shallow ↑in Shakspeare↓; or their college victories, like my friend U.[;] [215] or their religious conviction; each of these is a real development, hence its prominence[,] but is in nature one of a series, and to stop with it, or repeat it is suicide.

[224] Races. ⟨w⟩What Layard has to say on this subject especially on the art of the Shemitic race, is found Vol II p. 188 Nineveh[.] [216]
See Abdurahman's reflections on Layard's excavations.
↑Layard↓ Vol II [p]p. 70[–71] [217]

4 cents
12½
16½ [218]

[225] May 4, 1850.
It may be assumed that Nemesis is always levelling, & if by night you should chance to hear the burglar gathering your spoons into his bag, what is it but the caving in of a little sand or pebbles at the edge of the bank which is always falling. The levelling goes on surely at all hours, whether you watch it or no[.]

[226] Thackeray's "Vanity Fair" is pathetic in its name, & in his use of the name; an admission it is from a man of fashion in the London of 1850, that poor old Puritan Bunyan was ⟨wr⟩right in his perception of the London of 1650. And yet now in Thackeray is the

[215] Possibly Emerson's classmate Charles Wentworth Upham, who took part in the Harvard Commencement exercises, August 19, 1819.

[216] Austen Henry Layard, *Nineveh and Its Remains* . . . , 2 vols. (New York, 1849), p. 189.

[217] An open-ended oval line in ink is drawn above, down the left-hand side of, and below "Layard . . . 70".

[218] "4 cents . . . 16½" is in pencil. Above and to the left of these figures are two pencil drawings of boxes, with an oval knob sticking out at the top right corner of each box; "11¹" is written in pencil below the left figure, and "1¹" below the right.

added wisdom or skepticism, that, though this be really so, he must yet live in tolerance ↑of↓, & practically in homage & obedience to these illusions.

And there is in the book an admission, too, which seems somewhat new in literature, akin to [227] Froude's formula in the "Nemesis," that "moral deterioration follows on a diminished exchequer;" ↑See AZ 162↓ and State street thinks it is easy for a rich man to be honourable, but that, ⟨when a man is⟩ in failing circumstances, no man can be relied on to keep his integrity. And I felt in New York, that, from the habit of expense, the ⟨want of⟩ absence of religion, the absence of bonds, clanship, fellow-feeling of any kind, when a man ↑or a woman↓ is driven to the wall, there is less hope. It seemed as if Virtue was [228] coming to be *a luxury which few could afford*, ↑or↓ "at a market almost too high for humanity", as Burke said of "all that class of the severe & restrictive virtues."[219]

Is life coming to be a luxury which few could afford, or, as Burke said, "at a market almost too high for humanity?"

[229] For egotism, the continent is not wide enough. Is it coffee, he said, or is it pure intellect, pure of love, that makes this desart where I go? The world is not big enough to hide me.

Betaubende. Men want wine, beer, & tobacco, to dull or stupefy a little the too tender papillae. The body is sore with the too quick & harsh impressions of nature. The edge of ⟨them⟩all objects must be taken off. Close the eyes partly; they are painfully wide open. Drop them to the floor, & do not see every ugly man that goes by.

[230] It is the scholar's misfortune that his virtues are all on paper, & when the time comes to use them, he rubs his eyes & tries to remember what is it that he should do.

[219] "Speech on . . . A Plan . . . for the Economical Reformation of the Civil and Other Establishments." See *The Works of the Right Honorable Edmund Burke*, revised ed., 12 vols. (Boston, 1865–1867), II, 268. See *JMN*, VI, 163. "Thackerays 'Vanity . . . virtues.'" is struck through in ink with single, discontinuous vertical use marks on pp. [226], [227], and [228]; "State street . . . virtues.'" is used in "Wealth," *W*, VI, 91.

Hicks said, that to know what Allston was & was not, you should think of Michel Angelo, who, having to paint the Sistine Chapel, went down perhaps into the Pope's gardens behind the Vatican, & with a shovel dug out ochres, red & yellow, mixed them with glue, & water, &c. with his own hands, and, having[220] [231]–[232] [leaf torn out]

[233][221] ↑On Friday, 19 July,↓ Margaret dies on rocks of Fire ↑Island↓ Beach within sight of & within ⟨400 yards⟩ ↑60 rods↓ of the shore.[222] To the last her country proves inhospitable to her; brave, eloquent, subtle, accomplished, devoted, constant soul! If nature availed in America to give birth to many such as she, freedom & honour & letters & art too were safe in this ⟨wor⟩new world. She bound in the belt of her sympathy & friendship all whom I know & love, Elizabeth, Caroline, Ward, the Channings, Ellen Ho⟨p⟩oper, Charles K. N., Hedge, & Sarah Clarke. She knew more select people than any other person did & her death will interest more[.]

[234] Yet her taste in music, painting, poetry, character, would not be on universal, ⟨|| . . . ||⟩but on idiosyncratic grounds, yet would be genuine. ⟨Even⟩Then even the best people must have families, which they foolishly prefer.[223]

She had a wonderful power of inspiring confidence & drawing out of people their last secret.

The timorous said, What shall we do? how shall she be received, now that she brings a husband & child home? But ⟨if you⟩ she had only

[220] "Hicks said . . . having", struck through in ink with a vertical use mark, is used in "Power," *W*, VI, 72. Emerson may refer to the American painter Thomas Hicks (b. 1823).

[221] A poem, " 'On the Death of S. Margaret Fuller.' By G. P. R. James," cut out from a newspaper or magazine, is tipped in between pp. [230] and [233]. Matching marks on the clipping and the top of p. [233] show that it was attached at one time to p. [233] with a paper clip.

[222] Margaret Fuller, her husband, Giovanni Angelo Ossoli, and their child, Angelo Eugene Philip (born September 5, 1848), perished in the wreck of the merchantman *Elizabeth*, which sailed from Leghorn May 17. A gale on the night of July 18 off the New Jersey coast drove the ship off course; it sank about 4 o'clock the next morning. Only the body of the son was recovered.

[223] "Yet her . . . prefer.", struck through in pencil with a vertical use mark, is used in *Memoirs*, I, 268.

to open her mouth, & a triumphant success awaited her. [235] She would fast enough have disposed of the circumstances & the bystanders. For she had the impulse, & they wanted it. Here were already mothers waiting tediously for her coming, for the education of their daughters. ⟨S⟩Mrs Ripley thinks that the marriage with Ossoli was like that of De Stael in her widowhood with the young ↑*De Rocca*,↓ who was enamoured of her. And Mrs Barlow has ⟨|| . . . ||⟩an unshaken trust that what Margaret did, she could well defend.[224]

[236] Her love of art, like that of many, was only a confession of sympathy with the artist in the mute condemnation which his work gave to the deformity of our daily life; her co-perception with him of the eloquence of Form; her aspiration with him to a life altogether beautiful.

"Her ⟨love⟩ heart, which few knew, was as great as her mind, which all knew"—what ⟨young⟩ Jung Stilling said of Goethe, *E.H. says of Margaret; and, that she was the largest woman; & not a woman who wished to be a man.[225]

[237] ⟨This is ce⟩

It is the charm of practical men, that, outside of all their practicality, is a certain poetry & play, as if they led this good ↑war-↓horse "*Power*" by a bridle & preferred to walk, though they can ride so fiercely. Bonaparte is intellectual, as well as Caesar, so is Chadwick, & even seacaptains & railway-men have a gentleness when off duty.—↑A good natured admission that there are Illusions, & w⟨e⟩ho shall say he is not their sport?↓

We distinguish what we call "the cast-iron-men," who cannot so

↑* See E.H.'s remark *infra*, p 239↓ [226]

[224] Emerson could refer to either Sarah Alden Bradford Ripley, wife of Samuel, or Sophia Willard Dana Ripley, wife of George. Albert-Jean-Michel Rocca (1788–1818) married Mme de Staël in 1816—and perhaps earlier, secretly, in 1811. "And Mrs . . . defend." is used in *Memoirs*, I, 300.

[225] Jung Stilling's remark is quoted by Carlyle in "Schiller," *Fraser's Magazine*, III (March 1831), 138. See *JMN*, IV, 52. The entry on p. [236] is struck through in pencil with a vertical use mark; "Her love . . . beautiful." is used in *Memoirs*, I, 267; " 'Her ⟨love⟩ . . . man." is used in *Memoirs*, I, 300.

[226] The asterisks in the note and text, and "See . . . 239", are in pencil.

detach themselves, as dragon-ridden, thunder-stricken, & fools of fate, w⟨ho⟩ith whatever powers endowed.[227]

See AZ *226* ↑BO 37↓ Vanity Fair

[238] I have lost in her my audience. I hurry now to my work admonished that I have few days left. There should be a gathering of her friends & some Beethoven should play the dirge.
She poured a stream of amber over the endless store of private anecdotes, of bosom histories which her wonderful persuasion drew out of all ⟨of them⟩to her. When I heard that a trunk of her correspondence had been found & opened, I felt what a panic would strike all her friends, for it was as if a clever reporter had got und⟨r⟩erneath a confessional & agreed to report all that transpired there in Wall street.[228]

[239] O yes "Margaret & her Friends" must be written, but not post haste.[229] It is an essential line of American history

"Yes that is an example of a destiny springing from Character"
"I see your destiny hovering before you but it always escapes you" [230]

Elizabeth Hoar ⟨says⟩ quotes Mrs Barlow as saying, that Margaret never disappointed you. To any one whose confidence she had once drawn out, she was always faithful. She could (& she was alone in this) talk of persons & never gossip, for she had a fine instinct that

[227] The entry on p. [237], struck through in ink with a vertical use mark, is used in "Illusions," *W*, VI, 317.

[228] Underlying the ink entry on p. [238] is the same entry in erased pencil. "private anecdotes . . . it was" is struck through in ink with a diagonal use mark; "She poured . . . to her." is used in *Memoirs*, I, 312.

[229] In a letter to Caroline Sturgis Tappan on August 3, 1850, Emerson relates how the project of writing Margaret Fuller's biography was first suggested by William Henry Channing, who proposed calling it "Margaret and her Friends" (ms. Houghton Library). Emerson visited Channing and they agreed that Samuel Gray Ward, Channing, and Emerson should collaborate in collecting and editing materials, including the Sturgis-Fuller correspondence.

[230] "O yes . . . escapes you' ", in pencil, is struck through in ink with a vertical use mark; " 'Yes that . . . escapes you' " is used in *Memoirs*, I, 215; see *JMN*, IX, 297.

kept her from any reality & from any effect of treachery. The fact is she had large sympathies.[231]

[240][232] Dr ↑W.E.↓[n] Channing said to her, "Miss Fuller, when I consider that you are all that Miss P— wished to be, and that you despise her, and that she loves and honors you, I think her place in Heaven must be very high."[233]

Mrs Barlow has the superiority to say ↑of Margaret,↓ that the death seems to her a fit & good conclusion to the life. Her life was romantic & exceptional: So let her death be; it sets the seal on her marriage, avoids all questions of Society, all of employment, poverty, & old age, and besides was undoubtedly predetermined when the world was created.

[241] Our no
Lidian says, that, in the fly-leaf of ⟨M.'s⟩ ↑Margaret's↓ bible, was written a Hymn of Novalis.—

She had great tenderness & sympathy, as M[ary].M[oody]. E[merson]. has none. If M.M.E. finds out anything is dear & sacred to you, she instantly flings broken crockery at that.

"Nor custom stale
her infinite variety"[234]
[Shakespeare, *Antony and Cleopatra*, II, ii, 240–241]

Elizabeth Hoar says of Margaret, Her friends were a necklace of diamonds about her neck. The confidences given her were their best, & she held them to them;[235] that the honor of the ⟨c⟩Conversations was the high tone of sincerity & culture from so many consenting

[231] Underlying this ink entry, beginning "Elizabeth Hoar" is the same entry in erased pencil, with "E H says the quotes" for "Elizabeth Hoar ⟨says⟩ quotes". The entry, struck through in pencil with a vertical use mark, is used in *Memoirs*, I, 300.

[232] Underlying both ink entries on this page are the same entries in erased pencil.

[233] This sentence is used in *Memoirs*, I, 239.

[234] "Our no . . . Novalis.—" and "'Nor custom . . . variety'" are in pencil. Underlying "She had . . . that." are the same words in erased pencil, followed by a partially erased rule above "'Nor custom . . .'"

[235] "Elizabeth Hoar . . . them;" is used in *Memoirs*, I, 213.

individuals, & that Margaret was the Keystone of the whole. She was perhaps impatient of complacency in people who thought they had claims, & stated their contrary opinion with an air. For such she had no mercy. But though not agreeable, it was just. And so her enemies were made.[236]

[242]–[243] [blank]
[244] Cincinnati[237]
William Greene
Judge T[imothy]. Walker
Rev B[enjamin]. W. Barrett, Eighth St. 3d door east of Elm
A[insworth]. R[and]. Spofford
Davis B Lawler 113 Broadway
Manning F[erguson]. Force
J Mooder
Rev. A[bel]. A. Livermore
J[ohn]. C. Vaughan *Cleveland*
Mrs J. I[nman]. Haskins
J[oseph] B[rown] Ladd
C. H. Goddard
George Willey, *Cleveland*
J[ohn] B[ernhard] Stallo
J[ohn]. E. Goodson[238]

[236] Underlying "Elizabeth Hoar . . . made." are the same words in erased pencil.

[237] During his first lecturing in the west, Emerson gave eight lectures to the Cincinnati Literary Club between May 20 and June 3, 1850.

[238] William Greene (1797–1881) was a lawyer; Judge Timothy Walker, Harvard 1826, a founder of the Law School of Cincinnati College and editor of the *Western Law Journal*; Benjamin Fiske Barrett (1808–1892), Harvard Divinity School 1838, minister of Cincinnati's New-Church Society. Ainsworth Spofford (1825–1908) was a bookseller, publisher, and associate editor of the *Cincinnati Commercial*; Davis Lawler, a prosperous businessman; Manning Force (1824–1899), soldier, jurist, author, lawyer; Abel Livermore, minister of the First Unitarian Church. John C. Vaughan was a South Carolina abolitionist and editor of the free soil daily, *Free Democrat.* While in Cincinnati, Emerson saw Mrs. Inman Haskins and her famliy (*L*, IV, 204). Joseph Brown Ladd was a relative on the Haskins side of the Emerson family; Goddard, a school teacher; George Willey, an attorney, later trustee of the Cleveland Library Association. John Bernhard Stallo, whose *General Principles of the Philosophy of Nature* Emerson had read, was a

[245] *Chaucer* [239]

⟨Gentility⟩ Gentilesse. Wif of Bath's Tale

"But ⟨if⟩ ↑for↓ ye speken of such gentilesse" [I, 193; l. 1109]

Grisilde The Clerk's Tale
The Doctor's Tale

"Lo I ⟨n⟩Nature
Thus can I form & paint a creature" [I, 315; ll. 11–12]

pathos of the Man of Law's Tale—

"O my Custance, full of benignity,
O emperor's yonge daughter dear
He that is Lord of Fortune be thy stere!" [I, 151; ll. 446–448]

"The Destiny Minister general
That executeth in the world over all" &c

is in the Knightes Tale [I, 75; ll. 1663–1664*]

Abduction of the cock in the Nun's priest's Tale

Now wol I turn unto my tale agen,
The sely widow & her daughters two. [I, 436; ll. 4564–4565*]

[246] John E. Goodson

Ariadne's complaint of Theseus

"Meker than ye find I the beestes ⟨|| . . . ||⟩wild"

---

scientific writer and lecturer; John E. Goodson, otherwise unidentified, was knowledgeable in music (see Journal at the West, p. [24] below) and was introduced by Emerson to the Boston Athenaeum later in July, 1850. J. Mooder is unidentified.

[239] Emerson may or may not have quoted the lines that follow from *Chaucer's Canterbury Tales and Other Poems*, 2 vols. (London, n.d.), in his library; not a single line is copied exactly. Volume and page numbers in brackets are references to his edition; line numbers follow F. N. Robinson's edition. An asterisk means that a vertical line appears in the margin of Emerson's edition beside the quoted lines.

in the Legend of good women. ["The Legend of Ariadne," II, 165; l. 2198*]

In the Book of the Duchess the whole portrait of the ⟨Duchess⟩lady from

"⟨It⟩'Twere n better to serve her for nought
Than with another to be well." [II, 197; ll. 844–845*]

The Cuckow & the Nightingale
The Squire's Tale   Cambuscan
House of Fame   pictures of Chaucer himself

[247] [240] The elements have no nonsense of democracy; but at sea the need of life & death establishes a despotism the most complete the world knows. See *V 47* a fire breaking out in a village, &c.

A man of 45 does not want to ⟨take⟩ open new accounts of friendship. He has said Kitty kitty long enough.[241]

You look as if you had locked your trunk & lost the key[.]

[248] A larger dialectic, I said, conveys a sense of power & feeling of terror before unknown, & H[enry]. T[horeau]. said, "that a thought would destroy like the jet of a blowpipe most persons," & yet we ⟨turn⟩ apologise for the power, & bow to the persons. I want an electrical machine. Slumbering power we have, but not excited, collected, & discharged. If I should be honest, I should say, my exploring of life presents little or nothing of respectable event or action, or, in myself, of a personality. Too composite to offer a positive unity, but it is a recipiency, a percipiency.n [249] ⟨I⟩And I, & far weaker persons, if it were possible, than I, who pass for nothing but imbeciles, do yet affirm ⟨|| . . . ||⟩by their percipiency the presence & perfection of Law, as much as all the martyrs.

[240] P. [247] is in pencil.

[241] With this sentence, cf. *JMN*, VIII, 242: " 'Like the good Grandfather when they brought him the twentieth babe he declined the dandling, he had said "Kitty, Kitty" long enough.' "

Napoleon is of the other kind, aggressive, impatient to subdue, to appropriate, to plant his own quality. All sensible, all strong people are selfish (?)

"'Twere [n] better to serve her for nought
Than with another to be well."
Chaucer. [*The Book of the Duchess*, ll. 844–845]

---

[250] Every glance at society—pale withered people with gold--filled teeth, with scalps tied on, ghastly, & with minds in the same dilapidated condition, drugged with books for want of wisdom,—suggests at once the German thought of the Progressive God, who has got thus far with his experiment, but will get out yet a triumphant & faultless ⟨cre⟩ race.

[251] ⟨Government & a state is as natural to⟩ Men [n] as naturally make a state as caterpillars a web. They are born loyal, born to be governed, law abiding. I⟨t⟩f however they were more cultivated it would be less formal. It would be nervous, like the Shakers wh⟨ere⟩o all are inclined for a ride on the same day, & the horse comes up to the door.[242] ↑See *GH* 38
BO 17↓

The relation of men of ⟨genius⟩ thought to society is always the same. They abhor whiggism, they abhor rebellion. They refuse the necessity of mediocre men, that is, to take sides. They keep their own /equilibrium/self poise/, and the Ecliptic is never parallel [252] with the earth's equator.

Geniality, yes, very important, but so is substance. The ↑entrance of a↓ Scholar puts a whole insurance-office to flight. Every elegant loafer steals out when *he* comes in. He deplores this medusa-masque which scares every one from his side. The merchants he admires. ⟨L⟩See how long their conversation lasts in the rail-car! What can

[242] "men as . . . door.", struck through in ink with a vertical use mark, is used in "Worship," *W*, VI, 203. For the Shakers anecdote, see *JMN*, IX, 63.

they have to say, that is still so fresh, and so much? Yes. But they are unhappy as soon as they [253] are alone: And he is unhappy as soon as he is ⟨in company.⟩ ↑not alone.↓

In old ⟨boo⟩MS. I find—But the spiritualist needs a decided bias to the life of contemplation. Else, what prices he pays! poor withered Ishmaelite, Jew in his ghetto, disfranchised, odd one! what succors, what indemnities, what angels from the celestial side must come in to make him square! *GH* 75.

[254][243] Carlyle is the voice of London, a true Londoner with no sweet country-breath in him, & the instigation of the Pamphlets seems to be the night-walking in London streets.
⟨Re⟩ I fancy, too, that he does not wish to see any body whom he cannot eat & reproduce tomorrow in his pamphlet or pillory. A. ↑Alcott↓ was meat that he could not eat, & ⟨F⟩M[argaret]. F[uller], likewise, so he rejected them at once.[244]

But what a believer in laws[!]
Gravitation at 16 feet per second

[255] He shall have the book who has made its contents ⟨o⟩his own[.]

——

"Gaudent compositi cineres sua nomina dici" [245]
(Claudian)?

——

"Et Nati natorum, et qui nascentur ab illis." [246]
Virgil. [*Aeneid, III*, 98]

two mottoes for "*Genealogy*."

[256] 1850, August 25. I⟨t⟩n fifty or three hundred years, a poet; and the other demonstrations of the Divinity are as rare. In many

[243] P. [254] and "He shall . . . own" on p. [255] are in pencil.

[244] "Carlyle is . . . once." is struck through in pencil with a diagonal use mark; see *JMN*, X, 553.

[245] "Our dead ones laid to rest rejoice to hear their names." Ausonius, *Parentalia*, Bk. IV, l. 11; the Loeb text has "conpositi."

[246] "Even his children's children and their race that shall be born of them."

days, a pleasure; in many months, a concatenating thought; in years, a law, is discerned[.]

———

A few words ⟨are⟩ will give the curious the history of our age. What a fine subtle inward genius was C[harles].K[ing].N[ewcomb]., puny in body & habit as a girl, yet with an aplomb like a general's, never disconcerted. Yet he lived & thought in 1842 such worlds of life, all hinging too on the idea of Being or Reality, [257] on the one part, & Consciousness on the other; hating intellect with the ferocity of a Swedenborg, & valuing the Hero in ——— ——— Caroline! [247] Montaigne is his delight.

I find in Van Helmont the same thought which is the genius of Swedenborg too, & of Pascal, that piety is an essential condition of Science; that "the Soul understands in peace & rest, & not in doubting," and, one would say, that Van Helmont is a cross of Aristotle & Thomas A-Kempis.[248]

[258] [249] Yes the terror & repudiation of war & of capital punishment may be a form of materialism, as you say, & show that all that engages you is what happens to men's bodies.

See in M M E, too, the "sensitive Dr Channing's terror of war." [250]

[259] 1850

Sept. 1. Yesterday took that secluded Marlboro road with W[illiam]. E[llery]. C[hanning]. in a wagon. Every rock was painted "Marlboro." & we proposed to take the longest day in the year, & ride to Marlboro,—that flying Italy. We went to Willis's Pond in Sudbury & ⟨o⟩paddled across it, & took a swim in its water, coloured like sugarbaker's molasses. Nature, E. thought, is less interesting. ⟨I think⟩ Yesterday [n] Thoreau told me it was more so, & persons less. I think

[247] Probably a reference to one of Newcomb's manuscripts — see Journal TU, p. [251] above.

[248] The quotation is from van Helmont, *Oriatrike* . . . , 1662, p. 9. "I find . . . Science;" is used in "Progress of Culture," *W*, VIII, 228.

[249] P. [258] is in pencil.

[250] Emerson refers to his Notebook Mary Moody Emerson 1, pp. [18]–[19]; cf. also "Mary Moody Emerson," *W*, X, 422–423.

it must always combine with man. Life is ecstatical, & we radiate joy & honour & gloom on the days & landscapes we converse with.

[260] But I must remember a real or imagined period in my youth, when they who spoke to me of nature, were religious, & made it so, & made it deep: now it is to the young sentimentalists frippery; & a milliner's shop has as much reason & worth.[251]

At Latin School we found the longest word—honorificabilitudinibusque[.]

[261] I have often observed the priority of music ⟨in⟩to thought in young writers. And last night remembered what fools a few sounding sentences made of me & my mates at Cambridge, as in Lee's & John Everett's Orations.[252] How long we lived on "Licoo;"—on Moore's "Go where glory waits thee"; & Lalla Rookh; & "When shall the swan his death note singing."[253]

↑I still remember a sentence in Carter Lee's oration, "And there was a band of heroes, & round their mountain was a wreath of light, & in the midst, on the mountain top, stood Liberty, feeding her eagle."↓

[262] Mythology

Jove	Æther
Juno	Air
Neptune	Water
Vulcan	Fire
Metis	Counsel
Prometheus	Forethought
Epimetheus	Afterthought

[251] "Sept. 1 [p. [259]] . . . worth." is marked in pencil with a vertical line in the left margin, perhaps a use mark.

[252] Charles Carter Lee (1798–1871), a southerner, graduated from Harvard in the class of 1819. John Everett (1801–1826) was Edward's brother.

[253] Licoö occurs in "Song of the Tonga-Islanders"; see *JMN*, I, 352, 385. For " 'When shall . . . singing.' ", see Thomas Moore, "The Song of Fionnuala," l. 5.

[263] If we could be directly rich, namely, by insight; by relation to nature physical & metaphysical,—source of all wealth; by immense memory; by grandeur of thought; by imagination, & constructive power; ⟨f⟩by instant lead & sway of the spirits of men;—of course, we should not then need to be indirectly rich by farms, ↑mills,↓ goods, & money: nor need to remind others of our possible nobility, by showing that our father or uncle was rich & famous. But now the ⟨constant⟩ ↑⟨invincible⟩↓ habit of alluding to our wealth, or the wealth of our blood-relations [n] [264] ⟨shows the invincible belief⟩ ↑betrays an inveterate↓ persuasion that wealth is the natural fruit of nobility of soul.[254]

Hero.

How much Language thinks for us, witness that word *Hero.* What has Carlyle, what has Charles Newcomb added to the bare word, which has been the inspiration of them both, & will be of all the generous.

For an excellent specimen of the *nobile volgare eloquenza,* see Van Helmont, [*Oriatrike* . . . , 1662,] p. 34 the story of the poor woman.

---

[265] *My Method*

I write Metaphysics, but my method is purely expectant. It is not even tentative. ⟨I am r⟩Much less, am I ingenious in instituting *experimenta concis* to extort the secret, & lay bare the reluctant lurking law. No, I confine my ambition to true rep⟨e⟩orting, though I only get one new fact in a year.[255]

This, of course, is a corollary of the doctrine of Inspiration. But the Scholar may have the mechanical advantage of posting his observations, & so discovering Neptune by three records in his day book.

[254] "If we [p. [263]] . . . of our blood-" is marked in pencil with two wavy vertical use marks in the left margin; see Appendix I. The comma after "our possible nobility" is in pencil.

[255] This sentence is used in "Powers and Laws of Thought," *W*, XII, 11.

[266_1][256] I have, I think, in my letter to M[argaret]. F[uller]. an account of the negative method of the spirit[257] ↑AZ 36↓

↑H. W.↓ Convenient as money.[258]

Dreams. ↑Pr in Demonology?↓

⟨N⟩ A skilful man reads his dreams too, ↑for his self knowledge;↓ but not the ⟨particular⟩ details, but the quality. What part does he play in them? A cheerful, sufficient, manly part;—or, a poor, shuffling, disgraceful, & drivelling part.[259]

[267_1] "I use the word poet in the wide sense of the Germans, with whom the creator of Trim & Uncle Toby, though he never wrote a verse, is a greater poet than Cowper; and the Claims of Goldsmith to the high name are derived from the authorship of the Vicar of Wakefield."

Calvert.[260]

[266_2] *Vespucci of Florence.*

Everything must have its success, and lying also. And of impostors & false pretenders, I think Amerigo Vespucci's success in fastening his name on the New World, the flagrant example. He was a dealer in pickles & caterer for vessels at Seville, till 1499, when he embark↑ed↓ as a subaltern with Hojeda, in his second voyage. His highest ↑naval↓ rank was boatswain's mate in an expedition which never sailed.—[261]

Account of Viscount Santarem in "Daily Advertiser," Sept. 1⟨2⟩3, 1850[262]

[256] Emerson inadvertently repeated the page numbers [266] and [267]. The editors have supplied subscript numbers to identify the four pages.

[257] This sentence, and "H. W." below, are in pencil.

[258] "H. W." is possibly Hugh Whelan, a gardener and handyman who sometimes worked for Emerson.

[259] This paragraph, struck through in pencil with a diagonal use mark, is used in "Demonology," *W*, X, 9. "Pr in Demonology?" is in pencil.

[260] Perhaps George H. Calvert, Harvard 1823, poet, essayist, and friend of Margaret Fuller. The quotation is used in "Poetry and Imagination," *W*, VIII, 43.

[261] Except for the first sentence, this paragraph, struck through in ink with a vertical use mark, is used in "Cockayne," *W*, V, 152.

[262] Emerson refers to a review of E. V. Childe's translation of Manuel Francisco de Barros, 2nd visconde de Santarem, *Researches respecting Americus Vespucius, and*

↑*Geometer.*↓

A geometer is superior in pitching a camp, in laying out a garden bed, or in piling wood[.]

[267₂] In my romance, the lost prince shall be ⟨taught⟩sung to sleep & again taught to play *Quorum* by nonsense lullabies, which, when he comes to age, & to the mountains of his country, shall translate themselves into advertisement of those particulars he is to know.[263]

↑Geometer↓

In my romance, too, Talbot was to come as poor as Beranger's Romeo into town, yet was to build his plain cottage ⟨afterwards⟩ with such beauty as to eclipse the villas of the grandees, and to cut his walks in curves of inimitable beauty, curves too whose law he only knew; & to add a fountain-jet which tapped a mountain; [264]

[268] (BEN JONSON.)

Poetry

In "*Selection of Poems*" insert from Ben Jonson's Works Vol I p 11 lines from Geo. Chapman

7 lines from Ed. Heyward
286 Song
378 "Humour is now" &c
481.
512

His Voyages (Boston, 1850); the review appeared in the Boston *Daily Advertiser*, September 13, 1850. According to the reviewer, Santarem completely demolishes Vespucius' claims to a share in the discovery of any part of America and denounces the fraud by which he and his friends got his name imposed on the new world. Emerson's information in the preceding paragraph comes from the review.

[263] Edward Emerson notes that "*Quorum*", usually called "Corum," was a type of hide-and-seek game.

[264] "his plain cottage . . . grandees," and "jet which . . . mountain;" are struck through in ink with vertical use marks. For the story of Romeo, "minister of Raymond Berenger," and its source in Dante's *Paradise*, Canto VI, see *JMN*, VII, 478, and n. 560.

Vol II 115 *In Prose* the Dedication
236 Song
254
257
Vol III 131 On my first Son
137 To my Muse
141 To Lucy Countess of Bedford
153 The Club
164 The Child of Q Elizabeth's Chapel
166 *Uvedale* & Epitaph
177 To Penshurst
189 Song "Drink to me only"
⟨3⟩286 The Whole Masque of Beauty
303 Preface
393 Fame Song
394 Song
395 Lady of the Lake
427 Song
443 Song
453
[269] Ben Jonson; Vol. IV p 477
482
483
485
486
Vol V 142 Song
197 Poet's interest in beauty
NB. Vol. V contains more than any other [265]

[265] The continuation of the list of Ben Jonson's poems appears below a long rule across p. [269] after the entry "I praised . . . truth", which is written on the top third of the page. As the list is clearly a continuation of the one begun on p. [268], it is so printed here.

What Emerson meant by " '*Selection of Poems*' insert" is not known. All volume and page numbers apply to his edition of *The Works of Ben Jonson*, 1716, except for those to volume IV, which ends on page 455. Volume II is missing. Identifications where needed are preceded in the following description by volume and page number:

I, 11, begins with Chapman's "Now by the Shafts of the great Cyrrhan Poet"; I, 7, begins with Hayward's "To Ben Johnson [sic], on his Works"; I, 286, has a

I praised the rhymes of sun & shade, man & maid, in my Woodnotes.[266] ⟨How⟩But how far that can be carried! inasmuch as every substance is only the r⟨hyme⟩eflection or rhyme of some truth[.]

[270] The artist now should draw⟨n⟩ men together by praising nature, show them the joy of naturalists in famous Indian glens,—natural botanic gardens—in the profusion of new ⟨sp⟩genera,[n] that they could only relieve themselves by cries of joy; then the joy of the conchologist in his *helix pulcherrima*, whose elegant white pattern becomes invisible in water, visible again when ⟨taken⟩dry. ⟨Y⟩Let him unroll the earth & sky, & show the splendour of colour & of form: then let him, on the top of this delight, add a finer, by disclosing the secrets of intellectual law; tell them a secret that will drive them crazy; & things that require no system to make them pertinent, but ⟨make their own place, &⟩ make everything else [271] impertinent. I think, give me the Memory to tell of, or the Imagination,—& I could win the ear of reasonable people, & make them think common daylight was worth something.

---

song from *Cynthia's Revels*, I, ii, 65–75; I, 378, has lines from *Cynthia's Revels*, V, iv, 629ff.; I, 481, begins with *The Poetaster*, IV, ix, 98, and ends with V, i, 18; I, 512, begins with *The Poetaster*, "To the Reader," l. 209 and ends with l. 240, the last line; III, 141, has "On Lucy Countess of Bedford," not "To Lucy Countess of Bedford," which occurs later; III, 153, has "On Play-wright," and "Inviting a Friend to Supper," involving a kind of club for two; III, 164, has "An Epitaph on S. P., a Child of Queen Elizabeth's Chapel"; III, 166, has "To Sir William Uvedale" and "Epitaph on Elizabeth, L. H."; III, 303, has the preface to *Hymenaei*; III, 393, has a song about fame from *The Masque of Queens* beginning "Help, help all tongues to celebrate this wonder"; III, 394, has "Who, Virtue, can thy power forget," from the same masque; III, 395, begins with *The Speeches at Prince Henry's Barriers*, and the Lady of the Lake has the first speech; III, 427, has both "Nay, nay, you must not stay," and "Nor yet, nor yet, O you in this night blest," from the masque *Oberon, the Fairy Prince*; III, 443, has "How near to good is what is fair!" from *Love Freed from Ignorance and Folly*; III, 453, has from *Love Restored* "This motion was of Love begot," complete, and "Have men beheld the Graces dance," which ends on p. 454; V, 142, has "What he suffered" and "Her Triumph" from *Under-Woods*, but the second poem is marked by a penciled X in the left margin; V, 197, begins with "An Elegie" from *Under-Woods*, of which the first line is "Let me be what I am, as Virgil cold;".

Volume V contains *A Tale of a Tub*, *The Sad Shepherd*, *Under-Woods*, *Mortimer's Fall*, and eight masques.

[266] With this sentence, cf. "Woodnotes," *W*, IX, 54, ll. 160–161: "Primal chimes of sun and shade, / Of sound and echo, man and maid,".

Afterwards let him whisper in their ear the moral laws ⟨&⟩

> "more fair than heaven's broad pathway paved with stars
> Which Dion learned to measure with delight."
> [Wordsworth, "Dion," ll. 51–52]

[272] ↑*Quality and Amount*ⁿ See p 279↓

You must have fine disposition:—it is more essential than talent for the wor⟨d⟩ks of talent. Nothing will ⟨excuse⟩ ↑supply↓ the want of sunshine in peaches, and to make ⟨wisdom⟩ knowledge available or valuable, you must have wisdom.

But for the skepticism with which they charge us, I can well afford to us⟨t⟩e the inkhorn. I dip my pen in the blackest of the pot because I am not afraid of ⟨being⟩ falling into my inkpot, ↑like↓ Hathaway, who once told me that ⟨he⟩ in the[267] [273]–[276] [2 leaves torn out][268] [277] gain, which will jeopardize this social & secular accumulation[.][269]

William E. Forster of Rawden has married Jane M. Arnold of Foxhow[270]

Melioration

The Rosaceae in botany include, I believe, all our common fruit trees, as, the apple, pear, cherry, peach, & plum; & this gentle race does not appear in the fossil formations, being strict contemporaries with man.[271]

[267] The entries on p. [272] are struck through in ink with a vertical use mark. "You must . . . wisdom." is used in "Considerations by the Way," *W*, VI, 264; "But for . . . in the" is used in "Worship," *W*, VI, 201. Emerson's reference is possibly to Nathaniel Hathaway (d. 1836), Harvard 1818, or to the Hathaway mentioned in *JMN*, IX, 119.

[268] Emerson indexed p. [273] under Beauty and Genius, p. [274] under Culture, and p. [276] under Drill. In Notebook BO Conduct, p. [39], Emerson notes: "Genius is natural method, or real principle of order. Angelo Napoleon distribute chaos into beauty. AZ 273".

[269] "gain, which . . . accumulation", struck through in ink with a vertical use mark, is used in "Culture," *W*, VI, 165.

[270] The Quaker William Edward Forster entertained Emerson at Rawdon in 1847; Jane Arnold was Matthew Arnold's sister.

[271] This sentence, struck through in pencil with a vertical use mark, is used in "Country Life," *W*, XII, 145. For the next entry, see Journal TU, p. [145] above.

The Rose the only wild flower that is improved by culture

---

[278] *Beauty* ↑printed?↓

It is curious that we so ⟨tyrannically⟩peremptorily require beauty, and if it do not exist in any one, we feel at liberty to insult over ⟨it⟩ ↑that subject,↓ without end. Thus the poor Donkey is not handsome, & so is the gibe of all mankind in all ages, notwithstanding his eminent usefulness; whilst those handsome cats, the lion, leopard, tiger, are allowed to tear & devour, because handsome mischiefs, & are the badges of kings.[272]

[279] *Amount & Quality.*

Schelling's distinction, "Some minds speak about things, & some minds speak the things themselves"[n 273] remains by far the most important intellectual distinction, as the ⟨moral distinction or the⟩ quality is the important moral distinction. Amount and Quality.[n] Searching tests these! What does he add? and What is the state of mind he leaves me in? (For Quality, see p. 272)
For Amount, I look back over all my reading, & think how few authors have given me *things*⟨;⟩: Plato has, and Shakspeare, & Plutarch, & Montaigne, & Swedenborg.

[280] Goethe abounds in things, & Chaucer & Donne & Herbert & Bacon had much to communicate. But the majority of writers had only their style or rhetoric, their claudelorraine glass. They were presentableness, Parliamentariness, Currency, Birmingham. Wordsworth almost alone in his times belongs to the giving, adding class, and ⟨yet⟩ Coleridge also has been a benefactor.
I was looking lately at a new volume of Sermons of a preacher more intellectual [281] than most of his class, & thought, how wanting in ideas! How ill the whole printed ethics & religion, *now*, would compare with ⟨th|| . . . ||⟩books, in the same department, of Hooker, Donne, Herbert, Taylor, J[ohn]. Smith, Henry More! As ill would the Tribune Verses or the Lond. Athenaeum, or Fraser's Maga[zine].

[272] A pencil line is drawn across the top of p. [278] and down the left margin beside the entry — possibly a use mark.

[273] Quoted in Julius and Augustus Hare, *Guesses at Truth*, 2 vols. (London, 1827), II, 274. See *JMN*, VI, 195, and "Being and Seeming," *Lectures*, II, 307.

verses, compare with Donne; B Jonson; B[eaumont] & Fletcher; [274]

And all this in mere amount; in the modern, you can omit the whole without loss; in the old, somewhat is done & said in every piece.

[282] When I looked into Plutarch's Placita Philosophorum the other day, it was easy to see that Spinosa, Laplace, Schelling, & Oken, & Plato are /immortal/pre-existent/; [275] that these old men, in the beginning of Science, as we are apt to say, had little to learn from all our accumulation of facts.

Thales [*Plutarch's Morals* . . . , 1718] (Vol III 138)
Anaximenes [*ibid.*, p.] 138 Air is the Soul & source of things [276]
Empedocles

Pythagoras ([*ibid.*,] p 168) made the first discovery of the obliquity of the Ecliptic, but one *Oenipodes* of Ch⟨a⟩ios challenges to himself the invention of it.

Aristarchus ([*ibid.*,] p 174) "places the sun among the fixed stars; that the Earth is moved [283] about the sun by its inclination & vergency towards it; intercepts its light, & shadows its orb." What could Copernicus add?

[*Ibid.*,] p 175 *Thales* that the moon borrows all its light from the sun. (p 184 that the earth is globular)
[*Ibid.*, p.] 176 The moon's eclipse is perfectly known.[277]

[*Ibid.*, p.] 162 *Metrodorus*, infinite worlds in infinite space.[278]

[274] Emerson has left approximately 2 inches of space after "B & Fletcher;", undoubtedly so that he could add another name or two.

[275] "im-/mortal" is marked by ink lines, one resembling an opening parenthesis before "im-" and another forming a partial oval around "mortal", open on the left-hand side. "pre-existent" is written above the oval line.

[276] See *JMN*, X, 187–188.

[277] No such statement occurs on p. 176 of the 1718 edition; Emerson may have had in mind: ". . . and the *Moon* is then Eclipsed when she falls upon the shadow of the Earth . . . the Earth intercepting the Light of the Moon" (1718 ed., p. 176).

[278] With "When I [p. [282]] . . . space.", cf. "Fate," *W*, VI, 18: "No one can read the history of astronomy without perceiving that Copernicus, Newton, Laplace, are not new men, or a new kind of men, but that Thales, Anaximenes, Hipparchus, Empedocles, Aristarchus, Pythagoras, Oenipodes, had anticipated them;".

⟨Some of them⟩ There are in this motley list plenty of fancies, notions that lead nowhere but into corners; ⟨an⟩thoughts that have no posterity. Then comes one betraying a mind parallel to the movement of the world, &, as it is an aperçu of nature, so it can be applied again & again as an explanation.

[284] ↑Jenny Lind↓

Of what use for one to go to California who has a fine talent that ⟨address⟩reaches men? All the contents of California, Canton, India, Turkey, France, England, will be offered & urged on this Swedish girl with a fine voice.

↑*Leasts*↓

The man ⟨who⟩ under the hands of a dentist, thinks his mouth must comprise an extent of some acres.

⟨The three Horatii—Horace Greeley, Horace Mann, Horace Sumner⟩
↑Horatio Greenough
Horace Mann
Horace Greeley
Horace Bushnell↓

[285] Jenny Lind need not go to California, California comes to her. Jenny Lind needs no police. Her voice is worth a hundred constables, & instantly silenced the uproar of the mob.

Manners

My prayer to women would be, when the bell rings, when visitors arrive, sit like statues.[279]

I wrote that it is difficult to ⟨find⟩ begin the culture too young.[280] Mrs Barbauld said, they should never remember the time when they knew

[279] This sentence, struck through in pencil with a diagonal use mark, is used in "Social Aims," *W*, VIII, 85.

[280] See "Culture," *W*, VI, 164: "Let me say here that culture cannot begin too early."

not the name of God, [286] and a well born boy never did not know the names of the men of genius who are to be his escort & fraternity through life.[281] But the ⟨youths⟩ ↑young barbarians↓ I see ⟨&⟩knew nothing but footballs until they went to Latin School & to College, & at Cambridge first learn the names of the Laureates, & use them, as country editors do, awkwardly & barbarously. George Sand has the same thing in view when she points at the defective education of women. They learn casually & irregularly, [287] & are not systematically drilled from childhood to letters.

The Superlative. In the east, a war is as readily undertaken for an epigram or a distich, as in Europe for a duchy.[282]
The reader of Hafiz would infer that all the food was either candy or wormwood.

I learn from the Indian Agent that the Indian is now as keen a money-catcher as the white man.[283]

For the love of poetry, let it be remembered that my copy of Collins, after much search, was found smuggled away into the oven ↑in the kitchen.↓[284]

[288] Oct. 24.

A ride yesterday to Marlborough, though projected for years, was no good use of the day. That town has a most rich appearance of rural plenty & comfort; ample farms, good houses, profusion of apples, pumpkins, &c. Yellow apple heaps in every enclosure, whole orchards left ungathered, &, in the Grecian piazzas of houses, pumpkins ripening between the columns. At Gates's, where Dr C[hanning]. & Mr Jona. Phillips used to resort, they no longer keep a public house, closed it to the public last spring; —at Cutting's, though there

[281] Cf. *The Works of Anna Laetitia Barbauld*, 2 vols. (London, 1825), II, 333–334.

[282] This sentence is used in "Persian Poetry," *W*, VIII, 238.

[283] For Emerson's reading of a governmental Report on Indians, see p. [222] above.

[284] Emerson owned 2 copies of William Collins' *Poetical Works* . . . , London, 1815, and London, 1830.

were oats for the horse, there w⟨ere⟩as no dinner for men,—so we repaired to the chestnut woods & ⟨||...||⟩an old orchard, for ours. Ellery, who is a perpetual holiday, & ought only to be used like an oroflamme or a garland for Maydays & Parliaments [289] of wit & love, was no better today nor half so good as in some walks[.] [285]

It is wonderful how fast in politics cabbages ripen to pomegranates. Isaac Hill was the foulest of low libellous country newspaper editors, whose whole business was malignant lying, in Concord[,] New Hampshire, for money. Well, he has got into Congress, & into government-contracts, by his lying & subserviency. And he has been doing the same thing up to this day. But ⟨now⟩ his name has been before the public so long with "Honorable" attached to it, that Webster, who thoroughly knows what a dismal dog he is, now gravely has ⟨his⟩ ↑Hill's↓ letter in commendation of his ↑own↓ course, printed, as if it were Albert Gallatin's. ↑& the Daily Advertiser does not disdain to pick it up & print it.↓ [286]

[290] ↑*Practical Naturalist.*↓

↑Now that the ↑*civil*↓ Engineer is fairly established,↓ I think we must have one day a Naturalist in each ⟨of our⟩ village⟨s⟩ as invariably as a lawyer or doctor. It will be ⟨the⟩ ↑a new↓ subdivision of the ⟨doctor's⟩ ↑medical↓ profession. I want to know what plant this is? Penthorum What is it good for? in medical botany? in industrial botany↑?↓ Now [n] the Indian doctor, if there were one, & not the sham of one, would be more consulted than the diplomatic one. What bird is this? What hyla? What caterpillar? Here is a new bug on the trees. Cure the warts on the ⟨tree⟩ plum, & on the oak. How to attack the rosebug & the curculio. ↑Show us the poisons. How to treat the cranberry meadow?↓ The universal impulse toward natural science in the last twenty years promises this practical issue. And how beautiful

[285] This sentence is used in "Concord Walks," *W*, XII, 176.

[286] Isaac Hill (1789–1851), congressman, senator, and governor of New Hampshire, owned the *New Hampshire Patriot* and had been critical of Daniel Webster; the letter Emerson refers to is Hill's letter of April 17, 1850, to which Webster replied on April 20, reprinted in *The Writings and Speeches of Daniel Webster*, 18 vols. (Boston, 1903), VI, 550. The letter, signed "Isaac Hill," and Webster's reply were printed in the Boston *Daily Advertiser*, October 22, 1850.

would be the [291] profession. ↑C[harles]. T. Jackson,↓ John L. Russell, and Henry Thoreau, & George Bradford, ↑John Lesley↓ would find their employment. All questions answered for stipulated fees; and, on the other hand, new information paid for, as a newspaper office pays for news. To have a man of Science remove into this town, would be better than ⟨o⟩the capitalist who is to build a village of houses on Nashawtuck.[287] I would gladly subscribe to his maintenance. He is, of course, to have a microscope & a telescope.[288]

[292] [Index material omitted]
[inside back cover] [Index material omitted]

[287] Nawshawtuct, or Lee's Hill, is near the junction of the Assabet and Sudbury Rivers.

[288] With this paragraph, cf. "Country Life," *W*, XII, 161–162.

BO

1850–1851

Journal BO, a regular journal, follows chronologically after Journal AZ, beginning with entries in the same month, October, 1850, as Journal AZ ends with. Dated entries run from October 27, 1850 (p. [6]), to October, 1851 (p. [159]). In February and March, 1851, Emerson made two trips west to lecture, first, to Rochester, Buffalo, and Syracuse, later to Pittsburgh. Observations made on these trips are recorded in Journal at the West, pp. [43]–[60]. Beginning on p. [201] of Journal BO, heralded by the opening words "Bad times.", is a continuous sequence of entries, to the end of the book, on the Fugitive Slave Law, Daniel Webster, slavery and liberty, from which Emerson drew heavily for his two addresses on the Fugitive Slave Law, in May, 1851, in Concord, and March, 1854, in New York.

Journal BO is written in a hard-cover copybook, virtually identical to those designated TU and AZ. The cover, 17.7 x 21.2 cm, is of predominantly brown paper marbled with blue and yellow over boards, with a tan leather margin at the binding and forming two triangles at the top and bottom outer edges. The spine, of brown leather, now peeling, has traces of ink inscription. The front cover is inscribed "BO/1850" centered in ink on the upper portion of the marble paper, below which there is an ink rule, and "BO" is inscribed in ink in both upper and lower triangular corners. The back cover is not inscribed. The unruled pages measure 17.3 x 20.2 cm. The pages are numbered in ink except for the following 3 in pencil: 58, 59, 160. Fourteen pages are unnumbered: 61, 66, 121, 151, 205, 221, 223, 237, 247, 253, 255, 257, 269, 271; 6 pages are blank: 66, 131, 183, 251, 288, 289 (verso of flyleaf). Six leaves have been torn out, with fragments of the stubs still in the binding: pp. 91–92, 95–96, 113–114, 135–136, 137–138, 141–142. Page numbers 162, 163, 280, and 281 are repeated; after the latter, Emerson skipped the numbers 282 and 283, picking up his pagination again with 284. Five pages have been misnumbered, then corrected: 15⟨2⟩4, 22⟨2⟩4, ⟨259⟩260, 26⟨0⟩1, 28⟨4⟩5. Glued to the bottom left portion of page 53 is a newspaper clipping entitled "Growth of Massachusetts," reviewing the record of growth in dollars for several economic growth indices in Massachusetts for the ten-year period, 1840–1850.

[front cover] BO

BO
1850

BO

[front cover verso] ↑Examined throughout, May, 1878.↓

[Index material omitted]

"The wisdom of our laws," says Lord Coke, "is most apparent in this, that any departure from their established principles, although at the time wearing the specious appearance of advantage, never fails to bring ↑along↓ with it such a train of unforeseen inconveniences as to demonstrate their excellence, & the necessity of again having recurrence to them."

Speech of Sir F. Burdett, June, 1809, ap. Cobbett. [*Political Register*, vol.] XV. [January–June, 1809, p.] 973[1]

[i] ↑Gulistan lent —
see p. 94↓[2]

R.W. Emerson —
Oct. 1850

BO
Fara da se.

Higher Law.

Abp. Whitgift (of Canterbury), who had been Coke's tutor, sent unto his pupil, when the Queen's Attorney, a fair New Testament, with this message; "He had now studied Common Law enough: let him hereafter study the law of God."

Fuller's Worthies
II, 130.[3]

[1] Emerson apparently borrowed this volume of *Cobbett's Political Register* from the Boston Athenaeum October 25 to November 9, 1852; the quotation may have been entered here at that time. Kenneth W. Cameron lists the withdrawal of volume XVII twice, but the dates are identical. Elsewhere, he lists the withdrawal of volumes XV and XVII. See his *Ralph Waldo Emerson's Reading* (Raleigh, 1941), pp. 27 and 65.

[2] "Gulistan . . . 94" is in pencil.

[3] Thomas Fuller, *The History of the Worthies of England* . . . A New Edition . . . by J. Nichols, 2 vols. (London, 1811). Emerson borrowed volume 1 from the

[ii] ↑*Lord Mansfield*↓ [4]

Lord Mansfield said in the case of the slave Somersett, wherein *dicta* of Lords Talbot & Hardwicke had been cited to the effect of carrying back the slave to the W Indies,[n] "I care not for the supposed dicta of judges, however eminent, if they be contrary to all principle.[5] The dicta cited were probably misunderstood, and at all events, ↑they↓ are to be disregarded."
Campbell's Lives of Chief Justices
Vol II p 419 [6]

[1] *Blackstone's Commentaries.*
"The Creator has laid down only ⟨wa⟩such laws as were founded in those relations of justice that existed in the nature of things antecedent to any positive precept: these are, the eternal immutable laws of good & evil, x x xx. Such among others, are these principles, that we should live hones↑t↓ly, should hurt nobody, & should render to every one his due — to which three general precepts, Justinian has reduced the whole doctrine of law."
[2] "He has so intimately connected, so inseparably interwoven the laws of eternal justice with the happiness of each individual, that the latter cannot be attained but by observing the former." [7]

After this, he says of "Ethics or natural law,"

"This law of nature being coeval with mankind, & dictated by God himself, is of course superior in obligation [3] to any other. It is binding all over the globe in all countries & at all times. No human laws are of any validity if contrary to this; & such of them as are valid, derive all their force, & all their authority, mediately or immediately from this original." [Blackstone, *Commentaries on the Laws of England*, 1843, I, 27–28]

And he proceeds to say, that the enacting of human laws ↑annexing a

---

Boston Athenaeum September 6–11 and volume 2 September 11–October 27, 1852. The entry may have been made at this time.

[4] This index heading begins in the upper right margin of p. [ii] and continues onto the upper left margin of p. [1], breaking thus: "*Lord Ma/nsfield*".

[5] The paragraph to this point is used in "The Fugitive Slave Law" (1851), *W*, XI, 191.

[6] John Lord Campbell, *The Lives of the Chief Justices of England*, 2 vols. (London, 1849).

[7] Sir William Blackstone, *Commentaries on the Laws of England*, 2 vols. (New York, 1843), I, 27.

punishment to a crime, as *murder*↓[,] "do not superadd any fresh obliga[tion] n to abstain from its perpetration; nay, if any human law shd allow or enjoin us to commit it, we are bound to transgress that [4] human law, or else we must offend both the natural & divine." [*Ibid.*,] Vol 1. Section 2. [pp. 28–29]

Lord Coke. "That the common law shall control acts of Parliament & sometimes shall adjudge them to be merely void; for where an act of Parliament is against common right & reason, the Common law shall control it & adjudge it to be void."[8]

⟨S⟩ 8 Rep. f. 118a. *Apud* Lord Campbell's
Lives of ⟨Liv⟩the Chief Justices[, 1849].
Vol 1 p. 290 —

[5] Everybody forgets very fast, except those whose business it is to remember. I talked with Solomon W. Roberts at Pittsburgh —[9]

King James said to Coke C[hief]. J[ustice]. "My lord, I always thought, & by my soul I have often heard the boast that your English law was founded upon reason. If that be so, why have not I & others reason, as well as the judges?"

Lord Campbell's Lives
of Chief Justices[, 1849]
Vol. 1 p 272

↑*Higher Law*. See *infra* p. 7.↓

[6] October 27

No doubt, each man represents his set, and, if he have the accidental advantage of personal ascendency, which implies neither more nor less of talent, but merely the temperamental eye of a soldier or a schoolmaster, (as W. E.[10] had, & I had not; as E[benezer] R[ock-

[8] The entries on pp. [1], [2], [3], and on p. [4] to this point, are used in "The Fugitive Slave Law" (1851), *W*, XI, 190–191.

[9] Solomon White Roberts (1811–1882), canal and railroad engineer, was elected to the Pennsylvania State House of Representatives in 1848.

[10] Probably William Emerson.

wood] H[oar] has, & G. B.[11] has not,) then quite easily, & without envy or resistance, all his coadjutors & feeders will admit his right to absorb them. The Merchant lives by his clerks; the lawyer's authorities are ⟨all⟩ hunted up by his students. The geologist reports ⟨all⟩ [7] the surveys & discoveries of his subalterns: Commander Wilkes ⟨of the Exploring Expedition⟩ appropriates the results of all the naturalists attached to the expedition. Thorwaldsen's statue is finished by his stone cutters.[12] Dumas has journeymen, and Shakspeare, as I wrote long ago, & as W[illiam] E[llery] C[hanning]'s talk ran yesterday, was theatre manager, & used the labours of many young men as well as the playbooks.[13]

↑——↓

"Life is so short," E. ↑W[illiam]. E[llery]. C[hanning].↓ says, "that I should think everybody would steal."

"LEGĒS LEGUM ex quibus informatio peti possit quid in singulis legibus aut bene aut perperam positum aut constitutum sit."

Bacon.
De fontibus Juris. aph 6.[14]

[8] Rambling talk with H[enry]. T[horeau]. last night, in accordance with my proposal to hold a session, the first for a long time, with malice prepense, & take the bull by the horns. We disposed

[11] Possibly the Concord lawyer George Merrick Brooks, who lived opposite Emerson's house.

[12] When Dr. Charles T. Jackson, Emerson's brother-in-law, was studying the mineral wealth of the Lake Superior region in 1847, he was accused by the surveyor-general of Detroit of appropriating the work of his assistants without acknowledgment. While Charles Wilkes (1798–1877) wrote volumes I–V of the history of his expedition to the South Seas in 1838–1842 and received the general credit for the expedition, several assistants also wrote volumes of the history but without achieving Wilkes's fame. Bertel Thorvaldsen or Thorwaldsen (1768–1844) was a Danish sculptor.

[13] "No doubt . . . playbooks.", struck through in pencil and in ink with single vertical use marks on pp. [6] and [7], is used in "Power," *W*, VI, 58.

[14] Francis Bacon, *The Works* . . . , 10 vols. (London, 1824), VII, 440, in Emerson's library. Translated by Joseph Devey as: "[We shall, therefore, here offer, according to the best of our judgment,] certain laws, as it were, of laws; from whence an information may be derived as to what is well or what is ill laid down, or established by particular laws." Francis Bacon, *The Physical and Metaphysical Works* (London, 1853), p. 349.

pretty fast of America & England, I maintaining that our people did not get ripened, but, like the⟨se⟩ peaches & grapes of this season,[n] wanted a fortnight's more sun, & remained green,—whilst, in England, because of the density, perhaps, of cultivated population, ⟨th⟩ more calorie was generated, & more completeness obtained. Layard is good example, both of [9] the efficiency as measured by effect on the Arab, & in its reaction ⟨on him⟩ of his enterprise on him; for his enterprise proved a better university to him than Oxford or Sorbonne.

Henry thought, ⟨they, that is,⟩ the English, "all train⟨ed⟩," ⟨were⟩ ↑are↓ mere soldiers, as it were, in the world. And that the⟨re⟩ir business ⟨was⟩ ↑is↓ winding up, whilst our pioneer ⟨was⟩ ↑is↓ unwinding his lines.

⟨Seemed to me⟩ I like the English better than our people, just as I like merchants better than scholars; for, though on a lower platform, yet there is no cant, there is great directness, comprehension, health, & success. ↑So with English.↓

[10] Then came the difference between American & English scholars. H. said, the English were all bred in one way, to one thing, he had read many lives lately, & they were all one life, Southey, Campbell, Leigh Hunt, or whosoever, they went to Eton, they went to College, they went to London, they all knew each other, & never did not feel the ability of each. But here, Channing is obscure, Newcomb is obscure, & so all the Scholars are in a more natural, healthful & independent condition[.]

[11] My own quarrel with America, of course, was, that the geography is sublime, but the men are not; that the inventions are excellent, but the inventors, one is ashamed of; that the means by which events so grand as the opening of California, Texas, Oregon, & the junction of the two Oceans, are effected, are paltry, the filthiest selfishness, fraud, & conspiracy. As if what we find in nature, that the animalcule system is of ferocious maggot & hideous mite, who bite & tear, yet make up the fibre & texture of nobler creatures; so[n] all the grand results of history are brought about [12] by these disgraceful

tools.[15] I am afraid that the upper painters are not nice in their pencils.[16]

It was agreed, however, that what is called a success in America ⟨a⟩or in England is none; that their book or man or law had no root in nature, — of course!

But ⟨I demand an⟩in the face of the facts which appear as soon as a couple of meditative men converse, I demand another ⟨quest⟩ sort of biography than any of which we have experience, bold, experimental, varied, availing [13] itself of these unspeakable incomputable advantages which this meditative conversation at once discloses as within reach. Thus a man should do the feats he ↑so↓ admires. Why not suddenly put himself to the learning of tongues, &, like [George] Borrow, master in a few months, the dialects of Europe, Moor & gipsy, flash & patois: then, in another summer, put himself at the centre of Sciences, (which seems & is so easy when he meditates,) & read from simple arithmetic the activities of chemistry, of geology, of astronomy; paint out the beautiful botany, as Goethe wished, by figuring not only all actual, but all possible plants:
[14] then work out *apriori* politi↑c↓s,: then set himself, like Walter Raleigh, & Columbus, & Cabot, on the ⟨surve⟩finding & survey of new kingdoms or try, say rather, *and try*, after other months, all the melodies of music & poetry with the boldest ⟨& most undoubting⟩ adventure. Why ↑only↓ one Humboldt, one Crichton, one Pythagoras, one Napoleon, when every thinker, every mind, in the ascensions of conversation, sees his right to all these departments? We arm ourselves with a pretty artillery of tools now in our social national ⟨capacity⟩ ↑arrangements↓, ride four times as fast as our fathers did, ⟨write by [15] telegraph, weave & forge, steam the Atlantic in a week,⟩ ↑travel, grind,↓ weave, ⟨&⟩ forge, ⟨&⟩ plant, ⟨&⟩ till, & excavate by ⟨mighty⟩ formidable mechanical allies, — but we have yet not armed our selves with metaphysical ⟨weapons⟩ aids, with languages, sciences, calculi, ↑divination,↓ and a whole system of accomplish-

[15] "My own . . . tools.", struck through in ink with vertical use marks on pp. [11] and [12], is used in "Considerations by the Way," *W*, VI, 256.

[16] With this sentence, cf. *JMN*, VI, 126.

ments & culture tantamount to these new shoes & gloves & glasses & gimlets with which we have armed our bodies.[17]

Why are we so excellent at the humdrum of our musty household life, when quite aware of these majestic prerogatives? We do not try the ⟨po⟩virtue of the amulets we have. Thus we can think so much better, by thinking with a wise man. Yet we come [16] together as a pair of six footers, always as six footers, & never on the ground of the immensities, which we have ↑together↓ authentically & awefully surveyed. Why not once meet & work on the basis of the Immensities, & not of the six feet?
Yes, we have infinite powers, but cannot use them. When shall we attain our majority, & come to our estate? Henry admitted, of course, the solstice[.]

[17] I complain, too, that grandeurs do not ultimate themselves in grandeurs, but in paltriness. The idea of God ends in a paltry Methodist meetinghouse.[18]

Law-abiding, loyal, &c. O yes, the whole creation is made of hooks & eyes, of bitumen, of stickingplaster, &, whether your community is made in Rome, or in California; of saints, or of rogues & pirates, it coheres in one perfect lump.[19]

See AZ 251

Whiggism

"A stubborn retention of customs is a turbulent thing, not less than the introduction of new."

Lord Bacon [20]

[18] The consciousness of ⟨p⟩ wealth or of facility of obtaining

[17] "We arm [p. [14]] . . . bodies." is used in "Works and Days," *W*, VII, 163.

[18] With "I complain . . . meetinghouse.", cf. "Works and Days," *W*, VII, 160: "And there is no argument of theism better than the grandeur of ends brought about by paltry means."

[19] "creation is . . . lump." is struck through in ink with a vertical use mark. "Law-abiding . . . lump." is used in "Worship," *W*, VI, 202–203.

[20] Cf. "Of Innovations," *The Works*, ed. Basil Montagu, 3 vols. (Philadelphia, 1850), I, 32.

any article of pleasure or usefulness we want, will of course communicate, when habitual, a certain serenity to the features; &, when by experience, it is found to be the lot of few, a certain superiority also. But, much more, the consciousness of natural power as of an engineer, or of an excellent thinker & talker, to put ⟨the⟩ his thought & its proof before you, & compel belief & following, will, when habitual, communicate to the features that air of contentment & security which is the plume of victory.[21]

[19] The secret of eloquence is to realize all you say. Do not give us counters of base coin, but every word a real value[.]

[20] Scott had appreciation & ear, was a practitioner of poetry, or rightly equipped & facultied for a minstrel. Witness all his metrical romances, his minstrelsy of the Northern Border, Helvellyn, & Dinas Emlinn.[22] ↑See *CR* 64↓

[21] "But ha⟨f⟩lf of their charms with Cadwallon must die." [23]

[Scott, "The Dying Bard," l. 16, misquoted]

[22] "Truth needs no colour with his colour fixed
Beauty no pencil, beauty's truth to lay;
But best is best, if never intermixed."

[Shakespeare, Sonnet CI, ll. 6–8]

[23] ↑*Incapacity of melioration*↓

In experience, the narrowness of intelligent citizens irresistibly suggests the material hypothesis of mental acts, as of "channels often worn" of Locke, or, of the ruts of wheels. How many good people who can never understand a joke, or a trope, but remain staunch literalists after having been joked & poetised & musici⟨s⟩zed & rhetorized for eighty years.[24]

↑Days↓ [25]

And you think another day another scream of the eternal wail.

[21] This paragraph is struck through in ink with a vertical use mark; see Appendix I.

[22] This paragraph is struck through in ink with four diagonal use marks; see Appendix I.

[23] The quotation, struck through in ink with two diagonal use marks, is used in "Beauty," *W*, VI, 303.

[24] "How many . . . years." is used in "Culture," *W*, VI, 140.

[25] Added in pencil.

Dr Jackson's remedy for the headache is amputation.[26]

[24] Οι ρεοντες Beauty

"Ah! yet doth beauty, like the dial hand,
Steal from his figure, & no pace perceived." [27]
[Shakespeare, Sonnet CIV, ll. 9–10]

↑Printed in "Beauty" (Conduct of Life)?↓ [28]
Plutarch says, of the mechanics of Demetrius, "that they were of a princely kind, a certain grandeur of design appearing in all his works, and his very enemies were pleased with their beauty. They looked with admiration on his galleys of 15 or 16 banks of oars, as they sailed along; & his engines called helepoles (or towntakers,) were a pleasing spectacle to the very towns which they besieged."

Life of Demetrius Vol VII, p 20 [29]

[25] Οι ρεοντες
"Apollo is a god who defends or destroys, according to the nature of the case."

Muller, p. 195 [30]

"There is no rule in morals which does not bend to circumstances."

Frisbie.[31]

[26] "Pan is a god, and Apollo is no more." *Hazlitt*? [32]

[27] E[lizabeth] H[oar]. says, there are two kinds of love of our fellowmen; one, such as her mother has, of doing good to them;

[26] See Journal RS, p. [233] above.

[27] See *JMN*, VI, 42.

[28] Added in pencil and separated from the poetry above by a pencil line across the page.

[29] *Plutarch's Lives*, trans. John and William Langhorne, 8 vols. (New York, 1822). All but vol. VII are in Emerson's library.

[30] Carl Otfried Müller, *Introduction to a Scientific System of Mythology*, trans. John Leitch (London, 1844). See *JMN*, IX, 369.

[31] Levi Frisbie, *A Collection of the Miscellaneous Writings of Professor Frisbie . . .*, ed. Andrews Norton (Boston, 1823), p. 140.

[32] William Hazlitt, *Lectures on the Dramatic Literature of the Age of Elizabeth*, Lecture I (see *The Complete Works*, 21 vols. [London, 1930–1934], VI, 192). See *JMN*, VI, 69.

(a kind which she does not much value;) & the other, that of enjoying their talents & virtues & advantages.

[28] ↑Beauty↓
I saw a boy on the common seize an old tin milkpan that was rusting on a dirtheap & poising it on the top of a stick he held in his hand set it a turning & made it describe the most elegant imaginable curves.[33]

↑Printed I think?↓[34]
Beware of cheap wit. How the whole vulgar human race every day from century to century plays on the stale game of ⟨calling⟩ each man ↑calling↓ the other a donkey. The poor braying animal can never be mentioned [29] but all the company begin to rack their wits to make ⟨what they call their joke,⟩ their small joke in the ⟨wonderful⟩ intimation that their adversary is a donkey. This & the allusion that their adversary ⟨is going⟩ has gone or is going *to hell*, constitute the principal stock of wit of all companies in the known world.
↑E.g. Look at his picture,—how perfect!
Yes, it almost brays.↓

[30] *Columbus*
"While I was waiting for ships to convey me in safety, & with a heart full of joy, to your royal presence, victoriously to announce the news of the gold I had discovered,—I was arrested & thrown with my two brothers, loaded with irons, into a ship, stripped, & very ill treated, without being allowed ⟨to⟩ any appeal to justice. I was 28 years old when I came into your Highnesses' service, & now I have not a hair upon me that is not grey; my body is infirm, & all that was left to me as well as to my bothers has been taken

↑[turn to page 32]↓

[31] Astronomy
Kepler: 1. ⟨Elli⟩Orbits elliptical
2. Radius vector describes equal areas in equal times.
3. Squares of the periodic times as the cubes of their distances from the sun.

[33] This sentence, struck through in ink with a vertical use mark, is used in "Beauty," *W*, VI, 291.
[34] Added in pencil, then erased.

Newton. Every particle of matter gravitates to every other particle with a force inversely proportional to the squares of the distances.[35]

Newton "found that the weight of the same body would be twenty three times greater at the surface of the sun than at the surface of the earth."

Brewster [*The Life of Sir Isaac Newton*, 1831,] p 152

[32] away & sold, even to the frock that I wore.[n] ⟨(to my great dishonour.)⟩ I cannot but believe that this was done without your royal permission. x x x

With regard to temporal things, I have not even a blanca for an offering, & in spiritual things, I have ceased here in the Indies from observing the prescribed forms of religion. Solitary in my trouble, sick, & in daily expectation of death, surrounded by millions of hostile savages, full of cruelty, & thus separated from the Sacraments of our Holy Church, [33] x x x weep for me, whoever has charity, truth, & justice!" Letter to the K & Q Fourth Voyage of Columbus dated *7 July, 1503*.[36]

[34] The love of life is out of all proportion to the value set on a single day, and seems to indicate, like all our other experiences, a conviction in immense reserves & possibilities proper to us on which we have never drawn.[37]

↑printed in "Immortality"↓ [38]

Old age.

The world wears well. These autumn afternoons & well-marbled landscapes of green, & gold, & russet, & ↑steel-↓blue river, & smoke--blue New Hampshire mountain, are & remain as bright & perfect pencilling as ever[.]

[35] Sir David Brewster, *The Life of Sir Isaac Newton* (New York, 1831), p. 150, in Emerson's library.

[36] *Select Letters of Christopher Columbus, with Other Original Documents, Relating to his Four Voyages to the New World*, trans. and ed. R. H. Major (London, 1847), pp. 201–203.

[37] This sentence, struck through in ink with six diagonal use marks, is used in "Immortality," *W*, VIII, 337.

[38] "(Is not this paragraph used in 'Immortality'?" is written in pencil underlying "printed in 'Immortality' ", in ink.

[35] ↑Democracy↓

The objection of practical men to free institutions, is, that responsibility is shirked. Every power is exerted by a committee which is every moment comp↑o↓sed of new persons. If you should take an Irishman out of the street, & make him despotic in your town, he would try to rule it well, because it was his own. But these rotating governors & legislators go for their own interest, which is the only permanency they know. They go for their *party* [n] which is much more permanent than their office, & for their contract, or claim, or whatever private interest[.]

[36] ↑Fame↓

It is long before Tennyson writes a poem, but the morning after he ⟨prints it,⟩ ↑sends it to the Times,↓ it is reprinted in all the newspapers, &, in the course of a week or two, is as well known all over the world as the meeting of Hector & Andromache in Homer.

[37] ↑*Culture*↓

It occurred yesterday more strongly than I can now state it, that we must have an intellectual property in all property, & in all action, or they are naught. I must have children, I must have events, I must have a social state & history,—or my thinking & speaking will have no body & background. But having these, I must also have them not, (so to speak), or carry them as contingent and ↑merely↓ apparent possessions to give them any real value.[39]

See AZ 237

[38] The one thing we watch with pa⟨inful⟩thetic interest in our children is the⟨ir pos⟩ degree in which they possess recuperative force. When they are wounded by us, or by each other, when they go down at school to the bottom of the class, when they fail in competitions of study or of play with their mates, if they lose their spirit, & remember the mischance in their chamber at home,—it is all over with them, they have a check for life. ⟨So⟩But if they have that degree of buoyancy & resistance that makes light of these mishaps, & pre-

[39] This paragraph, struck through in ink with a vertical use mark, is used in "Culture," *W*, VI, 158.

occupies them with ever new [39] interest in the new moment, the scars rapidly cicatrize & the fibre is all the tougher for the wound.[40]

[40][41] To the plus man the frost is a mere colour[,] the rain[,] the wind is nothing[.][42]

W. Rice fancied that in the presence of certain persons the air smelled sweet and that when the milkman passed him on the road he perceived a certain odour, (as of animals)[;] also that when he & another youth occupied one chamber he used to hear knockings which he fancied made by other people, but now believed were occasioned by his companion & himself[.][43]

[41] Archimedes
Professor
Martial
Winckelmann

At Harrisburgh, 2 April, I met W[illiam]. L[ogan]. Fisher.[44] The good old Quaker believes in Individualism, still: so do I. Fourierism seemed to him boys' play; and so indeed did money; though he frankly admitted how much time he had spent about it: but a vital power in man, identical with that which makes grass grow, & the sweet breeze blow, & which should abolish slavery, & raise the pauper, that he believes in, against all experience. So we held sweet counsel together. A great curiosity he professed, & there again he met me, to know how the fact lies [42] in the minds of these poor men that were sitting in the front car. If there is a right statement, he felt & said, it

[40] This paragraph, struck through in pencil with a vertical use mark on p. [38] and a diagonal use mark on p. [39], and in ink with single diagonal use marks on pp. [38] and [39], is used in "Power," *W*, VI, 60–61.

[41] P. [40] is in pencil.

[42] "To the. . . . nothing", struck through in pencil with two diagonal use marks, is used in "Culture," *W*, VI, 154.

[43] "W. Rice . . . himself" is struck through in pencil with two diagonal use marks. W. Rice was probably a member of a Concord family.

[44] William Logan Fisher (1781–1862), a Quaker of Germantown, Pa., wrote *Pauperism and Crime* (Philadelphia, 1831), *History of the Institution of the Sabbath Day* (Philadelphia, 1846), and a family genealogy.

ought to satisfy Paddy too. We agreed that the power of Carolina over Massachusetts & the states, was in the personal force; and, therefore, it is a triumph of Individualism.

[43] Linnaeus. "Methodus naturalis ultimus finis Botanices est et erit." [45]

"Plantae omnes utrinque affinitatem monstrant, uti territorium in Mappa Geographica." [46] *Linnaeus*. Phil. Bot. 27

"Plantae quae genere conveniunt, etiam virtute conveniunt; qu[a]e ordine naturali continentur, etiam virtute propius accedunt." [47] *Phil. Bot.* 337

[44] ↑16 November.↓

Yesterday ⟨came⟩ I read Margaret's letters to C[aroline]. S[turgis].[,] full of ⟨n⟩probity, full of talent & wit, full of friendship, ardent affections, full of noble aspiration.[48] They are tainted with a female mysticism which to me appears so merely an affair of constitution that it claims no more respect or reliance than the charity or patriotism of a man who has just dined well & *feels good*. When I talked with G. H. I remember the eggs & butter seemed to have got into his eyes. In our noble Margaret her personal feeling colours all her judgments [45] of persons, of books, of pictures, & of the laws of the world. This is easily felt in common women & a large deduction is ⟨on⟩ civilly made on the spot, by whosoever replies to their remark. But when the speaker has such brilliant talent & literature as Margaret, she gives so many fine names to these merely sensuous & subjective objects, that the hearer is long imposed upon, and thinks so precise & glittering nomenclature cannot be of mere *muscae*

[45] "The natural method is and will be the ultimate goal in Botany" (Ed.). In this and the following two quotations, Emerson is quoting from *Caroli Linnaei Philosophia Botanica* . . . (Stockholm, 1751), p. 137, sec. 206; p. 27, sec. 77; p. 278, sec. 337.

[46] "All plants show a relationship, similar to a territory on a map, to each other" (Ed.).

[47] "Plants which are alike in genus are also alike in their medicinal virtues; those which are alike in their natural order are also more nearly alike in their medicinal virtue" (Ed.).

[48] In a letter to Caroline Sturgis Tappan dated "Concord, 17 Nov", Emerson acknowledges receiving from her a "parcel" of Margaret Fuller material (ms., Houghton Library).

volitantes,[49] but must be of some real ornithology hitherto unknown to him.

[46] This mere feeling exaggerates a host of trifles, as birthdays, seals, bracelets, ciphers, coincidences & contretemps, into a dazzling mythology; but when one goes to sift it, & ⟨see⟩find if there be a real meaning, it eludes all search. Whole sheets of warm fluent florid writing are here, in which the eye is caught by "carbuncle," "heliotrope," "dragon," "aloes," "Magna Dea," "limboes," "stars," & "purgatory," but can connect all this or any part of it with no universal experience.[50]

[47] Yet Margaret had her own mer↑i↓ts, & we shall not see her like. What a basis of earnest love of knowledge & ↑love↓ of character! Her ⟨s⟩decided selection so sagacious generally of her friends; in some instances, her election anticipates for some years any personal intercourse, & her fidelity to them, & generous forgiving appreciation. —She estimates society & its opinion, very well,—far better than so many people of talent. Her expensiveness creates tragic relation & feeling to it, [48] and thence with ill health comes all the unworthy sentimentalism of Destiny, Daemon, gold, & the cross.

Yet I draw from this warm refreshening [n] of faded tints on the canvas of the past admonitions always needed, that what spoke to the best minds among the young ↑in those years, 1838 to 1842,↓ was the spontaneous & solitary thought, & not the Birmingham ⟨Lustre⟩ Lacker,[51] and though Whiggism & cities condemn now, so did they then, & yet this somewhat [49] more real & strong than Whigs or cities, made itself a place & name, & compelled the reiterated visit & inquest of these, though they still pronounce it imposture, & will require new visit & inquest, until at last it is stamped as good whiggism & municipality.

It is curious that Margaret made a most disagreeable impression

[49] Literally, "flies flitting about"; technically, the term for spots before the eyes (see *JMN*, IX, 362).

[50] "Yesterday ⟨came⟩ . . . experience.", struck through in pencil with vertical use marks on pp. [44], [45], and [46], is used in *Memoirs*, I, 279–280.

[51] See Journal AZ, p. [27] above: "But Birmingham comes in, & says, 'Never mind; I have some patent lustre that defies criticism' ".

on her friends at first,—created a strong prejudice which she had then to conquer. It was so with Elizabeth H[oar]., with Sarah Clarke, & with me.

Sarah Clarke quotes Spenser's sonnet [50]

"Rudely thou wrongest my dear heart's desire
In finding fault with her too portly pride
The thing which I do most in her admire
Is of the world unworthy most envied;
For in those lofty looks is close implied
Scorn of base things & sdeign of foul dishonour
Threatning rash eyes which gaze on her so wide
That loosely they ne dare to look upon her.
Such pride is praise, such portliness is honor,
That boldened innocence bears in her eyes,
And her fair countenance like a goodly banner
Spreads in defiance of all enemies.
Was never in this world aught worthy tried
Without some spark of such selfpleasing pride." [52]

["Amoretti: or, Sonnets," Sonnet V]

[51] Alcott's bonhommie & sympathy would certainly have made him servile, but for his exacting ideal which makes the rich Bostonians & their belongings very commonplace.

A Journal is to the author a book of constants, each mind requiring, ↑(↓as I have so often said,↑)↓ to write the whole of literature & science for itself[.] [53]

[52] London
From London to Edinburgh 377 miles time of transit 8 hours
for ↑£↓3.5s.

↑47 miles per hour↓

---

[52] "It is curious . . . pride.' ", struck through in pencil with single vertical use marks on pp. [49] and [50], is used in *Memoirs*, I, 202, 239. The text of the sonnet in Emerson's edition, *The Works of Edmund Spenser* (London, 1844), differs considerably from the text he wrote down. He may have copied from another text or modernized from his own edition. "See my Spenser p. 425" has been added in the top margin of p. [50].

[53] The parentheses around "as I . . . said," are in pencil.

The sky of England is ashcoloured.[54]

Henry de Blois, ⟨was⟩⟨son⟩ nephew of Henry I., was made by him Bishop of Winchester A.D. 1128-9, & founded the ⟨Abbey⟩Hospital of St Cross, 1136.[55]

Winchester Cathedral has 556 ft of length by 290 of breadth of transept[.]

⟨T⟩In Winchester, Alfred was crowned & was buried.

The crypt in the Cathedral was ⟨partly⟩ built in part in the early part of the fourth Century.[56] The first story of the transept by Kenelwalch ⟨T⟩ A.D. $\frac{584}{648}$

Other parts of the Cathedral by Walkelyn in 1079; then Wykeham [57]

[53] ↑*Massachusetts.* *Boston.*↓

"A bag of coffee is as good as money at interest." [58]

Boston is within 15 hours of ⟨u⟩Upper Canada: [59]

in 2 or 3 years, Boston, N.Y., Phila., Baltimore, Charleston, Savannah, & Mobile, will be within 2 days of St Louis:

Then, in 10 years, St Louis within 4 days of San Francisco; & San Francisco within 17 days of ⟨rom⟩ China.

E H D
1850 [60]

[54] This sentence, struck through in ink with two vertical use marks, is used in "Land," *W*, V, 34.

[55] "& founded . . . 1136.", struck through in ink with two vertical use marks, is used in "Stonehenge," *W*, V, 289.

[56] "Winchester Cathedral . . . Century.", struck through in ink with a vertical use mark, is used in "Stonehenge," *W*, V, 289, 290.

[57] For "Henry de Blois . . . Wykeham", see *JMN*, X, 257–258.

[58] An ink line curves down in the left margin and underneath this sentence, resembling a large "C" with a long tail.

[59] "is" is preceded and followed by single vertical slash marks in ink.

[60] Glued to the lower left half of p. [53] is a newspaper clipping, "Growth of Massachusetts," giving statistics of the growth of property values, commerce, and manufactures in Massachusetts, 1840–1850, with boastful comparisons to Kentucky

[54] The best time is the present time.[61]

"Interest can not lie."

One thing at a time.

Store your wood as carefully as your hay.

[55] ↑το κινητικον↓ [62]

"All the rest of the Syracusans were no more than the body in the batteries of Archimedes, while he himself was the all moving & informing soul."

Plutarch. [*Lives*, 1822]
Marcellus p. 119 Vol III

Certain persons naturally stand for cities, because they will certainly build them; as, Erastus B Bigelow, Patrick Jackson, William Emerson of Bangor, Alvah Crocker, Samuel Lawrence, David Neal.[63]

↑See *CO* 88↓

[56] ↑*Leasts*↓

⟨We⟩ ↑Saint John & Fenelon↓ are made of ferocious animalcules; and Homer's poetry begins with whistle, jingle, & wordcatching; &

and Maine, the latter of which the "city of Boston alone could purchase . . . entire . . . and have the pretty sum of eighty millions left;".

[61] This sentence, struck through in ink with a diagonal use mark, is used in "Land," *W*, V, 37, and "Wealth," *W*, VI, 125.

[62] "the all-moving one" (Ed.).

[63] This sentence, struck through in ink with curved vertical and diagonal use marks, is used in "Fate," *W*, VI, 42–43. Of those listed who have not been previously identified, Patrick Jackson (1780–1847) was a Boston entrepreneur who built houses on Pemberton Square; William Emerson, a merchant and perhaps a distant relative, met Emerson first in 1834 and again in Bangor in October, 1846 (*JMN*, IX, 458); Alvah Crocker (1801–1874), manufacturer, politician, and railroad builder, helped found the Fitchburg Railroad in 1843; Captain David A. Neal of Salem was associated with the Reading and Illinois Central Railroads.

In the lower left-hand corner of p. [55] is a faint arrow in pencil, pointing downwards, as if to suggest that matter on p. [55] is continued on, or related to matter on, the next page.

revolutionary thoughts from single occasions & personalities; & the grandeur of centuries out of the paltriest hours; & the discoveries of stars & of gravity & of fluxions are attended by pitiful squabbles.

See Above p.11.

[57] ↑*Leasts*↓

En peu d'heure dieu labeure: "betwixt the stirrup & the ground I mercy asked, I mercy found" and drowning men have long moments.[64]

"But indeed to play well, takes up the whole man," says Evelyn speaking of the Irish harp.[65]

Architecture, the skeleton, the resistance to gravity & the elements —make one extreme;—florid petulant anthropomorphism which ⟨turns⟩ ↑carves↓ every ⟨ha⟩pumphandle & doorknob into a human face is the other; midway between these is the sobriety & grace of art.

↑See a passage on True Taste in *Art* p 27↓

[58][66] Manners
J[ohn] Q[uincy] A[dams] wavy iron li⟨a⟩mp band [GH 6]
Claverhouse feminine virility
English red dough full of culture & power [BO 61]
Sit like statues [AZ 285], if they come
never allude to sickness C 221

[64] "En peu . . . moments." is in pencil. The French sentence, from Goethe's *Dichtung und Wahrheit*, IV (in *Werke*, 1828–1833, XLVIII, 49) is used in "Works and Days," *W*, VII, 178. The quotation, from William Camden, *Remaines Concerning Britaine* . . . (London, 1636), p. 392, appears in Boswell's *The Life of Johnson* (see the Oxford, 1934, ed., IV, 212; *JMN*, V, 355).

[65] John Evelyn, *Diary and Correspondence*, ed. William Bray, 4 vols. (London, 1850–1852), II, 36, entry for Nov. 14, 1668.

[66] Except for "Creep-mouse manners.", which is added in ink, pp. [58] and [59] are in pencil.

people who are biped weeping willows
↑Creep-mouse manners.↓[67] [BO 59]

[59] 33000 miles seacoast in U S A
Pook's ship feat of intellect [TU 10]
love of beauty cannot be spared
Boston-Common-boys a kind of music or walking thro' the past in their earnest play. Music culture. Warren Burton —[68]

Rome 170 miles from Naples

Creep mouse manners of E S

boy to turn grindstone
Prof Wallraf of Cologne[69]

[60] ↑*Low tone.* Printed in Cultur[e]↓[70]
Mark of man of the world is the low tone, abates the brag,[n] dresses plainly; promises not at all; performs much; speaks in monosyllable & keeps close to the facts; conversation no more ambitious than the weather & the news; allows himself to be surprised into thought & learning & philosophy. How the curiosity is piqued by anecdotes of ⟨Rufus King⟩ a man in plain grey clothes being Rufus King; of General Taylor's slouching farmer dress & averseness to regimentals; of Webster in broad straw hat & fisherman's gear, at Marshfield; of Napoleon in plain suit in his glittering levee; of Beethoven, or Scott, or Wellington, or Newton, or any container of transcendant power passing for nobody. Of[n] Epaminondas who never says anything but will listen eternally.[71]

[67] Four items in the list are used in "Behavior," *W*, VI: "J Q A" (175–176), "Claverhouse . . . virility" (175), "never allude to sickness" (196), and "Creep-mouse manners" (185).

[68] Warren Burton (1800–1866), a member of Emerson's class at Harvard, was both a Unitarian and a Swedenborgian minister, once associated with Brook Farm.

[69] Ferdinand Franz Wallraf (1748–1824) bequeathed works of art to the Wallraf-Richartz Museum in Cologne. "E S" is unidentified.

[70] "Printed in Cultur" is in pencil, added perhaps by Edward Emerson.

[71] For "Of Epaminondas . . . eternally.", a paraphrase from "A Discourse

↑Goethe↓ prefers n trifling subjects & common expressions in intercourse with strangers, worse [61] rather than better clothes (a box-coat,) & behave a little more capricious than you are n See C 45 [72]

Go far & go sparing,
For, you'll find it certain,
The poorer & the baser you appear,
The more you⟨l⟩ look through still.[73]
B[eaumont]. & F[letcher]. [*The Woman's Prize, or, The Tamer Tamed,* IV, v]

Yet Montaigne thought to dress fine was a younger brother's ⟨tactics⟩ prudence. For the elder, his house & equipages sufficiently speak.

Call yourself preacher, pedler, lecturer, tinman, ⟨pen⟩grocer, scrivener, jobber, or whatever lowest name your business admits, & leave your lovers to find the fine name.

⟨See W's objection to being observed. *LM* 17⟩

In old countries a fine coat gets to be no distinction, & you find humourists. Englishman a face of red dough unexpectedly discloses wit, learning, personal intercourse with good men in all parts of the world, &c.[74]

[62] "for I know, King Harry would downweigh my best horse with gold, to know that I were condemned to die this day;" said Johnnie Armstrong to James V.[75]

Concerning Socrates's Daemon," *Plutarch's Morals . . .*, 1718, II, 411, see *JMN*, VII, 168.

[72] Emerson is in error; the cross-reference should read C 55 (*JMN*, V, 316), where he records Goethe's preferences in a quotation from *Briefe in den jahren 1768 bis 1832*, ed. Heinrich Döring (Leipzig, 1837), p. 66.

[73] "Mark of . . . still.", struck through in ink with a vertical use mark on p. [60] and two vertical use marks on p. [61], is used in "Culture," *W*, VI, 150–151.

[74] "⟨See W's . . . &c." is struck through in ink with two diagonal use marks; "In old . . . &c." is used in "Culture," *W*, VI, 152. See *JMN*, X, 428.

[75] Scott attributes the quoted matter to "*Pitscottie's History*, p. 145" in *Minstrelsy of the Scottish Border*, 1868, p. 254.

osafada
getinonimome
gikup [76]

Spell t*ea*p*o*t with two, & E*lderblow*tea with four letters.

Who is the first man named in the Bible? Chap. First.

[63] ↑*Games*↓
What reason to think Charles I consented to his execution?
They axed him whether he would or no.

Why is one playing blindman's buff, like sympathy? [77]
↑'Tis a↓ *Fellow feeling for a fellow creature.*

What reason to think the Carthaginians had domestic animals?
Virgil says, "*Dido et dux,*"
"*et pig-e-bit Elisa.*" [78]

How could the Children of Israel sustain themselves for forty days in the desart?
Because of the sand-wich-is there

Why is a kiss like a sermon?
two heads & an application

[64] *Where do the lines come from?* [79]

"Like angel visits, few, & far between."} ↑Blair &↓ ↑*Campbell*↓ [80]

[76] The same three words appear in Notebook OS, p. [121], under the heading "Hostler's Charges."

[77] Emerson recorded versions of this (and the above) question (but not the answers) in his journal for 1844 (*JMN*, IX, 91).

[78] The punning riddles are based, of course, on *The Aeneid*, IV, 124 or 165 — "Dido dux et Troianus," "Dido and the Trojan chief" — and IV, 335, "nec me meminisse pigebit Elissae," "nor shall my memory of Elissa be bitter."

[79] Evidence in the manuscript that the authors' names below were added at a later date suggests that this is another of Emerson's "games" — to write some lines and then look for, or later try to remember, the authors.

[80] Emerson's source is undoubtedly William Beattie, *Life and Letters of Thomas*

"There stands the statue that Enchants the world."
↑*Thomson.*↓ [*The Seasons*, "Summer," l. 1347, misquoted] [81]

"The feast of reason & the flow of soul."
↑I Satire of II Book of Horace↓
Pope ↑Vol III p 24↓ [82]

"Men are but children of a larger growth." [Dryden, *All for Love*, IV, i, 43]

Et nati natorum et qui nascentur ab illis. *Virgil*
↑Æneid↓ [III, 98] [83]

↑Eripuitque Jovi fulmen, s⟨v⟩ceptrumque tyrannis,↓ [84] ↑see *infra* p. 284↓

Eripuit que Jovi fulmen, viresque tonandi.[85]
Manilius [Astronomica,]
↑Lib. I, 104,↓

Of Caesar

Nil actum reputans dum quid superessit agendum.[86] [Lucan, *Pharsalia*, II, 657]

"Tu que tuis armis; nos te poteremur Achille!" [87] [Ovid, *Metamorphoses*, XIII, 130]

Campbell, 2 vols. (New York, 1850), I, 223, where a note compares the quoted line from Thomas Campbell's *Pleasures of Hope* (Pt. II, l. 378,) with a similar line in Robert Blair's "The Grave" (l. 589).

[81] See *JMN*, IV, 168.

[82] *Poetical Works of Alexander Pope*, 3 vols. (Boston, 1853), I. 128, in Emerson's library.

[83] See Journal AZ, p. [255] above.

[84] "And he snatched the lightning from Jove, and the scepter from tyrants" (Ed.). The quotation is enclosed by an oval line in ink. An adaptation of Manilius' line below, a variation of it was constantly associated with Franklin by the French. See *JMN*, VI, 208.

[85] "And he snatched the lightning from Jove, and power from the thunder" (Ed.).

[86] "[But Caesar] thought nothing done while anything remained to do."

[87] "And you, Achilles, would still have your own armour, and we should still have you."

Cited by Canning, *de* Percival,
and by Peel, *de* Canning.

Homo sum, nil humani &c [a me alienum puto.] [88]

↑*Terence*↓ [*The Self-Tormentor*, I, i, 25]

[65] *Readings for Ellen*

Archimedes in Plutarch

Professor Wallraf & the Medusa at Cologne

Lockhart's Count Alarcos.

"The Mighty Tottipottimoy," from Hudibras

Childe Dyring

Story of Belisarius [89]

[66] [blank]

[67] ↑Heat↓

In talking with Mr H↑oar,↓ last night, I found the advantage, as several times before in my life, of an inspiring subject. ⟨She⟩One likes in a companion phlegm that it is a triumph to dis⟨s⟩turb↑.↓ [90] ⟨& scatter.⟩ So when we find that our habitual aridity, incapacity, & egotism can be overpowered by a ⟨great⟩ ↑generous↓ cause, ⟨&⟩ all impediment brushed away, & our long unused faculties arouse in perfect array, &

[88] "I am a man. I hold that what affects another man affects me." See *JMN*, VI, 59.

[89] Plutarch's account of Archimedes is in his life of Marcellus. For Professor Wallraf, see p. [59] above; what "reading" Emerson may have intended about Wallraf is not identified; his bequest of works of art to the Wallraf-Richartz Museum in Cologne included a head of Medusa. "Count Alarcos and the Infanta Solisa" is the last ballad in J. G. Lockhart's *Ancient Spanish Ballads, Historical and Romantic* (London, 1842); "The Mighty Tottipottimoy" occurs in Samuel Butler's *Hudibras*, Pt. II, Canto II, ll. 421–422; "Child Dyring" is attributed to Scott in Emerson's *Parnassus* (Boston, 1874), pp. 336–337, but has not been located in Scott's works.

[90] This sentence is used in "Character," *W*, V, 135–136.

at last obedient to the will, so that we nobodies are ↑suddenly↓ great & eloquent, — we can forgive the long hybernation, & impute our past insignificance to the triviality of the game.

↑See what is said of logic of passion. *TU* 134
and *TU* 156, 155,↓

[68] Mr McLerque said, that the Englishman Wyatt told him, that Americans seemed to him to make a speech whenever they said any thing.[91]

[69] *Eloquence.* You shall not impoverish me. When Campbell he⟨re⟩ard ↑Joseph↓ Gerald defend himself in the court, at Edinburgh, he said to the stranger next him, "By heavens, sir, that is a great man." "Yes sir," he answered, "he is not only a great man himself, but he makes every other man feel great who listens to him."[92]

↑One might say this sometimes of Alcott.↓

---

barvatelle. *Rousseau*[93]

As soon as a man shows the power of expression like ↑Chatham,↓ Canning, or Erskine, or Choate even, all the great mass interests crowd to him to be their spokesman, so that he is at once a potentate.[94]

[70] Campbell

"His favorite maxim then was that a man accustomed to work was equal to any achievement he resolved on; & that necessity, not inspiration was the great prompter of his muse."[95]

[91] This sentence, struck through in ink with a vertical use mark, is used in "Culture," *W*, VI, 152. Wyatt may refer to the sculptor Matthew Cotes Wyatt; McLerque is unidentified.

[92] This anecdote occurs in William Beattie, *Life and Letters of Thomas Campbell*, 1850, I, 91. Joseph Gerrald (1763–1796), convicted of sedition in Edinburgh, 1794, defended himself in an address to the jury.

[93] For the anecdote about a roast barvatelle, in Rousseau's *Confessions*, see *JMN*, VI, 137.

[94] This sentence is used in "Eloquence," *W*, VIII, 117.

[95] William Beattie, *Life and Letters of Thomas Campbell*, 1850, I, 195. This sentence, struck through in pencil and in ink with single curved vertical use marks, is used in "Power," *W*, VI, 74.

Campbell received at the age of 20, in 1798, for the copyright of "Pleasures of Hope", sold out & out, sixty pounds in money & books. But the publishers for two or three years gave him £50, on every new edition.

For Goethe & Jean Paul's rec[e]ipts see N 43

[71] "Conversational powers are so much the rage in London, that no reputation is higher than his who exhibits them to advantage." [96] [Beattie, *Life and Letters of Thomas Campbell*, 1850, I,] 315

"I have been introduced to others of the nobility, but acquaintance with them I could never keep up. It requires a life of idleness, dressing, & attendance on ↑their↓ parties.[97] I exhausted a good deal of time & money in one London campaign. I got no object ↑attained↓ that I desired. I acquired certainly a very genteel circle of acquaintance, &c &c ↑x x x x↓ I have still retained acquaintance with one or two respectable families, but not in the highest rank. I think they are better hearted than the high gentry, & enter into one's affairs more in earnest." [*Ibid*.,] p. 414

———

"I feel as blithe as if the devil were dead." [*Ibid*., II, 50]

[72] "Dardis said, 'Tony spoke like a true Irishman, whose thoughts came always out of his head crooked, like a stick in a basin of water.'" [Beattie,] Life [*and Letters of Thomas Campbell*]. [1850,] Vol II p ⟨136⟩ 136

Horatio Nelson
Honor est a Nilo [98]

Napoleon Bonaparte
L e n o p o n e   b o n a r a p t a
5 6 1 4 3 7 8   9 10 11 2

Quid est veri⟨s⟩tas?
Est vir qui adest

[96] This quotation is struck through in ink with a vertical use mark; see Appendix I.

[97] "I have . . . parties.", struck through in ink with a vertical use mark, is used in "Aristocracy," *W*, V, 194.

[98] " 'Dardis said . . . Nilo" is struck through in pencil with a vertical use mark. "Horatio Nelson" and the remaining entries on p. [72] are in pencil.

N a p o l e o n Ναπολεων
α π ο λ ε ω ν
π ο λ ε ω ν
ο λ ε ω ν on
λ ε ω ν ο
ε ω ν ω
ω ν[99]

[73] Vernon semper viret

Ver non semper viret[100]

James Watt told Campbell in 1821 "that they had formed a plan for getting the king on board a steam vessel, on his voyage to Ireland. They watched him, & succeeded; and this little incident has raised the credit of this kind of vessels."[101] 'Tis like the way ⟨th⟩in which potatoes were introduced into France. The king was persuaded to wear a potato bloom in his buttonhole.[102]

↑Tools.↓

When will they arrive at manufacturing day out of night, time out of space & space out of time,[103]

For Mr M., — I will send my children to eat to him.
↑1878 And who was Mr M. & what his plan?↓[103a]

[99] The anagrams on p. [72] may be translated thus: "Honor is from the Nile" ("Honor . . . Nilo"); "Put it in wool, goods seized" ("Leno . . . rapta"); "What is truth? It is the man" ("*Quid* . . . adest"); "Napoleon, being a destructive lion, going about destroying cities" ("Ναπολεων . . . ων"). All four appear in *JMN*, VI, 149, which has "Lano" for "Leno"; for the third, see also *JMN*, I, 245.

[100] These two entries, in pencil, are partially overwritten by the paragraph in ink printed below. They were probably inscribed at the same time as the Latin and Greek anagrams on p. [72]. "Vernon semper viret" and "Ver non semper viret": literally, "the spring does not always flourish," but punned upon to mean "Vernon always flourishes" (Ed.). See *JMN*, VI, 67, where "vivet" should read "viret."

[101] William Beattie, *Life and Letters of Thomas Campbell*, 1850, II, 135.

[102] See *JMN*, VI, 211, 358.

[103] This entry is used in "Works and Days," *W*, VII, 161.

[103a] Added in pencil.

[74] *Superlative*

⟨Every⟩ ↑In the↓ newspaper ⟨describes the scorching⟩ every inve⟨n⟩ctive is scorching, every epithet withering, every argument annihilating, so it be directed against the newspaper's enemy.

Columbus

"Such is my fate that the 20 years of service thro' wh. I have passed with so much toil & danger, have profited me nothing, &, at this very day, I do not possess a roof in Spain that I can call my own. If I wish to eat or sleep, I have nowhere to go⟨,⟩ but to the inn or tavern, & most times lack wherewith to pay the bill."

Columbus, Letter describing his Fourth Voyage—to the King & Queen. p. 173[104]

[75] ↑*An Essay.*↓

One of the most agreeable surprises is to fall in with Mr ⟨Jackson⟩.[105] He comes in to borrow a light for his lamp or ⟨to⟩ a shovel of coals to kindle his fire, and finding you hunting up a law--case he happens, by the oddest coincidence, to know the very book & page where it is to be found: but when the conversation diverges to politics, he is so at home, that you think he must be a cabinet minister; & we should have set him down as such, but that there chanced to be a chemist in the room turning over Dr Black's pamphlet,[106] which drew ⟨Jackson⟩ to make an explanation of the new theory of heat, ⟨which drew⟩ ↑and the views he suggested inspired in↓ the whole company ⟨to⟩ a new interest in so wonderful a science; and I do not know how many crucibles & alembics would have been bought the next day, if Mr Unwin,[107] Mr [76] Cowper's friend, had not come in with some verses of that poet. These, being read aloud, led ⟨Jackson⟩ to warm praise, & then to discourse at large on modern & old poetry, which he esteemed the chief entertainment & ⟨a⟩the nobility of human wit, & drew from its flights a very curious evidence to the

[104] *Select Letters of Christopher Columbus . . . ,* 1847.

[105] Probably this name, also canceled twice more in this entry, below, is fictional.

[106] Perhaps a reference to the chemist Joseph Black, M.D. (1728–1799), author of chemical essays and *Lectures on the Elements of Chemistry*, 2 vols., (Edinburgh, 1809).

[107] Two curving lines are drawn down through this name, perhaps to cancel it. William Cawthorne Unwin (1745?–1786) was a confidant and correspondent of the poet Cowper.

existence of new & more penetrating senses, (to use his expression,) than ↑any↓ that metaphysicians reckoned as proper to the human subject. But glancing at my brother, — who is, you know, — a lover of mathematics, & ⟨especially⟩ ↑still more↓ of mechanics, he made a sudden transition in his talk to show [77] how extremes were likely to meet, & how all the ancient fables of poetry were likely to be realized by the French engineers, and, that he thought that ⟨all⟩ the fancy & imagination of the century to come would find sufficient food in following or predicting the progress of the useful arts, without any need of recourse to nursery giants, or ⟨bodiless⟩ ↑truncated↓ angels.[108] And ⟨p⟩for this opinion he gave such solid reasons & exhibited such a picture of the resources of the machine-shop & of the laboratory↑,↓ that we all felt as rich as kings↑,↓ & that the [78] human race were about to ⟨v⟩be [n] ⟨dism⟩ relieved henceforward from personal labor.

The Conversation afterwards took new & various directions, but our new friend was never at fault. He added so many vivid details that he seemed to have been present at every scene he described. It was certain that he had lived in many countries, & he seemed to have lived in different ages of the world, so intimate was his acquaintance with ↑so many↓ historical persons.

[79] *Charlestown Versatility*

Several years ago, how much we were entertained with Mr T↑yler.↓,[109] whom I knew only because he had rare books, & the only copy ↑in this country,↓ of Taylor's Aristotle in the "Nobleman's Edition." But when, one day, he stopped at my door, his feats were by no means exclusively platonic. He was hale, stout, & ruddy; said he could lift a barrel of flour, & carry it farther than any of his men. He was immersed in politics, & knew how the elections were going, & was stumping it every night for Gen. Harrison. He was an efficient member of an Engine-Company,[n] [80] was a ⟨rich & bustling⟩ ↑thriving↓ broker, & had lately been on a visit to some religious rela-

[108] The cancellation of "bodiless" and the added "truncated" are in pencil, as are the commas after "laboratory" and "kings" below.

[109] "yler" is added in pencil. Emerson's reference is probably to George Washington Tyler, a Boston merchant. See *JMN*, VIII, 91.

tions in New Hampshire, where ⟨having been mistaken by⟩ ↑he met with↓ a Baptist from Plaistow, who was so edified by his talk, that he mistook T. for a clergyman, & invited him to come over to Plaistow, & ⟨give them an evenin⟩ speak at a Conference; —an invitation, which T. accepted, to the horror of his cousins, went over on the appointed day, spoke an hour [81] & twenty minutes, left all the audience in tears, & heard, ⟨thr⟩two days after, that he had awakened a revival in the town!

Laomedon menacing the gods adds that he will cut off their ears.[110]
Feith[ius]. Antiq[uitatem]. Hom[ericarum]. *ii.* 20.
ap. ↑J.↓A. St John. [*The History . . . of Ancient Greece*, 1842,]
Vol 3. p 9

[82] Happy those, say I, who can live in the present moment! who do not use their memories, or sulkily reflect, "well, I shall have my revenge by & by, when you want a pilot, a shoemaker, a lawyer," or whatever craftsman ⟨|| ... ||⟩poor devil chances to be! Yet it must be, that strong determination of force into one practice, (which is essential to a good performance,) must leave the channels dry & unhandsome. Then it needs, that nature should add to the child, whom she has thus wronged for the good of the whole, [83] a comely marble front,—that when he is not a good *man*,[n] he may still be an agreeable statue, not ⟨impeding⟩ ↑encumbering↓ but adorning the room. An appletree bears fruit but once in a year; but, covered with ice, or under bare poles ⟨in⟩ rattling in the January wind, it is never offensive. How I hate these past & future birds, who frown & attitudinize in the cheerful parlour!

The great difference in men as in children is, that one class enter at once & cordially into the game, & whirl with the whirling world, & the other passive, cold-handed, ⟨h⟩cold-hearted, are & remain bystanders, do not [84] engage, & at most only suffer[n] themselves to be dragged on by the irresistible humor & vivacity of the rest, who can carry this dead weight.[111]

[110] This sentence, struck through in pencil with two vertical use marks, is used in "Worship," *W*, VI, 205. The anecdote occurs in Homer's *Iliad*, XXI, 455.

[111] "The great . . . weight.", struck through in pencil with a vertical use mark

The initiative, the affirmative, is in one, & ↑is↓ not in another, as one horse has the "go" in him, & another in the whip. "On the neck of the young man ⟨sits no⟩sparkles no gem so gracious as the spirit of adventure."[112] Import into the Dutch ↑of N. Y.↓ or the planters of Virginia a colony of Yanke⟨s⟩es with seething brains, whose heads are full of steamengines, triphammers, & all the combinations of pulley, crank, & toothed wheel, & every thing begins to shine with values. In every company there is not only the affirmative & negative sex, but in both men & women a deeper & more important[n] [85] sex of mind, namely the ⟨performing & the⟩ inventive ⟨&⟩ ↑or↓ creative class of both men & women, & the uninventive or accepting class.[113]

[86] ↑Canning said, "In the H of Commons you must repeat or you must expatiate. Choose which."↓

Mr Hoar told me that the lawyers said of Judge Prescott, that he repeated his argument once for each juror.[114]

One Idea *Monomaniacs.*
Monotones.

Kinds or specialties. Besides the genealogists; Besides sheriffs, like the Dartmouth man; and antiquaries or pamphlet-collectors like Mr Chandler; and Dead-men's-men like Mr Walker of London; — I recall the man who so amused the stagecoach once from Middleborough with his contrivances for defending ⟨an⟩his own coffin in his grave from bodysnatchers.[115] He had contrived a pistol to go off pop from this end, & a pistol pop from that end⟨,⟩ ↑(of the coffin,)↓ [87]

on p. [83] and in pencil and ink with single vertical use marks on p. [84], is used in "Power," *W*, VI, 55–56.

[112] Joseph von Hammer-Purgstall, *Geschichte der schönen Redekünste Persiens* . . . , 1818, p. 91. See "Translations," *W*, IX, 301.

[113] "The initiative . . . class.", struck through in pencil and in ink with single diagonal use marks on pp. [84] and [85], is used in "Power," *W*, VI, 57–58.

[114] William Prescott (1762–1844), father of the historian William Hickling Prescott, was judge of the Boston Court of Common Pleas, 1818–1819.

[115] For the sheriff who marshalled Dartmouth processions, see *JMN*, VII, 209; for the Unitarian minister Chandler of Lowell, Mass. (otherwise unidentified), see p. [110] below. "Graveyard Walker" is noted in Journal RS, p. [65] above.

& he was plainly spending his life in the sweets of ⟨vengea⟩ ⟨r⟩the revenge he was going to take hereafter on the ⟨an⟩young doctors that should creep to his graveyard.

The pounders on one string till it is heard.[116] *O* 163

⟨T⟩Like my ↑quaker↓ friend, Mr [William Logan] Fisher, who thinks the cause of crime in New England is the Churches.

Z[A] 103

And Mr Phillips in London who thought the ruin of England lay in Musical Concerts.[117]

See also *LM* 158, the ↑Mr↓ Lazarus that worshipped the sun.
Reid of ventilation. *LM* 9;

Brindley of navigable canals.[118]

"Aristomachus of Soli devoted to the study of bees 58 years" *J. St John* [*The History . . . of Ancient Greece*, 1842,] Vol II. p. 291

So Democratie Pacifique thinks the Lorrainen ↑not Normandic↓ is the pure Austrasian[,] the Frank of Franks, & that la pipée is the training of a revolutionist[.] [119]

[88] ⟨W⟩The selfish philosophy.

Après moi, le Déluge, was the legitimate expression of it. Who said this? Tallyrand or Metternich? ↑or Louis Quinze↓

"Mais, donc, c'était M. votre pere qui n'était pas si bien." [120]

[116] With this entry, cf. "Culture," *W*, VI, 132: "But worse than the harping on one string, nature has secured individualism. . . ."

[117] This sentence is used in "Culture," *W*, VI, 132. Emerson's reference may be to Samuel Phillips (1814–1854), English journalist, novelist, and owner of the newspaper *John Bull*. See *JMN*, X, 293, and Journal RS, p. [65] above.

[118] James Brindley (1716–1772) was an English engineer of canals; Emerson referred to him in his 1837 lecture, "Trades and Professions" (*Lectures*, II, 125).

[119] *Démocratie pacifique* was a daily paper published in Paris, 1843–1851.

[120] This, and the French quotation immediately below, Emerson attributes to Talleyrand in Notebook T (*JMN*, VI, 363).

"Il faut avoir connu Madame de Stael, pour connaitre tout⟨e⟩ le bonheur d'aimer une femme bête."

One Idea

"The air is full of poniards," said Fouché [121]

When Robt Owen crossed the French frontier, Dr Arnott said, he fell in with a sentinel, who cried out, "who goes there?" and he replied "the ⟨|| . . . ||⟩Creature of Circumstances." [122]

[89] Every saying & deed of his was marked by ⟨goo⟩wisdom,—great pieces of good sense, ⟨one⟩all of the same composition, one as like another as one basket of coals is like another basket; only this serves to keep us warm & boil the pot today, ⟨&⟩as that did yesterday.

↑*One Idea*↓

When Bonaparte saw David's picture of the straits of Thermopylae, he said; "A bad subject; after all, Leonidas was turned."

Lord Coke "values Chaucer only in as far as the Canon's Yeoman's Tale illustrates the statute 5 Hen. IV. c.4. against alchymy" Lord Campbell's Life of [Sir Edward Coke, *Lives of the Chief Justices*, 1849, I, 337]

Sanctorius passed 20 years in a Balance & proved [123] N 134
———— grew old in experimenting on yellow pigment [124]

[90] I thought last night that the right Conclusion of my

[121] Louis Antoine Fauvelet de Bourrienne, *Private Memoirs of Napoleon Bonaparte, During the Periods of the Directory, the Consulate, and the Empire*, 4 vols. (London, 1830), III, 99. See *JMN*, IX, 159. This sentence, struck through in ink with five diagonal use marks, is used in "Culture," *W*, VI, 132.

[122] Emerson heard this story when he dined with Neil Arnott (1788–1874), Scottish physician and inventor, on his English tour, May 4, 1848; see *JMN*, X, 253–254.

[123] "Lord Coke . . . proved", struck through in ink with a vertical use mark, is used in "Culture," *W*, VI, 132.

[124] In Journal GO, p. [14], Emerson writes: "M. Bouvieres, (I believe it is) spent his life in producing a good yellow pigment." M. Bouvieres is unidentified.

Chapter on polit. economy is the statement, that the merchant is right, —infinitely right; —all his rules are laws of the Universe, and there only needs a liberal expounding of them. He is a reduced copy,— you must give us a new draught of the size of life. The Merchant's economy is a coarse symbol, but a faithful one of the soul's economy. It is to spend for power & not for pleasure, it is to invest ⟨instantly all its⟩ income⟨s⟩, that is to say, to take up particulars into generals, days into integral eras—literary, emotive, practical,—[125] [91]–[92] [leaf torn out]

[93] man raised to his highest power.[126]

[94] Thomas Melloy, Berwick, Maine

To George H. Burleigh, Great Falls N. H I am to lend my Gulistan, to be forwarded by Express, Court St.[127]

Miss Anna ↑P.↓ Jones, 28 Chestnut Street.
Miss Lucy Howes Chestnut Street
Miss S[ally]. Gardiner at Mrs Talbot's—
Miss Edna Littlehale[128]

[95]–[96] [leaf torn out]

[97] Dec. 9— ↑*Economy*↓

As I read my lecture on *Wealth*, the other night, I came to a passage where I wished to insert something to the effect that our economics in house & barn rapidly show their relation to the laws of

[125] The entry on p. [90], struck through in pencil and in ink with vertical use marks, is used in "Wealth," *W*, VI, 125.

[126] This conclusion to a passage which included matter from the missing leaf is struck through in ink with a vertical use mark. Cf. "Wealth," *W*, VI, 126–127. See Journal TU, p. [148] above.

[127] Emerson has left approximately two inches of space between "by" and "Express," presumably to add matter later. See p. [i] above; Burleigh is unidentified.

[128] The four women in this list were probably students in Margaret Fuller's Conversation group in 1839–1840 (and perhaps at other times); see *Memoirs*, I, 338. Ednah Dow Littlehale (1824–1904), who married Seth Wells Cheney in 1853, was an author, abolitionist, and suffragette.

geometry, of morals, & of natural history—"The gods are to each other not unknown[.]"[129]

[98][130] It is strange that superior persons should not feel that they have some better resistance against Cholera, than avoiding green peas & sallads. Life hardly seems respectable, if it has no guaranteeing task, no duties, affections ↑that constitute a↓ ⟨&⟩ [n] necessit⟨ies⟩y ⟨of continuance⟩ of existing.

———

It seems as if the lime in their bones alone held them together. Y 245

[99] One should dignify & ⟨i⟩entertain & signalize each journey or adventure by carrying to it a literary masterpiece, & making thorough acquaintance with that, on the way, as, the Figaro of Beaumarchais; the Vita Nuova [n] of Dante; the Bride of Corint⟨t⟩h of Goethe; the 47th Proposition of Euclid; ode of Horace or of Hafiz; & so on, Clouds of Aristophanes, The trilogy of Æschylus.[131]

[100] December 1850
I thought, the other day, at Mr S.'s lecture, that Luther's religious movement was the fountain of so much intellectual life in Europe; that is, Luther's conscience animating sympathetically the conscience of millions, the pulse passed into thought, & ↑ultimated itself in↓ Galileos, Keplers, Swedenborgs, Newtons, Shakspeares, Bacons, & Miltons↑.↓ ⟨were produced⟩ The morale of New England makes its intellect possible. At the South, they are really insensible to the criminality of their laws & customs. They are still semibarbarous, have got but one step beyond scalping.

[101] But I like to see the growth of material interests here, as power educates its potentate. As long as our people quote (even in thought) English standards, they will miss the beauty of power.

[129] Homer, *Odyssey*, V, 79. The quotation is used in "Character," *W*, III, 112; see *JMN*, VIII, 177.

[130] The entries on p. [98] are struck through in ink with a vertical use mark; "It is strange . . . existing." is used in "Worship," *W*, VI, 232.

[131] "One should . . . Hafiz;" is struck through in ink with a vertical use mark; cf. "Inspiration," *W*, VIII, 295.

But let Benton, Clay, Houston, Freemont, or whatever hard head Wisconsin or Utah sends, half orator[,] half assassin, to represent its wrath & cupidity at Washington, and the disposition of territories of public lands, & the necessity of balancing & keeping at bay the snarling majorities of German, of Irish, & of native millions, will bestow promptness, address, & reason at last on our buffalo-hunter, & [102] authority & majesty of manners.[132]

Intellect

Identity

But what is the cause asked M[ary]. M[oody]. E[merson]. once, that, after the sleep of ages, the human mind should arouse like a giant refreshed by slumber? [133]

The analogy belongs to my series.

Intellect & morals "Illimitable prospects can best apply euphrasy to the understanding, &c." M M E p 149 [134]

"Religion, that home of genius, will strengthen the mind, as it does the character." p 31

[103] Make yourself necessary to somebody.[135]

Columbus. at Veragua 1503

"I was alone on that dangerous coast suffering from a fever & worn with fatigue. All hope of escape was gone. I toiled up to the highest part of the ship, & with a quivering voice & fast falling tears, I called upon your Highnesses' warcaptains from each point of the compass, to come to my succour; but there was no reply. At length, groaning with exhaustion, I fell asleep, & heard a compassionate voice address me thus. 'O fool, & slow to believe & serve thy God, the God of all. What did he do more for Moses [104₁] or for David, than he has done for thee? From thine infancy he has

[132] "But I . . . buffalo-hunter, &" is struck through in ink with a vertical use mark; "As long as . . . manners." is used in "Power," *W*, VI, 62–63.

[133] "after the sleep . . . slumber?" is struck through in ink with a vertical use mark; cf. "Religion," *W*, V, 216: "Man awoke refreshed by the sleep of ages."

[134] The page references here and in the next entry are to Notebook Mary Moody Emerson 1.

[135] This sentence is used in "Considerations by the Way," *W*, VI, 275.

kept thee under his constant & watchful care. He gave thee for thine own the Indies, & thou hast divided them as it pleased thee. He gave thee also the keys of those barriers of the Ocean sea which were closed with such mighty chains. [105_1] Turn to him & acknowledge thine error[,] his mercy is infinite. The privileges promised by God he never fails in bestowing, nor does he ever declare after a service has been rendered him that such was not agreeable to his intention or that he had regarded the matter in another light. His acts answer to his words, and it is his custom to perform [136] [106_1] all his promises with interest.' I heard all this as it were in a trance, but I had no answer to give in definite words, & could but weep for my errors. He who spoke to me, whoever it was, concluded by saying, [107_1] 'Fear not, but trust: All these tribulations are recorded on marble, & not without cause.' "

Letter to K. & Q⟨.⟩↑ueen-↓ [*Select Letters of Christopher Columbus* . . . , 1847,] Fourth Voyage↑.↓ 1503] Major p. 185 [137]

[104_2] *Music*

Ce qui ne vaut pas la peine d'être dit, on[n] *le chante;*[138] *et ce qui ne vaut pas la peine d'être chanté, on le danse.* ⟨T⟩So the *Courrier des Etats Unis* extends the *mot* of Beaumarchais.

[105_2] 18 Dec.

Charles Newcomb came, & yesterday ⟨‖ . . . ‖⟩departed, but I do not ask him again to come. He wastes my time. 'Tis cruel to think of. Destroyed three good days for me! The Pythagoreans would have built a tomb for him⟨.⟩↑—the unique, inspired, wasted genius!↓

[106_2] *Prudence.*

Qu'un ami véritable est une douce chose

Qu'un ami véritable est une douce chose

[136] An ink line in the right margin is drawn beside "The privileges . . . perform".

[137] This passage, which begins on p. [103], undoubtedly was written after the entries inscribed on the upper portions of pp. [104], [105], [106], and [107]; on each of these pages an ink line is drawn across the page and the Columbus entry is continued below each line, thus running continuously through the bottom halves of pp. [104]–[107]. "*Columbus*" is written below the line on the left side of pp. [106_1] and [107_1]. The Columbus entry is printed here as a continuous sequence, and the entries on the upper portions of pp. [104]–[107] follow below.

[138] Beaumarchais, *Le Barbier de Séville*, I, ii.

Qu'un ami véritable est une douce chose

"Qu'un ami véritable est une douce chose!"
[Jean de] La fontaine. [*Fables Choisies*, Livre Huitième, XI, "Les Deux Amis," l. 26]

[107₂] "je crois que le ciel se moque de nous, car il donne toujours au voisin le sort qui nous conviendrait."

Quand on paie, c'est pour ↑se↓ dispenser d'aimer.
"The word pay is immoral." [139]

---

[108] ↑*Travelling* Egypt↓

I have read that he who has once drunk of the water of the Nile, is restless until he can drink it again.

The "European Complaint."

[109] ↑*Friendship.*↓

My chief want in life, is, somebody who shall make me do what I can.[140]

[110] The encounter with Mr Chandler[,] a unitarian clergyman made out of a machinist, ⟦he said there were five of them together in the machine shop in Lowell who are now all ministers; one was George Bradburn, one was ⟧ and now specially is a collector of pamphlets,—having precisely the distemper of Dr Pierce & Dr Sprague, gave me to think how oddly Nature controuls or betrays us.[141] The methodic, the conserving, constructive, or architectural instinct is of that primal necessity, that, to make it sure, she daubs it on thick, till it overruns into these ridicules of collectors of ⟨t⟩all that other people throw away. Father Damon at West Cambridge (of whom I remember W. G. Swett [111] at the Water-

[139] See *JMN*, VIII, 84.

[140] This sentence, struck through in ink with two diagonal use marks, is used in "Considerations by the Way," *W*, VI, 272.

[141] William Buell Sprague (1795–1876), minister of the Second Presbyterian Church in Albany, made extensive collections of religious pamphlets and autographs. George Bradburn is unidentified.

town Association declared "that he should not make a speech, because he concurred in all that his Father Damon *was going* to say,"—) wasted whole days & nights in talking over a foolish pedigree of good for nothing uncles & aunts. Peter Force will give Mrs R. $15.00 for a copy of the first Edition of E. Everett's Concord Oration[.][142]

Mr C.[143] is most lucky in his monomania that people would gladly give him some thing to take off their hands the very rubbish he is so greedy to collect.

[112] *Laws of Work*

The manly part is to do what you can do, & with might & main. The world is full of fops who never did any thing, & who have persuaded ⟨men⟩ beauties & men of genius, too, to wear their fop livery, & ↑to↓ hiss with their hiss; & these will explicitly & impliedly deliver ⟨their⟩ ↑the fop-↓opinion, that it is not respectable to be seen earning a living; that it is much more respectable to spend without earning, & this doctrine of the devil will come from the Carlyles & the Macaulays[,] from the Newcombs & the Thoreaus almost, that is,[144] [113]–[114] [leaf torn out][145]

[115] Shakspeare's fancy never flagged. He never appears the anatomist, never with a mere outline, which is to be filled up in a

[142] David Damon, Harvard 1811, was pastor of the Congregational Society in West Cambridge until his death in 1843; William Gray Swett (1808–1843), pastor of the First Church of Lexington; Peter Force (1790–1868), an archivist and historian. Everett's *An Oration Delivered at Concord, April the Nineteenth, 1825* (Boston, 1825) is in Emerson's library.

[143] Probably the "Mr Chandler" referred to on p. [110] above.

[144] The entry on p. [112], struck through in ink with a vertical use mark, is used in "Wealth," *W*, VI, 91–92.

[145] Legible words and parts of words on the stub of p. [113] are: "the ‖ . . . ‖ Bu‖ . . . ‖ the ‖ . . . ‖ the ‖ . . . ‖ don‖ . . . ‖ tha‖ . . . ‖ ⟨all⟩ ‖ . . . ‖ The s‖ . . . ‖ tracts ‖ . . . ‖ &, on ‖ . . . ‖ mark‖ . . . ‖"; and on the stub of p. [114]: "‖ . . . ‖ting ‖ . . . ‖ive ‖ . . . ‖dges ‖ . . . ‖⟨tory⟩ ↑ficance↓ ‖ . . . ‖ttleton". The recoveries are insufficient for positive identification, but cf. "Wealth," VI, 92: "The *s*tatue is so beautiful that it con*tracts* no stain from the *mark*et . . . ." (NB: "tracts" begins a line; the previous line may well have ended with "con-".); "the determined youth saw in it an aperture to insert his dangerous we*dges*, made the insigni*ficance* of the thing forgotten, and gave fame by his sense and energy to the name and affairs of the Ti*ttleton* snuff-box factory." Italicized words or parts of words correspond to those on the stubs.

happier hour, but always gorgeous with new & shining draperies. As a dry thinker, too, he is one of the best in the world[.]

"Every action that hath gone before
Whereof we have record, trial did draw
Bias, & thwart; not answering the aim
And that unbodied figure of the thought
That gave't surmised shape." [146]
[Shakespeare, *Troilus and Cressida*, I, iii, 13–17]

[116] ⟨———⟩ Complained that life had lost its interest. 'Tis very funny, be sure, to hear this. For most of us the world is all too interesting, *l'embarras de richesses*. We are wasted with our versatility; with the eagerness to grasp on every possible side, we all run to nothing. I cannot open an agricultural paper without finding objects enough for Methusalem. I jilt twenty books whenever I fix on one. I stay away from Boston, only because I cannot begin there to see those whom I should wish, the men, & the things. I wish to know France. I wish to study art. I wish to read laws.

[117] Talleyrand at 15 years had discovered that the secret of governing ↑men↓ lay in selfcommand.

"Augustus Caesar at nineteen years put on the dissimulation, which he never put off." *Gibbon*.[147]

Napoleon III. acquired such skill in the art of lying, that "the journals complained you could not depend on the exact contrary of that which he stated[.]" [148]

[118] Poet,—no, prosewriter is un orateur manqué. Did not old Goethe say, that Byron's poems were, ⟨in his eyes,⟩ undelivered

[146] The entry on p. [115] is struck through in pencil with a wavy diagonal use mark.

[147] Cf. Edward Gibbon, *The History of the Decline and Fall of the Roman Empire*, chap. III. See *The Works of Edward Gibbon*, ed. J. B. Bury, 15 vols. (New York, 1906–1907), I, 90.

[148] In Notebook Sigma, p. [68], is a newspaper clipping reporting a *bon mot* of a French capitalist about Napoleon's speech at Auxerre: "It is said that the Emperor has carried deceit to such a point of refinement that one cannot even believe the contrary of what he says."

parliamentary speeches?[149] Much more is it manifest, my dear Carlyle, that your rage at stumporatory is inverted love.

Road from Trebizond to Erzr⟨oa⟩oom, 200 miles.—
"Whilst the attention of the crowd was diverted, the necessary graves were removed, & that part of the work completed beyond all undoing. The Turk is a fatalist, & when a thing becomes a fixed fact, he acquiesces without further ado."

[119] Ellery says that "he likes Stow; he is a very good character, there is only a spoonful of wit, and ten thousand feet of sandstone."[150]

Conduct of Life

Morning thoughts

"Sleep is like death, &, after sleep,
The world seems new begun,
Its earnestness all clear & deep,
Its true solution won;
White thoughts stand luminous & firm
Like statues in the sun.
Refreshed from supersensuous founts
The soul to blotless vision mounts."

Allingham.[151]

[120] In the heats of youth, we defend the stoical thesis,—faith without works,—the Platonic plenum, &c., & scorn to degrade our life by the trivial measures of practice. Of course, in the cardinal ⟨fact⟩ ↑instance↓ of love, the crimes of love are to be expiated & purified away only by more love,—the flame of love burning up all mortal taint, &c. But, later, ⟨in life⟩ we begin to see that some allow-

[149] *Conversations with Goethe in the Last Years of His Life*, trans. from the German of Eckermann by S. M. Fuller (Boston, 1839), in *Specimens of Foreign Standard Literature*, ed. George Ripley, 14 vols., 1838–1842, IV, 158. *Conversations* is in Emerson's library. See *JMN*, VIII, 249.

[150] The reference here is undoubtedly to Cyrus Stow (1789–1876), a farmer, butcher, and town clerk of Concord, 1840–1848.

[151] "Wakening," stanza 2, in William Allingham, *Poems* (London, 1850), p. 154, in Emerson's library. In the book, "blotless" is struck through with two diagonal pencil marks; "purer", in what looks like Emerson's hand, is inscribed in pencil in the left margin. Lines 1–2 and 5–8 are used in "Inspiration," *W*, VIII, 280.

ance, & always more & more, must be ⟨allowed⟩ ↑made↓ to the poor whiggish [121] facts; that is to say, the ⟨horrid⟩ carnage made in human relations, the breach of the order of society, & the stings of remorse, from a false position, in the actor, & the cruel false position given to the sufferer, together constitute such a mass of rancorous objection, that nothing but a supernatural magnanimity & aplomb in the hero, can confront, or make any head against; and all this is nothing but an expounding from facts of a↑n↓ ⟨latent⟩ occult law which the [122] strutting pagan Intellect had not descried, ⟨r⟩but which is integral part of theory, & which a Christian soul, ⟨r⟩to be sure, would have divined without aid of the offensive facts. ↑1850↓

↑(These last two pages read like nonsense. August 1873)↓ [152]

[123] Mais, Monsieur, il faut que j⟨e vive.⟩ ↑'existe.↓
Monsieur, je n'en vois pas la nécessité.[153]
Talleyrand.

[124] Talleyrand. ↑continued↓

"La France est capable du tout, selon qu'il est conduit." [154]
Richelieu

"Selon qu'il est conduit, le peuple Francais est capable de tout."
Richelieu.

"On peut être plus *Fin* qu'un autre, mais pas plus Fin que tous les autres."
"All the world is ↑a↓ wiser man than any man in the world"
See Life of Sterling p. 251 — [155]

[125] The "sickly sentimentalism"[,] the "trashy sentimentalism", as it is now called, of keeping the ten Commandments!

These taunts upon sentimentalism, & higher law, & the like, which our senators use, are the screens of their cowardice. See AZ 160[, 204]

[152] "1850 . . . 1873" is in pencil.

[153] This sentence is used in "Stonehenge," *W*, V, 287–288.

[154] This quotation is struck through in ink with four diagonal use marks. See Journal TU, p. [147] above.

[155] Thomas Carlyle, *The Life of John Sterling* (Boston, 1851), in Emerson's library.

[126] Tennyson's *In Memoriam* is the commonplaces of condolence among good unitarians in the first week of mourning. The consummate skill of the versification is the sole merit. The book has the advantage that was Dr Channing's fortune, ⟨to have no⟩ that all the merit was appreciable. He ⟨wa⟩ is never a moment too high for his audience. But to demonstrate this mediocrity I was forced to quote those moral sentences which make the fame of true bards [n] such as

"In whose pure sight all Virtue doth succeed,"

of Wordsworth; [156]

"'Tis crown enough to Virtue, still, her own applause,"

of Ben Jonson; or

"It was for Beauty that the world was made."
B. J.[157]

[127] or

"Unless above himself he can
Erect himself, how poor a thing is man." [158]

of Daniel ["To the Lady Margaret, Countess of Cumberland," ll. 95–96];

or

"The sum of Virtue is to know & dare;"

of Donne ["To the Countess of Bedford," l. 33, misquoted] [159]

and then to ask, Now show me one such line in this book of Tennyson?

"The recluse hermit oft times more doth see
Of the world's inmost wheels than worldlings can
⟨Th⟩As man is of the world, the heart of man
Is the epitome of God's great book
Of Creatures, & men need no further look."
Donne ["Ecclogue," ll. 48–52]

[156] The quotation is struck through in pencil with a diagonal use mark.

[157] The Wordsworth quotation is "Brave Schill," l. 14. The first Jonson quotation is l. 18 of "*An* ODE. To *himself*." (see *JMN*, VI, 231); the second is l. 8 of a song in THE SECOND MASQUE, Which was of BEAUTY, in *Works*, 1716, V, 175, and III, 297.

[158] This quotation is used in "Civilization," *W*, VII, 30. See *JMN*, VI, 103.

[159] See Journal TU, p. [18] above.

[128] ↑*Turner*↓

The fact that the creator of beauty in English art, the man who has all his life been shedding lustre & loveliness in profuse works of his industrious pencil, is a poor hunks sulking in a lonely house with his woman Jessica, a miser too, who never asked anybody to dine, & has made £300 000 by his works,—is not a dead fact, but significant of the compensations of nature; significant that every old crooked curmudgeon has a soft place in his heart; & not without comfort too, that when one feels the drawbacks & diseases & disgraces[n] of his temperament & activity, he recalls, that still he too may not be useless or pestiferous [129] if he steadily retires on his task of even a sad, ⟨solitary⟩ crusty, churlish, ↑⟨compensatory⟩ expiatory↓ devotion to art & beauty, like J.M.W. Turner's.[160]

Brave comme l'épée qu'il porte.[161]

The principal thing that occurs now is the might of the law which makes slavery the single topic of conversation in this Country. A great wrong is attempted to be done & the money power is ⟨n⟩engaged to do it. But unhappily because it is criminal the feeble force of conscience is found to set the whole world against it. Hallelujah!

[130] Edith says, Father, I have very bad dreams, that way that the houses grow larger & smaller.

Diamonds, I read, appear the same in a bowl of water, as out of it, whilst ⟨p⟩glass loses its light.[162]

---

[131] [blank]

[132] Reality

---

[160] Most of this paragraph, struck through in pencil with single vertical use marks on pp. [128] and [129], is used in "Character," *W*, V, 135. For Emerson's recollections of his seeing a group of Turner's pictures and of a visit to the painter's studio in London, see *JMN*, X, 527–528.

[161] This sentence is in pencil.

[162] See *JMN*, VI, 326.

Such is our instinctive value for reality in success, that we smile superior if our bedfellow dream of palaces, & murmur of gifts.

The courage of having done the thing before.[163]

[133] ↑*Education. Drill.*↓

It is better to ⟨sen⟩ teach the child arithmetic and Latin Grammar, than geography, or rhetoric, or moral philosophy; — because these first require an exactitude of performance in the pupil, — it is made certain whether the lesson is gotten: — and that power of performance is worth all the science⟨s⟩ of all the libraries. He can very easily learn any thing which is important to him now that the power to learn is secured; — as Mechanics say, when one has *once learned the use of tools*, it is very easy to work at a new craft, as at wheelwright, or cabinet maker, or painter, or smith.[164]

[134] *Man the inventor*

It is frivolous, of course, to fix pedantically the date of this or that invention, they have all been invented over & over fifty times, that is, man is ⟨a perfect machine,⟩ the archmachine of which all these ↑shifts drawn from himself↓ are petty machinules, & he helps himself in each emergency by copying his own structure just so far as the need is, ↑& no farther↓:[165] if he only wants fixed types for the nonce, he makes ⟨only⟩ fixed types. By & by, he wants moveable types, & ⟨as easily⟩ makes them: Then come⟨s⟩ all the mannikins of that day, & cry, who but we? ↑Ah our poor benighted grandfathers!↓ Lo! we have invented printing! It is hard to find the right Copernicus or Homer or Zoroaster. There are twenty in the field.[166]

[135]–[138] [2 leaves torn out][167]

[163] This phrase is used in "Culture," *W*, VI, 139. See *JMN*, X, 43.

[164] "It is better . . . *tools*," struck through in pencil with a diagonal use mark, is used in "Education," *W*, X, 147, as is "very easy . . . craft,".

[165] "It is frivolous . . . need is," struck through in ink with a curved vertical use mark, is used in "Fate," *W*, VI, 17.

[166] "It is hard . . . field.", struck through in ink with a vertical use mark, is used in "Fate," *W*, VI, 17.

[167] Emerson indexed p. [135] under Machine, p. [136] under Days, and p. [138] under Energy, Greatness, Magnet, and Power. See also Notebook BO Conduct,

[139] ⟨&⟩ commissar↑i↓es ↑& quarter masters.↓ Whilst oats & barley grow, whilst men, money, & iron, are to be found, with these men I shall be pretty sure to have them. Newton will not long be a stranger anywhere in the Copernican system. Every ⟨man becomes⟩ ↑peasant turns↓ sutler, every acre of ground yields corn, when the hero arrives. *Tout est soldat pour vous combattre.*[168]

[140] Merchants think, that, though there is so much wealth accumulated in the cities, Boston or New York could not bear their own weight. ⟨B⟩New York, until within a few years, was always an indebted city, being the factor for the country. Boston, too, is becoming indebted.—When we carried the trade of the world from 1800 to 1812, a seizure was now & then made of an American ship. Surely the loss was great to the owner, but the country was indemnified at once, for we charged 3 d a pound for carrying cotton; 6 d for tobacco; & so on, which paid for the risk & loss, &, after the war was over, we got payment over & above, for[169] [141][170] all the ||msm|| grew r||msm||

---

p. [1]: "Unity in human structures pervasive: hump appears in intellect, too. *BO*, 137.", and BO Conduct, p. [9]: "Give me the leader, you may have the baggage. *BO* 138".

[168] This sentence, from the fourth verse of "La Marseillaise," is used in "The Fugitive Slave Law" (1854), *W*, XI, 237.

[169] "When we carried . . . for", struck through in ink with a vertical use mark, is used in "Wealth," *W*, VI, 109–110.

[170] The leaf bearing pp. [141]–[142] is torn away approximately one and one-half inches from the binding. The entry on pp. [141]–[142] is used in "Wealth," *W*, VI, 110–111 (words and parts of words corresponding to those in the ms. are italicized: ". . . *all the* seizures. Well, the Americans *grew r*ich and great. . . . Britain, France and *Germ*any, which our extraordinary profits had impoverished, *send o*ut, attracted by the fame of *our a*dvantages, first their thousands, then their millions *of poo*r people, to share *the cr*op. At first we employ them, and *incr*ease our prosperity; but *in the* artificial system of society and of protected labor, *whic*h we also have adopted and *enla*rged, there come presently *check*s and stoppages. Then we refuse *to em*ploy these poor men. But *they w*ill not be so answered. They go into the poor-rates, and *though we* refuse wages, we must now pay the same amount in the for*m of* taxes. . . . *It is* vain to refuse this payment. We c*annot* get rid of these people, and w*e cannot* get rid of their will to be sup*ported*. That has become an inevita*ble ele*ment of our politics; and, for *their* votes, each of the domin*ant* parties courts and assists *them* to get it executed. Moreo*ver, we* have to pay, not what *would* have contented them at hom*e, but* what they have learned to *think* necessary here; so that *opinion*, fancy and all manner of *moral* considerations complicate *the pro*blem."

turn mu||msm||
& Germ||msm||
send o||msm||
our a||msm||
of poo||msm||
the cr||msm||
& incr||msm||
in the ||msm||
whic||msm||
& enla||msm||
check||msm||
to em||msm||
they w||msm||
stantly, ||msm||
though w||msm||
[142] ||msm||m of
||msm|| It is
||msm||annot
||msm||e cannot
||msm||ported.
||msm||ble ele-
||msm|| their
||msm||ant
||msm|| them
||msm||ver, we
||msm|| would
||msm||e, but
||msm|| think
||msm|| opinion,
||msm|| moral
||msm|| the pro-

[143] *Rotation.*

What an excellent principle our favourite rule of rotation in office would be if applied in industrial matters. You have been watch-maker long enough, ⟨& I am tired of being baker⟩ now it is my turn to ⟨be⟩ make watches, & you can bake muffins. The carpenter is to make glass this year, & the glassblower staircases. The blacksmith is to ⟨make⟩ cut me a coat, & the tailor to take charge of the machine shop. Mr Benton has served an apprenticeship of thirty years to the Federal Senate, has learned the routine, has opened his views to a national scope, & must now retire ⟨bef⟩ to give place to Johnny Raw.

[144] The odious inequality must be borne. A superintendent at the mills must have 2000 dollars, whilst the most industrious operative has only 400. Because, order & faculty are r⟨e⟩are & costly. Why should not the wheels of the loom say, "see me, I whirl & buzz with ⟨a⟩ ↑two↓ hundred revolutions in a minute, whilst that great lazy waterwheel down below there, only turns five times. I will not go faster than he."

I learned also that the valuations of Massachusetts, of Boston, of New York, are nowise reliable for direct comparison. As for example the saying that Boston could buy Maine & have $80,000,000. left.[171] Because the values of Boston are artificial values, [145] the value of luxuries, furniture, books, pictures, inflated prices of land & houselots & houses, &c. whilst the values of Maine are primary & necessary, & therefore permanent under any state of[?] society.

This consideration of inflation goes ⟨directly⟩ into all farming value. The farmer gets 200, whilst the merchant gets 2000 dollars. But the farmer's 200. is far safer, & is more likely to remain to him. It was heavy to lift up from the soil, but it was for that reason more carefully bestowed, & will stay where it was put; so that the two sums turn out at last to be equivalent.[172]

[146] In the streets I have certain darkenings which I call my nights.

I found when I had finished my new lecture that it was a very good house, only the architect had unfortunately omitted the stairs.

---

[171] For the source of these figures, see pp. 296–297, n. 60 above.
[172] With this paragraph, cf. "Wealth," *W*, VI, 102.

[147] — If immortal, how rich the joy of that aspiring soul whose competitors find him higher than earthly hopes! If "*not to be*", how like the bells of a fool the trump of fame! [173] But what renders this idle, the spirit is framed for endless happiness in its origin, without one other object or pursuit — writes my antique Saint-sibyl.[174]

[148] *The Morning.*

Hear what the morning says, & believe that.[175] The house is full of noise, & contradicts all that the morning ⟨says⟩ ↑hints↓: Worse, it distracts attention from what the morning ⟨says, to⟩ ↑beams on us to↓ all the ⟨base⟩ [176] nonsense which the house ⟨says⟩ ↑chatters↓. But there is one good child in the house who furtively eyes from time to time the east, through the window, & so keeps his mind steadily fixed on that which it speaks, & defends his ears from the rattle around him.

[149] Diamonds

"A lady in the rei⟨n⟩gn of Q. Elizabeth would have as patiently digested a lie as the wearing of false stones, or pendants of counterfeit pearl, so common in our age."

Thomas Fuller's
Worthies II 294 [177]

[150] *Low tone*

⟨The true⟩ Biography [n] & history make us gape. But the true biography & history is that which is heard over the tavern stove, & ⟨in the⟩ overheard in the railroad train. Thus of my distinguished friend, I was told, "he is no lawyer, he cannot get you out of a scrape: ⟨L⟩little K. or W. is worth two of him for that, — he is too just." [178]

[173] This sentence is used in "Immortality," *W*, VIII, 336. For "'*not to be*'", see Shakespeare, *Hamlet*, III, i, 56.

[174] Probably Mary Moody Emerson.

[175] This sentence is used in "Country Life," *W*, XII, 157.

[176] The cancellations of "says" (twice) and "base" are in pencil, as are the added words "hints" and "beams"; "base" is also canceled in ink.

[177] *The History of the Worthies of England* . . . , 1811. The quotation is used in "Truth," *W*, V, 119.

[178] Emerson's "distinguished friend" is probably either Samuel Hoar (1778–1856) or Ebenezer Rockwood Hoar (1816–1895).

↑15 January↓ [179]

Last night, at the ⟨Social Circle⟩ ↑Club↓ it was urged that persons were ⟨very⟩ much hurt who had failed to be elected, &c. & the committee of nominati⟨n⟩on which brings one candidate, out of all the list, before the Club, was thought most invidious.[180] And much was said on the natural [151] indignation which the rejected candidates feel at having a better man preferred to th⟨em⟩ose who stood prior to him in ⟨the⟩ time of ⟨their⟩ application; &c. To which, two conclusive answers seemed to rise. If, ↑when a vacancy occurs,↓ there be several names and the first in order of time is a ⟨young but a⟩ blameless candidate, but young & nowise ⟨commanding in claim⟩ ↑clubable↓; &, next below him, is the name of a man who ⟨is the⟩ tells the best story in the county, & is as full of fun & information as Judge Warren or Harry Lee, or the like excellent talker,—is it not a cruel wrong to the Club to deprive it, perhaps for years, of such a member? [181]

Then, secondly, I have no sympathy[n] [152] with the wounded feelings of candidates who wish to be preferred to a better man, or who count themselves injured when an older or better man is chosen. Let them sympathize with the Club, & with good sense, instead of sympathizing with themselves.

⟨a⟩ ↑Say for a Boston↓ Club—

⟨W. P. ⟨a⟩Atkinson, J. E. Goodson,⟩ J. P. Lesley. Cabot, Ward, Bangs, Bradford, ⟨Simmons, Bemis⟩ Alcott, Lowell, ⟨Shackford, S. Cheney, Watson⟩ H. James, ⟨Parker, H. Greenough, Weiss, Higginson, O. Frothingham, W. B. Greene,⟩ Whipple, Hale, Curtis, Norton, ⟨Matthews,⟩ Whittier, ⟨Hawthorne⟩ [182]

[179] A line is drawn across the page above this date, and "*1851*" is written in the left margin, both in pencil, perhaps added by Edward Emerson.

[180] The Social Circle, a club of Concord's leading citizens, grew out of the Committee of Safety of Revolutionary days; Emerson became a member in 1839.

[181] Charles Henry Warren (1798–1874) was judge of the Common Pleas Court, Suffolk County, from 1839 until 1844. Harry Lee is unidentified.

[182] The cancellations of names in this list are in pencil. Of those who are not previously identified or easily recognizable, William Parsons Atkinson, Harvard graduate, was principal of the high school in Brookline; Seth Wells Cheney (1810–1856), an engraver and crayon artist; Benjamin Marston Watson of Plymouth, a close friend of Thoreau and husband of Waldo's teacher, Mary Russell. Emerson

[153] Low tone

The proof of literary genius is the *nobil volgar eloquenza*,[183] or, ↑with large views,↓ the low tone, ⟨or with large views⟩ and humour to show its unaffectedness. Burns & Goethe & Carlyle, with great difference of power, understand it well. Goethe is in this way a great success.

M[ary] M[oody] E[merson] & Henry James are both proficients, & C[harles]. K[ing] N[ewcomb]., H[enry]. D[avid]. T[horeau]., & W[illiam]. E[llery]. C[hanning].

↑See BO 60, 150, 175.↓

bring[?] in 175[184]

[15⟨2⟩4] To the Chapter on the Superlative belongs all the matter on the *Low tone* ⟦see BO pp 60, 150, 153,⟧ and also the matter ⟨a⟩of Egotism, Conceit, elephantiasis, on which one collects so many texts. The words "I am on the eve of a revelation," sound sad & insane.—Perhaps the whole may fitly come into the Chapter on *Culture*.[185]

[155] Culture

The secret of Culture is to interest the man more in his public than in his private quality.[186]

The poet has a brilliant talent ⟨o⟩f↑or↓ writing. His poem elicits a multitude of critiques in journals & newspapers & in conversations everywhere. From all these ⟨or from the⟩ it is, after a time, quite easy to eliminate the real judgment or verdict which mankind passed upon his poem. And that is in the main unfavorable. Now the poet as

probably refers to Charles Eliot Norton (1827–1908) rather than to his father and earlier critic of Emerson, Andrews Norton. Matthews is unidentified. Emerson may be pondering founding another club to replace the Town and Country Club which ceased to exist in June, 1850.

183 For the italicized words, see Journal TU, p. [125] above.

184 "bring in 175" is in pencil.

185 "Conceit, elephantiasis . . . *Culture*." is struck through in ink with a vertical use mark; " 'I am . . . revelation,' " is used in "Culture," *W*, VI, 133. See *JMN*, V, 322.

186 This sentence, struck through in ink with a vertical use mark, is used in "Culture," *W*, VI, 157.

a craftsman is only interested [156] in the praise that is accorded to him & not in the censure, though it be just. And, in ordinary, the ↑poor little↓ poet hearkens only to that, reads only that, believes only that, & rejects the censure, as ⟨inc⟩ only proving incapacity in the Critic. But the poet *cultivated* becomes a stockholder in both companies, ↑in↓ the Tennyson stock, & ↑in↓ the Humanity stock; and his interest in the last exults as much in the demonstration of the unsoundness of Tennyson, as his interest in the former gives him pleasure in the currency of Tennyson. For the depreciation [157] of his Tennyson stock, only shows the immense values of the Humanity stock, & what

As soon as he sides with his critic against himself with joy, he is cultivated man.[187]

[158] *Eloquence*

Bad air, unfriendly audience, faint heart & vacant thought in the orator are things of course, and incident to Demosthenes, to Chatham, to Webster, as inevitably as to the gentlemen who address the stifling Concord Vestry this week. But here & there fell the bolt of genius astounding & dazzling out of this very fog & stench, burned them all up, melted away bad air, rowdy mob, coldness, aversion, part⟨y⟩isanship, sterility, in one blaze of wonder, sympathy, & delight, and ⟨these⟩ the total consumption of all this fuel, is the proof of Eloquence.

[159] *Helix oblonga*, from Rio Janeiro, I saw in Salem at Mrs Barstow's, with white eggs, about the size of a robin's egg, which the fish lays.[188]

[October, 1851] *Littaea geminiflora*, a beautiful plant of the agave species, looking like a gigantic orchis 11 or 12 feet high, I saw in full flower at the Horticultural Shop.

Oct 1851

[187] "The poet . . . man.", struck through in ink with vertical use marks on pp. [155], [156], and [157], is used in "Culture," *W*, VI, 157–158.

[188] Emerson's reference is perhaps to Mrs. Nancy Forrester Barstow, wife of the physician who attended Nathaniel Hawthorne in his young Salem days and who later became a merchant, shipowner, and congressman.

[160] *Affirmative.* All depends on the battery. If it can give one shock, we shall get no farther than the fish form, & there the development will be arrested; if 2 shocks, to the bird; if 3, to the quadruped; if four, to man.[189]

[161] Mr ↑Rogers↓ of Gloucester who owns the rocking stone ⟨which the tide moves—at about 1½ mile from G. village⟩ ↑about half a mile from Gloucester village, which stone the tide moves,↓ told me a good story of Jarvis of the Sandwich Glass Company, who ⟨went⟩ ↑came↓ down there with his gun, & bonded all the farms, the farmers thinking him a crazy man with a pocket full of money: so they followed him, & got each man 10.00 from him for a bond, &, last of all, his landlord also got a gold watch & 5.00. Then J. went up to Boston, put himself in funds, came down & demanded a deed of all these lands & houses, to the terror of the owners.[190]

[162_1][191] To every reproach, I know now but one answer, namely, to go again to my own work.
"But you neglect your relations."
Yes, too true; then I will work the harder.
"But you have no genius." Yes, then I will work the harder[.]
"But you have no virtues." Yes, then I will work the harder[.]
"But you have detached yourself & acquired the ⟨the c⟩aversation of all decent people. You must regain some position & relation." Yes, I will work harder.

[163_1] *Tools*

As an *instantia flagrans*[192] of the more mechanical character of our surgery I must not forget the transfusion of blood lately experimented in Paris and   remark that a man would change his blood as often as his shirt.[193]

[189] This paragraph, in pencil, is used in "Poetry and Imagination," *W*, VIII, 72.

[190] George H. Rogers, a merchant of Gloucester, laid out plans for a summer colony at Bass Rocks (where the rocking stone was), but died before the development was completed. Jarvis is unidentified.

[191] Page numbers [162] and [163] are repeated, as the subscript numbers indicate.

[192] "flagrant instance" (Ed.).

[193] This sentence is used in "Works and Days," *W*, VII, 160.

Everyman is careful to keep his tool-chest in order. The good order & connexion of the wires is essential to the telegraph. The lawyer is impotent without his library of precedents, & without Court Street. The Merchant without his Banks & his Brokers[.]

[162_2] Columbus's Letters. H Major. 1847[194]
His dream p 184
and the high irony of his description of the Heavenly King p 185
His complaints p. 200 201 202 203
p. 173.
He possesses the secret of his course to Veragua
p. 190–1
His poverty p. 173[195]

"The men with me were 150, — many fit for pilots & good sailors, but none of them can explain whither I went.[196] I started from a point above the port of Brazil, x x x x storms x I put into an island called Isla de las Bocas, & then steered for terra firma . . . but impossible to give correct account, because of currents. x
I ascertained however by compass & by observation, that I moved parallel with the coast of terra firma. No one could tell under what part of the heavens we were, nor at what period I bent [163_2][197] my course for the island of Espanola[198] The pilots thought, we had come to the island of St John, whereas it was the ⟨co⟩land of Mango, 400 leagues to the westward of where they said. Let them answer & say if they know where Veragua is situated. I assert that they can give no other acc[oun]t than that they went to lands where there was an abundance of gold; this they can certify: but they do not know the way to return thither for such a purpose; they would be obliged to go on a voyage of discovery, as much as if they had never been there before. There is a mode of reckoning derived from astronomy, which is sure & safe, & a sufficient guide to any who understands it.[199] This resembles a prophetic vision" [*Select Letters of Columbus*, 1847] p[p.189–]191

194 The heading "Columbus's . . . 1847" refers to *Select Letters of Christopher Columbus*.

195 Emerson quotes from p. 173 of *Select Letters of Christopher Columbus* . . . , 1847, on p. [74] above.

196 " 'The men . . . sailors,' " is used in "Success," *W*, VII, 285.

197 The index heading "*Columbus*" is written in the top margin of p. [163_2].

198 "~" has been added in pencil under the "n" of "Espanola", probably not by Emerson.

199 " 'Let them answer . . . it.' " is used in "Success," *W*, VII, 285.

[164] I think there is a prose in certain Englishmen which exceeds in woody deadness all possibility of rivalry, & seems to say, like the gates of the Inferno, "*Leave all hope behind*".[200] And it is not very uncommon. Two obscure Unitarian ministers I have seen, were faithful examples, & might tempt one to suicide, Mr Harding & Mr Doherty.

It is a nation where mediocrity is ⟨funded & decorated⟩ ↑entrenched↓ & consolidated, & ⟨entrenched & decorated⟩ funded & decorated in an adamantine manner.[201]

[165] I must try to recall here where I sit by the ⟨t⟩edge of Seneca Lake, my conversation yesterday with Albert H. Tracy of Buffalo.[202] He believed that Europe was effete beside America & fancied that the office of men here was in many ages to bring the material world into subserviency to the moral. And, that, if one should expect only such a future as the past, nations & man might well despair. Nor that yet were even the means of change apparent and that it was utterly futile to hope anything from such arrangements or philanthropies as might now organize; for [n] they begin by saying, now let us make a compact, which is a solecism inasmuch as it implies a sentimental [166] res⟨s⟩istance to the gravities & tendencies which will steadily by little & little pull over your air-castle. There is nothing to tie it to. He believes in a future of great equalities; but all our experience↑,↓ ⟨is⟩he sees, is of inequalities.

Mrs L M Drury
Canandaigua N Y
Care of Commodore William Mervine U.S.N.
Utica N.Y.[203]

[200] This sentence, struck through in ink with a vertical use mark, is used in "Manners," *W*, V, 111–112. The allusion is to Dante, *Inferno*, III, 9. See *JMN*, X, 238, 511.

[201] This sentence, struck through in ink with a vertical use mark, is used in "Manners," *W*, V, 112.

[202] Margaret Fuller's father wanted her to marry Tracy, an attorney, according to a letter from her to Tracy in the Overbury Collection, Barnard College Library.

[203] "Mrs L M Drury . . . Utica" is in pencil; "Commodore . . . Utica" is

[167] Some persons are thrown off their balance, when in society; others are thrown on to balance; the excitement of company & the observation of other characters corrects their biases. Margaret Fuller always appeared to unexpected advantage in conversation with a circle of persons, with more commonsense & sanity than any other,—though her habitual vision was through coloured lenses.[204]

[168] Mr Moseley at ⟨Alb⟩Buffalo described Webster's attitude when in the senate seeking for a word that did not come. "He pauses, puts his hand to his brow,—you would think then there was a mote in his eye. Still it comes not; then he puts his hands—American fashion ↑first into his breast under his waistcoat, deeper than I can, then, ↓—to the bottom of his fobs, bends forward,—then the word is bound to come, he throws back his head, & out it comes with a leap, &, I promise you, it has its full effect on the Senate." [205]

[169] All national brag in English or American is mean, & betrays want of real power. Just as far as the sympathy of the company goes with you, you may value your English, French, or Dutch traits, but when old Dr Gardiner or Fanny Kemble or my little Kingston begins to assume airs on modern England, ↑going beyond any perception of facts that we have,↓ it is about as respectable as the admiration of a Freshman at College of his class. "My country," forsooth, makes me sick, Madam or Sir.[206]

[170] ⟨Our poor little Mulchinock⟩ [207]

---

traced in ink. Emily Mervine Drury, with whom Emerson was later a frequent correspondent, was the daughter of the navy Captain William Mervine (1790–1868), later a rear admiral. Emerson met them on a Mississippi steamboat in 1850 (*L*, IV, 210).

[204] This paragraph, struck through in pencil and in ink with single vertical use marks, is used in *Memoirs*, I, 216.

[205] William Abbot Mosely (1799–1873), a Buffalo lawyer, was a congressman from 1843 to 1847. Emerson lectured in Buffalo February 10 and 11, 1851.

[206] This paragraph is struck through in pencil with a curved vertical use mark. Emerson's reference is probably to William Gardiner (1770–1853), English musicologist, whom he "just missed seeing" in England (*L*, III, 455).

[207] In Account Book 5 (1849–1853), Emerson records a $1.00 payment for *The Ballads and Songs of William Pembroke Mulchinock* (New York and Boston, 1851) and, a few pages later, a $10.00 loan to Mulchinock.

⟨s⟩Safe to ⟨s⟩lay all this stress on Energy & stomach (in Power lecture) because Nature has provided ↑for↓ each his own issues. His existence is a perfect answer to all cavils; if he *is*, he is wanted; & has the precise peculiarities that are required; only do not let his sympathies with mobs lead him away from his sacred strengths.[208] He is created antidote to the mob, & he is doing all he can to ⟨n⟩ be mob, & succeeds just so far as to neutralize his own quality. He does not become mob, & he deserts himself & is nobody.

A. H. Tracy & G[eorge]. B[arrell]. E[merson]. both said, & plumed themselves on saying, "Why he will [171] be a pin-maker, if he does the one thing he can, & he must resist that with might & main!" Well, yes, if ⟨he⟩ you want decent debility, ↑inoffensive insignificance.↓ But I think this; —there are seven or eight of us rolled up in each man's skin, seven or eight ancestors, ⟨to say the⟩at least, and they constitute the variety ⟨a⟩of notes required for a new piece of music.[209] Let him obey, listen & obey, & by wise passiveness accept & use his ⟨own⟩ ↑several↓ powers, & health & symmetry will be kept for him, ↑sufficient↓ variety of power & of expression, joy to himself & utility to men.[209a]

[172] Chasles thinks the rage for *illustrated Journals* all over Europe & the United States, a decided symptom of the decline of literature.[210] Exciting novels, & pictures, in the room of ideas, have made literature a sensual pleasure.

[173] Fourier's Criticism on modern civilization, is, "An accountant was required, & a dancer got the place."

[208] "his own issues . . . required;", struck through in ink with two vertical use marks, is used in "Considerations by the Way," *W*, VI, 252.

[209] This sentence, struck through in ink with a diagonal use mark, is used in "Fate," *W*, VI, 10. See Journal AZ, p. [82] above.

[209a] "Wise passiveness" is from Wordsworth, "Expostulation and Reply," l. 24.

[210] Philarète Chasles (1798–1873), French scholar and writer, was interested in American literature; in 1844 he included Emerson in an article on literary tendencies in England and America in *Revue des Deux Mondes*, and in 1852 his *Anglo-American Literature and Manners* was published in New York. Emerson's source was a review of Chasles' *Etudes sur les Hommes et les Moeurs au Dix-neuvième Siècle* in the *Westminster Review*, LIV (Jan. 1851), 264 (vol. XXXI, No. II, in the American edition).

For Fourier's laws, &c. see AZ 197

'Tis the best piece of land there is out of doors, says Gowan.

[174] Fisher brought his diagram of climate showing Philadelphia & Rome to be iso-thermal & the true climate of empire, to Boston & found the people inconvertible to his thesis; then to Charleston, & still people could not accept it. But at Philadelphia, not a word of objection was heard.[211]

[175] ↑Printed↓ [212]

The farmer is eager to buy land, but one does not find how it lies in his mind, he is not vain or proud. His strongest phrase is, "Why, I don't work quite so hard as I ⟨used to,⟩ ↑once did,↓ & I don't mean to." [213]

⟨The farmer⟩The country boys & men have in their mind the getting a knowledge of the world as a thing of main importance. The New Hampshire man in the cars said that. ⟨V⟩Somebody grew up at home & his father whipped him for several years,—he would fall on him in the field & beat him [176] as he would his cattle. But one day the boy faced him, & held his hands. Then the boy had never been to school, & he thought he would go to California. There he was, a man grown, good, stout, well-looking fellow, six feet, but as ignorant as a horse; *he had never had any chance*; how could he know anything? ⟨W⟩So he went to California, & stayed there a year, & ⟨now he⟩ has come back.—⟨And⟩ He [n] looks ⟨very⟩ well, he has much improved [177] in his appearance, but he has not got a ninepence.

And really New Hampshire & Vermont look on ⟨c⟩California, & railroads, ⟨|| . . . ||p⟩as formerly they did on a peddling trip to Virginia,

[211] This paragraph, struck through in ink with a vertical use mark, is used in "Land," *W*, V, 40–41. Emerson's reference may be to Thomas Fisher (1801–1856), Philadelphia poet, member of the Academy of Natural Sciences, and author of *Dial of the Seasons . . .* (Philadelphia, 1845).

[212] Added in pencil.

[213] This paragraph is used in "The Superlative," *W*, X, 169–170.

—as their education, as *giving them a chance* to know something.[214]

"The demoralizing feeling of their own incapacity."

"Bravery is half victory." Heimsk[ringla, 1844, III, 101]

[178] The difference between Americans & English in the love of money, is, that, in the first, ambition unites with it, and they mean to be powerful, as well as rich. But nothing can be more foolish than this reproach which goes from nation to nation of the love of dollars. It is like ↑oxen↓ taxing each other with eating grass or a society of borers in an oaktree accusing one another of eating wood; or in a great society of cheese-mites, if one should begin making insinuations that the other was eating cheese.[215]

[179] And yet there stand the two creations[,] of Greek sculpture & of Italian painting.

[180] Women carry sail, & men rudders. Women look very grave sometimes, & affect to steer, but their pretended rudder is only a masked sail. The rudder of the rudder is not there.[216]

[181] ↑*Thermometers.*↓

There are men who are as sure indexes of the equity of legislation & the sane state of public feeling, as the thermometer that hangs at your door is of the heat. It is a bad sign if they are discontented.[217]

[182] Passion is logical[218] ↑Abandon↓

"The formation of barricades in July, shows how by a blind passion we

[214] "And really . . . something.", struck through in ink with two diagonal use marks, is used in "Culture," *W*, VI, 146.

[215] This paragraph is struck through in pencil with a diagonal use mark.

[216] This paragraph is used in "Woman," *W*, XI, 407.

[217] This paragraph, struck through in ink with a curved vertical use mark, is used in "The Fugitive Slave Law" (1851), *W*, XI, 179–180.

[218] See Journals RS, p. [131], and TU, p. [134] above.

can do rapidly & in perfection that which in cool blood ⟨&⟩would require much more time, & be executed in worse style."

Hugh Doherty p 35 [219]

Barricades is crystallization, still.

"The man who is his own master knocks in vain at the doors of poetry."

Plato.[220]

[183] [blank]

[184] Mr Choate is an excellent singer

1.	State of the Question		
2.	Power		
3.	Wealth		
4.	Economy		
5.	Culture	Books	Superlative
6.	Worship		Instinct & Inspiration

———

Natural Aristocracy

———

England

———

Eloquence [221]

———

[219] In *Charles Fourier's Theory of Attractive Industry, and the Moral Harmony of the Passions*, trans. Hugh Doherty (London, 1841). The title page in the Houghton Library copy is inscribed "A Bronson Alcott Esq with the Author's kind regards".

[220] The quotation is used in "Inspiration," *W*, VIII, 274–275. Emerson's immediate source is unknown. Compare, in the Loeb edition of the *Phaedrus*, 245A, "he who without the divine madness comes to the doors of the Muses, confident that he will be a good poet by art, meets with no success. . . ."

[221] The numbers and the headings following them, in the left-hand column, are in pencil; "Books" and "Superlative . . . Eloquence" are in ink. The list in pencil is apparently the first attempt at organizing the titles of the lecture series "Conduct of Life," delivered in Boston December–January, 1851–1852, and thereafter until 1856 in the United States and Canada, though Emerson frequently varied the lectures in the series. The ink titles on the page were possibly added later; the lectures were written and delivered at various times from 1846 (Eloquence) to 1850 (Instinct and Inspiration). Taken collectively, the titles constitute pretty much the

[185] The poet ⟨writes a fair copy of his verses, &⟩[222] sends ⟨it⟩ ↑a copy of his verses↓ to the printer. Thenceforward, ↑he is relieved,↓ the human race take charge of it. & it flies from land to land, from language to language. ⟨But If he should need,⟩ ↑It happens that they are in a new style, &↓ he may even ⟨have⟩ ↑be forced↓ like Coleridge, or like Campbell, to prove painfully that he wrote the verses; — they have become so entirely the World's property, that it is hard to prove that he had anything to do with them. ⟨But⟩ But the poetaster, as our poor little Mulchinock,[223] having made [186] what he calls verses, goes about reading them to you, & me, & all who ⟨will⟩ can be made to listen; begs them to befriend them; to quote them; to sign a certificate that they are verses; to subscribe to his book, to write it up; and, in short, devotes himself to the business of nurse or attendant to these poor ⟨poems⟩ ↑rhymes↓, which, God knows, need all this backing, & will go to the devil in spite of it.[224]

[187] An Epic of a poet who ↑has↓ taken great pains to get favorable notices of his work in public prints.

"Such notices," said Goethe, "have appeared in various papers. But at last comes the *Halle Literary Gazette*, telling plainly what the poem is really worth, & thus all the compliments of the other papers are nullified."

Eckermann. Vol II p 158[225]

[188] *Genial heat* *Imagination.*

There is ⟨&⟩ ↑and↓ must be a little air-chamber, a sort of tiny Bedlam in even the naturalist's or mathematician's brain who arrives at great results. They affect a sticking to facts; they repudiate all

---

series Emerson gave in New York, March 14–April 2, 1850; in Philadelphia, April 3–April 11, 1850; and in Cincinnati, May 20–June 3, 1850 (with some changes or omissions of lectures and changes in order).

[222] The ampersand, not included in the original ink cancellation, is canceled in pencil.

[223] See p. [170] above.

[224] The cancellation of "poems" and the inserted "rhymes" are in pencil. The inserted "has" in the first sentence on p. [187] below is also in pencil.

[225] *Conversations of Goethe with Eckermann and Soret*, trans. John Oxenford, 2 vols. (London, 1850).

imagination & affection, as they would disown ⟨incest⟩ ↑stealing↓.[n] But Cuvier, Oken, ⟨S⟩Geoffrey-St-Hilaire, Owen, Agassiz, (Audubon), ⟨Agassiz,⟩ must all have this spark of fanaticism for the generation of steam, & there must be that judicious [189] tubing in their brain that is in the boiler of the locomotive, or wherever steam must be swiftly generated.[226] ⟨Goethe, That⟩ They[n] all deny it, ⟨is a thing⟩ of course. Goethe had it very large. Goethe had this air--chamber so large, that, like Pericles, he must ⟨have⟩ ↑wear↓ a helmet to conceal the dreaded infirmity. But he never owned it, he even persuaded the people that it was the county jail.[227] If you have never so much faculty of detail without this [190] explosive gas, it makes the ↑Dr↓ Prichards & ⟨↑Dr↓ Wymans⟩ ↑Dr Worcesters↓ & ↑Dr↓ Warrens, ↑men that hold hard to facts, Dr Dryasdusts,↓[n] the most tedious & dreaded of mankind.[228] But add this fanaticism, & you have Buffons & Davys. Dr ⟨J's⟩ ↑Jackson's↓ misfortune is that he has none, &, like his class, is imposed upon by the loud disclaimer of the fanatics, & ⟨believes that Goethe's⟩ ↑takes Goethe at his word that his↓ air--chamber is the county jail.[229]

[191] Nothing so marks a man as bold imaginative expressions. A complete statement in the imaginative form of an important truth arrests attention & is repeated & remembered. A phrase or two of that kind will make the reputation of a man. Pythagoras's golden sayings were such; and Socrates's, & Mirabeau's & Bonaparte's; and, I hope

[226] "for the generation of steam," [p. [188]], is enclosed in an oval pencil line. With "judicious tubing . . . locomotive," cf. "The Superlative," *W*, X, 178.

[227] Emerson originally wrote: "Goethe had this . . . infirmity. Goethe had it very large, but he never owned it . . ." He then enclosed "Goethe had it very large," in an oval pencil line and attached an arrow pointing up to between "course." and "Goethe had". The editors have followed this revision, changing the comma after "large" to a period and capitalizing "but".

[228] Emerson is probably referring to Dr. John Collins Warren (see Journal RS, p. [194] above) and Dr. Jeffries Wyman (1814–1874), Hersey Professor of Anatomy and Surgery at Harvard. A Jonathan Fox Worcester had taken an M.D. at Harvard in 1832; Emerson apparently referred to James Cowles Prichard, English physician and ethnologist, in Journal TU, p. [209] above, but the reference is favorable.

[229] The cancellation of "believes that Goethe's" and the insertion "takes . . . his" are in pencil.

I shall not make a sudden descent, if I say, that, Henry Thoreau promised to make as good sentences in that kind as any body.[230]

[192] Bettine is the most imaginative person in our day.

[193] ↑*Power*↓
Equal to whatever may happen.[231]

[194] The French call one class of malcontents with the present order o⟨r⟩f things,—those who espouse the ⟨cau⟩ liberal side in respect to the poor, the slave, &c. but who do not propose a remedy,—*Les Stériles*.[232]

[195] The Greeks "contemplated death only as the distributor of imperishable glory." J.A. St John. [*The History . . . of Ancient Greece*, 1842,] I. 309

"A maxim of Greek philosophy that a magnanimous man is seldom under any circumstances disturbed." [*Ibid.*,] p 308
"Hence even the battlepieces of the Greeks are beautiful."[233]

"in whatever actions engaged, retain a sel⟨p⟩f possessed & serene aspect."[234]
[*Ibid.*,] p. 308

[196] *Beauty*
"For there is a language in looks & gestures, there is a fountain of joy & delight concealed deep in the physical structure, & its waters laugh to the eye of intellect, & reflect into the hearts of those who behold it a sunniness & exhilaration greater than we derive from gazing on the summer sea." St John [*The History . . . of Ancient Greece*, 1842,] Vol II, p. 191.

[197] [↑Printed in "Farming." in Society & Solitude↓][235]

[230] "Nothing so . . . Bonapartes;", struck through in pencil with a vertical use mark, is used in "Poetry and Imagination," *W*, VIII, 12.

[231] This phrase is used in "Power," *W*, VI, 56; cf. "Worship," *W*, VI, 232: "Thus man is made equal to every event."

[232] The dash after "remedy," has been added in pencil.

[233] " 'A maxim . . . beautiful.' " is struck through in ink with a diagonal use mark; cf. "Culture," *W*, VI, 159.

[234] This quotation is struck through in ink with a wavy vertical use mark; cf. "Culture," *W*, VI, 159.

[235] This heading, in the left margin, is enclosed in an oval ink line.

Among the 19 or 20 things which make the test questions at the Egyptian funeral, is the question, How did he stand on the world? The brave Therien stands well in the world; — very inconspicuous in Beacon street, — absolutely unknown & inadmissible, living & dying, he never shall be known there. But he stands well in the World; as Adam did, as an Indian does, as a bull or a lion or as one of Homer's heroes, Agamemnon or Ulysses do, very fitly compared to bull & lion. Is my friend a [198] person whom a poet of any clime[,] Milton or Saadi & Ammar & Firdausi & Chaucer[,] would see & appreciate, as being really pieces of the old nature, comparable to sun & moon, to rainbow & flood, to tiger & lightning, because he is, as all natural persons are, only metamorphoses of these things, & not secondary & tertiary formations, the slops & rinsings of ⟨s⟩ city society.[236]

[199] He stands well in the world. He has so much out-of-door nature & life, & so much self subsistency in him, that he does not need consideration, & a whole ⟨chorus of puffing anecdotes & paragraphs⟩ ↑chronicle of tells & puffs↓ from Miss Peabody & Miss Lynch [n] to prepare the mind for him.[237]

[200] *The Nineteen or Twenty Tests.*[238]

"Who *now* waits in the antechamber, — Johnson, or Chesterfield?"
[London?] Examiner.

Sickness & poverty test the heart of the witness.

[201] ↑65
35 -100-↓

Bad times. We wake up with a painful auguring, and after exploring a little to know the cause find it is the odious news in each day's paper, the infamy that has fallen on Massachusetts, ⟨&⟩ ↑that↓

[236] "How did he . . . persons are," struck through in ink with double vertical use marks on pp. [197] and [198], is used in "Farming," *W*, VII, 153.

[237] Emerson's references are probably to Elizabeth Peabody and Anne C. Lynch (for the latter, see Journal AZ, p. [191] above).

[238] Cf. Journal AZ, p. [152] above: "That, there are not one or two, but six or seven, nay, nineteen or twenty things, that must be considered⟨,⟩ & ⟨,⟩ had."

clouds the daylight, & takes away the comfort out of every hour. We shall never feel well again until that detestable law is nullified in Massachusetts & until the Government is assured that once for all it cannot & shall not be executed here.[239] All I have, and all I can do shall be given & done in opposition to the execution of the law.

[202] Mr. [Samuel] H↑oar↓. has never ⟨b⟩ raised his head since Webster's speech in last March, and all the interim has really been a period of calamity to New England. That was a steep ⟨d⟩step downward. I had praised the tone & attitude of the Country. My friends had ⟨doub⟩ mistrusted it. They say now, It is no worse than it was before; only it is manifest and acted out. Well I think *that* ⟨a very important evil.⟩ ↑worse.↓ It shows the access of so much courage in the bad, so much check of virtue, terror of virtue, withdrawn. The tameness is shocking. Boston, of whose [203] fame for spirit & character we have all been so proud. Boston, wh⟨ere⟩ose ↑citizen↓ intelligent people in England told me they could always distinguish ⟨advantageously⟩ ↑by their culture↓ among Americans. Boston, which figures so proudly in Adams's diary, which we all have been reading: Boston, through the personal influence of this New Hampshire man, must bow its proud spirit in the dust, & make us irretrievably ashamed. I would hide the fact if I could, but it is done, it is debased. It is now as disgraceful to be a Bostonian as it was hitherto a credit.

[204] Boston, we have said with so much lofty confidence,—no fugitive slave can be arrested here—. And now we must transport our vaunt to the country, & say with a little less confidence, no fugitive man can be arrested there, at least we can brag so until tomorrow, when the farmers also are corrupted, & the cowardice & unabashed selfishness of New York & Boston ⟨is f⟩ has infected the total population.

[205] The tameness is edifying. There is not a gentleman left in Massachusetts. I am told the only haste in Boston is who shall first sign the list of volunteers. The One is only reminded of the Russian poltroonery,—a nation without character where when they cheat you, & you show them that they cheat, they reply—"Why you did not think we were Germans surely; we are only Russians;"

[239] The paragraph to this point is struck through in ink with a wavy vertical use mark; "Bad times . . . hour." is used in "The Fugitive Slave Law" (1851), *W*, XI, 179.

that is, *we all cheat.* I met an episcopal clergyman, & allusion being made to Mr Webster's ⟨fall,⟩ treachery, he replied [206] "Why, do you know I think that the great action of his life?" I am told, they are all involved in one hot haste of terror, presidents of colleges & professors, saints & brokers, insurers, lawyers, importers, jobbers, there is not an unpleasing sentiment, a liberal recollection, ↑not↓ so much as a snatch of an old song for freedom ⟨lef⟩ dares intrude.

I am sorry to say it, But New-Hampshire has always been distinguished for the servility of its eminent men. Mr Webster had resisted for a long [207] time the habit of men of ⟨th⟩ his ⟨countrymen⟩ ↑*compatriots*, I mean no irony,↓ & by adopting the spirited tone of Boston had recommended himself—as much as by his great talents to the people of Massachusetts; but blood is thicker than water, the deep servility of New Hampshire politics which have marked all ↑prominent↓ statesmen from that district, with the great exception of Mr Hale, has appeared late in life with all the more strength that it had been resisted so long, & he has renounced what must [208] have cost him some perplexity all the ⟨pa⟩ great passages of his past career on which his fame is built. ⟨He has lived⟩ His great speeches are, his discourse at Plymouth denouncing ⟨Northern⟩ Slavery; his speech against Hayne & Southern aggression; his ⟨speech⟩ Eulogy on Adams & Jefferson; a speech which he is known by & in which he stands by the Fathers of the Revolution for the very resistance which he now denounces; [209] and lastly his speeches & ↑recent↓ writings on Hungarian liberty. At this very moment ↑attitude assumed as foreign secretary in↓ his letter to Mr Hulsemann ⟨stands⟩ ↑is printed in all newspapers↓ before the people in the ⟨au⟩most aukward contradiction to his own domestic position, precisely like that of the French President ⟨in⟩ between French liberty & Roman ⟨Slav⟩ tyranny; or like *Hail Columbia*, when sung at a slave-auction.[240]

I opened a paper today in which he pounds on the old strings in a letter to the Washington Birth Day feasters at N. Y. "Liberty!

[240] When Chevalier J. G. Hülsemann, Austrian chargé d'affaires in Washington, accused the United States of being hopeful for the downfall of the Austrian monarchy, Secretary of State Daniel Webster replied, defending America's support of democracy.

liberty!" Pho! Let Mr Webster for decency's sake shut his lips once & forever on this word. The word *liberty* in the mouth of Mr Webster sounds like the word *love* in the mouth of a courtezan.[241]

[210] The fame of Everett is dear to me, & to all his scholars, & I have watched with alarm his derelictions. Whenever his genius shone, it of course was in the instinct of freedom, but ⟨the⟩ one ⟨cannot see without mortification that he has no heart to break from his leader.⟩ ↑of his old Scholars ⟨who heard⟩cannot but ask him whether there was no sincerity in all those apostrophes to freedom & adjurations of the dying Demosthenes: was it all claptrap?↓ And as to the name of New England Societies, which Mr Choate, Mr Webster, & Mr Foote, Mr Clay, & Mr Everett address, & are responded to with enthusiasm, it is all a disgusting obsequiousness.

[211] Their names are tarnished: what we have tried to call great, is little; and the merely ethnographic fact remains that an immense external prosperity is possible, with pure c⟨a⟩owardice & hollowness in all the conspicuous official men. I cannot read longer with any comfort the local good news[,] even "Education in Massachusetts."
Art union
Revival of religion[242]

[212] E[lizabeth]. H[oar]. finds the life of Campbell to send her back with new force of attachment to her Temperance friends in America. Every life of an European artist shows her that they have no self-command. Their tears are maudlin, for they are the tears of wine. ⟨And⟩ ↑But↓[243] the ocean & the elements are at the back of the brave old puritans of the world when all the Websters are putrid.

[241] This entry on Webster and the Fugitive Slave Law, beginning "Mr. Hoar." on p. [202], is struck through in ink with single vertical use marks on pp. [202], [203], [204], [205], [206], [207], [208], and [209]; "The tameness is [p. [205]] . . . dares intrude." [p. [206]] is used in "The Fugitive Slave Law" (1851), *W*, XI, 180–181.

[242] "I cannot . . . religion", struck through in ink with a vertical use mark, is used in "The Fugitive Slave Law" (1851), *W*, XI, 181.

[243] "And" is canceled and "but" inserted in pencil.

[213] The little fact comes out more plainly that you cannot rely on any man for the defence of truth who is not constitutionally of that side. Wolf, however long his nails have been pared, however neatly he has been shaved, & tailored, & taught & tuned to say 'Virtue' & 'religion', cannot be relied on when it comes to a pinch, he will forget his morality, & say morality means ↑sucking↓ blood. The man only can be trusted to defend humanity. And women are really the heart & ⟨asylum⟩ sanctuary of our civilization.[244]

[214] The impudence of this pretension is enormous. Mr Choate[,] whose talent consists in a fine choice of words which he can hang ⟨upon⟩ indiscriminately on any offender, has pushed the privilege of his profession so far as to ⟨say⟩ ↑ask ⟨brazen-facedly⟩ hypocritically↓ "What would the puritans of 1620 say to the trashy sentimentalism of modern reformers?" And thus the stern old fathers of Massachusetts who ↑Mr Choate knows↓ would have died at the stake for freedom ↑before soiling themselves with this damnation↓ are made to repudiate the trashy sentimentalism of the Ten Commandments. The joke is too impudent[.] [245]

[215] The profession of the law has the old objection that i⟨s⟩t makes the practitioner callous & skeptical. The practice of defending criminals of all dyes of guilt & holding them up with vehement protestations that they are injured but honest men, firm Christians, models of virtue only a little imprudent & open to practices of [246]

[216] It is the need of Mr Webster's position that he should have an opinion; that he should be a step in advance of everybody else, & make the strongest statement in America; that is vital to him. He cannot ⟨live⟩ ↑maintain himself↓ otherwise.[247]

[217] Mr Webster has deliberately taken out his name from all

[244] The entry on p. [213] is struck through in ink with a wavy vertical use mark; "The little . . . blood." is used in "The Fugitive Slave Law" (1851), *W*, XI, 183.

[245] The entry on p. [214] is struck through in ink with a vertical use mark. For "the trashy sentimentalism of the Ten Commandments.", see p. [125] above.

[246] The entry on p. [215] is struck through in ink with two vertical use marks.

[247] This paragraph is struck through in ink with a vertical use mark.

the files of honour in which he had enrolled it, from all association with liberal, virtuous, & philanthropic men, and read his recantation ↑on his knees at Richmond & Charleston↓. He has gone over in an hour to the party of ⟨tyranny⟩ ↑force↓, & stands now on ↑the↓ precise⟨ly the footing⟩ ↑ground↓ of the Metternic⟨h⟩ks, the Castlereaghs, & the Polignacs, without the excuse of hereditary bias & of ⟨of⟩an ancient name & title which they had. He has undone all that he has spent his years in doing; he has discredited himself[.]

[218] ⟨What right has⟩ He[n] to talk of liberty, & to rate an Austrian?[248] He would dragoon the Hungarians, for all his fine words. ⟨He would Let them not trust him⟩ ↑⟨Kossuth⟩↓ ↑I advise Kossuth after his experience of Gorgey not to trust Webster↓. He would in Austria truckle to the Czar, as he does in America to the Carolinas; and hunt the Hungarians from the Sultan as he does the fugitives of Virginia from the Massachusetts. ⟨Yes⟩ He may bluster.[n] ⟨He has taught⟩ ↑It is his tactics.↓ We shall make no more mistakes. He has taught [219] us the ghastly meaning of liberty[n] in his mouth. It is kidnapping & hunting to death men & women, it is making treason & matter of fine & imprisonment & armed intervention of the resistance of[249]

[220] N

I said the subject of education, of art, of religion, had come to appear bitter mockeries. The newspaper is only a proclamation & detail of our shames. The very question of property, the house & land we occupy, have lost all their sunlight. And a man looks gloomily on his children & ⟨s⟩ thinks what have I done that you should begin life in dishonour[?][250]

I may then add *the Union.* Nothing seems to me more bitterly futile than this bluster about the Union. A year ago we were all lovers & prizers of it. Before the passage of [221] that law ⟨to⟩ which Mr

[248] In the manuscript, "What right has he" is canceled, but the cancel line through "he" is finger-wiped.

[249] "⟨What right . . . resistance of" is struck through in ink with single vertical use marks on pp. [218] and [219].

[250] "I said . . . dishonour", struck through in ink with a vertical use mark, is used in "The Fugitive Slave Law" (1851), *W*, XI, 181–182.

Webster ⟨gave his⟩ made his own, we indulged in all the dreams which foreign nations still cherish of American destiny. But in the new attitude in which we find ourselves, the degradation & ⟨dish⟩ personal dishonour which now rests like miasma on every house in Massachusetts, the sentiment is entirely changed. No man can look his ne↑i↓ghbor in the face. We sneak about with the infamy of crime in the streets, & cowardice in ⟨the⟩ourselves and frankly once for all the Union is sunk[,] the flag is hateful[,] & will be hissed.

[222] The Union! o yes, I prized that, other things being equal; but what is the Union to a man self condemned, with all sense of self respect & chance of fair fame cut off,—with the names of conscience & religion become bitter iro⟨in⟩nies, & liberty the ghastly ⟨kidna⟩ ↑no↓thing which Mr Webster means by that word? The worst ⟨evils⟩ ↑mischiefs↓ that could follow from secession, & new combination of the smallest fragments of the wreck were ⟨blessings⟩ ↑slight & medicable↓ [223] to the ⟨curse⟩ ↑calamity↓ your Union has brought us. Another year, and a standing army ↑officered by Southern gentlemen,↓ to protect the Commissioners & to hunt the fugitives ⟨officered by Southern gentlemen⟩ will be illustrating the ⟨further⟩ ↑new↓ sweets of Union in Boston, Worcester, & Springfield. ⟨From the⟩ It did not appear & it was incredible that ⟨even⟩ the passage of the Law would make the Union odious; but from the day it was attempted to be executed in Massachusetts, this result has appeared [22⟨2⟩4] that the Union is no longer desireable. Whose deed is that? [251]

[225] One more consideration occurs[—]the mischief of a legal crime. The demoralization of the Community. Each of these persons who touches it is contaminated. There has not been in our lifetime another moment when public men were personally lowered by their political action. But here are gentlemen whose names stood as high as any, whose believed probity was the confidence & fortification of all who by fear of public opinion, or by that dangerous ascendency of Southern manners have been drawn into the support of this [226] nefarious business, and have of course changed their relations to men.

[251] "I may . . . that?" is struck through in ink with single curved vertical use marks on pp. [220], [221], [222], [223], and [224].

We poor men in the country who might have thought it an honor to shake hands with them, would now ⟨not⟩ shrink from their touch; nor could they enter our humblest doors. Can the reputed wealth of Mr Eliot restore his good name? Can Mr Curtis reinstate himself, or could Mr Webster obtain now a vote in the state of Massachusetts [n] [227] for the poorest municipal office? [n 252] Well, is not this a loss inevitable to a bad law⟨;⟩?↑—↓ a law which no man can countenance or abet ⟨in ex⟩the execution of, without loss of all self respect, & forfeiting forever the name of a gentleman.[253] We therefore beg you to stand so far the friends of yourselves & of poor well meaning men, your constituents, as not to suffer them to be put in a position where they ⟨must⟩ cannot do right without breaking your law or keep the law without corrupting & dishonouring the community.

[228] The College, the churches, the schools, the very shops ↑& factories↓ are discredited. ⟨One can look at no⟩ ↑Every↓ [n] kind of property & every branch of industry & every avenue to ⟨lab⟩ power suffers injury, and the value of life is reduced.—I had hardly written this before my friend said, "If this law should be repealed, I shall be glad that I have lived; if not, I shall be sorry that I was born." What kind of law is that ↑which extorts this kind of language↓ for a free civilized people? [254]

[229] I am surprised that lawyers can be so blind as to suffer the law to be discredited. The law rests not only in the instinct of all people, but, according to the maxims of Blackstone & ⟨other⟩ ↑the↓ jurists[,] on equity, and it is the cardinal maxim ⟨of law⟩ that a statute contrary to natural right is illegal, is in itself null & void. The practitioners should guard this dogma well, as the palladium of the profession, as their anchor in the respect of mankind.

[252] Samuel Atkins Eliot (1798–1862) was Mayor of Boston, 1837–1839, treasurer of Harvard, statesman, and man of letters. George Ticknor Curtis (1812–1894), United States Commissioner in Boston, ordered the return of fugitive slave Thomas Sims to slavery in April, 1851.

[253] "One more . . . gentleman.", struck through in ink with single vertical use marks on pp. [225] and [227] and two vertical use marks on p. [226], is used in "The Fugitive Slave Law" (1851), *W*, XI, 197–198.

[254] The entry on p. [228], struck through in ink with a vertical use mark, is used in "The Fugitive Slave Law" (1851), *W*, XI, 182.

Against this all the⟨ir⟩ arguments ↑of Webster↓ ⟨are like⟩ ↑make no more impression than↓ the spray of a child's squirt.[255]

[230] The fame of Webster ends in this nasty law.

And as for the Andover & Boston preachers, Dr Dewey & Dr Sharpe ⟨if⟩ who ⟨uphold kid⟩ deduce kidnapping ⟨o⟩from [n] ⟨the law⟩ their Bible, ⟨we say⟩ ↑tell the poor dear doctor↓ if this be Christianity, it is a religion of dead dogs, let it ⟨be infamous, &⟩ never pollute the ears & hearts of noble children again.[256] O bring back then the age when valour was virtue, since what is called morality, [231] means nothing but pudding. Pardon the spleen of a professed hermit.

[232] Mr Webster cannot choose but regret his loss. Tell him that those who make fame, accuse him with one voice: those ⟨who⟩ to whom his name was once dear & honoured as ⟨the one type of⟩ the manly statesman, to whom the ⟨g⟩choicest gifts of nature had been accorded,—eloquence with a simple greatness; those who have no points to carry that are not those of public morals & of generous civilization, [233] ⟨M⟩ the obscure & private who have no voice & care for none ⟨in⟩ as long as things go well, but who feel the infamy of ⟨this⟩ his nasty legislation creeping like a fever into all their homes & ⟨making them weary of their life.⟩ ↑robbing the day of its beauty.↓ Tell him that he who was their pride in the woods & mountains of New England is now their mortification; that they never name him; ↑they have taken his picture from the wall & torn it—dropped the pieces in the gutter[;] they have taken his book of speeches from the shelf & put it in the stove.↓ & he cannot choose but feel [234] the change; and all the fribble of the Daily Advertiser & of its model

[255] The entries on p. [229], struck through in ink with a vertical use mark, are expanded in "The Fugitive Slave Law" (1851), *W*, XI, 190–193.

[256] Emerson is probably referring to Reverend Orville Dewey and to Reverend Daniel Sharp, pastor of the Charles St. Baptist Church, 1812–1853. On the first Thanksgiving Day after President Fillmore signed the Fugitive Slave Law, Sharp preached a sermon calling for obedience to the law on constitutional grounds and arguing that "free citizens of the United States, living under the protection, and enjoying the benefits of our blessed laws, with all the advantages of the national compact, [cannot] be justified in encouraging poor fugitive slaves to acts of resistance. . . ." See Parker Pillsbury, *Acts of the Anti-Slavery Apostles* (Concord, N.H., 1883), pp. 471–472.

the N. Y. Journal of Commerce will not ⟨be able⟩ quite compensate him. I have no fear that any roars of New York mobs will be able to drown this voice in Mr Webster's ear. It can outwhisper all the salvos of their cannon. If it were Mr Cass, it might be different; but Mr Webster ⟨know⟩ has the misfortune to know the voice of truth from the stupid hurrahs of New York.

[235] It will be his distinction to have changed in one day by the most detestable law that was ever enacted by a civilized state, the fairest & most triumphant national escutcheon the sun ever shone upon, the free, the expanding, the hospitable, the irresistible America[,] home of the homeless & pregnant with the blessing of the world, into a jail or barracoon for the slaves of a few thousand Southern planters & all the citizens of this hemisphere into kidnappers & drivers for the same. Is that a name [236] will feed his hungry ambition? [257]

[237] I question the civilization when I see that the public mind had never less hold of the strongest of all truths. I cannot think the most "judicious tubing" a compensation for metaphysical debility.[258]

inconceivable levity of the public mind, an unbroken prosperity the cause.[259]

[238] There are or always were in each country certain gentlemen to whom the honour & dignity of the community were confided, persons of elevated sentiments, ⟨w⟩ relieved perhaps by fortune from the necessity of injurious application to ⟨business⟩ arts of gain, and who used that leisure for the benefit ⟨th⟩of their fellow citizens in the study of elegant learning, the learning of liberty & in their forwardness on all emergences to lead with courage & magnanimity against any [239] peril in the state. I look in vain for such a class

[257] This entry, beginning "Mr Webster cannot . . .", is struck through in ink with single vertical use marks on pp. [232], [233], [234], [235], and [236]; "Mr Webster cannot . . . of their cannon." is used in "The Fugitive Slave Law" (1851), *W*, XI, 201–202.

[258] For " 'judicious tubing' ", see pp. [188]–[189] above.

[259] "I question . . . cause.", struck through in ink with a curved vertical use mark, is used in "The Fugitive Slave Law" (1851), *W*, XI, 183, 184.

among us. And that is the worst symptom in our affairs. The↑re↓ ⟨eleg⟩are persons of fortune ⟨an⟩enough and men of breeding & of elegant learning but they are the very leaders in vulgarity of sentiment. I need call no names. The fact stares us in the face. They are full of sneers & derision &[n] their reading of Cicero & of Plato & of Tacitus has been drowned under grossness of feeding and the bad company they have kept. [240] It is the want perhaps of a stern & high religious training, like the iron Calvinism which /made/steeled/ their fathers seventy five years ago. But though I find the names of old patriots still resident in Boston, it is only the present ↑venerable↓ Mr Quincy who has renewed the hereditary honour of his name by scenting the tyranny in the gale. The others are all lapped in after dinner dreams [241] and are as obsequious to Mr Webster as he is to the gentlemen of Richmond & Charleston. The want of loftiness of sentiment in the class of wealth & education ↑in the University too↓ is deplorable. I am sorry to say I predict too readily their feeling. They will not even understand the depth of my regret & will find their own supercilious & foppish version. But I refer them back to their Cicero & Tacitus & to their early resolutions.

[242] It was always reckoned even in the rudest ages the distinction of the gentleman[,] the oath of honour of the knight[,] to speak the truth to men of power or to angry communities, and ⟨to defend the helpless & avenge⟩ ↑uphold↓ the poor ↑man↓ against ⟨the savage selfishness of⟩ the rich oppressor. Will the educated people of Boston ⟨who imagine themselves gentlemen⟩ ask themselves whether they side with the oppressor or the oppressed? Yet I know no reason why a gentleman, who is I take it a natural formation, should not be [243] true to his ⟨order⟩ ↑duties↓ in Boston ⟨as⟩ in 1850, as haughtily faithful & with as sovereign superiority to all hazards as his fathers had in 1770, or as Mr Hampden ⟨had⟩ or Mr Eliot in London in 1650, or Arundel, or More, or Milton,[260]

[244] I do not value any artificial enthusiasm of protest got up by individuals in corners, which, however vehement, tells for nothing on

[260] This entry, beginning "There are or always were", is struck through in ink with single vertical use marks on pp. [238], [239], [240], [241], [242], and [243].

the public mind; but I look eagerly ↑and shall not have to look long↓ for a spontaneous expression of the ⟨wild animal⟩ injured people,—in fault of leaders creating their own, & shaking off from their back these degenerate & unworthy riders. I make no secret of my intention to keep [245] them informed of the baseness of their accustomed leaders. It is well to quote Cicero & Tacitus when doing the deed of Chiffinch & of Buckingham[.] [261]

The first act ↑as it was very natural↓ was a little hesitating, but the next was easier, & the glib officials will ↑I daresay↓ in a few weeks be quite practised & handy at stealing men. When the session is over Mr Webster on his return to Boston can have call at the wardroo [262]

[246] In the weakness of the Union the law of 1793 was framed, and much may be said in palliation of it. It was a law affirming the existence of two states of civilization or an intimate union between two countries[,] one civilized & Christian & the other barbarous[,] where cannibalism was still permitted. It was a little gross[,] the taste for boiling babies[,] but as long as ⟨the oper⟩ this kind of cookery was confined within their own [247] limits, we could agree for other purposes, & wear one flag. The law affirmed a right to hunt their human prey within our territory; and this law availed just thus much to affirm their own platform,—to ⟨claim⟩ fix the fact, that, though confessedly savage, they were yet at liberty to consort with men;—though they had tails, ⟨&⟩ & their incisors were a little long, yet it is settled that they shall by courtesy be called men; we will all make believe they are Christians; & we promise not to look at their tails or incisors when they come into company. [248] This was all very well. The convenient equality was affirmed, they were admitted to dine & sup, & profound silence on the subject of tails & incisors was kept. No

[261] Both George Villiers, second Duke of Buckingham (1628–1687), and the royal closet keeper William Chiffinch (1602?–1688) were associated with scandals and abuse of power in the court of Charles II.

[262] The increasing lightening of ink in the last word here suggests that Emerson ran out of ink, intending, probably, to write "wardroom." "The first . . . wardroo" is struck through in ink with a vertical use mark; "When the session . . . wardroo" is struck through in ink with vertical and curving oval use marks. "The first . . . stealing men." is used in "The Fugitive Slave Law" (1851), *W*, XI, 196.

man in all New England spoke of Ghilanes in their presence.[263] ⟨b⟩But of course ↑on their part↓ all idea of boiling babies in our caboose was dropt; all idea of hunting ↑in our yards↓ fat babies to boil, ⟨in our yards,⟩ was dropt; & the law became, as it should, a dead letter. It was merely ↑there in the statute-book↓ ⟨written⟩ [249] to soothe the dignity of the maneaters. ⟨But now⟩ And we Northerners had, on our part, indemnified & secured ourselves against any occasional eccentricity of appetite in our confederates by our own interpretation, & by offsetting state-law by state-laws. It was & is penal here in Massachusetts for any sheriff or town[-] or state-officer to lend himself or his jail to the slavehunter, & it is also settled that any slave brought here by ⟨the co⟩his master, becomes free. All this was well. What Mr Webster has [250] now done is ↑not only↓ to re↑-↓enact the old law, ⟨and to *reinforce it*; which and⟩ ↑but↓ *to give it force*, which it never had before, or to bring down the free & Chr↑i↓stian state of Massachusetts to the cannibal level.

They'll say[264]

[251] [blank]

[252] Now this ⟨dem⟩ conspiring to hold up a bad law, and intimate correspondence of leading gentlemen ⟨to⟩ ↑⟨to⟩ mutually engaging to↓ run to New York & to Cambridge, & dine in public on poor Wash↑i↓ngton's birthday, & the reading of the riot-act & ⟨the⟩ of Washington's Legacy, & obtaining the preaching of Rev. Drs. Sharpe & Dewey, seems for the moment successful; & I do not know but Mr Fillmore & Mr Webster & Everett flatter themselves that the difficult Massachusetts is somehow[n] [253] managed, & that they had really overestimated the traditionary rebellion of the town of Boston. Once for all ⟨it⟩ ↑the best lie↓ has this insuperable objection. They are always at the mercy of a truth speaker. It does very well as long as all the spectators agree to make believe with them, but the first unlucky boy that calls things by their names will ruin the cheat. Unless they can coax the good Creator not to ⟨blab⟩ make any more men

[263] "Scientific Gossip" in the *Athenæum* (Sept. 8, 1849) reported on a paper given to the Académie des Sciences by the African traveler, M. E. Du Couret, describing an African tribe of Ghilânes with small tail-like appendages.

[264] These two words are in pencil.

[254] or to make them of the pattern of the Ghilanes unless he will hoodwink them all[.]

⟨There is no⟩My dear sir, ↑Thomas Melville is gone↓,[265] Mr Cabot is dead, ⟨the old⟩ ↑Mr↓ Otis ↑of the Hartford Convention↓ is dead, ↑Mr Quincy is old;↓ ↑the turbulent↓ Quincy Adams is at last ⟨well dead⟩ ↑still;↓ and though there is an unlucky book of the old Adams printing about these times, yet, north or south, we don't hear of any body who will not be peaceable. I think you may venture it.
Ah ⟨my dear sir⟩ ↑Mr President↓ trust not the information. The [255] ⟨burly⟩ ↑gravid↓ old Universe goes ⟨grinding⟩ ↑spawning↓ on; the ⟨spawning generation hurls out ↑to↓⟩ [n] ↑wombs conceive & the breasts give suck to↓ thousands & millions of ⟨English-speaking souls,⟩ ↑hairy babes↓ ⟨no⟩formed not in the image ⟨& likeness⟩ of your ⟨law⟩ ↑statute↓, but in the image ⟨& likeness⟩ of the Universe, too many to be bought off, too many than that they can be rich, & therefore peaceable, and necessitated to express ↑first & last by one or another↓ every truth of nature. You can keep no secret, for whatever is true, some of them will say, [256] however unseasonably. You can commit no crime for they are created in their ⟨bone &⟩ nature & sentiments conscious of & hostile to it: and unless you can suppress the English tongue in America, & hinder boys from declaiming Webster's Plymouth speech, & pass a law against libraries,—
This dreadful English speech is saturated with songs, proverbs & speeches that flatly contradict & defy every [257] line of Mr Mason's Statute.[266] Then sir there is England itself,—fault⟨y⟩s of her own undoubtedly,—but unhappily now so clean on this question,—that she will give publicity to every ⟨stain⟩ vice & trick of ours. ↑There is France,—There is Germany, but worst a thousand times worse than all, there is this yeaning America[,] the yeaning northwest, millions of souls to accuse us.↓ If the thing were to be carried in a close corpora-

[265] Herman Melville's grandfather (1751–1832), revolutionary patriot and soldier.

[266] "Now this . . . Statute." is struck through in ink with single vertical use marks on pp. [252], [253], [254], [255], [256], and [257]; "Ah . . . Mr President [p. [254]] . . . Statute." is used in "The Fugitive Slave Law" (1851), *W*, XI, 194.

tion, all the persons might be sounded & secured ⟨before the attempt was made⟩. ⟨I⟩Even in a senate, even in a House, they can ⟨know the⟩ calculate the exact amount of resistance; but ⟨not⟩ ↑this is↓ quite impossible in a country. For one, only one truth speaker will ruin them.[267]

[258] This affectation of using sacred days & names,—Washington's birthday forsooth, & the Pilgrims' day, for the effusion of all this rancid oil of eloquence on compromises[268] seems to be a hint borrowed from the adepts at Rochester, where Mrs Tubbs & Mr Potts very familiarly summon the Spirit of the deceased Dr Channing's & of Goethe, & of Swedenborg, [259] to affirm the respectability ↑& transparent honour↓ of Madam Tubbs & of Master Potts.[269]

What is the use of logic & legal acumen if it be not ⟨to⟩ to demonstrate to the people what is metaphysically true? [n] The fact that a⟨n inequitable⟩ ↑criminal↓ statute is illegal—is admitted by lawyers ⟨but⟩ and, that fact once admitted by the people, the whole structure of this new tyranny falls to the ground.[270] Why do not the lawyers who are professionally its ⟨expositors⟩ interpreters put this home to the people? [n] There is for every man a statement possible of that [⟨259⟩260] truth which he is most unwilling to receive, a statement possible, so pungent & so ample that he cannot get away from it, but must either bend to it or die of it. Else, there would be no such word as eloquence, which means this. Mr Webster did that thing in his better days for Hayne. Mr Hayne could not hide from himself that something had been shown him & shown the whole world which

[267] "If the . . . them." is struck through in ink with a curved vertical use mark.

[268] The tail of the "n" in "on" is joined to the "c" of "compromises"; a vertical pencil line is drawn between the words to separate them.

[269] "This affectation . . . Master Potts." is struck through in ink with single vertical use marks on pp. [258] and [259]. In Mrs. Tubbs and Mr. Potts, Emerson is obviously ridiculing the spiritualist movement in Rochester, N.Y., which began in 1847 when mysterious rappings were heard in houses occupied by the Fox sisters, and grew into a pseudoreligion in which the practitioners insisted they could communicate with spirits.

[270] "The fact . . . ⟨but⟩ and," is marked in the left margin by a pencil line, possibly a use mark.

he did not wish to see.[271] He left public life & retired, &, it is said, [26⟨0⟩1] died of it. Mr Webster has now in his turn chosen ⟨the wrong horse⟩ ↑evil for good,↓ & ⟨more⟩ less ⟨un⟩innocently than Mr Hayne, and Mr Hayne is avenged. For it is ⟨as⟩ certain ⟨as that water will boil at 212° or stones fall, or sap rise,⟩ that he will be cast & ruined. He fights with an adversary not subject to casualties.

Tout est soldat pour vous combattre[.]

Everything that can walk, turns soldier to fight this down.[272]

[262] It is said, that, events within a few years have shown a levity in the morals of the population; that the pe⟨ro⟩rsons who can be relied on to stick to what they have said & agreed ⟨is⟩are few & fewer.[273]

Mr Webster unfortunately is the most remarkable example. The Whig Conventions plead his example & almost come up with it.

But Aristotle's reply ⟨w⟩to the question, What ⟨is the disadvantage of⟩ ↑advantage a man may gain by↓ lying? is still true; "not to be believed when he speaks the truth," ⟨I should say,⟩ ↑much more,↓ 'not to be believed when he lies again.'[274]

[263] Webster & Choate think to discredit the higher law by personalities[;] they insinuate much about transcendentalists & ab-

[271] "*Printed in Eloquence Society & Solitude*" is written in ink in the left margin; "There is . . . see.", struck through in ink with four vertical use marks on p. [259] and a single vertical use mark on p. [260], is used in "Eloquence," *W*, VII, 91–92. "truth which . . . means this." is also struck through in pencil with a vertical use mark.

[272] This sentence is marked in the left margin with a pencil line; "Tout est . . . down." is used in "The Fugitive Slave Law" (1854), *W*, XI, 237. For "Tout est . . . combattre", see p. [139] above.

[273] This sentence is struck through in ink with a wavy vertical use mark.

[274] The cancellation of "I should say" and the inserted "much more," are in pencil, traced in ink. See Diogenes Laërtius, "Aristotle," *The Lives and Opinions of Eminent Philosophers*, V, 17: "To the question, 'what do people gain by telling lies?', his answer was, 'Just this, that when they speak the truth they are not believed.' "

stractionists & people of no weight. It is the ⟨easy⟩ ↑cheap↓ cant of lawyers & of merchants in a failing condition, & of rogues. These classes usually defend an immorality by the practice of men of the world, & talk of dreamers & enthusiasts; every woman has been debauched by being made to believe that it is the mode, it is custom & none but the priest & a few devout visionaries ever think otherwise. [264] People never bring their history into politics, or this thin smoke would deceive nobody[.]
It is the most impolitic of all steps, this demoralization of the people. "Poets are the guardians of reverence in the hearts of the people." [275] It must always happen that the guiding counsels of ages & nations should come not from ⟨presidents of nations⟩ ↑statesmen↓ or political leaders, always men of scared consciences, 'half villains', who, it has been said, are more dangerous [265] than whole ones, ⟦Mr Webster would be very sorry if ⟨any⟩ this country should take his ↑present↓ counsel, ⟨c⟩for any but this particular emergency⟧ but from contemplative men aloof by taste & necessity from these doubtful activities, and really ⟨aware of competent⟩ aware of the truth long bef⟨roe⟩ore the contemporary statesman because more impressionable. Mr Webster never opened a jury case without praising the law-abiding disposition of this people. But he knows that they owe this [276]

[266] Mr Everett[,] a man supposed aware of his own meaning[,] advises ⟨a⟩pathetically a reverence for the Union. Yes but hides the other horn under this velvet? Does he mean that we shall ⟨take⟩ ↑lay hands on↓ a man who has escaped from slavery to the soil of Massachusetts & so has done more for freedom than ⟨an⟩ten thousand orations, & tie him up & call in the marshal, and say,—I am an orator for freedom; a great many fine sentences have I turned,—none has turned finer, except Mr Webster,—in favour of ⟨l⟩plebeian [267] strength against aristocracy; and, as my last & finest sentence of all, to show the young men of the land who have bought my book & clapped my sentences & copied them in their memory, how much I mean by them,—Mr Marshal, here is a black man of my own age,

[275] Quoted in *Memorials of Mrs. Hemans*, ed. Henry F. Chorley, 2 vols. (New York, 1836), II, 225. See *JMN*, VII, 154.

[276] "People never . . . this" is struck through in pencil with single vertical use marks on pp. [264] and [265].

& who does not know ⟨as much⟩ ↑a great deal↓ of Demosthenes, but who means what he says, whom ⟨I⟩ we will now handcuff and commit to the ⟨cl⟩custody of this very worthy gentleman who has come on from Georgia in search of him; I have no doubt he has much [268] to say to him that is interesting & ⟨I will use the opportunity to send⟩ [277] ↑as the way is long I ⟨will not⟩ don't care if I give them↓ a copy of my Concord & Lexington & Plymouth & Bunker Hill addresses to ⟨r⟩beguile their journey from ⟨here⟩ ↑Boston↓ to the plantation whipping post? [n] Does Mr Everett really mean this? that he & I shall do this? Mr Everett understands English, as few men do who speak it. Does he mean this? Union is a delectable thing, & so is wealth, & so is life, ⟨y⟩ but they may *all* [n] cost too much, if they cost honour. If

[269] It is very remarkable how rare a bad law, an immoral law, is. Does Mr Everett know how few examples in Civil history there are of bad laws? I do not think it will be easy to parallel the crime of Mr Webster's law. But the crime of kidnapping is on a footing with the crimes of murder [278] & of incest and if the Southern states should find it necessary to enact the further law in view of the too great increase of blacks that every fifth manchild should be boiled in hot water,—& obtain a majority in Congress ⟨b⟩ with a speech by [270] Mr Webster to ⟨en⟩ add an article to the Fugitive Slave Bill,—that any fifth child so & so selected, having escaped into Boston should be /boiled there/seethed in water at 212°/ ⟨by Rev. Mr Sharpe,⟩ will not the mayor & alderman boil him? Is there the smallest moral distinction between such a law, & the one now enacted? How can Mr E. put at nought all manly ⟨d⟩qualities,[n] all his claims to truth & sincerity, for the sake of backing up this cowardly nonsense? [n]

[271] ⟨O⟩Does he mean this, that he & I shall do this, or does he ⟨mean⟩ ↑secretly know↓ that he will ⟨suffer damnation⟩ ↑die the death↓ sooner than lift a finger in the matter, he or his son, or his son's son,

[277] "here are copies" is inserted, beginning above "send". It does not seem to fit into the syntax of Emerson's revision.

[278] "It is . . . law, is." and "examples in Civil . . . to parallel" are each struck through in pencil with two vertical use marks; "It is . . . of murder" is used in "The Fugitive Slave Law" (1851), *W*, XI, 187.

and only ⟨w⟩hopes to persuade certain truckmen & constables to do this, that ⟨he & his⟩ ↑rich men↓ may enjoy their estates in more security? [n]

↑The historian tells us that↓ "Thrasymachus's sophistry was political, & his aim the destruction of freedom, by extinguishing that sense of justice, on which it must ever be based."
J. A. St John [*The History . . . of Ancient Greece*, 1842, I,] p[p. 257–]258

[272] If [?]
Mr Webster is fond of fame. His taste is likely to be gratified. For there is not a man of thought or ingenuity, but at every dinner table, in every private letter, in every newspaper I take up, is ⟨racking his brain⟩ ↑forced↓ to say some thing biting of this enemy of the honour of Massachusetts. ⟨All⟩ He has the curse of all this Country which ⟨d⟩he [n] has afflicted.
[273] ⟨N⟩ One way certainly the Nemesis is seen. Here is a measure of pacification & union. What is its effect? that it has made one subject, one only subject for conversation, & painful thought, throughout the Union, Slavery.[n] [279] We eat it, we drink it, ↑we breathe it,↓ we trade, we study, we wear it.[n] ⟨we spew it out⟩ We are all poisoned with it, & after the fortnight the symptoms appear, purulent, making frenzy in the head & rabidness

[274] What a moment was lost when Judge [Lemuel] Shaw declined to affirm the unconstitutionality of the Fugitive Slave Law! [280]

⟨I concede that it is not quite analogous⟩ The [n] present crisis ↑is not analogous↓ to the Revolution. No liberty of the controlling classes is now threatened. If the South, or if the Federal Government threatened the liberty of any class, ⟨or any⟩ I doubt not, there would

[279] "Here is . . . Slavery," is used in "The Fugitive Slave Law" (1851), *W*, XI, 199.

[280] On April 7, 1851, in Boston, Judge Lemuel Shaw (1781–1861) refused to release from jail, on habeas corpus, the fugitive slave Thomas M. Sims, who was returned to slavery.

be as violent reaction as was then. [275] This is merely a case of conscience, not of ⟨resis⟩ anger, a call for compassion, a call for mercy,

That is one thing; now it is not less imperative that this nation should say, this Slavery shall not be, it poisons & depraves everything it touches[.]
There can never be peace whilst this devilish seed of war is in our soil. Root it out. Burn it up. Pay for the damage & let us have done [276] with it. It costs a hundred millions. Twice so much were cheap for it. Boston is a little city, & ⟨wo⟩yet is worth near 200 millions. Boston itself would pay a large fraction of the sum, to be clean of it. I would pay a tithe of my estate with joy; for this calamity darkens my days. It is a local accidental distemper, & ⟨will⟩ the vast interests of a cont↑i↓nent cannot ⟨long⟩ be sacrificed [277] for it.

[278] Lord John Russell ⟨said⟩ ↑in Parliament, spoke↓ to this effect; "I know there are gentlemen in this House who think that the conquests of England cost too much, that the colonies ⟨of E⟩ ought to be abandoned, and the army & navy reduced, & the whole expense of this Empire put on the narrowest economy. Perhaps they are right; but let not me be the instrument of bringing down the glories of England to this humiliation." [281]

⟨If for⟩ ↑I wish↓ Mr Webster could have had the like ↑fine↓ sense of personal honour,—he who had asked "if there was not to be a North," he who had pledged himself [279] to resist all extension of slave area, all Compromise.[282]

[280₁] It is contrary to the sense of Duty; and therefore all human beings, in proportion to their power of thought & their moral sensibility, are, as soon as they are born, the ⟨irreconcileable⟩ ↑natural↓ enemies of this statute.

[281] Cf. Lord Russell's speech to the House of Commons, March 13, 1848, *Hansard* (Third Series), vol. 97, p. 519.

[282] In a speech at Marshfield, September 1, 1848, Webster had said: "I think there will be a North; but up to the recent session of Congress there has been no North . . . in which there has been found a strong, conscientious, and *united* opposition to slavery." *Writings* . . . , 1903, IV, 135. "Lord John . . . Compromise." is struck through in ink with single vertical use marks on pp. [278] and [279].

⟨I am⟩

⟨Dangers⟩ ↑Evils↓ of a bad law are sure to appear. Fitchburg Road evades the manifest intention of their Charter, & calls what is merely *its second track from Acton to Concord* a part of the *Sterling Branch Road*. Well, it obtains a sanction in the legislature for this fraud. [281_1] Now comes a ⟨no⟩ petition for a North⟨r⟩boro & Sterling Road infringing the Fitchburg privileges by a ruinous competition & lapping, & the Fitchburg men say, "This is robbery." But their case excites no pity, but only a sneer of "*Aha! Robbery is it, this time?*"

[280_2] Hosmer says, Sims came on a good errand; ↑for↓ Sumner is elected, Rantoul & Palfrey are likely to be; ⟨&⟩ the state of Massachusetts ought to buy that fellow.[283]

I find ↑it has made↓ every student ⟨is⟩ a student of law[.] [284]
The destiny of America, the Union, yes, great things, dear to the heart & imagination, & not to be put at risk by every young ranter.

⟨W⟩But a larger state, a prior union, still dearer to heart & imagination, & much longer to be our country is the World. We will not levy war against that, to please this New Hampshire strapper, ⟨i⟩nor the Carolinas.

[281_2] We will buy the slaves at a hundred millions. It will be cheaper than any of our wars. It will be cheap at the cost of a national debt like England's.—

But we must put out this poison, this conflagration, this raging fever of Slavery out of the Constitution. If Webster had known a true

[283] Emerson's reference is probably to Edmund Hosmer. Sumner's election and news of the Thomas Sims fugitive slave case in the newspapers both occurred in April, 1851, the likely date of this entry. John Gorham Palfrey (1796–1881), Unitarian clergyman, editor, historian, and abolitionist, was a congressional candidate for the Free Soil party. Emerson spoke against the Fugitive Slave Law in Palfrey's campaign in May, 1851. For Rantoul, see Journal AZ, p. [212] above.

[284] With this sentence, cf. "The Fugitive Slave Law" (1851), *W*, XI, 199: "It has . . . made every citizen a student of natural law."

& generous policy, this would have made him. He is a spent ball. It is the combined wealth behind him that makes him of any avail. And that is as bad as Europe[.]

[284][285] "The doctrine of ⟨m⟩*Manilius* is, that the earth is at rest, prest on all sides by equal forces: Yet his language is remarkably coincident with the Newtonian theory of gravitation."

> Imaque de cunctis mediam tenet undique sedem.
> Id circoque manet stabilis, quia totus ab illa
> Tantundem refugit mundus: fecitque cadendo
> Undique ne caderet. Medium totius et imum est,
> Ictaque contractis consistunt corpora plagis.[286]
> Lib. I. 167 170[287]

[28⟨4⟩5] "Eripuit que Jovi fulmen, viresque tonandi."[288]
↑Manilius,↓ [*Astronomica*,] Lib. I. l. 104

> ↑Eripuit coelo fulmen, sceptrumque tyrannis.
> *Algernon Sydney*.↓[289]

[285] For explanation of the gap in pagination, see the bibliographical note.

[286] "[So the earth, a ball, endures and fashions the universe,] and in respect to the lowest point of all things it holds a central place in all respects. It remains stable in the center, because in respect to it, the whole turns just as much and the earth does this in every respect when it falls, but the center of the whole and the lowest point do not fall. The bodies, by impulses, contain themselves in narrow zones" (Ed.). The "est" after "imum" does not appear in the A. E. Housman text of Manilius, and l. 167 follows l. 214. Emerson was evidently copying from one of the many corrupt texts.

[287] The last four letters of "contractis" are canceled, "#ictis" is written below the canceled letters, in pencil, and probably not by Emerson. "Manilius (?)" is written to the left of "Lib." in pencil, perhaps by Emerson.

[288] See p. [64] above.

[289] "And he snatched the lightning from heaven, and the scepter from tyrants" (Ed.). See p. [64] above. An adaptation of Manilius, *Astronomica*, I, 104 (see the entry immediately above), these words were applied by Turgot to Benjamin Franklin and were printed on portraits and medallions of the American statesman when he was "Ambassador" to France. See *JMN*, VI, 208, where the quotation is followed by one from "*Sidney*"; apparently Emerson copied the "Eripuit coelo" quotation from his Notebook Encyclopedia and wrongly ascribed it to Sydney. Underlying "Eripuit . . . *Sydney*." are traces of erased pencil writing, apparently an earlier inscription of the same words.

[286] Think, you rascal! "Réfléchissez. Rappelez vous du mot que j'ai dict⟨is⟩é, et écrivez le. Je ne repéterai pas le mot."

↑*Napoleon.*↓[290]

History of liberty

'Tis idle to complain of abolitionist [&] Free Soiler. See-saw, up & down, tilts the pole, ⟨j⟩swings the pendulum of the world. Violen⟨t⟩ce is followed by collapse, cruelty by pity. You cannot get rid of women, you cannot cut the heart out, & leave the life in. The atrocities of Savages exasperated Christianity into being[n] [287] & power. Christianity lived by love of the people. "Bishop Wilfrid, on receiving the grant of Selsey from the Caedwealha of Wesse⟨y⟩x, immediately manumitted 250 serfs whom he found attached to the soil. The clergy obtained respite from labor for the boor on the Sabbath, on certain festivals, &c. The lord who compelled his (boor) to labor between sunset on Saturday & sunset on Sunday, forfeited him altogether."

See Kemble I. 211.

Saxons[291]

"A nation never falls until the citadel of its moral being has been betrayed & become untenable." Kemble [*The Saxons in England* . . . , 1849, I, 307]

[288]–[289] [blank]
[290] [Index material omitted]
[291] [Index material omitted]
[292] [blank]
[inside back cover] [blank]

[290] Henry Richard Vassall Fox, Baron Holland, *Foreign Reminiscences* (New York, 1851), p. 186. See *JMN*, VI, 356–357.

[291] John Mitchell Kemble, *The Saxons in England. A History of the English Commonwealth till the Period of the Norman Conquest*, 2 vols. (London, 1849), I, 211–212. "The atrocities . . . altogether.'", struck through in ink with two vertical use marks on p. [286] and one vertical use mark on p. [287], is used in "Religion," *W*, V, 216.

CO

1851

Journal CO, a regular journal, covers the period from May to November, 1851, thus overlapping entries in Journal BO, kept concurrently up through October, 1851. Dated entries run from July 22 (p. [107]) to November 1 (p. [287]). (For the dates of Emerson's two western trips in 1851, during which he recorded entries in Journal at the West, see the headnote to Journal BO.) Although there are no unusually heavy concentrations of entries devoted to one or more topics (as in Journal BO, on the Fugitive Slave Law question, for example), slavery and notes on Margaret Fuller are preoccupations here in addition to other eclectic journal matter.

Journal CO is written in a hard-cover copybook, virtually identical to those designated TU, AZ, and BO. The cover, 17.7 x 21.1 cm, is of predominantly brown paper marbled with blue, black, and yellow over boards, with a tan leather margin at the binding and forming two triangles at the top and bottom outer edges. The spine, of brown leather, now cracked and peeling, has "CO" in ink on the upper portion, the "C" barely visible. The front cover is inscribed "CO" centered in ink on the upper portion of the marbled paper, "CO/1851" in ink on the upper leather triangular corner, and "CO" in ink on the lower triangular corner. The back cover is inscribed in ink "CO" on the lower triangular corner. The unruled pages measure 17.3 x 20.3 cm. The pages are numbered in ink except for the following 35 in pencil: 80, 86, 91, 109, 112, 113, 120, 122, 124, 126, 130, 132, 134, 136, 138, 140, 141, 142, 144, 150, 156, 160, 162, 168, 169, 178, 179, 180, 182, 184, 190, 192, 206, 208, 244. Fifteen pages are unnumbered: 127, 133, 137, 139, 143, 145, 149, 159, 177, 183, 185, 189, 209, 263, 294 (verso of flyleaf). Only two pages are blank, 177 and 189, and only one leaf is missing — that bearing pages 269–270 has been torn out. Page 49 is mistakenly numbered 21, and seven pages have been misnumbered, then corrected: 1⟨9⟩09, ⟨304⟩204, ⟨305⟩205, 21⟨0⟩2, 21⟨1⟩3, 21⟨2⟩4, 21⟨3⟩5. Fifteen pages, originally numbered in pencil, are renumbered in ink: 100, 101, 118, 119, 121, 128, 148, 163, 164, 166, 167, 170, 186, 187, 188. Glued to the bottom of page 214 is a newspaper clipping, "The Passage of the Baltic."

[front cover]

CO
1851

CO

CO

[front cover verso] [Index material omitted]

↑Examined this book throughout, Nov. '77.↓[1]

[i] [Index material omitted]

1851.

R. W. Emerson

CO

1851

Speak as you find.
[Tacitus, *Histories*, Bk. 1, i]

θεοῦ θέλοντος κἂν ἐπὶ ῥιπὸς πλέοι.[2]

[ii] [blank]

[1] Audubon saw the great Eagle first over one of the great lakes at a vast distance; and never got another sight of it, until ten years afterwards, at a place 3000 miles away from the first.

American Authors.
⟨I⟩Œhlenschlager said, that, when he wrote in Danish, he wrote to no more than two hundred ⟨per⟩readers.[3]

[1] "Examined . . . '77." is written in pencil and enclosed in a penciled oval line.

[2] The proverb may be translated, "If God wanted him to, he'd go to sea on a mat" (Ed.).

[3] This sentence, struck through in ink with a vertical use mark, is used in "Ability," *W*, V, 100.

[2] ↑*Lecturing.*↓

Experimentum in corpore vili.[4] The barber learns his art on the orphan's face. Cobden & Phillips learned their art at the expense of many a poor village Lyceum & country church.[5]

↑*House of Fame*↓

"Hearest thou not the great swough?
Yes perdie, quoth I, & well enow.
And what sound is it like? quoth he⟨?⟩.

Like the beating of the sea,
Quoth I, against the rocks hollow
Whe⟨r⟩n tempests do their ships swallow,
And that a man stand out of dou↑b↓t
A mile thence & hear it route." [Chaucer, *The House of Fame*, ll. 1031–1038]

[3] George Minott thinks that it is of no use balloting, for it will not stay, but ⟨if you do⟩ what you do with the gun will stay so.[6] ↑printed↓ [7]

[4] Dante said, when invited to go to Rome, "If I go, who will stay? and, if I stay, who will go?" [8]

I sat at the table at ——— House & said each of these men has one privilege, but some hold two, some three, some ten tickets, or, are here by so many several rights.[9] That man by his political importance;

[4] "Experiment on a worthless body" (Ed.).

[5] With this sentence, cf. "Power," *W*, VI, 78: "Stumping it through England for seven years made Cobden a consummate debater. Stumping it through New England for twice seven trained Wendell Phillips."

[6] This sentence, struck through in ink with a vertical use mark, is used in "Courage," *W*, VII, 260.

[7] Below this word and slightly right of the center of the page is a pencil drawing of an oval, with three small circles, one at the top of and two within the oval; several straight lines extend from the circles and the outer left side of the oval.

[8] This sentence, struck through in ink with two vertical use marks, is used in "Society and Solitude," *W*, VII, 8. A famous anecdote about Dante, c. 1300, it is his answer to those who asked him to head an embassy to the Pope. See C. A. Dinsmore, *Aids to the Study of Dante* (Boston, 1903), p. 101.

[9] An entry in Notebook BO Conduct, p. [8], identifies Emerson's reference here as "the American House", a hotel in Boston.

he must be courted, & his weight in the St⟨eig⟩ate House is not mentally forgotten for a moment; he can talk, or sulk, as he chooses. That next man, by his knowledge & business talent; the next to him, by his jovial fellowship; the next, by his entire selfsubsistency & preoccupation with his own affair; & next was a spirited boy, perfectly at home; & next, a ⟨good⟩bon vivant.

[5] ↑Superlative↓
Vasari does not hesitate to say "Nature herself was surpassed by the colours of Raphael" Bohn's Vasari Vol II p 362 [10]

He tells us, that the ancient masters vanquished nature herself ⟨but⟩most gloriously; but that Michel Angelo Buonaroti vanquished them. [Vasari, *Lives* . . . , 1850–1852, II,] p 364

[6] Vasari's life of Piero di Cosimo[,] the eccentric painter ↑is excellent↓, & reminds me in its traits of tragic figures well known to me. [*Ibid.*, II, 412–425]

For the old Italian ↑homage &↓ hospitality to ⟨& rev⟩ Art, there is a good anecdote in the life of Leonarda Da Vinci. *Bohn's Vasari.* [*Ibid.*,] II. 382–3.

[7] Correggio painted in the Church of San Antonio at Parma a Virgin & Magdalen "& near them a boy representing a little angel with a book in his hand, who is smiling so naturally, that all who look on him are moved to smile also; nor is there any one, however melancholy his temperament, who can behold him without feeling a sensation of pleasure." Vasari [*ibid.*,] II. *406*

[8] No answer could be better to most of the proslavery eloquence than our unscrupulous Mr Foster's to Cheney at the Post Office, "Fiddlestick." [11] See *C*. 161

[10] Giorgio Vasari, *Lives of the Most Eminent Painters, Sculptors, and Architects* . . . , trans. Mrs. Jonathan Foster, Bohn edition, 5 vols. (London, 1850–1852), in Emerson's library.

[11] With this sentence, cf. "Art and Criticism," *W*, XII, 287. Stephen Symonds

The worst of antislavery, like war, I find, is, that it spoils conversation; and it is disgraceful to find one's self saying after the newspapers.[12] ⟨See⟩

[9] The old woman who was shown the telegraph & the railroad, said, "Well, God's works are great, but man's works are greater!"

The wonderful machinery has inspired old Tantalus with a new hope of somehow contriving to ⟨waylay &⟩ bottle the wave.[13]

↑printed↓

[10] "The man who is his own master knocks in vain at the doors of poetry." [14] Plato [*Phaedrus*, 245]

The old guide knows the passes from mountain to mountain, the bridges over gorge & torrent; & the salvation of numberless lives is in his oaken staff: and my guide knew not less the difficult roads of thought, the infinitely cunning transitions from ⟨one⟩ law to law in metaphysics; in the most hopeless mazes, he could find a cheerful road, leading upward, & lighted as by the midday sun.

[11] A topic of the "Conduct of Life" under the head of *Prudence*,[n] should be how to live with unfit companions: for, with such, life is, for the most part, spent: and Experience teaches little better than our earliest instinct of selfdefence, namely, not to engage, not to mix yourself in any manner with them, but let their madness spend itself unopposed; You are You, & I am I.[15]

Another topic under the same head should be the practice of

Foster (1809–1881) was an antislavery lecturer. Emerson may refer to John Milton Cheney, a classmate at Harvard and cashier in a Concord bank.

[12] With this sentence, cf. "War," *W*, XI, 156: "Fontenelle expressed a volume of meaning when he said, 'I hate war, for it spoils conversation.'" See also *JMN*, II, 369, and VI, 137.

[13] This sentence, struck through in ink with three vertical use marks, is used in "Works and Days," *W*, VII, 163.

[14] See Journal BO, p. [182] above.

[15] This sentence, struck through in ink with a vertical use mark, is used in "Considerations by the Way," *W*, VI, 270.

↑D.↓ S↑hattuck↓.,[16] who ⟨wh⟩ reads his sentence in the newspaper three times over, before he speaks of it. ↑and who ⟨gave⟩at the Cattle Show ⟨in Concord⟩ Dinner in Concord after a bad Discourse ⟨of the Orator of the day ↑Mr↓⟩ [n] offered the toast. "The Orator of the Day,—his subject deserves the attention of every farmer."↓ [17]

[12] [↑Printed in *Essays & Social Aims.*↓]

I notice, in the road, that the landscape is uninteresting enough, but a little water instantly relieves the monotony. For it is no matter what objects are near it;—a grey rock, a little grass, a crab-tree, or alder-bush, a stake,—they instantly become beautiful by being reflected. It is rhyme to the eye, & explains the charm of rhyme to the ear, & suggests the deeper rhyme or translation of every [13] natural object into its spiritual sphere.[18]

↑And is crazy about Mr Tompkins↓ [19]

"Wood is faith" according to Swedenborg.

When R. don't care for Julius, suddenly Julius comes round & ⟨&⟩cares for ⟨him⟩ ↑R.↓; & shows the involuntary revelation which character makes of itself.

↑Manners↓ [20]

I think all solid values run directly into manners[.]

This floor holds us up by a fight with agencies that go to pull us down. The whole world is a series of balanced [14] antagonisms[.]

[16] "hattuck" is added in pencil.

[17] An asterisk is attached to "it." and evidently refers to Emerson's footnote, "See bottom of page 10." "and who . . . farmer.' ", written upside down on the bottom of p. [10], belongs with the Shattuck entry on p. [11] and is here so inserted by the editors. For the Cattle Show anecdote, see *JMN*, VII, 459. Col. Daniel Shattuck was president of the Concord Bank. "and who . . . farmer.' " is used in "The Superlative," *W*, X, 171.

[18] This paragraph, struck through in ink with a single vertical and three diagonal use marks on p. [12] and two diagonal use marks on p. [13], is used in "Poetry and Imagination," *W*, VIII, 45.

[19] Added in pencil.

[20] Added in pencil.

You can't write up what is ⟨done down⟩ ↑falling by natural gravity↓.[21] You can't write up Fourier↑ism,↓ whilst one man overlays, uses, eats up another, as an animal eats the vegetable. Yes, but when the Socialistic Idea stirs in the mind, it causes writing, with efforts of all kinds[.]

[15] I like much in Allingham's poetry, but you must not remember the Masters. Chaucer, Milton, Shakspeare, have seen mountains, if they speak of them. The young writers seem to have seen pictures of mountains. The wish to write poetry they have, instead of the poetic fury; and what they write is studies, sketches, fantasies, & not yet the inestimable poem. The vein is too poor to be worth working: it affords ⟨ingots⟩specimens, but not ingots. It is therefore a mere luxury, their work, amateur poetry; but[n] whenever I meet true poetry, [16] ↑and though it appear only in a single mind,↓ I shall sit down to it as the result & justification of the Age, & think very little of histories & statutes.

↑none of your p⟨ian⟩arlor & piano poetry.↓[22]

[17] Concord is "sma' mercies."

Characters ⟨are⟩ and talents are complemental or suppletory and the ⟨flo⟩ house & the world stands by balanced antagonisms[.][23]

↑See above. p. 13
See p. 24 repeated↓[24]

[18] Prudence. One of the cardinal rules is Timeliness. My neighbor the carriage maker, all summer is making Sleighs, and all winter is making light gay gigs & chariots for June & August; & so, on the firs↑t↓ days of the new season is ready with his carriage, which is

[21] This sentence is used in "Eloquence," *W*, VIII, 131, and "The Man of Letters," *W*, X, 256–257.

[22] This phrase is used in "Poetry and Imagination," *W*, VIII, 63.

[23] "Characters . . . antagonisms", struck through in ink with a diagonal use mark, is used in "Powers and Laws of Thought," *W*, XII, 53.

[24] "above." is struck through in ink with a diagonal line. "See Ext. from Manilius at end of BO" is written in pencil to the left of "See p. 24"; "repeated" is also in pencil.

itself an invitation. And the putting the letter into the post one minute before the mail-bag is closed, is a great triumph over Fate. And in all our affairs the sense of being ready & [19] up with the hour imparts to a man's countenance & demeanour a wonderful air of leisure & success. A man who is always behind time, is careworn & painful.

Prudence

"Les bons comptes font les bons amis."

[20] Where is nature? Where shall we go to study her interior aspects? She is hard to find. The botanist after completing his herbarium remains a dry doctor, no poet. The lumberer in Maine woods by Moosehead Lake does not get into the forest to any purpose, ⟨but⟩ ↑though he↓ drives logs with his feet in the water all day. The poet goes ⟨ignorantly⟩ ↑untimely↓ into a ⟨hundred⟩ ↑dozen↓ inviting dells, & finds himself not yet admitted, but a poor excluded dilettante. [21] He makes many desperate attempts to throw the brush at the picture, but rarely ⟨rarely⟩ makes a good hit.[25] Ah when! Ah how rarely! ⟨does⟩ ↑can↓ he draw a true Aeolian note from the harp.—And then comes some fine ↑young↓ gentleman like Milton or Goethe, ↑⟨or Scott even⟩↓ who draws on his good London boots, ↑and in coat of newest tailoring,↓ ⟨takes his gentleman's coat &⟩ ↑with↓ gold--headed cane, ⟨&⟩ marches forth into the groves & straight ↑as if he were going to his Club,↓ to the secret sacred dell, where all the Muses & ⟨all⟩ the shyest gods, fauns, & naiads, [22] have their home. So also did Collins, & so did Spenser: nay, Walter Scott himself ⟨was a⟩ sheriff of Selkirkshire, ⟨was⟩is admitted in full suit to the crag & burn.

My texts are

Moonlight caves when all the fowls
Are safely housed save bats & owls[26]
&c &c

[25] With this sentence, cf. the anecdote about Protogenes, from Montaigne, in *JMN*, VIII, 55.

[26] Beaumont and Fletcher, *The Nice Valour, or The Passionate Mad-man*, III, i; see *JMN*, I, 382, and *Parnassus*, pp. 138–139. The couplet is used in "Poetry and Imagination," *W*, VIII, 55, and "Love," *W*, II, 177.

Mountains on whose barren breast &c
[Milton, "L'Allegro," l. 73]

Bubbling runnels joined the sound
[Collins, "The Passions: An Ode for Music," l. 63][27]

——

Shakspeare's threnes

——

[23] The railroad & telegraph are great unionists. Frank Browne told me that, whilst he was at Savannah, they were telegraphing ↑to↓ the President at Washington, every hour, news of the Cuban invaders.[28]

New man, new method.
Every man is a new method, & distributes all things anew. If he could attain complete development, he would take up first or last atom by atom all the world into a new crystal hitherto undescribed.[29] But, fault of time, & of ⟨cor⟩ stamina in himself, he is compelled to let Homer & Horace, Arts & Sciences, religions & governments be, & confine his [24] creation to some one or two poor specialties. ↑Well, characters & talents are complemental & suppletory, & the house & the world stand by balanced antagonisms.↓[30]

A thought comes single like a foreign traveller, but find out its name, & it is related to a powerful & numerous family. B 90, 334
See also Φ p. 45.

[27] Both the Milton and Collins lines quoted here appear in *Parnassus*, pp. 4 and 129, respectively. See *JMN*, IX, 376.

[28] Emerson's reference is probably to his nephew, Francis Charles Browne of Concord, a freshman at Harvard in 1847–1848. Narciso Lopez led armed Cuban revolutionists and some American annexationists on two unsuccessful expeditions (April, 1850, and August, 1851) to free Cuba from Spanish domination. Both expeditions drew recruits and funds from the United States.

[29] The paragraph to this point is used in "Powers and Laws of Thought," *W*, XII, 29–30.

[30] See p. [17] above.

Treat drastically

The scholar goes into the attorney's office, or the carpenter's shop, &, however civilly, is treated as a trifler. Here is real business, & he is soon set aside: but Archimedes & Kant are as much realists as blacksmiths are: and ↑t↓he↑y↓ ⟨is⟩ ↑are↓ to deal with intellections as rigorously & drastically as the joiner with his chisel & board; & set carpenter & merchant aside.[31]

[25] I do not forgive any one for not ⟨standi⟩ knowing & standing by his own order. Here are clergymen & scholars voting ↑with the world, the flesh, & the devil,↓ against Sumner & freedom↑.↓ ⟨with the world the flesh & the devil.⟩ New genius always flees to old. ⟨Uncommon boys follow uncommon men.⟩ [32] ↑printed↓
↑Sampson Reed! thinks Webster was never greater than now, &c Sept. 1851↓

[26] Why need we answer catechism in words whilst the fact to be translated never disappears? N 34, E ⟨1⟩26

The new John Baptist

It is not to be disguised that all our contemporaries[,] scholars as well as merchants[,] feel the great Despair, are mere Whigs, & believe in nothing. Repent ye, for the Kingdom of heaven is at hand.[33]

[27] Ellery says, What a climate! One day, they take the cover off the sun, and all the Irishmen die of drinking cold water; &, the next day, you are up to your knees in snow.

↑American Climate CD 82, 36,↓

He admires, as ever, the greatness in "Wilhelm Meister". "It is no

[31] The cancellation of "is" and the inserted "t" and "y" in "they" are in pencil.

[32] This canceled sentence, struck through in ink with four vertical use marks, is used in "Eloquence," *W*, VIII, 115. See *JMN*, VI, 125.

[33] For this sentence, see Matt. 3:2.

matter what ⟨he⟩ ↑Goethe↓ writes about. There is no trifle: much superior to Shakspeare in this elevation."

[28] *Lecturing*

Danger of doing something. You write a discourse, &, for the next weeks & months, you are carted about the Country at the tail of that discourse simply to read it over & over[.] ↑See p 27⟨3⟩ 4↓[34]

Too much guano. The German & Irish nations, like the Negro, have a deal of guano in their destiny. They are ⟨l⟩ferried over the Atlantic, & carted over America to ditch & to drudge, to make the land fertile, & corn cheap, & then to lie down ↑prematurely↓ to make ⟨the grass⟩ [29] a spot of greener grass on the prairie.[35]

But it does not seem to me much better, when the gross instincts are a little disguised, and the oestrum, gadfly, or br⟨‖ . . . ‖⟩ize of sex takes sentimental forms. I like the engendering of snails better than the same ⟨rut⟩ masquerading in Watts's psalms to the Church[,] the bride of Christ, or an old girl forming sentimental friendships with every male [30] thing that comes by, under the pretence of ↑"↓*developing a new side.*↑"↓[36]

In feeble individuals, the sex & the digestion are all, absorb the entire vitality; and, the stronger these are, one would say, the individual is only so much the weaker. Of course, the more of these drones ⟨that⟩ perish, the better for the hive. Later, ↑perhaps↓ they give birth, to some [31] superior individual who has ⟨a⟩ sufficient ⟨amount of⟩ force to add to this animal a new ⟨existence of consistent⟩ aim, & a ⟨complete⟩ apparatus of means to work it out. Instantly all the ancestors become guano.[37] Thus most men are mere bulls & most women cows; ⟨but, one day⟩ with however ⟨in each⟩ now & then an individual who has an Æolian attachment or an additional cell opened in his brain [32]

[34] The cancellation of "3" and the added "4" are in pencil.

[35] This paragraph, struck through in ink with a vertical use mark on p. [28] and a diagonal use mark on p. [29], is used in "Fate," *W*, VI, 16–17.

[36] The quotation marks have been added in pencil.

[37] The paragraph to this point, struck through in ink with single vertical use marks on pp. [30] and [31], is used in "Fate," *W*, VI, 11.

as an architectural or a musical or a philological knack; some stray taste or talent, as, a love of flowers, or of chemistry, or pigments, or a narrative talent, a ⟨great⟩ ↑good↓ hand for ⟨telling stories,⟩ ↑⟨cards,⟩↓ ↑chess,↓ ⟨or⟩ ↑or a good foot↓ for dancing, &c.—which skill nowise alters the life of ⟨the⟩ himself or the people, nowise alters their rank in the scale of nature, but merely ⟨beguiles the time,⟩ serves to pass the time,—the [33] bulling & milking going on as before. At last, however, these tastes or talents, which nature has hitherto exhibited only as hints & tendencies, get⟨s⟩ fixed, & in one or in a succession of individuals ↑each↓ appears[n] with steadiness, & absorbs so much food & force as to become itself a new centre & counteraction. The new talent draws off so rapidly the whole spirit & life of the plant, that nothing remains for animal functions, & hardly enough for health, [34] so that, though in the first instance, these individuals have reserved enough juice for digestion & for reproduction, yet, in the second generation, if the like genius appear, the ill health is visibly deteriorated, & the generative force ⟨is⟩ impaired.[38]

[35] M[argaret]. F[uller]. to C[aroline]. S[turgis]. Prov[idence]. 2 Nov., 1837. "I could not but laugh at your catalogue of the things you must not have,—nothing striped, diamonded, or (above all things) *square*. That is driving me to close quarters I think."

[36] *Dualism.*

I see but one key to the mysteries of human condition, but one solution to the old knots of Fate, Freedom, & foreknowledge;—the propounding, namely, of the double consciousness. A man is to ride alternately on the horses of his private & his public n⟨i⟩ature, as the Equestrians in the circus throw themselves nimbly from horse to horse, or plant one foot on the back of one, & the other foot on the back of another: so, when a man is the victim of his fate, has a hump-back, and a hump [37] in his mind; a club foot & a club in his wit; (for there is nothing outward that was not first within) or is ground to powder by the vice of his race;—he is to rally on his relation to

[38] "as an architectural . . . impaired." is struck through in ink with single vertical use marks on pp. [32], [33], and [34]: "Thus most . . . impaired." is used in "Fate," *W*, VI, 11–12.

the Universe, which his ruin benefits. From the demon who suffers, he is to take sides with the God↑.↓ ⟨who damns him.⟩ [39]

↑See CO. 221↓

[38] Excellent texts of the artist's life in Vasari's Life of Fra Angelico (Giovanni da Fiesole)

He said, "⟨n⟩he who practised the art of painting had need of quiet, & should live without cares or anxious thoughts." ↑⟨See Jones Very⟩↓

"He altered nothing ↑(of a painting once finished)↓ but left all as it was done the first time, believing, he said, that such was the will of god." [Vasari, *Lives* . . . , 1850–1852, II, 34, 35]

↑like Jones Very.↓ [40]

"He would never take a pencil in hand until he had first offered a prayer." [*Ibid.*, p. 35]

| Not impartable |

Jones Very
C[harles] K[ing] N[ewcomb]
A[mos].B[ronson].A[lcott].
M[ary].M[oody].E[merson]
C[aroline].S[turgis].
M[argaret].F[uller].
W[illiam].E[llery].C[hanning].
P[hilip].P[hysick].Randolph [41]

[39] Lidian proposes to found a Dormitory, and to preach on

[39] This paragraph, struck through in ink with vertical use marks on pp. [36] and [37], is used in "Fate," *W*, VI, 47. "See CO. 221" below has been added in pencil.

[40] A line under "like Jones Very." slants up and underlines "was the will of god.", suggesting that the Very insertion belongs with the matter above it.

[41] "Not impartable . . . P. P. Randolph" is in pencil. Philip Randolph, grandson of the surgeon, Philip Syng Physick Randolph, probably met Emerson in Philadelphia in January, 1854, after which he appears as an occasional correspondent. These penciled names may have been added after that meeting.

almshouses, from the text, "The tender mercies of the wicked are cruel."[42] Abraham, Isaac, & Jacob, are to adorn the walls *couchant*, & in night caps, and the portrait of the Foundress is to be taken fast asleep.

[40] "Has not S. the requisite number of stamens?" ↑said Ellery—↓[43]

It is probable that the election always goes by avoirdupois weight, and that if you could put ⟨the⟩ any ten of the leaders of either party in a town ⟨into⟩ on the Dearborn Balance, as they passed the hay-scales, you could predict with certainty which party would carry it. [41] I have thought it would be a good plan to have the hayscales at the door of the Town Hall, as the issue of the canvas could be so much quicker determined by this than by the common method.[44]

Vote in the Fourth District 26 May 1851
↑Forty towns↓

For Palfrey	6270
For Thompson	6365
For Frothingham	693

In Concord,	For Palfrey	169
	Thompson	101
	Frothingham	28[45]

[42] ↑*Imbecility of the good party.*↓

Speak very modestly of the country, & of its virtue. Any action of the well-disposed & intelligent class in its affairs is uniformly

[42] Prov. 12:10.

[43] "Ellery—" is followed by "(Sumner?)" in pencil, probably added by Edward Emerson. The query may refer to the "S." in Ellery's question.

[44] This paragraph, struck through in ink with two vertical use marks on p. [40] and one vertical use mark on p. [41], is used in "Fate," *W*, VI, 14.

[45] In this special election for Congress, the Whig, Benjamin Thompson, defeated the Free Soil candidate, John Gorham Palfrey, by a plurality of 87 votes out of 13,000. Emerson repeated his May 3, 1851, speech on the Fugitive Slave Law several times in support of Palfrey's campaign. Frothingham is probably Richard (1812–1880), historian and state legislator, who ran several times as Democratic candidate for Congress.

reckoned an impertinence, & they are presently whipped back into their libraries & churches & Sunday Schools.

There is one benefit derived from the movement lately. The most polite & [43] decorous whigs, all for church & college & charity, have shown their teeth unmistakeably. We shall not be deceived again. We believed, & they half believed that they were honest men. They have been forced to take prematurely their true & ignominious place.

I find a text for ⟨the⟩ ↑our↓ very fact in an English paper speaking of their 10 April 1848. "It precipitated the Whigs into Toryism, making them rush into that [44] political infamy for which they seem to have a constitutional predilection."

[The] Leader [vol. II, no. 58,]
May 3, 1851, [p. 422]

Our people mean, that men of thought shall be dilettanti; ornamental merely; if they dare to be practical with their ideas of beauty, ⟨wo to them!⟩ it is on their peril. Everett is ornamental with liberty & ↑dying↓ Demosthenes, &c. but when he acts, he comes with the planter's whip in his buttonhole[n] ↑—↓& El↑i↓ot writes "history [45] of liberty," & votes for South Carolina. & the University, Mr Sparks, & Mr Felton carry Demosthenes & General Washington clean for Slavery.[46]

The Boston letter to Webster was ↑a↓ shop-till letter, & the Union Party is a shop-till party.[47]

I like that Sumner & Mann & Palfrey should not be scrupulous

[46] Samuel Eliot (1821–1898), historian, educator, and philanthropist, published *Passages from the History of Liberty* . . . (Boston, 1847), but it was Samuel Atkins Eliot (1798–1862), statesman and man of letters, who served in the House of Representatives in 1850–1851 and voted for the Fugitive Slave Law. Emerson may be confusing the two. Jared Sparks (1789–1866), historian and president of Harvard, published *The Writings of George Washington*, 12 vols. (Boston, 1834–1837); Cornelius Conway Felton (1807–1862) was Eliot Professor of Greek literature and the first Regent of Harvard under President Sparks.

[47] For Webster's Boston letter, see Journal AZ, p. [208] above.

& stand on their dignity but should go to the stump. They should not be above their business.

[46] The young ⟨farmer⟩ ↑minister↓[48] did very well, but one day he married a wife, &, after that, he noticed, that, though he planted corn never so often, it was sure to come up tulips, contrary to all the laws of botany.

[47] ↑Arthur Helps↓

↑A.↓ Helps should not have made all his interlocutors alike, but should have made one an extreme humorist, a believing Fakeer or Buddhist, for example, who saw, through ↑the↓ disguise of gener⟨is⟩ation↑,↓ ⟨the⟩ firm in the flowing, flowing in the firm, the unexpended unexpendable energy that we call God, ⟨genius⟩ goodness, beauty, or genius, as we see it in divers modes.[49] Thus Jarno is a flat heavy fellow beside a bright Buddhist.[50] It would be easy to tell fortunes, if you can read characters. You are schoolmaster, you will next be born a ratcatcher, and a bishop afterwards.

[48] [51] ↑⟨the dread of⟩ Man is dreadful to man↓.

Every god is still there sitting in his sphere. The young mortal comes in & on the instant & incessantly fall snowstorms of illusions. Among other things he fancies himself nobody & lost in a crowd. There is he alone with them alone,—they pouring their grand persuasions—proffering to lead him to Olympus—he baffled, dazzled, distracted by the snowing illusions and when, by & by, ⟨the⟩ for an instant the air clears, & the cloud lifts a little, there they are still sitting around him on their thrones.[52]

[48] Added in pencil.

[49] "unexpended" is circled in pencil. Each essay (e.g., "Truth," "Conformity," "Despair") in Arthur Helps, *Friends in Council: A Series of Readings and Discourse Thereon* . . . , 2 vols., 1847–1849, is followed by discussions by interlocutors.

[50] Jarno (or Iarno) undoubtedly refers to the man of the world in Goethe's *Wilhelm Meister*. See *JMN*, VIII, 346.

[51] P. [48] is in pencil, except for "Every god . . . thrones.", which is in ink, written over a similar entry in pencil, with "god still" for "god is still"; "leading him" for "proffering to lead him". The pencil version ends with "snowing illusions".

[52] This paragraph, struck through in ink with a vertical use mark, is used in "Illusions," *W*, VI, 325.

I expect rewards ⟨a⟩like Lord Clive for having volunteered as an author. I wrote up

---

The muskrat on the deluge brought up the grain of dry land[.]

---

[49][53] It will hereafter be noted that the events of culture in the nineteenth century were, the ↑new↓ importance of the genius of Dante, Michel Angelo, & Raffael, to Americans; the reading of Shakspeare, &, above all, the reading of Goethe. Goethe was the cow from which all their milk was drawn. They all took the "European complaint" & went to Italy.[54] Then there was an uprise of Natural History and in London ⟨(& in B⟩ if you would see the fashionable & literary celebrities, you must go to the [50] soirées of the Marquis of Northampton, President of the Royal Society, or, to the Geological club at Somerset House.[55]

It seems, however, as if all the young gentlemen & gentlewomen of America spent several years in ↑lying on the grass &↓ watching "the grand movements of the clouds in the summer sky," during this century.

[51] and *how* he looked! ⟨&⟩ *so* sweet!
& *such* an hour! ↑Oh!↓

Don't expect that every shower will wash away the Alleganies.

[52] *Politics*

Bear in mind the difference between the opponents & the defenders of the shameful statute, that the opposition will never end, will never relax, whilst the statute exists: ⟨whilst⟩as long as grass

[53] This page was erroneously numbered "21", in ink, perhaps because Emerson may have been recently reading p. [21] and is here expanding on the Goethe allusion there.

[54] See Journal BO, p. [108] above.

[55] Spencer Joshua Alwyne Compton, second Marquis of Northampton (1790–1851), was president of the Royal Society, 1838–1848.

grows, as long ⟨i⟩as there is summer & winter, night & day, world & man, so long the sentiments will condemn this. But your statute & its advocacy is a ⟨shortlived⟩ thing; is a phantasm, is a contrivance, a cat's cradle, a petty trap, a jackstraw that has no root in the world. ↑Turn to p. 54↓

[53] [56] 'Tis ||msm||
au||msm||
capacities ||msm||
needs a new Da||msm||
& ⟨grad⟩ guage, & grade new ||msm||
for them.

Manners

The manners & refinement of the navy & of the travellers to Italy, is not real & in the character. It is the polish of a button compared to the polish of a gem.

[54] ↑*Patience*↓ See p. 52 [57]

||msm||ave
||msm|| expected
||msm||, we saw that
||msm|| were many ideots & imbeciles,
& poor rowdies in the county; the whole population was poor, pitiful, uncultured, not worthy yet of being the instruments of justice & freedom. But we saw longevity in our cause. It can well afford to wait; for ages & worlds, [55] the stars of heaven & the thoughts of the mind are the editors & vote-distributors of ⟨F⟩*the free soil*.

⟨The sun borrows his beams⟩ [58]

---

flamboyant idealism [59]

[56] A triangular piece has been cut out of the top third of the leaf bearing pp. [53] and [54].

[57] Because of the triangular piece cut away, the first few lines of the entry below are fragmentary.

[58] This sentence is used in "Illusions," *W*, VI, 318.

[59] These two words are in pencil.

[56] "There is no happiness in this life but in intellect & virtue." [60] *Wordsworth, letter to Beaumont.*

[57] It fitted exactly,↑—↓that shipwreck,↑—↓thought Ellery, to the life & genius of the person. 'Twas like Socrates' poison, or Christ's cross, or Shelley's death. For goodness is a sad business, and, if he was insurer, he would never insure any life that had any infirmity of goodness in it.[61] It is Goodwin * who will catch pickerel; if you have any moral traits, you'll never get a bite.

[58] Low tone. Box coat
Beranger
Beaumont & F
Milnes [62]

⟨C⟩Beranger's answer to those who asked about the "*de*" before his name[:]

"Je mis vilain
Vilain vilain
Je honore une race commune
Car sensible, quoique malin,
Je n'ai flatté que l'infortune." [63]

[59] The bitterness of the crisis is that the violation of ⟨the⟩ morals is not felt as such.

* a felon in Concord who had been a convict in the state's prison.[64]

[60] This sentence, struck through in ink with three vertical use marks, is used in "Works and Days," *W*, VII, 178–179. For Wordsworth's letter to Sir George Beaumont, July 20, 1804, see Christopher Wordsworth, *Memoirs of William Wordsworth*, 2 vols. (Boston, 1851), I, 269.

[61] Above "insurer" in a copy of this passage in Notebook OP Gulistan, p. [17], Emerson has written "Mr Bowditch", presumably J. Ingersoll Bowditch.

[62] "Box coat . . . Milnes" is struck through in ink with two vertical use marks; cf. "Culture," *W*, VI, 151: "There are advantages in the old hat and box-coat.", followed by quotations from Beaumont and Fletcher and from Milnes.

[63] P. J. Béranger, "Le Vilain," *Oeuvres Complètes* . . . (Paris, 1844), pp. 157–159. "⟨C⟩Beranger's answer . . . l'infortune.'" is used in *Memoirs*, I, 260–261.

[64] The asterisk in the text and in Emerson's note and "a felon . . . prison." are added in pencil.

The absence of moral feeling in the ⟨country⟩ ↑whiteman↓ is the very calamity I deplore. The ⟨loss of⟩ captivity of a thousand negroes is nothing to me[.]

[60] Aristocracy

Make yourself useful. That is the secret to clear your complexion, & make you desired.

The four degrees of lordship

1. protection
2. hospitality
3. invention & art
4. moral aid.

[61] Webster truly represents the American people just as they are, with their vast material interests, materialized intellect, & low morals. Heretofore, their great men have led them, have been better than they, as Washington, Hamilton, & Madison. But Webster's absence of moral faculty is degrading to the country.

Of this fatal defect of course Webster himself has no perception. He does, as immoral men usually do, make very low bows to the Christian [62] church, & goes through all the decorums of Sunday[,] but when allusion is made to Ethics, & the sanctions of morality, he very frankly replies, as at Albany the other day,↑—"Some higher law somewhere between here & the third heaven, I do not know where[.]"↓[65]

[63][66] We are all opium eaters[.]

The daguerrotypist sets his /boy/sitter/ in freedom & expression by a lively song[.]

[65] ", —'Some higher . . . where'" has been added in pencil, as have the commas after "Ethics," "morality," and "replies,". "church, & . . . third heaven," is struck through in pencil with a vertical use mark. "He does [p. [61]] . . . where'" is used in "The Fugitive Slave Law" (1854), *W*, XI, 228. For the quotation, see Daniel Webster, "Speech to the Young Men of Albany," *Writings* . . . , 1903, IV, 275.

[66] P. [63] is in pencil.

Artists

The art of playing on men

Why should we who believe in the Intellect ever speak ⟨or lecture⟩ to a public meeting without yielding them a spark of lightning[,] /a/some/ word ↑of↓ transforming[,] upbuilding truth[?]

Our poor parlor & piano poetry ⟨u⟩never draws on this ⟨hi⟩ deep spring[.] [67]
The Hoods & Longfellows, Milneses, & even Tennysons, are content to amuse. Let ⟨n⟩your poetry taste the world & report of it instead of some miserable clique or school[.]

[64] ↑*Politics*↓

In this age of tools, one of the best machines is certainly this governing machine, which we have brought to such mechanical perfection: the distributing political electricity over a vast area, so as to make the highest energy consistent with perfect safety. Thus, yesterday was election day; and a revolution, (for every election is a revolution,) went off with the quietness of a pic-nic or a ⟨church⟩ sermon. This by means of universal suffrage, & town-meetings & ward-meetings.

[65] ——

I believe so much in metamorphosis, that I think the man will find the type not only in ⟨qual⟩kind, but in quantity, of all his moral & mental properties in the great world without⟨,⟩. He is to hold to his purposes with the tough impracticability of gravitation itself: "no power nor wheedling on earth could have made" him give up his point.[68]

[66] Margaret had the attributes of a lady, a courtesy so real & sincere that it reached the chambermaid, the mantuamaker, and all who served her for money[.]

The use made of Fate in society is babyish[;] put your finger in your

[67] See p. [16] above.

[68] "He is to . . . point.", struck through in ink with a vertical use mark, is used in "Fate," *W*, VI, 24.

eye. ⟨But I wish that⟩ It should rather be to bring up our conduct to the loftiness of nature.[69] The Englishman & Frenchman may have the November desolation emptiness which cannot see a lamp post or a dangling rope without temptation to suicide, but to a charged, healthful, preoccupied manly mind, night & storm & cold [67] are not grim, but sternly cheerful even. Rude & invincible except by themselves (or their own law) are the elements. So let him be. Let him empty his breast of all that is superfluous & traditional, of all dependence on the accidental, on money, on false fame, falsehood of any kind; & speak wild truth, & by manners & actions as unaffected as the weather, let him be instead of God to men, full of God, new & astonishing & nothing of the Edinburgh Review, of England, of France, or Greece, or Rome, or Fine Arts, or Church, or American Constitution, or any other bit of old hypocritical trumpery.[70]

[68] I suppose I need not go to St Louis to know the flavor of Southern life; there is not only St Louis, but all Avernus, in a fiery cigar. Goethe kept his Acherontian experiences in a separate bag; & said, if he himself should happen to fall into that bag, he should be consumed, bones & all.

[69] ↑*London*↓

I read that Sir John Herschel had found London to be the centre of the physical globe. What does that mean? the centre of the ⟨Lo⟩ terraqueous hemisphere perhaps? The Greeks looked upon Delphi as the navel of the Earth.[71]

[69] "The use . . . of nature.", struck through in ink with single vertical and curved vertical use marks, is used in "Fate," *W*, VI, 24.

[70] "Rude & invincible . . . weather," struck through in ink with a diagonal use mark, is used in "Fate," *W*, VI, 24.

There are penciled commas after "Review", "France", "Greece", "Rome", "Arts", and "Church". The editors have accepted these because they fall within the rubric of silent punctuation of elements in a series. They have also added silent commas after "England" and "Constitution" under the same rubric. The "t's" in "Constitution" and "hypocritical" are crossed in pencil and the i's in the same two words are dotted also in pencil.

[71] Cf. Sir John F. W. Herschel, *Outlines of Astronomy* (Philadelphia, 1849), p. 172: "It is a fact . . . that London occupies nearly the centre of the terrestrial hemisphere." The paragraph is struck through in pencil and in ink with single diagonal use marks; the first and last sentences are used in "Land," *W*, V, 40.

I read also that the Crystal Palace was built in six months, & cost £150 000.[72]

[70] Fate

The intellect conquers fate,—and it is the property of men of insight to be serene, for their faith in law has become sight. But they who talk much of destiny, their birth star, &c. are ⟨i⟩on a lower, dangerous, vertiginous plane, & seem to invite the evils they fear.[73]

[71] *Fate*

"That which we wish when young, comes to us in heaps when we are old."
Goethe [*The Auto-biography* . . . , 1848–1849, I, 181]

Because ⟨what⟩ we are sure to have what we ⟨ask⟩ wish, let us beware that ⟨a⟩ we ask for high things.[74] *Charles Newcomb*

"Cursed with every granted prayer." [75] [Pope, *Moral Essays*, Epistle II, 147]

[72] "Rien ne réussit mieux que le succès." [76]

Heterogeneity ↑Character↓

Men are miscellanies, rag-bags, unannealed glass, utter discontinuity; and all their power absorbed in their individual antagonisms. "Hot, cold, moist, & dry, four Champions fierce," contend within the man.[77] 'Tis Newton's heterogeneous body, which *loses* the ray of light. Now if a fire, as, ⟨of Love⟩ for example, Love's, could kindle & melt them over, recast the whole mass, then you should have logic,

[72] Emerson's source is perhaps an article in the *Athenæum* for Aug. 31, 1850, where the £150,000 figure is given as "the total value of the building, were it to be permanently retained" (pp. 924–925).

[73] "But they . . . fear.", struck through in ink with a diagonal use mark, is used in "Fate," *W*, VI, 23.

[74] With this sentence, cf. *JMN*, IX, 338.

[75] " 'That which . . . granted prayer.' ", struck through in ink with a curved vertical use mark, is used in "Fate," *W*, VI, 46–47. For " 'Cursed . . . prayer.' ", see *Memoirs*, II, 266, and *JMN*, VIII, 130.

[76] This proverb is used in "Success," W, VII, 289.

[77] For the quotation, see Milton, *Paradise Lost*, Book II, 898.

unity, & power; a man that would be felt to the centre of the Copernican system.[78]

[73] I noticed a little boy in the company whose speech in talking with his mates never went out as a mendicant from him, engaging him to what was said, but he remained quite entire when his speech was gone. So will it be when he is a man. ↑[[Compe. with passage from Dr A. Carlyle in *GL* 101,]]↓ [79]

Wealth

The world is babyish, & the use of wealth is: it is made a toy. Men of sense esteem wealth to be the assimilation of nature to themselves; the converting the sap & juices of the planet to the nutriment ⟨of their⟩ & incarnation of their design. Power is what [74₁] [80] they want, not candy, & they will pay any prices. Power for what? power to execute their idea,—which, in any well constituted man, of course, appears the end to which the Universe exists & all its resources might be well applied.[81] ⟨The Education of each goes on well as he begins to draw⟩ Each of the elm trees that you see over the land sends its roots far & wide, ⟨a⟩every great one to some river or water course. Its roots will run a mile, and the Education of each vascular man goes on well in proportion as his masculine roots draw from all the natures around him their tribute. Columbus thinks & thinks rightly, [75₁] that the sphere is a problem for navigation as well as for geometry, & looks on all kings & subjects as cowardly landsmen, until

[78] With this paragraph, cf. "Beauty," *W*, VI, 283.

[79] "[[Compe. with . . . *GL* 101,]]" is partially enclosed by a rectangular ink line forming a box open at the top. In Journal GL, p. [101], Emerson indicates that his source is Alexander Carlyle, *Autobiography of . . . Dr. Alexander Carlyle . . .* (London, 1860), p. 28.

[80] Emerson originally wrote the "English aristocracy", and the "Raffaelle" and "*Feats*" entries, printed below, on the upper portions of pp. [74] and [75], respectively: then, having begun the "*Wealth*" entry on p. [73] (apparently at a later date), he drew lines across pp. [74] and [75] below the inscribed entries and continued the "*Wealth*" entry below the lines, here printed as a continuous sequence. The original entries on pp. [74] and [75] are printed below as on pp. [74₂] and [75₂]. "*Wealth.*", an index heading, is written above "not candy,".

[81] "The world . . . applied.", struck through in pencil and in ink with single vertical use marks on p. [73] and in ink with a vertical use mark on p. [74₁], is used in "Wealth," *W*, VI, 92–93.

they dare fit him out. Few men on the planet have so truly belonged to it as he. He has had ⟨many worthy⟩ successors, who have inherited his map, & have felt all his fury to complete what he left incomplete, Captain Cook for one, Captain Laya⟨j⟩rd with his Nineveh, Sir C Fellowes with his marbles[.] [82]

The doctrine of currents
of storms
of anatomy.

↑[turn to p. 82↓

[74₂] English aristocracy It is very condescending in them surely to pray to God.[83]

[75₂] Raffaelle *Feats*

"They studied in his workroom the wonders of his genius who so 'Pingere posse animum atque oculis praebere videndum.' " [84]

---

[76] Never was truer fable than the Sibyl's writing on leaves which the wind scatters. ↑See p 118 infra.↓ [85] A. asked me if the thought clothes itself in words? I answer, yes; but they are instantly forgotten. The difference between man & man is, that, in one, the memory with inconceivable swiftness flies after & *re-collects* thes⟨s⟩e leaves;—flies on wing as fast as that mysterious whirlwind; & the envious Fate is baffled.[86]

[77] The excellence of fairies is to be small. ↑See p 85↓ The king & the queen are the least of all. Nature works in leasts.[87] The

[82] "Columbus thinks . . . kings & subjects" is struck through in pencil with single vertical use marks on pp. [74₁] and [75₁]; "as well as for geometry . . . marbles" is struck through in ink with a vertical use mark; "Columbus thinks . . . marbles" is used in "Wealth," *W*, VI, 93.

[83] "English . . . God." is in pencil.

[84] See *Lives of the Italian Painters: Michel Angelo*, by Richard Duppa . . . ; *Raffaello*, by Quatremère de Quincy; trans. William Hazlitt (London, 1846), p. 425. Despite the double quotation marks before "They" and after videndum' " ", only the Latin is quoted (with "animam" for Emerson's "animum"). The Latin is translated as the "[art] of representing to the eye the feelings of the soul."

[85] "See p 118 infra." is partially enclosed in an oval ink line, open on the right-hand side.

[86] This paragraph is used in "Memory," *W*, XII, 95.

[87] With the entry to "of all.", cf. *JMN*, IX, 297. For "Nature works in leasts.", see *JMN*, IX, 410, and "*In minimis natura.*", p. [85] below.

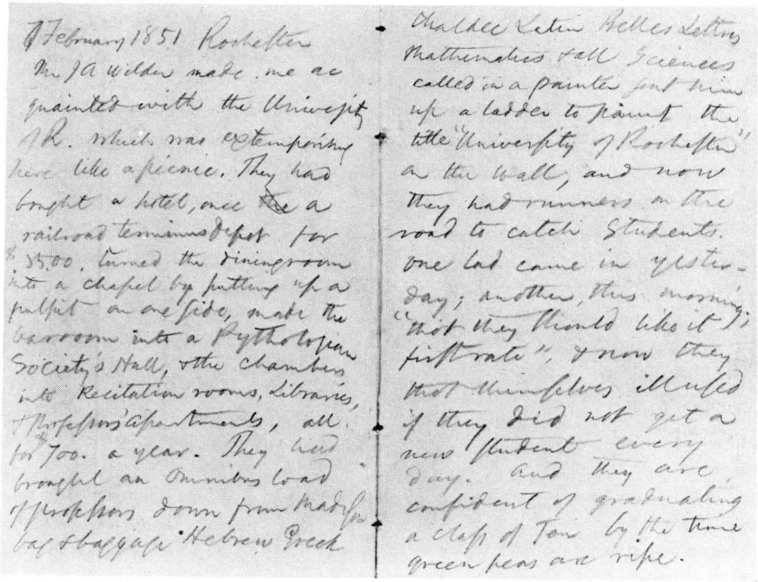

7 February 1851 Rochester
Mr J A Wilder made me acquainted with the University of R. which was extemporized here like a picnic. They had bought a hotel, once a railroad terminus depot for $8500, turned the diningroom into a chapel by putting up a pulpit on one side, made the barroom into a Pythologian Society's Hall, & the chambers into Recitation rooms, Libraries, & Professors' apartments, all for 700. a year. They had brought an Omnibus load of professors down from Madison bag & baggage Hebrew Greek Chaldee Latin Belles Lettres Mathematics & all Sciences called in a painter sent him up a ladder to paint the title "University of Rochester" on the wall, and now they had runners on the road to catch Students. One lad came in yesterday; another, this morning; "thought they should like it first rate", & now they thought themselves illused if they did not get a new student every day. And they are confident of graduating a class of Ten by the time green peas are ripe.

Plate I   Journal at the West, pages 46–47   Text, pages 519–520
Emerson's dry Yankee wit

144 We are glad at last to get a
clear case, one on which no shadow
of doubt can hang. This is not
meddling with other peoples
affairs,—this is other people
meddling with us. This is not
going crusading after slaves who
it is alleged are very happy &
comfortable where they are. all that
amiable argument falls to the
ground, but defending a human being
who has taken the ~~most frightful~~
risk of being shot or burned alive,
or cast into the sea, or starved

Plate II

Journal CO, page 144
On the Fugitive Slave Law

Text, page 411

to death or suffocated in a wooden box,—
taken all this risk to get away from
his driver ~~that lothsome~~ home & recover the
rights of man. And this man
the Statute says, you men ~~Children~~ of
Massachusetts shall kidnap &
send back ~~home~~ again ~~to the dog hutch~~
a thousand miles across the sea
to the Dog-hutch he fled from.
And this filthy ~~ferocious~~ enactment was
made in the 19th Century, by people
who could read & write.
I will not obey it, by God.

Plate III *Journal CO, page 145* *Text, pages 411–412*

On the Fugitive Slave Law

36 Dualism.

I see but one key to the mysteries of human condition,
but one solution to the old
knots of Fate, freedom, & foreknowledge;—the propounding,
namely, of the double consciousness. A man is to ride alternately on the horses of his private
& his public nature, as the
equestrians in the circus throw
themselves nimbly from horse
to horse, or plant one foot on
the back of one, & the other foot
on the back of another: So, when
a man is the victim of his fate,
has a hump-back, and a hump

Plate IV *Journal CO, page 36* *Text, page 377*

Emerson's solution to a profound philosophical problem

in his mind; a club foot & a club in his 37
wit; (for there is nothing outward that
was not first within) or is ground
to powder by the vice of his race; —
he is to rally on his relation to the
Universe, which his ruin benefits.
From the demon who suffers,
he is to take sides with the God.
who damns him.

See CO, 221

Plate V *Journal CO, page 37* *Text, pages 377–378*

Emerson's solution to a profound philosophical problem

250 Every glance at society — pale withered
people with gold-filled teeth, with
scalps tied on, ghastly, & with minds
in the same dilapidated condition,
drugged with books for want of
wisdom, — suggests at once the
German ~~thought~~ of the Progressive
God, who has got thus far with
his experiment, but will get out
of it a triumphant & faultless
~~[illegible]~~ race.

Plate VI *Journal AZ, page 250* *Text, page 263*

A skeptical comment on race

121

ΜΕΛΕΤΗ ΤΟ ΠΑΝ. I took my hoe & watering pail
& fell upon my sleepy pear trees,
broke up the soil, pulled out the
weeds & grass, I manured, & mellowed,
& watered, pruned, & washed, &
staked, & separated the clinging boughs
by shingles covered with list: I killed
every slug on every leaf. The detestable pear worm, which
mimics a twig, I detected & killed.
The poor tree tormented by this
excessive attention & industry, must
do something, & began to grow

My pear saplings were well favoured as
long as I did not go beyond my own hedge:
but if I went down to Edmund's farm,
his trees were three stories high, & high
up in the air hung a harvest of fruit.

Plate VII *Journal TU, page 121* *Text, page 132*

Emerson cares for his pear trees

Games (63

What reason to think Charles I consented to his execution?

They axed him whether he would or no.

Why is one playing blindman's buff, like sympathy?

'Tis a Fellow feeling for a fellow creature.

What reason to think the Carthaginians had domestic animals?

Virgil says, "Dido et dux,"

"et pig-e-bit Elisa."

How could the Children of Israel sustain themselves for forty days in the desert?

Because of the sand-wich-is there

Why is a kiss like a sermon?

two heads & an application

Plate VIII *Journal BO, page 63* *Text, page 301*

Riddles

pride of England is, to rule the world in the little plain chamber of St Stephen's.[88] ⟨So⟩ ↑In like manner↓, the whole battle of the world is fought in ⟨these⟩ ↑a↓ few heads: a little finer order, a little larger angle of vision commands centuries of facts & millions of stupid people.[89] We shall not long go on reckoning prosperity by the census, —the more fools you have the worse,—but, by the competent heads.

The power of assimilation. Swedenborg took up the whole underworld into his [78] head & gave it a tongue. Fourier is immensely rich & joyous with his ranges & gradations of power. It suffices him to say, Nature has made it; so I know there is a turnpike[-]way out. ↑Is the thing really desireable? then there *is* a way to it.↓ [90]

↑go on (Vishnu) p 85↓

[79] In the youth I heard last Sunday a sort of rattle of thunderbolts behind there in the back of his head. He threatened in every sentence to say somewhat new, bright, fatal. And that is the charm of eloquence, its potency. Here is mere ⟨de⟩play, play of genius, improvisation for the artist's own delight, & out of the midst of it he hurls a winged word that becomes a proverb of the world & conquers kings, & clothes nations in its colours.

[80] I liked that M↑argaret Fuller↓. should see in Napoleon's head his mighty future, &, ⟨even in⟩ ↑for all↓ the beautiful[,] even voluptuous mouth, should find mountains ⟨&⟩ ↑of the slain & the↓ snows of Russia not irrelevant[.] [91]

[81] I read somewhere that Dalton did not wait for empirical confirmation of his "law," but promulgated it, struck ⟨but⟩ ↑by↓ its internal evidence.[92]

[88] "The excellence . . . St Stephen's." is struck through in ink with two diagonal use marks; "The pride of . . . St Stephen's." is also struck through in ink with a diagonal use mark. "The excellence . . . leasts." is used in "Works and Days," *W*, VII, 176; also cf. "Swedenborg," *W*, IV, 104, 114.

[89] This sentence is used in "The Celebration of Intellect," *W*, XII, 121.

[90] This sentence is marked in the left margin by two vertical lines in pencil, possibly use marks. "go on . . . 85", below, is added in pencil.

[91] Emerson is recalling, or had been recently consulting, some ms. notes Margaret Fuller sent him in 1840 on the Athenaeum Gallery of Sculpture; cf. *Memoirs*, I, 270.

[92] For Dalton's law, see Journal TU, p. [279] above.

⟨Wh⟩Probably Kepler's laws were so seen.
Newton's was.
And the transcendental anatomy stands so, the *one animal* or the thoughts of God written out —
And Knox's law of races,

that nature loves not hybrids, & extinguishes them.

that the ⟨race⟩ ↑colony↓ detached from the race deteriorates to the crab[93]

It would be a great comfort in Metaphysics to establish a good collection of these instances of *accepted ideas*, as a table of constants.

[82] *Wealth*
Everybody knows these exaggerating schemers, maniacs who go about in marts & insurance offices & railroad cars, talking up their project, & entreating the world to subscribe. How did your factories get built? how did your New England get traversed with iron rails, except by the ⟨eloquence of &⟩ importunity of these ⟨madmen⟩ ↑orators↓ who dragged all the prudent men in? ↑Is↓ "Party ⟨is said to be⟩ the madness of many for the gain of a few?"[94] This is the madness of a few, for the gain of the world. The projectors are hurt, but the public is immensely a gainer.[95]

[83] "After all[n] *Canova* had seen, he was astonished at the Elgin marbles, & happy in finding them real flesh, nothing geometrical, nothing conventional, but a *vera carne*: & satisfied of what he had always believed, that, the works ⟨that⟩ which want this excellence, are only copies from the great masters." *M. F⟨'s⟩uller's Journal*

The best works are

[93] See Robert Knox, M.D., *The Races of Men; A Fragment* (Philadelphia, 1850), pp. 52, 86, 107, 317. "that nature . . . hybrids," is struck through in ink with one diagonal and three vertical use marks; "that nature . . . crab" is struck through in ink with a vertical use mark. "And Knox's . . . crab" is used in "Fate," *W*, VI, 16.

[94] Alexander Pope, "Thoughts on Various Subjects," *The Works of Alexander Pope, Esq.* (London, 1807), p. 117; this is a "Supplementary Volume" to *The Works* . . . , ed. Joseph Warton, 9 vols. (London, 1797).

[95] This paragraph, struck through in ink with two vertical use marks, is used in "Wealth," *W*, VI, 93–94.

/slanci/ dartings/ *spontanei d'una musa é d'una eloquenza ispirata*, but these swift flashings are from minds full of heaped up fuel well on fire acted on by the muse, perfect births.

[84] *England*

"hommage instinctif, continuel, feroce, au dieu de tous; l'or.— la nation animée de la fureur de *paraitre*. Paraitre quoi? Riche, audessus ⟨le⟩du rang qu'on occupe réellement." [96]

Jules Lecomte
Courrier des Etats Unis

[85] *In minimis natura.*

Vishnu in his avatar came as a dwarf, & asked for as much earth as he could cover with three steps. The evil power was duped, & granted it; and the dwarf took in a world with each step.

We ⟨esteem⟩ ↑think↓ a man unable & desponding. It is that he is misplaced & mistimed. Put with him new companions & they will bow to his wonderful genius, & paradise will begin for them, & for him. The circumstance of circumstance is ⟨jump⟩timing & placing.

It is however also true, that the chronology has its own law, pervasive, & he is not despondent or isolated without cause[.] [97]

[86] There is ⟨in⟩a thick skull, that is fate. The crustacia, the birds, the tortoises, are fatalists, yet amelioration must be assumed. These very walls & jails must be believed to be charity & protection; & meanness the preparation of magnificence: as madness is assumed to be a scre⟨n⟩en of a too ↑much↓ tempted soul.

The gross lines are legible to the dull; the cabman is ph[r]enologist so far; he looks in my face to see if his shilling be sure. A dome of brow denotes one thing, a pot belly another, a squint and mats of hair betray character.[98]

---

[96] " 'hommage . . . réellement.' " is struck through in pencil with a vertical use mark. See *JMN*, X, 519–520, where the arrangement differs.

[97] "We ⟨esteem⟩ think . . . without cause" is in pencil. "We ⟨esteem⟩ think . . . also true," is struck through in pencil with single diagonal and curved diagonal use marks; "We . . . think . . . placing." is used in "Social Aims," *W*, VIII, 83.

[98] This paragraph, struck through in pencil and in ink with single vertical use marks, is used in "Fate," *W*, VI, 9.

[87] ⟨It is true that i⟩In each town you ⟨go into⟩ ↑visit↓,[99] there is some man who is in his brain & performance a↑n↓ explanation of all that meets the eye there,—of the tillage, production, factories, banks, meetinghouse, ways of living, & tone of society, of that town. When you go to a prospering new city, you are conscious there is such a person, who is an abridgment or key to the prosperity. You may not meet him, ⟨&⟩ but he is there; &, if you do not chance to meet him, all that you see will [88] leave you a little puzzled: if you see him, all will become plain. Mr ↑Erastus↓ Bigelow, Mr M'Elrath, Mr Lawrence, Mr Crocker, Mr Vanderbilt, the old Rotch & Rodmān, Jackson & Lowell, the Dwights at Springfield, Mr Mills, Mr Forbes, are each ⟨a city⟩ a walking city, &, wherever you put them, will build one.[100] See *BO*. 55

[89] ↑All this page printed, I believe↓

Also, I believe, that ⟨as⟩ nothing can be done except by inspiration. The man's insight & power is local; he can ⟨d⟩ see & do this, but it steads him not beyond: he is fain to make that ulterior step by mechanical means. It can ⟨never⟩ ↑not↓ be done↑.↓ ⟨so.⟩ That ulterior step is to be ⟨done⟩ also by inspiration; if not thro' him, then through another man. ⟨Cl⟩Every real step is by *lyrical glances*, by lyrical felicity, & never by main strength & ignorance. Years of mechanics will only seem to do it; it will not be done.[101]

[99] The cancellation of "go into" and the inserted "visit" are in pencil.

[100] This paragraph is struck through in pencil and in ink with vertical use marks on pp. [87] and [88]; "In each town . . . of that town.", and "you do not . . . build one.", struck through in pencil with vertical use marks on pp. [87] and [88], are used in "Fate," *W*, VI, 42–43. Of those not previously identified or easily recognizable, M'Elrath is perhaps Thomas McElrath (1807–1888), partner of Horace Greeley in publishing the New York *Tribune* and Whig member of the New York Assembly; Joseph Rotch moved to Dartmouth on Buzzard's Bay in 1765 and became a founder of New Bedford; Rodman may refer to an ancestor of Emerson's friend and correspondent, Benjamin Rodman, also of New Bedford; Lowell, Mass., received its name from Francis Cabot Lowell (1775–1817); Jonathan Dwight and his son Edmund (1780–1849) were prominent businessmen of Springfield. Along with his partner James K. Mills, Edmund Dwight helped establish the manufacturing towns of Chicopee and Holyoke. John Murray Forbes (1813–1898), later father-in-law of Emerson's daughter Edith, was a prominent businessman and financier of western railroads.

[101] This paragraph, struck through in pencil with a vertical use mark, is used in

[90] ↑Who was↓ that [n] foolish man ↑who↓ yet said truly that the mystic never discusses↑?↓

[91] ⟨The mayor of Bost⟩ It will happen easily that twenty mistakes will be made. People often talk most of that which they do not represent. Boston talks of Union, & fevers into proslavery, but the genius of Boston is seen in her real independence, productive power, & *northern* acuteness of mind, πολυτροπος Οδυςςευς, which is ⟨y⟩generically antislavery.[102] Boston Common, Boston Athenaeum, Lowell Institute, Railroads, & the love of German literature[—] these are the true Boston, & not an accidental malignity, or [92] a momentary importance of a few pugnoses, people too slight to sail in any but the fairest weather, and therefore by their very importance praising the great prosperity of Boston. "If it were always such weather as this," my Captain Ellis used to say, "Women might take his ⟨|| ... ||⟩ship to sea."[103]
Vasari affirms ↑of the city of Florence,↓ that "the desire for glory & honour is powerfully generated by the air of that place in the men of every profession, & whereby all who possess [93] talent are impelled to struggle that they may not remain in the same grade with those whom they perceive to be only men like themselves," &c, &c, which see, *Bohn's Vasari,* [*Lives . . . ,* 1850–1852,] *Vol. II, p. 308*[104]

[94] I recall today in conversation with W[illiam]. H[enry]. C[hanning]. the impression made by Wilkinson.[105] He seemed full of ability, power of labor, acute vision, marvellous power of illustration, of great learning in certain directions, ⟨but spoile⟩having also the

"Inspiration," *W*, VIII, 271. For "*lyrical glances*", see Notebook Margaret Fuller Ossoli, p. [237] below. The added inscription, "All this . . . believe", is in pencil.

[102] The Greek means "a versatile Ulysses." See p. [195] below. "the genius . . . antislavery." is used in "Boston," *W*, XII, 208.

[103] This sentence, struck through in pencil with a vertical use mark, is used in "Wealth," *W*, VI, 108. Cornelius Ellis was captain of the brig *Jasper* on which Emerson sailed to Europe from Boston, Dec. 25, 1832.

[104] "Vasari affirms . . . possess" is struck through in pencil with a vertical use mark on p. [92]; "Vasari affirms . . . themselves,' " is used in "Boston," *W*, XII, 185–186.

[105] Reverend William H. Channing was visiting Emerson in July to work on their memoir of Margaret Fuller. On his trip to England in 1848 Emerson met the Swedenborg scholar John James Garth Wilkinson.

power I so value & so rarely meet of *expansion*, expansion, such as Alcott shines with; —but all this spoiled by a certain levity. He held himself cheap. There was no sacredness, no poetry, about him. He was changing his sphere from Swedenborg-mysticism [n] [95] to French Fourierism, with shocking levity, & had forgotten or did not care longer for his past studies. He was surrounded by inferior people, doctors, socialists, Educationists, &c. whom he seemed to value. I fancied I read "For Sale", on all his great talents, & was not flattered even by his kind & encomiastic reception of me. He was tall & large-limbed, looking like our ↑Rev. Thos.↓ Worcester, and wanted the expression of refinement.[106] He was a man of that kind of waste strength that he could [96] easily run for diversion into Icelandic literature, as it seems he is doing.

I should say of him that as we see children at school often expend a prodigality of memory & of arithmetical power, which, occurring in an adult subject, would make a Porson, Parr, or Lacroix[107] — & see it in such children without respect, — mere boarding school rattle, — because it does not [97] seem solid & enduring or known to the mind itself, & so secured, but merely as this year's grass, or annual plants, which a single ⟨frost⟩ ↑night in November↓ will annihilate. So I believe that all this unrealized ability seemed insecure. As soon as he himself has said, These weapons are mine, and lo↑!↓ by them I possess the Universe, as yonder Astronomer does the stars by his tube & ⟨his⟩ chart: O joy, I cannot live, I am too happy. Hold back thy thunderbolt, Jove, envy me not my near approach: — then we should sympathize with [98] the terror & beauty of his gifts & he would be sacred to himself & to us.
It did not seem that he was enamoured of his thoughts, as all good thinkers ought to be. A fair ample house with excellent windows, but no fireplace.

This experience is surely very familiar, that things are valued by

[106] Reverend Thomas Worcester, D.D. (1795–1878) was the first pastor of the Boston Society of the New Jerusalem, 1818–1867.

[107] Richard Porson (1759–1808) was an English classical scholar; Samuel Parr (1747–1825), an English Latin scholar; Sylvestre François Lacroix (1765–1843), a French mathematician.

pairs, & that either alone is naught.[108] Salt enhances the egg, which ↑without it↓ is naught. Money is good for nothing at Juan Fernandez, but ⟨in⟩ London is not London without it. Refinement of person & manners [99] ⟨are⟩ ↑is↓ inestimable to a person of real force: But ⟨only a temporary re↑c↓ommendation to⟩ one who wants that ↑is only a nice man↓. And ⟨that⟩ ↑force↓ fails, & is ever in Coventry, for want of refinement. ↑A remarkable example of a man of great proportions failing yet to be great.↓

[100] Edward Everett had in my youth an immense advantage in being the first American Scholar who sat in the German Universities & brought us home in his head their whole culture, method, & results,—to us who did not so much as know the names of Heyne, Wolf, Hug, & Ruhnken. He dealt out his treasures too with such admirable prudence, so temperate & abstemious [n] ⟨&⟩ that our wonder & delight were still new. It seems to me as if our new lecturer [101] had the like advantage.[109] He has a deal of talent, reads well, distributes well, & keeps fast to the central thesis of his discourse, has a good deal of *popular profoundness*, shall I say, or just that degree of depth which his audience can swim in, without any real originality ↑except in his rhetoric;↓ but suggests to me continually the conjecture, or the probability, that he is repeating after some good master or masters, to us unknown, in Halle, or Gottingen. I think his lectures excellent ⟨&⟩ for our young men, & instructive [102] to old craftsmen, as specimens of good lecturing.

Edward Everett was a Manco Capac.[110]

America. Emigration.

In the distinctions of the genius of the American race it is to be considered, that, it is not indiscriminate masses of Europe, that are ⟨transported⟩ shipped hitherward, but the Atlantic is a sieve through which only or chiefly the liberal adventurous sensitive *America-loving*

[108] With this sentence, cf. "Clubs," *W*, VII, 230: "Things are in pairs: a natural fact has only half its value until a fact in moral nature, its counterpart, is stated."

[109] Emerson's reference is to the German exile Emmanuel Vitalis Scherb. See Journal AZ, pp. [9]–[10] above, and p. [202] below.

[110] Manco Capac is traditionally considered the founder of the Inca dynasty in Peru.

part of each city, clan, family, are brought. It is the light complexion, the blue eyes of Europe that come: the black eyes, the black drop, the Europe [103] of Europe is left[.] [111]

↑*Prudence*↓

Opere peracto lude⟨re⟩mus [112]

Among the men made for work, *dura ilia*,[113] & seemingly not of flesh & blood, but of brass & iron, Coke, & Mansfield, Gibbon, Johnson, ↑& John Adams↓ [114]

[104] ↑*Bias.*↓

I have said so often, & must say once more, the first fortune is a controlling determination of genius, that leaves ↑Hauy no choice but to be mineralogist,↓ Paxton no choice but to be landscape gardener & architect, & Jackson a chemist.[115] That abolishes so many perplexities. But that is not enough. He must have adaptation, besides, to men; or else, that magazine of sufficiency, that makes him indifferent to other men, like a statue of a Roman Emperor, in a crowd.

[105] *Prudence*

I was to have quoted respecting money, Lord Mansfield's saying, that the funds gave interest without principal; the land principal without interest; but mortgages both principal, & interest.

Sept., 1851.

↑Mr↓ Eben. Francis told me, twenty years ago, that it was easy to invest a million, but by no means so easy to invest the second million.[116] And I heard the other day that with all his care of his

[111] "In the distinctions . . . left" is struck through in pencil with single vertical use marks on pp. [102] and [103]; see Appendix I and *JMN*, X, 462, 463. "of Europe is left" is written on p. [103] below a rule drawn across the middle of the page following the entry "Among the . . . Adams".

[112] "In completed work we shall take pleasure" (Ed.).

[113] "tough stomachs" (Ed.). See *JMN*, IX, 339.

[114] "Among the . . . Adams" is struck through in pencil with a vertical use mark. There is approximately an inch space between "Johnson," and "& John Adams", left, probably, for another name to be added.

[115] René Just Haüy (1743–1822), French mineralogist, was one of the founders of crystallography; Sir Joseph Paxton (1801–1865) was superintendent of the Duke of Devonshire's gardens at Chatsworth and architect of the Crystal Palace.

[116] Ebenezer Francis was a former treasurer of Harvard. The paragraph appears to have been added; the entry on p. [107] is dated July 22, 1851.

property, &, with all the high rates that money rents at in Boston, h⟨e⟩is property has not increased faster than six per cent for many years past.

[106] That the Event & the Person meet, we must believe, & that Dante is Italian because, ⟨he could most live⟩ at that moment, he could most live as an Italian. At this moment he would be born American.[117]

[107] 1851, July 22. Yesterday, Eddy & Edie going with me to bathe in Walden, Eddy was very brave with a sharp bulrush, & presently broke into this rhyme—

"With my sharp-pointed sword
I will conquer Concórd."

[108] ——

Kleinstadtisch thinks all the rest of the world is a heap of rubbish.[118]

——

Nationality[n] is babyishness for the most part.[119]

——

[1⟨9⟩09] Is it not a convenience to have a person in town who knows where penny royal grows, or sassafras or punk for a slow-match; or Celtis⟨;⟩,—the false elm; or cats-o-nine-tails; or wild cherries; or wild pears; where is the best appletree, where is the Norway pine, where the beech, or Epigaea, or Linnaea, or sanguinavia, or orchis pulcherrima, or drosera, or lauras benzoin, or pink huckleberry, or shag barks, where is the best chestnut grove, hazelnuts, where are trout, where woodcocks, where wild bees, where pigeons, or who can tell where the stakedriver (bittern) can be heard, who ⟨can⟩ has seen & can show you the Wilson's plover[?][120]

[117] With this paragraph, struck through in ink with a diagonal use mark, cf. "Fate," *W*, VI, 39.

[118] In Journal FOR, p. [68], Emerson associates "Kleinstadtisch" with "provincial, village politics".

[119] "Kleinstadtisch . . . part." is struck through in ink with a vertical use mark.

[120] "Is it not . . . plover", struck through in pencil with a vertical use mark, is used in "Country Life," *W*, XII, 161–162.

[110] *Culture*
"The masters have now brought our art to a degree of perfection which renders it possible for him who possesses design, invention, coloring, to produce six pictures in one year, whereas, formerly, those earlier masters could produce only one picture in six years. While /the/our/ paintings are more highly finished than were those"

Vasari [*Lives* . . . ,]
Bohn [1850–1852,] II. 363.

[111] Thoreau wants a little ambition in his mixture. Fault of this, instead of being the head of American Engineers, he is captain of a huckleberry party.[121]

[112] "I had formed an opinion that courage & reading were all that were necessary to the formation of an officer." (Soldier-)
"I had met with an observation among regular officers, that mankind were naturally divided into three sorts; one third of them are animated at the first appearance of danger, & will press forward to meet & examine it; another third are alarmed by it, but will neither advance nor retreat, ⟨but⟩till they know the nature of it, but stand ⟨full⟩to meet it. The [113] remaining third will run or fly upon the first thought of it."

John Adams
Vol III p 86[122]

He proceeds — "If this remark is just, as I believed it was, it appeared to me, that the only way to form an army to be confided in, was a systematic discipline, by which means all men may be made heroes."[123]

[*The Works* . . . , III, 86–87]

[114] John Adams in 1782 (aetatis suae 46) told the Duke of Vanguyon he was going to Paris to treat of peace with the British Commissioners &c. "He replied, that he rejoiced to hear it, for he believed Mr Jay & I were cordial, & he thought it absolutely neces⟨a⟩-sary that I should be there, for, that the immoveable firmness ⟨which⟩that Heaven had given me would be useful & necessary upon this occasion."

[*Ibid.*,] Vol. III. p. 281,

[121] This paragraph, struck through in pencil with one wavy diagonal use mark and two diagonal use marks, is used in "Thoreau," *W*, X, 480.

[122] *The Works of John Adams*, ed. Charles Francis Adams, 10 vols. (Boston, 1850–1856). Volume III was published in 1851.

[123] "He proceeds . . . heroes.' ", struck through in pencil with a vertical use mark, is used in "Culture," *W*, VI, 139.

[115] Culture.

——"The genius of the people" "What is the genius of people"? said I.

"It is," replied Count Sarsfield, "a manufacture: it is the effect of government & education."

[*Ibid.*,] Vol III p 291

"a systematic discipline by which all men may be made heroes."[124]

See above, p 113

[116] *Loadstone.* "This substance is in the secret of the whole globe. It must have a sympathy with the whole globe." *J Adams* [*ibid.*, p. 378]

Viny [n] says, Franklin said to him, "Mankind are very superficial & dastardly. The⟨n⟩y begin upon a thing, but, meeting with a difficulty, they fly from it discouraged; but they have capacities, if they would employ them."[125]

J Adams [*ibid.*, p. 395]

[117] I think Horace Greeley's career one of the most encouraging facts in ⟨these⟩our Whiggish age. A white haired man in the city of New York has adopted every benevolent crotchet, & maintained it, until he commands an army of a million now in the heart of the United States. Here we stand shivering on the North wall of opposition, we New-England idealists,—& might have taken Boston long ago, "had we had the pluck of a louse," to use the more energetic than elegant expression of my travelling friend.[126]

[118] *Conversation.*

Whenever the Muses sing, Pan spirts poppy-juice all about, so that no one who hears them ↑can↓ carry any word away.

True of fine conversation. See *supra* p. 76

[119][127] I don't like linear but spheral people; but discontent

[124] " 'a systematic . . . heroes.' " is struck through in ink with a vertical use mark.

[125] " 'Viny says . . . them.' ", struck through in ink with a diagonal use mark, is used in "Considerations by the Way," *W*, VI, 248.

[126] For " 'pluck of a louse,' " see *JMN*, X, 215.

[127] This page is in pencil.

merely shows incompleteness, as you measure yourself by times & events; as soon as you express yourself, you will round.

[120][128] assaults on heaven our tools
echo
we shall decompose him   vice conservative
day will come when Hercules cannot be organized[129]
Criticism describes critic
Complaint announces incomplete unfolding
When we read metaphysics, we ⟨shall⟩ jump out of our skin.
Bonaparte & Moscow

[Art.]
Two ideas, Greece & Jewry, sway us; look at our apish buildings.

We pass from thought to thought easily, but not from realization to realization.
Eloquence should
⟨This is not slavery here⟩ ↑What have we to do with slavery↓, they said
It seems they had everything to do with it
Pan spirts poppy juice all about.

[121][130]
Conservative literal.
All the rest rhetoric of youth.
Webster's daylight statement has no voluntary composition no ingenuity but they lie like strata of cloud or of geology[131]

We can't protest against half a thing

[128] The entries on p. [120] are in pencil; "When we . . . metaphysics, we", "jump out . . . skin.", "Art.", "Two ideas . . . to realization.", and "Pan spirts . . . about." are traced over in ink. For the last sentence, see p. [118] above.

[129] This is quoted in Notebook Amos Bronson Alcott, p. [27].

[130] The entries on p. [121] are in pencil; "Conservative literal. . . . of youth." and "One of these days . . . be leisure." have been traced over in ink, with minor differences in punctuation.

[131] "Websters daylight . . . geology", struck through in pencil with a diagonal use mark, is used in "The Fugitive Slave Law" (1851), *W*, XI, 202.

How to make generation an art

They all ride together in the eye & in the brain.
One of these days we shall do without this[132] dismal multitude[n] — the paddy period, [—][133] the human race will no longer spawn like vermin or fishes: instead of the mob, we shall be a family. The earth is getting subdued, friable, roaded, & telegraphed, gas-lighted, sun-painted, & echoed: labor disused, and the paddy problem will no longer come up. There will be leisure.
[122][134] & the tinkering of politics or this after-work, superseded by education, which anticipates crimes by virtues, anticipates events by men,
We are always a little late[135]

In rare moments there seems to have been a fusion of all the bloods of the world; as, in Italy, in the fall of Rome; and in the Crusades.

We are always outgeneralled by tacticians[,] choked off by the previous question or by insidious assistance or by sly amendments or by false friends[.]

[123] "We shall sink at last into the arms of a vast conservatism embracing even the fiends in its charity yet without losing sight of the immutable laws"

Now the earth takes up him,
he plants his brain. By & by he will take up the earth & have his gardens & vineyards there

↑See p 241↓[136]

[132] "They all ride . . . this" is struck through in pencil with two diagonal use marks.

[133] In the pencil version underlying the ink tracing, "the paddy period", without punctuation, is an insertion.

[134] Except for "in the fall . . . Crusades.", which is in ink only, the entries on p. [122] are in pencil; "In rare moments . . . in Italy," has been traced over in ink.

[135] "& the tinkering . . . little late" is struck through in pencil with a vertical use mark; "& the tinkering . . . after-work," and "We . . . late" are used in "Culture," *W*, VI, 140.

[136] " 'We shall sink . . . See p 241" is in pencil. "Now the earth . . . vine-

Two boys pushing each other on the curbstone of the sidewalk. Everything is pusher or pushed, & Matter & mind are in perpetual tilt & balance so. Whilst the man is weak, the earth takes up him. He plants his brain, his affections. By & by, he will take up the earth, & have his gardens & vineyards in his brain.[137] ↑See p 241↓

[124][138] It turns out at last that this stupid iron Whiggery which he has cursed, is ⟨his b⟩ much his friend; that he has owed sacred benefits & salvations to ⟨its⟩ this poor musty hencoop decorum[.]

In Boston this is a mere scramble for pistareens[.]

[125] H[enry]. T[horeau]. will not stick
he is not practically renovator. He is a boy, & will be an old boy. Pounding beans is good to the end of pounding Empires, but not, if at the end of years, it is only beans.[139]

I fancy it an inexcusable fault in him that he is insignificant here in the town. He speaks at Lyceum or other meeting but somebody else speaks & his speech falls dead & is forgotten. He rails at the town doings & ought to correct & inspire them[.]

[126] In Webster the past the ⟨leter⟩ letter[140]
the animal orgies, falls back on that
protection of property
lucky all that was written when he came
nothing else can go

Simply he has no faith in the power of selfgovernment. In

yards there" is struck through in pencil with a diagonal use mark; see the next entry immediately below.

[137] This paragraph, struck through in ink with a diagonal use mark, is used in "Fate," *W*, VI, 43.

[138] Pp. [124]–[130] are in pencil.

[139] "H. T. will . . . only beans." is struck through in pencil and in ink with single vertical use marks; "Pounding beans . . . beans." is used in "Thoreau," *W*, X, 480.

[140] "In Webster . . . letter" is struck through in pencil with a vertical use mark, which has been erased.

extemporizing gov.t not ⟨a⟩ the smallest municipal provision would ever receive his sanction, but only conformity to the old.
'Tis inevitable in him, he has animal & animal-intellect powers, but no morals. ⟨has a hole⟩ His [n] religion is literal, calvinistic, formal. His minister ↑I know↓ esteems him a religious man[.]

But morals he has none, but a hole in his head. No hope, no liberty, no forward foot, no inception.
[127] All the liberty is merely rhetoric & juvenile enthusiasm[,] sentimentalism. He can celebrate it in the past, but it means as much with him as it would from Metternich or Talleyrand. Hungarian speech is claptrap. In Concord in 1776 he would without a question have been refugee.[141]

His rhetoric has got purged of the word liberty for Fate has been too strong for him.
⟨In⟩ All the drops of his blood have eyes that ↑look downward↓[.]
But not by such as he have the steps for mankind been taken.[142] But by

We want an exploding Bonaparte who could take forward steps instead of these crabs[.]
Webster values the Union then only as a large farm property.[143]

[128] Now Columbus was no crab, nor John Adams, nor Patrick Henry, nor Jefferson,
nor Martin Luther nor Copernicus

And the American idea is no crab but a man incessantly ad-

[141] "the animal orgies . . . refugee.", struck through in pencil with a curved vertical use mark on p. [126] and three vertical use marks on p. [127], is used in "The Fugitive Slave Law" (1851), *W*, XI, 203–205.

[142] "All the drops . . . taken." is struck through in pencil with a vertical use mark; "All the drops . . . downward" is used in "The Fugitive Slave Law" (1851), *W*, XI, 204.

[143] "We want . . . property." is struck through in pencil with three vertical use marks. "We want . . . crabs" is used in "The Fortune of the Republic," *W*, XI, 536–537; "Webster values . . . property." is used in "The Fugitive Slave Law" (1851), *W*, XI, 204.

vancing as ⟨a sha⟩ [n] the shadow of the dial or the heavenly body that casts it.[144]

America is the ↑idea of↓ emancipation[.]

abolish kingcraft, Slavery, feudalism, blackletter monopoly, pull down gallows, explode priestcraft, ↑tariff,↓ open the doors of the sea to all emigrants. Extemporize government, California, Texas, Lynch Law. All this covers selfgovernment. All proceeds on the belief that as the people have made a gov.t they can make another[,] [129] that ⟨if they⟩ their Union & law is not in their memory but in their blood. If they unmake the law they can easily make it again. The imagination of Mr Webster thinks this Union is a vast Prince Rupert's drop which i⟨t⟩f an acre should fall ⟨off⟩out anywhere the whole would snap into a million pieces. He does not see that the people are loyal, law-abiding, have no⟨t⟩ taste for drunken soldiering or misrule or uproar, but prefer order[.]

Mr Everett tells of a bloody line of castles along the frontier. On the contrary the people are all cousins, traders, partners, ra
The only castles they know or care for are Depots & ↑the↓ express ⟨riders⟩ ↑-man↓ ⟨are⟩ ↑is↓ the only dragoon⟨s⟩ & instead of a bloody line of castles there is a white line of flour barrels[.] He has been reading in his Robertson instead of in the faces of the people.[145]

[130] ↑It amounts to this——— nakedly.↓

I will give you a pistareen or a mountain of pistareens, if you will be quiet about this.

[131] The Crisis has shown

1. The Fug↑itive↓ Law contravened
2. The broader question of the Union [146]

---

[144] This sentence, marked in the left margin by two vertical pencil lines, is used in "The Fortune of the Republic," *W*, XI, 537.

[145] "Now Columbus . . . people." is struck through in pencil with single vertical use marks on pp. [128] and [129]; "Now Columbus . . . order" is used in "The Fortune of the Republic," *W*, XI, 537, 528; "The imagination . . . order" is used in "The Fugitive Slave Law" (1851), *W*, XI, 205.

[146] "The Crisis . . . Union" is in pencil; "2. The broader . . . Union" is erased, overwritten by "Keep the . . . run.", below.

Economy

Keep the air. ↑Nature says, 'Thou shalt↓ walk,[n] ↑skate, swim,↓ ride, run.'[147] When you have worn out your shoes, the strength of the sole leather has passed into the fibre of your body. I measure your health by the number of shoes & hats & clothes you have worn out. He is the richest man who ⟨has⟩ ↑pays↓ the largest debt to his shoemaker.

[132][148]

The Crisis has shown
the nature & impracticability of this Statute
Mr Webster
his support
& the opposition

The American Idea
Emancipation selfreliance selfhelp advance

These thirty nations are equal to any work. They are to become 50 millions presently & should achieve something just & generous. Let them trample out this mischief before it has trampled out them.[149] For the future of slavery is not inviting. But the destinies of nations are too great for our spanning & what are the instruments no policy can show[,] whether Liberia, whether flax[,] cotton, whether the working them out by Irish & Germans [133] none can tell; ⟨B⟩ or by what scourges God has guarded his law. But one thing is imperative[,] not to do unjustly, not to steal a man, or help steal him, or to call stealing honest.[150]

Constitution guards
without due process of law[151]

[147] " 'Thou shalt" is in pencil.

[148] Pp. [132]–[145] are in pencil.

[149] "These thirty . . . them trample", struck through in pencil with a vertical use mark, is used in "The Fugitive Slave Law" (1851), *W*, XI, 209–210.

[150] "of nations . . . honest." is struck through in pencil with single vertical use marks on pp. [132] and [133]; "of nations . . . imperative" is used in "The Fugitive Slave Law" (1851), *W*, XI, 209–210.

[151] This and the preceding line were written at the top of p. [133]; a pencil rule was drawn across the page and followed by "none can tell . . . honest."

[134] ↑1851.↓

Mr T. ⟨H⟩W. old merchant sees what he foresaw[,] ⟨thinks⟩ ↑knows↓ Yankees can make everything, as soon ⟨|| . . . ||⟩as it is certain to pay, & has found one nostrum sovereign, not free trade, not laws, not morals, not antislavery, but only the natural growth of the thirty nations.[152] ⟨T⟩One way or another they arrive at the same thing which you would compass with your law. Thus they have got free trade in substance, tho' not in form; free trade with thirty nations. They wanted tariff to protect their iron. Well, they did not get it; but instead of 20 000 tons, last year they manufactured 800 000: which is getting it. So peace, so abolition of Slavery will be got by lying quiet a little.

But liberty & land are the nostrum.

[135] "Two wrongs don't make a right."

S. W↑ard↓ thinks 'Twill do for Carolina to be unreasonable & nullify. But not so with Massachusetts, which is the head: the toe may nullify, but the head must not nullify.

thinks that the confidence of financiers proves nothing; proves everything ⟨f⟩ in reference to old & known dangers, but nothing in reference to new dangers. The /stocks/French/ stood firm until Louis Philippe fell.

The Union is part of the religion of this people. Its dissolution has not been contemplated.

⟨It⟩His private opinion is, that Disunion is inevitable. The North & South are two nations. It is not slavery that separates them, but climate. ⟨T⟩ Without slavery they do not agree. The South does not like the North, ↑& never did,↓ slavery apart. The North likes [136] the South well enough.[153]

But he reckons abolition ⟨im⟩ by purchase impossible. Thousand million of dollars.[154] A financial measure so gigantic not to be thought of.

[152] According to Edward Emerson, the reference here is to Thomas Wren Ward, father of Samuel G. Ward.

[153] This paragraph is used in "The Fugitive Slave Law" (1851), *W*, XI, 206.

[154] With "But he . . . dollars.", cf. "The Fugitive Slave Law" (1851), *W*, XI, 208–209: "'Tis said it will cost two thousand millions of dollars."

In a common financial measure such an onerous infinity of particulars, so many heart burnings, so many sacrifices of character, conflict of interests.——What would it be then with a complication so vast as this? It cannot be done[.]

⟨Thusly⟩ ↑Nothing but putting money in our pockets & having every[n] thing we want↓[;] there must come an end of this too much prosperity of ours, or it would go on to madness.

They are morally injured. Tone of the ⟨Massa⟩ press not lower on Slavery than on everything else,—criminal on that point, ready to be criminal on every other.

[137] ⟨I⟩⟨n⟩No measures to be relied on; no concert; it will come by chance. ⟨Somebody will get pushed⟩ We stand on a brink & somebody will get pushed ↑further than he meant↓, and when the fat is on the fire, we shall see the blaze.

⟨He⟩
a good deal of indifferentism,
a good deal of respect for law,
and, however hot people may get, when they come to the street & have to resist the law, it is cold & ridiculous.

My Philadelphia desperadoes cowed down instantly by the touch of a policeman on the shoulder.

Thirty Years' War, says Schiller, made Germany a nation.[155] What Calamity will make us one?

[138] Webster low, has no character, could not conceive a great design & put it through, lives with little people, & is easily led.

"finds nonsense very refreshing."[156]

We thought we had guards for liberty in the careful provision of the Constitution that
without due process of law
and on claim

[155] This sentence is used in "Considerations by the Way," *W*, VI, 254.

[156] " 'finds . . . refreshing.' " is used in "Considerations by the Way," *W*, VI, 269, where it is attributed to Prince Talleyrand. See Charles Maxime Catherinet de Villemarest, *Life of Prince Talleyrand* [trans. from the French], 4 vols. (London, 1834–1836), III, 233, and *JMN*, IX, 360.

but the slavish spirit of the people has made these guards of none effect [157]

[139] As soon as the Constitution enacts a criminal law, disunion already exists. "'*Tis you that say it, not I; you do the deeds*[.]" [158]

---

old law ↑of 1793↓ affirmed slavery in Massachusetts *pro honoris causa*, just as K. James was styled King of Great Britain, *France*, & Ireland,

city & country morally injured

That law must be made inoperative

[140] M[argaret]. F[uller] said one day to S[amuel] W[ard] & A[nna] W[ard] "I have not seen any intellect that would compare with my own." [159]

If these ⟨‖ . . . ‖⟩30 nations cannot do what they would, who can? Is it not time for them to do something beside ditching & draining? beside making land friable, & ↑hay &↓ corn cheap? beside getting money?
Every race has done somewhat generous. What have you done? [160]

[141] One thing or the other.[n] If it is ascertained that the commissioner is only a notary to ⟨deliver⟩ surrender the black man to his hunter, then infamy attaches to the post. No man of right sentiments can sit on that bench. It belongs to a class from which ⟨the jailer &⟩ the turnkey & the hangman ↑& the informer↓ are taken. ⟨If law means

[157] With "We thought . . . effect", cf. "The Fugitive Slave Law" (1851), *W*, XI, 184.

[158] " '*Tis you . . . deeds*' " is used in "The Fugitive Slave Law" (1851), *W*, XI, 193. For the quotation, see Sophocles, *Electra*, l. 624, and *JMN*, VII, 187.

[159] This sentence, struck through in pencil with a diagonal use mark, is used in *Memoirs*, I, 234.

[160] This paragraph is struck through in pencil with a vertical use mark; "If these . . . cheap?" is used in "The Fugitive Slave Law" (1851), *W*, XI, 210.

↑slavery,↓⟩ [n] ⟨Let⟩ The [n] ↑dislike &↓ contempt of Society very properly attaches to the officer.[161]

[142] People will not stick to what they say & the number increases
They cannot remember 1775
Their fathers were seditious. ↑They kept↓ those [n] ten seditious commandments which god gave on Sinai.[162]

literary blackguard
hatchetfaced cadaverous philosopher

[143] The fugitives
You may say the slaves are better off as they are,[n] ⟨You will not⟩ & that nothing will tempt them to exchange their condition. This amiable argument falls to the ground in the case of the fugitive. He has certified, as distinctly as human nature could, his opinions.
And to take him back is ⟨s⟩to steal[.] [163]

[144] We are glad at last to get a clear case, one on which no shadow of doubt can hang. This is not meddling with other people's affairs,—this is other people meddling with us. This is not going crusading after slaves who⟨m⟩ it is alleged are very happy & comfortable where they are: all that amiable argument falls to the ground, but defending a human being who has taken the ⟨most frightful⟩ risks of being shot or burned alive, or cast into the sea, or starved [145] to death or suffocated in a wooden box,—taken all this risk to get away from ⟨that loathsome home⟩ ↑his driver↓ & recover the rights of man. And this man the Statute says, you ⟨children⟩ ↑men↓ of Massachusetts shall kidnap & send ⟨home⟩ ↑back↓ again ⟨to

[161] This paragraph, struck through in pencil with a diagonal use mark, is used in "The Fugitive Slave Law" (1851), *W*, XI, 198.

[162] "People will . . . Sinai." is struck through in pencil with a curved vertical use mark; "Those ten . . . Sinai." is struck through in pencil with a vertical use mark and marked in the left margin with a vertical pencil line.

[163] This paragraph is struck through in pencil with a vertical use mark; cf. "The Fugitive Slave Law" (1851), *W*, XI, 187–188. It would appear that this paragraph is expanded in the one immediately following.

the doghutch⟩ a thousand miles across the sea to the dog-hutch he fled from. And this ⟨ferocious⟩ ↑filthy↓ enactment was made in the 19th Century, by people who could ⟨wr⟩ read & write.
I will not obey it, by God.[164]

[146] A voyage! yes; but I do not like that ⟨boat⟩ ↑craft↓ which requires that we should stand all hours at the pump.

Intellect strips, affection clothes. If the good God would perfect his police on any day he has only to open that upper chamber in each man's & woman's brain wh⟨ere⟩ich is his or her determinate love, & on the instant chastity is secured by an impregnable guard, ⟨though⟩ as if all the population lived like naked children in one nursery.

[147] ↑*Doctrine of Leasts.*↓

Nature makes everything Cheap: the smallest amount of material; the low-price, the ⟨b⟩low-fare system, is hers. ↑least action, least pain.↓ [165]

[148] [166] ↑Liberty.↓

I think this matter of liberty is one of those rights which requires fine sense to appreciate, & with every degree of civility it will be more truly felt & defined. A barbarous tribe will by means of their best heads secure ⟨the li⟩ substantial liberty, but where there is any weakness in a race as is in the black race & it ⟨is⟩ ↑becomes in any degree↓ matter of concession & protection from the↑ir↓ stronger neighbours, ⟨it will⟩ the incompatibility & offensiveness of the wrong will of course be most evident to the most cultivated[.]

[149] For it is, is it not, the very nature of courtesy, of politeness, of religion, ↑of love,↓ to prefer another, to postpone one's self, to protect another from one's self. That is the distinction of the gentle-

[164] These entries are struck through in pencil with single vertical use marks on pp. [144] and [145]. They are used, except for the last two sentences, in "The Fugitive Slave Law" (1851), *W*, XI, 187–188.

[165] With this entry, cf. p. [77] above.

[166] Except for the index heading "Liberty." added in ink, pp. [148] and [149] are in pencil.

man,—to defend the weak & redress the injured, as it is of the savage & the brute, to usurp & use others.[167]

[150] Fate stands opposed to intellect, & so to science. Its motto is, "Let all drive." Science says, make a footpad, a weapon, a valet, of these passions & their power.[168]

"There are points from which we can command our life,
When the Soul sweeps the future like a glass,
And coming things, full freighted with our fate,
Jut out dark on the offing of the mind."

Festus.

↑"And his five fingers made five nights in air"↓ [169]

[151] The peculiarity of our School system, is, that the poor man has acquired the right to vote the money of the rich for the education of his own children. Dives pays a tax of $1000, has but one child, & sends him to a private school. Lazarus pays only his poll-tax, & has twenty children, & wishes to send them all to college. Having thus got his hand once into the rich man's pocket, why not again? In Maine, they spill the barrel of brandy, by law. It is not property, by their law. It is but one step, now, to say to the drinker of the brandy, 'You are a barrel of poison, & shall not be allowed to infect the state with your *virus*. You shall not marry. Go into the street; go to Poneropolis.' [170]

[152] Dante was very bad company, & never invited to dinner.

[167] "I think . . . others.", struck through in pencil with single vertical use marks on pp. [148] and [149], is used in "The Fugitive Slave Law" (1854), *W*, XI, 229–230.

[168] "Fate stands . . . power." is struck through in pencil with a vertical use mark.

[169] Philip James Bailey, *Festus, A Poem*, 3d ed. (London, 1848), in Emerson's library. The first four lines are on p. 16 and marked in the left margin by a pencil line. On the inside of the back cover Emerson wrote "p. 16" and "There . . . life". The fifth line, added in pencil, is unlocated in Emerson's edition; it is on p. 366 of the Boston, 1849, edition. See *JMN*, X, 538.

[170] This paragraph apparently draws on information Emerson sent the Irish politician and educational reformer Edward Turner Twisleton (1809–1874), who had sent him questions on the common school system in Massachusetts. See *L*, IV, 261, and Notebook ML, p. [3]: "Letter to Twistleton. CO 151".

The ministers of Beauty are not beautiful in the coach & the saloon[.] [171]

Nature never makes us a present of ⟨the⟩ [n] a fine fruit or berry, pear, peach, or plum without also packing up ⟨in it⟩ along with it a seed or two of the same[.] [172]

[153] ↑*Faith*↓

We are born believing. A man bears beliefs, as a tree bears apples.[173] ↑also GH, 38↓

[154] In England, the Crystal Palace is not considered successful, until it pays. No matter how much ⟨eclat beauty⟩ convenience, beauty, or eclat; it must be selfsupporting. That wise nation ⟨are⟩ ↑is↓ contented with their slower Cunard steamers, as long as they know that the swifter Collins boats lose money to their owner with every trip, because, ⟨the⟩ beyond a certain limit, the ⟨p⟩ speed does not increase in proportion to the power.[174] The same rule ⟨is⟩ strictly holds in the economy of a man. Every man must be selfsupporting [175] [155] or

[156] The apple is our national fruit, &, in October, the country is covered with this most ornamental harvest. The beautiful colour of the apple heaps, more ⟨var⟩ lively & varied than the orange,—balls of ⟨fir⟩ scarlet fire,—give a gaiety & depth to our russet Massachusetts.[176]

[157] October, 1851

I believe in Society, in grace & courtesy, and mean therefore to

[171] "Dante . . . saloon", struck through in ink with a vertical use mark, is used in "Society and Solitude," *W*, VII, 7.

[172] "Nature . . . same" is in pencil.

[173] This entry, struck through in pencil and in ink with single vertical use marks, is used in "Worship," *W*, VI, 203.

[174] "In England . . . every trip," struck through in pencil and in ink with single vertical use marks, is used in "Wealth," *W*, V, 156.

[175] "because, ⟨the⟩ . . . selfsupporting" is marked in the left margin with a vertical pencil line.

[176] "The apple . . . & varied than" is struck through in pencil with a vertical use mark; "The apple . . . harvest." is used in "Country Life," *W*, XII, 145.

write answers to my letters, & not rely longer on mere brute force of duty.

[158] [Chaucer,] *House of Fame* [ll. 43–52]

"Or if the soul of proper kind
Be so perfect as men find
That it wot what is to come,
⟨&⟩And that he warneth all & some
Of every of their aventures,
By ⟨a⟩ ↑pre↓visions, or ⟨by⟩ figures,
But that our flesh hath no might
↑It↓ ⟨T⟩to understand ⟨it⟩ aright,
For it is warned too darkely;
But why the cause is, not wot I." [177]

[159] [Chaucer,] Book of the Duchess [ll. 1155–1158, 1160–1166]

"Me to keep from idleness
Truely I did my business
To make songes as I best ⟨could⟩ coude
And of↑t↓ time I sung them loude;
Although I coude not make so well
Songes, nor knew the Arte all⟨.⟩
As coude Lamek's Son Tubal,
That found out first the art of song,
For as his brother's hammers rung
Upon his anvil up & down,
Thereof he took the first sowne."

[160] *Chaucer*
↑House of Fame↓ [ll. 643–660]

And also, bean fire, of other things
That is, thou hast no tidings
Of Love's folk, if they be glad,
Ne of nothing else that God made,
And not only fro some countree
That no tidings come to thee
Not of thy very neighbours,
That dwellen almost at thy doors,

[177] The quotation, struck through in ink with a vertical use mark, is used, except for the last line, in "Fate," *W*, VI, 46.

Thou hearest neither that nor this,
For when thy labor all done is
And hast made all thy reckoning,
Instead of rest & of new things
Thou goest home to thy house anon
And also dumb as a stone
Thou sittest at another book
'Till fully dazed is thy look
[161] And livest as an hermite
Although thy abstinence is lite

[162] Politics is an afterwork, a poor tinkering. We are always a little late. When shall we learn to supersede politics by education, which an↑t↓icipates crimes by virtues, anticipates events by men? [178]

[163] [179] Fate
Fate Passion. antagonist force is Science & Intellect & Reason
The man & his things are all of one piece, the man & his history. He thinks his fate alien, ⟨not seein⟩ because the copula is hidden, but some people, being fatal, are made up of rhyme, & coincidence, & omen, & period.[180]

We go to Herodotus & Plutarch for examples of Fate; but we are examples.[181] Toss up a pebble & it falls. And the soaring of your mind & the magnanimity you indulge will fall↑.↓ ⟨as fast⟩ [182] But cannot we ride the horse which now throws us?

[164] An expense of ends to means is fate, organization tyrannizing over character[.]
The Menagerie or forms & powers of the spine is a book of fate; so is the scale of ↑races;↓ temperaments; so is sex; ↑⟨races;⟩↓ so is climate; so is the reaction of talents concentrating[,] imprisoning the vital power[.]

[178] This paragraph, struck through in ink with a vertical use mark, is used in "Culture," *W*, VI, 140.

[179] Pp. [163]–[167] are in pencil.

[180] "He thinks . . . period.", struck through in pencil with vertical use marks, is used in "Fate," *W*, VI, 40, 46.

[181] This sentence, struck through in pencil with a vertical use mark, is used in "Fate," *W*, VI, 41.

[182] "The man . . . fast⟩" is struck through in pencil with a vertical use mark.

Every spirit makes its house; but neither must the spirit's house cost too much any more than a merchant's who ruins himself ⟨to live⟩ on Beacon St[.] [183]

[165] The ⟨Pythag⟩ ancients most truly ⟨rep⟩ & poetically represented the incarnation or descent into nature of Pythagoras, his condescension to be born, as his first virtue.
It is indeed a perilous adventure[,] this serious act of venturing into mortality[,] swimming in a sea strewn with wrecks, where none indeed go undamaged,
It is as bad as going to Congress[;] none comes back innocent.

↑Those who conquer,—the victory was born with them. They may well be serene. They seem to fight, but their lives are insured & their victories. You like better to hear what they say. Well you may, for they announce this success in every syllable.↓

[166] As Vishnu in the Vedas ⟨follo⟩ pursues Maya in all forms, when, to avoid him, she changes herself into a cow, then he into a bull; she into doe, he into a buck; she into a mare, he into a stallion; she into a hen, he into a cock, & so forth; so our metaphysics should be able to follow the flying force through all transformations, & name the new pair, identical[n] thro' all variety. For Memory, imagination, Reason, sense, are only masks of one power; as physical & spiritual laws are only new phases of limitation[.] [184]

[167] The poet is the lover loving; the critic is the lover advised.

For the rest of men remains only the stoic resignation. They ⟨fill⟩ ↑bridge↓ up by their dying bodies the path of their successors. They are the Corallines who make the new world, theatre of new Redemption & find their wages in an immense faith[.] [185]

[183] The entry on p. [164], struck through in pencil with a vertical use mark, is used in "Fate," *W*, VI, 8–9.

[184] With this paragraph, struck through in pencil with a vertical use mark, cf. "Fate," *W*, VI, 20. With "For Memory . . . power;", cf. Journal AZ, p. [182] above.

[185] "the lover advised . . . faith" is marked in the left margin with a vertical pencil line.

[168] A great man ought to see his character (& will see) emitted in the events that seem to meet, but which really accompany & exude from him. The events grow with the character. As he expands, they are colossal; as once he found himself among toys.[186]

Is not time a pretty toy to play with? [187]

[169][188] Wonderful constancy this harumscarum life admits. We wonder how the fly finds its mate. And yet year after year we find two men or two women, without legal or carnal tie, spend a great part of their best time within a few feet of each ⟨ea⟩other.[189]

Aunt Mary thinks that you never enjoy so much as ↑in↓ solitude with a book that met your feelings.

[170] But people are stupid, & when you speak of realities, it seems to them conjuring. Most of soci[e]ty is barbarous. S. Carolina is but a short remove from scalping.[190]
Which are the realities,—the thoughts, or the iron spikes? And who is truly wanted,—the railroad engineer, or the philosopher; David Neal, or Bronson Alcott? It is a mere question of Time. These roads & roadmakers must be had, I suppose, & are wanted now for fifty years good. The men of thought, & of truth to thought, are always wanted, & for all ages. You are to stand for that which is always good, and the same. There is never a fine aspiration but is on its way to its body or institution.

↑Continued on p. 175.↓

[171] ↑*Rhyme*↓ [191]

[186] This paragraph, in pencil, and struck through in pencil and in ink with single vertical use marks, is used in "Fate," *W*, VI, 42.

[187] This sentence, struck through in ink with two vertical use marks, is used in "Illusions," *W*, VI, 318.

[188] P. [169] is in pencil.

[189] This paragraph, struck through in pencil with a diagonal use mark, is used in "Fate," *W*, VI, 46.

[190] "But people . . . scalping." is in pencil.

[191] This index heading is in pencil.

We are lovers of rhyme & return & period & reflection. Metre ⟨is⟩ begins with pulsebeat. Young people like rhyme, drum, tune, things in pairs, and in alternations. Then they like to transfer that rhyme to life, & to see a melody as coarse as "April June & ⟨Sept⟩November"
"Thirty days hath September" in
their life. Hence come omens, signs, coincidences, sortilege, prophecy & fulfilment, anniversaries, amulets, rix dollar providences, & so forth. By & by when they see real rhymes, man & maid, Nature & art, Nature [172] & mind, ⟨man⟩Character & History, they do not value any longer these rattles & dingdongs[,] rudest barbaric rhymes of Superstition. Astronomy, botany, Chemistry, Hydraulics, & the Elemental forces ⟨r⟩of Magnetism &c, are grander strains of harmony not less exact.[192]

When oaks are in the grey,
Then Farmers plant away.[193]

At Candlemas,
Have half your ⟨hay⟩ ↑wood↓ & half your grass.

"The Ram, the Bull, the heavenly Twins [194]
And next the crab the lion shines
The Virgin & the Scales;
The Scorpion, Archer, & He goat,
The man that holds the waterpot
And fish, with glittering scales."
↑And the Philadelphia Rhyme↓ [195]

[173] [196] Fate

[192] "We are lovers . . . exact.", struck through in pencil with a discontinuous vertical use mark on p. [171] and a vertical use mark on p. [172], is used in "Poetry and Imagination," *W*, VIII, 46, 47, 48–49.

[193] This couplet is used in "Samuel Hoar," *W*, X, 448. See *JMN*, VIII, 240.

[194] This and the following lines of quoted poetry are from Isaac Watts, *Works* . . . , ed. D. Jennings and P. Doddridge, 6 vols. (London, 1753), IV, 706–707; see *JMN*, X, 86. " 'The Ram . . . Twins' " is used in "Poetry and Imagination," *W*, VIII, 46.

[195] Added in pencil. The "Philadelphia Rhyme" may refer to the couplet made up of Philadelphia street names in Journal AZ, p. [199] above or to the earlier version in *JMN*, VIII, 334.

[196] This page is in pencil.

"Hell so presses on him as the sea does on every part of a dike ; which pressure it is impossible for man by his own strength to resist."[197]
Swedenborg
Arc II. 242

[174] Dante interests by incessant power[;] now he is Pindar & now Archimedes. ↑Euclid↓[198]

[175] ↑*Continued from p. 170*↓

These people that are made now, & for the day's wants, journeymen, will be impossible to be organized in a more advanced society, & if they should there appear ⟨but⟩would shock by their barbarism.[199] The world was once a rock, & peopled itself with lichen, moss, & sponge, the ↑first↓ disintegrators. Afterwards it was a cold swamp; sponge, sphagnum, fly, fish, lizard, multiplied. By & by came men, but rude men; after all, came Englishmen, & planted America; but the wheel is not scotched, but rotates still, & the men of today cannot live in the warm aerial future any more than the Sauri can escape extirpation [176] in the man[-]bearing granite of Massachusetts & New York.[200]

[177] [blank]

[178][201] Autobiography too. I am never beaten until I know that I am beaten. I ⟨hear⟩ meet powerful people to whom I have no skill to reply. They think they have defeated me. It is so published in the ⟨newspapers⟩ journals. I am defeated in this external way, perhaps, on a dozen different lines. My Leger may show that I am in debt, cannot make my ends meet, & vanquish the enemy so. My race may be not prospering, we are sick, ⟨|| . . . ||⟩ugly, obscure, unpopular: My children may be worsted; I seem to ⟨have I⟩ [n] fail in my protegés too. That is to say in all the encounters that have yet chanced I have not

[197] This sentence is struck through in pencil with a diagonal use mark. The reference to Swedenborg, immediately following, is to *Heavenly Arcana* . . . , 12 vols. (Boston, 1837–1847).

[198] Added in pencil.

[199] With this sentence, cf. "Culture," *W*, VI, 166: "The time will come when the evil forms we have known can no more be organized."

[200] With "The world . . . New York.", cf. "Fate," *W*, VI, 15.

[201] P. [178] is in pencil.

been weaponed for that particular occasion, & have been historically beaten, & yet I know all the time that I have never been beaten, have never yet fought, shall certainly fight when my hour comes, & shall beat.[202]

[179] All eloquence is a war of posts. What is said is the least part of the oration. It is the attitude taken, the unmistakeable sign never so casually given [in the tone of voice, or manner, or word,] that a greater spirit speaks from you than is spoken to in him.[203]

S

I believe in the Fable that the /Fates/Destinies/ fell in love with Hermes.[204]

Ηστραπτεν, ἐβρόντα, ξυνεκύκα την Ἑλλάδα.[205]

See ⟨Cart⟩Wheelwright's Translation
Vol II. p. 126
Acharnians[206]

[180] ↑Baring is↓ a walking pocketbook[207]

⟨of assertion⟩

Concord is "small mercies"[208]

---

[181] In "Natural Aristocracy," or in "Culture," it needs to say, that the instinctive belief of mankind in melioration is plainly indicated in

202 The entry on p. [178], struck through in pencil with a diagonal use mark, is used in "Worship," *W*, VI, 234–235.

203 This paragraph, struck through in pencil with two diagonal use marks, is used in "Eloquence," *W*, VIII, 131.

204 This sentence is used in *Memoirs*, I, 236. See Notebook Margaret Fuller Ossoli, p. [254] below. "All eloquence . . . Hermes." is in pencil.

205 "Thundered and lightened and confounded Hellas."

206 *The Comedies of Aristophanes, Translated into Familiar Blank Verse . . .*, by C. A. Wheelwright, 2 vols. (Oxford, 1837), in Emerson's library.

207 P. [180] is in pencil. Emerson dined with William Bingham Baring, 2nd Baron Ashburton, in London in March, 1848.

208 See p. [17] above.

the care which each *auto* ↑or *allo*-↓biographer takes to show that /the/a/ hero came of good blood, ⟨that⟩ came of "kenned folk"; that his ancestor was a gentleman two hundred years before.

[182][209] This crisis demonstrative
People judge of the politics by their nature & not of their part from the party[.]

We ⟨are⟩ have got a better enemy than ever we had. Perhaps that was all we wanted. That may accelerate the slow crystallizations of the new men against the antiquated, against the old dead folks. Thirty years' war made Germany a nation.[210]

[183] But when will your law get legs?

The state stands for property; & the slave as the highest kind of property, is fitly made the question between the party of light, & the party of darkness.

[184] We are not such pedants as to suppose a king comes only with a crown on his head. The moment a man says "give up your rights, here is money",—there is tyranny. It comes masquerading in monks' cowls, & in citizens' coats, ↑comes savagely or comes politely.↓ But it is tyranny.[211]

☞ Nay the ⟨shading⟩ ↑gradation↓ is endless, & the family resemblance /meets/runs/ us throughout creation.[212]

[185] It is not so strange as we say that races mix. We make a great ado about pure races, but ⟨we are struck with⟩ strange resemblances ⟨& proofs of mixture⟩ ↑meet us everywhere↓. Not strange that Malay & European, Celt & Saxon, Roman & Tartar should ⟨breed⟩

[209] Pp. [182] and [183] are in pencil.

[210] For this sentence, see p. [137] above.

[211] This paragraph and the rule across the page, immediately below it, are in pencil.

[212] The alternate word "runs" in this sentence is in pencil.

↑mix↓, ⟨when we see that white & black, nay⟩ when we see the /descent/rudiments/ of the beasts of the forest in our human form, that the barriers of the races are not so firm but that some spray sprinkles us from the most distant seas.[213]

[186] We are superstitious[.]

What we think & say is wonderfully better for our spirits & trust, *in another's mouth.*[214]

Of course, the fact of my discontent with Webster's speech, which reaches to total aversion, does not yet advertise me that it weakens his position, until I hear another man say "it is base."[215]

We think the event severed from the person, & do not see the inevitable tie. It is like the nudicaulis plant,—the leaf invariably accompanies it, though the stems are connected underground.

[187] I am always taught that not the topic,—the subject,—is important,—but the angle of vision only. A↑llcot↓ astonishes by the grandeur of his Angle. I tell him he is the Bonaparte of speculators, born to rout the armies of ghosts, the Austrians of the Soul.[216]

[188][217] Dreams

[213] This paragraph, struck through in ink with two diagonal use marks, is used in "Race," *W*, V, 49–50. Of the corrections in the paragraph, the following are in pencil: the cancellations of "& proofs . . . mixture", "breed", and "when we . . . nay"; the insertion "mix", and the alternate "rudiments".

[214] This sentence, struck through in pencil with two vertical use marks and marked in the left margin with two vertical pencil lines, is used in "Quotation and Originality," *W*, VIII, 190.

[215] P. [186] is in pencil to this point, as is the rule drawn across the page below "'it is base.'" "Of course . . . base.'" is marked in the left margin with two vertical pencil lines. For an earlier reference to Webster's speech at Albany, see pp. [61]–[62] above. The entry below the rule, beginning "We think . . .", is in ink, written over the same entry in erased pencil.

[216] This is an ink version of an almost identical passage in erased pencil written upside down on the bottom half of the page. For "not the topic, — the subject, — is important, —" Emerson originally wrote "the subject is not important,".

[217] P. [188] is in pencil. "My dreams . . . corners." is written upside down beginning in the bottom margin.

My dreams are somewhat arch & sat↑i↓rical if I dare give them all the meaning they will bear. If they mean anything, they are surprising hits, yet by no means from a divine plane, but from a great sagacity on the Franklin level. This confusion in counting New Hampshire bills was an example. They had a varying value, twenty different figures on the corners.

[189] [blank]

[190] "How the names of the Willeys have been preserved, & every stage company lives over the adventure! The dullest can conceive that poem, as they look at the mountains, & one thinks the people must have had lives worth living, in the midst of so much beauty."[218] M. F↑uller↓. 29 July 1842.

[191][219] H[enry]. D[avid]. T[horeau's]. theory of sickness was the excess of ambition. A man says, I will remove that mountain; but he cannot. That is, he is sick.

[192] Mediator mediation There is nothing else[;] there is no Immediate known to us. Cloud on cloud, degree on degree, remove one coat, one lamina, and another coat or lamina just like it is the result,—to be also removed. When the symbol is explained the new truth turns out to be only a symbol of ulterior truth. The Judgment Day is in reality the Past. We have all been judged & we have judged⟨.⟩↑all.↓

We would gladly think highly of Nature & Life but what a country--muster, what ⟨an egg-pop⟩ Vanity-Fair full of noise, squibs, & egg pop, it is! ⟨Rev⟩ Pass your last week in review, & what figures move on the swelling scene! Mr Potter, Mr Minott, Mr Garfield, Tom Hazel, & the ticket master, are among the best.[220] 'Tis a one-cent

[218] Samuel Willey, an early settler of Conway, N.H., perished with his family in an avalanche, August 28, 1826. The incident is the basis of Hawthorne's story "The Ambitious Guest."

[219] Pp. [191] and [192] are in pencil.

[220] Emerson's references are undoubtedly all to Concord residents—Potter, a store keeper, George Minott his neighbor, farmer Daniel Garfield, and an Irish youngster, Tom Hazel, who went to school across the street from Emerson's house and played with the Emerson children on occasion (*L*, IV, 421).

farce. ↑Am I deceived, or is the low & absurd a little predominant in the piece?↓

[193] ↑Tools. The Age.↓

The age is marked ↑by↓ this wondrous nature Philosophy as well as by its better chisels & road & steamers but the attention of mankind is now fixed on ⟨the⟩ ruddering the balloon, & probably the next war,—the war of principles, is to be fought in the air.[221]

M. Petin [222]

The naturalist can carry us no farther than the vesicle which has the capacity of change into oak, ape, man, & God.[223]

[194] He did not grow old, because though his mind was ardent & laborious, when in action,—it immediately collapsed, &, in the intervals, he was not remarked for any vigour or sprightliness, ⟨n⟩but was a dull companion.

[195] Alcott thinks the American mind a little superior to English, German, Greek, or any other. It is a very amiable opinion, & deserves encour[a]gement; and certainly that is best which recommends ⟨the⟩ his home, & the present hour to every man[.]

↑Shall I say, it has the confirmation of having been held of his own country by every son of Adam?↓

---[224]

The "many turning Ulyssean culture" of this country, ⟨"⟩ Margaret quotes.

---

[221] This sentence, struck through in ink with a vertical use mark, is used in "Wealth," *W*, V, 161, and "Works and Days," *W*, VII, 163. See *JMN*, X, 464.

[222] "M. Petin" and the short rules above and below the name are in pencil. Petin is unidentified.

[223] This sentence, struck through in ink with a vertical use mark, is used in "Fate," *W*, VI, 14.

[224] Emerson undoubtedly drew the short rule after completing his original entry, ending "every man". Later, he wrote the added sentence "Shall I . . . Adam?" above and below the rule. The editors here print it below the added sentence.

A writer in the London Times, says, that "America is better fitted to shine in a famine, than in a fair."

[196] ↑*Shakspeare.*↓

⟨In⟩One listens to the magnifying of Goethe's poem by his critic, & replies, "Yes, it is good, if you all agree to come in, & be pleased;" and you fall into another company & mood, & like it not. It is so with Wordsworth. But to Shakspeare alone God granted the power to dispense with the humours of his company: They must needs all take *his*. He is always good; & Goethe [197] knew it, & said, "It is as idle to compare Tieck to me, ⟨&⟩ as me to Shakspeare."[225] I looked through the first part of Faust today, & find it a little too modern & intelligible. We can make such a fabric at several mills, though a little inferior.[226] The miraculous, the beauty which we can manufacture at no mill, can give no account of, it wants; —the[n] cheerful, radiant, profuse beauty of which Shakspeare, of which Chaucer, had the secret. —[227]

The Faust on the contrary abounds in the disagreeable. [198] The vice is prurient, learned, Parisian. In the presence of Jove, Priapus may be allowed, but he should have the least to say. But here he is an equal hero. The egotism, the wit is calculated. The book is undeniably made by a great master, & stands unhappily related to the whole modern world, but it is a very disagreeable chapter of history, & accuses the author.[228] Shakspeare [199] could, no doubt, have been as disagreeable, had ||msm||[229]

[225] *Conversations with Goethe*, 1839, p. 100. "'It is . . . Shakspeare.'" is marked in the left margin with two vertical pencil lines.

[226] This sentence is struck through in ink with a diagonal use mark; "I looked . . . inferior." is used in "Poetry and Imagination," *W*, VIII, 69.

[227] "The miraculous . . . secret. —", struck through in ink with a diagonal use mark, is used in "Literature," *W*, V, 256.

[228] "The vice . . . author.", struck through in pencil with a vertical use mark, is used in "Poetry and Imagination," *W*, VIII, 69.

[229] Most of the leaf bearing pp. [199]–[200] is torn away approximately an inch from the top margin. The matter on p. [199] is undoubtedly a continuation of the entry on p. [198] and is used in "Poetry and Imagination," *W*, VIII, 69 (words and parts of words corresponding to those in the ms. are italicized): ". . . he less *genius, and i*f ugliness had *attracted* him. In short, *our E*nglish nature and *gen*ius has made us the *wors*t critics of Goethe, —

'We, who speak the tongue

[200] In Ben Jonson's Masque ||msm|| [230]

[201] It is impossible to detach an individual from the mass without injustice & caricature. Do not pity Tom because he is low & will remain low all his life, but replace him in the circles & systems wherein he belongs, & there is reaction, compensation, old aboriginal neces[s]ity, far-reaching universal connection whose good as well as evil he shares, & in the scope of all of which only can he be rightly seen.[n]

[202] I listen with great pleasure to the masterly lectures of Mr Scherb, & with none the less that I reserve my opinion, & by no means accept his national estimates. But it is a most gratifying monument of culture, his lecture. Such a regnant good sense, such a calm high generalizing criticism, so sane, so superior, so catholic, so true to religion & reason; if at all I feel that they are [203] not his own, but that he is the good scholar of better masters,—my joy is not the less ↑in the reality of the benefit,↓ or my satisfaction in the conveyance of these healthy waters into our American fields[.]

He has more selfpossession than I have seen in any literary man, & read his lecture to these twelve persons ⟨in⟩& the empty benches of the little orthodox vestry with an elegance & finish as if he were addressing an audience of lords & duchesses in London, as C[hanning?]. remarked. C. said, too, that this elegance of his could not be preserved if he had ever once spoken to a [⟨304⟩ 204] labourer here on ↑such↓ a footing as we all use.

If the tree, the mountain, the lake, would only give a token,—were it only a ↑waving↓ leaf, a sigh, a ripple,—that it knew the man who was born by them, & carried them always in his blood & manners!—[231]

---

*Th*at Shakspeare spake, the faith and manners hold
*W*hich Milton held.' "

[230] Words and parts of words remaining on the stub are: "other entertainments ||msm||rance performed ||msm||e country ||msm||e need ||msm||h kitchens ||msm||n was ||msm|| by ||msm||nd ||msm||ral ||msm||p,". P. [200] is indexed under Lidian. In Notebook WA, p. [215], Emerson records: "Inaugural address to the Cook *CO* 200."

[231] This sentence is struck through in pencil with a vertical use mark.

[⟨305⟩205] ↑*Books.*↓
It is absurd to rail at books: it is as certain ↑that↓ there will always be books, as that there will be clothes.

Jenny Lind is once for all the standard which every artist & scholar thinks of as the measure of remuneration ↑and Gorgias, who erected a statue of Apollo of massy gold, at Athens enriched by his pupils & his embassies.↓

↑1855

Jenny Lind's net receipts for 93 concerts in America were $176, 675. 09 — ↓

[206] "Do not think now ↑that↓ the postage is changed that I have forgotten its existence. ——— I like honesty, the ground work of all virtues."
July 1845 ↑C[aroline] S[turgis]↓ [232]
"I will forgive you that you do so much, & you me that I do nothing." [233]
↑printed↓ ↑C S↓

[207] "Always believe Ellery in everything with regard to me. He understands me better than you do," &c
↑C. S.↓ [234]

[208] "I am sorry he is not satisfied who wd like to have me pleased thro' his acts, but everything must take its own way. Even the daemons cannot interfere among men, but that they are here close to us, all must believe, who see the circles of life. All above, as below, is organised, & into the innermost being man ⟨can⟩ ↑may↓ not enter. So let us return the smiles of the angels who look upon our sports, as children return those we so condescendingly bestow. But let the angels [209] know as we also know for the children, that our place in the universe holds good with theirs, & our games are a part of its music." ↑Caroline Sturgis.↓ [235]
July 10

[232] The initials here, and following the next two entries below, and "Caroline Sturgis," on p. [209] are added in pencil.

[233] This sentence, struck through in ink with two vertical use marks, is used in "Success," *W*, VII, 312.

[234] From a Caroline Sturgis letter to Emerson, Aug. 23, 1845 (letter in Houghton Library).

[235] From a letter to Emerson, July 10, 1845 (letter in Houghton Library).

"No secret can be kept in the civilized world." [236]

[210] We hold of the party of the Universe, though we live in the states, & in Boston. ⟨Mr Webster holds⟩ As [n] Fenelon said, "I am more a Frenchman than a Fenelon, & more a man than a Frenchman." [237]

I wish I could get the fact about ⟨horse⟩ shoe nails, which, after being hammered & worn & recast & hammered & worn, are made up into Damascus steel, which is thus a result & simmering down, & last possibility of iron. I believe the tradition is fabulous but such in nature are men made up of monads, each of which has held governance of fish or fowl or worm or fly, & is now promoted to be a particle of man.

[211] A noble woman is moral, is a Beatrice, &, in the choice of universal aims, her lover is really courting her. But he dares not believe, that, in this her religion, she has not excepted herself. He believes, she will delight in his uniform preference of virtue to joy, with the solitary exception of preferring total union with her to the virtue of the Universe.

[21⟨0⟩2] Expansions is still the name for that game which Alcott's talk permits, more than anybody's. Other people, all good people, give you leave,—give you hint, & scope; ⟨B⟩but he more purely. One would use him for that, tho' others would afford it; just as we prefer ⟨phosp↑h↓orus⟩ ↑litmus↓ as a chemical reagent, tho' other substances will do.[238]

[21⟨1⟩3] ↑*Prudence*↓

Half measures fail.
Don't be leaky.[239]

---

[236] This sentence is used in "Worship," *W*, VI, 223.

[237] Joseph Spence, *Anecdotes, Observations and Characters of Books and Men* . . . (London, 1820), p. 27. See *JMN*, VI, 325.

[238] This paragraph is struck through in pencil with a wavy diagonal use mark.

[239] With this sentence, cf. "Behavior," *W*, VI, 195–196: "you shall not be facile, apologetic, or leaky, . . ." See Notebook BO Conduct, pp. [16] and [29].

↑*Power.*↓ ↑*Bias.*↓

The French papers say that somebody is revolutionizing mechanics by ⟨making⟩ ↑converting↓ the ⟨pendulum⟩ come & go force of the pendulum into a perpetual push, as has been done by steam in the rotation of the paddle↑-↓wheel, instead of the oar. Well, this power of perpetual push instead of the push spasmodic ⟨o⟩is the differencing power of men. ⟨A⟩ However mild & gentle the nature, if it has a steady push in one direction, it is ⟨b⟩soon a recognized element in society, and is entitled to shake its head at twenty times as much genius or force of the intermittent kind.

[21⟨2⟩4 214] ⟨Pa⟩ Steamers

⟨E⟩Aug 18⟨4⟩51
Arrived *Europa* from Liverpool, at Halifax,
8 days 18 hours.
Aug. *Baltic*, at Liverpool from N. Y
9 days 22 hours
Aug 12 *Africa*, at N. Y from Liverpool—
10 days 6 hours
Aug 11 Arctic at N. Y. from Liverpool
11 days 18 hours
Aug 16 Baltic at N. Y. from Liverpool
9 days 13 hours[240]

[21⟨3⟩5] [blank]

[216] Goethe is the pivotal man of the old & new times with us. He shuts up the old, he opens the new. No matter that you ⟨live sin⟩ were born since Goethe died,—if you have not read Goethe, or the Goetheans, you are an old fogy, & belong with the antediluvians.

The old Adams & Jay, ↑as Nelson & Wellington,↓ think⟨s⟩ ⟨‖ . . . ‖⟩as I think about the French, that they have no *morale*.

---

[240] Glued to the bottom right-hand side of p. [214] is a newspaper clipping, "The Passage of the Baltic.", giving the recent record-breaking ocean-crossing time of the *Baltic* (9 days, 13 hours) and a table of previous records listing the ships, captains, days, and hours, from 1848 to 1851.

A French man may possibly be clean, but an Englishman is conscientiously so.[241]

———

[217] The shape in which Providence appeared to me, was in ⟨bills⟩ tradesman's bills, & to my dame in derangements of her domestic establishment, — cook — chambermaid, & sempstress. —

———

—— *Manners.*

The ⟨Greek⟩ Athenian & Roman call all outside of the city bounds, *barbarian*; and the Londoner thinks that fine manners are not seen beyond London & Paris. But when he crosses the seas, he learns that broad lands make great interests, which are knotted up into results somewhere, &, in whatever town or place, these results educate these manners. Broad lands, great interests, dealing with results, make⟨s⟩ high manners. From New York round the world eastward to Peru, 'tis all alike.[242]

[218] E[lizabeth]. P[almer]. P[eabody]. ransacks her memory for anecdotes of Margaret's youth, her selfdevotion, her disappointment↑s↓ which she tells with fer⟨f⟩vency, but I find myself always putting the previous question. These things have no value, unless they lead somewhere. If a Burns, if a De Stael, if an artist is the result, our attention is preengaged; but ⟨no⟩ [243] quantities of rectitude, mountains of merit, ⟨or⟩ chaos of ruins, are of no account without result, — [n] ↑'tis all↓ mere nightmare; false instincts; wasted lives.

[219] Now, unhappily, Margaret's writing does not justify any ⟨b⟩ such research. All that can be said, is, that she represents an interesting hour & group in American cultivation; then, that she was herself a fine, generous, inspiring, vinous, eloquent talker, who did

[241] This sentence, struck through in pencil with a wavy diagonal use mark and in ink with a diagonal use mark, is used in "Manners," *W*, V, 107. See *JMN*, X, 514.

[242] This paragraph is struck through in pencil with a vertical use mark; "But when . . . alike." is struck through in ink with a vertical use mark which originally extended through the first sentence of the paragraph but was then finger-wiped down to "But when". For "The ⟨Greek⟩ . . . *barbarian*;", see Appendix I.

[243] Canceled in pencil as well as in ink.

not outlive her influence; and a kind of justice requires of us a monument, because crowds of vulgar people taunt her with want of position.

[220] ↑*Novels*↓

⟨I⟩The ⟨t⟩merit of Bulwer's Caxtons ↑as of Ward's novel↓ [244] is that his character has a basis of probity.[245] Thereby he is a gentleman. The vulgar novelist does not give a natural basis to a hero, but one of manners & fortune. It seems a cheap secret: yet it is the secret of the Most High.[246]

[221] Culture.

The secret is to learn that a few great points steadily reappear, alike in the poverty of Arabia, & in the immense miscellany of London life, & that these few are alone to be regarded. The escape from all false ties, courage, ⟨& love⟩ to be what we are, & love of what is simple & beautiful, independence & cheerful relation[,] these are the essentials. — [247] *See CO 36*

But we must accept our friends even in disguises of terror. The Calamities are our friends. We try hard to learn the lesson & be accomplished by learning philosophy by rote, & *playing* the hero. But the wiser God says[,] In with you, never baulk water, do the right & take the shame & the poverty & the ↑enforced↓ solitude.[248]

[222] M. Michel de Bourges who speaks for the revision of the Constitution in the French ⟨a⟩Assembly, is a good realist, & his truisms (if they be) sound well in French phrase. "Vous le savez, les partis vivent de leur principe. Si vous appliquez votre principe, vous tombez dans l'Orléanisme. (Dénégations diverses) Ces dénégations vous honorent. Je sais que vous voulez mieux que ce que vous

[244] Added in pencil.

[245] Emerson's references are to Bulwer-Lytton's *The Caxtons* (1849) and, probably, Robert P. Ward's *De Clifford; or, The Constant Man* (1841), which he referred to in 1841 (*JMN*, VIII, 92).

[246] This sentence is marked in the left margin with two vertical pencil lines.

[247] This paragraph, struck through in ink with a vertical use mark, is used in "Considerations by the Way," *W*, VI, 278.

[248] This paragraph, struck through in ink with a vertical use mark, is used in "Culture," *W*, VI, 161, 162.

avez fait: mais je sais aussi que vous seriez entrainés. Vous ne sauriez être meilleurs que votre principe."[249]

He spoke of three men there present, who had governed the kingdom during the last reign; M. Molé, M. de Broglie, & M. Thiers, [223] & whom he compares to three artists, who, playing on the same instrument, always finish, however they call it, with playing the same air. Pourquoi ces hommes d'Etat ont ils conservé et perdu tour a tour le pouvoir? Parce qu'il n'y avait entre eux que des nuances imperceptibles: ce ne sont pas eux qui ont perdu le pouvoir; c'est le pouvoir qui ↑les↓ a laissés: le pouvoir né⟨at⟩tait pas à eux; il était aux majorités.

Marchez sans le peuple, et vous marchez dans les tenebres. La Providence n'est pas avec vous.[250]

↑"The pit rose to me"↓[251]

[224] Concord, 11 August—

I remember that Bernhard, one of the redactors of the "Deutche Schnellpost," told Margaret Fuller↑;↓ ⟨that the difficultly with female writers was that in everything they wrote, said, or thought, they were thinking of a husband. Women are all alike: ⟨&⟩ he never knew one exception⟩ ↑there could be no conversation with women:↓ whatever they write, say, or think,—they are ⟨du⟩always thinking of a husband;—every one of them.

[225] A[mos] B[ronson] A[lcott] said of W[illiam].E[llery]. C[hanning]. that he had the ⟨greatest⟩ ↑keen↓ appetite for society with extreme repulsion, so that it came to a kind of commerce of cats, ⟨alternate⟩ love & hate, embrace↑s↓ & fighting.

[226] Carlyle is a better painter in the Dutch style than we have had in literature before. It is terrible—his closeness & fidelity: he

[249] " 'Vous le . . . principe.' " is struck through in ink with two discontinuous vertical use marks.

[250] This sentence is used in "Power," *W*, VI, 70. Here, as on p. [222] above, the quoted matter is both quotation and paraphrase of Michel de Bourges, *Révision de la Constitution; Discours de Michel de Bourges et de Victor Hugo* (Paris, 1851), pp. 10–11, 21, 23.

[251] Added in pencil. See Journal AZ, p. [4] above.

copies that which never was seen before. It is like seeing your figure in a glass. It is ⟨th⟩ an improvement in writing, as strange as Daguerre's in picture, and rightly fell in the same age with that; and yet, there is withal an entire reserve on his own part, & the hiding of his [227] hand. What do we know of his own life? The ⟨grand⟩ courage which is grand, the courage to feel that nature who made me may be trusted, & ⟨my⟩ ↑one's↓ self painted as also a piece of nature, he has not.[252]

[228] *Beauty.*

Once open the sense of beauty,—& vulgar manners,—tricks, bad eating, loud speaking, yelps, and all the miscreation of ugliness, become ⟨so⟩ intolerable, ⟨that⟩ ↑and↓ we are reconciled to the intense selfishness & narrowness of "good society," ⟨and⟩ think↑ing↓ that, bad as it is, the better alternative, as long as health lasts.

[229] Privilege. Beauty.

It is a privilege. The handsome youth may stoop as from the clouds, & snatch up the fairest maid. Indeed, all privilege is that of Beauty, for there are many Beauties: 1. of face; 2. of form; 3. of manner, not less prevailing. 4. of brain or method:[253] the sphere changes with the mode, and the sphere of brain or method is elemental, & lasts long: —Shakspeare's, Raphael's, Michel Angelo's is this Beauty of Brain or Method.

[230] In my memoirs, I must record that I always find myself doing something less than my best task.[254] In the spring, I was writing politics; now am I writing a biography, which not the absolute command, but facility & amiable feeling prompted.[255]

---

[252] This paragraph is struck through in pencil with single vertical use marks on pp. [226] and [227].

[253] "Indeed, all . . . method:", struck through in pencil and in ink with single vertical use marks, is used in "Beauty," *W*, VI, 287.

[254] "that I always . . . task.", marked in the left margin with two vertical pencil lines and struck through in ink with three vertical use marks, is used in "Works and Days," *W*, VII, 173.

[255] Emerson's "biography" undoubtedly refers to his collaboration on Margaret Fuller's *Memoirs*.

↑See "Works & Days"
printed↓

[231] Fate ↑printed on p 16↓[256]

Jesus said, "When he looketh on her, he hath already committed adultery"⟨;⟩.[257] ⟨b⟩But he is an adulterer already, *before yet he has looked on the woman*, by the superfluity of animal, & the weakness of thought, in his constitution. Who meets him, or who meets her, in the street, sees at once, they are ripe to be each other's victim.[258]

[232] George Minot says, that old Abel Davis went up ⟨into⟩to Temple, N.H. & was one day fishing there, & pulled out a monstrous pickerel; "Wal," said he, "who'd ever have thought of finding *you* up here in Temple? You & a slice of pork ⟨of⟩will make Viny & me a good breakfast."[259]

For George Minot again see *RS* 109

[233] ↑Symbol↓

Yes, History is a vanishing allegory, ⟨the⟩ and repeats itself to tediousness, a thousand & a million times. The *Rape of the Sabines* is perpetual, and the fairest Sabine virgins are every day pounced upon by rough ↑victorious↓ Romans, masquerading under ⟨U⟩mere New Hampshire & Vermont & Boston names, as Webster, Choate, Thayer, Bigelow or other obscurity[.]

[234] Ellery thinks these waterside cottages of Nahant & Chelsea & so on, never see the sea. There, it is all dead water, & a place for dead horses, & the smell of Mr Kips' omnibus stable. But go to Truro, & go on to the beach there, on the Atlantic side, & you will

[256] Added in pencil, probably by Edward Emerson. The passage appears in "Fate," *The Conduct of Life* (Boston, 1884), p. 16.

[257] Matt. 5:28, misquoted.

[258] This paragraph, struck through in pencil with a wavy diagonal use mark and in ink with a vertical use mark, is used in "Fate," *W*, VI, 11.

[259] Abel Davis, Concord resident and soldier at the Concord fight in 1775, was 79 years old when Emerson visited him in 1835 (*JMN*, V, 62).

have every stroke of the sea like the cannon of the "Sea-Fencibles".[260] ⟨You cannot⟩ There is a solitude, which ⟨he⟩ ↑you↓ cannot stand more than ten minutes.

[235] He thinks the fine art of Goethe & company very dubious, & 'tis doubtful whether Sam Ward is quite in his senses in his value of that book of prints of old Italian School, Giotto & the rest.[261] It may do for very idle gentlemen, ↑&c &c.↓ I reply, There are a few giants who gave the thing vogue by their realism,↑—↓Michel Angelo & Ribiera & Salvator Rosa, and the man who made the old Torso Hercules, & the Phidias,↑—↓man or men, who made the Parthenon reliefs, ↑—↓ had a drastic style which a blacksmith or a stonemason [236] would say, was starker than their own. And I adhere to Van Waagen's belief, that there is a pleasure from works of art, which nothing else can yield.[262]

[237] A woman never so trim & neat does not please by inoffensiveness, while she only complies [n] with the exactions of our established decorum, but is coarse. But, as soon as her own sense of beauty leads her to the same perfect neatness, & we ascribe to her secret neatness, then is she lovely, though sick, poor, & accidentally squalid.

[238] *Art.*
Art lies not in making your object prominent, but in choosing objects that are prominent.

To describe adequately, is the high power, & one of the highest enjoyments of man See *IT* 28

[260] The "Sea-Fencibles" may refer to the old gunhouse on Boston Common, erected in 1814, or to the soldiers organized in 1813 for coastal defence.

[261] Emerson may refer here to a portfolio of prints of Salvator, Guercino, Raphael, and Michelangelo which Ward lent him in 1839 and from which Ward gave him a copy of "Endymion" as a gift; see *Letters from Ralph Waldo Emerson to a Friend*, ed. Charles E. Norton (Boston, 1899), pp. 13, 14, 15, 17; "Ode to Beauty," ll. 52–55, *W*, IX, 89; *JMN*, VII, 314; *L*, II, 228, 230.

[262] See *JMN*, VIII, 174, where Emerson quotes this sentence more accurately from Gustav F. Waagen, *Works of Art and Artists in England*, trans. H. E. Lloyd, 3 vols. (London, 1838), II, 199–200. "Ellery thinks . . . yield." is struck through in pencil with single vertical use marks on pp. [234], [235], and [236].

↑See p 246↓ [263]

↑You can't write up gravitation↓[.] [264]

[239] ⟨A⟩When one arrives at a new place, say a watering place, it takes a long time to dissipate the superstition that hangs over it. ↑⟨T⟩New objects daunt us.↓

[240] Our culture or art of life is sadly external. It is certain that the one thing we wish to know is, where is power to be bought. I think it was Watt who told King George, that, "he dealt in an article of which kings are said to be fond,—power." But we want a finer: and 'tis plain, that I & every reasonable man would give any price of house & land, & future provision, for condensation, concentration, & the recalling at ⟨liberty⟩ will high mental energy. But we do not know where the shop is.[265]

[241] I take it to be law ⟨of the universe⟩ that every solid in the universe is ready to become volatile on the approach of the mind; and that the power to volatilize is the measure of the mind. Whilst the wall remains adamant, it accuses the want of thought. ↑To↓ a [n] subtler force, ⟨will⟩ the adamant will peel off in laminae, will exhale in gas.[266]

Our money is only a second best, or *pis aller*. We would jump to buy power with it, or first principles, or *first best*.[267]

[242] Shakspeare astonishes by his equality in every play, act, scene, & line. One would say, he must have been a thousand years old, when he wrote his first piece, so thoroughly is his ⟨every⟩ thought familiar to him, so ⟨exactly &⟩ solidly worded, as if it were

[263] Added in pencil, as is "You cant . . . gravitation" immediately below. For "To describe . . . man", see Journal AZ, p. [16] above.

[264] See p. [14] above.

[265] Except for the first sentence, this paragraph is used in "Inspiration," *W*, VIII, 269.

[266] This paragraph, struck through in ink with a vertical use mark, is used in "Fate," *W*, VI, 43.

[267] "Our money . . . *first best*." is used in "Inspiration," *W*, VIII, 269.

already a proverb, & not only hereafter to become one. Well, that millennium, in effect, is really only a little acceleration in his process of thought:[268] his mill, his loom, is better toothed & [243][269] cranked & pedalled than other people's. & he can turn off a hundred yards to their one. It is just as we see at school, now & then, a boy or girl who is a wonderful cipherer, wonderful remembering-machine of geography, ⟨& chronology⟩ Greek grammar, history, &c.

One chamber more, one cell more is opened in this brain, than is opened in all the rest, & what majestic results.[270] I admire Thoreau, too, with his powerful arithmetic, & his whole body co-working. He can ⟨walk⟩ pace sixteen rods more accurately than another man can measure it by tape.[271] ⟦How much better this than Fourier's cane meted into inches, or Hobbes's cane inkstand!⟧[272]

[244][273] The man of men, the only man you have ever seen—(if you have seen one,) is he who is immovably centred. Yet there are all degrees of aplomb, & most kinds turn out to be reliance on companies less and larger, &, what does not yet threaten the company, ⟨he⟩ does ⟨d⟩not disconcert him.

Where is the New Metaphysics? We are intent on Meteorology to find the law of the Variable Winds to the end that we may not get our hay wet. I also wish a Farmer's Almanac of the Mental Moods that I may farm my mind.[274] There are undulations of power & imbecility & I lose days sitting at my table which I should gain to my body & mind if I knew beforehand that no thought [245] would come that day. I see plainly enough that ordinarily we take counters for gold, that our eating & trading & marrying & learning are mistaken by us for ends & realities, whilst they are only symbols of

[268] "Shakspeare astonishes . . . thought:", struck through in pencil with a vertical use mark, is used in "Powers and Laws of Thought," *W*, XII, 50.

[269] "H T to find the telegraph wd follow the wires not advertisement" is written in pencil in the top margin of p. [243].

[270] With this sentence, cf. Journal BO, p. [188] above.

[271] "I admire . . . tape.", struck through in ink with two vertical use marks, is used in "Thoreau," *W*, X, 453, 461; "He can . . . tape." is used in "Works and Days," *W*, VII, 157.

[272] For "Fourier's cane", see Journal AZ, p. [197] above.

[273] This page and the first four words on p. [245] are in pencil.

[274] This sentence is used in "Powers and Laws of Thought," *W*, XII, 11.

true life; and, as soon as we have come by a divine leading into the inner firmament, we are apprised of the unreality or representative character of what we had esteemed solidest. Then we say, here & now! We then see that before this terrific beauty nature too is cheap; that geometry & astronomy also are ⟨bagatelles⟩ ↑its cheap effects↓, before this pure glory. Yet Ah! if we could once come in & plant our instruments, & take some instant measurement & inventory of this Dome, ⟨where in⟩ ↑in↓ whose light forms, & substances, & sciences [246] are dissolved. ⟨—⟩ But we never ⟨get⟩ so much as enter,[n] — 'tis a glimpse; 'tis a peep↑ing↓ ⟨as⟩ through a chink; the dream in a dream. We play at Bo-peep with Truth, and cannot write the Chapter of Metaphysics. We write books, "How to Observe," &c yet the Kant or the Plato of the Inner World, which is Heaven, has not come. To describe adequately, is the high power ⟨of man⟩ & one of the highest enjoyments of man. This is Art. ↑See p 238↓[275]

[247][276] 'Tis indifferent whether you say, all is matter, or, all is spirit; & 'tis plain there is a ⟨c⟩tendency in the times to an identity philosophy. You do not degrade man by saying, Spirit is only finer body; nor exalt him by saying, Matter is phenomenal merely; all rests on the affection of the theorist, — on the question whether his aim be noble.

Here & there were souls which saw through ⟨apples & pears⟩ ↑peaches & wine,↓ politics, money, & women, saw that these as objects of desire were all alike, & all cheats; that the finest fruit is dirty, [248][277] & must be seen by the soul as it is seen by the provision-dealer; and that all the other⟨s⟩ allurements that infatuate men, & which they play for, are the selfsame thing, with a new ⟨web⟩ ↑gauze↓ or two of ⟨finer gauze⟩ ↑illusion↓ overlaid.[278] But the soul is distinguished by its aim, — what is its end? This reacts, this far future consummation which it seeks, reacts through ages, & ⟨enno⟩enobles & beatifies every modern moment, [249] & makes the individual grand among ⟨its⟩ ↑this↓

[275] Added in pencil.

[276] "Sept 1851" is written in pencil in the top margin of p. [247], probably by Edward Emerson.

[277] "Sept 15 1851" is written in the top margin of p. [248].

[278] "infatuate men . . . overlaid.", struck through in ink with three diagonal use marks, is used in "Fate," *W*, VI, 40.

coevals, though they had every advantage of skill, force, & favor. Here & there is a soul which is a seed or principle of good, a needle pointing to the true north, thrown into the mountains of foolishness, & desarts of evil, & therefore maligned & isolated by the rest. This soul has the secret of power, this soul achieves somewhat new & beautiful which endears heaven & earth to mankind, & lends a domestic grace to the sun & the stars.[279]

[250] *Edith's opinion*

Edith, when a little girl, whimpered when her mother described the joys of Heaven. She did not want to go there, she wanted to "stay" (& she looked round the room,) "where there was a *door*, ↑& folks,↓ and *things*."

[251] E↑llery↓ thinks that he is the lucky man who can write in bulk, forty pages on a hiccough, ten pages on a man's sitting down in a chair; like Hawthorne, &c, that will go.

I have lately in E[lizabeth]. P[almer]. P[eabody].'s letter this passage. "Hawthorne always said, that Lloyd F[uller]. explained the faults of Margaret.[280] I don't know if you ever saw that creature. He seems to be the Fuller organization, Fullerism unbalanced, unmixed with the oversoul, which sweetens & balances the original demon, & yet he is unquestionably what the Scotch people call an "innocent;" for he is so self sufficient, & exacting, & insolent, unawares, unconsciously, & in the purest good faith. He acts & feels according [252] to his Constitution, & God is responsible for his ugliness. He was sent, perhaps, as a sign what original ugliness could be overcome by a glorious spirit, which had a vision of the good & true & beautiful, with a will & determination to conquer. Margaret's life was the result of this strange association[."]

[253] ↑Printed?↓ End of Culture, Self-creation.

In some sort, the end of life, is, that the man should take up the

[279] "But the soul . . . stars." is marked in the left margins with two vertical pencil lines on p. [248] and one wavy vertical pencil line on p. [249].

[280] James Lloyd Fuller (b. 1826) was Margaret Fuller's youngest brother.

universe into himself, or, out of that quarry leave nothing unrepresented, and he is to create himself. Yonder mountain must migrate into his mind. Yonder magnificent astronomy he is at last to import, fetching away ⟨star & system⟩ ↑moon & planet↓ ⟨s⟩lunation, solstice, period, ⟨galaxy⟩ comet, ↑&↓ binal star, ⟨& galaxy,⟩ by comprehending their relation & law. Instead of the timid stripling he was, he is to be the stalwart Archimedes, Pythagoras, Columbus, Jesus, of the physic, metaphysic, & ethics of the design.[281]

[254] *Skill in packing ⟨a party.⟩an evening party.*

The Editor of Korner & Schiller says, he was present at an evening party, in Germany, when a lady—a very fascinating woman, —& her three husbands,—two divorced, & one in office,—were among the guests,—how judiciously selected! [282]

Trifles. Les Mirmidons of Beranger and Goethe's remark, that a gold teaspoon constrains us, if we are used to silver.[283]

[255] The Americans accept any work that falls in their way, & will be sailors, farmers, judges, presidents, or authors, as need & opportunity command⟨s⟩, just as the farmer makes no choice of his work because he likes to husk or to ⟨winnow⟩ ↑thresh↓ or to plant, but accepts the task of the day from the state of the crop & the weather,—hays in a hay day, gathers each fruit when it is ripe, winnows in a windy day, fishes in a wet one, goes on to his meadow in ⟨a frosty day⟩ ↑December↓.[n]

[256] The housewife's proverb is "There are a thousand things to everything[.]"

Such is the mechanical perfection or result of a large city that the most

[281] "Yonder mountain . . . mind." is struck through in ink with a diagonal use mark; the paragraph is used in "Education," *W*, X, 131.

[282] Emerson's source is a footnote by the editor in *Correspondence of Schiller with Körner, Comprising Sketches and Anecdotes of Goethe, the Schlegels, Wieland, and other Contemporaries* . . . , ed. Leonard Simpson, 3 vols. (London, 1849), II, 220.

[283] Goethe's remark occurs in *Conversations with Goethe*, 1839, p. 244.

casual things, & things whose beauty lies in their casualty, are produced as punctually, & to order, as the baker's loaf and[n] coffee for breakfast. Thus Punch makes one capital joke a week, & the Journals contrive to furnish one event every day.[284]

[257] Strong thinking dissolves the material universe, and these ↑two↓ things are in perpetual balance, the power of inertia & the power of thought.[285]

↑*Experience.*↓

I know that men are meteorous, & the world is, & that the truisms of morals are the Eternal law: but ⟨I⟩ my experience gives me no ground to believe that I can rashly realize my aspirations, and with ⟨my powers⟩ these hands & feet & head obey the poetic rule.

Providence has a wild, rough, incalculable road to its end, & it is of no use to try to whitewash its huge mixed instrumentalities, or to dress up that terrific benefactor in ⟨a⟩ clean shirt & white neckloth of an Unitarian parson.[286]

[258] Once again in celebration of the Intellect, it is true, that the world is wrong, & we are right; that ⟨we have conversed⟩ our conversation once or twice with our mates has apprized us, that we belong to better circles than we have yet beheld; that there is a music somewhere awaiting us, that shall make us "forget the taste of meat;"[287] ⟨an intellectual⟩ ↑a mental↓ power whose generalizations are more worth for joy & for ⟨power⟩ ↑avail↓ than anything that is now called philosophy or literature; that the poets, that Homer & Milton & Shakspeare, do not content us; they have not dared [259] to offer us this food. No, the most they have done is to ⟨p⟩have put themselves in symmetry with this, to betray their belief that such discourse ⟨is⟩as this is possible to the like of them.

[284] "Such is . . . day.", struck through in ink with a vertical use mark, is used in "Fate," *W*, VI, 18.

[285] This sentence, struck through in ink with a vertical use mark, is used in "Fate," *W*, VI, 28.

[286] This sentence, struck through in ink with a vertical use mark, is used in "Fate," *W*, VI, 8.

[287] In *JMN*, IX, 282 and 362, Emerson associates forgetting "the taste of meat" with the "sweet drunkenness" produced by eastern storytellers.

There is something,—our brothers over the sea do not know it or own it,—Scott & Southey, Hallam & Macaulay, Carlyle & Dickens would all deny & blaspheme it,—which is setting them all ⟨e⟩aside, & the whole world also, & planting itself forever & ever.[288]

[260] All men know the truth, but what of that? it is rare to find one that knows how to speak it. A man tr⟨y⟩ies to speak it, & his voice is like the hiss of a snake; the truth is not spoken, but injured. The same thing happens in power to do the right. His rectitude is ridiculous. His organs do not play him true. By & by comes by a facility, a walking facility. He can move the mountain, & carry off yonder star, as easily as he carries the hair on his head.[289] [261] Yet who is he, & whence? God knows; his brother is an ideot, his father is a ↑pawn-↓broker, his mother is a cow.

Culture. Plainly, a man can spare nothing; he wants blackest night & whitest day, sharp eye, fleet foot, strong hand, head of Jove, health, sleep, appetite, & conscience like a clock. The finest artist, the tenderest poet, wants the ferocity of cannibals,—only transmuted into ⟨their⟩ ↑this↓ milder instruments,—as battery or magazine to furnish out ⟨their⟩ ↑this↓ long drawn sweetness.[290]

↑Mr Ro⟨w⟩land Edwin Cotton advises to engage John Harlow to visit L[idian]. E[merson].'s woodlands in Plymouth. Nov. '77—↓ [291]

[262] Michel Angelo & Raphael in the next age ↑re-↓appear↑ed↓ as Milton & Shakspeare[.]

Oct. 14. Today is holden at Worcester the "Woman's Convention." [292]

[288] "a mental power [p. [258]] . . . ever." is used in "Poetry and Imagination," *W*, VIII, 63.

[289] The paragraph to this point is used in "Powers and Laws of Thought," *W*, XII, 46–47.

[290] With "Plainly, a man . . . sweetness.", cf. "Culture," *W*, VI, 166.

[291] "Mr Ro⟨w⟩land . . . Nov. '77—", as well as the rule across the page immediately above it, is in pencil; the entry is marked in the left margin with two vertical pencil lines.

[292] In a letter to Lucy Stone, Concord, October 7, 1851, printed in the New

I think that, as long as they have not equal rights of property & right of voting, ⟨tis a sign that⟩ they are not on a right footing. But this ↑wrong↓ grew out of the savage & military period, when, ⟨it⟩ because a woman could not defend herself, it was necessary that she should be assigned to some man who was paid for guarding her. Now in more tranquil & decorous times it is plain she should [263] have her property, &, when she marries, the parties should ↑as regards property,↓ go into a partnership full or limited, but explicit & ⟨well known⟩ ↑recorded↓.

For the rest, I do not think a woman's convention, called in the spirit of this at Worcester, ⟨could⟩ can much avail. It is an attempt to manufacture public opinion, & of course repels all persons who love ↑the↓ simple & direct method. I find the Evils real & great. If I go from Hanover street to Atkinson street,—as I did yesterday,—what hundreds of extremely ordinary, paltry, hopeless women I see, whose ⟨case⟩ plight [293] [264] is piteous to think of. If it were possible to repair the rottenness of human nature, to provide a rejuvenescence, all were well, & ⟨w⟩ no specific reform, no legislation would be needed. For, as soon as you have a sound & beautiful woman, a figure in the style of the Antique Juno, Diana, Pallas, Venus, & the Graces, all falls into place, the men are magnetised, heaven opens, & no lawyer [265] need be called in to prepare a clause, for woman moulds the lawgiver.[294] I should therefore advise that the Woman's Convention should be holden in the Sculpture Gallery, that this high remedy might be suggested.

"Women," Plato says, "are the same as men in faculty, only less." [295]

York *Daily Tribune* October 17, p. 7, Emerson regretted that his work on the Margaret Fuller Memoir would keep him from attending the Woman's Rights Convention, and said that he had in the previous year signed the call for such a meeting and that he still supported the Convention's objectives (*L*, IV, 260–261).

[293] A rule is drawn across the bottom of p. [263] below which is written "inscribed on their forms, 'Leave all hope behind' ", both apparently added later than the original entry. See Journal BO, p. [164] above.

[294] "& no lawyer [p. [264]] . . . lawgiver." is used in "Woman," *W*, XI, 425.

[295] This sentence, struck through in pencil with two vertical use marks, is used in "Woman," *W*, XI, 406. Emerson may have had in mind *The Republic*, Book V, sect. 455: "All the pursuits of men can naturally be assigned to women also, but in all of them a woman is weaker than a man" (Jowett translation, Oxford, 1953, p. 310).

I find them all victims of their temperament.[n] "I never saw a woman who did not cry," said E[lizabeth Hoar?]. Nature's end of maternity, —maternity for twenty years,—was of so supreme importance, that it was to be secured at all events, even to the [266] sacrifice of the highest beauty.[296] Bernhard told Margaret that every woman ⟨was thinking o⟩ (whatever ⟨they⟩she says, reads, or writes) ⟨was⟩ ↑is↓ thinking of a husband.[297] And this excess of temperament remains not less in Marriage. Few women are sane. They emit a coloured atmosphere, one would say, floods upon floods of coloured light, in which they walk evermore, & see all objects through this warm tinted ⟨enveloping⟩ mist ↑which envelopes them.↓ Men are not, to the same degree, temperamented; [267] for ⟨they l⟩ there are multitudes of men who live to objects quite out of them, as to politics, to trade, to letters, or an art, unhindered by any ⟨reference⟩ influence of constitution[.] [298]

I remember meeting with a misogynist, who looked on every woman as an impostor.

---

[268] *Doctrine of Degrees*

A tent is good, & so is a cathedral. Know first what you want, whether a ↑make-↓shift, or whether an institution. ⟨Wheth No⟩ There is a time ⟨for⟩ ↑to get up↓ a pic-nic, and a time to found an university. A wisk or a duster is good to cleanse with, but if there is more dust, we want a broom; ⟨perhaps⟩ if more, a mop & soapsuds; & if more,—chlorine, & lime, & perhaps fire.

[269]–[270] [leaf torn out] [299]

[271] The agents in politics & colonization whose paltriness is wrenched & twisted by irresistible in⟨ward⟩ner tendencies ⟨into grand

[296] "'I never saw . . . even to the" is struck through in pencil with two vertical use marks on p. [265]; "Nature's end . . . beauty." is used in "Woman," *W*, XI, 418.

[297] See p. [224] above.

[298] "Men are not . . . constitution", struck through in pencil with a vertical use mark on p. [266] and two vertical use marks on p. [267], is used in "Woman," *W*, XI, 418.

[299] Emerson indexed p. [269] under Marriage. In Notebook S Salvage, p. [88], he records: "Life is miscellaneous, hazardous, spotty, &c. CO 269". For summations of matter on p. [270], see Notebook BO Conduct, pp. [20] and [30].

result⟩ ↑to proud↓ historical results.

The Italians complained that the King of Naples had "erected the negation of God into a system of government." [300]

---

[272] ↑Fenimore↓ Cooper said to a lady in conversation, "I can make any woman blush." The lady blushed⟨.⟩ ↑with natural resentment.↓ "I can lay it on deeper than that, madam," said the pitiless talker. Out of vexation at her own selfdistrust the lady crimsoned again to her neck & shoulders. ↑—the power of impudence.↓
Mr Mackay said to little Marny Storer, "Why, Marny! What is the matter with your eyes?" "Nothing is the matter with my eyes," said the little beauty, looking up earnestly. "Why Marny," said Mr Mackay, "they are getting to look deeper & deeper, and, by & by, I fear, [273] they will be so deep, that somebody will fall in." [301]

A man serves his work, and loves to feel his liberty. ⟨I think⟩ He [n] likes his dram & his segar for that, because they make him kick & fling, & the strait jacket is loosened a little. A man serves his work. A man is a housekeeper,—yea, verily, he builds a house, & it is his task thenceforward whilst he lives to paint, shingle, repair, enlarge, & beautify that house. The house finds him in employment as long as he lives. A man ⟨I knew⟩ buys a piece of land:—Who buys? who is bought? Is it the land? or the man? Year by year will testify[.]

[274] I knew a man who had a claim on Mexico. He was a ⟨l⟩good Quaker, &, like the liberal of his sect, a little transcendental in his notion↑s↓. But he left all, & prosecuted this claim, & it took him no whither. He learned to lie & steal, & to take the name of ↑his↓ God, ⟨& man⟩ in vain. ⟨I⟩ A man writes a lecture, & is carted round the Country at the tail of his lecture, for months, to read it.[302]

[300] This sentence, struck through in ink with a vertical use mark, is used in "Worship," *W*, VI, 209.

[301] With this sentence, cf. "Behavior," *W*, VI, 180: "There are eyes. . . . liquid and deep,—wells that a man might fall into;—". Marny Storer is possibly Elizabeth Hoar's niece, Margaret Woodbury Storer (1845–1922), daughter of Robert Boyd Storer and Sarah Sherman Hoar.

[302] With this sentence, cf. p. [28] above.

A man inherits a fortune, & leaves all his ideas & tenden⟨a⟩cies [n] [275] to husband & spend it; & it spends him. It makes him a fribble.

Roots are made by trees best, when the leaves & wood are made best. Saliency & inertia ⟨are the two principles⟩

⟨Peo⟩ I believe in the flowing power. Whigs believe only in the stagnant.

[276] 27 October

It would be hard to recall the rambles of last night's talk with H[enry]. T[horeau]. But we stated over again, to sadness, almost, the Eternal loneliness. I found, that, though the stuff of Tragedy & of Romances is in a moral Union of two superior persons, and the confid⟨a⟩ence of each in the other, for long years, out of sight & in sight, and against all appearances, is at last ⟨vic⟩justified by victorious proof ↑of probity,↓ to gods & men, causing a gush of joyful emotion, tears, glory, or whatnot,—though there be for heroes this *moral union*,—yet they too are still as far off as ever from an intellectual union, & [277] this moral union is ⟨co⟩for comparatively low & ⟨fo⟩ external purposes, like the cooperation of ↑a↓ ship's /company/ crew/,[303] or of a fir↑e↓-club. But how insular & pathetically solitary, are all the people we know! Nor ⟨could⟩ ↑dare↓ we tell what we think of each other, when we bow in the street. ⟨We⟩ ↑'Tis mighty fine for us to↓ taunt men of the world with superficial & treacherous courtesies↑.↓ [304] ⟨,but [n] are ours any better?⟩ I ⟨told my⟩saw yesterday ↑Sunday↓ whilst at dinner my neighbor H[osmer]. creeping into my barn. At once it occurred, 'Well, men are lonely, to be sure, & here is this able, social, intellectual ⟨man⟩farmer under this grim day, as grimly, sidling into my barn, in the hope of some [278] talk with me, showing me how to husband my cornstalks. Forlorn enough!' [n]
It is hard to believe that all times are alike & that the present is also rich. When this annual project of a Journal returns, & I cast about to

[303] "crew" is in pencil.

[304] "Nor ⟨could⟩ dare . . . courtesies." is struck through in ink with six vertical use marks; "I found [p. [276]] . . . courtesies." is used in "Society and Solitude," *W*, VII, 9.

think who are ⟨the⟩ ↑to be↓ contributors, I am struck with a feeling of great poverty; my bareness! my bareness! seems America to say.

There are several persons who would be inestimable to it, if you could attach to them a selfacting siphon, that would tap & draw them off, as ↑they↓ cannot do by themselves. Alcott & Channing, in chief. Lane would be valuable, year in, & year out, in spite of his bad writing; for he is real sturdy, quantitative, & his sharp speaking creates dramatic situations, & brings out good things from himself & others. ↑Unspeakable meannesses, to be sure—but he can afford them.↓ [305]

[279] Certainly concert exasperates people to a certain fury of performance, they can rarely reach alone. A Journal can behave well, when a man cannot behave well. The same sentence is more weighty from the ↑old↓ Journal, than from a new writer. And a truth-speaking institution thus seems possible, out of a society of editors who singly cannot ↑quite↓ speak the truth.

[280] Beware of Engagements. Learn to say no, & drop resolutely all false claims↑.↓ ⟨on you.⟩ [306] I suppose, I have a letter, each week, asking an autograph; one, each quarter, asking antislavery lecture; one yesterday asking particulars of the life of Mr Carlyle, &c. &c. And every day is taxed by the garden, the orchard, the barn,

[281] Faith shall be justified. Live for the year, not for the day. Let logic, let character rule the hour. That is never vulgar.

But can really every man afford to procure his proper tools?

[282] ⟨September⟩October

In reading Carlyle's "Life of Sterling," I still feel, as of old, that the best service C. has rendered is to Rhetoric, or the Art of Writing. Now here is a book in which the vicious conventions of

[305] This sentence is written on the bottom of p. [279], opposite the sentence "Lane would . . . & others.", which is crowded into the bottom of p. [278]. The editors have interpreted it as the concluding sentence to the paragraph on p. [278] beginning "There are several . . .".

[306] Canceled in pencil.

writing are all dropped; you have no board ⟨or screen⟩ interposed between you & the writer's mind, but he talks flexibly, now high, now low, in loud hard emphasis, then in undertones, then laughs ⟨aloud⟩ outright, then calmly narrates, then hints or ⟨winks⟩ raises an eyebrow, & all this living [283] narration is daguerr↑e↓otyped for you in his page. He has gone nigher to the wind than any other craft. No book can any longer be tolerable in the old husky Neal-on-the-Puritans model. But he does not, for all that, very much uncover his secret mind.[307]

[284] A personal influence ⟨is⟩ ↑towers up in memory↓ the only ⟨memorable⟩ ↑worthy↓ force [n] ⟨not a disguise for⟩ ↑when we would gladly forget↓ numbers or money or climate, gravitation, & the rest of Fate. Margaret, wherever she came, fused people into society, & a glowing ⟨c meeting⟩ company was the result. When I think how few persons can do that ⟨thing⟩ ↑feat↓ for ↑the↓ intellectual class, I feel our squalid poverty.

[285] Massive figures, sitting never so poorly clothed or sheltered, not ashamed of themselves, or of their hands, or feet, or faces.

Undoubtedly if a Concord man of 1750 could come back, ⟨into⟩ & walk ↑in our street, today,↓ from the meetinghouse to the Depot, he would recognize all the people as if they were his own Contemporaries. Yes, that is a Buttrick; and that a Flint; & that Barrett or Minot: Here an Erskine, there a Rowe, for no doubt a regent atom or monad [n] constrains all the other particles to take its feature & temperament[.]

[286] But ⟨is⟩no [n] man outsees another. No man's verdict is final on another; the reserves, the remains, are immense. ⟨He,⟩ ↑The observer↓ has really, though he were Socrates, no sense to apprehend the other's peculiarity. Every gas is a vacuum to every other gas.[308]

[307] This paragraph, struck through in pencil with single vertical use marks on pp. [282] and [283], is used, except for the last sentence, in "Art and Criticism," *W*, XII, 297, 298. Daniel Neal (1678–1743) wrote *The History of the Puritans*, which appears in an Emerson booklist in *JMN*, II, 213.

[308] This sentence is used in "Resources," *W*, VIII, 149; see Journal TU, p. [279] above.

[287] November 1.—

I suppose, at last, Culture will absorb the hells also. There is nothing that is not wanted for bone or for fibre, for shade or for color.[309]

⟨Exercise⟩ ↑Practice↓ is as much wanted for metaphysical, as for weaving or ploughing skill. It is not until ↑after↓ a long time exploring this dim field in Conversation that we begin to see well what is there.

We believe that men will not all or always be local, spotty, trifling, but that men will come native to all districts of nature, all related,— who will suck the [288] earth, the air, the sea;—be solidly related to the forest & the mineral; amphibious, with one door ↑down↓ into Tartarus, & one door upward into light, belonging to both; & when such men are possible some of the meaner kinds will become impossible, & pass into the fossil remains.

———

"You may be sure Kossuth is an old woman, he speaks so well." Said H[enry].D[avid].T[horeau].

[289] Two boys pushing each other on the curb stone, two races contending like Celt & Saxon, two ideas like Feudalism & Democracy, Everything is mover or moved, and each in turn is moved, (see p 241) and the growth of man is measured by the appropriation of new weapons.[310] There is no thing that is not for him. The victorious Soul, the victorious intellect, can touch all with power. The more formidable mischief ⟨the⟩ will only make the more useful servant,— ↑he↓ will convert the Furies into Muses, & the hells into benefit.[311] War, party, luxury, avarice, Whiggery, ↑Radical↓ are ⟨all⟩ ↑so many↓ asses with loaded panniers, to serve ↑the kitchen of↓ the King, who is

[309] "I suppose . . . color." is struck through in ink with a vertical use mark; "I suppose . . . also." is used in "Culture," *W*, VI, 166.

[310] "Two boys . . . Saxon," is struck through in ink with a curved vertical use mark; the sentence is used in "Fate," *W*, VI, 43. See p. [123] above.

[311] "There is no thing . . . benefit.", struck through in ink with discontinuous curved vertical use marks, is used in "Culture," *W*, VI, 166. For "convert . . . Muses," see *JMN*, IX, 361.

Intellect.[312] There is nothing that does not pass into lever or weapon, masses of men, Christianity,[313]

[290] Omnipresence. Omnipotence.

With Culture, too, the self direction develops. In the fables, the disk Chakra(?), the weapon of Hari, is self directing, & leaps upon his enemies. In the /Voluspa/Edda,/ ? the ship of the gods is self steered.[314] In the ⟨(Shah Nameh)⟩ Persian fables, the Divine horses refuse any rider but their own hero. A man might as ⟨well⟩ ↑easily↓ mount a lion, as Kyrat, if Kyrat's master have not laid the bridle on his hands; and the ⟨g⟩God Freye has a sword so good that it will itself strew a field with carnage, when the owner ↑so↓ ordered it.[315]

---

[291] ——————

When a man frequents an opiumshop, the whole world becomes an opiumshop[.]
↑tobacconist pouring out smoke ⟨st⟩ ↑as↓ from a chimney —↓

The malignity of parties betrays the want of great men. If there were a powerful person to be the Belisarius of Free Soil, ⟨it⟩ ↑he↓ would strike terror into these rich Whigs, & these organized vulgarities called the Democracy.

The puzzle of currency remains for rich & poor. I never saw a rich man who thought he knew wh⟨y⟩ence the hard times came.[316]

[312] In this sentence, "Radical" and "so many" are added and "all" is canceled in pencil.

[313] "War, party . . . Christianity," is marked in the right margin with two vertical pencil lines.

[314] Emerson's source of information about Vishnu's discus, or chakra, is probably *The Vishńu Puráńa* . . . , trans. H. H. Wilson (London, 1840), in his library. The "Vǫluspá" is a poem in *The Prose or Younger Edda* . . . , 1842.

[315] Emerson borrowed *The Sháh Námeh of the Persian Poet Firdausi*, trans. and abridged . . . by James Atkinson (London, 1832) from the Harvard College Library in 1846 and 1847. Kyrat was the horse of Kurroglou; see *JMN*, X, 86, 92, 93, 117. For "the ⟨g⟩God Freye . . . it.", see *JMN*, X, 55.

[316] This paragraph is struck through in ink with a vertical use mark; cf. "Wealth," *W*, V, 168–169.

[292] But Free Trade must be right, & the annexation of England to America, and, as for the tariff, that interests only a few ↑rich↓ gentlemen in Boston ↑& Philadelphia↓. The railroad Capital vastly exceeds the manufacturing Capital in Boston, too. But I think we shall never understand Political Economy, until we get Beranger, or Burns, or some poet, to teach it in songs.[317]
Hooke's discovery, "Ut pendet continuum flexile, sic stabit contiguum rigidum inversum."[318]

[293] I think that a man should compare advantageously with a river, with an oak, with a mountain, ⟨the⟩ ↑endless↓ flow, ⟨of the one⟩ expansion, & grit.

[294] [Index material omitted]
[inside back cover] [Index material omitted]

[317] This sentence is used in "Poetry and Imagination," *W*, VIII, 37.

[318] Loosely, "as it hangs continuously pliant, so inverted it will stand nearly rigid" (Ed.). This was Hooke's solution to the problem of building any kind of arch. He meant that "an inverted catenary — a catenary being the curve of a flexible chain hanging freely from two points of suspension — would provide a stable arch" (Margaret 'Espinasse, *Robert Hooke* [Berkeley, 1956], p. 71). Emerson drew two vertical lines at the left of the quotation; at the right he apparently tried to draw a catenary, though he has lines instead of a chain, and a pendant at the base of the curve.

PART TWO

Miscellaneous Notebooks

Margaret Fuller Ossoli

1851

Margaret Fuller Ossoli and her husband and child died in a shipwreck July 19, 1850. In this notebook Emerson wrote original biography and collected quotations from Margaret's diary, letters from her and letters of her friends as the basis for his contribution to a memoir. The writing and editing were to be shared by William Henry Channing and James Freeman Clarke. Most of Emerson's materials went into those chapters for which he is given credit in the Table of Contents in volume I, but some 2000 words, none of them original with Emerson, went into volume II, mostly in the section on Europe. *Memoirs of Margaret Fuller Ossoli* was published in Boston in February, 1852.

Notebook Margaret Fuller Ossoli is written in a hard-cover copybook, virtually identical to those journals designated TU, AZ, BO, and CO. The cover, 17.8 x 21.1 cm, is of predominantly brown paper marbled with blue, black, and yellow over boards, with a tan leather margin at the binding and forming two triangles at top and bottom outer edges. The spine, of brown leather, now cracked and peeling, has "OSSOLI" written horizontally and centered. The front cover is inscribed "OSSOLI" centered in ink in the upper portion of the marbled paper and "M.F." in ink in the upper triangular corner. The back cover is inscribed in ink "OSSOLI" in top and bottom triangular corners. The unruled pages measure 17.2 x 20.3 cm. The pages are numbered in ink except for the following in pencil: 48–50, 60, 70, 74, 76, 78, 80, 81, 90, 91, 100, 101, 105, 108–110, 120, 130, 140, 150, 160, 165, 170, 180, 190, 200, 210, 220, 230, 250, 260, 261, 266, 268–271, 280, 290. Ninety-five pages are unnumbered: 40, 52, 53, 55, 61, 66–69, 71, 77, 84, 85, 87, 92, 93, 103, 106, 107, 111–115, 121–123, 126, 127, 138, 142–145, 151–153, 162, 163, 168, 169, 171, 174, 175, 178, 179, 186–189, 193–199, 202, 203, 206–208, 215–219, 221, 229, 233, 237, 239, 241–247, 249, 257, 275, 281–283, 288, 289, 291–298 (verso of flyleaf). One hundred are blank: 17, 18, 31, 32, 52, 53, 55, 56, 61, 62, 68, 69, 71, 79, 84, 85, 89, 93, 94, 96, 99, 110–115, 119, 121–123, 125–127, 142–145, 151–153, 157, 162, 163, 167–169, 171, 172, 174, 175, 178, 179, 185–189, 194–199, 202, 203, 205–208, 215–219, 221, 224, 239–247, 255, 257, 263, 264, 269, 275, 276, 279, 281–283, 287–289. Three leaves have been cut out, those bearing pages 35–36, 63–64, and 97–98. The bottom third of the leaf bearing pages 23–24 has been cut out, and the leaf bearing pages 61–62 is partially cut out, undoubtedly by the instrument used to cut the leaf bearing pages 63–64. Three pages have been misnumbered in ink and corrected in pencil: ⟨143⟩43, ⟨144⟩44, ⟨145⟩45. 28⟨5⟩6 was misnumbered and corrected in ink. Page 72 is numbered both in ink and pencil. The folded sheet forming two leaves bearing pages 233–236 is loose from the binding; although it matches the pages in this book, there is no evidence of stitch holes and it was probably never sewn in. Laid in between pages 96 and 99 (pages 97–98 have been cut out) is a blue sheet titled "*Table of Contents*" for the *Memoirs,* in Emerson's hand. Laid in between pages 130 and 131 is a white sheet with ink inscription titled "Gerus. Lib. / XII 17 or 37/ 16 or 36" probably in Emerson's hand, and pencil writing, not in Emerson's hand. Laid in between pages 148 and 149 is a folded sheet, a letter, apparently in Margaret Fuller's hand. Laid in between pages 176 and 177 are two folded white sheets and one folded blue sheet — letters, in Margaret Fuller's hand.

[front cover] OSSOLI M.F.

[front cover verso] Life & death of
1851? [1] *Margaret Fuller Ossoli.*

Et quae tanta fuit Romam tibi causa videndi?
Libertas.[2]

Virgil.
Ecl[ogues]. 1, l[1]. [26–]27

[1] Margaret Fuller Ossoli.

"Do not scold me, — they are guests of my eyes. Do not frown; — they want no bread; they are guests of my words." [3]

"A flame tormented by the wind." [4]

---

[2] Madame Arconati writes from Bellagio 2 September ↑1850↓[:] [5]

Que je serais contente de passer l'hiver avec vous! je vous aime, et

[1] By Emerson?

[2] "And what was the great occasion of your seeing Rome? Freedom."

[3] " 'Do not . . . words.' " is used in *Memoirs*, I, 317. See "Turkman Songs," *Specimens of the Popular Poetry of Persia* . . . , 1842, p. 391.

[4] Beginning below the first entry on p. [1], and underlying " 'A flame . . . wind.' ", is, in erased pencil writing, " 'Do not scold . . . words.' ", the same as the entry above.

[5] Added in pencil. The Marchesa Costanza Arconati Visconti (d. 1870), was Margaret Fuller's mentor and close friend in Florence.

j'ai la plus grande admiration pour vous. La présence du vrai mérite et de la grandeur véritable a fait peu a peu impression sur mon ame. J'ai [n] ouvert les yeux par degrés. Ce n'est pas seulement une jouissance que je vous dois, c'est un bienfait. Le spectacle de la beauté morale élève l'âme.[n] Je vous embrasse avec reconnaissance, ma chere amie.

[3] "Je n'ai point rencontré dans ma vie de femme plus noble, ayant autant de sympathie pour ses semblables, et dont l'esprit fut plus vivifiant. Je me suis tout de suite sentie attirée par elle. Quand je fis sa connoisance, j'ignorais que ce fut une femme remarquable." [6]
Constance Arconati de Visconti.

[4] taste for gems, ciphers, talismans, omens, coincidences↑, birthdays↓. Her name, Margarita, a pearl. She never forgot. Leila she thought her own name from the first sight of it. Sortilege she valued. *Sortes biblicae* she tried, & her hits were memorable. As happens to such persons, these guesses are justified by the event.[7] Her forebodings at embarcation in the "Elizabeth" to Mme Arconati.
This catching at straws of coincidence where all is geometrical, where man rhymes with maid, sea with sky, action with reaction, man with event, & heaven with earth, seems the luxury of nearsightedness.[8]

↑"When I first read the name of Leila, I thought from its very look & sound it was mine. My heart knew that it meant *Night*"↓ [9]

[5] ↑"night brings out stars as sorrow brings out truths."↓ [10]

To C[aroline] S[turgis]

Slow wandering on a tangled way
To their lost child pure spirits say,
The diamond marshal thee by day,
By night the carbuncle defend,
Heart's blood of a bosom friend;

[6] This entry is used in *Memoirs*, I, 200.

[7] P. [4] is in pencil. "taste for . . . event.", struck through in pencil with two vertical use marks, is used in *Memoirs*, I, 219.

[8] This sentence is used in *Memoirs*, I, 221. With "taste for . . . nearsightedness.", cf. Journal CO, pp. [171]–[172] above and "Poetry and Imagination," *W*, VIII, 48–49.

[9] " 'When I first . . . *Night*' ", struck through in pencil with a vertical use mark, is used in *Memoirs*, I, 219.

[10] Philip James Bailey, *Festus, A Poem* (London, 1848), p. 7. This sentence, in pencil, is used in *Memoirs*, I, 219.

On thy brow the amethyst
    Violet of secret earth
When by fullest sunlight kissed,
    Best reveals its ⟨sec⟩regal [n] worth;
And when that haloed moment flies
Shall keep thee steadfast, chaste, & wise.

"Cary says the amethyst is her stone." The ancients considered this gem a talisman to dispel intoxication, give good thoughts & understanding; the Greek meaning is *antidote against drunkenness.*[11]

[6] ↑To Marchesa Arconati Visconti.↓

Florence, Evg. of 25 Apr. 1850.

I have written to introduce my friends, the ⟨|| . . . ||⟩ Storys, to Madame Mohl.[12] I hope she will like them. ⟨i⟩It was an odd combination. I had intended, if I went by France, to take the packet ship "Argo," from Havre. I had just written to Mrs Story that I should *not* [n] do so, &, at the same time, requested her to find from Madame M: (Miss Clark) the address of Miss Fitton, in order to getting my muff, &c. Having closed the letter, I took up Galignani, & my eye fell on these words, [7] "Died, 4 April, at her house, no. 10, Rue Ville l'Evéque, Miss E. Fitton." This was the elder of the two sisters. Turning the leaf, I read of the wreck of the "Argo," returning from America to France. There were also notices of the wreck of the "Royal Adelaide" a fine Eng. steamer; & of the John ⟨Nu⟩Skiddy; —one of the fine American packets. I shall embark more composedly in my merchant ship, praying indeed fervently that it may not be my lot to lose my babe at sea, either by unsolaced sickness, or amid the howling waves; or, that if I should, it may be [8] brief anguish, & Ossoli, he, & I, go together.[n 13]

To Marchesa Arconati Visconti
Palazzo Prini.
Lung Arno. Pisa.

Florence, 6 April, 1850.

I would not for the world have your last thoughts of me mingled with the least unpleasantness, when mine of you must always be all sweet. I say,

[11] The entries on p. [5], struck through in pencil with a vertical use mark, are used in *Memoirs*, I, 220, 219–220.

[12] William Wetmore Story (1819–1895), Boston lawyer turned poet, sculptor, and essayist, went to Italy in 1847 with his wife, Emelyn Eldredge of Boston; they became close friends of Margaret Fuller. The home of Mary Clarke (1793–1883), wife of the German orientalist, Julius von Mohl, became a popular intellectual center in Paris for English men and women after her marriage in 1847.

[13] This paragraph is used in *Memoirs*, II, 336.

LAST *thoughts*. I am absurdly fearful about this voyage. Various [9] little omens have combined to give me a dark feeling. Among others just now, we hear of the wreck of the ship Westmoreland, bearing Powers's Eve.[14] Perhaps we shall live to laugh at these; but in case of mishap, I should perish with my husband & child perhaps to be transferred to some happier state; [15] and my dear Mother, whom I so long to see, would soon follow, & embrace me more peaceably elsewhere. You, loved friend, God keep & cherish here & hereafter! is the prayer of your loving & grateful

Margaret

[10] *R.W.E. to M.F.*

And here I may quote a letter of my own addressed to Margaret, 6 January, 1844, after reading a piece of hers on the Drama.[16] "It is the least like writing & the most like vital affluent Communication that can be. It is an infinite refreshment to me to see it in the dry stone ↑'↓Dial.↑'↓ [n] The hardened sinners will be saved for your sake, o living friend! I think, that, when, (if you should ever do such a thing, & many many years hence may it be!) you shall lay your body in the ground, the dust will beat & palpitate above, & the flowers that grow there thrill & tremble to the eye."

[11] From separate torches flames arise
Whose half-seen summits mingle in the air; —
Before each one a summoning spirit flies;
And thus we part — to meet — we know not where.

S.M.F. from C.S.

She writes in her Journal, July, 1844, to the planet Jupiter, ⟨th⟩ "I have ever loved thee better than any created thing." [17]

Certain dreams she has periodically, — as one of her mother's death & burial.[18] See *Journal* July, 1844. p. 130.

[14] Hiram Powers, American sculptor (1805–1873), did two versions of "Eve Before the Fall," or "Eve Disconsolate," as it is sometimes called, one in 1843, one in 1850. Since the second is in the Cincinnati Art Museum, Margaret must be referring to the first.

[15] "I am . . . dark feeling." and "but in case . . . state;" are used in *Memoirs*, II, 337.

[16] "The Modern Drama," *The Dial*, IV (Jan. 1844), 307–349.

[17] This sentence, struck through in pencil with a vertical use mark, is used in *Memoirs*, I, 219.

[18] This sentence, struck through in pencil with a vertical use mark, is used in *Memoirs*, I, 221.

[12] Anniversaries

May /22/23/ M's birthday & that of M[argaret] F[uller] Channing[.] [19]
1844, 3 Oct. anniversary of the most moving event in my life, when the Ideal seemed nearest an earthly realization⟨. alas!⟩↑.↓[20]

1844, July 4. It is the anniversary of that Ganymed day last year[.] [21]

1841, Oct. 3. Only a year today since the event that I felt so sure was an era on the earth of the same kind as the union of the Red Cross Knight & his spotless maid. All has vanished.[22]
3d. Oct. is S[amuel]. G[ray]. W[ard].'s birth & marriage day.

⟨29⟩30 August. {C.S. birthday she remembers at Rieti
and ( ) wedding. day 1849

Oct. 1. Nov., 1849, she writes to her mother she had thought all that day of her father & mother[.] [23]

1843, Jan. 28.

[13] To Marchesa Arconati Visconti at Milan
Rome 22 June.

"There is something fatal in my destiny about correspondence.[24] The loss of two successive letters from the man on earth I have most loved, broke our relation at the time it might have become permanent."

Writing so much is why I write so ill. I have a hundred correspondents[.] [25]

[19] Margaret Fuller's niece, daughter of Ellery Channing and her sister, Ellen Fuller Channing.

[20] Undoubtedly a reference to the marriage of Anna Hazard Barker and Samuel Gray Ward, one of Margaret Fuller's self-acclaimed protegés, on October 3, 1840.

[21] Margaret Fuller composed "Ganymede to his Eagle" on a cliff, the "Eagle's Nest," in Oregon, Rock River, Illinois, July 4, 1843; see *Summer on the Lakes, in 1843* (Boston, 1844), pp. 54–57.

[22] The allusion is to the betrothal of the Red Cross Knight and Una in Spenser's *The Faerie Queene*, Book I, Cantos XXXVI–XXXVII.

[23] "Oct. 1 . . . mother" is in pencil.

[24] This sentence is used in *Memoirs*, II, 242.

[25] "Writing so . . . correspondents", struck through in pencil with a vertical and two diagonal use marks, is used in *Memoirs*, I, 231.

"I write such a great number of letters, having not less than a hundred correspondents." [26]

Letter from *Casa Libri,* 3° piano
piazza San Maria Novella Florence
1 Oct. 1849.

[14] May, 1844, Heartsease to Carrie, with verses.

Content in purple lustre clad,
Kingly serene & golden glad,
No demi-hues of sad contrition,
No pallors of enforced submission,
Give me such content as this,
And keep awhile the rosy bliss.[27]
↑M F↓

[15] Friends.

She told William Story in Italy, that she spent one day in every week in looking after her friends. If she had not less than a hundred correspondents, it needed no less time.

Too many friends./Journal July, 1844. "After dinner, read the Western letters. Yes, they are beautiful, & moved me deeply. The birth of a soul, it looks like. But I loved *thee, fair rich* EARTH, and all *that* is gone forever. This that comes, we know in much ↑(farther)↓ [28] stages. But there is silver sweet in the tone, generous nobility in the impulses." [29]

↑To C.S., Apr., 1842.↓ "It is somewhat sad that two friends must become ⟨somewha⟩uninteresting to one another, because they have arrived at [16] a mutual good understanding, yet this very thing makes the beauty as well as the sadness of music."

To C.S. Oct., 1838, "My museum is so well⟨f⟩-furnished that I grow lazy about collecting new specimens of human nature." [30]

---

[26] " 'I write . . . correspondents.' ", struck through in pencil with a vertical use mark, is used in *Memoirs*, II, 242.

[27] The entry on p. [14] is struck through in pencil with a vertical use mark; the poetry is used in *Memoirs*, I, 221.

[28] Added in pencil.

[29] P. [15] to this point is struck through in pencil with a vertical use mark. "She told . . . time." is used in *Memoirs*, I, 231; " 'Yes, they are . . . impulses.' " is used in *Memoirs*, I, 286–287.

[30] This sentence, struck through in pencil with a vertical use mark, is used in *Memoirs*, I, 286.

[17]–[18] [blank]

[19] ↑To Marchesa Arconati. Apr. 6. 1850.↓

"When you write by post, please direct *Marchesa Ossoli*, as all the letters come to that address. I might lose yours without it. I did not ex⟨press⟩plain myself on that point. The fact is, it seems to me silly for a radical like me, to be carrying a title; and yet, while Ossoli is in his native land, it seems disjoining myself from him not to bear it. You spoke of my always addressing you in form: now for you, it seems appropriate, &, though the least of your honors, it would [20] pain me to have it omitted. You were born so. You are really the lady of large lands: you & your husband both feel the duties that come with position of command, &, I am sure, if you look back with pride to ancestors, it is not, as many do, to lean upon their merits, but to emulate them. For me, it is a sort of thing that does not naturally belong [21] to me, &, unsustained by fortune, is but a souvenir even for Ossoli. Yet it has seemed to me for him to drop it, — an inherited title, — would be in some sort to acquiesce in his brothers' disclaiming him, & dropping a right he may possibly wish to ⟨|| . . . ||⟩maintain for his child. How does it seem to you? I am not very clear about it. If O. dropt the title, it would be a suitable moment in becoming an inhabitant of republican America." [31]

[22]	I	Youth autob.		80	440
	II	Cambridge J[ames]. F[reeman]. Clarke.		70	
	III	Groton Prov[idence]		50	
	IV	Concord	R.W.E.	180	
	V	Boston		60	
	VI	Jamaica Plains	W[illiam] ⟨h⟩H[enry] C[hanning]	180	
	VII	Highlands		50	
	VIII	New York	H[orace] Greeley	100	
	IX	Europe	Letters	100	
	X	Wreck		20	[32]

[31] Except for " 'You spoke . . . emulate them.' ", " 'When you [p. [19]] . . . America.' " is used in *Memoirs*, II, 317.

[32] The "Table of Contents" for both volumes of *Memoirs* follows this draft closely in terms of the chapter numbers and titles, though the final pagination varies considerably, both higher and lower, than estimated here. The chapter numbers and titles for volume I, chapters I–V, follow exactly the list here; volume II has only four chapters: "VI. Jamaica Plain", "VII. New York", "VIII. Europe", and "IX. Homeward".

[23] *From Journal May, 1844.*

"I remembered our walking in the garden avenue between the tall white lilies, & Ellen's appletree. She was a lovely child then, & happy; but my heart ached, & I lived in just the way I do now. Father said seeing me at a distance, 'Inced⟨o⟩it Regina' " &c [33]

[24] *Marriage*

W.H.C. fancied that M had not married: that a legal tie was contrary to her view of a noble life. I, on the contrary, ⟨think⟩ believed that she would speculate on this subject as all reformers do; but when it came to ⟨the⟩ ↑be a↓ practical question to herself, she would feel that this was a tie which ought to have every solemnest sanction; that against the theorist was a vast public opinion, too vast to brave; an opinion of all nations & of all ages.
See what she says in *Aglauron & Laurie*; which is as follows. "||msm|| [34]

[25] ↑Journal. *Concord July, 1844.*↓

⟨I walked here with Hawthorne⟩At present, it skills not. I am able to take the superior view of life, & my place in it: but, I know, the deep yearnings of the heart & the bafflings of time will be felt again, & then I shall long for some dear hand to hold. But I shall never forget that my curse is nothing compared with that of those who have entered into those relations, but not made them real; who only *seem* husbands, wives, & friends. W. was saying as much the other evening.[35]

[26] To Mary Rotch. Canton 1842.[36]

I have enjoyed the solitude & silence. It has been a thoughtful, tho' not a thinking time. I incline thus to characterize the two phases of life. At such

[33] Virgil, *Aeneid*, I, 46: "Ast ego, quae divum incedo regina": "Yet, I, who move as queen of gods". " 'I do now . . . Regina' &c" is struck through in pencil with a vertical use mark; with the paragraph, cf. *Memoirs*, I, 235.

[34] The bottom third of the leaf bearing pp. [23]–[24] has been cut out. Margaret Fuller's "Dialogue," *The Dial*, IV, (April 1844) concerns the characters Aglauron and Laurie.

[35] This paragraph, struck through in pencil with a diagonal use mark, is used in *Memoirs*, I, 292.

[36] Mary Rotch, an esteemed friend of Emerson, was a liberal Quaker of New Bedford.

times, however, with the great subjects lying mountainous & distant as ever in the horizon, it seems a farce to pretend one has ever been thinking or living at all, or, far more, that one has ever been fatigued with such child's play as that of last year. The growths of the past year which seemed at [27] the time a rich & various mantle, have recurred to mother ⟨e⟩Earth, &, all that remains is some pictures, seeds, & a few more hieroglyphics indicating the way to truths that promise a perennial spring.[37]

Journal, May, 1844. at Frank Shaw's.[38]

Looking out on the wide view, I felt the blessings of my comparative freedom:[n] I stand in no false relations: who else is so happy? Here are these fair unknowing children⟨,⟩ envying the depth of my mental life. They feel withdrawn by sweet duties from Reality. Spirit, I accept, teach me to prize & use whatsoever is given me.[39]

[28] 3 May 1844.

"⟨Why⟩ ↑Ah!↓ you can sleep now, C., why, you are still. It is because you are loved; the stream of love flows full & free enough to upbear your life, for the present. The keel does not grate against the rocky bottom. x x x

Love is a nursing mother to cradle the child on her breast: it can sleep, & sleeping grow. I am glad ⟨you are⟩ ↑she is↓ largely loved; it brings a few days' sweet repose. I know [29] not the full price demanded for this night's lodging ↑in our journey↓:[n] no doubt, heavy. We are not housed in that way for nothing: but in what coin must it be rendered? I know not, but I think she will be willing to pay; she needed repose so much."

[30] Travelling. MS.

I doubt there is no pleasant or natural mode of life except travelling.
Reasons why.

Wordsworth says, "Books were Southey's passion, Wandering was mine." [40]

[37] This entry is struck through in pencil with single vertical use marks on pp. [26] and [27].

[38] Francis George Shaw (1809–1882), philanthropist and translator of George Sand, Fourier, and Zschokke, moved in 1841 to West Roxbury near Brook Farm, in which he was interested.

[39] This entry, struck through in pencil with a vertical use mark, is used in *Memoirs*, I, 292.

[40] See "On the Leading Characters and Scenes of the Poem [*The Excursion*]," *The Prose Works of William Wordsworth*, ed. A. B. Grosart, 3 vols. (London, 1876), III, 195–196.

[31]–[32] [blank]

[33] "Italy is one of the fairest thoughts of the mind which made heaven & earth."

"Ital. autumn not so beautiful as expected neither in the vintage of Tuscany, (the best of the vintage was really to eat the grapes,) nor here."[41]
Rome

Florence was all flowers. I had many magnolias & jasmines,——garden full of immense oleanders in full bloom.[42]

———

To C[harles].K[ing].N[ewcomb]. Rome, 25 Nov. 1848.

I lived, ↑in autumn,↓ on the bank of a river which becomes, in the storms, a wild torrent, & lit up almost constantly by flashes of lightning. Opposite my window was a vineyard, whose white & purple clusters [34] were my food near three months. It is pretty to see the vintage: The asses & wagons loaded with this wealth of amber & rubies, the nutbrown maids & naked boys singing in the trees in which the vines are trained, as they cut the grapes; the women in their red corsets, & white head-cloths, receiving them below, while their babies crow amid the grass, where they have laid them.

[35]–[36] [leaf cut out]
[37] To RWE Rieti, July 11, 1848.

I hear at this moment, the clock of the church del Purgatorio telling noon in this mountain solitude. Snow yet lingers on these mountain tops, after 40 days of hottest sunshine last night broken by a few clouds prefatory to a thunderstorm this morning. It has been so hot ↑that↓ even the peasant in the field, says *non porro piu resistere*, & slumbers in the shade rather than the sun.[n] I love to see their patriarchal ways of guarding the sheep, & tilling the fields. They are a simple race, remote from the corruptions of foreign travel, they do not ask for money, but smile [38] upon & bless me as I pass; for the Italians love me: they say, I am so "*simpatica*". I never see any English or Americans, & now think wholly in Italian, only the surgeon who bled me the other day was proud to speak a little French, which he had learnt at Tunis! The ignorance of this people is amazing. I am to them a divine visitant, an instructive Ceres, telling them wonderful tales of foreign customs & even legends of their own saints. They are people

[41] This sentence is used in *Memoirs*, II, 222.

[42] Underlying "Florence . . . had" are the same words in pencil. "Florence . . . bloom." is used in *Memoirs*, II, 212.

whom I could love & live with⟨,⟩. Bread & grapes among them would [39] suffice me, but I have no way of earning these from their rich soil.[43]

[40] She gave Harro $500, I believe.[44]

"I see ⟨why⟩ ↑how↓ family men come to be so mean"

[41] *To Marcus Spring*. Florence 12 Dec. 1849.
x x x"In answer to what you say of Harro I wish indeed the little effort I made for him had been wiselier applied. Yet these are not the things one regrets. It does not do to calculate too closely with the affectionate human impulse⟨s⟩. We must consent to make many mistakes or we should move too slow to help our brothers much. I am sure you dont regret what you spent on Miàni & other worthless people. As things looked then, it would have been wrong not to risk the loss."[45]

[42] Mrs Story relates that at in [46] she loaned to an artist in distress unsolicited her last fifty dollars, which sum was afterwards happily re⟨t⟩-paid[.]

[⟨143⟩43] Italy To E[lizabeth] H[oar]

I cannot begin to speak of the magnificent scenes of nature, nor the works of art that have raised & filled my mind, since I wrote from Naples. Now I begin to be in Italy. But I wish to drink deep of this cup, before I speak my enamoured words. Enough to say, Italy receives me as a long lost child, & I feel myself at home here; & if I ever tell any thing about it, you will have something real & domestic.[47] [⟨144⟩44] [48] Among strangers I

[43] This paragraph is used in *Memoirs*, II, 244. The semicolon after "pass", the quotation marks around *simpatica*, and the comma after "Ceres" are in pencil.

[44] P. [40] is in pencil. Harro Paul Harring (1798–1870), Danish exile, came to America bearing a letter of introduction from Margaret Fuller to Emerson. For Emerson's accounts of Harring's difficulties in publishing his South American novel *Dolores* (New York, 1846–1847) and his attempts to help him, see *L*, III, 381–383, 385–386.

[45] "Miani" is possibly an error for (Count) Mamiani (1799–1885), head of the provisional government in Rome in 1848. This paragraph, struck through in pencil with a vertical use mark, is used in *Memoirs*, I, 302–303.

[46] Emerson has left approximately an inch of space after "at" and after "in", undoubtedly for adding place and time. The incident is expanded in *Memoirs*, II, 228; the artist is not named.

[47] "I cannot . . . domestic." is used in *Memoirs*, II, 219–220.

[48] "Madame Arconati", enclosed by an oval line open at the top, is written in the top margin of p. [44].

want most to speak to you of ⟨Mar⟩a friend I have made in Italy, the Marchioness Arconati Visconti. She is a Milanese, but I knew her first at Rome. She is now here. She is a specimen of the really high-bred lady, such as I have not known, without any physical beauty. The grace & harmony of her manners produce all the impression [⟨145⟩45] of beauty. She has also a mind strong, clear, precise, & much cultivated by intercourse both with books & men. She has a modest nobleness that you would dearly love. She is intimate with many of the first men. She seems to love me much, & to wish I should have whatever is hers. I take great pleasure in her friendship.[49]

[46] Mme Arconati writes, Florence, 22 Nov.

Oui un peu de célébrité aurait été commode pour faire des connaisances, mais j'ai vu que vous attirez les personnes par une attraction naturelle et elles se présentent plus simplement comme cela.

Florence, 18 Mai. Si les momens que j'avais [n] passés avec vous a Rome m'avaient inspiré la plus vive sympathie et une admiration réelle pour vous, vos tendres adieux m'ont confirmé ces sentimens. Vous m'avez fait grand plaisir quand vous m'avez dit, je vous aime beaucoup. Ces mots ne m'ont jamais semblé aussi vrais que dans votre bouche.

[47] To EH ⟨2⟩Rome 29 Oct. 1847.

I have taken rooms here until 1 April, happy in the prospect of some tranquil time here, very happy. I have been getting better every hour since I came back to Rome.

Mme. Arconati writes *Florence, 18 May,*

"Toujours les plus grandes jouissances me sont venues par la rencontre que j'ai [n] faite de quelque personne distinguée; et je ne suis pas blasée sur ce plaisir: au contraire, c'est celui que je recherche avec le plus d'empressement."

[48] Saw Rossini, Manzoni, Nicollini. ↑née↓ Princess Radzivill (Valued Mazzini Montanelli Guerazzi[50]

[49] "Among strangers . . . friendship." is used in *Memoirs*, II, 220.

[50] Saw Rossini . . . Guerazzi" is in pencil. Gioacchino Antonio Rossini (1792–1868) was an operatic composer; Alessandro Francesco Manzoni (1785–1873), a novelist and poet; Giovanni Battista Niccolini (1782–1861), a playwright and

The tone of the letters to Mme. Arconati is dignified, but respectful. M. seems to have felt a certain awe of her, and in no wise to have assumed the tone of superiority which Mme Arconati's expressions would seem to have warranted her in taking. Mme Arconati's language quoted above p. is very significant when one reads all her letters & observes how true, sensible, [49] & dignified she invariably is[.] —

[50] In Margaret's [n] MS. dated *25 March*

Love

"He only loves who loves without hope," says *Schiller*.

"The best & highest love never is, &, from its very nature, never can be requited in full measure by its object," says Rafaello. (S.G.W?) [51]

Of a disposition that requires the most refined, the most exalted tenderness, without charms to inspire it. Poor Mignon! fear not the transition through [51] death. No hell can ⟨|| . . . ||⟩have in store ⟨for thee⟩worse torments than thou art familiar with already.[52]

Of her own marriage M.F. writes to C.S. Rome, 11 Jan. 1848.

"The beautiful forms of art charm no more, & a love in which there is all fondness, ⟨&⟩but no help, flatters in vain." [53]

[52]–[53] [blank]

[54] June, 1844 Journal

"I remain fixed to be, without churlishness or coldness, as much alone as possible. It is best for me. I am not fitted to be loved; & it pains me to have close dealings with those who do not love; to whom my feelings are 'strange'. Kindness & esteem are very well. I am willing to receive & bestow them; but these alone are not worth feelings such as mine; & I wish I may make no more mistakes, but keep chaste for mine own people." [54]

---

devoted patriot; Radziwill, a Polish princess; Giuseppe Mazzini (1805–1872), an Italian patriot and reformer; Giuseppe Montanelli (1813–1862), a writer and statesman; Francesco Domenico Guerrazzi (1804–1873), a historical novelist.

[51] "Rafaello" was Margaret Fuller's name for Samuel Gray Ward.

[52] This paragraph, struck through in pencil with single vertical use marks on pp. [50] and [51], is used in *Memoirs*, I, 291.

[53] This sentence is used in *Memoirs*, II, 233.

[54] This entry, struck through in pencil with a diagonal use mark, is used in *Memoirs*, I, 292–293.

[55]–[56] [blank]
[57] To E.H. Jamaica Plains. May 15↑, 1839↓.[55]

"It is Blossom Sunday. The apple trees are full of blossoms, the golden willows too. I have found new walks, & a waterfall, and a pond with islands. But my feeling of beauty is superficial now. All these fair things are dumb compared with the last year. I long to feel them too. I feel near a faithful breast, yet gently put back by an irresistible power. I am like Ulysses near the loved shades. Write to me, dear E. I like when a friend has left me, to take up the next links. Since you went away, I have thought [58] of many things I might have told you, but I could not bear to be eloquent & poetical. It seems all mockery thus to play the artist with life, & dip the brush in one's own heart's blood. One would fain be no more an artist, or a philosopher, or a lover, or a critic, but a soul ever rushing forth in tides of genial life, or retiring evermore into precious crystals, too pure to be lonely.[56] A life more intense, you say, we pine to have. But we mount [59] the heights of our being, only to look down into darker colder chasms. It is all one earth, all under one heaven — but the moment — the moment."

---

10 Oct. 1841.

"O Carrie! what a poor first sketch this life is, — all torn & thrown aside too. Were it not for the muse who peeps in, now & then, at the window, how lonely here at home! I wish she would come & light my candles, it is dark here, except one little rush-candle in the corner, that only serves to show how many silver [60] branches there are that might be lit up."

[61]–[62] [blank][57]
[63]–[64] [leaf cut out]
[65] Mme Arconati writes from Milan.

Arconati, 25 Septre [n]

Promettez moi, je vous prie, de venir me voir a votre retour de Rome. Ce que je vous ai ecrit de Bellagio ↑e↓tait la sincere expression de mes sentimen⟨ts⟩s, et je crois être sure que quelque difference qui puisse se declarer entre nous, je ne changerai pas. Je ne puis pas me tromper sur ⟨t⟩l' élévation [n] et l'énergie de votre ame et vos opinions ne peuvent pas l'altérer.[n]

[55] ", 1839" is added in pencil.

[56] "Since you [[p. 57]] . . . lonely.", struck through in pencil with a vertical use mark, is used in *Memoirs*, I, 294.

[57] The leaf bearing pp. [61]–[62] has a clean cut near the inner edge and running approximately half-way down from the top; it was apparently made when the following leaf was cut out.

Je serais bien fache que vous fussiez telle que Mickiewitz vous désire. Ce n'est pas seulement sa foi plus profonde qui le rend [66] exclusif, — c'est[n] que son horizon est ⟨borné⟩plus borné. Je crois en verité que cela tient à sa race. Avez vous trouvé beau coup de Slaves d'un esprit étendu? Je le respecte pourtant, mais je me sens profondement etrangère a coté de lui, et je ne le sens point à coté de vous, qui appartenez à une autre nation que moi, et qui êtes de plus separée de moi par les croyances, et par une supériorité extraordinaire.

Vous êtes une enigme ici pour les personnes qui vous ont vu, mais [67] qui vous ignorent. Elles se doutent qu'il y a quelque chose qui leur est caché et cherchent en vain a déviner. Je ne leur dis rien, et on dit alors que vous ⟨avez⟩m'avez ensorcelé. Avez vous vu M. Thomar? ——

[68]–[69] [blank]

[70] a note to the Diva Triformis of Horace[:]

Terret, lustrat, agit, Proserpina, Luna, Diana,
Ima, superna, feras, Sceptro, fulgore, sagitta.[58]

[71] [blank]

[72] Writing

How can I ever write with this impatience of detail? The first suggestion of a thought delights; — to follow it out, wearies & weakens me.

I am like Sterling. I shall never be an artist. I have no patient love of execution. I am delighted with my sketch, but the moment I try to finish it, I am chilled. Never was there a great sculptor who did not love to chip the marble.[59]

[73] Writing

Her pen was a nonconductor[.]

I find in her Journal of May, 1833 this motto on the inside cover[:]

"*Scrivo sol per sfogar l'intern⟨a⟩o.*"

↑Journal, ⟨Apr⟩Apr., 1840.↓

[58] "She terrifies, she illuminates, she compels — Proserpina, Luna, Diana, — the lower and the upper worlds, and the wild animals, by a sceptre, by lightning, by an arrow" (Ed.). The Latin is an annotation to Horace, *Odes*, Bk. III, XXII, l. 4 ("diva triformis"); it appears in *Quinti Horatii Flacci Opera . . .* (Philadelphiae, 1824), p. 195.

[59] "How can . . . marble.", struck through in pencil with a curved vertical use mark, is used in *Memoirs*, I, 295.

"Then a woman of tact & brilliancy like me, has an undue advantage in conversation with men. They are astonished at our instincts. They do not see where we got our knowledge, &, while they tramp on in their clumsy way, we wheel, & fly, & dart hither & thither, & seize with ready eye all the weak points, like Saladin in the desert. It is quite another thing when we come to write, [74] and without suggestion from another mind, to declare the positive amount of thought that is in us. Because we seemed to know all, they think we can tell all, &, finding we can tell so little, lose faith in their first opinion of us, *which, nathless, was true.*
Then these gentlemen are surprized that I write no better, because I talk so well. But I have served a long apprenticeship to the one, none to [75] the other. I will write well yet; but never, I think, so well as I talk; for then I feel inspired, and the means are pleasant; my voice excites me; my pen never.—I shall by no means be discouraged, nor take ↑for final↓ what they say, ⟨for gospel,⟩ but try to sift from it all the truth, & use it. I feel within myself the strength to dispense with all illusions, & I will manifest it. I will stand steady, & rejoice in the severest probations." [60]

(Continued on p. 88)

[76] Margaret was a sentimentalist. That hitherto odious ⟨n||...||⟩ malformation nature in her case adopted, & was to make respectable. Just as the fictions of the law are defended on their eminent convenience; or, as the arbitrary Linnaean classification of plants affords wonderful facilities for students; or, as we are fed on superstitions, & live by illusions, & houses are built by scaffolding; ⟨so here was a head wh⟩ or as the [77] Alexandrian Platonists[n] clothed their master in brocade & spangles that have drawn more eyes to him than his own diamonds; so here was a head which [was] so creative of new colours, of wonderful gleams⟨,⟩ so iridescent, that it piqued curiosity, ⟨&⟩ stimulated thought, & communicated mental activity to all who approached her, though her perceptions were not to be compared with her fancy, & she made [78] numerous mistakes. Her perceptions are not accurate, but her integrity was perfect, and she was followed by love, and was really bent on truth, but continually deceived by her fancy.[61]

[60] " 'Her pen was . . . probations.' ", struck through in pencil with single curved vertical use marks on pp. [73] and [74], and a curved diagonal use mark on p. [75], is used in *Memoirs*, I, 294, 295–296.

[61] "Margaret [p. [76]] . . . by her fancy." is used in *Memoirs*, I, 280.

[79] [blank]
[80][62] *Gems again*

"Carbuncles,"[n] says Southey, "are male & female. The female casts out light. The male has his within himself. Mine is the male."[63]

June, 1844, p.

⟨Sh⟩M signalized every anniversary like Henry Hedge, every birthday; her trinkets; her sealring.[n]
[See the verses to it [in 1844, June, p 39] [64]

The coincidence again or preestablished harmony of the names of Michel Angelo, & of Raffaelle, she felt, & the Rosencrantz, Rosicrucians. See *Journal* ⟨*May*⟩*June, 1844* p. 96[65]

She put on the carbuncle & bracelet to write to her friend.

[81][66] The same dream returns to her four times, on her birthday, on All Souls' or All Saints' day, &c[.]
Journal May, 1844. p 34— "Eighteenth of April," &c. ↑*Ib.*↓ p. 39

---

[62] The entries on p. [80] are struck through in pencil with single discontinuous vertical use marks. " 'Carbuncles . . . male.' " is used in *Memoirs*, I, 219; "M signalized . . . sealring." is used in *Memoirs*, I, 221; "The coincidence . . . Rosicrucians." is used in *Memoirs*, I, 220; "She put . . . friend." is used in *Memoirs*, I, 219.

[63] See *Southey's Common-Place Book*, ed. J. W. Warter, 4 vols. (London, 1850), IV, 47. Southey is quoting from Camillus Leonardus, *The Mirror of Stones* (London, 1750).

[64] With this sentence, cf. *Memoirs*, I, 221: "She had a series of anniversaries, which she kept. Her seal-ring of the flying Mercury had its legend." The verses, under the title "My Seal-ring," begin

Mercury has cast aside
The signs of intellectual pride. . . .

See Margaret Fuller Ossoli, *Life Without and Life Within* . . . (Boston, 1860; reprinted 1970), p. 378.

[65] Emerson evidently derived his judgment from the entry from Margaret's journal which he copied on p. [83] below. Margaret thought that Christian Rosencrantz was the founder of the Rosicrucians; the name was Christian Rosenkreutz. Some scholars consider it a pseudonym for Johann Valentin Andreä.

[66] The entries on p. [81] are struck through in pencil with a vertical use mark, in addition to the use marks described in note 68 below; "The same . . . day, &c" is used in *Memoirs*, I, 221.

And dreams. Her journals pertinaciously record her dreams, pertinacious dreams, too; for they seem also to have re⟨turned⟩↑curred↓ periodically, annually, & with marvellous aptness. Thus also, in Journal 1842⟨2⟩

"In C.S., I, at last, distinctly recognize the figure of the early vision whom I found after I had left Amelia, who led me on the bridge towards the city glittering in sunset, but midway the bridge [82] went under water.[67] I have often seen in her face that it was she, but refused to believe it." [68]

1840

I build on our friendship now with trust for I think it is redeemed from "the search after Eros." We may commune without exacting too much, one from the other.⟨"⟩ [69]

July, 1839.

Could a word from me avail you, I would say that I have firm faith that Nature cannot be false to her child who has shown such an unalterable piety towards her.[70]

[83] *Names* Journal 1844, June.

If Christian Rosencrantz is not a made name, the genius of the age interfered in the baptismal rite, as in the ⟨n|| . . . ||⟩cases of the Archangels of Art, Michel & Raffaello. & in giving the name of Emanuel to the Captain of the New Jerusalem. *Sub rosa crux* [71] I think is the true derivation, & not the chemical one, *Generation Corruption* [n] &c[.] [72]

[84]–[85] [blank]

[86] June, 1844 p 95 at Hawthorne's

[67] "⟨To⟩ C. S." is written in ink in the top margin of p. [82].

[68] "Her journals . . . it.' ", struck through in pencil with single vertical use marks on pp. [81] and [82], is used in *Memoirs*, I, 221.

[69] "I build . . . other, ⟨"⟩", struck through in pencil with two vertical use marks, is used in *Memoirs*, I, 282, and comes from a letter from Margaret Fuller to Caroline Sturgis, 184[?], ms., Houghton Library.

[70] "I build . . . her." is struck through in pencil with a vertical use mark; "Could a word . . . her." is used in *Memoirs*, I, 282.

[71] "The cross under the rose" (Ed.). A poem of Margaret's in *Memoirs*, II, 114–116, has this title and this theme. Webster's Dictionary finds the derivation of Rosicrucian in NL Rosae Crucis.

[72] "If Christian . . . &c", struck through in pencil with a vertical use mark, is used in *Memoirs*, I, 220.

"After they were all in bed, I went out & walked till near 12↑, o.clock.↓ The moonlight ⟨was beautiful &⟩ filled my heart. I feel the beauty of the↑se↓ embowering elms: they stood in holy blackness[,] the praying monastics of this holy clear night, full of grace, in every sense; their life so full, so hushed, not a leaf stirred." [73]

In verses to the moon, 1844, she writes

> "But, if I steadfast gaze upon thy face,
> A human secret like my own I trace,
> For, through the woman's smile looks the male eye." [74]

[87] To C.K.N. Rome, 24 Nov. 1848 —

"I have watched every day & night the skies & the earth. I know all their expressions." [75]

[88] *Talking* — continued from p. 75

To RWE Apr., 184⟨6⟩0.

When I look at my papers I feel as if I had never had a thought that was worthy the attention of any but myself, & some fond friend; & 'tis only, when, on talking with people, I find I tell them what they did not know, that my confidence at all returns.[76]

[89] [blank]
[90] Paris. *To Mary Rotch. Rome, 184⟨3⟩7.*

All winter in Paris. Paris is the focus of the intellectual activity of Europe: there I found every topic intensified, clarified, reduced to portable dimensions. There is the cream of all the milk.

Paris Dec. 26, 1846. To Mrs M Fuller

In Paris, I have been obliged to give a great deal of time to French, in

[73] This paragraph, struck through in pencil with a curved vertical use mark, is used in *Memoirs*, I, 264.

[74] "In verses . . . eye.", struck through in pencil with a diagonal use mark, is used in *Memoirs*, I, 229.

[75] This entry, struck through in pencil with a diagonal use mark, is used in *Memoirs*, I, 263.

[76] This entry is struck through in pencil with a diagonal use mark.

order to get the power of speaking, without which I might ⟨be⟩ as well be in a well, as here.[77]

---

[91] I have been asked to remain in correspondence with "La Revue Independante," after my return to the U.S. which will be very pleasant & advantageous to me.

Madame Pauline Roland I find an interesting woman, an intimate friend of Beranger & of Pierre Leroux[.]

We occupy a charming suite of apartments *Hotel Rougement, Boulevard Poissonnière*, a new hotel.[78]

To R.W.E. In France, among the many persons that brought me some good thing, it was only with Mickiewicz, that I felt any deep-founded mental connection.[79]

[92] [80] I have been presented at Court, & been to the Court Ball. Was in the Chamber of Peers. I heard Arago lecture; ↑have↓ seen Considerant, Doherty, Mme. Vigoureux, also, the friend of Fourier.
Beranger, Lamennais, Le Francois,[81]

[93]–[94] [blank]
[95] Ellery Channing To E.H. Cambridge 1842

⟨W⟩E. has written to you. We have had several good ⟨times⟩ ↑hours↓ together. He is unequal & uncertain, but in his good moods, of the best for a companion, absolutely abandoned to the revelations of the moment, without distrust or check of any kind, unlimited, & delicate, abundant in thought, & free of motion, he enriches life, & fills the hour.[82]

[77] This sentence is used in *Memoirs*, II, 191.

[78] "I have been asked . . . hotel." is used in *Memoirs*, II, 192.

[79] With this sentence, cf. *Memoirs*, II, 207: "He came, and I found in him the man I had long wished to see, with the intellect and passions in due proportion for a full and healthy human being, with a soul constantly inspiring."

[80] P. [92] is in pencil, with "have" and scattered punctuation added in ink.

[81] With this entry, cf. *Memoirs*, II, 201, 202, 205. François Arago (1786–1853) was a regular lecturer on astronomy at the Paris Royal Observatory; Victor Prosper Considérant (1809–1893), a social reformer and disciple of Fourier; Hugh Doherty, a Fourierist and editor of the *London Phalanx*; Clarisse Vigoureux, an early follower of Fourier; Félicité Robert de la Mennais (1782–1854), a French abbé and socialist philosopher; Nicolas-Louis-Edouard Lefrançois (1803–1854), a Belgian mathematician.

[82] "had several good . . . hour." is struck through in pencil with a vertical use mark; "He is . . . hour." is used in *Memoirs*, I, 210.

[96] [blank]
[97]–[98] [leaf cut out] [83]
[99] [blank] [84]

[100] "The best talker since De Stael."

Letter to RWE [85]

1839, Nov. 12. Had ⟨my⟩ the first meeting with my class last Wednesday & gave them a brief statement of my views & aims apparently not without success for they were intent & many (some strangers to me) said words of faith & cheer to me afterwards. But tomorrow comes the real trial of whether they will talk themselves. There are some fine faces.

[101] 26 Dec., 1839.

Yet I could not make a good statement this morning on the subject of *Beauty*.[86]

25 Nov., 1839.

My class is singularly prosperous I think. I was so fortunate as to rouse at once the tone of simple earnestness which can scarcely, when once awakened, cease to vibrate. All seem in a glow & quite as receptive as I wish. They question & examine, yet follow leadings; & thoughts (not opinions) have been trumps every time. There are about 25 members, & every one, I believe, full of interest. The first time, ten took part in the conversation; the [102] last still more. Mrs Bancroft came out in a way that surprized me. She seems to have shaken off a wonderful number of films. She showed pure vision, sweet sincerity, & much talent. Mrs Josiah Quincy keeps us in good order & takes care that "Xy"[Christianity] & "morality" are not forgotten. The first time was the genealogy of heaven & earth, then the Will (Jupiter); the Understanding, (Mercury) [.]
Second, the celestial inspiration of genius, perception & transmission of divine law (Apollo), the terrene inspiration, [103] the impassioned abandonment of genius (Bacchus) [;] of the thunderbolt, the caduceus, the ray, (?) & the grape having disposed of as well as might be, we came to

[83] Emerson indexed p. [97] under Greeley H.

[84] Tipped in between the stub of the missing leaf bearing pp. [97]–[98], and p. [99], is a blue sheet, folded, written on one side in ink, with the title "Table of Contents for Volume Second": "VI. JAMAICA PLAIN. W. H. CHANNING —", "VII. NEW YORK — LETTERS AND JOURNALS", "VIII. EUROPE", and "IX. Homeward". Under VI and VII are a number of subheadings. None of the material on the sheet is in Emerson's hand.

[85] "Letter to RWE . . . *Beauty.* [p. [101]]" is in pencil.

[86] This sentence is used in *Memoirs*, I, 231.

the wave⟨s⟩, & the seashell it moulds; to Beauty, & Love, her p⟨resent⟩-arent [n] & her child[.]

I assure ↑you↓, there is more Greek than Bostonian spoken at the meetings, & we may have pure honey of Hymettus to give you yet. I have been happy *a mourir*. Four hundred & seventy designs of Raffaelle in my possession for a week.[87]

[104] ↑Margaret [n] Fuller↓ To RWE Nov., 1839.

I could not make those ladies talk about Beauty: they would not ascend to principles, but kept clinging to details. I have let it drop, & shall take it up again by & by, if they get in train.[88]

↑M G. Fuller↓
To W[illiam]H[enry]C[hanning] Sunday 8 Nov., 1840.

Wednesday, I opened with my class. It was a noble meeting. I told them the great changes in my mind, & that I could not be sure they would be satisfied with me now, as they were when I was in deliberate possession of myself. I tried to convey the truth, &, though I did not arrive at any full expression [n] [105] of it, they all with glistening eyes seemed melted into one love. Our relation is now perfectly true, & I do not think they will ever interrupt me. A. sat beside me, all glowing, & the moment I had finished, she began to speak. She told me afterwards, she was ⟨as⟩all kindled, & none there could be strangers to her more. I was really delighted by the enthusiasm of Mrs F. I did not expect it. All her best self seemed called up, & she feels that these meetings will be her highest pleasure. E.H. too was most beautiful. I went home with Mrs F. & had a long attack of nervous headache. She attended anxiously on me, & asked if [106] would it be so all winter? I said 'if it were, I did not care;' & truly I feel now such an entire separation from pain & illness, such a calm consciousness of another life, while suffering most,—that pain has no effect but to steal some of my time.[89]

She defined the *daimonische* "Energy for energy's sake."[90]

[87] "I have . . . week.", struck through in ink with five diagonal use marks, is used in *Memoirs*, I, 266. "My class is [p. [101]] . . . give you yet." is used in *Memoirs*, I, 331–332.

[88] Perhaps the entry refers to the "class of ladies assembled at Miss [Elizabeth] Peabody's rooms, in West Street, on the 6th November, 1839." *Memoirs*, I, 328.

[89] "Wednesday, I opened [p. [104]] . . . my time." is used in *Memoirs*, I, 339–340.

[90] "She defined . . . sake.'" is in pencil, written on the top of p. [105], followed by a page-wide rule in ink separating it from the continuation of the letter to William Henry Channing of 8 Nov.

To W[illiam].H[enry]C[hanning]. Cambridge, 28 Apr. 1844.

It was the last meeting of my class. We had a most animated meeting. On bidding me goodby↑e↓, they all & always show so much goodwill & love, that I feel I must really have become a friend to them. I was then [107] loaded with beautiful gifts, accompanied with those little delicate poetic traits of which I should delight to tell you, if we were near. Last, came a beautiful bunch of flowers, passion flowers, heliotrope, & soberer flowers. Then I went to take my repose on C.'s sofa, & we had a most sweet afternoon together.—[91]

To EH. 20 Feb. 1841.

It is proposed that I have an evening class in Boston & a few gentlemen my friends are to be members. There are to be only 5 or 6 meetings.[92]

[108][93] Conversations Nov., 1842.

To EH

Both the Conversations since you were here have been spirited. Miss S. Burley has joined the class, & hers is a presence so positive as to be of great value to me[.][94]

Oct., 1843.

Will not Lidian come to our Conversations ↑this winter if I get a class↓ the subject Health[?]

[109] To E. H. ↑without date↓[95]

I send you 3 papers written for my class, two by S Clarke, one by Marianne Jackson. ⟨T⟩Our last meeting yesterday was beautiful: how noble has been ⟨our⟩my experience of such relations for six years now, & with so many, & so various minds! Life *is* worth living—is it not?[96]

[91] This paragraph is used in *Memoirs*, I, 351.

[92] "*To EH* . . . meetings." is written at the top of p. [107] followed by a page-wide rule separating it from the continuation of the letter to William Henry Channing. With "It is proposed . . . meetings.", cf. *Memoirs*, I, 347.

[93] P. [108] is in pencil.

[94] This sentence is used in *Memoirs*, I, 350. Miss Susan Burley was known for her literary salons in Salem, where she lived.

[95] Added in pencil.

[96] "how noble . . . not?" is used in *Memoirs*, I, 351.

[110]–[115] [blank]
[116] Sing Sing. ↑;S.M.F.↓ To EH Oct. 20, 1844.

"We have just been passing Sunday at Sing Sing. We went with William Channing: he staid at the chaplain's; we at the prison. It was a noble occasion for his eloquence, and I never felt more content than when, at the words 'Men and Brethren,' all those faces were upturned like a sea swayed by a single wind, and the shell of brutality burst apart at the touch of love divinely human.[97] He visited several of them in their cells & the incidents that came, were moving.[98]
[117] On Sunday they are all confined in their cells after 12 at noon, that their keepers may have rest from their weekly fatigues. But I was allowed to have some of the women out to talk with, & the interview was very pleasant. They were among the so called worst, but nothing could be more decorous than their conduct, & frank too. All passed much as in ⟨my⟩one of my Boston classes. I told them I was writing about Woman, & as my path had been a favoured one,[99] I wanted to ask some information of those who had [118] been tempted to pollution & sorrow. They seemed to reply in the same spirit in which I asked. Several however expressed a wish to see me alone, as they could then say *all*, & they could not bear to ⟨to || . . . ||⟩ before ↑one↓ another: and I intend to go there again, & take time for this. It is very gratifying to see the influence these few months of gentle & intelligent treatment have had on these women: indeed it is wonderful, & even should the ⟨s⟩State change its policy, affords the needed text for treatment of the subject." [100]

[119] [blank]
[120] Concord [101]
To EH Groton 14 July 1836.

I will come to Concord, next week, on Friday, 22 July, if that will be agreeable to Mrs Emerson.[102]

[97] " 'We have . . . human.' " is used in *Memoirs*, II, 144.

[98] In this paragraph the following are in pencil: the semicolon after "chaplain's", the period after "prison", and the commas after "eloquence", "wind", and "came". Numerous i's have been dotted and t's crossed in pencil.

[99] On p. [117] the following commas are in pencil: after "noon", "with", "Woman", and "one", and numerous i's have been dotted and t's crossed in pencil.

[100] " 'On Sunday . . . subject.' ", struck through in pencil with vertical use marks on pp. [117] and [118], is used in *Memoirs*, II, 144–145.

[101] This word is in pencil.

[102] Margaret Fuller's visit to the Emersons in Concord in late July and early August, 1836, marked the beginning of their friendship.

[121]–[123] [blank]
[124] Dial
To RWE Florence June, 1847.

⟨The⟩ I am glad to hear of the new Journal ↑[Mass Quarterly]↓, which will answer to a deep want, though I doubt by the list of names you send me, the danger there will not be a sufficient range & diversity of power to make it a fair Journal.[103] Yet how precious was the old Dial, with all its faults. I felt this indeed after being in England. It had been manna in the wilderness to people there.

[125]–[127] [blank]
[128] To Mary Rotch Boston *Apr., 1842.*
↑*Happy days/*↓ [104]

My winter has indeed been very pleasant. Destiny, which still cross-biases me,[105] refusing me what I desired, solitude & quiet, in which to concentrate my powers, has rewarded my submission to her guidance, with more & fairer gifts than I could have deemed the due of any one,—with ⟨new⟩many new & sweet thoughts, an extending hope, & a clearer faith.

[129] *Journal May, 1844.*
While hearing him (Ole Bull) I was happy, & felt overpaid for existence by that degree in which I possess the power of apprec[i]ating genius.[106]

Rome, 16 Dec. 1847. My life at Rome is thus far all I hoped. I have not been so well since I was a child, nor so happy ever as during the last six weeks.

I wrote you about my home. It continues good, perfectly clean; food wholesome; service exact.—[n] I pay but not immoderately. The sum total of my expenses here for 6 months will not exceed 400, or, at most, $450.[107]

[103] In a letter to Margaret Fuller, 30 April, 1847, Emerson mentioned Bronson Alcott, William Henry Channing, Theodore Parker, Charles Sumner, James Elliot Cabot, John Sullivan Dwight, and Thomas Treadwell Stone as "filled with rage to institute" the new journal, the *Massachusetts Quarterly Review* (*L*, III, 394).

[104] Added in pencil.

[105] Cf. George Herbert, "Affliction," l. 53: "Thus does thy Power cross-bias me . . . ,".

[106] The violinist Ole Bull gave several concerts in Boston between May 21 and June 4, 1844, one of which Emerson attended (*JMN*, IX, 98).

[107] "Rome, 16 Dec. . . . $450." is used in *Memoirs*, II, 223, where the letter is headed "To Her Mother." The comma after "Rome" and the periods after "Dec" and "1847" are in pencil.

The air of Rome agrees with me as it did before and Rome is so dear [130] I do not know how I can ever be willing to live any where else.

To RWE. White Mts. ⟨A⟩July 25, 1842.

You say that Nature does not keep her promise⟨s⟩: but surely she satisfies us now & then, for the time. The drama is always in progress, but here & there she speaks out a sentence, full in its cadence, complete in its structure, it occupies for the time the sense & the thought. We have no care for promises. Will you say, it is the superficialness of my life, that I have known hours with men & nature [131][108] tha↑t↓ bore their proper fruit, all present ate, & were filled, & there were taken up of the fragments twelve baskets full. Is it because of the superficial mind, or the believing heart that I can say this?[109]

[132][110] *The West* To Mary Rotch Cambridge 1844.

I wrote you one letter while at the West. I ⟨sent m⟩ know not if my letter was ever received. I sent it by a private opportunity,—one [of] those traps to catch the unwary. I had never so clear an idea of the capacity to bless of mere earth, merely the beautiful Earth, when fresh from the original breath of the creat⟨ive Spirit⟩or.[n] To have this impression one must see large tracts of wild country where the traces of man's inventions are too few & slight to break the harmony of the first design. It will not [133] be long even where I have been now. In three or four years those vast flowery plains will be broken up ⟨in⟩for tillage; those shapely groves converted into logs & boards. I wished I could have kept on now two or three years, while yet the first spell rested on the scene.

[Chicago Aug., 1843. The characters of persons are brought out by the little ↑wants &↓ adventures of country life, so that each one awakens a healthful interest & the same persons who if you saw them

[108] Tipped in between pp. [130] and [131] is a folded white half sheet, with "Gerus. Lib.

XII 17 or 37
16 or 36"

in ink in Emerson's hand on one outside page, and, in pencil, not in Emerson's hand, an index with page numbers under the heading "De placitis philosophorum" on two pages. In *Memoirs*, I, 223–224, Emerson reproduces Margaret's quotations from Tasso's *Gerusalemme Liberata*, Canto XII, stanzas 76 and 77.

[109] With "all present . . . full.", cf. Matt. 14:20; Mark 6:42–43; Luke 9:17. "You say . . . this?" is struck through in pencil with single vertical use marks on pp. [130] and [131].

[110] The entries on pp. [132] and [133] are struck through in pencil with single vertical and diagonal use marks.

at these hotels, would not have a word to say that could fix the attention, [134] become most pleasing companions; for their topics are before them, & they take the hint. You feel so grateful too for the hospitality of the log-cabin,—such gratitude as the hospitality of the rich, however generous, cannot inspire; for these wait on you with domestics & money, & give of their superfluity only. But here, the master g⟨i⟩ives you his bed, his horse, his lamp, his grain from the field, his all, in short, & you see that he enjoys doing so thoroughly, [135] & takes no thought for the morrow. So that you run in fields full of lilies, perfumed with pure kindness.

[136] Miss Peabody's letter

"Not counting myself among her intimate friends, as she decidedly wished I should not———I ⟨knew⟩ ↑heard of↓ her in 1822, as a wonderful child at Dr Park's school, talking pure mathematics with her father, at 12 years, 'had no religion'[,] made a covenant with her father to educate her brothers & sisters, & she should have $3000 to go to Europe.[111]

In 1827–8 first saw her. Margaret said almost nothing, but I thought she was laughing at me, for which there seemed good cause. I was impressed strongly with her perfect good nature. It seemed to me her eyes overflowed with fun, & this fun was a pure sense of the comic,—inevitable [137] to an intellect⟨,⟩ sharp as a diamond; the conviction was irresistible that she had no malice in her ⟨|| . . . ||⟩heart.

I saw her again: she spoke of M.A.M. who was my scholar ⟨i⟩on whom I hoped to make an impression, 'She never will improve,' & she never did."

[138] ↑*Margaret's Friends.*↓

F. H. Hedge
Amelia Greenwood
Almira Barlow
George Davis
W. H. Channing
E Randall
Sarah Clarke
James Clarke
Anna Barker
Sam G. Ward

↑Mary Rotch
⟨Miss⟩Susan Burley
A. H Tracey↓

[111] With this paragraph, cf. *Memoirs*, I, 204–205.

Caroline Sturgis
Jane Tuckerman
Mary Soley
George Calvert
Charles K Newcomb
Sarah Russell
Sarah Shaw
Anna Shaw
George Ripley
Elizabeth Hoar
Mrs S. A. Ripley
Nathaniel Hawthorne
⟨J⟩Giuseppe Mazzini
Horace Greeley
Dr Channing
Ellen Hooper
Mrs Farrar
Harriet Martineau[112]

[139] To RWE 5 July 1840.

Do not think because persons are intimate with me, that they know this or any of my other friends' affairs. I know how to keep relations sacredly separate. I should never have let you know anything about this, if we had been intimate forever, unless A. had.[113]

To RWE Nov., 1841.

The papers we spoke of I have again looked over, & they, I believe finally, refuse to be shown. Let all that lie apart. If you enter into an

[112] Of those not previously identified or easily recognized, Amelia Greenwood was an acquaintance of the Peabody sisters; George Davis (1810–1877), with whom Margaret apparently had an unhappy love affair, became a lawyer and member of Congress; Jane Tuckerman, daughter of Gustavus Tuckerman, a Boston merchant, was a member of one of Margaret's conversation classes; Sarah Shaw was the wife of Francis G. Shaw, the mother of Colonel Robert Gould Shaw, and a member of one of Margaret's conversation classes; Anna B. Shaw was also a member of one of the classes, and Mrs. Eliza Ware Farrar (1791–1870) was an author and the wife of the Harvard professor of astronomy. E. Randall, Mary Soley, and Sarah Russell are unidentified.

[113] More of this letter to Emerson is in *L*, II, 309–310. "A." may be Anna Barker, Samuel Gray Ward's future wife.

intimate relation with him my sometime son it will be of quite [140] another character, let it bear its proper fruit. The scrolls of the past burn my fingers. They have not yet passed into literature. The dry leaves clog the stream & the wind sighs amid the despoiled groves. Gladly would I wash off the whole past for a little space; the sympathetic hues would show again before the fire, renovated & lively.

[141] Her first notice of S[amuel].G[ray].W[ard]. in the journey of July 27, 1835, is on board the boat to N.Y.

"About six, came out, & had a walk & a talk with Mr Ward: did not like him much."

[142]–[145] [blank]

[146] To E.H. 20 March 1842.

Ill health

Head can only be soothed by keeping it wet with cold water: pain in the spine & in the side,—languor, grass hopper a burden—and though as each task comes, I borrow a readiness from its aspect, as I always do brightness for the moment from the face of a friend, yet, as soon as the hour is past, I sink.[114]

I do not suffer keen pains & spasms, as formerly; but neither have I ⟨the⟩ half the energy in the intervals. Probably, *then*,[n] I [147] did not get well, but was always in a state of tension of nerves; whilst now I am not. *Then*, I constantly looked forward to death. Now, I feel there has been a crisis in my constitution. It is a subject of great interest to me ⟨i⟩as connected with my mental life for I feel this change dates from the era of illumination in my mental life. If I live, I shall write a full account of all I have observed. Now that my mind is so calm & sweet, there seems to be no fire in me to resist or to consume, & I can neither bear nor do what I could⟨,⟩ while much [148] more sick, but am very weak. No doubt, this finds its parallel in what we know of the great bodily strength of the insane.

My childhood was full of presentiments. In childhood I was a somnambulist. I was subject to attacks of delirium;—I perceive now I had spectral illusions.

When I was twelve, I had a determination of blood to the head.[n] My parents were much mortified to see the fineness of my complexion de-

[114] "—and though . . . sink.", struck through in pencil with a vertical use mark, is used in *Memoirs*, I, 231.

stroyed. My own vanity was for a time severely wounded, but I recovered [n] [149] [115] & made up my mind to be bright & ugly.

Goethe's "Notes to W. O. Divan," — I read them [n] in bed ⟨today⟩ for I was very ill today. I can always understand anything better when I am ill.[116]

[150] To E. H. Jan.
Of Charles Lane

I like him much & should find profit in talking with him, for he speaks nobly, & is also precise, & full of resource. When he speaks, I attend not only to the thing, but to all the words. Thus I am not tired, as with most talkers.

[151]–[153] [blank]
[154] ↑*Margaret's Letters.*↓

I have plagues about me, but they don't touch me now. I thank nightly the benignant Spirit for the unaccustomed serenity in which it enfolds me.
Ellery is very wretched, almost hopeless now, & once I ⟨|| . . . ||⟩could not have helped taking on me all his griefs, & through him the griefs of his class, but now I drink only the wormwood of the minute, & that has always equal parts, a drop of sweet to a drop of bitter.

But I shall never be callous, never unable to understand *home-sickness*. Am not I too one of the band who [155] know not where to lay their heads? [n] Am I wise enough to hear such things? Perhaps not, but happy enough surely; for that Power which daily makes me understand the value of the little wheat amid the field of tares, & shows me how the kingdom of heaven is sown on earth like a grain of mustard seed, is good enough to me, & bids me call unhappiness happy[.] [117]

[115] Laid in between pp. [148] and [149] is a folded sheet of white paper containing ink writing on all four sides in Margaret Fuller's hand. It is composed of comments on philosophical subjects and on the writer's state of mind. One page is dated "28th Jany".

[116] "My childhood . . . ill.", struck through in ink with single vertical use marks on pp. [148] and [149], is used in *Memoirs*, I, 228–229.

[117] "I have plagues . . . happy", struck through in pencil with single vertical use marks on pp. [154] and [155], is used in *Memoirs*, I, 309. With "Am not I . . . heads.", cf. Matt. 8:20 and Luke 9:58; with "the value of . . . tares," cf. Matt. 13:28–30; with "the kingdom of heaven . . . seed," cf. Matt. 13:31–32, Mark 4:31, and Luke 13:19.

Cambridge 26, 1842. Ellery is here, but he is too much harassed by anxiety for companionship. I can do nothing so will not take the possible tragedy to heart. I am inclined to say with Mephistopheles, "*He is not the first*!"[118] Ay, [156] surely, it is the enigma of my time that no genius shall bear both flower & fruit; may as well trouble myself for a thousand as one — so I am not troubled.

[157] [blank]

[158] I remember, on one occasion, when she found ↑her old friend↓ H[enry]. H[edge]. with me, she looked at him attentively, and seemed hardly to know him. ⟨T⟩She thought he had had a paralytic shock. But, in the afternoon, he invited her to go with him to Waltham, and the moment he was in the gig, she said, his face changed, he lost the stony aspect which he had worn here, & her old friend of many years came back. "And you fancy," she said, "that you know him. You have never seen him."[n 119]

[159] May, 1844.

We ↑(S[arah]. Shaw & MF)↓ had a long & deep conversation happy in its candor. Truth, truth, thou art the great preservative. Let free air into the mind, & the pestilence cannot lurk in any corner.

I have the satisfaction of knowing that in my counsels, I have given myself no air of being better than I am.[120]

In the chamber of death, I prayed in very early years, Give me truth: Cheat me on by no illusion. Oh the granting of this prayer is sometimes terrible to me. I walk over the burning ploughshares & they [160][121] do sear my feet. Yet nothing but truth will do; no love that is not eternal, & as large as the universe; no philanthropy in executing whose behests I myself become unhealthy; no creative genius which bursts asunder my life, to leave it a poor black chrysalid behind.

[118] Goethe, *Faust*, Part I, "A Gloomy Day." Mephistopheles says, "She is not the first."

[119] This paragraph, struck through in pencil with a vertical use mark, is used in *Memoirs*, I, 312–313.

[120] "We (S. Shaw . . . am.", struck through in pencil with a vertical use mark, is used in *Memoirs*, I, 304, 303.

[121] A canceled subject heading, "Macaria", is written in the top margin of p. [160]. The name Macaria, from Goethe's *Wilhelm Meister*, is explained by Margaret Fuller in a note to her article on Goethe in *The Dial*: ". . . the daughter of Hercules, who devoted herself a voluntary sacrifice for her country. She was adored by the Greeks as the true Felicity" (II, July 1841), 27.

And yet this last is too true of my life.[122]

To S.G. W. ↑?/↓ Oct. 1839. My own entire sincerity in every passage of life gives me a right to expect that I shall never be met by unmeaning phrases or attentions.[123]

[161] *Macaria*

[162]–[163] [blank]

[164] ↑1842 July to C S↓[124]

"it is because of the recoils & positive repulsions which have attended every stage of your development & been most manifest in my direction."

[165] Caroline Sturgis

To EH March, 1842.

Carrie I see little. I have not time. And we were so much together in the summer, that it needs not, at present. She, however, has come forth into life, seeking in the details of study & observation, fuel for her flame. But neither love nor duty offer yet with any bounty, occasions which can much aid her, & she is learning, at present, I believe, grain of sand on grain of sand, as Schiller said. She is much with Anna Shaw, whose free & noble ardour suits her now. &c.&c. Thus the orbs weave their dance.

[166] Sam & Anna I see little, but take more pleasure in them when I do than before. They are more open to genial & inspiring themes. Still we are in different regions. Just as I put off the operation on Arthur's eye till they set off on their bridal tour, & ↑on↓ that first day of divine October beauty was with him & the surgeon, while they were together, so is it now, as to circumstances between us.[125] I do not like to tell them what I am thinking & doing; they can tell one another what they think & do. It is all well, if they will live worthily.

[167]–[169] [blank]

[170] To C S Feb., 1839.

[122] This paragraph, struck through in pencil with single vertical use marks on pp. [159] and [160], is used in *Memoirs*, I, 303–304.

[123] This sentence, struck through in pencil with a vertical use mark, is used in *Memoirs*, I, 304. "To S.G. W." is enclosed by an oval line in ink.

[124] Added in pencil.

[125] With this sentence, cf. *Memoirs*, I, 301: "She went, from the most joyful of all bridals, to attend a near relative during a formidable surgical operation." Arthur is undoubtedly her brother.

—my verses—I am ashamed when I think there is scarce a line of poetry in them; all "rhetorical & impassioned," as Goethe said of Mme de Stael. However, such as they are, they have been overflowing drops from the somewhat bitter cup of my existence.[126]

[171]–[172] [blank]

[173] In verses which have been shown me of late, I see a higher faith, a higher inspiration, than has breathed from lives for a long time back.[127] They mourn not over the blight of external disaster, the rebuff of the world, or the crash of affections; but for nobleness unachieved, high faculties left inert, & the circle of beauty broken, which we feel we ought to reunite. Such thoughts seem to announce a flux of waters which may one day pile up Miltonic peaks on the shore.

[174]–[175] [blank]

[176] S.G.W. says How can you describe a Force? How can you write the life of Margaret?
Well, the question itself is some description of her.

[177] [128] ↑June, 1868.

I find in my old journal, *F*[2]⟨6⟩57, a page describing a Conversation with Margaret.↓

[178]–[179] [blank]

[180] To EH March, 1842.

My inward life has been rich & deep, & of more calm & musical flow than ever before. It seems to me, that Heaven, whose course has ↑ever↓

[126] This paragraph, struck through in pencil with a vertical use mark, is used in *Memoirs*, I, 295.

[127] As Emerson indexes p. [173] under Caroline Sturgis, Margaret Fuller is undoubtedly referring to her poetry here.

[128] Laid in between pp. [176] and [177] are three loose, folded sheets, one light blue and two white, each bearing ink writing by Margaret Fuller, each appearing to be a letter, or portions of letters. One of the white sheets contains the three passages "He only . . . with already" which Emerson records on pp. [50]–[51] above. The "of a disposition . . . with already" passage on this laid-in Fuller letter is struck through in pencil, and also appears on p. [248] below. The other white sheet includes the passage "He always . . . *ame*" which Emerson records on p. [237] below.

been to crossbias me, as Herbert said, is no niggard in its compensations.[129] I have indeed been forced to take up old burdens, from which I thought I had learned what they ⟨w⟩could teach. The pen has been snatched from my hand just as I ↑most↓ longed to give myself to it. I have been forced to dissipate, when I most wished to concentrate; ⁿ [181] to feel the hourly presence of others' mental wants, when it seemed I was just on the point of satisfying my own. &c &c. But a new page was turned, & an era begun, from which I am not yet sufficiently remote to describe it, as I would. I have lived a life, if only in the music I have heard,—& one development seemed to follow another therein, as if bound together by destiny, & all things done for me. All minds, all scenes have ministered to me; nature has seemed an ↑ever↓ open secret; the Divine, a sheltering love; Truth, an always springing [182][130] fountain, & my own soul more alone & less lonely, more hopeful, more patient, &, above all, more gentle, & humble, in its living.

New minds have come to reveal themselves to me, though I do not wish it, for I feel myself inadequate to the ties already formed. I have not strength or time to meet the thoughts of those I love already.ⁿ But these new have come with gifts too fair to be refused, & which have cheered my passive mind.[131]

[183] ↑*To EH* March 1842↓

I ⟨was⟩wish ⁿ I could write you often, to bring before you the varied world scene you cannot so well go out to unfold for yourself. ⟨I think⟩ But it ⟨is⟩ ↑was↓ never permitted me even where I wished it most. I think less than a daily offering of thought & feeling would not content me[,] so much seems to pass unspoken each day.[132] But the forest leaves fall unseen & make a soil on which shall be reared the growths & fabrics of a nobler era. This thought rounds off each day. Your letter was a little golden key to a whole volume of thoughts & feelings. I cannot make the one bright drop, like champagne in ice, but must pour a full gush if I speak at all, & not think [184] whether the water is clear either.[133]

Richard read me something from the Greek, for he did not wish to talk about little Waldo. It was to this effect: "All things return to thee, o Proserpine! But all things that go to the earth become beautiful. Venus poured out her tears for Adonis's wounds, yet all was turned to flowers; for each drop of blood, a rose; for each tear, an anemone." [134]

[129] With this sentence, cf. p. [128] above.

[130] "*to EH* March 1842" is added at the top of p. [182].

[131] "My inward life . . . mind.", struck through in pencil with single vertical use marks on pp. [180], [181], and [182], is used in *Memoirs*, I, 309–310.

[132] This sentence is marked in the left margin with a vertical pencil line.

[133] "I . . . wish . . . either.", struck through in pencil with single vertical use marks on pp. [183] and [184], is used in *Memoirs*, I, 285–286.

[134] "Richard read . . . anemone.' " is struck through in pencil with a vertical use mark.

[185]–[189] [blank]
[190] to RWE April, 1841.

I am glad Henry T[horeau] is coming to you; *that*[n] seems feasible. No, I have not heard the result of your projects, but I thought you were not sufficiently in light as to what you wanted, to succeed. Cela n'est pas votre metier, je crois. All you could hope would be some instructive blunder. Let others cook the *potage*, and you examine the recipe.

[191] The only solution to be given of the impression she made was some intrinsic grandeur[.]

Her features were dis⟨g⟩agreeable to most persons so long as they were little acquainted with her, that is until the features were dissolved in the power of ↑the↓ expression;[135]

[192] So I should say of this repeated account of sumptuousness of dress, I think *that*,[n] like her beauty seen by some persons, was simply an effect of general impression of magnificence made by her ⟨—⟩& mistakenly attributed to some external ⟨p⟩ elegance for I have ⟨inquired of⟩ ↑been told by↓ one ⟨who should be exactly informed⟩ ↑of her most intimate friends who knew↓ ⟨of⟩ every particular respecting her at that very time, & learn that [193] there was nothing of special expense or splendour in her toilette.[136]

[194]–[199] [blank]
[200] ↑Margaret Fuller Ossoli↓
Economics[137] *To Mary Rotch*[n] Tivoli 1848
"My uncle in his will left me no legacy. After the legacies were paid, I came in, with 62 other heirs, for my share of what was left,—less than a thousand dollars, of which I owed at that time ⟨f⟩near four hundred."

What was the agreement with Mr Greeley?[138]

[135] With "Her features . . . expression;", cf. *Memoirs*, I, 202, 337, and Journal BO, p. [49] above.

[136] This paragraph is used in *Memoirs*, I, 337.

[137] This word is in pencil, underlined in ink.

[138] Horace Greeley engaged Margaret Fuller to write travel letters for his paper at $8.00 per dispatch; see Joseph Deiss, *The Roman Years of Margaret Fuller* (New York, 1969), p. 20.

What with the Springs? [139]

⟨S⟩O

1835, October 25. After her father's death.—"It appears there will not be more than 21 000 & that we children shall not have above 2000 each." [140]

[201] Rome 16 Dec., 1847. Sum total of my expenses here for 6 months, will not exceed 400, or at most, $450: with the Marchesa.[141]

In 1837, she engaged with Hiram Fuller of the Greene Street School in Providence. She was to have $1000. a year, for services in the school, of four hours daily.— [142]

---

[202]–[203] [blank]

[204] To Ellen Channing, Florence, Dec. 11, 1849.

During the siege of Rome I could not see my little boy. In the burning sun I went every day to wait in the crowd for letters about him. Often they did not come. I saw blood that had streamed on the wall close to where Ossoli was. I have here a piece of bomb that burst close to him. I sought solace in tending the suffering men, but when I saw the beautiful fair young men bleeding to death or mutilated for life, I felt all the wo of all the mothers who had nursed each to that full flower to see it thus cut down.[143]

[205]–[208] [blank]

[209] Others lean on this arm which I have found so frail. Perhaps it was strong enough to have drawn a sword, but no better suited to be used as a *bolt*,[n] than that of Lady Catherine Douglas of loyal memory.[144]

[139] "What was . . . Springs?" and the three short rules are in pencil. Marcus and Rebecca Spring of New York proposed that Margaret Fuller join them on a tour of Europe, to be paid for in part by her taking care of their twelve-year-old son, Eddie.

[140] Margaret Fuller's father, Timothy, died on October 1, 1835.

[141] See p. [129] above.

[142] Colonel Hiram Fuller (1814–1880), not a relative, founded the Greene Street School to which he invited Emerson to give the dedicatory address, 10 June, 1837; later, he was connected with the New York *Mirror* and became editor of the London *Cosmopolitan*. With this entry, cf. *Memoirs*, I, 176.

[143] This entry is used in *Memoirs*, II, 278–279.

[144] This paragraph, struck through in pencil with a vertical use mark, is used in *Memoirs*, I, 286.

[210] ↑*To Lewis Cass, Jr.*↓

Fate./

Your letter was dated 5 Sept ⟨on the anniversary of⟩ ↑which is↓ [the] birthday of my little boy.[145] ⟨5 Sept⟩ "I wish I had received it then. I had, instead, the letter of the London publishers, which, indeed, I had foreseen, from previous advices, or rather perhaps, from a feeling of fate. It has been my fate, that when I worked for others, I ⟨should⟩ ↑could always↓ succeed; when I tried to keep the least thing for myself, it was not permitted."

From Georgiana Bruce to Mrs W.E.C.[146] *Santa Cruz Apr., 1851.*

"When I first met Miss Fuller, I was[n] already cut from my moorings, & was sailing the broad sea of [211] experience, conscious that I possessed unusual powers of endurance, & that I should meet with sufficient to test this strength. She made no offer of guidance, & once or twice, in the succeeding years, alluded to the fact that she 'had never helped me.' This was in a particular sense, of course; for she helped who knew her. She was interested in my rough history, but could not be intimate with one so unbalanced⟨;⟩,—a soul so inharmonious as mine then was: &, on my part, I reverenced her. She was to me the embodiment of wisdom & tenderness. I heard her converse, [212] & in the rich & varied intonations of her voice, I recognized a being to whom every ⟨h⟩shade of sentiment was familiar. She knew, if not by experience, then by unquestionable intuition how to interpret the inner life of every man & woman, &, by interpreting, she could soothe & strengthen. To her, psychology was an open book. When she came to Brook-Farm, it was my delight to wait on one so worthy of all service, to arrange her late breakfast in some remnants of ancient china [213] & save her, if it might be, some little fatigue or annoyance during each day." [147]

To C.S. 16 March 1849.

"All life that has been or could be natural to me, is invariably denied." [148]

[145] Margaret Fuller's son, Angelo Ossoli, was born September 5, 1848. She wrote Lewis Cass, Jr., U.S. envoy, asking for help in getting out of Rome shortly after the French entered the city in 1849.

[146] Georgianna Bruce, an English girl, had been a governess in Dr. Ezra Gannett's household before joining Brook Farm.

[147] " 'When I first . . . day.' ", struck through in pencil with single vertical use marks on pp. [210], [211], [212], and [213], is used in *Memoirs*, II, 79.

[148] This sentence, struck through in pencil with a vertical use mark, is used in *Memoirs*, I, 226.

To CS Rome 11 Jan. 1848.

My days at Milan were not unmarked. I have known some happy hours, but they all lead to sorrow, & not only the cups of wine but of milk seem drugged with poison for me. It does not seem to be my fault,—this destiny: I do not court [214] these things, they come. I am a poor magnet with power to be wounded by the bodies I attract.[149]

[215]–[219] [blank]

[220] I have no good reason to give for what I think of M. It is a demoniacal intimation. Every body at W. praised her, but their account of what she said gave me the same ↑unfavorable↓ feeling.[150] This is the first instance in which I have not had faith, if you liked a person. Perhaps I am wrong now; perhaps, if I saw her, a look would give me a needed clue to her character, & I should change my feeling. I do not judge her till I have seen her for my self: yet I have never been mistaken in these intimations that I recollect. I hope I am now.[151]

[221] [blank]

[222][152] ↑Of *M.M.E.*↓ To E.H. *Newbury, Oct., 1841.*

Your Aunt Mary too has been to see us, but the best I have got from her is to understand as I suppose W[aldo]. better. Knowing such a person who so perpetually defaces the high by such strange mingling of the low, I can better conceive how the daily bread of life should seem to him gossip, & the natural relations sheaths from which the flower must burst & never remember them. It certainly is not pleasant to hear of God & Miss ⟨Gage⟩ ↑Biddeford↓ in a breath.[153] [223] Still some sparkles show where the

[149] "My days . . . attract.", struck through in pencil with single vertical use marks on pp. [213] and [214], is used in *Memoirs*, I, 226. In addition to the use marks struck through individual passages on p. [213], as described above, the full page is struck through with a single vertical use mark in pencil.

[150] The ms. of this letter, from Margaret Fuller to Caroline Sturgis, Groton, February 2, 1839, is in the Houghton Library. "M." is Maria White, a member of one of her conversation classes, and later wife of James Russell Lowell, and "W." is Waltham.

[151] This paragraph is struck through in pencil with a vertical use mark.

[152] Pp. [222] and [223] show unusual pencil markings. "Your Aunt Mary too" is enclosed in a penciled box; "I can better . . . remember them." is enclosed in penciled square brackets, joined by a pencil line; "Still some . . . the rubbish." is also enclosed in penciled square brackets. The cancellations of "Gage" and "dipping" are in pencil, as are the insertions "Biddeford" and "skimming".

[153] Miss Gage is unidentified. Emerson may be supplying "Biddeford", a town in Maine, to conceal the real person's name.

gems might in better days be more easily disengaged from the rubbish. She is still valuable as a disturbing force to the lazy. But, to me, this hasty attempt at ⟨dipping⟩ ↑skimming↓ from the deeps of theosophy, is as unpleasant as the rude vanity of reformers. Dear Beauty! where, where amid these morasses & pine barrens shall we make thee a temple? Where find a Greek to guard it⟨!⟩ Clear-eyed, deep-thoughted, & delicate to appreciate the relations gradations which Nature always observes.[154]

[224] [blank]

[225] ⟨She⟩ ↑Margaret Fuller↓ was every where a welcome guest. The houses of her friends in town & country were open to her, & every[n] hospitable attention was eagerly offered. Her arrival was a holiday, & so was her abode. She stayed a few days, ⟨son⟩ often a week, more seldom a month and all tasks that could be suspended were put aside to catch the favorable hour in walking, riding, or boating to ⟨accompany &⟩[155] talk with this joyful guest who brought wit, anecdotes, lovestories, tragedies, oracles, with her, & with [226] her broad web of relations to so many fine friends, seemed like the Queen of some parliament of love, who carried the key to all confidences, & to whom every question had been finally referred. ⟨Every fine person⟩[156] Persons were her game; a marked person—marked by fortune or character,—these were her victims; to these was [227] she sent. She addressed them with a hardihood, almost haughty assurance, queenlike: indeed they fell in her way, where the access might have seemed difficult, by wonderful casualties; and the inveterate recluse, the coyest maid, the most wayward poet, disappointed all the bystanders by making no resistance, but yielding at discretion, as if they had been waiting for her,—all doors to this imperious dame. She drew them at once to the most surprising conf⟨idences⟩essions [228] ⟨they⟩.[n 157] She was the wedding guest to whom the long-pent story must be told,[158] and they were not less astonished on reflection ⟨than⟩ at the suddenness of the friendship which had established in one day

[154] This entry, struck through in pencil with single vertical use marks on pp. [222] and [223], is used in *Memoirs*, I, 315. The exclamation point after "Beauty", the comma after "where", and the question mark after "temple" are in pencil.

[155] Canceled in pencil.

[156] Canceled in pencil.

[157] See Journal AZ, p. [234] above.

[158] Undoubtedly a reference to Coleridge's "The Ancient Mariner."

new & permanent relations. She ⟨called⟩ extorted the secret of life which cannot be told without setting heart & mind in a glow, & thus had the best of those she saw. Whatever romance, whatever virtue, [229] whatever impressive ⟨lines fate or genius had written⟩ ↑experience↓[—]this came to her and she lived in a superior circle,—for they forgot or suppressed all their commonplace in her presence.

She was perfectly true to this confidential trust. She never confounded relations, but kept a hundred fine threads in her hand without crossing or entangling any. Total intimacy.
⟨T⟩An absolute all-confiding intimacy ⟨with one⟩ ↑between her & another,↓ which seemed to make ⟨them⟩ ↑both↓ sharers of the whole horizon of each [230] other's & of all truth, did not yet make her false to any other friend,[n] gave no title to the history that an equal trust of another friend had put in her keeping. In this reticence was no prudery & no effort, for[n] so rich her mind,—that she was never ⟨drawn⟩ tempted to treachery by the desire of entertaining: f⟨i⟩or her opulent mind the day was never long enough to exhaust, & I who have known [231] her intimately for ↑ten↓ years from ↑July 1836↓[n] till ↑Aug 1846↓ when she left this country never saw her without some surprise at her new powers.[159]

The same power followed her into all circles. In England ↑& Scotland↓, I met people who gave the same testimony to her eloquence & in ⟨France⟩ Paris though more than usually tormented by finding herself dispossessed of her natural weapon in the embarrassment of ↑speaking↓ a new language, she yet learned French fast enough[160] [232] to establish the like commanding interest in a circle of superior people. She had a day with Madame Sand. She became intimate with Micievickski, she saw Lamennais, & Beranger, Francois, the Editor of La Revue Independante.[161]

[159] In this sentence, "ten", "July 1836" and "Aug 1846" are added in pencil. In addition to the page-length vertical use mark indicated in note 160, "her intimately for . . . powers." is struck through in pencil with six diagonal use marks.

[160] "Margaret Fuller was . . . enough" is struck through in pencil with single vertical use marks on pp. [225], [226], [227], [228], [229], [230], and [231]; "Margaret Fuller was . . . new powers." is used in *Memoirs*, I, 213–215.

[161] Margaret Fuller met George Sand in Paris, January 18, 1847, and in Naples, March 17, 1847; Adam Mickiewicz (1798–1855) was a Polish poet; Ferdinand François was coeditor of *La Revue Indépendante*, in which Margaret Fuller published an essay on American literature. For La Mennais, see p. [92] above.

⟨When she pass⟩ She had already in London made the acquaintance of Mazzini, & at Rome she found herself his friend, his Counsellor. Here too Madame Arconati who relates that ⟨the⟩ her friends think she has bewitched her [See letter, p 67].

[233][162] ⟨Q⟩The ⟨r⟩test of this eloquence too was its range. It was efficacious on children & on old people, it was felt by people of the world as well as by sainted maids. She could hold them all by her honied tongue. Mrs Ripley said, "she stood herself in certain awe of her monied neighbors, the manufacturers, &c. knowing they would have small interest in Plato or in Biot, but that ⟨when they⟩[163] she saw them approach Margaret with perfect security, for *she* could give them bread that they could eat."[164]

[234] And of the ⟨s⟩ conversations above described, namely, with recluses & scholars, ⟨the⟩ I meant to say the substance of them was whatever was suggested by her passionate wish for noble companions, to the end of making life altogether noble. With the firmest tact she led the conversation into the midst of their daily living & working, recognising the goodwill & sincerity which each man has in his aims, & treating so playfully & intellectually all the points, that one seemed to see his life *en beau* [235] or in a fine mirage, & was flattered by seeing what was ordinarily so tedious in its workday ⟨c⟩ weeds shining in ⟨so⟩ glorious costume. He delighted to see ⟨all⟩ each of his friends in the new light, and hope seem⟨d⟩ed to spring under his feet, & life was worth living. The auditor could not conceal his delight & surprise or his thirst for unlimited draughts: What,—is this the dame whom I heard was sneering & critical, this the [236] bluestocking of whom I stood in terror & dislike,—this wondrous woman full of counsel, full of nobleness, who carries an atmosphere, before whom every mean thing is ashamed & hides itself—

wondrous woman of manifold gifts, sportive, eloquent, who seems to have learned all languages,—heaven knows when or how:

[162] Pp. [233]–[236], comprising one folded sheet of two leaves, are loose; though in texture, size, and color the leaves appear identical to those in the notebook, there is no evidence that this sheet was ever bound into the sewn book.

[163] Canceled in pencil.

[164] The entry on p. [233], struck through in pencil with a vertical use mark, is used in *Memoirs*, I, 215–216.

I should think she was born to them, magnetic, im⟨|| . . . ||ing⟩plying so much more than she says, magnificent —[165]

[237] She was a heroine to her chambermaid[.][166]

lyrical glances was a favorite expression. It came from George Sand, who speaks of an artist whose ambition outwent his genius; — "He always found himself obliged at last to translate into the vulgar language '*les élans lyrique*↑*s*↓ *de son âme*.ⁿ' "[167]

↑and from Campbell↓[168]

[238] ——

"Cursed with every granted prayer."[169]

[Pope, *Moral Essays*, Ep. II, l. 147]

——

"Many harps are tuned to sing one lay."

——

"A flame tormented by the wind."[170]

[239]–[247] [blank]

[248] I find the following detached fragment of M.'s on a loose bit of paper[:]

"Of a disposition that requires the most refined the most exalted tenderness, without charms to inspire it. — Poor Mignon! fear not the transition through death. No hell can have in store worse torments than thou art familiar with already."[171]

23 March, 1840.

[165] The entries on pp. [234], [235], and [236], struck through in pencil with single vertical use marks, are used in *Memoirs*, I, 215.

[166] This sentence is in pencil.

[167] See n. 128 above; Journal CO, p. [89] above; and Margaret Fuller to Emerson, June 3, 1839, in Houghton Library: "nor could I utter it forth again unless I had the gift of doing so by 'lyrical glances.' "

[168] Added in pencil. Margaret Fuller discusses Campbell's poetry in her essay "Modern British Poets" in *Papers on Literature and Art*. See *The Writings of Margaret Fuller*, ed. Mason Wade (New York, 1941), p. 315.

[169] This quotation is used in *Memoirs*, II, 266, and "Fate," *W*, VI, 46–47; see Journal CO, p. [71] above.

[170] See p. [1] above.

[171] See pp. [50]–[51] above.

[249] *May, 1844.*

I cannot help wearying myself of this ugly cumbrous mass of flesh. When all things are blossoming, it seems so strange not to blossom too; that the quick thought within cannot remould its tenement. Man is the slowest aloes, & I am such a shabby plant, of such coarse tissue. I hate not to be beautiful, when all around is so.[172]

[250] Her confidence in herself was boundless, & was frankly expressed. She told S.G.W. that she had seen all the people worth seeing in America, & was satisfied that there was no intellect comparable to her own.—

"With the intellect I always have—always shall overcome, but that is not the half of the work. The life, the life, o my God! shall the life never be sweet?" [173]

Journal May, 1844
p. 118

"Incedo Regina" see ⟨above⟩ p 23 of this *Ossoli* Book.
And the passage on Education in Journal May, 1844, p. 78—[174]
↑Ellen Fuller & Belinda Randall complained that she put herself on them & allowed them no chance. B. R. resisted this & still does with petulance, jealous [251] of another's influence;↓ [175]

⟨She⟩ ↑M.↓ could easily astonish any company by such a speech ↑as that to S[amuel].W[ard].↓ but the tone of her journals is humble, religious, prayerful.[176]

"Last year, I wrote of Woman, & proudly painted myself as Miranda." [177]

[172] Except for the first sentence, this paragraph, struck through in pencil with a vertical use mark, is used in *Memoirs*, I, 291–292.

[173] "Her confidence . . . sweet?'" is struck through in pencil with a vertical use mark; "She told . . . sweet?'" is used in *Memoirs*, I, 234, 237; see Journal CO, p. [140] above.

[174] "'Incedo . . . p. 78—" is struck through in pencil with a diagonal use mark; see p. [23] above and p. [251] below.

[175] Ellen Fuller was Margaret's sister; Belinda Randall was a singer who gave recitals in Concord.

[176] "⟨She⟩ M . . . prayerful.", struck through in pencil with a diagonal use mark, is used in *Memoirs*, I, 238.

[177] Margaret Fuller's reference here is undoubtedly to her article "The Great Lawsuit," *The Dial*, IV (July 1843), 1–47, where Miranda appears.

Journal May, 1844.

May, 1844.

Mrs ↑H[enry].↓ Ware talked with me about education, (I mean wilful education) in which she is trying to get interested. I talk with a Goethean moderation on this subject, which rather surprizes her, & Anna Lowell, who are nearer the entrance of the studio.[178] I am really old on this subject, in near 8 years' experience. [252] I have learnt as much as others would in 80, from my great talent at explanation, tact in the use of means, & immediate & invariable power over the minds of my pupils. My wish has been more & more to purify my own conscience when near them, give clear views of the aims of this life; show them where the magazines of knowledge lie, & leave the rest to themselves, & the spirit, who must teach & help them to self impulse. I told Mrs W. it was so much if we did not injure them, [253] if they were passing the time in a way that was *not bad*, so that good influences have a chance. Perhaps people in general must expect greater outward results, or they would feel no interest.[179]

Tolga il ciel che alcuno
Piu altamente di me pensi ch'io stesso.[180]
[Alessandro] *Manzoni's* [*Conti di*] *Carmagnola.*
[III, iii, 178–179]

I feel within myself an immense power, but I cannot bring it out. A barren vinestock, no grape will swell, tho' richest wine is slumbering at its root. I never doubt my eventual perfection, though I doubt whethe⟨th⟩r this climate will ripen my fruit.

[254] I said, I felt an immense power. It may seem a joke, but I do feel something correspondent to that tale of the Destinies falling in love with Hermes.[181]

[178] Mary Lovell Pickard Ware (1798–1849) went to Milton, Mass., in 1844, after the death of her husband, to instruct small children. Anna Lowell is probably the daughter of John Lowell, "the little Rebel" (1769–1840), Boston lawyer, political writer, and philanthropist.

[179] This entry, struck through in pencil with single vertical use marks on pp. [251], [252], and [253], is used in *Memoirs*, I, 236–237.

[180] "Tolga il . . . stesso.", struck through in pencil with a vertical use mark, is used in *Memoirs*, I, 238.

[181] "I said . . . Hermes.", struck through in pencil with a vertical use mark, is used in *Memoirs*, I, 236. For the last sentence, see Journal CO, p. [179] above.

[255] [blank]

[256] To RWE Groton 1st Sept., 1836.

I was entertained by the discussions at the Institute, particularly by Mr Frederick Emerson's horror at the idea of this common earth being peopled by gods, "an idea upon which he would not dilate —" [182]

[257] [blank]

[258] The unlooked for trait in all these journals to me is the Woman, poor woman: they are all hysterical. She is bewailing her virginity and languishing for a husband.

"I need help. No, I need a full, a godlike embrace from some sufficient love." &c. &c.

See too Journal June, 1844 p 67 [183]
and p ⟨5⟩49 May, 1844. "Where is Hector?"
This I doubt not was all the more violent recoil from the exclusively literary & "educational" connections ⟨w⟩in which she had lived.
Mrs Spring ⟨said⟩told me that Margaret said to her, "I am tired of these literary friendships, I long to be wife & mother."

[259] A tone of sadness was in her voice like the wail of the ocean. And from my earliest acquaintance I had a feeling as if some one cried *Stand from under!* [184]

[260] The feeling she excited among good sort of people like Mary R[otch] &c was that she was sneering, scoffing, critical, disdainful of humble people, & of all but ↑the↓ intellectual, I had, I remember, some feeling in my early acquaintance with her of the unprofitableness of all this derision & joking & crackling of thorns under a pot. It was a superficial judgment. Her journals are throughout religious, tearful, tragic in their ⟨comparis⟩ tenderness & compunction at shortcomings, and the tone of [261] conversation was

[182] "I was . . . dilate —' " is struck through in pencil with a diagonal use mark.

[183] "See too . . . p 67" is in pencil.

[184] This sentence, struck through in pencil with a vertical use mark, is used in *Memoirs*, I, 228.

only the pastime & necessity of her talent.[185] Miss Gardiner & the rest all testify to her extreme candour & tenderness, to every feeblest expression of opinion from any member of her class. She made the most of it, & with what goodness of heart.

[262] I fear that M.'s eyes were ⟨so prismatic⟩ not achromatic, but so affectionate, active, & radiant, that, though I have perfect confidence in her integrity, I have none in the accuracy of her vision. When she gives a judgment on any music, picture, statue, book, or genius, I have no belief that I should in the same place see what she saw.[186]

[263]–[264] [blank]
[265] *Note from M.M.E.* to RWE. *Aug., 1850.*

"I think if she had survived only her husband and been impressed with that kind of grief which gives a sort of immortality to certain minds we read about.[n] ⟨h⟩Her expression &c &c — I may as well confess — that in taking an interest in her fate, I do not love to remember her want of beauty. She looked very sensible, but as if contending with ill health & duties. Had I been favored with one sparkle of her fine wit, — one argument for her dissent[n] ⟨from her fine mind⟩, — what a treasure to memory. She lay all the day & eve. on sofa, & catechised me, who told my literal traditions [266] like any old bobbin woman." [187]

---

[267] ↑Counsel↓

"Be to the best thou knowest ever true." [188]

[268] 1844, July 3.

Passed the morning in Sleepy Hollow with E. H. very profitably. What fine just distinctions she ma⟨kes⟩de. Worlds grew clearer as we talked. She said she would have for a motto,

[185] "The feeling . . . talent." is struck through in pencil with vertical use marks on pp. [260] and [261].

[186] This entry is struck through in pencil with a diagonal use mark; cf. *Memoirs*, I, 267–268.

[187] " 'She looked [p. [265]] . . . woman.' " is used in *Memoirs*, I, 315.

[188] "Counsel" is added in pencil. " 'Be to . . . true.' ", struck through in ink with a vertical use mark, is used in *Memoirs*, I, 282, and also occurs in a poem by Margaret Fuller, "Sub Rosa Crux," l. 44, *Memoirs*, II, 115.

"In Arcady I too was born [189]
Tho' now a maiden all forlorn
I milk the cow with the crumpled horn."

[269] [blank]

[270] *Sex.* Journal July, 1844.

How all but infinite the mystery by which sex is stamped on the germ! By what modification of thought is this caused? Impossible to trace. Here am I the child of masculine energy, & Eugene of feminine loveliness; & so in many other families.

A man's ambition with a woman's heart,—'tis an accursed lot.[190]

[271] Her life was concentrated on certain happy days, happy hours, happy moments. ⟨S⟩The rest was a mere blank. She had read in DeVigny that a ⟨literary⟩ man of letters must lose many days to work well on one. Much more must a Sappho or a Sibyl. She remembers, in June 1844, a moment, years before, when S[amuel]. W[ard]. ⟨brot he⟩ & she saw snowdrops at the foot of a rock. "It passed quick, as such beautiful moments do, & we had never such another." [191]

[272] May, 1844.

"If I had wist"—I am a worse self-tormentor than Rousseau, & all my riches are fuel to the fire. My beautiful lore, like the tropic Clime, hatches sc⟨r⟩orpions to sting me. There is a verse Annie of Lochrayan s⟨ing⟩ays about her ring, that torments my memory, it is so true of my conduct.[192]

[189] Schiller, "Resignation," l. 1: "Auch ich war in Arkadien geboren"; *Sämmtliche Werke*, 12 vols. (Stuttgart, 1853), I, 84, and the motto of Goethe's *Travels in Italy*. In Notebook OP Gulistan, p. [49], Emerson records this line and the poetry following.

[190] This sentence, struck through in pencil with a vertical use mark, is used in *Memoirs*, I, 229.

[191] This paragraph is struck through in pencil with a vertical use mark; "Her life . . . Sibyl." is used in *Memoirs*, I, 227–228.

[192] "'If I had . . . conduct.", struck through in pencil with a vertical use mark, is used in *Memoirs*, I, 228. The "verse Annie of Lochrayan s⟨ing⟩ays about her ring" is quoted in *Memoirs*, I, 293, and is from Sir Walter Scott's "The Lass of Lochroyan," ll. 77–80.

[273] ⟨Whe⟩
In Italy, ⟨‖ . . . ‖⟩Miciwicski[193] wished to divorce himself in order to marry Margaret; Mazzini, it is reported, offered marriage: & Ossoli[,] a young nobleman[,] prosecuted his suit against all denial, & married her. When I expressed surprise at this series of conquests,[n] E[lizabeth]H[oar] replied, It is not at all wonderful. Any ⟨of⟩one of those fine girls of sixteen she had known here, would have married her, if she had been a man. For she understood them.[194]

To W[illiam].H[enry].C[hanning]. she writes, Rome, March 10, 1849, "I have been, since we parted, the object of great love from the noble & the humble. I have felt it [274] towards both. Yet a kind of chartered libertine, I rove pensively always, in deep sadness often; 'O God help me,' is all my cry."[195]

[275]–[276] [blank]
[277] "I have talent & knowledge enough to furnish a dwelling for friendship, but not enough to deck with golden gifts a Delphos for the World."[196]

[278] A gallery was a home to her.

[279] [blank]
[280] To RWE Nov., 1841.

My little eyrie promises well & is at this moment made beautiful by the presence of a bouquet of roses, geraniums, & heliotrope. The neighborhood of Sarah Clarke casts the mildness & purity, ⟨of⟩too, of the moonbeam on the else particoloured scene.[197] I have three pupils for my afternoons,—Carrie, Marianne Jackson, & Anna Shaw.

[193] The word is preceded by what looks like an earlier attempt to spell "Mickiewicz," plus three to four more words; all are finger-wiped and overwritten by "Miciwicski wished to".

[194] "In Italy . . . them.", struck through in pencil with a curved, discontinuous vertical use mark, is used in *Memoirs*, I, 281.

[195] " 'O God . . . cry.' " is used in *Memoirs*, II, 302.

[196] This sentence, struck through in pencil with a vertical use mark, is used in *Memoirs*, I, 295.

[197] This sentence, struck through in pencil with a vertical use mark, is used in *Memoirs*, I, 207.

[281]–[283] [blank]

[284] At Blackwell's Island, Ma⟨g⟩rgaret was left alone with a female prisoner who was in bad health & likely to die.[198] She ⟨w⟩ bore a very bad character[,] a hardened ⟨impracticable⟩ ↑cold sulky↓ person.

Margaret asked her if she was willing to die? She answered, "⟨y⟩Yes," —and then, with her usual bitterness, added, "not on religious grounds, though." Margaret replied,[n] "That is well, to understand one's self." Presently ⟨the⟩she began to talk with her about her health & condition with increasing interest, and, on rising to go, [285] said, "Is there not anything I can do for you?" The woman said, "I should be glad if you would pray with me." Margaret was ⟨tou⟩ surprised & touched. She stayed & prayed with her.

There was in our house a handsome Catherine who had been a vicious street girl in Boston, & was brought here ↑to do housework↓ by Mrs Goodwin, after an attempt by C. to kill herself. M. asked Elizabeth H. if she could not help her. [28⟨5⟩6] E replied, no, she could do nothing for her. She should be so conscious of what she had heard about her in talking with her, that it would be painful to the girl.—M. was quite indignant at this weakness. The girl you know is now taken away from all her life, & will feel the vacuity. ⟨She⟩ ↑Her mind↓ must be employed & she led to know & feel her powers.[199] And it was easy to see that if this girl had ⟨f⟩ been in M.'s neighborhood she would have devoted herself to her education & in this way she served many souls.[200]

[287]–[289] [blank]

[290] *Chronology* ↑of Margaret Fuller↓ [201]

[198] In 1828 New York City purchased Blackwell's Island, site of a workhouse and prison, in the East River; its name was later changed to Welfare Island.

[199] "At Blackwell's . . . powers." is struck through in pencil with single vertical use marks on pp. [284] and [285] and with two vertical use marks on p. [286]. "At Blackwell's . . . with me.'" is used in *Memoirs*, II, 149; "There was . . . powers." is used in *Memoirs*, II, 130–131.

[200] "that if . . . souls.", struck through in pencil with a vertical use mark, is used in *Memoirs*, II, 131.

[201] "of ⟨M. F.⟩" in pencil underlies "of Margaret" in ink.

Born
1810 May ⟨22⟩ ↑23↓

1822 a wonderful child at Dr Park's School.

1827–8 Miss Peabody knew her with Amelia Greenwood

1832–3 "Began German," & "read in a year incredible number of books" E[lizabeth]P[almer]P[eabody]

1835 July 27. Set out on a journey with Mrs Farrar, Mrs Thorndike, Miss Dana, & S.G. Ward, to N.Y. & Trenton Falls. saw Anna Barker at Newport.

Aug. Harriet Martineau at Cambridge.

Oct. 1. Her father, Hon. Timothy Fuller died

1836 July 22. First visit at Concord

[291][202] 1837 Jan. Gave instruction in Mr Alcott's School. & reported. ↑May S.G.W. in Rome.↓ June. Green St School Providence R.I. ↑Anna B sailed for Europe.↓

1837 July. Sept. Oct. Nov. at Providence
Nov. 16. Letter to C[aroline].S[turgis]. on her father's misbehaviour

1838 Jan. At Providence. School very successful

July at Newport. Happiest
Sept. Walk with Calvert at Newport

1839 Jan. Groton. Feby. partook of Sacrament 3d time.
Translation ↑of Eckermann published June.↓

[202] Underlying the ink entries on p. [291] is erased pencil writing, covering the full page, an early version of the "chronology" on pp. [290] and [291], beginning "1835 July 27 . . ." and concluding "Translat⟨ed⟩ing Gunderode". One entry in the erased pencil writing is substantially different from the ink version: "[date?] Angry letter to CS on her father's treatment".

Apr. 1. Removed to Jamaica Plains
June. October. Correspondence with C.S.
↑June —— November. Occupied on *Goethe's Life*
20 Oct. with Mr Alcott at Concord
Nov. 6. Wednesday First Conversation on Mythology.↓

1840 July 5. Jamaica Plains
Aug. At Concord with Anna B., ↑&↓ Caroline S.
Sept. 26 } New mental states
Oct. 22 }
Oct. 3 S. G. W's marriage
Nov. class for Conversation. ↑⟨H⟩In her own hired house.↓

1841 Jan. unhappy. At Cambridge
May. at Concord
Aug. 31 at Cambridge. perfectly happy
⟨3.⟩ July 30 at Newport with C.S.
Sept. 29 W.E.C.'s marriage
Oct. 10 Translat⟨ed⟩ing Gunderode
Nov. Conversations began *P.M.*—3 pupils, CS., M.J., A.S—

[292] 1842 March Letter to E.H. see p.180
Apr. parting with C.S.
July. White Mountains—
Aug. 30, at Concord, with W.E.C. & R.W.E.
Sept.[203]

1843 ⟨Feb⟩ Died Waldo E. 27 Jan.[204]
1843 May 25 Set out on journey to the West
28 Niagara to 4 June
June 10 Chicago
24 left for Rock River
25 Geneva

[203] Underlying "1842 March . . . Sept" is erased pencil writing, an earlier version of the overlying matter in ink.

[204] "1843" and "Died . . . Jan." are in pencil, traced over in ink; "⟨Feb⟩" is in pencil only. Beginning with "1843 May 25 . . ." below, the remainder of p. [292], and pp. [293]–[297] are in pencil. Waldo died Jan. 27, 1842.

July 1 Hazelwood 9 30 1 July
happy time
8 Chicago full happy time
11 Milwaukee
Aug. 5 Back at Chicago
18, 19, Mackinaw
amiable Josephine
29 Sault St Marie
↑30 On River St Mary↓
Sept. 8 Buffalo
10 N. Y
12 Staten Island
16 Concord

[293] Margaret Fuller's Notes.

March 27 "time of almost unbearable anguish"

1844 May at Concord with W & S Clark & Caroline
May 23 wrote the last line of Summer on the Lakes [205]

Oct. Fishkill Singsing,
2⟨7⟩8 Nov. Left Fishkill
30 Nov. At Mr Greeley's N.Y. to reside
10 Nov. ⟨1⟨0⟩7⟩ Finished "*Woman in the XIX Century.*"

1845 NY July happy in her experience

Feby. Attempts cure of spine by magnetism
Dr Leger [206] March

Wom⟨e⟩an in XIX Cent.

[294] 1845
22 Nov. Year 1845 "has rent from me all I cherished, but

[205] *Summer on the Lakes* was announced for publication by Little & Brown in the Boston *Courier* of June 5, 1844.

[206] Théodore Léger, author of *Animal Magnetism; or, Psycodunamy* (New York, 1846), had an office at 74 Broadway in New York City.

has given me instead such great revelations. I have lived at last not only in rapture but in fact."[207]

1846 1 Jan. N.Y. fever⟨ish⟩ till 18th
Cassius Clay, Halleck

[295] 1846 1 August sailed for Europe ⟨in Cambria⟩in the Cambria.

16 Aug. writes from Liverpool. *Made the shortest passage ever known.* Stewardess said "Any one who complained this time tempted the Almighty."

Nov. 25 Paris, half dead with fatigue
Nov. 28 Paris
Dec. 26 Paris

↑1847↓ Jan. 31 Paris

1847 ↑Apr. 15 Rome May 7
1 July Florence↓
10 July Venice
Aug. 9 Milan
26 Bellaggio Lake of Como

Sept. 15 Florence at Mr Mozier's[208]
Oct. 28 Rome 29 Oct. *happy*, *alone*, & *free.*
Nov. 2 Rome

[296] 1847. ⟨26 Aug. Bellaggio, Lake of Como⟩
Rome 9 Dec., 47 had spent sweetly 2 of the 6 mos. she would pass in Rome
House expenses $50 per month
16 Dec. Rome
⟨Came to Rome 10 Oct., 1847⟩
Married ⟨perhaps⟩ in Oct. Nov. or Dec.

[207] Undoubtedly a reference to Margaret's unhappy love affair with James Nathan in New York.

[208] Joseph Mozier (1812–1870), American sculptor, had a studio in Rome from 1845.

1848 Jan. 11 Rome
Rome, 25 Feb. 1848
17 March ⟨Fr⟩Pains & headach from 16 Dec.
20 May 21 May goes to Rieti

July 3 Rieti
Rieti
Sept. 5, Angelo Eugene Ossoli was born/

Nov. 17 Rome 23 Nov.

Dec. 30 Rieti

1849
Feb. 23 Rome
[297] 1849 June 10 Rome ↑Since 30 April I go almost daily to the hospitals
1849 Aug. 28 Rieti 30 Apr. named Regolatrice F[ate-] B[ene] F[ratelli] Hospital↓
March 8 Rome

Nov. Florence police permit residence

Dec. 12 Florence
17

1850
Feb. Florence

May 14 Florence last letter to her mother

June 3 Gibraltar

July 19, Friday, dies on the rocks at Fire Island

[298][209]
[inside back cover] [Index material omitted]

209 Erased pencil writing, a preliminary index, covers this page.

Journal at the West

1850–1853

Emerson used this pocket notebook not only to keep track of expenses on several lecture tours to the West but also to make perceptive notes on places like the Mammoth Cave in Kentucky, the geography of the Mississippi, the state of agriculture and the local economy, and the quality of life and people in the West. Perhaps the best example of his terse observation and dry Yankee wit is the description of the beginnings of the University of Rochester, on pp. [46] and [47] below.

Journal at the West is a small pocket notebook with a black leather cover measuring 9.2 x 14.4 cm. A small label, marked in ink "Journal at the West / 1850", not in Emerson's hand, is pasted onto the cover. The pages, faintly ruled, measure 9.2 x 14.4 cm. They have two columns on the left and one on the right, for accounts. Including the front flyleaf there are 121 pages; none of them are numbered. Twelve pages are blank: 2–8, 13, 31, 32, 42, 44. Leaves bearing the following pages are torn out: 21–22, 65–66, 73–76, 95–96; and so is the back flyleaf. Glued to the inside back cover is a newspaper clipping with the title "Curiosities of the West."

[front cover]

[front cover verso] 1850

Cincinnati
Mammoth Cave
1851
Rochester
Niagara

1852–3
Cincinnati
St Louis
Springfield, Illinois

[i] [1] "At mihi succurrit pro Ganymede manus." [2]

Quum primum pavido custos mihi purpura cessit [3]
Persius [*Saturae*, Satura V, l. 30]

ap "My novel" p 121 [4]

[ii] *Vischer, Aesthetik oder Wissen⟨c⟩schaft des Schönen, Vol.* II. p 248. says, "that the virtues of the German race point specially ⟨in⟩to the family, & friendship, respect to w⟨‖ . . . ‖⟩omen; so that this winterly man shows his taste more in the apartments of a house, thro' beauty of private life, than on the street, through ⟨t⟩life abroad. This inwardness is the *eigensinn* of individuality, which does not reach to a whole. Also the race holds not loyally together. Many of them serve disloyally in Roman armies. Truth in private life, & untruth in public life, is very apparent in German peoples.↘" [5]

[1] 375 ft

From Boston to Albany	200 miles
Albany to Buffalo	325
Buffalo to Sandusky	250
Sandusky to Cincinnati	218 miles
Cincinnati to St Louis	350
	1343 [6]

---

deep & aukward

[1] "688" is inscribed in green pencil in the upper right corner of p. [i].

[2] For the line from Martial's *Epigrams*, see Journal TU, p. [105] above. The line is repeated in pencil just below.

[3] "When first as a timid youth I lost the guardianship of the purple".

[4] "At mihi . . . p 121" is in pencil. Emerson found the second quotation in Sir E. Bulwer-Lytton, *My Novel; or, Varieties in English Life*, 2 Parts (New York, 1852), Part I.

[5] Friederich Theodor Vischer, *Aesthetik oder Wissenschaft des Schönen, zum Gebrauche für Vorlesungen*, 5 vols. (Reutlingen and Leipzig, 1846–1854). Vischer is apparently summarizing from Tacitus.

[6] "375 ft . . . 1343" is in pencil.

[2]–[8] [blank]

[9][7] 1850, 25 May at Fort Ancient, Warren County, Ohio. All these alleged *remains* of the departed American race of 3000 years ago seem at first nothing more than the familiar "ridges" of Massachusetts such as I know in Concord woods, in Mount Auburn Cemetery, or, on the Ridge Road in Groton. ⟨T⟩Geologists call them *Osars* or *horsebacks*. Here, however, they are continued to a great extent, [10] between 4 & 5 miles in circuit, & return into the system; keep too about the same elevation from the interior plane or level of the Fort, & so present a very fort-like appearance. Very old trees stand on the very summit of this long-drawn parapet. A few well-⟨enough⟩ defined mounds [11] are here & there in the line of the works, and two or three piles of stones are found. No other trace of man is here. The forest is a magnificent colonnade of tulip-trees, rock maple, white oak, shagbark, black walnut, & beech. The fallen columns form natural bridges over every ravine, and enormous grapevines [12] depend like cables from the trees. In this sylvan Persepolis, I spent my birthday with a very intelligent party of young men, ⟨Mr⟩ James, Blackwell, Goddard, Spofford, Mathews, Collins, & was often reminded of my visit to Stonehenge with Carlyle in June 1848[.][8]

[13] [blank]

[14] The ⟨i⟩Kentuckian sits all day on his horse. You shall see him at the door of a country store. There he sits & talks & makes his bargains for hours, & never dismounts. When all is done, he spurs up his steed, & rides away.—The path of a tornado is traced through the forest, of the same width for [15] miles. They tell of a child wh⟨ich⟩o was carried five miles by one. This was too good to leave alone. So we presently heard of a tornado which drove a plough through a field, & turned as pretty a furrow all round the field as you ever saw. This, of course, suggested ⟨to another [16] of the company a⟩ ⟨the⟩ ↑a↓ storm in Havana where the wind blew so hard,

[7] Pp. [9]–[12] are in pencil.

[8] Of those not previously identified, Charles P. James was a Cincinnati judge; Henry B. Blackwell, an abolitionist; Stanley Matthews, a lawyer; Isaac C. Collins, a law student studying under Matthews.

that a man was left clinging to an iron lamp-post, with nothing on him but his stock & his spurs.[9]

[17] In riding from Sandusky to Cincinnati, I saw a great deal of rich bottom-land lying in single fields of a hundred acres & more, wheat & corn. Much of this land is never manured, & the proverb is that when the manure-heap grows very large, the farmer removes the barn [18] to get rid of it.[10]
Mr W. Greene tells me of a single field belonging to Mr Enoch, on the Big Miami River, which contains a thousand acres, & which yields 100 bushels of corn per acre. But he says when he told this story in [19] New England, gentlemen would always take wine with him.

At Cleveland, Mr Freese showed me a boy in his school, named ⟨Henry⟩ ↑Kennedy↓ Clinton, who was the best scholar, and who could give a good lecture ⟨i⟩on geology, chemistry, or algebra.[11] Today, 30 May, Mr Storer [20] showed me a boy in a Cincinnati public School named William Heinking, a German by birth, & who has been in this country but two years, who was at the head of his school, &, as his masters agreed, of unusual promise. In the German quarter of the city, the city employs German as well as [21]–[22] [leaf torn out]

[23] ⟨Mary E Herring ↑now↓
240 McAsker
75 Michael M'Asker
———
315 Appleton House
Lowell ⟨m⟩Mass⟩ [12]

⟨W. Goodman 4th St west of Smith⟩
⟨Dr I. Wilson, Fourth E of Broadway⟩
by MacAllister

[9] In this paragraph, the commas after "done", "steed", "field", "This", and "course" are in pencil.

[10] Emerson relates this same anecdote to his wife in a letter of May 20, 1850 (*L*, IV, 203).

[11] Andrew Freese became principal of the high school, superintendent of schools, and author of the first history of the schools of Cleveland.

[12] Michael McAsker wrote to Emerson from Lowell, March 16, 1850, regarding the estate of Mary E. McAsker (*L*, IV, 205).

⟨Dr Mitchell⟩
⟨Mr Barrett 8th 3d door east of Elm⟩
Mr Lawler 113 Broadway
Mr Storer n e corner 6 & Race
Mr Urner
Mr Brooks [13]

Why don't you go to Church? said Dr Chan[ning]
Because the ministers take too much for granted, saith H[are].[14]

[24] J. E. Goodson reads his favourite scores without any piano, & says, that, lying on his bed, he thinks them over, & enjoys them more than in any performance, so many faults belong to any execution. "Bach's music has the stability of a spur of the Rocky mountains;" Beethoven always verges on the supernatural. Do not believe too much, it seems to say, in the force of gravitation. I will lift you presently.

[25] Nothing is deep without religion.

The people do not let the Ohio river go by them without using it as it runs along. The waterworks supply the city abundantly, &, in every street, in these dusty days, it is poured on to the pavement. The water offered you to drink is as turbid as lemonade, & of a somewhat greyer hue. Yet it is freely drunk, & the inhabitants [26] much prefer it to the limestone water of their wells.

---

stoves
coal
iron

[13] "⟨Mary E . . . Brooks" is in pencil. Of those not previously identified, conjectural identifications are that William Goodman was president of an insurance company in Cincinnati; Ormsby MacKnight Mitchel (1809–1862) was director of the Cincinnati Observatory; Bellamy Storer (1798–1875), attorney, congressman 1835–1837, was judge of the Supreme Court in Cincinnati; Benjamin Urner was an insurance agent. "Mr. Brooks" may be either E. S. Brooks, educator, or Moses Brooks, bank director and member of the Board of Trustees of Wesleyan Female College. Dr. I. Wilson is otherwise unidentified.

[14] Robert Hare was a Philadelphia doctor.

corn
machinery
pork
room
blackeyes

---

drama indebted to

↑the↓ Catholic church

Church bells.

---

agre⟨a⟩eable churches

---

cholera resisted, limestone [15]

---

vineclad hills

---

lose a day [16]

---

beauty stowed away

---

river on fire [17]

---

obscurities

Star cave [18]

---

disposition to exaggerate [19]

[15] Cholera, widespread in St. Louis in the summer of 1850, was causing death in Emerson's hotel (*L*, IV, 216–217). Cf. Journal BO, p. [98] above.

[16] Emerson wrote Lidian from St. Louis, June 16 and 17, 1850, about how his trip to Kentucky's Mammoth Cave "lost one of the 'days'" of his life (*L*, IV, 213); cf. "Illusions," *W*, VI, 309.

[17] In a letter to his wife, Emerson describes the fires which occur on the Green River (*L*, IV, 211–212).

[18] The "Star Chamber" of Mammoth Cave is described in "Illusions," *W*, VI, 310, and in a letter to Lidian (*L*, IV, 213–214).

[19] "stoves . . . exaggerate" is in pencil. Pp. [27] and [28] following are also in pencil.

[27] 4 June. Took passage on board the Ben Franklin for Louisville with a party of ladies & gentlemen[,] Mr & Mrs Ward, Mr & Mrs Donaldson, Mr Gallagher, Miss K. Greene, Miss L. Briggs, Mrs I. Wilson, Miss F. ⟨W⟩Goodman, Mr Wiltsen, Mr Partridge, Mr Blackett, & Messrs Marshalls, Mr Shepard, & Miss Smith. Arrived at night safely at Louisville. No stage on the morning of 5th June for us to Mammoth Cave, no coaches nor horses for such a party. The regular coach was full & went at 5 AM[,] no other would go till Friday[,] nor then could accommodate us. [28] So we took passage by the ↑"↓Mammoth Cave"-Boat [n] which goes to Evansville & up the Green River and with many petty delays & breakages but no important misfortune we have come thus far to Cloversport, Ky, 130 miles from Louisville on this fine morning of 6 June.[20]

[29] outside of the cave is the best side
volutes and acanthus or celery formations [21]
We lost a day [22]

E Shepard
J R Wiltsie
F Donaldson
C A Partridge
W D Gallagher
J. W. Ward & Lady
Mrs George Donaldson

[20] The *Daily Cincinnati Gazette*, June 5, 1850, reported that Emerson visited the Mammoth Cave "with a number of the Literati of our city" (*L*, IV, 208). James Warner Ward (b. 1817), poet and botanist, later taught at the Female College of Ohio and edited the *Botanical Magazine*; William Davis Gallagher (1808–1894) was an editor, poet, and public official of Philadelphia; Katey Greene later married the German physician Friedrich Roelker; Mrs. Israel Wilson wrote Emerson from Cincinnati in December, 1850, asking permission to make a bronze bust of him, which she did when he returned in 1852; Fanny Goodman later married Learner Harrison; John R. Wiltsie, a harness and saddle dealer from Newburgh, N. Y., was visiting his sister in Cincinnati; Edwin Shepherd was a stereotyper and member of the Western Art Union.

[21] Writing to Lidian June 16 and 17, 1850, Emerson said he'd learned from "Cleveland's Cabinet" in Mammoth Cave that "the volutes & foliations of the capitals of columns were not learned from any basket of acanthus, but from the efflorescence of caves" and that "outside of the cave is the best side," (*L*, IV, 213).

[22] "outside . . . day" is in pencil.

Miss F Greene
Miss Smith
Miss Fanny Goodman
Miss Louisa Briggs
J. W. Marshall
G. H. Marshall
Montagu Blackett

[30] Mammoth Cave Hotel 10 June.[23]

[31]–[32] [blank]
[35] [24] All gov't is brought into disrepute. The governor is not worth his own cockade[;] he sits there to see the laws broken, every peaceable citizen endangered, & the best citizens[—]those who throw themselves on the part of the weak[—]insulted, hustled, & hurled to the wall by the riff raff[.]

[34] I thought he would have exhausted the means of legal ingenuity for the security & honor of those citizens whose sovereignty he represented. If he found no guard, no reserve of liberty, no security to the liberty of Mass. in her capital city, I thought he would have convened the legislature or made his proclamation [33] to the people that he found himself powerless & called on them to strengthen his hands or else consulted his honor as a man & resigned a chair he could not fill.[25]

[36] [26] Green River
Turkey duck sheldrake [27]

[23] "Mammoth . . . June." is in pencil.

[24] The following entry, "All govt . . . fill.", written upside down and in pencil, beginning on p. [35] and ending on p. [33], was probably written later than June, 1850, after Emerson's return home from one of his western trips.

[25] Emerson could be referring to any of several episodes after passage of the Fugitive Slave Law on September 18, 1850—the rescue of Shadrach in February or the return of Sims to slavery in April, 1851, when George S. Boutwell was governor; or the attempted rescue of Anthony Burns in May, 1854, when Emory Washburn was governor.

[26] Pp. [36]–[41] are in pencil.

[27] In a letter to his wife, Emerson writes: "In the Green River, we disturbed the ducks all the way before us . . . & wild turkeys flew before us from tree to tree" (*L*, IV, 211).

[37] Missisippi River
14 June
Cairo
Finished villages
Fever & ague shook the panes out
lonely river, no boats, no settlements
2/3 mile deer.
Ohio River, buffalo & catfish
gaming
Missisippi River about ½ a mile wide at St. Louis[;] above that, a mile to ¾ generally.

⟨E⟩On board the "Excelsior"

[38] At St Louis only Missouri water is drunk. The waters of the two streams are kept unmixed[,] the Missisippi on the east bank[,] the Missouri on the west until 40 miles below St Louis.
18 June. Under a bright moon about 9 o'clock pm I reached the mouth of the Missouri. Very sorry not to see this confluence by day. But at night it was very easy [39] to see the two volumes of water by their different colour, one muddy, & one black, & the force with which from its mighty mouth the Missouri drove the Missisippi towards ⟨its own⟩ ↑the Illinois↓ bank. I asked the Captain if the mouth of the Ohio were not as wide? "Perhaps it is but there is not so much water comes out of it. [40] It[n] pours in a high water, but it does not last but a little while." How deep is the water here? "From 20 to 50 feet." How fast ⟨d⟩is the current? "Three miles an hour." How fast do you go against it? "Six, six and a half, and seven." And ten miles down stream? Can you keep ten all day? "Yes."[n]

[41] Steamboat disasters are as common as musquitoes. At St Louis, 47 boats were burned between 17 May, 1849, and 17 May 1850[.]

In 1834–8 when Captain Ward first went up the Missisippi he carried *produce*.[n] Now the River loads him with exports.[28]

[28] James Ward was captain of the steamer *Excelsior*.

[42] [blank]

[43][29] 1851. Feb. 4.

	Left Boston at	7.30 AM
	Worcester	8.09
	Arr Springfield	10.50 AM
	Left S	1.15 pm
	Albany	6.
	left Albany	7 pm
	arrived Utica	11.30 pm
5	left Utica	11.30 AM
	Arrived at Rochester	6 30 pm
8	Left Rochester at	7.30 AM
	arrived at Buffalo	10.

[44] [blank]

[45] Cinder in the iron. Yes, but there was cinder in the pay.[30] 'Twas bought with bonds & shares & nobody knows what all. Cheap, cheap--iron.

[46][31] ⟨6⟩7 February 1851. Rochester

Mr J A Wilder made me acquainted with the Unive[r]sity of R. which was extemporising here like a picnic.[32] They had bought a hotel, once ⟨the⟩ a railroad terminus depot[,] for $8,500,[n] turned the diningroom into a chapel by putting up a pulpit on one side, made the barroom into a Pythologian Society's Hall, & the chambers into Recitation rooms, Libraries, & professors' apartments, all for $700. a year. They had brought an Omnibus load of professors down from Madison bag & baggage [—] Hebrew, Greek, [47] Chaldee, Latin, Belles Lettres, Mathematics, & all Sciences, called in a painter, sent him up a ladder to paint the title "University of Rochester" on the wall, and now they had runners on the road to catch students. One lad came in yesterday; another, this morning; "thought they should like it first rate", & now they thought themselves ill used if they

[29] P. [43] is in pencil.

[30] "Cinder in . . . pay." is used in "Considerations by the Way," *W*, VI, 276.

[31] Pp. [46]–[50] are in pencil.

[32] John Nichols Wilder was a founder and for nine years president of the Board of Trustees of the University of Rochester.

did not get a new student every day. And they are confident of graduating a class of Ten by the time green peas are ripe.

[48] Went to Kidd's Foundry & saw Dr Boyntons put his hand through a jet of liquid iron.[33] He told me Wightman's speech to Paine[:] "Mr P. this is good grease gas." ⟨n⟩And at the jet when hydrogen should come[:] "no hydrogen here," smelling it—

[49] At the Falls. 10 Feby., 1851.
Saw Father Hennepin's picture of the Falls in 1698, apparently they have receded 200 feet.[34] The ⟨bas⟨e⟩s note⟩ bass note of the fall is very distinguishable from the noise of the rapids. ⟨A blade⟩ Stick a penknife into a tree[,] the knife will vibrate. Porter has crossed to the Canada side on an ice bridge; has been on all the "Three Sisters" islands.[35] Best point they told me was a mile above the falls on Canada side.

[50] skeleton of the Umbrella pluviosa, and[n] the American sarcophagus. ⟨Wo⟩⟨Th⟩Goat Island is worth $5000 a year to the Porters. & Buffalo 10,000 to Mr P—

[51] Cincinnati Dec., 1852.
Population 125 000
Every mile of the Little Miami gives a mill[.]
Dr Lee says no storms in Ohio, wind on the lake[,] wind to the south from the gulf, up to Kentucky[,] wind to the Cumberland Mountains and Atlantic winds but never a gale at Cincinnati. Mr Longworth came here in 1804[,] bought land at $25 per acre. Judge Burnet kept of all his land only [52] 32 acres, which was his cow pasture &

[33] The foundry of William Kidd (1806–1880), on Brown's race, manufactured machinery and castings. Dr. John F. Boynton of Syracuse was lecturing on geology and related subjects in February, 1851.

[34] Jean Louis Hennepin (1640–1705), Flemish Recollet friar, published a picture of Niagara Falls in his *Nouvelle Découverte* . . . , 1697; see *A New Discovery of a Vast Country in America*, reprinted from the second London issue of 1698 . . . 2 vols. (Chicago, 1903), I, 54.

[35] Peter Augustus Porter (1827–1864), Harvard graduate, 1845, was a trustee of Hobart College in Geneva and DeVeaux College in Niagara Falls. Porter later had a distinguished military career in the Civil War.

when Longworth offered to buy it for 5000, said, "Pretty story in Jersey, that you came to study law with me, & I made you a slave for life. No, you shall not buy it."
L's 13½ acres which he bought for two old stills, the fee for which he cleared a horse thief.[36] Judge B. might have been worth 20 000 000, had he bought land instead of bankstock[.]

[53] Kentucky

Their eyes are all dangerous, & I wonder that life is so safe as it is. They announce in the St Louis papers that only two men were killed in the streets during the last week. But this morning I notice a fatal affray the last night. They are made of sulphur & potash. Yet Memphis is the gunpowder point.[37]

An age or generation in Ohio, is 3 years.
Mr Greene says, "Sir I have held that opinion three weeks."

[54] [38] How did you get on with your goods? [n] "O you know the Pawnees pitched into me & I was glad to get off with my scalp." Well, you know he was humbugging me but only that word Pawnee was enough & I thought I had just as lief be killed by a Pawnee, as sit here at a desk every day, from 9 o'clock till 7.[39]

[55] He only is great who makes me great. Do not care then for jesuit or doctrinaire, Mrs D, but consider whether the influence be expansive & aggrandising or no.

[56] I answer ⟨n⟩too swift anthropomorphism with the sensible horizon. Men would put a deity into the mind that their very eyes

[36] Nicholas Longworth (1782–1863), horticulturist, studied law in Cincinnati in Judge Jacob Burnet's office. Land exchanged for the two stills rose in value to over one million dollars in Longworth's lifetime. Longworth became a lawyer, millionaire, and patron of the arts, and a skilled horticulturist who made grape-growing a commercial succcess. Jacob Burnet (1770–1853), lawyer and senator, became a judge of the Supreme Court of Ohio.

[37] "Kentucky . . . point." is in pencil.

[38] Pp. [54]–[58] are in pencil.

[39] This sentence is used in "Power," *W*, VI, 68.

would ⟨o⟩rebel against. Their very eyes require a providence ⟨as⟩ big enough to float a steamboat in, & they would put on their *minds* something less. I insist on not being cornered,—searoom[.]

[57] St Louis

Here they already smell the Pacific. A certain largeness in the designs & enterprize of the people, generosity. They had a boat drawing so little water that they said it would sail in a heavy dew. & when it got aground, they took out the crew, got out, & put their shoulders under [58] the boat & lifted it along[.][40]

	Left Boston 1⟨1⟩5 March [1851][41]		
	Fare of L E & self to Boston	1.50	
	L E & self to N. Y	9.00	
	Coach in Boston	50	
	Coach in N Y	1.00	
	⟨dinn⟩ supper on boat	.65	
	porter	.25	
Mar. 16	Coach to S. I. Ferry	50	
	Coach to W E	1.00	14.
17	Bixbys[42]	2.72	
	porter	25	
	Railroad to Phila	3.00	
	Coach	⟨6⟩75	
		12	
18.	to Pittsburg	10.	
19.			
20	Expenses 50.50	1.00	
	Phila	1.00	
	Canalboat	1.50	
			2034
			34.34

[40] "the boat . . . along" is written on the bottom of p. [58], separated from the schedule of costs by a short rule.

[41] Emerson and his wife traveled to New York City where they stayed with the William Emersons; Emerson then went on to Pittsburgh via Philadelphia; Lidian remained in New York. See *L*, IV, 245.

[42] A hotel at 1 Park Place, New York.

[59]

key	75
C	
Sundries	2.⟨1⟩00
M⟨l⟩onongahela[43]	23
porters &c	1.
cab	.62
⟨Canal⟩ ↑ticket to Phil/↓[44]	10.

In the pews at St Louis are cards pasted on which is written "Gentlemen are requested by the ladies not to spit on the floor."[45] In the boats; "Gambling not permitted in the saloon"

[60][46] Pittsburgh, March 20⟨1⟩, 1851.

Coal at $1.40 pr ton delivered 3 to 5 cents a basket, at the mine.[47] The land containing it worth near Pittsburgh $1000 per acre.

---

3 bottoms; land, coal, salt.[48]

---

coal strata 5 ft thick

---

two strata below, ⟨1⟩9[,] 12 or 14 ft thick

---

one in six of the coal boats lost in getting to N. Orleans

Coal reaches from [Pittsburgh?] to Pomroy in Ohio
[61] horse 1250 lb

[43] Emerson stayed at the Monongahela House in Pittsburgh, March 20 to approximately April 2 (*L*, IV, 245–247).

[44] "key . . . Phil/" is in pencil.

[45] With this sentence, cf. "Behavior," *W*, VI, 173–174: ". . . in the same country [on the banks of the Mississippi], in the pews of the churches little placards plead with the worshipper against the fury of expectoration."

[46] Pp. [60] and [61] are in pencil.

[47] On March 21, 1851, Thomas McElrath of the New York *Tribune* apparently showed Emerson through his coal mine in Pittsburgh (*L*, IV, 246).

[48] "Thus at Pittsburgh . . . every acre of land has three or four bottoms, first of rich soil; then nine feet of bituminous coal; a little lower, fourteen feet of coal; then iron or salt . . ." (*CEC*, 470).

his foot is a sledgehammer of 1250 lb. pounding stones all day

[62] Ohio	Buckeye	
Indiana	Hoosier	
Illinois	Sucker,	prairie,
Kentucky	Corncracker	
Missouri	Puke	
Arkansaw	Wolverine	
Wisconsin	Badger	State?
Iowa	Hawkeye	

The emblem or arms of Canada is a maple leaf & a beaver.

[63] "The longest pole takes the persimmon."
"coming the huckleberry over the persimmon."

Saint Louis looked better on the map than in the town. On the map, it must grow; in the town, 'twas going to ruin.

---

[64] Wait for new men
Undulation
Safe to trust an air line
You can't help serving truth
nor they their pot
But it becomes a duty to protest
Railroad & telegraph better unionists than 10 000 Websters.

[65]–[66] [leaf torn out]
[67] *St Louis*
1852 Population, 95 000
1840

---

114 bushels of corn to the acre in Missouri.

The bound⟨s⟩ of a deer measures 28 feet

---

[68] ↑*St Louis*↓
Mr & Mrs Dean at St Louis, told me, that they never knew what it was to live in a free country, until they came here. Here they are free.
A cheat is a coward.

⟨5⟩60 000 miles of river navigation are tributary to St Louis.

---

[69] ↑*St Louis.*↓

The two great axes of river trade in America are, the Missisippi, running north & south; &, the Ohio & Missouri, running east & west. These meet here, & St Louis is at the intersection. ↑"'Tis the greatest cross-roads the world ever saw." *Benton.*↓

The River is now half a mile wide. In freshets it extends from bluff to bluff, or, here, 10 to 15 miles wide, & is crossed in steamboats so far. They think the river here unconquerable, [70] & that man must follow & not dictate to it. If you drive piles into it to construct a dam or pier you only stir the bottom which dissolves like sugar & is all gone. Very laborious & costly constructions have been carried off. Real estate on the shores of Missouri is very floating capital. The river is low in winter, & fullest in May & June.

[71] Capt. Douglass gave me some ⟨e⟩details concerning the Pawnees, Rapahoes, Crows, Sioux & Delawares.[49] The Delawares (& Shawnees) removed hither from the State of New York, are the ablest of the ⟨races⟩tribes. Five Delawares will go from Missouri to the Pacific & no man who knows them to be Delawares will meddle with them. Five Delawares armed with rifles were attacked by a hundred Pawnees. They threw themselves into a thicket, killed [72] 16 or 17 of them & the Pawnees retreated & left them. The Mexicans ⟨co⟩when they make a caravan from Santa Fe hitherward, usually ⟨secure⟩ take care to have fifteen or twenty Americans in the party. Then the Indians will not attack them. A few years ago the Pawnees fancied

[49] In December, 1852, Emerson was apparently staying at the house of John T. Douglass in St. Louis. Douglass had been chairman of the lecture committee of the St. Louis Mercantile Library Association (*L*, IV, 332).

"left Buffalo 9:45" is inscribed in pencil beneath "Delawares. The".

that the Americans were but a handful[,] some poor fellows [73]–[76] [two leaves torn out] [49a]

[77₁] who had nothing to live on & were forced to come out into their country to get something to eat. Col. Kearney was instructed by government to make a demonstration of force, & carried howitzers. The Pawnees hovered about them for a time but seeing them on a hill he threw a s⟨a⟩hell among them. They stared & went up [78] to it, & saw it spinning about, & some of the chiefs tried to take hold of it, when it exploded, & killed four or five men. For two years after, no Indian was ever seen on that trail. ⟨The⟩ White-Cloud told Capt. D. that "he did not like those *wagon-guns*."

[77₂] Keystone State Capt Stone
Chicago to Buffalo

8	48
8	56
12	96
4	32
51	357
5⟨‖ . . . ‖⟩	300
	60
	325
	100

13⟨6⟩74
4 50
1.00
3 00
22 24 [50]

[79] ↑*St Louis*↓

↑"Nearly↓ all [n] the business here is done by Eastern men."
"There is no difference here between boy & man. As soon as a boy is that high, (high as the table) he contradicts his father."

[49a] Despite the missing leaves, the prose on p. [77₁] may be continuous with that on p. [72]. The stubs of pp. [73]–[75] are blank; the stub of p. [76] contains some botched multiplication by Emerson.

[50] "Keystone . . . 22 24" is in pencil; it underlies the ink inscription on p. [77₁]. "Keystone . . . Buffalo" is partially encircled by a penciled line.

[80] Dr Wing of Collinsville, Ill. ⟨o⟩remarked that the strength of Slavery consisted in the support it found in the New England States.[51]

He said, what I have heard from others, that ⟨a man's⟩ you can form no conclusion to depend upon, from what a man says, he will do, in this country. He says he will come, he will not come; he says he will bring twenty hands; perhaps he will bring three.

[81] ⟨A⟩Entire want of punctuality & business habit. One principal cause of this is the uncertainty of health. The miasma takes the laborers.

The Illinoi⟨s⟩ans were called *Suckers*, from the circumstance, that the first settlements were in the ⟨Nor⟩Southern part of the state, ⟨at Galena⟩ & the settlers used to come up to ⟨the mines at⟩ Galena, to work in the mines, about the ⟨s⟩time when the Suckers came up the river, in the spring & return when they returned.

[82] ⟨D⟩Jan. 8. 1853. Left St Louis, & came up the river to Alton, 25 miles, at the rate of 10 miles ↑the hour↓ on the steampacket Cornelia. The other boat, the Altona, is faster, & has made it in 1h. 40′.[n] The meeting of the Missouri & Missisippi is a noble landscape & the town of Alton (6 or 7000 pop.) on the high limestone bluff shows well over the widewatered shore[.]

[83] At Alton, we took the train for Springfield, 72 miles. Senator Breese & Mr Young of U. S. Congress, ↑Gov. Edwards,↓ & other railroad men were in the train, & made an agreeable party *in the baggage car*, where they had a box of brandy, a box of buffalo tongues, & a box of soda biscuit.[52] They showed me eight or ten deer flying across the prairie, with their white tails erect, disturbed by the

[51] Dr. Henry Wing, a graduate of Illinois College in 1844, later became a member of the State Board of Medical Examiners and a professor in Chicago Medical College.

[52] Sidney Breese (1800–1878) served in the Illinois Senate from 1843 to 1849. Timothy Roberts Young (1811–1898) was a congressman from Illinois from 1849 to 1851. Emerson may have confused Ninian Wirt Edwards (1809–1889), first superintendent of public instruction in Illinois, with his father, Ninian Edwards, who had been governor of Illinois Territory (d. 1833).

train; then, presently, one who stood & looked at us; then a fire on the prairie.[n] The corn was not yet gathered, & a farmer told us, that they had not yet been [84] able to get upon the land to gather it,—too much mud for horse & wagon.—[n] It does not usually get all gathered until March. Gov. Edwards had been at St Louis in 1815 or 1816 when there was but one brick house in the place. And until lately any man arriving there & seeing the dilapidated old ⟨f⟩French houses[,] their posts all rotted away at bottom & swinging from the piazza above[,] would have [85] been more struck with the air of decay than of growth.

At Springfield, found the mud of the deluge. Mr B. had said of a bread & butter pudding at the hotel, "It was a fraud upon Lazarus;" & told the story of the London milk-man, who, being indicted for adulterating milk, got off by proving that there was no particle of milk in the composition. A man brought ⟨churns⟩ patent churns here, & somebody [86] there[n] ↑said, "↓You take Peters's milk, & if you can make a particle of butter out of that, you shall ⟨n⟩have not only a patent, but a deed of the State of Illinois!" Meanness of politics, low fillibusterism, dog-men, that have not shed their canine teeth; well, don't be disgusted; 'tis the work of this River, this Missisippi River that warps the men, ↑warps the nations,↓ they must all obey it, chop down its woods, kill the [87] alligator, eat ⟨e⟩the deer, shoot the wolf, "follow the river," mind the b⟨a⟩oat, ⟨c⟩plant the Missouri-corn, cure, & save, & send down stream the wild foison harvest tilth & wealth of this huge mud trough of the 2 000 miles or 10 000 miles of river. How can they be high? How can they have a day's leisure for anything but the work of the river? Every one has the mud up to his knees, & the coal of the country dinges his shirt collar. How can he be literary or grammatical? The people are all kings: ⟨U⟩out on the prairie [88] the sceptre is the driving-whip. And I notice an extraordinary firmness in the face of many a drover, ⟨what⟩an air of independence & inevitable lips, which are worth a hundred thousand dollars: ⟨But the polit⟩No holding a hat for opinions. But the politicians in their statehouses are truckling & adulatory.

[89] In California, there is much insanity. A man is getting out of his digging 20.00 a day, &, next beside him, another is getting out $1000. per day, and the men in the one work like dogs, because

they are expecting every hour that they will strike on the same vein. How can their heads or bodies stand such excitement[?]

[90] As soon as one is sick all is over with him, he pays an ounce to the doctor for every visit, say three times a day[,] then for nursing at high rates, so that he pays 50 to 75 dollars a day while he is sick, which soon empties his pocket.
A man goes to the tavern & says to the landlord "I have no money." [n] [91] "It makes no difference" says the landlord, "go to the table." For the case is common & they know that every man who ⟨c⟩will work will soon "make a raise," as they call it, as any mechanical work will pay six dollars a day. Judge Shattuck of Pennsylvania with his two sons tried law, but got no money.[53] Judge Henry lent him some. Then he [92] said, "I only lose so. Here is a man advertises that he wants a cellar dug. I shall take that job" & he & his sons went to work & dug the hole. Somebody came & found him there digging, & told him what a case he had in court. "Now, do you let your sons finish that hole, & you come to court." He went, & tried it, & won it. Then he ⟨w⟩bought land, & ⟨v⟩raised vegetables for the market, with his sons, and now [93] is worth half a million. San Francisco is as well built a town as Saint Louis; has 60,000 people, & as good living at the Oriental, or Tehama hotels, as at any hotel in the States; —[n] says my Californian doctor, who means to go to the Sandwich Islands to live. The energy of the States is there, & the humanity too. 5,000,000, a month in gold comes to the States[.]

[94] Church members are apt to misbehave in San Francisco, & free-thinkers are apt to ↑be↓ very moral men there.
And he believes himself safer ⟨in⟩with money about him in San F. than in St Louis or New York because of the summary justice that is executed ⟨here⟩there.

[95]–[96] [leaf cut out]

[97] Springfield is set down here in a prairie bottom in the richest corn-belt, but in a bottom land, & not a rolling prairie. There-

[53] A David Olcott Shattuck of Connecticut went to San Francisco in April, 1850, with two sons, David O. and Frank W.

fore, they cannot build cellars ⟨&c⟩under the houses, & there is mud such as I never beheld. The Capitol, a costly limestone building, sinks & cracks its walls. I walk to the end of the streets on each side the [98] town, & look out, but dare not step into the immeasureable mud. After walking the deck, thus, for a sufficient time, as I hope, to secure sleep, I remove some pounds of mud from my overshoes, & creep into my cabin.

Yesterday I went over to the Statehouse, with Judge Breese (U. S. Senator.) & called on the Governor. (French)[54] Whilst I was paying my respects to his Excellency [99] the Secretary of State[55] came into the room, & the Governor introduced me to him. "Governor," said the Secretary, "did you ⟨borrow⟩ ↑take↓ my screw-driver[n] ↑out of my room?↓" The Executive of Illinois acknowledged the fact, & asked the clerk in the room to find it. They are all poor country people & live hard.

Senator Douglass ↑(newly ↑re-↓elected,)↓ gives an entertainment to his friends in the Representative Chamber on Thursday night, for which [100] 800 cards have been issued. Mr Douglass is at Washington, but is to pay the bills, &, 'tis said here, the entertainment is to cost $3000. Tomorrow night the Legislature is invited to Alton, to celebrate the new road, & the desired improvements of that town. The old heroes came in ↑with↓ 100 cannon & 10 000 troops, the leaders of today ⟨⟨h⟩come w⟩ conquer with 100 champagne bottles & 20 boxes segars.

[101] ⟨S⟩At St Lou⟨s⟩is, they talk St Louis incessantly, in all companies. And 'tis said, that, after people have been out here in the West for ten years, nothing would induce them to live in one of the old states. Mr Wolcott of ⟨S⟩Jacksonville says, his eyes ache for mountains, but when, ten years ago, he went back to Connecticutt, he found he could not [102] breathe there, or, as he persisted in saying, a man was nothing there, could not make his mark.[56] He has the care of keeping the track in order between Springfield & Jacksonville, he in working-clothes, and is a graduate of Yale College. At Springfield

[54] Augustus C. French (1808–1864) was governor of Illinois from 1849 to 1853, his second administration.

[55] David L. Gregg.

[56] Elihu Wolcott left Connecticut in 1830 to settle in Jacksonville. He was a leader in the Congregational Church and an abolitionist.

the American House is a poor house enough but was full of governors, [103] judges, senators, secretaries, & treasurers, Gov French, the retiring Gov, Matteson, the acceding Executive, Gov Reynolds, the new Speaker of the House, & Gov. Edwards, an old pioneer.[57] When I visited them at their rooms, I found them allowanced with no more square inches of chamber than myself, & with only one chair apiece.

[104] The whole government of the state was all piggled together in dingy condition. Snyder & Denio of the Senate appeared to be men of considerable power. The last is a working mason.[58]
At Jacksonville, 35 miles, by strap-rail-road,[59] I found an excellent man in Dr David Prince, & ⟨in⟩a man of much natural polemic talent in John or Jonathan B. Turner.[60] [105] At Springfield my friend & inviter was F. A. Moore, formerly of Manchester, N. H. And the best of his friends was also one of mine, Cornelia Kegwin; to whom I must send one of my books; and, above all, *George Herbert's*.[61]

[106] Between Jacksonville & Springfield I passed a field of corn containing 1000 acres. A little to the north of us was a field as large belonging to Mr Strawn, who lives 4 miles out of J[acksonville]. & who owns ⟨28⟩ ↑40↓ 000 acres, lives in the saddle, manages all himself, & is of course a man of prodigious energy.[62] They said he eats mush & [107] milk with two spoons & his idea↑l↓ of beauty is a fine

[57] Joel Aldrich Matteson (1808–1873) was governor of Illinois from 1853 to 1857; John Reynolds (d. 1865) was speaker of the House of Representatives from 1853 to 1854.

[58] William H. Snyder and Cyrenius B. Denio were members of the Illinois House of Representatives from 1853 to 1854.

[59] The railroad had been built in 1838 and named the Northern Cross R.R. The trains ran on strips of flat iron laid on wooden stringers. It ran the 33½ miles from Springfield to Jacksonville in two hours and eight minutes.

[60] Dr. David Prince was a community leader and later an Army surgeon. Jonathan Baldwin Turner (1805–1899) graduated from Yale in 1833, became a professor at Illinois College in Jacksonville, and in 1850 formulated the plan for land-grant colleges, enacted into law in 1862.

[61] On January 11, 1853, Emerson wrote Lidian from Springfield, "Here I am in the deep mud of the prairie, misled . . . by a young New Hampshire editor. . . ."; this was F. A. Moore, who had written Emerson twice urging him to lecture in Springfield. In 1853 Cornelia Kegwin wrote to thank Emerson for books he had sent her.

[62] Jacob Strawn (d. 1865) was known as the great cattle dealer of Morgan County, Illinois.

steer & his ideal of a great man the man who stands in the gap when a great herd of cattle are to be separated[,] these for market & those to remain for ⟨f⟩pasture. Of course the man who stands in the gap is to choose on the instant by their looks which to let through the gate & which [108] to keep off the other way as they come up and he must be of such a size & look too as that the cattle shall not run over him. His picture at full length, in his house, exhibits him as standing among cattle with a huge driving whip under his arm. The work is done here [109] by a roving tenantry of natives, of Irish & of Dutchmen, one man being able to till 30 to 40 acres. Mr King represented the whole State as being used for nothing but to raise the greatest quantity of grease. — [63] They raise vast amounts of corn to feed millions of hogs.

[110] [64] ⟨3⟩4 Feb. [1851]	Fare to Boston	50	
	Hack	25	
	American	1.00	
	Hack	25	
	Ticket to Albany	5.00	
	Warrener[?]	50	
	Coach ⟨porter⟩	25	
	Albany Supper	25	
	Ticket	9.00	
	porter	25	
	Utica	1 25	37
		12	
	Syracuse	25	
			18 88
	Expense at Rochester		
		5.50	
	porter	25	
	Sh.	10	
		5 85	5 85
			24 73

[63] Mr. King may be Turner R. King, who migrated from Massachusetts to Springfield in 1840.

[64] Pp. [110]–[112] are in pencil. At various points on p. [110] is a series of irregular marks, a line, and a doodle, which appear to have no meaning.

To Niagara 1.25

[111] To Albany ticket 9.
Expense at Geneva 2.25 [n]
25
Syracuse porters &c 25
Albany expense 1.50
Springfield ⟨12⟩50
Concord 12
⟨———⟩
Ticket to Worcester 4.25
to Concord 1.30
18.42
25 98
44 4⟨8⟩0

[112] 315
133
82

From Boston to Albany 200
Albany to Buffalo 325
Buffalo to Sandusky 250
Sandusky to Cincinnati 218
Cincinnati to Louisville 133
Louisville to Evansville 182
Evansville to Bowling Green 150 [65]
Bowling Green to Mammoth Cave 30

Mamm↑o↓th Cave to Bell's 7
Bell's to Bowling Green 23 [66]

[65] See p. [1] above.

[66] Emerson walked the seven miles to Bell's Tavern, and, the next day, fourteen of the twenty-three miles to Bowling Green (*L*, *IV*, 214).

Bowling Green to Hopkinsville	65
Hopkinsville to Eddyville	40
To Paducah	72
↑To Cairo	45↓
To St Louis	175
To Galena	457
To Chicago	167
To ⟨Detroit⟩ new Buffalo	6⟨0⟩5
T	

[113]

To Detroit by M C Railroad	224
To Buffalo	330
To Niagara	22
To Lewiston & Oswego	
To Syracuse	
To Albany	
to Worcester	
to Concord [67]	

My companions Messrs Page & Pettes told me they never take their clothes off[,] hardly their boots[,] on the Missisippi: when they get into the Ohio, they go calmly to bed.[68]

45 [69]

4.65
34 00
38.65

[67] "To Detroit . . . Concord" is in pencil. "To Lewiston . . . Concord" is overwritten in ink by "My companions . . . their boots", which is printed below.

[68] In the lecture "The Anglo-American," Emerson identifies his companions only as western merchants. A Samuel Pettes, Jr., wrote a letter to Emerson September 18, 1854.

[69] This figure, in pencil, is some four page-lines above the next figures and appears to have no relation to any other figures on the page. It may be a rounding off of the figure "44 4⟨8⟩o" on p. [111].

[114][70]	Framingham		1.50
	To Albany		5.
	Dinner Springfield		.75
	Carriage		37
14	Congress Hall ↑at night↓		1.50
	porter↑s↓		37
15	Tickets to Buffalo		9.75
	Expenses		75
	Phelps's Buffalo		1.00
	Ticket to & from Falls		1.00
	Ticket at Falls	25	
	d[itt]o	25	
	suspension	25	
	⟨T⟩Cab	25	
	ferry	6	
	dinner	50	1.56
	Niagara book		.25
	Tickets to Cincinnati		1⟨7⟩0.⟨25⟩00[71]
	Porter at Phelps		.25
			↑34.05↓

[115]		↑Brought up	34.05↓
16	Porter at Cleveland, for care of baggage in the fire.		.50
	porter again		.50
17	Expense at Weddell House		2.00
18	Expense at Sandusky		
	lodging		.50

[70] On pp. [114]–[119] the daily entries and some totals are in pencil; "34.05" and the rule above (p. [114]), and "Brought up 34.05" (p. [115]) are in ink; "47 60" (p. [115]) and the rule above are in ink, inscribed on top of the same figures in pencil; so is "112 36" on pp. [116] and [117]. On p. [117] Emerson wrote "132 01" in ink on top of "130.01" in pencil — an error. He did the same at the top of p. [118]; at the bottom of that page he wrote "171.96" in ink on top of "170.26" in pencil, to correct another error. At the top of p. [119] he wrote "171.26" in ink over "170.26" in pencil. At the bottom of the column on p. [119] he wrote "191.80" in ink on top of "190.80" in pencil — his final correction of error.

[71] Emerson seems to have changed "7.25" to "10.00".

porters & omnibus				.30
Breakfast at Tiffon				.25
Dinner at Springfield				.30
Supper at Morrow				.30
			38.65	

Envelopes	10			
Western Guide	1.00			
pencil	5			
		1.15	1.20	
ice		5		
Visit to Fort Ancient			3.40	
map of Minesota			.75	
baths			.50	
sack			2.25	
gloves			25	
porter			20	
tolls			↑ 40	
				47.60↓

[116] 1850		47.60
May 30	Post Office stamps	1.00
	comb	.25
	cap	1.00
	3 pencils	.15
	wine	.10
	ice, &c. & fair	.45
	visiting cards	.40
	Pendennis	⟨1⟩1.25
	Burnet House	37.25
	porter	.50
	Chambermaid	.25
	barber & ⟨c⟩hairdresser	.35
	Fare to Louisville on the Ben Franklin	2.50
	portage to Bowling Green	.30
	Ale	.25

	Expenses to Mammoth Cave & there	6 00	
		6 66	
		4.00	
			1⟨0⟩6.66
	Expense at Bell's		1.50
	additional fees at Cave		.60
			↑112.36↓

[117]	↑*Brought up*	112.36↓
	From Bells to Bowling Green	1.25
	Bowling Green Inn	.50
	Fare to Hopkinsville	4.50
	Breakfast	.50
	dinner	40
	Supper & lodging at Hopkinsville	.50
13	Fare to Eddyville by stage	3.00
13	Breakfast at Oakland	.25
	Dinner at Eddyville	.25
14	Fare to Paducah — boat —	2.50
	Fare to St Louis	5.00
	Bottle of fish	1.00
		↑132.01↓

1270	
1365	
26.35	1465
6.	2291
	⟨19⟩
	3756

[118]		↑132.01↓
June 18	Planters' House at St Louis	6.17
	Pendennis	1.25
	White pantaloons	3.00
	Fare to Galena in boat Excelsior	6.00
	Cabman in St Louis	1.00

	porter		.50
	wine &c		.50
19	wine		10
	barber		20
	Galena Fare to Chicago		9.00
	breakfast		25
	dinner		25
	extras		30
	breakfast		37
	Elgin expenses		1.00
	porter		
	Chicago Inn		75
	porter &c		31
	Fare to Buffalo		9.00
			↑171.96↓

[119]

	↑171.26↓
Breakfast	50
Fare to Niagara	75
At Niagara	2.00
To Oswego	3.50
⟨To⟩Breakfast	.37
To Albany	3.⟨2⟩75
To Worcester	4.50
⟨T⟩Springfield	.50
Am. House Worcester	.75
To Concord	1.30
	12
Sundries	1.00
Indian toys	1 50
	↑191.80↓

[120]

Feb.	6	Thurs. Rochester	9
	7	Fri.	10
	8	S	11
	9	S	12
	10	Buffalo	13

	11	Buf			14
	12				15
	13		35		16
	14	S	103		17
	15		20		18
	16		158		19
	17				20
	18				21
Wed.	19	⟨Clinton⟩			22
	20	Canton			23
Fri.	21	Newb[ur]yp[or]t			24
	22	Waltham			25
	23				26
	24				27
	25		33		28
	26		191		29
	27				30
	28			Mon.	31
	⟨29⟩March				
Sat.	1				
	2				
	3				
	4	E Boston			
	5				
	6				
	7				
	8				

[inside back cover] [72]
||msm||
||msm||rn acres in one field
28 000 acres
Stand in the gap
Strong. 4 miles out

[72] Glued lightly to the back cover is a newspaper clipping headed "Curiosities of the West." It quotes a gentleman traveler as having seen such things as "a Kentuckian seven feet ten inches high," "prairie flies nearly as large as humming birds, and musquitoes about the size of yellow wasps."

of Jacksonville
lives in the saddle
manages all himself
1 man till 30 or 40 acres
eats mush & milk with two spoons [73]

100
300
450

[73] The notes relate to entries on pp. [106]–[107] above.

Appendix

Textual Notes

Index

Appendix

The following table shows which of Emerson's journals and miscellaneous notebooks are already printed in the Harvard University Press edition (*JMN*, I–X), and where they may be found, by volume and volume page numbers. Because this edition prints Emerson's manuscript page numbers of the journals and notebooks in the text, the reader should have no difficulty in locating cross-references to previously printed journals or notebooks. These are listed alphabetically, as designated by Emerson or others; the dates are supplied by Emerson, or the editors, or both. Since some passages are undated and some dates are doubtful, scholars should look at individual passages before relying on their dating.

Designation	Harvard edition
A (1833–1834)	IV, 249–387
AB (1847)	X, 3–57
B (1835–1836)	V, 3–268
Blotting Book I (1826–1827)	VI, 11–57
Blotting Book II (1826–1829)	VI, 58–101
Blotting Book III (1831–1832)	III, 264–329
Blotting Book IV (1830, 1831? 1833)	III, 359–375
Blotting Book IV[A] (1830, 1832–1834)	VI, 102–114
Blotting Book Psi (1830–1831, 1832)	III, 203–263
Blotting Book Y (1829–1830)	III, 163–202
Blue Book (1826)	III, 333–337
Books Small [I] (1840?–1856?)	VIII, 442–479
Books Small [II]	VIII, 550–576
C (1837–1838)	V, 277–509
Catalogue of Books Read, 1819–1824	I, 395–399
CD (1847)	X, 58–123
Charles C. Emerson (1837)	VI, 255–286
Collectanea (1825–1828?)	VI, 3–10
College Theme Book (1819–1821, 1822? 1829?)	I, 161–205
Composition (1832?)	IV, 427–438
D (1838–1839)	VII, 3–262
Dialling (1825? 1841? 1842)	VIII, 483–517

Designation	Harvard edition
E (1839–1842)	VII, 263–484
ED (1852–1853)	X, 494–568
Encyclopedia (1824–1836)	VI, 115–234
England and Paris (1847–1848)	X, 407–445
F No. 2 (1840–1841)	VII, 485–547
France and England (1833)	IV, 395–419
G (1841)	VIII, 3–77
Genealogy (1822, 1825, 1828)	III, 349–358
GH (1847–1848)	X, 124–199
H (1841)	VIII, 78–145
Italy (1833)	IV, 134–162
Italy and France (1833)	IV, 163–208
J (1841–1842)	VIII, 146–197
JK (1843?–1847)	X, 365–404
Journal 1826 (1825, 1826, 1827? 1828)	III, 3–41
Journal 1826–1828 (1824, 1825, 1826–1828)	III, 42–112
K (1842)	VIII, 198–247
LM (1848)	X, 288–362
London (1847–1848)	X, 208–287
Maine (1834)	IV, 388–391
Memo St. Augustine (1827)	III, 113–118
Meredith Village (1829)	III, 159–162
N (1842)	VIII, 248–308
No. II (1825)	II, 413–420
No. XV (1824–1826)	II, 272–351
No. XVI (1824–1828?)	II, 396–412
No. XVII (1820)	I, 206–248
No. XVIII (1820–1822)	I, 249–357
No. XVIII[A] (1821?–1829)	II, 355–395
Notebook 1833 (1833–1836)	VI, 235–254
O (1846–1847)	IX, 355–470
Platoniana (1845–1848)	X, 468–488
Pocket Diary 1 (1820–1831?)	III, 338–348
Pocket Diary 1 (1847)	X, 405–406
Pocket Diary 2 (1833)	IV, 420–426
Pocket Diary 3 (1848–1849)	X, 446–457
Q (1832–1833)	IV, 3–101
R (1843)	VIII, 349–441
RO Mind (1835)	V, 269–276
Scotland and England (1833)	IV, 209–235
Sea 1833 (1833)	IV, 236–248
Sea-Notes (1847)	X, 200–207

Designation	Harvard edition
Sermons and Journal (1828–1829)	III, 119–158
Sicily (1833)	IV, 102–133
T (1834–?)	VI, 317–399
Trees[A:I] (1843–1847)	VIII, 518–533
Trees[A:II] (1847)	VIII, 534–549
U (1843–1844)	IX, 3–92
Universe 1–7, 7[A], 8 (1820–1822)	I, 358–394
V (1844–1845)	IX, 93–181
W (1845)	IX, 182–255
Walk to the Connecticut (1823)	II, 177–186
Warren Lot (1849)	X, 489–493
Wide World 1 (1820)	I, 3–32
Wide World 2 (1820–1821)	I, 33–58
Wide World 3 (1822)	I, 59–90
Wide World 4 (1822)	I, 91–113
Wide World 6 (1822)	I, 114–158
Wide World 7 (1822)	II, 3–39
Wide World 8 (1822)	II, 40–73
Wide World 9 (1822–1823)	II, 74–103
Wide World 10 (1823)	II, 104–143
Wide World 11 (1823)	II, 144–176
Wide World 12 (1823–1824)	II, 187–213
Wide World XIII (1824)	II, 214–271
Xenien (1848, 1852)	X, 458–467
Y (1845–1846)	IX, 256–354
Z (1831? 1837–1838, 1841?)	VI, 287–316
Z[A] (1842–1843)	VIII, 309–348

Textual Notes

RS

5 him⟨self⟩to | it. **7** banker. **8** benefactors: [dot added to original period to make colon] **9** ⟨Tholml[?]⟩ | a **12** Activity **14** criticism. **16** lives;" **17** clouds. **23** country. **24** school. | vac*uum* **25** him;" **27** myth, **28** each **30** But | was,↓ from **32** Sewells' **35** t⟨‖ . . . ‖⟩o **36** ridges?) ↑*osars*,↓ **44** ⟨in[?]⟩ **45** just **52** But **53** heaven.— | Sylves-[177]ter, **55** Let | kin⟨d⟩g⟨im⟩dom **57** times. **58** Add **60** th*a*t | ⟨w⟩voulût [circumflex canceled] **61** ⟨never⟩$_2$ dare$_1$ **62** It **65** But **66** Asalanders↓ **69** his **72** Yes, | ⟨‖ . . . ‖⟩homes **75** ⟨t[?]⟩hundred **81** Dundee,

TU

88 *r*oad, | And **89** he **92** *Macro*cosm," R*ea*son, Co*nscie*nce, Su*bsta*nce Ac*cid*ence, N*atu*re, *Relati*on, F*ortune*, F*a*te, | Fortune,. **94** the artist [badly smudged] **95** Man **96** home; **106** Inte*llect* **109** Who **110** ↑i↓⟨th⟩t **111** ⟨farmers[?]⟩roarers. **117** ⟨understands⟩ & **118** sees & ↑the same & haply↓ **119** C'ant **121** [period canceled by ampersand] **122** them, ↑.↓ **126** secundus." Says **127** wh⟨en the⟩ich **128** man." | T⟨'s⟩↑aylor's↓ **132** ⟨dra[?]⟩pulled | "Is'⟨s⟩nt **140** ⟨fictions[?]⟩ **143** ⟨warm⟩ & | ↑& a↓ **145** lubberland. life **146** Road. **148** Prussia. **152** of ⟨wine⟩ **157** Des Cartes,$_2$ Keplers,$_1$ **158** Hid | th⟨r⟩irteenth **161** it. **164** occupation. **167** ex-[244]hausted **168** But **172** then **179** other." **180** When **181** ⟨yes[?]⟩

AZ

185 th*ey* | *th*ey . . . ar*tist*↑*i*↓cally **190** costs **192** Ticknor[?]⟩ **193** pleasures **194** ⟨hold[?]feel⟩ **195** in*teresti*ng S*und*ays . . . o*ve*r, **197** Nothing **198** ⟨Like my⟩as | enough, **199** *Schell*ing's **201** scorns, [comma in pencil] **203** ⟨out[?]⟩is | finds,↓ **204** houses, . . . tombs, [commas in pencil] | It **206** tale's | *ty*pe, **208** I⟨a⟩↑'↓m **211** the↑m↓ ⟨Simorg⟩selves **212** Shelterless **218** ⟨an[?] **227** expres-[140]sion, **228** sympa-[143]thized **234** qui⟨l⟩e⟨e⟩tly | substitute, [comma in pencil] **235** ballroom. **236** ⟨we m[*3–4 letters*]rs⟩the **238** reflec⟨‖ . . . ‖⟩tion **241** C.↑ommons.↓ **242** Fl⟨e⟩am⟨ing⟩mock **244** ⟨it[?]⟩ **246** h*i*s **251** tedious-[213]-ness, | t*hei*r **259** D⟨r⟩↑r W.E.↓ **262** "⟨It⟩T'were | percipi[249]ency. **263** "T'were | men **265** yesterday **267** blood-[264]relations **271** ⟨sp[?]⟩genera **272** *and* Amount **273** themselves." | Quality$_2$ and Amount$_1$ **277** botany↑?↓⟨, in⟩Now

BO

281 Indies. **282** obliga- **284** season; | So **290** wore, **291** p*ar*ty **294** ⟨re⟨a⟩fresh⟨ing⟩ening⟩ ↑refreshening↓ **299** brag. | of **300** Prefers | are" **308** ⟨v[?]⟩be | Engine-[80]Company, **309** m*a*n | suffer, **310** im-[85]portant **314** & | Nuova$_2$ Vita$_1$ **316** on **322** bard's **323** disgraces$_2$ & diseases$_1$ **328** biography **329** sympa[152]thy **334** For **337** he **341** ↑stealing↓; | they | facts Dr Dryasdusts↓ **343** Lymch **348** he | he may bluster. ↑is↓ | liberty. **350** Massachu-[227]setts | office. | ↑every↓ **351** ⟨o[?]⟩From **353** & and **355** some-[253]how **356** ↑to↓ [uncanceled] **357** true. | people. **360** post. | a*ll* | ⟨d[?]⟩qualities, | nonsense. **361** security. | ⟨d[?]⟩he | Slavery, | it, | the **365** being.

CO

370 Pr*ude*nce, **371** ↑Mr↓ [not canceled] **372** But **377** appear⟨s⟩ [Emerson finger-wiped out the canceled "s"] **380** buttonhole? **392** all — **395** That **396** Swedenborg-[95]mysticism **397** abstemious$_2$ & temperate$_1$ **399** Nationality. **401** 'Viny **403** multitude. **405** his **406** a ⟨sha⟩ **407** Walk, **409** every, **410** other, **411** means⟩ ↑slavery,↓ | the | Those | are. **414** the **417** idemtical **420** ⟨to have I⟩ **426** The **427** seen$_2$ rightly.$_1$ **429** as **431** result. — **436** complies$_2$ only$_1$ **437** A **439** ↑to↓ enter, **441** a ⟨frosty day⟩. December **442** ⟨at⟩nd **445** temper-ament, **446** he **447** tenden-[275]⟨a⟩cies | ↑.↓, ⟨but | enough! **449** ⟨force⟩ | m↑o↓mad [the "o" cancels the third upstroke of the first "m"; the second "m" is apparently an error for "n".] | No

Margaret Fuller Ossoli

457 j ai | ame **458** ⟨sec[?]⟩regal | not | together." **459** ↑"↓Dial↑"↓ **464** freedom↑:↓, | journey.↓: **465** sun, **467** j avais | j ai **468** Margarets' **469** Sep^{tre} | l élévation | l'altérer **470** c est **471** Platonists$_2$ [77] Alexandrian$_1$ **472** " 'Car-buncles," | sealring.; **473** G*e*n*erat*ion Cor*rup*tion **477** p⟨resent[?]⟩arent [or] p⟨refect[?]⟩arent | ↑Margaret, | ex-[105]pression **480** exact,. — **481** creat⟨ive⟩or ⟨Spirit⟩ **484** t*he*n, | head, **485** recover[149]ed | then | heads. **486** And . . . fancy, . . . that . . . him. **489** concentrate. | already, | ⟨was[?]⟩wish **490** t*ha*t | t*ha*t | *R*otch **491** *bo*lt **492** was [finger-wiped] **494** ewery | ⟨they⟩ **495** friend. | For | 1836.↓ **497** *ame.* **501** about, | dissent, **503** conquests. **504** replied.

Journal at the West

516 Cave,↑"↓-Boat **518** "It | Yes. | pro*duce.* **519** $85.00 **520** pluviosa⟨.⟩↑,↓ And **521** goods. **526** All **527** 1^{h}. 40↑'↓ **528** prairie, | wagon, — | there, **529** I . . . money | States — ; — **530** screw-driver? **533** ⟨2⟩2.25

Index

This Index includes Emerson's own index material omitted from the text. His index topics, including long phrases, are listed under "Emerson, Ralph Waldo, INDEX HEADINGS AND TOPICS"; the reader should consult both the general Index and Emerson's. If Emerson did not specify a manuscript page or a date to which his index topic referred, the editors have chosen the most probable passage(s) and added "(?)" to the printed page number(s). If Emerson's own manuscript page number is an obvious error, it has been silently corrected. If leaves are torn out but Emerson has indexed them, the index topic is listed and followed, in parentheses, by the journal title and page number, in square brackets.

References to materials included or to be included in *Lectures* are grouped under "Emerson, Ralph Waldo, LECTURES." References to drafts of unpublished poems are under "Emerson, Ralph Waldo, POEMS." Under "Emerson, Ralph Waldo, WORKS" are references to published versions of poems, to lectures and addresses included in *W* but not in *Lectures*, and to Emerson's essays and miscellaneous publications. Kinds of topics included under "Emerson, Ralph Waldo, DISCUSSIONS" in earlier volumes are now listed only in the general Index.